Echoes in the Canyons:
The Archaeology of the
Southeastern Sierra Ancha,
Central Arizona

Richard C. Lange

With

Richard S. Ciolek-Torrello

Lisa W. Huckell

Lynn S. Teague

and

Christine H. Virden-Lange

Arizona State Museum
THE UNIVERSITY OF ARIZONA

IN COLLABORATION WITH STATISTICAL RESEARCH, INC.

Arizona State Museum Archaeological Series 198

Arizona State Museum
The University of Arizona
Tucson, Arizona 85721-0026
(c) 2006 by the Arizona Board of Regents
All rights reserved. Published 2006
Printed in the United States of America

ISBN (paper): 978-1-889747-80-4
Library of Congress Control Number: 2007920237

ARIZONA STATE MUSEUM ARCHAEOLOGICAL SERIES

General Editor: E. Charles Adams
Technical Editor: Sarah Luchetta and Melanie Dedecker

The *Archaeological Series* of the Arizona State Museum, The University of Arizona, publishes the results of research in archaeology and related disciplines conducted in the Greater Southwest. Original, monograph-length manuscripts are considered for publication, provided they deal with appropriate subject matter. Information regarding procedures or manuscript submission and review may be obtained from the General Editor, *Archaeological Series*, Arizona State Museum, P.O. Box 210026, The University of Arizona, Tucson, Arizona, 85721-0026; Email: ecadams@u.arizona.edu.

Distributed by The University of Arizona Press, 355 S. Euclid Boulevard, Suite 103, Tucson, Arizona 85719

Contents

Figures Only Available in the Companion Materials located at:
http://www.statemuseum.arizona.edu/pubs/archseries/companion_materials.shtml

Tables

Preface and Acknowledgments

PREFACE

The following chapters present the most important data and summaries of information collected by the Sierra Ancha Project, June 1,1981 to July 1, 2004. Many, many people assisted during the course of the project. For the first decade, Richard C. Lange and Barbara A. Murphy assumed the principal roles in pursuing the project. Richard S. Ciolek-Torrello and Lange have cooperated on many endeavors over the years, Richard's contributions of time, scholarship, and to the final chapter of this report have been especially valuable. Thanks to everyone, it has been a tough, memorable, and hopefully, upon reflection, a fulfilling experience for all.

Technical Issues

Many of the sites discussed in the text have no site names, only their assigned number. Sites recorded by the Gila Pueblo Archaeological Foundation are indicated in the following format: GP C:1:36. Sites recorded into the Arizona AZSITE inventory are formally designated with their Arizona State Museum site numbers: AZ V:1:136(ASM). However, this can become cumbersome in the discussion, so the site numbers are shortened to: V:1:136. Site numbers from other institutions (for example, Arizona State University) are given in the complete format for the few times they are cited: AZ V:5:61 (ASU).

A compact disc (CD) was originally included with this publication. On the CD were folders that contain the majority of figures from the text. Figures that are primarily graphics (graphs, illustrations) were not put on the CD. Figures not on the CD are identified in the Table of Contents. All figures that were originally in color (slides or digital photographs) and that are rendered in grayscale in the text were presented in color on the CD. All photographs originally in black-and-white were also included on the CD. A set of figures was also included on the CD that are cited in the text, but do not appear in the text (labeled "CDxx"). These CD-only figures are additional examples of architecture and details presented in the figures in the text and comparative materials from other sites. The CD-only figures are listed in the Table of Contents. There was a document in a "Look_At_Me" folder on the CD that reiterated these details, and described the structure and contents of the folders on the CD. All of these materials are now available with the same parameters and names as on-line "Companion Materials" available at: http://www.statemuseum.arizona.edu/pubs/archseries/companion_materials.shtml.

Project records, materials, and artifacts are curated under Arizona State Museum Accession 2004-1733. Additional project and architectural details, photographs, and notes may be found in folders and computer records related to this accession. A draft of this report (Lange 2005) contains some additional memories and anecdotal information and is also in the archives of the Arizona State Museum, University of Arizona.

ACKNOWLEDGMENTS

The interest and participation of the public and professionals are what made this project possible. Their assistance, both physically and financially, is gratefully acknowledged.

Technical Assistance

Thanks to Ron Beckwith for drafting and preparing the maps for publication, and to Rick Karl, Skip Hooe, Christine Markussen, and Stephen McElroy and SRI, Inc. for assistance and preparation of GIS related figures. Thanks to the following for the various analyses: Lisa Young, lithics; Linda Pierce, faunal; Lisa Huckell, macrobotanical; Rich Lange, Virginia Hansen, students, and summer lab camp participants, ceramics; Lynn Teague, textiles; Dennie Bowden and Dick Warren, wood; Craig Howe, architecture; and Chris Lange, shell and rock art. The assistance of Jeff Dean is also gratefully acknowledged. Richard W. Lord photographed the artifacts, providing a service now well known throughout the Southwestern archaeological community. Elaine Hughes was a great help in the periodic monitoring and data retrieval from the temperature dataloggers. Katie and Drake MacFarland worked hard to improve the figures for publication by cleaning and editing the images. Thanks to Sarah Luchetta for assembling all of this and getting into print.

Hiking and Documentation

Thanks especially to Ken Gates for sharing our campfires and leading us to so many sites. Thanks for John Murray, Merry Austin, Grace and Paul Schoonover, Joan Clark, Charlie Gilbert, and other members of the Arizona Archaeological and Historical Society and the Arizona Archaeological Society in the early years. Ken Fite, Elaine Halbedel, Cherie Freeman, Mary Cuming, Bob Conforti, Pete Yonsetto, and Mark Conti were of great assistance in the later years—always willing to take a hike here or there and do any needed mapping or documentation.

Volunteers, whether formally or informally recruited, students or members from the general public at large, have been the backbone of this project over its many years. The companionship around the campfire has been welcome and wonderful, and the extra company, even just to have another person along, has been indispensable. Volunteers have endured some brutal hikes in cold, rain, snow, and heat. They have helped take tedious notes and measurements, and lent their enthusiasm and curiosity to the tasks at hand. To those who came to the project through Earthwatch or other means during the 1995 and 1996 years, the SAP owes a particular helping of gratitude. Not only did they participate in person in many important phases of the project, but also their financial assistance made it possible to purchase equipment, hire the personnel to supervise and feed them, and conduct other aspects of the project that were impossible without funding.

Thanks particularly to the crew chiefs and cooks during the 1995 and 1996 seasons, for adapting so well to a difficult situation and making it all such a great success.

Logistics

Thanks to personnel from the Tonto National Forest for providing permits and other critical support and interest in the project—Martin McAllister, J. Scott Wood, Steve Germick, and Howard Okamoto. The Mercer family at the Rock House Gas and Grocery has been of immense help over the years—a last fill-up, emergency supplies, a welcome shower, fixed flats, and a food freezer to reduce the number of trips all the way into Globe. Thanks to the Ellison family for providing food storage and water, and for pulling various vehicles and people out of Cherry Creek, and for being there in case of a serious emergency. Rebecca and Richard Bernal of El Rey Motel in Globe provided us a base to regroup and meet people, a home from time to time, and gave freely of ice, water, and hospitality. Thanks to Roger Irwin, Carla Van West and the Amaterra group for setting up the fabulous base camp in 1995 and 1996. Jeff Altschul assisted by supporting the project and permitting staff from Statistical Research, Inc., to participate. Thanks to Agnese Haury for her support and interest in the project over the years, and finally, thanks to Emil Haury for blazing the trails!

Professional Assistance

Bob Scarborough was an immense help in creating our understanding of the local geology. Craig Howe provided invaluable assistance in understanding the engineering and capacity of the cliff dwelling roofs. Bruce and Lisa Huckell interpreted the environmental potential for us. Many others, including Rick Ahlstrom, Mike McComas, Stephanie Whittlesey, John Welch, William Deaver, and John Madsen shared their thoughts and expertise with us.

Supporting Cast

Finally, thanks to Chuck Adams for allowing me to pursue this research, and for understanding how important it is to me. And, most gratefully, thanks to my wife, Chris, for the care, love, help, and support she has given over the long period of time she has endured the creation and completion of this report. She has contributed to this report in so many ways.

Chapter One
Previous Work and Project History

The Sierra Ancha (Spanish for "wide mountain") is in central Arizona, east of a mid-line in the state (Figs.1.1-1.2). It is a high mountain range below the Mogollon Rim, and is north and east of the confluence of Tonto Creek and the Salt River—present day Roosevelt Lake. Vegetation zones on the mountain vary from Lower and Upper Sonoran desert communities on the southern and western flanks and lower elevations to ponderosa pine forest and Canadian and Hudsonian Life Zones at the highest elevations (Lowe 1964). The name "Sierra Ancha" appears on maps as early as 1879, but "no one can say how the range came to be so called"(Barnes 1988:404).

The Sierra Ancha is located in an interesting position with respect to the major prehistoric cultures recognized by archaeologists. From one extreme to the other, the southeastern Sierra Ancha either lies in the "no-mans" land between traditionally recognized Hohokam, Salado, and Mogollon "culture areas" or within boundaries claimed by one or more. Redman (1993:12) sees the area as being at the junction of Mogollon and Salado and nothing. Reid and Whittlesey (1999:4) believe the area is totally Salado and Mogollon. Stark (1995:346) indicates no particular association for the area, but it is close to Mogollon and Salado. Finally, Wood (1985a: Figure 1) shows lower and middle Cherry Creek at the junction of Hohokam, Mogollon, and "Anchan" cultures.

In the history of US Southwestern archaeology, the Sierra Ancha is significant because it is the area where tree-ring dating was first successfully applied away from areas above the Mogollon Rim where the technique and chronology had been established. Archaeologically, the Sierra Ancha is important for addressing the confusion just noted. How does the Sierra Ancha fit into local and regional chronologies, who were the people living there, and how, if at all, do the boundaries and people change through time? The tree-ring dates from cliff dwellings in the Sierra Ancha should make it possible to provide some refinement of timing, changes, and boundaries in the regional chronology.

It must be clearly stated that the Sierra Ancha Project (SAP) described in this report is focused heavily on the cliff dwellings in the southeastern portion of the Sierra Ancha. Other site types in this area are considered, but there is no attempt to address the archaeology and culture history of the entire mountain range. The work presented here provides another piece of the puzzle for understanding the ebb and flow of history in this portion of east-central Arizona.

Cliff dwellings and romanticized cliff dwellers have been in the national psyche since the early descriptions of places such as Bandelier and Mesa Verde national monuments (Bandelier 1971; Nordenskiold 1973), and the cliff dwellers of the Mexican Sierra Madre (Blackiston 1905, 1909). There is also a common misperception in the general public that cliff dwellings are a cultural stage in the

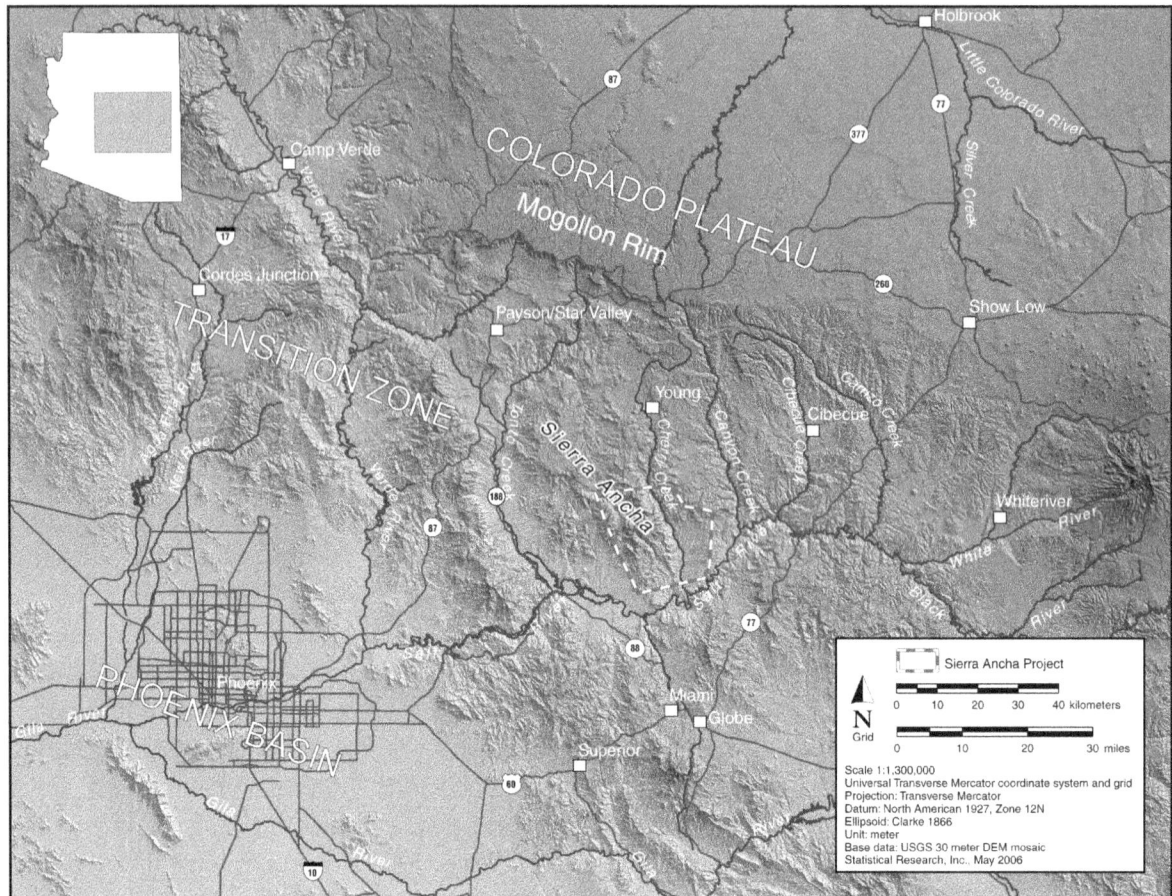

Figure 1.1. General Location of the Sierra Ancha (2004-1733-image4153) This figure is the sole property of Statistical Research, Inc., and may not be reproduced without its permission.

prehistoric occupation of the US Southwest (see also Smith 1973:xi-xiv, and Snead 2001: xxiii, 5, 7). Understanding the history and roles of such sites anywhere in the Southwest is certainly a challenge—in terms of placing them into regional contexts, as well as the basic logistics of studying them. The following sections detail previous archaeological work in the southeastern Sierra Ancha and the beginnings and evolution of the SAP.

ARCHAEOLOGICAL WORK IN THE SOUTHEASTERN SIERRA ANCHA AND VICINITY

Earliest Visitors and Descriptions

The earliest recorded visitors or descriptions

begin in the late 1800s. Several of the visitors were scientific observers, but most were just curious and adventuresome souls, many of whom lived in the local area.

Hope, Nordhoff, and USGS

The earliest record, and in fact the earliest inscription other than the prehistoric rock art, was found in one of the cliff dwellings (V:1:170 [see Preface: Technical Issues]) in Coon Creek, a drainage on the southern slopes of the Sierra Ancha. William Hope and Walter Nordhoff scratched their names and a date of November 19, 1880, on the back wall of a room in the cliff (Fig. 7.31b). They were on a reconnaissance for the newly formed US Geological Survey (USGS) to identify and map various mineral resources. Nordhoff was the official USGS

Figure 1.2. View of the Southeastern Sierra Ancha (2004-1733-image1036)

representative and probably employee; Hope seems to have been a local more familiar with the area. They appear to have been particularly interested in identifying potential gold prospects. No formal report has been located from their work on the south slopes of the Sierra Ancha, and there is no evidence that they sketched or photographed anything they may have seen. There is also no indication that they visited any of the other cliff dwellings or sites in the southeastern Sierra Ancha.

Adolph Bandelier

During his travels throughout the US Southwest, Bandelier passed through the Tonto Basin and spent several days visiting and describing the sites there. On May 24, 1883, he visited the upper and lower ruins at what would become Tonto National Monument (Bandelier 1890-92; Lange and Riley 1970:112-113). In the journal entries for his time in the Tonto Basin, Bandelier notes, in terms of sites in the area, that "while there are some around the Sierra Ancha, the heart of the Sierra itself is too rugged and precipitous to leave room for human abodes" (Lange and Riley 1970:116). However, other entries clearly contradict this. The entries also indicate that he was getting information from a wide variety of local residents regarding sites in the Sierra Ancha. Bandelier (Lange and Riley 1970:124) cites a Mr. Marbaix for information that "in the Sierra Ancha, north of the canyon of the Salt River, there are still ruins of large houses several stories high." Clearly, many sites were well known and were probably regularly visited by a significant number of people, even at this early point in time.

Other Tourists and Visitors

Travis "Buster" Ellison (Slim Ellison's younger brother) and Emil Haury told the author that Dewey Peterson (see below) guided "dudes" into the cliff dwellings, even before he toured Haury to the same dwellings. There are dates of 1914 and 1919 in pencil and charcoal among the modern signatures in Pueblo Canyon.

One of the more important visits to the cliff dwellings during this early period was by Victor L. Ackland and a small party in April, 1921. Ackland was a Hollywood cinematographer with several silent films to his credit (International Movie Database 2006). In the Sierra Ancha, he shot a silent film, making a movie that was never publicly released entitled *The Ancient Cliff Dwellings of America*. His descendants have recently contacted the Arizona State Museum about conserving the film and donating the still photographs derived from the film. As is evident from his signature in several cliff dwellings, and as seen in one of the still photographs, Ackland visited many of the cliff dwellings along Cherry Creek -- in Pueblo Canyon, Cooper Forks, and across from Pottery Point (Fig.1.3).

Gila Pueblo and Emil W. Haury

The Gila Pueblo Archaeological Foundation

Figure 1.3. Cinematographer Victor L. Ackland (light pants) and party at GP C:1:30, 1921 (2004-1733-image4163)

was founded by Harold S.Gladwin and Winifred MacCurdy in 1928 (Haury 1988). The foundation immediately took up the task of investigating the prehistoric cultures of the Globe/Miami and Tonto Basin areas. Gladwin had also acquired a great interest in tree-ring dating. In the winter of 1929-30, Gladwin, his wife to be (Winifred MacCurdy), and the Foundation secretary, Edith Sangster, drove down from Globe once a week to take A.E. Douglass's tree-ring course at the University of Arizona (Lange 1982a). Gladwin had received reports from local cowboys of ruins with timbers in them in the Roosevelt Lake area and was intent on having someone investigate them.

Gladwin had hired a local, George Dennis, to assist with Gila Pueblo activities in the Globe/Tonto Basin areas. George Dennis was probably responsible for Gladwin hiring Dewey Peterson, and for making the arrangements through Peterson for Haury's trip into the Sierra Ancha and Canyon Creek Ruin (Lange 1982a). Dewey Peterson was a cowboy whose family lived near Aztec Peak on the top of the Sierra Ancha (Lange 1982a). Dewey Peterson recorded sites primarily on the south face of the Sierra Ancha, around Coon Creek Butte, and on the southeastern corner of the mountain range. He recorded very little to the east of Cherry Creek, and in fact, a group of sites north of Cooper Forks was not recorded by him at all. Peterson's recording may have been limited to the cattle range he knew well. To the east and north were the ranges used by the Ellisons from the Flying V and Q ranches.

Emil W. Haury joined the staff of Gila Pueblo in June of 1930, and the Sierra Ancha trip was his second assignment (Lange and others 1983: 4). Haury first visited the cliff dwellings in the Sierra Ancha and Canyon Creek Ruin between October 2 and October 17, 1930 (see SAP archives). Dewey Peterson was his guide (Fig. 1.4).

Haury described this first trip as follows (Lange and others 1983:8):

> From [the Peterson Ranch] we went north to McFadden Horse Mountain, and several other parts of the crest of the Sierra Ancha. Then we dropped off the east side of the range, north of Pueblo Canyon and into Cherry Creek where we established camp. From our camp in Cherry Creek, we went back up into Pueblo Canyon, into Devils Chasm, and into Cold Spring Canyon. After collecting wood in ruins in each of those canyons, we set out to the east, passing south of Sombrero Butte, and on into lower Canyon Creek. After inspecting a prehistoric turquoise mine, we went up Canyon Creek to the Canyon Creek Ruin, which Dewey knew about but had not seen. We returned cross-country, almost due west, and dropped back into Cherry Creek to the Ellison Ranch where we ended the adventure.

Gila Pueblo's purpose for recording sites in the southeastern Sierra Ancha area, as well as the purpose of Haury's subsequent trip, was to evaluate the sites and assess their potential for tree-ring dating. The "gap" in the tree-ring chronology between the prehistoric and modern sequences had just been bridged in the summer of 1929 (Haury 1986).

Haury was asked if they had been able to take animals into the sites in the Sierra Ancha. Haury replied no and that he could not imagine getting animals to those sites. Peterson must have done it though, because there is a belly of a mule or donkey showing in one of the photographs from Pueblo Canyon (Fig. 1.5).

Based on this reconnaissance, Gila Pueblo, under Haury's direction, conducted excavations at Canyon Creek Ruin in 1932. However, the expedition was not outfitted by Dewey Peterson, it was handled by Slim Ellison (Ellison 1968; Fig. 1.6; CD01). Buster Ellison remembered marveling at how Haury had calculated everything down to the last strip of bacon! Haury, Russell Hastings, Solon T.

Figure 1.4. Dewey Peterson at GP C:1:8 (ASM Negative 71107)

Figure 1.5. Pack Animal in AZ V:1:131 (ASM), Pueblo Canyon (ASM Negative 71116)

Figure 1.6. Gila Pueblo Pack Train Enroute to Canyon Creek (ASM Negative 71179)

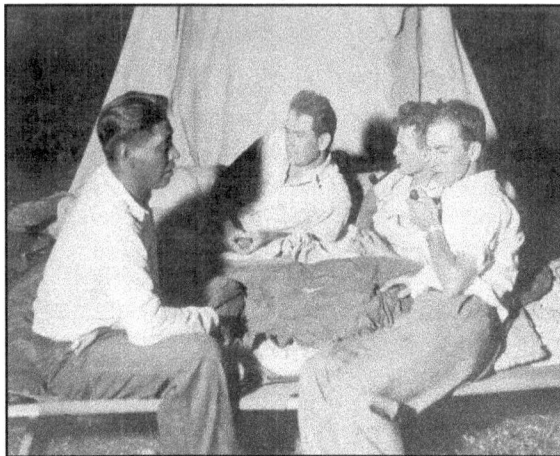

Figure 1.7. Gila Pueblo Crew at Canyon Creek Ruin (L to R: Jones Williams, Emil Haury, Solon Kimball, Russell Hastings) (ASM Negative 71190)

Kimball, and Jones Williams (a Pima Indian working at Gila Pueblo) were the excavation crew (Fig. 1.7). This work, and some of the basic information gathered by Dewey Peterson and Haury in the Sierra Ancha sites, was published as Gila Pueblo Medallion Paper #14 (Haury 1934). The reporting was limited, however. Only the first 22 of the 173 pages in the report concern the Sierra Ancha sites. This was the only formal publication concerning the archaeology of this area until the Cholla Project reports were published in 1982 (see below and Reid 1982a).

Byron Cummings

Byron Cummings became the Director of the

Arizona State Museum (ASM) and the founder of the Department of Archaeology at the University of Arizona in 1915. Haury gained his first exposure to archaeology with Cummings at Cuicuilco in the Valley of Mexico in 1925 (Haury 2004), and was among the first masters students in the department. Haury ultimately left the University of Arizona to join Gladwin and Gila Pueblo. Within months after Haury's initial trip into the southeastern Sierra Ancha, Byron Cummings followed. Cummings (1930: 43) journal notes from the trip mention that Haury had taken tree-ring samples from many of the beams in Pueblo Canyon. Haury acknowledged that he was probably aware of the trip, but did not know any specific reason for it (Lange and others 1983:9).

Cummings' group visited rock art on Cherry Creek (V:5:160 and 161 and other sites), Granite Basin Pueblo (V:1:26), the cliff dwellings in Horse and Willow canyons (V:2:64 and V:1:49), Rock House Pueblo (V:1:33), and 6 Caves Ruin (V:1:144), in Buster Canyon. Before completing the trip, the group also visited cliff dwellings in Grindstone (Cold Spring) and Pueblo canyons.

On the way between Granite Basin and Willow Canyon, Cummings camped for two nights below Mustang Ridge (Soldier Creek). In what he called the Sombrero Butte Ruins, they excavated one room completely and another partially. There are three principal cliff dwelling sites at this location (GP C:1:38, GP C:1:47, and GP C:1:50), but it is unclear where the excavations occurred. Buster Ellison stated that Cummings also excavated at Pottery Point (GP C:1:31; Lange and Murphy 1982:9-10), but this is not confirmed in Cummings' notes.

Correspondence continued for several years between Slim Ellison and Cummings (1931-1936:Item 15). They discussed possible protection of Granite Basin Pueblo through an Ellison mining claim, Ellison's monitoring of the ruin and nearly continual efforts to run off pothunters, and Cummings potentially paying Ellison to monitor and perhaps even dig in the ruin. Cummings clearly hoped to return to Granite Basin Pueblo, but work at Kinishba and many other endeavors and life events apparently prevented this from happening.

Arizona State University Field Schools

Arizona State University archaeological field schools were based in the Vosberg/Walnut Creek area west of Q Ranch in upper Cherry Creek. Students conducted survey and excavations at sites in the area from 1967 to 1970, with additional work in 1974. One of the striking discoveries is apparently side-by-side Hohokam and Anasazi/Mogollon architecture at Walnut Creek Village (AZ P:13:1 [ASU]; Morris 1970). Work at this locality is summarized in a number of papers and publications (Cartledge 1976, Chenhall 1972, Dittert n.d., Harris 1974, and Morris 1969, 1970).

Helga Teiwes and the US Forest Service

Helga Teiwes, ASM photographer, and several personnel from the US Forest Service made a trip into the Tonto Basin and southeastern Sierra Ancha in October 1969. They hiked into Pueblo Canyon by going up the bottom of the canyon, and visited sites on a lower terrace (V:1:124-127) as well as the main sites on the north side (V:1:130-132). It was a wet day, with mixed rain and hail. Not being able to get back up Cherry Creek the following day due to the storm and runoff, they concentrated on visiting sites in the Tonto Basin. Helga Teiwes photographs from this trip are ASM negative numbers 24805 to 24867.

Haury's Second Trip

Haury's second trip into the southeastern Sierra Ancha was in May, 1970. The group visited Hematite House (V:5:61) on Coon Creek, V:1:136 in Cold Spring Canyon, and the sites in Devils Chasm (V:1:167 and V:1:168), all places that Helga Teiwes and her group had been unable to get to during the during the previous October trip. Helga Teiwes produced a number of photographs from this trip as well--ASM negative numbers 27083 to 27148.

The SAP obtained copies of the Gila Pueblo and Helga Teiwes photographs of the sites. These photographs proved valuable for comparing site condition from 1929-30 to 1969-70 to 1981, and sometimes for locating sites using the surrounding landforms visible in the photographs.

Wesley Wells

Wells conducted a survey along the first terraces of lower Cherry Creek in 1970-71. This produced an oft-cited student paper (unpublished: Wells 1971) describing the sites and settlement history in that part of Cherry Creek and how those sites may relate to regional prehistory.

The Cholla Project

In the 1970s, archaeological work was done for an Arizona Public Service (APS) and Salt River Project (SRP) powerline passing through east-central Arizona. The line runs from the Cholla Plant near St. Johns AZ to south of Roosevelt Lake, where the SRP portion of the line splits off and runs to Phoenix. The APS portion continues to the Saguaro Station near Red Rock AZ.

Archaeological survey and mitigation work was done under contract to APS by the ASM Cultural Resource Management Division. The archaeological survey was done between 1974 and 1977 (Teague and Mayro 1979), and mitigation fieldwork was done from 1977 to 1979 (Reid 1982a). The author became successively involved as a crewmember (1977), crew chief (1977-78), and writer (1978-79) for the archaeological mitigation crews.

The author worked in the area of the line between Roosevelt Lake and the Mogollon Rim. The field work involved survey of areas to be impacted by roads, towers, and center span clearing, and of nearby areas to collect comparative information; testing of small sites and scatters; and mapping and documentation of numerous surface ruins as well as several cliff dwellings. The field crews lived in camps on private land in the Tonto Basin and later at the Rock House, south of the Q Ranch. This was the beginning of the author's interest in and curiosity about this area.

Specific interests in the Sierra Ancha cliff dwellings arose because of the Cholla Project. Richard Ciolek-Torrello and the author sought to tie together two project areas along the power line as reports were being prepared for the Q Ranch and Black Mesa segments of the project. Survey records and artifacts from the Gila Pueblo Foundation surveys (1929 and 1930) in the southeastern Sierra Ancha and middle Cherry Creek areas became part of the comparative materials. The Gila Pueblo materials had been transferred to ASM upon the closing of Gila Pueblo in 1950-51 (Haury 1988).The information from the Gila Pueblo surveys and the small survey on lower Cherry Creek (Wells 1971) was all that was available for the area between the two Cholla Project areas. The Gila Pueblo information was summarized and the ceramics in the survey collections were analyzed and presented as part of the final reports for the Cholla Project (Ciolek-Torrello and Lange 1982). The information was later reworked as a journal article (Ciolek-Torrello and Lange 1990).

Beginnings of the Sierra Ancha Project

The Gila Pueblo data for the southeastern Sierra Ancha contained artifacts, site records, and photographs. Summarizing the Gila Pueblo records had highlighted the shortcomings of these records. A plan was developed to visit the Gila Pueblo cliff dwellings in the middle Cherry Creek/southeastern Sierra Ancha area in June of 1981. This would be a chance to verify and update site information (particularly by mapping the sites in detail and getting a photographic record of the current condition of the sites). A small grant was received from the University of Arizona Vice-President for Research Office to support nearly three weeks of work in June, 1981. This initial work was done by Lange and Barbara Murphy.

The original plan was to visit all of the main canyons, but it became clear that each site required more time than initially anticipated, so the focus shifted to Pueblo and Cold Spring canyons (see Appendix I: Table 1). Return trips were made soon after the first trip, and were repeated frequently to finish up one aspect or another of the documentation or to get to sites not yet visited. Work was done as time was available, and often in conjunction with leading hiking tours to various sites. This piecemeal approach continued to the end of the project, with the exception of two major undertakings in the 1990s (see below).

Beam replacement (V:1:136), 1983

Repairs were made to the cliff dwelling labeled V:1:136 in Cold Spring Canyon. The site was constructed in a narrow cleft in a cliff in the Mescal Limestone (see Fig. III.15). A main roof beam along the hatch in Room 1 was severely damaged by insects and water.

A proposal was made to the Tonto National Forest that this beam be replaced in order to preserve the entire site. An initial inspection was made in September, 1982, and the beam was replaced in late October, 1983. The replacement beam was dragged up the old mine road behind a horse. The haul up the last slope was done with a pulley tied into a small tree, and a rope around the beam at one end and tied to the horse at the other. The final task of getting the new beam into the cliff dwelling had to be done manually by four people (Fig. 1.8).

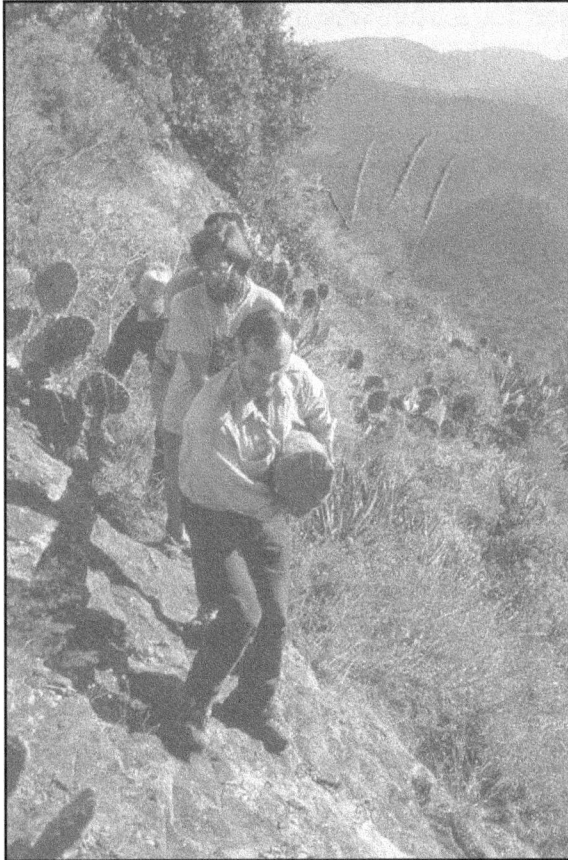

Figure 1.8. Carrying Replacement Beam for AZ V:1:136 (ASM) (2004-1733-image1747)

Two important pieces of information were learned from this experience. First, none of the original beams in these cliff dwellings had been dragged on the ground. Dragging leaves many gouges and scars that are lacking on the roof beams in the Sierra Ancha. Second, moving a moderate-sized beam around on the hillside was a major undertaking. Two people might be able to carry a beam on the flat or in the open, but working around rocks and bushes on a steep slope requires more hands for support and balance. This would have required most members of one nuclear family or the coopera-tion of members of several families.

Statistical Research, Inc., October 1991

The Tonto National Forest solicited proposals in July 1991 for work in four of the cliff dwelling sites in the southeastern Sierra Ancha. The goals of the project involved photography and architectural assessments, and preparation of exhibits and brochures for the trailheads. The contract was awarded to Statistical Research, Inc. The author was hired as a consultant to guide the crew into the sites and to provide information and maps that had been produced by the SAP. The four sites were V:1:167 in Devils Chasm, V:1:136 in Cold Spring Canyon, V:1:134 in Pueblo Canyon, and V:1:130-132 in Pueblo Canyon (Note: V:1:130-132 are grouped under a single site number in both the Gila Pueblo site numbering system [as GP C:1:16] and the Tonto National Forest system [AR-03-12-05-25]). A final summary of this work was prepared by Robert Vint (1993).

Earthwatch 1995 and 1996

A documentation project involving volunteers from Earthwatch was in the field in 1995 and 1996. The plan was for two teams of 10-12 volunteers per team, two weeks for each team, for a total of four weeks of fieldwork each season. About half of the team each week were independent volunteers, half were from Earthwatch in 1995. In 1996, the teams were mostly Earthwatch volunteers.

A Challenge Cost-Share grant from the Tonto National Forest was also secured for the first season. For the 1996 field season, help was supplied in the form of two US Government vehicles and a high-volume water pump to lift water up to camp from Cherry Creek.

The 1995 and 1996 Field Seasons
With Earthwatch and independent volunteers,

the SAP was finally able to mount a large and sustained project to document the Sierra Ancha cliff dwellings and other sites. An ambitious work plan was developed, not knowing how well volunteers and staff would hold up to the rigors of a primitive camp and extremely challenging logistics of getting into and out of the sites.

A base camp ("Camp Gladwin") was established on a terrace on the west side of Cherry Creek, north of the Ellison Ranch. This was a relatively "central" location for the anticipated work, and was in one of the few flat locations for a camp of the anticipated size (CD02; CD03).

The goals of the 1995 and 1996 field seasons were to revisit all cliff dwellings documented by the SAP to check maps and do additional documentation with new recording forms, to formally survey new areas in middle Cherry Creek, and to map the new sites and many of those not already mapped. The proposed 1995 work plan and the actual fieldwork are compared in Appendix I: Table 2. The shift away from the work plan began relatively early in the field season, as the emphasis shifted to completing work in Pueblo Canyon before moving on to other sites. Between the 1995 and 1996 seasons, several trips were made into the area. The primary purpose was to retrieve data from the temperature recording devices (dataloggers) that were put in place in late 1995. The second season was more flexible, allowing for completion of sites begun in 1995 or not yet addressed at all, as well as survey in areas along Cherry Creek. The purpose of the survey was to locate new sites on the landscape, and as an additional benefit, to evaluate the completeness of the recording of surface sites by Gila Pueblo. The 1996 original work plan and subsequent adjustments to it are presented in Appendix I: Table 3.

1996 To Present

After the 1996 field season, trips were made to monitor the dataloggers, and to tie up loose ends in documenting the various sites. This report covers project activities and data up to July 1, 2004. Any additional activities that may occur will be added to the project archives and summarized in other formats.

Chapter Two
Project Activities

This project was stimulated by the mapping and documentation work conducted on the Cholla Project in the cliff dwellings in Horse and Willow canyons (V:1:49 and V:2:64) and for sites like Castle Peak (V:1:34) and Gunsight Butte (V:1:74) (Reid 1982b). The SAP began with the goals of relocating the cliff dwellings recorded by Gila Pueblo, mapping them in detail, doing basic architectural documentation, and creating a photographic record of their condition. It was quickly apparent that there were other sites to be recorded; more information that could be gained from each site, particularly in terms of tree-ring studies; and that it would take longer to relocate and document the sites than initially planned.

The relatively long timeframe over which the SAP was conducted led to numerous trips into the area (see SAP archives). The trips occurred at different times of year and under varying weather conditions. The variations in season, temperature, precipitation, and daylight encountered have given a better understanding of this area and the human occupation there than could be gained from a single visit.

The following sections describe the activities done by the project: hiking and camping, site recording, mapping, photography, tree-ring studies, architectural documentation, collecting, and temperature studies. All of these activities have been important in documenting and preserving each of these different kinds of information about the sites. The data collected are the greatest legacy of the SAP. Copies of project records and data are curated in the ASM Archives, and also have been provided to the Tonto National Forest, Phoenix.

HIKING

Getting to or finding the sites requires hiking. Even with primitive roads providing access, the southeastern Sierra Ancha is one of the most remote areas of Arizona. At Tonto National Monument or the Gila Cliff Dwellings, visitors arrive by vehicle, park in a space near a visitor center, and follow a paved or prepared trail to the sites. Some, like Tonto National Monument, actually involve some elevation gain. Keet Seel and Betatakin, cliff dwellings at Navaho National Monument in northeastern Arizona, are serious hikes, with one steep, sandy, 180m elevation change in particular. However, apart from this obstacle, the hike is on relatively level ground. Haury described his trip into Devils Chasm in the southeastern Sierra Ancha as "the most difficult of access I have ever been to" (Gila Pueblo site form for GP C:1:44).

Moving around in the canyons and on the general landscape of the southeastern Sierra Ancha was instructive in terms of where various resources were located, particularly water and seeps, and the effort required to get from one place to another. In the sense of the prehistoric residents of this area, this knowledge can be projected to include a better understanding of the effort required to collect and transport a variety of resources—from clay to wood, water, and stone.

The cliff dwellings in the main canyons are a minimum of two to two-and-a-half hours one-way from the nearest parking locations. These two hours involve ascending over 400m in elevation. For a modern-day, sessile office worker, hikes of this magnitude and effort are rather onerous undertakings. If one is in good shape, however, or has become conditioned to such activities, the hikes are not so difficult. Through personal observation and documented travel and load data for Tarahumara in Mexico (Fisher 2003: Search for the Horizon Line) and Nepalese porters (Malville 2003: Long-distance Transport of Goods in Prehistoric North America), it is clear that distances covered and loads carried are often far greater than is assumed for prehistoric peoples (Lightfoot 1979). These data are in no way intended to minimize the accomplishments of the prehistoric builders of the Sierra Ancha cliff dwellings. Their efforts and accomplishments were at a level difficult to imagine.

For the 1995 and 1996 field seasons, most of the staff tried to get into shape beforehand. Many of the volunteers did, too, but some staff and volunteers struggled anyway. At the beginning of the second team (after two weeks of hiking for the staff), it was noticeable how much better conditioned the staff had become. On the other hand, even with good boots and socks and a day or two of rest every week, after four weeks of hiking in 1995, it was time for a break. Although the prehistoric residents could move around the landscape with relative ease, they probably did so no more frequently than was necessary.

Water can be readily found in the canyons and at many seeps. The seeps in Pueblo Canyon proved to be the most reliable. Without clearing vegetation and moss to increase the flow, it is possible to collect 300ml of water within 1.5 to 4 minutes (V:1:132 and V:1:134, respectively) essentially any time of the year. Pueblo Canyon has an additional water source at the elevation of the principal sites, only 10 to 15 minutes from the sites—the waterfall and pool at the head of the lower canyon. At the waterfall, there is generally water flowing except during occasional severely dry periods.

SITE RECORDING

At the time of the Gila Pueblo survey (1929-30), there were no 15- or 7.5-minute topographic maps of the area. Site locations recorded in the ASM site files were not accurate, and other sources were inaccurate as well. In Haury's publication (1934:2), Cooper Fork [sic] is located too far north, sites GP C:1:8 and C:1:14 are reversed, and GP C:1:46 should be up-canyon from GP C:1:36 in Cold Spring Canyon. Devils Chasm is noted as the north fork of the major canyon south of Cold Spring Canyon, and Dripping Springs is the south fork. This is the reverse of these canyon names on modern USGS maps. In Bannister and Robinson (1971:7) sites GP C:1:8 and 14 are reversed, and sites GP C:1:46 and C:1:36, like in Haury (1934:2), are not located properly relative to each other. Determining accurate site locations is important for understanding settlement patterns, and for managing the archaeological resources.

At the time of the initial work (1981), there were no global positioning (GPS) units. In 1996, GPS units were tested, but with the scrambled signals and limited views to the horizon, the coordinates obtained were not satisfactory. An attempt to use altimeters to better control elevation was also unsuccessful, because of being unable to track temperature and pressure fluctuations in two locations at once during the course of the day. Some rough triangulation with a surveying instrument generally confirmed elevations that were suspected for sites in the major canyons, but plotting the sites was done using 7.5-minute USGS topographic maps and the landscape.

Site recording was done initially by completing ASM site cards. Later, Tonto National Forest site forms were used. Sites were given field numbers (SA – x) and ASM site numbers (AZ V:1:x [ASM]). Many of the sites had Gila Pueblo numbers (GP C:1:x) as well as Tonto National Forest numbers (AR-03-12-05-x). Site number concordances and other site data are given in Appendix II. ASM site numbers and site names are used in the discussions that follow (but are abbreviated, see Preface: Technical Issues).

Surveying

The early part of the project involved informal surveys. Sites were found and recorded while going from one place to another or while looking for a particular site. Binocular surveys were also done across canyons and to other exposed cliffs, trying to locate standing walls or suspicious rubble that would lead to an actual visit to the location. No cliff dwellings or other sites were located in this manner. Two more formal surveys were done early in the project.

One was to locate Pottery Point Pueblo; the other was done on the flats, terraces, and ridges west of Cherry Creek, across from Banning Wash. A relatively small area was examined, and approximately a dozen sites were recorded. The latter survey was the precursor to a more formal survey done in conjunction with the 1996 field season. In 1996, surveys were conducted around Granite Basin Pueblo, and on the east and west sides of Cherry Creek above and below Banning Wash. These surveys were systematic, with transects formally covering the larger slopes and terraces, until the mesquite and prickly pear cactus made

it impossible (roughly at the break in slope between the terraces and steeper slopes leading up to higher ridges). Over 40 new sites were recorded by the 1996 surveys. With the SAP surveys and Wells (1971) earlier survey, a representative picture of sites and settlement patterns is beginning to emerge. However, 100 percent survey coverage is lacking for most of the Cherry Creek drainage.

MAPPING

Haury's 1934 publication contained maps of several of the cliff dwellings—derived from sketches and measurements done during his visit to the sites in 1930. These maps convey the basic plan of the sites, but they were not formally measured. Accurately mapping sketched and unmapped sites was one of the major activities of the SAP.

Mapping was usually done with a Brunton compass mounted on a tripod and a 30-m or 50-m measuring tape. This set up had the advantage of being accurate, highly portable, and the tripod could be used as a photographic tripod as well. Tape triangulation was occasionally used in particularly tight areas. Eventually, a theodolite and electronic distance meter (EDM) were used to map two large sites with extensive relief (Cock's Comb Ridge, V:1:145, and Elephant Rock Fortress, V:1:160). The theodolite and EDM were also used to tie together the compounds near the Ellison Ranch, and to map the compound with the small mound (Cherry Creek Mound Site, V:1:191).

Measurements to corners, walls, door edges, and the cliff face can be thought of as baseball "strike-zone" measurements. That is, distances were recorded to points at these various features somewhere between the knees and chest-high. Doing the measurements in this manner is the best approximation of usable space available to a standing person. Significant undercuts in the masonry walls or in the cliff faces were noted as encountered. All the points measured at a site were plotted by hand on graph paper at a scale of 1 in = 2m or 1 in = 4 m. Conventions were developed that indicate bonded or abutted corners, filled and open doorways, and existing or suspected wall locations (Fig. 2.1). The SAP generated more than 90 site maps.

After the pencil draft maps were done, inked copies of the maps were created on alba-nene. These were then scaled and converted to

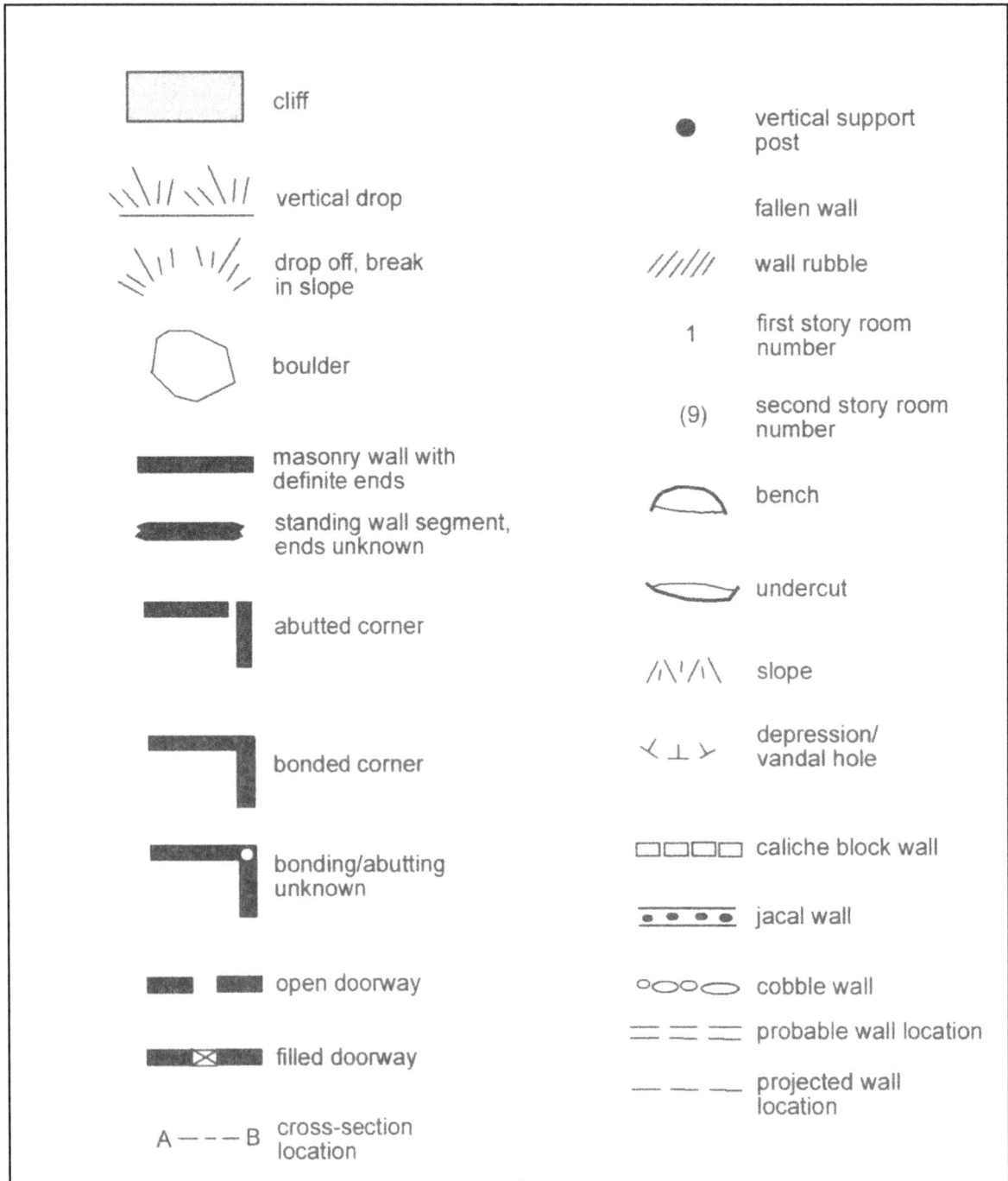

Figure 2.1. Key for Site Maps (2004-1733-image3981)

Photo Mechanical Transfers (PMTs) in an 8½ x 11 in format or smaller. The PMT versions of the maps were scanned, making them available as digital images (see Appendix III).

The SAP undertook two other mapping projects. After working in the Sierra Ancha cliff dwellings, where the majority of the room corners are abutted walls, and an earlier trip to Canyon Creek Ruin where this also seemed to be the case, it was interesting to see a map of Canyon Creek Ruin (V:2:1) indicating mostly bonded corners. During a subsequent trip to the site with the University of Arizona Grasshopper Field School during the summer of 1988, the site was formally mapped. A slight adjustment in number of rooms was made, and a more realistic map of the rooms and walls was achieved. It is uncertain if the new map (see Fig. III.23a) would alter any of the conclusions reached by Graves (1982).

During a visit to the Upper Ruin (U:8:48) at Tonto National Monument, it was clear that the map in Steen and others (1962) did not match the architecture there. Walls had been added during the National Park Service stabilization process, and one wall, in particular, was depicted as at least twice its actual width. This distortion was probably the result of the original mapping, most likely done with a plane table and alidade. Ironically, remapping the Upper Ruin produced exactly the same result, but this time the distortion was due to differential floor elevations and a very tall, leaning wall that exaggerated the wall width when measured from opposite sides at different elevations (Fig. 2.2). The distortion was corrected and the new map is included as Fig. III.24a.

PHOTOGRAPHY

Photographic documentation is another important aspect of the SAP. There were several goals for the photography. One was to replicate the Gila Pueblo photographs and those taken by

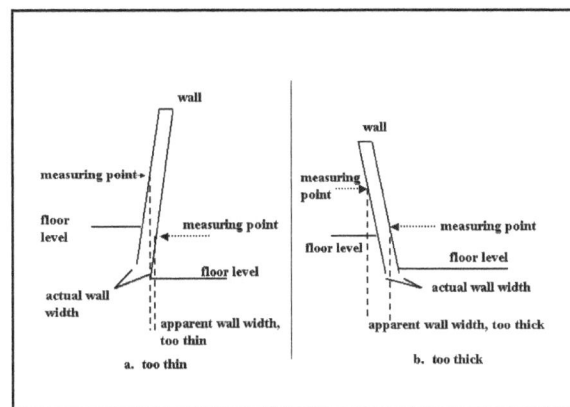

Figure 2.2. Leaning Wall Measurements (a = Too Thin, 2004-1733-image3982; b = Too Thick, 2004-1733-image3983)

Helga Teiwes in 1969 and 1970. Comparing the new to the older photographs would reveal any changes in site condition or integrity. Another goal was to provide documentation of current site condition. This was accomplished with general, overall views as well as wall-by-wall photography, with interior and exterior views, and close-ups of interesting details.

The SAP photography primarily involved standard formats and films. The majority of the photography was done with Olympus OM-1, 35mm cameras by Barbara Murphy. Films used were usually Kodak Plus-X Pan (ASA 125) film for the black and white photography, and Kodak Kodachrome (ASA 64) film for the color slides. Work at the SAP sites, since 1981 (excluding the 1995 and 1996 work), generated over 1000 black and white photographs and over 1000 color slides. The 1995 and 1996 field seasons created 1677 black and white shots and 1153 color shots (see SAP archives for photographic roll and shot inventories).

WOOD STUDIES

The Sierra Ancha played an important role in the early days of tree-ring dating. Samples collected from beams in the Sierra Ancha cliff dwellings proved that the newly established tree-ring chronology (1929, see Haury 1986:55-60) was applicable in areas outside of the plateau and Four Corners area where it was first developed (Haury 1934:iii-iv). There was a lot of wood that had never been sampled. Gila Pueblo sampling had been done by Dewey Peterson with a hand saw—removing wedges or whole ends of beams. Haury's sampling for Gila Pueblo had been done with a 1-inch (2.5 cm) hollow tube coring bit, powered by hand with a carpenter's brace.

Exhaustive sampling was critical for several reasons. First, all visible wood needed to be sampled before it decayed further due to insects and weathering, was totally destroyed by fire (campers' fires or forest fires), or was lost by removal. There is a story that a fir log from a cliff dwelling in Devils Chasm had been removed by a California "fiddle maker" (see Haury's Supplemental Site Form for GP C:1: 45). Second, the Gila Pueblo samples had focused on only the major (primary) beams, and were usually recorded only by site, not by room. By re-sampling beams, the SAP hoped to match previously dated samples to particular beams and rooms, and perhaps extend the ring sequence available for particular beams to provide better dates. Third, by sampling all visible wood, the project might gain additional dates, and at the very least, could identify species used to better understand construction preferences and procurement strategies.

Fortunately for the SAP, the University of Arizona Laboratory of Tree-Ring Research (UALTRR) was involved in a re-assessment of all materials from this general geographical area, and was glad for the opportunity to get better proveniences for earlier samples in order to fine tune the dating of these sites. Over 500 (N=505) samples were submitted to the UALTRR (see SAP archives). Many matches between the earlier and SAP samples were made, therefore providing better proveniences

for the Gila Pueblo samples. Unfortunately, few new dates were obtained, because many of the smaller beams had less than the 25 rings required to satisfy the UALTRR dating criteria. Species identifications were made for all of the SAP wood samples.

McGehee (1983, 1984) conducted a study of living trees in Pueblo Canyon as a class project. The purpose was to determine if ring-growth patterns in the living trees were similar to patterns in the archaeological beams. Although the study was unable to compare the actual ring-growth patterns, the tree-ring sequences from living trees in the lower portion of the canyon (at the elevation of the cliff dwellings) and the sequences from trees in the upper portion (near to and above the water fall) were both sensitive climatic recorders. Thus, the sensitive archaeological trees could have come from these relatively close-by locations, as well as from other locations farther away and higher on the mountain.

Punzmann (1982, 1986) assisted in the collection of tree-ring samples and data from Pueblo Canyon. His studies provided the basic analysis and interpretation of the tree-ring materials for V:1:130-132 in Pueblo Canyon. Punzmann's dates confirmed many of the earlier Haury (1934) dates, and were further confirmed by the UALTRR. In an effort to increase the number of dated samples, Punzmann (1986) used "tentative" dates (from short ring-count sequences) to add additional dates and bolster date clusters. Although these sequences are suggestive of additional dates, the use of tentative dates is not standard practice and only the officially accepted dates are reported and used in discussions here.

ARCHITECTURAL DOCUMENTATION

Understanding architecture and the use of materials involved in building a structure allows for a more complete view of past technologies. Architectural data are also important for future needs involving management, stabilization, and preservation (Metzger and others 1989).

General Documentation

Documenting the architectural units (rooms) was done by the mapping and photographic techniques discussed above, and by completing a form (see "Recording Forms" folder on CD: OldArchtx). Data recorded on the form included measurements for the room and its walls; the presence of rock art or painting on the walls; the presence, location, and dimensions of doorways, niches, and windows; and the relationships of walls to each other at the room corners. The form also recorded if the room was first or second story, the general condition of the room, and where it was located in the site.

Early in the project, walls were referred to by their relationships in the structure to the cardinal directions. However, as one swings around the curve of most caverns, the cliff face that was once the north or northwest wall, for example, can become the east wall. Thus, the relationships of the walls to the cliff and cavern are lost with this terminology. To clarify the wall orientations, walls were designated based on their relationship to an observer "floating" in the canyon, looking into the cliff dwelling. The first wall the observer encounters is the Front wall, the farthest away (often the cliff) is the Back wall (Fig. 2.3). On the observer's left is the Left wall, and on the right, the Right wall. Corners are therefore designated as Left Front or Right Back and so on, avoiding the difficulties with designations such as the "southeast" or "northwest" corner.

The original architecture forms (Lange 2005:Appendix VI.8) were filled out for all rooms in all sites until the 1995 and 1996 field seasons. For these field seasons, forms were used that were based on documentation

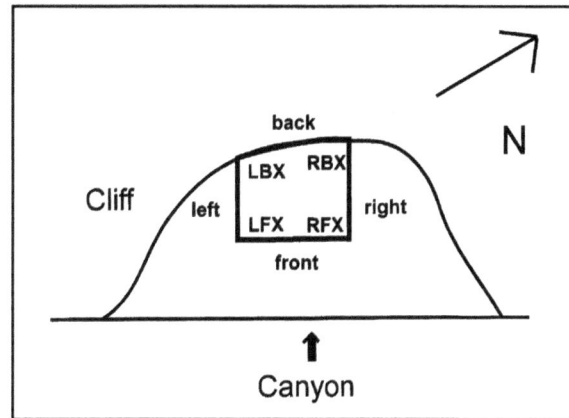

Figure 2.3. Key for Architectural Orientations and Terminology (LFX = Left Front Corner, RBX = Right Back Corner, etc.) (2004-1733-image3984)

procedures and goals used by the National Park Service (Metzger n.d., Metzger and others 1989) for sites such as Pecos and Wupatki national monuments. All of these data, except for the wall condition data, have been entered into computerized databases. Six forms were developed to record the data for six separate databases or data tables. These tables contain data for 235 structures, 840 wall surfaces, 204 features, and 63 roofs. The forms are described below:

(1) a General Structure form that records the general information about the room: condition, location in the site, type of construction, presence of roof, and so on (see "Recording Forms" folder on CD: GENSTRUC).

(2) a Wall Recording form (see "Recording Forms" folder on CD: WALLREC), with one form used for each wall and each surface (interior or exterior) of the wall. Wall dimensions, types of plastering and coursing, and presence of features in the wall are among the attributes recorded by this form.

(3) a Wall Feature form records details for features in the walls, such as doors,

vents, and niches (see "Recording Forms" folder on CD: WALLFEAT).

(4) a Roof Data form records data about a structure's roof (see "Recording Forms" folder on CD: ROOF). This can be done from actual beams still present in the room (in place or loose in the room), and also from beam holes present in the walls. From the holes, the beam sizes can be measured, beam placement can be discerned (butt vs. tip alignments), and the orientation of the primary and secondary components can be determined (Lange, Howe, and Murphy 1993).

(5) a Beam Location form that documents and provides measurements for locating primary and secondary beams (see "Recording Forms" folder on CD: BEAMLOC).

(6) a Wall Condition form (see "Recording Forms" folder on CD: WALLCOND) was completed. It details the existing condition of a wall, factors affecting its condition, and how active these factors are.

For documenting a room, with the original or any of the above forms, the perspective of the observer is moved to the interior of the room. All wall surfaces facing the inside of the room are the interior surfaces, those facing outside or belonging to the adjacent room(s), are exterior surfaces (for the subject room; what is the exterior wall surface to one room may be the interior to another). Measurements and observations are done on a wall by wall basis. Again, with the observer on the inside of the room, when documenting the Left wall, for example, the left side of that wall is at the Left Front Corner (designated "LFX") of the room, the right side or end is at the Left Back Corner (LBX)(see Fig. 2.3). When documenting the Front wall, the left end is at the RFX of the room, the right end at the LFX. A field manual

was devised for the crew chiefs and volunteers with additional definitions and guidelines for documenting the architecture and architectural features (see SAP archives).

Roofing Study

Data pertaining to the roofs were pursued further. An article about roofing a Great Kiva (Lightfoot 1988) raised questions about roofs in the Sierra Ancha. Were they built in standard ways and how sound were the engineering principles used in their construction? A study of the Sierra Ancha roofs was ultimately published in the Journal of Field Archaeology (Lange, Howe, and Murphy 1993). Roofs are also included in architectural discussions in later chapters.

COLLECTIONS

Gila Pueblo had collected small grab samples, primarily ceramics, from the Sierra Ancha sites as part of the on-going surveys and definition of cultures (Gladwin and Gladwin 1928). Most of the collections averaged less that 50 sherds per site (Ciolek-Torrello and Lange 1990:133). The ceramics were analyzed and discussed as part of the studies conducted by the Cholla Project (Ciolek-Torrello and Lange 1982) and were reconsidered in a later article as well (Ciolek-Torrello and Lange 1990). The Gila Pueblo ceramic data are included here as part of Table 4.1.

In some cases, decorated ceramics were few or missing altogether. For example, GP C:1:16W (V:1:132, the Ring-Tail Site), one of the largest cliff dwellings in the Sierra Ancha, had no decorated ceramics in the Gila Pueblo collections. Ironically, sitting in the Ring-Tail Site one evening, someone scuffed up a small piece of Gila Polychrome pottery. After passing it around, it was tossed into a nearby bush or a little downslope to prevent it from being collected illegally. The SAP ceramic collections are discussed in Chapter 4. The SAP ceramic coding conventions and raw ceramic data are in the SAP archives.

In addition to ceramics, the SAP collected other artifacts that might be removed by visitors, or, in the case of textiles and cordage, be destroyed by exposure to weathering and rodents. Collections included steatite, projectile points and other lithic artifacts, fragments of textiles and cordage, macro-botanical remains and artifacts (for example, quids, squash peduncles and rinds, corn cobs, ties, sandals, and fragments of arrows and mats), shell, and adobe pot plugs. Inventory numbers were assigned to 623 items or lots of material (see SAP archives). Included in these collections are three nearly complete vessels salvaged from pothunters' holes in V:1:174 in Cold Spring Canyon (CD21-24).

TEMPERATURE STUDIES

Cliff dwellings are often constructed in east, southeast, or south facing shelters and caves. This is said to be due to interest in passive solar heating during the winter. This reason seems to be intuitively correct, but there is little long term data with which to evaluate this hypothesis (see Adams 1979, and Christenson 1991 for additional data).

Funding circumstances for the 1995 field season made it possible to purchase three temperature recording units (dataloggers). A datalogger unit is approximately the size of a deck of cards, ideal for tucking into concealed locations. One datalogger had two channels so that a probe could be attached to record temperature up to 3m away. With a lithium battery, the dataloggers are capable of collecting data for many months before the data need to be downloaded. Downloading can be done with a laptop at the datalogger location.

Dataloggers were placed in seven different locations, with a one year long recording cycle sought from each location (Fig. 2.4). The recording interval was set at one-half hour.

The "control" datalogger was in a juniper tree on a ridge top about 1160m elevation on the south side of Pueblo Canyon (Location 1). It was not in the bottom of Cherry Creek, but was still susceptible to cold air drainage from Pueblo Canyon and the Cherry Creek valley. The other two dataloggers were moved around

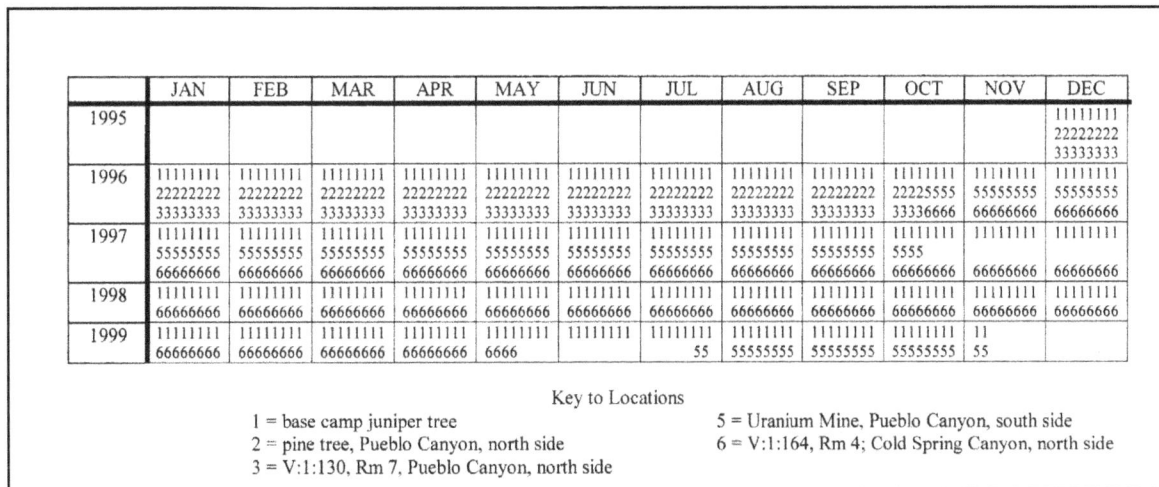

	JAN	FEB	MAR	APR	MAY	JUN	JUL	AUG	SEP	OCT	NOV	DEC
1995												11111111 22222222 33333333
1996	11111111 22222222 33333333	11111111 22222222 33333333	11111111 22222222 33333333	11111111 22222222 33333333	11111111 22222222 33333333	11111111 22222222 33333333	11111111 22222222 33333333	11111111 22222222 33333333	11111111 22222222 33333333	11111111 22225555 33336666	11111111 55555555 66666666	11111111 55555555 66666666
1997	11111111 55555555 66666666	11111111 55555555 66666666	11111111 55555555 66666666	11111111 55555555 66666666	11111111 55555555 66666666	11111111 55555555 66666666	11111111 55555555 66666666	11111111 55555555 66666666	11111111 55555555 66666666	11111111 5555 66666666	11111111 66666666	11111111 66666666
1998	11111111 66666666	11111111 66666666	11111111 66666666	11111111 66666666	11111111 66666666	11111111 66666666	11111111 66666666	11111111 66666666	11111111 66666666	11111111 66666666	11111111 66666666	11111111 66666666
1999	11111111 66666666	11111111 66666666	11111111 66666666	11111111 66666666	11111111 6666	11111111	11111111 55	11111111 55555555	11111111 55555555	11111111 55555555	11 55	

Key to Locations

1 = base camp juniper tree
2 = pine tree, Pueblo Canyon, north side
3 = V:1:130, Rm 7, Pueblo Canyon, north side

5 = Uranium Mine, Pueblo Canyon, south side
6 = V:1:164, Rm 4; Cold Spring Canyon, north side

Figure 2.4. Datalogger Temporal Coverage By Location (2004-1733-image3985)

to varying locations. The one with the external probe was set up to measure interior temperatures in a nearly intact room (first in Pueblo Canyon, in V:1:130 about 1585m [Location 3]; later in Cold Spring Canyon, in V:1:164 about 1880m [Location 6]), with the probe placed in the interior surface of the front wall to measure heat transfer from the exterior to the interior of the wall. The third datalogger was placed in an open canyon setting, first on the north side of Pueblo Canyon at approximately 1585m (Location 2); and later on the south side of the canyon at approximately the same elevation (Location 5).

Recording began in December, 1995 and the dataloggers were all removed in November, 1999. Over 137,000 lines of temperature data were recorded at the seven locations. Due to the massive amount of data collected by the temperature studies, the data are not presented as part of this document. However, the implications of the temperature data are discussed and representative graphs are presented in Chapter 6.

Chapter Three
Physiography

The Sierra Ancha lies between the Salt River and the Mogollon Rim in east central Arizona. The mountain range is in Gila County and mostly under the jurisdiction of the Tonto National Forest, US Department of Agriculture, but it does include some private land and several incorporated and unincorporated communities. The geology and elevation of the Sierra Ancha and surrounding areas below the Mogollon Rim, as well as the physiographic setting, will be considered in this chapter. First, it is important to determine how similar or different the Sierra Ancha is compared to nearby areas. Second, geology and elevation are among the factors that have profound effects on water, plant, and animal resources. Third, certain geological resources in the area are important for architectural materials and flaked stone tools, and also contain some exotic minerals.

The Sierra Ancha is near the western end of several large blocks of land defined by north-south trending streams on their eastern and western margins, and lying between the Mogollon Rim to the north and the Salt River to the south. These blocks of land are formed by large geological faults that have divided and shifted the land lying between the deserts and the Colorado plateau. Each of these blocks also has numerous internal faults as well. On the western end of this series is the Mazatzal block, lying between the Verde River and Tonto Creek. Next, moving eastward, are the Sierra Ancha block, between Tonto and Cherry creeks; the Q Ranch block, between Cherry and Canyon creeks; the Grasshopper block, between Canyon and Cibecue creeks; and the Cibecue block, between Cibecue and Carrizo creeks (Fig. 3.1).

The Sierra Ancha is the second largest of these blocks in spatial extent (Table 3.1), and has the highest average elevation (Fig. 3.2). The blocks are similar geologically, but the geological units occur at different elevations.

GEOLOGY AND ELEVATION

Table 3.1 summarizes the dimensions, area, and elevations of each of the blocks. The Mazatzal block is the farthest west and is the largest block of those considered here. This block is the only one of the five not fully bounded by the Mogollon Rim, Salt River, and creeks on the west and east. Because the Mogollon Rim is not well defined west of the Strawberry/Fossil Creek area, the block was arbitrarily cut off at the latitude of Taut Creek. The Verde River continues much farther to the north and west. If this area were also included, it would make the Mazatzal block even larger.

The Mazatzal block has the highest individual elevation point among the blocks. Along the Mogollon Rim, both above and below the rim, elevations are relatively similar. Along the southern edge of the blocks, the rising gradient

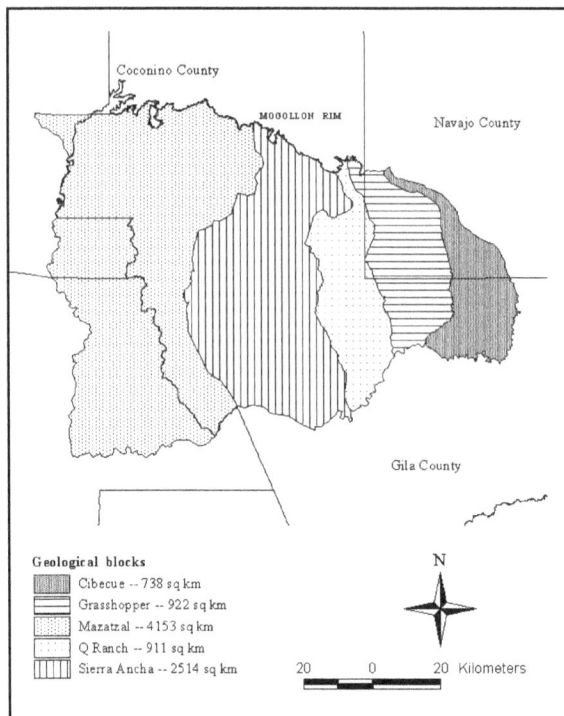

Figure 3.1. Boundaries of Selected Physiographic Units Below the Mogollon Rim (2004-1733-image3986)

of the Salt River is very clear.

The Sierra Ancha block is the second largest block (Table 3.1). It contains the second highest individual elevation point, but as noted (Fig. 3.2) has the highest average elevation of any of the blocks. Moving eastward, the Q Ranch block is the fourth largest of the five blocks, and lies in the middle of the five blocks considered here. Farther to the east, the Grasshopper block is the third largest, and finally, the Cibecue block is the farthest to the east and is the smallest of the five blocks.

Geologically, the blocks contain many of the same units, but there are differences in what constitutes the principal exposures and surface geology. Table 3.2 lists the geological units, rock types (sedimentary or igneous/metamorphic), and formations characteristic of this region below the Mogollon Rim in stratigraphic order (from younger to older down the table). Table 3.3 lists the formations present on each

block, subdivided by location on the block. The Mazatzal and Sierra Ancha blocks are geologically similar and most diverse, with 18 different formations present on each. The Q Ranch block is slightly less diverse, whereas the Grasshopper and Cibecue blocks are more homogeneous. In general, younger sediments and formations occur closer to the Mogollon Rim, where less overall erosion has occurred. With the exception of Quaternary and Quaternary-Tertiary sediments and igneous/metamorphic formations, most geological units in these blocks are of Permian or older time periods.

The surface geology in the northern section of the Sierra Ancha block is a complex mixture of Quaternary-Tertiary sediments, Quaternary-Tertiary basalt, Older Precambrian igneous rocks including granite and rhyolite, Older Precambrian metamorphic rocks in the form of schist, Younger Precambrian to Tertiary diabase, and Mescal Limestone from the Younger Precambrian Apache group. The dominant exposures are the Quaternary-Tertiary sediments, diabase, and Mescal Limestone. In the slopes below the Mogollon Rim are exposures of Carboniferous-Devonian limestone, shale, and sandstone, including the Naco and Supai formations.

The central portion of the Sierra Ancha block is dominated by diabase and Apache

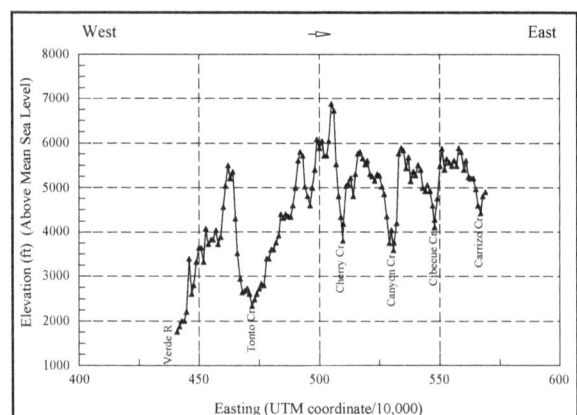

Figure 3.2. Elevations Along the N3750000 Line (2004-1733-image 3987)

Table 3.1. Dimensions and Elevation Data for Physiographic Blocks Defined

| Physiographic Characteristic | | BLOCKS | | | |
| | west | <----- | ----- | -----> | east |
	Mazatzal Block	Sierra Ancha Block	Q Ranch Block	Grasshopper Block	Cibecue Block
relative size	largest	second	fourth	third	fifth
north-south dimension	94 km (58 mi)*	78 km (48 mi)	65 km (41 mi)	49 km (30 mi)	57 km (35 mi)
east-west dimension	44 km (27 mi)*	36 km(22 mi)	13 km (8 mi)	18 km (11 mi)	16 km (10 mi)
block area	4153 sq km* (1604 sq mi)	2514 sq km (971 sq mi)	911 sq km (352 sq mi)	923 sq km (356 sq mi)	738 sq km (285 sq mi)
elevation at Mogollon Rim, west side		2377 m (7800 ft)	2316 m (7600 ft)	2256 m (7400 ft)	2316 m (7600 ft)
elevation at Mogollon Rim, east side	2377m (7800 ft)	2316 m (7600 ft)	2256 m (7400 ft)	2316 m (7600 ft)	2316 m (7600 ft)
elevation below Mogollon Rim, west side	701 m (2300 ft)	1890 m (6200 ft)	2134 m (7000 ft)	1981 m (6500 ft)	2256 m (7400 ft)
elevation below Mogollon Rim, east side	1890 m (6200 ft)	2134 m (7000 ft)	1981 m (6500 ft)	2256 m (7400 ft)	2316 m (7600 ft)
elevation at Salt River, west side	427 m (1400 ft)	640 m (2100 ft)	753 m (2470 ft)	885 m (2905 ft)	964 m (3163 ft)
elevation at Salt River, east side	640m (2100 ft)	753m (2470 ft)	885m (2905 ft)	964 m (3163 ft)	1244 m (4080 ft)
highest point(s)	Mazatzal Peak –2404m (7888ft)	Aztec Peak (2352m, 7718 ft), McFadden Peak (2175 m, 7135 ft), Turkey Peak (2153 m, 7063 ft)	Sombrero Peak (1962 m, 6436 ft), Colcord Mtn (2301 m, 7550 ft)	Chediski Peak (2274 m, 7462 ft), Blue House Mtn (1956 m, 6147 ft), Bear Mtn (1958 m, 6424 ft)	unnamed (2046 m, 6712 ft), Cibecue Peak (1983 m, 6507 ft), Ragged Top Mtn (1894 m, 6213 ft)

group rocks, including Mescal Limestone and Dripping Springs Quartzite. Some Barnes Conglomerate is also present. There are small pockets of Quaternary-Tertiary sediments in the center of this block, however, a major exposure of these sediments occurs along the western slopes, along Tonto Creek. Small pockets of Older Precambrian granite also occur, in exposures under the Mescal Limestone. Higher elevations in the central portion (such as Aztec Peak) are remnants of Carboniferous-Devonian limestone, shale, and sandstone (Naco formation) and are underlain by large exposures of Cambrian sandstone and quartzite, particularly Troy Quartzite.

The southern portion is largely Quaternary-Tertiary sediments, with a small pocket of Quaternary-Tertiary lake deposits (Chalk Creek area) and a Quaternary-Tertiary basalt intrusion—Black Mesa. Along the Salt River is an exposure of Older Precambrian diorite porphyry. The importance of particular formations for construction materials and for stone tools and ornaments is considered below.

WATER RESOURCES

Water availability in the Sierra Ancha can be viewed from several perspectives, and again, in comparison to the nearby blocks of land defined above. To understand the water resources of the area, drainages and drainage patterns, stream flow, precipitation, and seeps and springs will be examined.

Drainages

The flow rates and extents of floodplain and terraces in drainages compared to narrow canyon

Table 3.2. Geological Units Represented in the Below-Rim Geological Blocks

Time Period	Sedimentary	Igneous/Metamorphic
QUATERNARY	1 Silt, sand, and gravel	2 Basalt: flows, tuff, and agglomerate 3 Dikes and Plugs: mainly andesitic to basaltic in composition
QUATERNARY-TERITARY	4 Sand, silt, gravel, and conglomerate	5 Basalt: flows, tuff, and agglomerate 6 Volcanic flows, plugs, and dikes: rhyolitic to andesitic in composition
TERTIARY	7 Sandstone, shale, and conglomerate: includes some basalt	8 Andesite: flows, dikes, plugs, tuff, and agglomerate 9 Dikes and Plugs: mainly basaltic in composition 10 Dacite
CRETACEOUS	11 Mesa Verge group: includes Yale Point sandstone, Wepo formation, and Toreva formation 12 Mancos shale 13 Dakota sandstone	
JURASSIC	14 Morrison formation 15 San Rafael group: includes Summerville formation, Cow Springs sandstone, Bluff sandstone, Entrada sandstone, and Carmel formation	
JURASSIC/TRIASSIC	16 Glen Canyon group: includes in descending order, Navajo sandstone, Kayenta formation, Moenave formation, and Wingate sandstone	
TRIASSIC	17 Chinle formation 18 Shinarump conglomerate 19 Moenkopi formation	
PERMIAN	20 Kaibab limestone: includes Toroweap formation 21 Coconino sandstone 22 Hermit shale	
PENNSYLVANIAN AND PERMIAN	23 Supai formation: includes sandstone and shale	
MISSISSIPPIAN AND DEVONIAN	24 Redwall and Martin limestones	
CAMBRIAN	25 Tonto group: includes Muav limestone, Bright Angel shale, and Tapeats sandstone, Troy quartzite	
YOUNGER PRECAMBRIAN	26 Diabase (Younger Precambrian to Tertiary) 27 Grand Canyon series: includes Chuar and Unkar groups 28 Apache group: Mescal limestone, Dripping Spring quartzite Barnes conglomerate, Pioneer shale, Scanlan conglomerate	
OLDER PRECAMBRIAN		29 Granite and related crystalline intrusive rocks 30 Mazatzal quartzite, schist, greenstone 31 Rhyolite 32 Diorite porphyry, Pyroxenite 33 Granite gneiss

Table 3.3. Geological Units Present in the Below-rim Geological Blocks*

Block	Mazatzal	Sierra Ancha	Q Ranch	Grasshopper	Cibecue
northern portion	2, 4, 21, 23, 25, 29, 30, 31	4, 5, 21, 24, 26, 28, 29, 30, 31	4, 21, 23, 25, 26, 28	7, 21, 23, 24	5, 7, 21, 23, 24, 25
central portion	4	4, 25, 26, 28, 29		5, 7	23, 24
southern portion	4, 10, 24, 25, 26, 28, 29, 30, 32	1, 2, 4, 32	7, 10, 29, 32	26, 28	23, 24

*Note: numbers refer to geological formations outlined in Table 3.2

areas are critical factors for farming. Drainages have also often been frequently linked to means of access from area to area (for example, see Triadan and Zedeño 2004). Drainages and tributaries discussed here are the permanent and ephemeral streams indicated in blue on the USGS 1:250,000 (200 ft. [61m] contour interval) Holbrook (1960) and Mesa (1978) maps. Most drainages discussed here can be characterized as classic dendritic or trellis drainages (Stokes and Judson 1968:163). The tributaries join the main stream in a step or ladder fashion, alternating from west to east. Relatively few streams from the east and west meet at the same point on the main stream. Tonto Creek seems to have more instances of the latter pattern than the other watercourses.

All of the streams considered here tend to have rocky streambeds. Farming in the main channels would be limited to occasional sand bars. Most farming would occur on the terraces flanking the stream course, with the possibility of diverting water into canals along the lower terraces present along some of the streams.

If drainages provide routes for travel within a particular region, the drainages associated with these geological blocks certainly provide the means for travel along north-south axes as well as along east-west axes. Travel may not be confined to the actual streambeds,

however. The streambeds can contain standing and flowing water, making footing wet and slippery, and requiring crossing and re-crossing the streambed. The stream courses also tend to wind back and forth, not providing the most direct course between two points. Travel may have followed the drainages, but probably actually occurred on the adjacent terraces and ridges.

Verde River
The Verde River drains the largest area of any of the streams considered here (Fig. 3.3, Table 3.4). Stream flow data are not reported here for the Verde River, because there are numerous dams and irrigation systems that store or otherwise remove water from the normal flow of the river.

Tonto Creek
The Tonto Creek drainage is the second largest drainage system in this area, and it drains the eastern slopes of the Mazatzal block and the western slopes of the Sierra Ancha block. On the west side of Tonto Creek, the major drainage is Rye Creek, flowing from northwest to southeast from the watershed boundary with the East Verde River.

From the east side of Tonto Creek, and at its northern end, are two principal drainage sys-

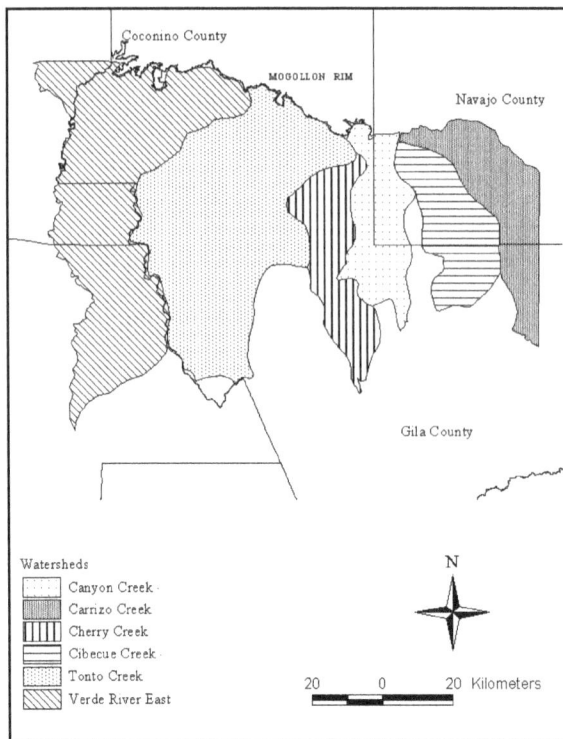

Figure 3.3. Watershed Boundaries for Selected Physiographic Units Below the Mogollon Rim (2004-1733-image3988)

tems. The Haigler Creek system collects runoff from the slopes of the Mogollon Rim and flows generally from northeast to southwest. Spring Creek enters Tonto Creek approximately 15 km downstream from Haigler Creek, but its headwaters are in the middle of the Sierra Ancha block. It flows to the north/northwest. South of the confluence of Rye and Tonto Creeks, is Gun Creek. It, too, originates in the middle of the Sierra Ancha block, and like Spring Creek, flows first to the north/northwest before hooking back to the southwest to flow into Tonto Creek. Greenback Creek heads up in the same area as Spring and Gun creeks, but flows from northeast to southwest directly into Tonto Creek. A large portion of the south-central area of the Sierra Ancha block flows directly into the Salt River, principally via Salome Creek.

Cherry Creek

The Cherry Creek drainage is the smallest of the drainages considered here (approximately 518 sq km). Only about one-eighth of the landmass of the Sierra Ancha block drains into Cherry Creek. The largest areas flow into Tonto Creek or drain directly into the Salt River. Cherry Creek also receives approximately half of the drainage from the Q Ranch block to the east.

The Q Ranch block, like the Mazatzal block, has a high ridge running approximately north-south through the middle of the block, creating roughly equal run-off to the east and west. However, the number of tributaries draining to the west off of the Q Ranch block (14) is double the number draining to the east into Canyon Creek. At the southeast corner of the Q Ranch block is a small area that drains directly into the Salt River.

Canyon Creek

The Canyon Creek drainage (818 sq km) is larger than the Cherry Creek drainage (518 sq km) and slightly larger than the Cibecue Creek drainage (764 sq km) as well. Canyon Creek gathers its flow from the Mogollon Rim, the east slopes of the Q Ranch block, and the west slopes of the Grasshopper block. Except for the area near the Rim, Oak Creek is the major tributary from the east side of Canyon Creek. Horse Canyon and Willow Creek join to form a major tributary from the west.

Somewhat less than the western one-third of the Grasshopper block contributes runoff to the Canyon Creek drainage. A large area in the center of the block drains southward through Salt River Draw directly into the Salt River. Unlike the Mazatzal and Q Ranch blocks that are elevated in the middle, the Grasshopper block is depressed in the middle.

Cibecue Creek

The Cibecue Creek drainage is the second smallest and is fed principally by Salt Creek and another Spring Creek from the eastern

Table 3.4. Stream Flow Data for Selected Streams Below the Mogollon Rim

a. General Stream Flow Data

Stream	Area (sq mi)	Area (sq km)	Average discharge (cu ft/sec)	Average discharge (cu m/sec)	Maximum discharge (cu ft/sec)	Maximum discharge (cu m/sec)	Date of Max Discharge
Verde River	6600	17,090					
Tonto Creek	675	1750	134.0	3.8	55,800	1580	1/17/79
Cherry Creek	200	518	39.7	1.1	8300		10/19/72
Cherry Creek					15,700	445	1/17/79
Canyon Creek	316	818			21,100	598	3/1/78
Cibecue Crk	295	764	43.6	1.2	22,200	629	9/2/77
Carrizo Creek	439	1137					
Salt River	4306	11,153	865.0	24.5	95,800	2710	12/19/79
Salt River					117,000	3343	3/14/41

b. Comparison of Maximum Flows

Stream	Maximum flow (cu ft/sec)	Size (sq mi)	Mean Flow (cu ft/sec)
Salt River	95,800 – 117,000	4306	865
Tonto Creek	55,800	675	134
Carrizo Creek	----	439	----
Canyon Creek	21,100	316	----
Cibecue Creek	22,200	295	44
Cherry Creek	8300 – 15,700	200	40

slopes of the Grasshopper block. Six tributaries enter from the west and eight from the east.

Carrizo Creek
The Carrizo Creek drainage is the farthest to the east of the streams discussed here, and like the Verde River drainage, is only partially represented in the Cibecue block. It is the third largest of the drainage systems, and receives the majority of its flow via numerous tributaries directly from the Mogollon Rim. The Cibecue block also contains an area along its southern edge, between the Cibecue and Carrizo creek drainages, that drains directly into the Salt River.

Stream Flow

Maximum and average stream flows have been recorded for varying numbers of years for the streams discussed here (U.S. Department of Commerce 1956). Both average and maximum flows reflect the size of the drainage system to a considerable degree (Table 3.4). The maximum flows represent from 135 to over 500 times the water volume of the average flows, quite remarkable for these relatively small drainages. The flow in each stream is derived principally from snowmelt and rain; either as runoff or after filtering into the ground and emerging at seeps and springs. Stretches of even the main tributaries to the Salt River (Verde, Tonto, Cherry, Canyon, Cibecue, and Carrizo) can go dry seasonally and in drought years. On Cherry Creek, in the area between the two road crossings on the FS 203 road, the author has seen parts of this area dry in June only once or twice during the period 1977-2000. Flows in these tributaries, and the tributaries feeding them, frequently run below the surface until forced back to the surface by the bedrock. For example, certain parts of Devils Chasm, Cold Spring Canyon, and Pueblo Canyon, all tributaries of Cherry Creek, are regularly dry even when there is considerable flow up or downstream from these areas.

The high flow volumes in the small drainages, particularly where confined to narrow canyons, can be very destructive. Five events witnessed by the author over the years illustrate the destructive potential in the Cherry Creek drainage.

First, in Devils Chasm, a large culvert was introduced to keep the roadbed (FS 203) safe above the stream. The first one was put in place in the early 1980s. It did not last long, and now there are three culverts downstream from the road crossing. During high flows, water and debris stack up behind the culvert and roadway (acting like a dam), eventually causing water to flow over the roadway. This erodes the roadbed and exposes the culvert, allowing it to be pushed downstream.

Second, the first (lower) crossing of the FS203 road across Cherry Creek has been problematical in creating a reliable crossing. Originally, the crossing was just bladed through the cobbles in the streambed. This tended to erode and become choked with new deposits of cobbles from upstream during higher flows. Unfortunately, there are no detailed records of the work and repairs at this crossing, so dates are approximate. The first-hard bottomed crossing was built after 1981. It was only a matter of a couple of years before the high flows undercut this crossing and moved it several hundred meters downstream. A new hard-bottom crossing was constructed in the late 1980s, a block of concrete and steel over 9m deep. This crossing has remained mostly intact, so far.

Third, in the area between the road crossings, parts of the FS 203 road ran in the bottom of Cherry Creek (near Pottery Point, for instance). Floods in the late 1970s forced this road to be moved up onto the hillsides and terraces, back from the stream channel. Slightly south in the same area, during the high flows, the main channel of Cherry Creek began to migrate from the west side to the east side. One private inholding lost part of a terrace to one flood. A large part of a nearby ridge was pushed out to "reclaim" that portion of land. The next flood removed that, too.

Fourth, only a day or two before the start of the first Earthwatch project in early October, 1995, central and southern Arizona received significant rain. In the area between the FS 203 road crossings, south of Banning Wash and east of the road, there had been a fire during the previous year that had burned off much of the vegetation. There were two washes about 50m apart that were normally just small trickles across the road. Both were 3 to 5m wide and over 1m deep.

The fifth instance notes some remarkable changes in one particular wash. Banning Wash entered Cherry Creek as a broad, flat stream course until a major flood event in fall of 1977. Hurricane Heather brought torrential rains to parts of central Arizona. Heavy rainfall must have occurred around Sombrero Peak in the southern part of the Q Ranch block. The resulting runoff cut a channel 10m wide and 2m deep.

These observations serve to indicate that although farming and some diversion and irrigation could be done in the bottoms of the major tributaries, there was also considerable risk to such practices. Smaller, ephemeral stream courses, used either as field areas themselves or diverted into nearby flats, may have been the preferred areas for agriculture. However, these areas, too, are obviously susceptible to severe flooding and erosion.

Precipitation

The Sierra Ancha, in particular, and the area defined by these geological blocks, in general, receive some off the highest precipitation totals in the state (see Table 3.5 for averages from selected sites, US Department of Commerce). The Sierra Ancha station, with the highest precipitation average of any station reported here, is located on the southern slopes of the mountain range, at the Arizona Department of Transportation maintenance yard. Average annual precipitation there is in excess of 610 mm (24 in) per year.

In the northern and central higher elevation portions of the geological blocks, winter precipitation is often in the form of snow. Snow can accumulate from a few centimeters to 60 cm deep, and can last on the ground for several days. Snowfall in the Tonto Basin is rare, but it can occur (see Ellison 1968: 28 for an account of snow in the Tonto Basin in the late 1800s – over one meter!).

Even during a droughty year (for example, 1956, see Table 3.6, US Department of Commerce 1956), the higher elevation areas receive more precipitation than surrounding lower areas. The precipitation at the station on the south slopes of the Sierra Ancha was more than 11 inches (279mm) below average, but still totaled over 13 inches (330mm). Rainfall in the area below the Mogollon Rim is subject to the patterns that affect Arizona and most of the US Southwest. The basic pattern is "a bi-seasonal regime characterized by winter precipitation, spring drought, summer precipitation, and fall drought" (Lowe 1964:8-10).

Seeps and Springs

As noted in the earlier discussion, the Sierra Ancha and surrounding areas are geologically complex. Tectonics (uplift), igneous intrusions, faulting and erosion have all contributed to the landscape seen today. Also, as just discussed, the Sierra Ancha receives some of the highest rainfall averages in the state.

The geological faulting and the permeability or porosity of the various formations combine to create pockets of water and seeps or springs where the water emerges from the mountain. Numerous seeps and springs occur throughout the Sierra Ancha, particularly in the cliffs at the contacts between the Troy Quartzite, basalt, argillite, and Mescal Limestone. Bob Scarborough, a geologist, characterized the Troy Quartzite and basalt as giant sponges—the quartzite because it is relatively porous, the basalt because of internal faulting. The dozens of vertical meters of mountain create quite a storage reservoir.

Some of the seeps run only during wetter periods, or ephemerally after storms. After a storm, there can be water everywhere, dripping out of nearly every nook and cranny. After one storm in Pueblo Canyon in early October 1984, there were 17 waterfalls coming over the cliffs. Some seeps are perennial, and even in the driest times, continue to produce at least a trickle. One good indicator of drought is the waterfall at the head of lower Pueblo Canyon. It is usually running water steadily, but has been totally dry a couple of times since 1981. The presence of seeps and springs at various elevations and locations means that water is available at locations other than the major streams or tributaries. And, many of these seem to be reliable sources of water, even in drier periods.

CLIMATE
Temperature

Although extreme highs and lows can occur throughout the area of the five geological blocks, temperatures are generally mild (Tables 3.7 and 3.8). Monthly average low temperatures in Young, located on top of the

Table 3.5. Monthly Average Precipitation (in inches) for Selected Sites In and Around the Sierra Ancha

YEAR(S)	PLACE	Elevation (ft)	JAN	FEB	MAR	APR	MAY	JUN	JUL	AUG	SEP	OCT	NOV	DEC	Total
1948-70	Phoenix	1117	0.73	0.57	0.70	0.27	0.09	0.16	0.72	1.10	0.65	0.50	0.44	0.81	6.74
1941-70	Globe	3550	1.56	1.00	1.41	0.53	0.21	0.27	2.38	3.00	1.31	1.10	0.86	1.90	15.53
1941-70	Roosevelt	2205	1.78	1.11	1.56	0.61	0.24	0.25	1.30	1.93	1.43	0.97	0.95	2.02	14.15
1948-70	Payson	4913	2.11	1.43	1.78	0.96	0.43	0.50	3.10	3.30	1.86	1.64	1.45	2.21	20.77
1941-70	Sra.Ancha	5100	2.85	2.06	2.59	1.15	0.41	0.45	2.66	3.90	2.11	1.68	1.73	3.16	24.75
1941-70	Young	5050	1.95	1.27	1.75	0.92	0.46	0.46	2.87	3.48	1.68	1.30	1.24	1.99	19.37
1941-70	Cibecue	5000	1.91	1.17	1.52	0.72	0.36	0.46	2.38	2.83	1.65	1.70	1.15	1.78	17.63
1950-70	Flagstaff	6993	1.87	1.50	1.87	1.33	0.59	0.65	2.50	2.81	1.69	1.11	1.58	2.20	19.80
1948-70	Winslow	4895	0.44	0.41	0.48	0.32	0.26	0.35	1.23	1.50	0.75	0.64	0.39	0.60	7.37
1949-70	Showlow	6400	1.40	0.96	1.25	0.60	0.31	0.50	2.47	2.25	1.22	1.46	1.06	1.87	15.35

Table 3.6. Monthly Average Precipitation (in inches) from 1956 for Selected Sites In and Around the Sierra Ancha

YEAR(S)	PLACE	Elevation (ft)	JAN	FEB	MAR	APR	MAY	JUN	JUL	AUG	SEP	OCT	NOV	DEC	Total	DFN
1956	Phoenix	1117	0.53	0.61	0.00	0.00	0.00	0.00	0.64	1.42	0.07	0.06	0.00	0.00	3.33	-3.79
1956	Globe	3550	2.26	1.00	0.00	0.27	0.00	0.08	1.78	1.83	0.02	0.80	0.00	0.18	8.22	-7.18
1956	Roosevelt	2205	1.44	1.42	0.00	0.65	0.17	0.00	1.45	0.55	0.00	1.10	0.00	0.08	6.86	-8.55
1956	Payson	4913	1.48	1.12	0.00	1.07	0.08	0.49	4.99	0.93	0.13	1.49	0.00	0.41	12.19	-8.32
1956	Sra. Ancha	5100	2.27	2.58	0.00	2.32	0.99	0.00	1.93	0.51	0.62	1.45	0.00	0.45	13.12	-11.63
1956	Young	5050	1.65	1.65	0.00	1.74	0.20	0.03	2.99	3.32	0.00	1.93	0.00	0.25	13.76	-6.48
1956	Cibecue	5000	2.13	0.95	0.00	1.45	0.00	0.00	2.61	1.47	0.14	0.57	0.00	0.00	9.32	-9.60
1956	Flagstaff	6993	1.62	1.06	0.12	0.86	0.17	2.79	1.19	1.42	0.02	0.68	0.84	0.39	10.37	-8.16
1956	Winslow	4895	0.64	1.01	0.21	0.42	0.20	0.37	1.55	1.04	0.01	0.21	0.09	0.00	5.75	-2.08
1956	Showlow	6400	1.44	1.70	0.19	0.94	0.13	0.18	2.60	1.62	0.00	1.24	0.02	0.28	10.34	-5.01

Sierra Ancha, are slightly warmer than mean lows in Flagstaff, but lower than at the recording station on the south face of the Sierra Ancha. Mean monthly highs at Young are higher than those at Flagstaff, but lower than the highs on the south face of the mountain. In 1956, a severely droughty year in terms of total precipitation, average monthly highs and lows (Tables 3.9 and 3.10) do not differ greatly from the overall averages (Tables 3.7 and 3.8). In general, higher elevation areas are cooler, but other factors such as facing, exposure, and surrounding topography also play important roles in influencing temperature at any particular location.

Growing Season

The growing season for much of the Sierra Ancha is expected to be around 140 days, based on a value for the nearby Grasshopper area (Holbrook and Graves 1982:5). Compare this number to 90 days in the higher elevations around the Little Colorado River basin to the north, and as many as 180 frost-free days around Winslow in the middle of the basin (Lange 1998:8). A baseline for growing corn is 120 frost-free days (Carter 1945, Hack 1942, Schoenwetter and Eddy 1964). Thus, the growing season would seem to be adequate, although there is not that much of a buffer.

Table 3.7. Monthly Average Low Temperatures (°F) for Selected Sites In and Around the Sierra Ancha

YEAR(S)	PLACE	Elevation (ft)	JAN	FEB	MAR	APR	MAY	JUN	JUL	AUG	SEP	OCT	NOV	DEC	Mean
1948-70	Phoenix	1117	38.0	41.1	45.3	52.4	60.2	68.9	78.3	76.4	69.7	57.5	45.9	39.0	56.1
1941-70	Globe	3550	29.5	32.0	35.6	42.3	48.9	57.2	66.7	64.6	58.1	46.8	36.0	30.4	45.7
1941-70	Roosevelt	2205	37.0	39.9	44.2	52.3	60.9	69.3	75.9	73.6	68.2	57.4	45.3	38.7	55.2
1948-70	Payson	4913	23.7	25.8	28.4	34.7	41.2	49.0	58.5	57.0	49.8	40.0	30.5	24.5	38.6
1941-70	Sra.Ancha	5100	31.1	33.2	35.7	42.6	49.9	58.2	63.5	62.4	59.4	49.9	39.1	32.9	46.5
1941-70	Young	5050	18.8	21.6	23.1	28.0	34.3	40.6	55.0	53.5	45.4	33.7	26.0	19.3	33.3
1941-70	Cibecue	5000	22.7	24.7	27.5	32.7	38.2	45.8	56.5	55.1	48.3	38.0	27.5	23.3	36.7
1950-70	Flagstaff	6993	14.6	16.9	20.1	26.5	33.1	40.6	50.6	49.0	40.7	30.5	21.6	16.0	30.0
1948-70	Winslow	4895	19.1	24.3	29.2	37.2	45.3	54.2	63.2	61.4	53.5	40.9	28.3	20.1	39.7
1949-70	Showlow	6400	17.7	21.0	25.4	32.1	38.5	47.6	55.5	54.1	47.6	35.7	24.8	18.9	34.9

Table 3.8. Monthly Average High Temperatures (°F) for Selected Sites In and Around the Sierra Ancha

YEAR(S)	PLACE	Elevation (ft)	JAN	FEB	MAR	APR	MAY	JUN	JUL	AUG	SEP	OCT	NOV	DEC	Mean
1948-70	Phoenix	1117	64.6	69.0	74.2	83.5	92.7	101.5	104.4	102.1	98.0	87.9	74.7	66.2	84.9
1941-70	Globe	3550	57.0	62.3	67.1	76.8	86.1	95.3	98.7	95.2	91.7	80.8	67.3	58.3	78.1
1941-70	Roosevelt	2205	58.9	64.6	69.7	79.5	89.0	98.2	102.1	99.3	95.4	84.2	70.1	60.1	80.9
1948-70	Payson	4913	53.1	57.2	61.4	70.0	79.0	88.9	92.5	89.2	85.2	75.5	63.3	55.2	72.5
1941-70	Sra.Ancha	5100	54.0	57.4	61.2	70.2	78.9	88.4	92.3	89.4	86.0	75.5	63.4	55.5	72.7
1941-70	Young	5050	52.7	56.7	59.6	67.7	77.7	85.6	90.3	87.3	82.0	74.9	62.7	53.3	70.9
1941-70	Cibecue	5000	52.1	56.7	60.5	69.9	78.7	88.0	90.6	87.8	84.6	74.5	62.0	53.9	71.6
1950-70	Flagstaff	6993	42.2	44.7	48.6	57.5	67.1	76.8	81.1	78.3	73.8	64.3	51.4	44.0	60.8
1948-70	Winslow	4895	45.5	52.9	60.3	70.5	80.2	90.4	93.9	90.9	85.6	73.8	58.5	46.5	70.8
1949-70	Showlow	6400	44.2	48.3	53.8	63.9	73.0	82.8	85.8	82.9	79.4	68.5	55.3	45.6	65.3

Hack (1942:7-9, 19-21) indicates that corn agriculture depends upon a balance between elevation and growing season. The effects of elevation and cold-air drainage are accentuated in a setting like the Sierra Ancha (see also Adams 1979). In the Sierra Ancha, facing and length of time the sun is on a particular parcel of land should also be considered as critical variables.

Climatic History

Climatic histories specific to Cherry Creek have not been done. However, detailed summaries for the Tonto Basin and southern Colorado Plateau have been done (Lange 1996:239-258; Lange 1998:138-145; Van West 1994, 1996:15-35; Van West and Altschul 1994:361-435). Van West and Altschul (1994:426) tested the relationship between the Tonto Basin and Colorado Plateau data and found good congruence. Thus, the Cherry Creek valley, just over the Sierra Ancha from the Tonto Basin, should be very similar to the Tonto Basin. Their discussion is focused on evaluating agricultural productivity and population trends in the Tonto Basin. However, they also make comments on basic climatic conditions through time, and those comments and conditions are summarized here. Similarly, the discussion here also involves

Table 3.9. Monthly Average Low Temperatures (°F) from 1956 for Selected Sites In and Around the Sierra Ancha

YEAR(S)	PLACE	Elevation (ft)	JAN	FEB	MAR	APR	MAY	JUN	JUL	AUG	SEP	OCT	NOV	DEC	Mean
1956	Phoenix	1117	45.2	40.0	47.6	54.0	65.0	74.9	78.4	74.5	72.5	58.0	44.3	40.3	57.9
1956	Globe	3550	34.3	29.1	34.5	42.6	50.6	63.9	66.4	62.8	59.5	46.9	31.3	27.3	45.8
1956	Roosevelt	2205	39.2	36.0	44.1	52.0	61.7	73.8	75.5	71.9	67.7	53.8	36.2	32.8	53.7
1956	Payson	4913	20.9	18.8	23.7	30.4	36.7	48.1	55.5	49.7	46.2	33.9	18.1	16.1	33.2
1956	Sra.Ancha	5100	38.1	28.7	39.1	41.8	52.2		62.9	61.9	63.6	49.9	36.3	32.4	46.1
1956	Young	5050													
1956	Cibecue	5000	23.4	18.6	25.3	31.0		51.6	53.8	51.2	46.7	34.1	22.0	18.6	34.2
1956	Flagstaff	6993	19.7	12.9	19.2	25.5	33.0	41.4	49.2	54.7	42.5	27.3	16.0	15.3	29.7
1956	Winslow	4895	28.2	17.6	28.4	36.5	46.3	58.0	60.9	58.0	54.7	40.1	18.9	16.0	38.6
1956	Showlow	6400	25.4	13.6	23.8	30.3	39.8	49.9	51.0	51.0	49.2	36.3	15.8	15.5	33.5

Table 3.10. Monthly Average High Temperatures (°F) from 1956 for Selected Sites In and Around the Sierra Ancha

YEAR(S)	PLACE	Elevation (ft)	JAN	FEB	MAR	APR	MAY	JUN	JUL	AUG	SEP	OCT	NOV	DEC	Mean
1956	Phoenix	1117	70.3	64.4	80.0	81.4	94.5	103.8	103.1	101.8	102.5	86.7	75.4	69.2	86.1
1956	Globe	3550	62.0	58.0	74.2	75.8	89.7	99.3	98.6	95.7	98.4	83.4	66.3	59.8	80.1
1956	Roosevelt	2205	61.6	58.1	75.2	78.0	91.5	101.9	100.6	99.1	100.6	84.8	67.4	62.5	81.8
1956	Payson	4913	57.3	50.6	69.0	67.2	81.3	92.6	90.5	86.9	93.1	76.0	64.1	58.4	73.9
1956	Sra.Ancha	5100	57.3	50.9	67.3	67.8	81.0		90.4	89.6	91.7	76.1	62.7	56.7	72.0
1956	Young	5050													
1956	Cibecue	5000	58.6	50.4	67.9			92.9	89.7	87.5	89.6	74.7	61.4	55.2	66.2
1956	Flagstaff	6993	46.6	39.7	54.5	55.7	70.3	80.5	79.4	90.3	80.5	63.9	51.7	45.2	63.2
1956	Winslow	4895	54.5	45.8	64.7	68.1	83.2	94.0	92.6	90.1	90.6	74.6	53.5	48.9	71.7
1956	Showlow	6400	51.0	41.6	60.1	60.3	75.9	86.7	85.6	82.7	86.0	71.8	53.5	47.6	66.9

climatic history as it affects agricultural productivity.

Climatic conditions during the period for which data are available (AD 740 to 1370) are quite variable (Van West and Altschul 1994:430), and agriculture becomes a "risky endeavor" due to the number, sequence, and severity of extreme fluctuations from wet to dry years. Van West and Altschul (1994:402-404) posit nine "natural" temporal periods to compare to archaeological periods defined by differences in material culture. Dates and characteristics of each natural period are given in Table 3.11.

Period II has the highest percentage of extreme variation, Period V the least. Period III has the highest ratio of dry-to-wet years, Period V the lowest. And finally, with Period I removed because it is somewhat arbitrary, Period VII is the time of least predictability; Period V has the greatest predictability. The general variability is highlighted across these periods, and the presence of high and low extremes, even within one decade, is not unusual (Table 3.12).

Period V, with the lowest percentage of extreme variation, lowest dry-to-wet year ratio, and greatest predictability, falls in the Sedentary Period in the Tonto Basin (see Fig. 10.3). It is seen as likely to be the most predictable era of agricultural productivity in the Tonto Basin (Van West and Altschul 1994:404). This

Table 3.11. Dates and Climatic Characteristics for Nine Natural Periods, AD 740-1370

Period	Dates (AD)	Characteristics
I	740-751	Beginning is somewhat arbitrary, ends with extreme drought in 750 and 751
II	752-809	Begins with moderate times and ends with serious drought in 808 and 809
III	810-925	Begins with moderate times after drought in 808 and 809 and lasts through 925, the end of almost eight continuous years of drought, 918 -925
IV	926-1041	Return to better conditions in 926, ends with another eight-year dry period, 1033-1041
V	1042-1121	Has an isolated severe drought at 1067, ends with another at 1121
VI	1122-1217	A period of frequent drought, including 6 years at the end, ending with very severe years of 1216 and 1217
VII	1218-1299	Contains many drought years and is a period of great interannual fluctuation
VIII	1300-1352	1352 is the end of a nearly continuous six-year drought
IX	1353-1370	A return to wetter years, with 1356 and 1358 extremely wet, and an extremely dry year of 1360

Table 3.12. Decadal Summary of Extreme Dry and Wet Years

Decade (AD)	Extreme Dry	Extreme Wet	Decade	Extreme Dry	Extreme Wet	Decade	Extreme Dry	Extreme Wet
740-750	2	0	951-960	3	1	1161-1170	1	1
751-760	1	0	961-970	0	0	1171-1180	2	1
761-770	1	2	971-980	1	1	1181-1190	1	1
771-780	1	0	981-990	2	1	1191-1200	1	2
781-790	1	0	991-1000	2	0	1201-1210	0	2
791-800	2	1	1001-1010	1	1	1211-1220	2	0
801-810	2	5	1011-1020	1	1	1221-1230	1	1
811-820	1	0	1021-1030	0	0	1231-1240	0	1
821-830	3	1	1031-1040	0	0	1241-1250	0	2
831-840	1	0	1041-1050	1	0	1251-1260	2	1
841-850	1	0	1051-1060	0	2	1261-1270	1	0
851-860	0	0	1061-1070	1	0	1271-1280	1	1
861-870	0	0	1071-1080	0	1	1281-1290	3	0
871-880	0	0	1081-1090	2	2	1291-1300	2	1
881-890	2	1	1091-1100	0	0	1301-1310	0	3
891-900	1	1	1101-1110	0	1	1311-1320	1	1
901-910	2	0	1111-1120	0	0	1321-1330	1	1
911-920	1	0	1121-1130	1	2	1331-1340	0	0
921-930	2	1	1131-1140	1	0	1341-1350	2	0
931-940	0	0	1141-1150	2	1	1351-1360	3	2
941-950	1	2	1151-1160	2	0	1361-1370	0	0

period was followed by 80 years of average conditions with rapid fluctuations of wet and dry years, followed by another 80 years of extremely poor conditions for agriculture. The last 80-year period ends at AD 1300.

The same period of time (631 years) can be divided into five archaeologically defined phases, periods, and sub-periods (see Van West and Altschul 1994:399). Their Table 14.15 is modified and presented here as Table 3.13. Again, the Sedentary Period is seen as the most moderate and predictable. The earlier Late Pioneer and Colonial periods are important, but climatic conditions are somewhat less critical to settlement and agriculture because population is still small and the landscape presents a number of opportunities to solve year-to-year problems of subsistence. As population increases, the need for sustainable production becomes more critical and there are fewer locations available to any one group because someone else is likely to already be using them. The Early and Late Classic periods have the highest percentages of extreme years of any periods, exacerbating the problems of subsistence for even greater numbers of people.

All of the agricultural strategies, including possible canal irrigation, available to the residents of the Tonto Basin, would also have been available to those living in Cherry Creek. The agricultural potential for those living in Cherry Creek would have been subjected to the same possibilities, limitations, and variability as the residents of the Tonto Basin.

NATURAL RESOURCES

This section details natural resources other than water available in the Sierra Ancha and nearby areas. Caves and shelters, stone material, clay, certain exotic stone materials, and plants and animals will be described here.

Caves and Shelters

The faulting and erosion in the sub-Mogollon Rim region has led to vast expanses of cliffs. Faults or pockets in the formations create caves. In the Sierra Ancha, cliff dwellings occur in caves in the Troy Quartzite, Mescal Limestone, and Dripping Springs Quartzite formations.

Shelters and overhangs are created when the forces of wind and water combine to work against the geological formations. Numerous shelters in the southeastern Sierra Ancha are created at the contact between the basalt and argillite layers that occur between the Troy Quartzite and Mescal Limestone. Water passes through the Troy Quartzite and basalt relatively easily, but is forced out by the argillite above the Mescal Limestone. The argillite in this context is extremely hard, somewhat brittle, and bluish-grey. This is unlike softer red argillite available around Jakes Corner and in the

Table 3.13. Extreme Events in the Lower Tonto Basin by Archaeological Periods (z-score < -1.29 and > 1.29)*

Years in Period	Period	Dates (AD)	Number of Dry Years	Number of Wet Years	Total Years	Percent of Period
35	Late Pioneer	740-774	4	2	6	17
200	Colonial	775-974	24	14	38	19
175	Sedentary	975-1149	15	12	27	15
150	Early Classic	1150-1299	20	14	34	23
71	Late Classic	1300-1370	8	7	15	21
631	(All)	740-1370	71	49	120	19

*This table is modified from Table 14.15 in Van West and Altschul (1994:399)

Prescott area that was used prehistorically for beads and other objects. The water is driven to the cliff faces by internal pressure where it emerges as seeps and is continually acting to weaken the cliff face. Under freezing conditions and the force of gravity, rocks break off from the cliffs, enlarging and deepening the shelters.

Stone—Construction Materials

As the cliffs erode and the shelters are created, lithic material usable for construction is left behind. In the Sierra Ancha, the Troy Quartzite, basalt, argillite, Mescal Limestone, and Dripping Springs Quartzite tend to break off in blocks or tabular pieces that can be used without modification and all were selected as building material. The stone construction materials could have been gathered from the cavern where construction occurred, from nearby shelters in the canyon, and from talus slopes that occur in faults and below less resistant cliffs or outcrops. Some material may have been carried several hundred meters to where it was used for construction.

Whether cliff dwelling or surface pueblo, the architectural units seem to have been made of the readily available materials. For the surface sites, this means they are often built of rounded cobbles, collected from the erosional terraces made up of the same materials as in the canyons. In the case of one surface pueblo (Pottery Point Pueblo, V:1:166), blocks of caliche were also used. The caliche is eroding out of exposures near the site.

Stone—Materials for Tools

Erosion of the various geological formations over the millenia has left behind a wealth of suitable materials for stone tools. Some of these materials seem to be derived from the Dripping Springs Quartzite and Mescal Limestone and include fine-grained chert, jasper, silicified limestone, and chalcedony. For heavier chopping and scraping tools, there is quartzite and fine-grained rhyolite.

The grinding tools (handstones, manos, and metates) are most commonly made of quartzite, probably mostly Troy Quartzite. Some igneous material is available, for example, the basalt associated with Troy Quartzite and argillite or in intrusions such as Black Mesa at the eastern end of the Tonto Basin. These basalts tend to be too fine-grained to make effective grinding equipment and too hard to shape effectively, so were not used for grinding tools.

Clay

Clay is needed for architectural uses—mortar, and floor and wall plaster—and for ceramics. Clays derived from intrusive diabase seem to have been used for all four purposes. Some color variation is noticeable in the wall plaster (evident in Fig. 6.2, V:1:130), indicating multiple sources for the plaster and mortar. Diabase units are common throughout the southeastern Sierra Ancha, but none are particularly close to the cliff dwellings. Clay may have been hauled over several hundreds of meters in both horizontal and vertical dimensions. For example, at one road cut on the old jeep road and trail to Cold Spring and Pueblo canyons, and higher up at Rattlesnake Crossing (the flat where the roads divide), there are extensive exposures of diabase clays. Much of the roadbed of the FS 203 road is also in a diabase unit as it passes through the southeastern Sierra Ancha area. All of the exposures just noted are outside the main canyons and well below the elevations of the cliff dwellings. Unlike Canyon Creek Ruin, where borrow-pits were obvious in the slopes below the site (Haury 1934:25,32), no evidence of such pits near the Sierra Ancha cliff dwellings has been noted.

Stone—Exotic Materials

A number of rare mineral types occur in the Sierra Ancha and nearby. These stone types include hematite, turquoise, steatite (soapstone), serpentine, and crystals.

Hematite, including specular hematite, is occasionally found in the erosional gravels and terraces of Cherry Creek. A major source, however, is located east of Canyon Creek and northwest of Grasshopper Pueblo, at and around a place called Iron Mine. Hematite, of course, is an important mineral for pigment, particularly for painting pottery.

Turquoise is also known from Canyon Creek, but farther south. This is a source that was exploited prehistorically (Haury 1934: 15-16; Welch and Triadan 1991).

Steatite or soapstone and serpentine are minerals that can occur in a variety of circumstances, but in this area are generally associated with Mescal Limestone. In addition to a major source area near Rock House on the Q Ranch block, steatite and serpentine have been observed in the gravels of Cherry and Coon creeks. Steatite is found on the south side of Pueblo Canyon and in the canyon sides of Workman Creek, above and below the falls.

Steatite and serpentine are both used for ornaments and carving by groups in the mountains (Mogollon) and in the desert (Hohokam). Steatite tends to be gray and is commonly used for beads. Serpentine is green or greenish white, and is more commonly used for pendants or figurines.

The Q Ranch block, particularly in the area from Rock House to Vosberg, may have been responsible for much of the steatite that occurs in the Phoenix Basin. The association of steatite bead production and Hohokam ceramics is unmistakable in the Rock House to Vosberg area (Lange 1982b, 1988). After the Hohokam ceramics drop out of the local inventory, steatite use seems to shift to larger ornaments and objects, such as arrow shaft straighteners.

Crystals are occasionally found on site surfaces and, of course, also in excavated contexts (Hohmann and Kelly 1988). Chris Lange (personal communication) has said they are present at Q Ranch Pueblo. The principal source for these crystals is the Diamond Point area, east of Payson.

Another mineral that occurs in association with the Mescal Limestone, but with modern implications, is asbestos. The asbestos industry began in Arizona about 1913 (USGS and Arizona Bureau of Mines 1969). In the 1940s and 1950s, numerous asbestos mines and mills occurred throughout Gila County. However, beginning about 1953, longer-fibered asbestos from northern British Columbia, Canada, started the demise of the industry in Arizona (USGS and Arizona Bureau of Mines 1969). Serpentine and asbestos are often associated geologically.

Finally, another mineral with modern implications that occurs in the area is uranium. Deposits of uranium are indicated in the Dripping Springs Quartzite and in higher formations, that is, near the contact of the basalt and argillite above the Mescal Limestone. Uranium salts are visible on the mineshaft walls in Pueblo Canyon, for instance. Many claims were filed and a few test adits were excavated in the period after World War II. This exploration activity was the reason for many of the roads and jeep trails cut into the southeastern Sierra Ancha area

Plants

The complex geology that produces a variety of rocks and soils, coupled with rapid elevation changes and differences in facing, creates a diversity of environmental situations that are reflected in the plant communities. This is particularly true in the southeastern Sierra Ancha area. Over a 6 km distance elevation rises from 940 to 2350m. The lower elevations are characterized by Lower Sonoran desertscrub (paloverde, saguaro, mesquite, prickly pear, and other cacti)(Lowe 1964:18). The distribution and density of species has been heavily affected by grazing over the last century—creating less grass and more scrub vegetation than before. Ironically, it was the lush grassland that originally brought cattle into the area. Buster Ellison, whose family has lived in the area since before 1900, related that, in the decades around 1900, there were 10,000 head of cattle in the Tonto Basin and Cherry Creek areas.

Moving upward in elevation, Upper Sonoran Oak Woodland and Chaparral and Oak-Pine Woodland communities are found. Pinyon pine, juniper, Gambel's and Emory oak, sotol, manzanita, and cliff rose are the most prominent members of these communities. The Oak Woodland and Oak-Pine communities occur from approximately 1370 to 2130m.

Higher still, above 2130m, is the Ponderosa Pine Forest. This plant community dominates the upper slopes and mountaintops in the Sierra Ancha. At the highest points (for example, Aztec Peak) and in wetter, colder drainages (for example, upper Workman Creek), there are also small stands of Canadian and Hudsonian communities. Dominant plant species in these communities include Douglas fir, ponderosa pine, quaking aspen, and blue spruce (Lowe 1964:69-76).

The well-watered canyons, in particular those of the southeastern Sierra Ancha, also support lush riparian communities. Here are found many other species, including cottonwood, sycamore, netleaf hackberry, Arizona walnut, Arizona wild grape, maple, red bud, ferns, and mosses.

The plant diversity available in the relatively small area of the southeastern Sierra Ancha is tremendous. In close proximity are a variety of woods for construction, tools, weapons, and fuel; and a variety of plants for food (cactus fruits and beans or nuts from trees) and other uses (such as for mats, sandals, basketry, ties, snares, and dyes).

Animals

Like the plants, the animals reflect the variability of the landscape. Many of the animal species have economic importance to prehistoric as well as modern peoples. From cone-nosed kissing bugs to bears, the Sierra Ancha has a little bit of everything.

Birds are represented by species such as turkeys, blue heron, canyon wrens, and red-tail hawks. Among the mammals are mice, rabbits, fox, coyote, skunk, whitetail and mule deer, javelina, elk, bear, ringtail cats, raccoon, mountain lion, and bobcat. Javelina and elk are part of the present-day environment, but javelina would not have been present prehistorically. Elk are present today on the Q Ranch block to the east, and perhaps in the northern part of the Sierra Ancha block, and may or may not have been present in these areas prehistorically. Elk would have been present in the higher portions of the White Mountains to the east. There are fish in Cherry Creek, including native dace, sucker, and chub species (Tonto National Forest data).

The rich variety of animals means that within relatively short distances are resources that can satisfy any need. There are a variety of bones, teeth, and claws for tools and ornaments, and there are many species that can provide meat, hides, feathers, and sinew.

SUMMARY

The preceding review of the physical setting of the Sierra Ancha and other nearby blocks of land below the Mogollon Rim indicates basic similarities between the Sierra Ancha and these other landmasses. There is similar geology, stream flow, precipitation, ranges of elevation, and diversity of natural resources from block to block. The southeastern Sierra Ancha, though, concentrates these resources into a tighter area than in the other blocks, due to the extreme differences in elevation. The southeastern Sierra Ancha has diverse exposed geology, higher precipitation levels, and a variety of geological, plant, and animal resources concentrated into a limited area ($\pm$ 440 sq km).

Chapter Four
Ceramics

In the US Southwest, ceramics tend to be well preserved and abundant, and are "perceived to be endowed with a host of behavioral information" (Triadan 1997:xiii, 1). Almost uniquely among all the classes of artifacts and data analyzed by archaeologists, ceramics have the potential to inform on a number of factors, including chronology, technology, trade, exchange, population movement, and cultural interaction.

Ceramics have been a focus of study from the earliest archaeological studies in the American Southwest onward (Zedeño 1994:1). Studies of Southwestern ceramics have involved a number of assumptions, some of which have held up over time, others of which have been called into question. Zedeño (1994:1-8) provides an effective review of assumptions and trends in Southwestern ceramic studies, as well as the contexts that led to the application and occasional misuse of particular approaches to Southwestern prehistory through ceramics. Zedeño (1994:1) characterizes US Southwestern ceramic studies from the 1920s to the 1950s as largely involving the delineation of cultural boundaries, establishing regional chronologies, and inferring ethnicity and cultural relationships. The resulting temporal and spatial reconstructions of culture history were based on two assumptions: (1) prehistoric communities were autonomous and self-sufficient, and (2) ceramic manufacture was a household activity conducted in all communities using ceramics. Ceramic traits, such as color, design style, firing preferences, and manufacturing technology, were used to determine the cultural affiliation of a site, along with architecture and burial practices. There were also early attempts at establishing where ceramics were made through petrographic analyses.

In the 1960s and 1970s, what turned out to be highly controversial studies were produced by archaeologists seeking to apply concepts from processual archaeology (Zedeño 1994:4). These studies have been discredited due to poor control over chronology and sourcing of the ceramics, and the failure to account for how ceramics come to be in archaeological deposits or how they move through and between villages.

Current analyses of Southwestern ceramics rely on a multi-dimensional approach for describing ceramic assemblages and variability (Zedeño 1994:11, Simon and others 1992:61-62). These analyses often involve traditional emphases on stylistic and technological attributes, and more recent ventures into compositional and performance characteristics. Stylistic attributes involve things such as design styles and elements, and layouts of design fields. Technological attributes involve the clay, tempering, and painting materials selected, how the vessel was formed (for example, paddle-and-anvil or coil-and-scrape), and control of the firing atmosphere and temperature. Compositional studies seek to describe components of the clay and tempering materials through thin sections and sophisticated probe techniques such as instrumental neutron activation (INAA), inductively coupled plasma emission spectroscopy (ICP), and x-ray diffraction (XRF). Performance characteristics such as hardness, strength, and porosity are determined by physical testing of vessels and sherds.

As noted in Chapter 1, the southeastern Sierra Ancha is in a geographical area where archaeologists assign cultural affiliation to no one or to almost all major Southwestern prehistoric cultures. The collections of ceramics from southeastern Sierra Ancha sites, however, clearly indicate closer ceramic ties to the north and east rather than to the south and west (Ciolek-Torrello and Lange 1982, 1990). Thus, studies such as those of Crown (1994), Lyons (2003), Simon and others (1992), Triadan (1997), and Zedeño (1994) will be the most informative on the sources and dating of the ceramics found in the southeastern Sierra Ancha.

THE SIERRA ANCHA COLLECTIONS

Ceramics tabulated in this report were collected from sites in the southeastern Sierra Ancha on three separate projects: the Gila Pueblo survey, ASM's Cholla Project (see Chapter 1), and the SAP.

The Gila Pueblo survey collections were part of a general plan to collect sherds from areas across Arizona and surrounding regions in order to determine the extent and relative abundance of different wares and types (Gladwin and Gladwin 1928). Haury confirmed that the general strategy was to recover about 50 sherds from each site, roughly in proportion to their occurrence there (Lange, Ferg, and Hohmann 1983:10). These collections were made by Haury and other Gila Pueblo staff, as well as by other employees, such as the cowboy

Dewey Peterson.

The Gila Pueblo collections from the southeastern Sierra Ancha total 2685 sherds from 61 sites. This is an average of 44 sherds from each site. These ceramics have been analyzed and discussed by Ciolek-Torrello and Lange (1982, 1990), and are dominated by sherds representing White Mountain Red Ware (Carlson 1970). There are also Roosevelt Red Ware (Salado polychromes); Cibola, Little Colorado, and Tusayan white wares; and miscellaneous brown, plain, and red wares in the collections (Table 4.1). In this report, "Roosevelt Red Ware" will be used to label the exterior red-slipped, black-and-white interior bowls and polychrome red, black, and white jars that some label "Salado polychromes." This is not intended to ignore the widespread production of these ceramics or the potential social and economic implications as documented by Crown (1994). In reviewing the work of other researchers, if they used "Salado polychromes" as the primary label, that label is retained here.

The Cholla Project collected 172 sherds from vandals' backdirt at one particular site of concern here—Granite Basin Pueblo (V:1:26). These sherds were tabulated by Ciolek-Torrello and Lange (1982, 1990), and are reported again here (also in Table 4.1).

The SAP collected a total of 3910 sherds from 64 sites, an average of 61 sherds per site (totals ranged from 1 to 728). The collection strategy focused on finding decorated ceramics as well as collecting examples of the undecorated and utilitarian wares. The generally extremely low densities of surface ceramics precluded a more formal or systematic collection strategy. The SAP also recovered three nearly complete vessels (CD21-24) from vandals' backdirt at V:1:174. The results of the analysis of the SAP sherds are presented in Tables 4.2 and 4.3. Ceramic types by site are tabulated in Chapter 7.

Like the Gila Pueblo collections, the SAP collections can be used as indicators of the period of occupation for the sites. Decisions about temporal placement are made according to the criteria described by Ciolek-Torrello and Lange (1990:138). These criteria involve the determination of the dominant ceramic group represented and evaluating the presence, absence, or proportions of other ceramic characteristics (Table 4.4). The SAP collections can also be compared to the Gila Pueblo collections to determine if the recent collections indicate a need to modify earlier temporal classifications of the sites (Ciolek-Torrello and Lange 1990:139-143). The SAP collections confirm the basic patterns seen in the Gila Pueblo collections, that is, the ceramic assemblages of the sites in the southeastern Sierra Ancha represent time periods from approximately AD 1100 to 1400 [or Pueblo III and IV] (Ciolek-Torrello and Lange 1990:138), and are dominated by types and wares from geographical areas to the north and east: White Mountain Red Ware, and Cibola, Little Colorado, and Tusayan white wares. Wares represented in low proportions and numbers include Roosevelt Red Ware (less than 3 percent of the total, Gila Pueblo; 4.88 percent, SAP) and Hohokam buff wares (0.04 percent, Gila Pueblo; 0.0 percent, SAP).

COMPARISONS AND DISCUSSIONS FOR THE SAP COLLECTIONS

The SAP ceramic collections can be compared to other collections from the same general region. These other collections involve the earlier Gila Pueblo collections from the same sites, later collections from Granite Basin Pueblo in Cherry Creek, the collections from the Upper and Lower Tonto cliff dwellings, collections from sites in the eastern Tonto Basin, and collections from the Grasshopper area. Each is considered below.

Gila Pueblo Collections and Granite Basin Pueblo

As noted, the SAP and Gila Pueblo collections from the same area and many of the same sites are similar (see Tables 4.1, 4.2, and 4.3). The Cholla Project collection from Granite Basin Pueblo, however, stands out. Roosevelt Red Ware from the Cholla Project collection at Granite Basin Pueblo makes up about 40 percent of the collection compared to only 5 percent in the original Gila Pueblo collection. The Gila Pueblo collection was made when the site was undisturbed; the Cholla Project collection was made after extensive vandalism at the site, including disturbance of mortuary contexts.

Functional differences in the use of particular ceramic types can probably explain the change in proportions seen at Granite Basin Pueblo. Roosevelt Red Ware is relatively abundant in mortuary contexts at Grasshopper Pueblo (Whittlesey 1978), and in general in such contexts below the Mogollon Rim (Crown 1994:100; Wood 1985a: 10). Unpublished research has shown that Roosevelt Red Ware is rare in room floor assemblages in this area below the Mogollon Rim (Ciolek-Torrello and Lange 1990:137). If the same pattern is true at Granite Basin Pueblo, the different proportions seen for Roosevelt Red Ware in the Gila Pueblo and Cholla Project collections can be explained. Such contextual differences may also explain the generally low proportions of Roosevelt Red Ware in most of the Gila Pueblo collections from the sites in the southeastern Sierra Ancha (Ciolek-Torrello and Lange 1990 :137). Alternatively, these pottery types just may not be present in significant quantities in these sites.

Upper and Lower Tonto Ruins

From other cliff dwellings in the region, Upper

Table 4.1 Gila Pueblo and Cholla Project Ceramic Collections from Southeastern Sierra Ancha Sites

Wares and Types	Gila Pueblo Collections	Gila Pueblo Percents	Cholla Project Collections*	Cholla Project Percents
White Mountain Red Ware				
Unidentifiable	104	3.9	12	7.0
Fourmile Polychrome	170	6.3	51	29.7
Fourmile Black-on-red	13	0.5	0	0
Showlow Polychrome	12	0.4	4	2.3
Cedar Creek Polychrome	9	0.3	2	1.2
Pinedale Polychrome	31	1.2	0	0
Pinedale Black-on-red	41	1.5	1	0.6
St Johns Polychrome and Black-on-red	16	0.6	0	0
Wingate Polychrome and Black-on-red	7	0.3	0	0
Subtotal	403	15.0	70	40.7
Roosevelt Red Ware (Salado Polychromes)				
Unidentifiable	17	0.6	0	0
Tonto Polychrome	20	0.7	24	14.0
Gila Polychrome	30	1.1	39	22.7
Pinto Polychrome and Black-on-red	13	0.5	5	2.9
Subtotal	80	3.0	68	39.5
Other Polychrome				
Unidentifiable	13	0.5	3	1.7
Kinishba Polychrome	1	0.04	0	0
Cibicue Polychrome	1	0.04	4	2.3
Subtotal	15	0.6	7	4.1
Cibola White Ware				
Unidentifiable	110	4.1	2	1.2
Pinedale Black-on-white	15	0.6	1	0.6
Tularosa Black-on-white	38	1.4	4	2.3
Reserve Black-on-white	54	2.0	0	0
Puerco Black-on-white	19	0.7	0	0
Snowflake Black-on-white	89	3.3	0	0
Red Mesa Black-on-white	8	0.3	0	0
Kiatuthlanna Black-on-white	1	0.04	0	0
Subtotal	334	12.4	7	4.1
Little Colorado White Ware				
Unidentifiable	30	1.1	0	0
Holbrook Black-on-white	20	0.7	0	0
Subtotal	50	1.9	0	0
Tusayan White Ware				
Unidentifiable	1	0.04	0	0
Flagstaff Black-on-white	1	0.04	0	0
Kana-a Black-on-white	1	0.04	0	0
Subtotal	3	0.1	0	0

Table 4.1 Gila Pueblo and Cholla Project Ceramic Collections from Southeastern Sierra Ancha Sites, cont'd

Wares and Types	Gila Pueblo Collections	Gila Pueblo Percents	Cholla Project Collections*	Cholla Project Percents
Unidentified White Ware				
Subtotal	57	2.1	0	0
Brown Ware				
Brown Obliterated Corrugated	634	23.6	9	5.2
Plain rough	287	10.7	0	0
Plain smooth	127	4.7	0	0
Subtotal	1048	39.0	9	5.2
Red Ware				
Salado Red Corrugated	461	17.2	6	3.5
Salado Red Plain	123	4.6	0	0
Salado White-on-red	5	0.2	0	0
Salado Black-on-red**	1	0.04	0	0
Subtotal	590	22.0	6	3.5
Unidentified Plain Ware				
Subtotal	88	3.3	5	2.9
Other				
Tusayan Corrugated	1	0.04	0	0
Hohokam Buff Ware	1	0.04	0	0
Gila Plain	5	0.2	0	0
Gila Red with white	1	0.04	0	0
Apache Plain	9	0.3	0	0
Subtotal	17	0.6	0	0
TOTAL	2685	100	172	100

*Note: Cholla Project Collections reported here are from one site: Granite Basin Pueblo (AZ V:1:26 [ASM]).
**Note: originally typed in Haury 1934 as El Paso Polychrome; similar "Salado Black-on-red" also found at Tonto National Monument at the Upper Ruin (Steen 1962:17).

Table 4.2. Sierra Ancha Project Ceramics by Vessel Form and Ware

Form\Ware*	Jar	Jar %	Bowl	Bowl %	Ladle	Ladle %	Other	Other %	Indet	Indet %	Total	% of total
Jeddito YW	1	0.03	0	0	0	0	0	0	0	0	1	0.03
Alameda BW	256	6.55	0	0	0	0	3	0.08	116	2.97	375	9.59
Wht Mt RW	66	1.69	549	14.04	0	0	1	0.03	109	2.79	725	18.54
Tusayan WW	3	0.08	8	0.20	0	0	0	0	6	0.15	17	0.43
Lil Colo WW	3	0.08	9	0.23	0	0	0	0	4	0.10	16	0.41
Cibola WW	98	2.51	135	3.45	0	0	0	0	66	1.69	299	7.65
Roosevelt RW	47	1.20	129	3.30	0	0	1	0.03	14	0.36	191	4.88
Mogollon BW	1011	25.86	110	2.81	8	0.20	8	0.20	1039	26.57	2176	55.65
Unk Ware	2	0.05	0	0	0	0	0	0	0	0	2	0.05
Zuni Types	1	0.03	1	0.03	0	0	0	0	0	0	2	0.05
Vosberg Series	67	1.71	0	0	0	0	0	0	35	0.90	102	2.61
Apache	1	0.03	0	0	0	0	0	0	3	0.08	4	0.10
Subtotals	1556	39.80	941	24.07	8	0.20	13	0.33	1392	35.60	3910	100.00

*Note: Jeddito YW = Jeddito Yellow Ware; Alameda BW = Alameda Brown Ware; Wht Mt RW = White Mountain Red Ware; Tusayan WW = Tusayan White Ware; Lil Colo WW = Little Colorado White Ware; Roosevelt RW = Roosevelt Red Ware; Mogollon BW = Mogollon Brown Ware; Unk Ware = Unknown Ware; Indet = Indeterminate vessel form.

and Lower Tonto to the southwest and Canyon Creek Ruin to the east, detailed data are only available from the sites at Tonto National Monument (see Table 4.5). The ceramics from the Upper and Lower Tonto ruins were analyzed by two different people, thus the categories and groupings are somewhat different. Five times as many sherds were recovered from the Upper Ruin compared to the Lower Ruin. However, the general character of the assemblages is similar, with two minor exceptions. One exception is that Tonto Red seems to be more prevalent in the Lower Ruin than in the Upper Ruin (78% compared to 65%). The second exception is that although Gila and Tonto polychrome are the dominant decorated ceramics in both collections, the relative proportions are different (5% and 17.5%). Otherwise, the proportions of Salado Red Corrugated are similar (5% and 6%). All other decorated ceramics, including Cibola White Ware and White Mountain Red Ware types, are rare in both collections (less than 0.4%).

Assuming contemporaneity of the Upper and Lower Tonto cliff dwellings with some of the Sierra Ancha sites, the ceramic assemblages of the two areas could not be more different, in terms of the proportions of wares present in both areas (compare Tables 4.1, 4.3, and 4.5). White Mountain Red Ware and Cibola White Ware dominate the Sierra Ancha collections and Salado Red Corrugated is present in greater proportions as well. Roosevelt Red Ware is far less common in the Sierra Ancha sites, as represented in the Gila Pueblo collections. In the SAP collections (Table 4.2), the dominant decorated ware is White Mountain Red Ware (18.5%), followed by Cibola White Ware (7.6%) and Roosevelt Red Ware (4.9%). At the Lower Ruin at Tonto National Monument, White Mountain Red Ware and Cibola White Ware together comprise less than one percent (0.6%) of the total assemblage, Salado Red Corrugated is 5 percent of the assemblage,

while Gila and Tonto polychromes (Roosevelt Red Ware) make up 5 percent of the assemblage (Table 4.5). At the Upper Ruin, White Mountain Red Ware types are 1.27 percent of the decorated types (0.32% of the total), Cibola White Ware is 0.3 percent of decorated types (0.07% of total), and Salado Red Corrugated is 6.2 percent of the total. Roosevelt Red Ware, almost exclusively Gila Polychrome, make up 71 percent of decorated types (17.5% of total).

Tonto Basin

Heidke (1995) discusses the ceramics recovered from the Roosevelt Community Development Study. From all contexts at 27 sites in the eastern arm of the Tonto Basin, over 90,000 sherds were recovered (N = 90,316). Figures 6.3 and 6.4 in Heidke's report (1995:16-17) show the proportion of various types and wares for utility and decorated wares. In the utility wares, nothing other than plain ware and red ware are present until the Miami/Roosevelt phase. The Miami/Roosevelt and Roosevelt phases add Tonto Corrugated, Salado Red Corrugated, and Salado White-on-red (Heidke 1995:16). In the decorated wares, only Hohokam buff ware and Cibola White ware occur before the Miami/Roosevelt phase (Heidke 1995:17). Buff ware proportions decrease and Cibola White ware proportions increase over time. In the Miami/Roosevelt and Roosevelt phases, Little Colorado White Ware, Roosevelt Red Ware, White Mountain Red Ware, and McDonald Corrugated are present with Cibola White Ware still the dominant ware.

Table 4.6 summarizes the Tonto Basin ceramic proportions from the eastern Tonto Basin collected by Desert Archaeology's Roosevelt Community Study project (Elson, Stark, and Gregory 1995; Heidke 1995). The assemblages are dominated by plain wares—unslipped utility plain ware (52%) and Tonto Basin corrugated, Salado Red Corrugated, and

Cibola White Ware in roughly equal proportions (8 to 9%). Hohokam buff wares are next (approximately 5%), and Mogollon Brown Ware, Roosevelt Red Ware, and White Mountain Red Ware all occur as less than one percent of the assemblages. The rest of the ceramics (22 wares) each constitute less than 0.5 percent of the collection.

The vast majority of the plain wares, as well as Salado Red Corrugated, appear to have been made in the Tonto Basin (Simon and others 1992). In contrast, most of the decorated wares (Little Colorado White, Cibola White, and White Mountain Red wares) are made in areas to the north and east of the Tonto Basin above and below the Mogollon Rim (see the following discussion of the Grasshopper area ceramics for more details).

Grasshopper Area

Raw data concerning ceramic types, wares, and counts from sites in the Grasshopper area are difficult to find. Studies by Crown (1981), Montgomery (1992), and Zedeño (1994) all report types and wares for only whole or nearly complete vessels with an emphasis on the decorated types. Some proportions of decorated wares can be calculated from Montgomery and Reid, Table 3 (1990:93), and provide some baseline values for comparisons with the Sierra Ancha sites. Montgomery and Reid (1990) present data from Chodistaas from surface and floor contexts. Chodistaas was probably abandoned in the AD 1290s. They also present data from surface collections at Grasshopper pueblo. Percentages for all categories reflect only "rim sherds identified to individual vessels," individual complete vessels," or "rimsherds" (Montgomery and Reid 1990:93). These data are summarized here in Table 4.7.

Chodistaas is certainly earlier than most of the Sierra Ancha cliff dwellings (see Chap-

ter 5), and so it is predictable that proportions of certain wares will vary. Grasshopper was founded about the same time as most of the Sierra Ancha cliff dwellings (AD 1275-1330), but was occupied longer (after AD 1340)(Reid and Shimada 1982:16-17; Reid and Whittlesey 1999). Thus, if there are general changes in proportions of wares in the area simply based on whether a site dates before 1295, between 1295 and 1330, and after 1330, then that alone would be sufficient to explain the differences. However, the surface and floor contexts from Chodistaas also reveal different proportions. The greater proportion of Roosevelt Red Ware in floor contexts at Chodistaas is interesting, and is thought to represent a rapid shift to Roosevelt Red Ware in the later years of occupation there (after 1285 [Montgomery and Reid 1990]). In the case of Granite Basin Pueblo (see above and Table 4.1) and at Grasshopper, the higher proportions of Roosevelt Red Ware (mostly the types Gila and Tonto Polychrome) are thought to reflect mortuary contexts. The mortuary contexts were discovered by disturbance (vandalism) in the case of Granite Basin Pueblo (Ciolek-Torrello and Lange 1990:137) and through excavation in the case of Grasshopper (Whittlesey 1978).

ROOSEVELT RED WARE, CIBOLA WHITE WARE, AND WHITE MOUNTAIN RED WARE

Three principal decorated wares represented in the Sierra Ancha collections have received attention in recent years by researchers using combinations of various compositional analysis techniques. These are ceramics identified as Roosevelt Red, Cibola White, and White Mountain Red wares. One other type, Salado Red Corrugated, is also considered in the following studies and occurs commonly in the Sierra Ancha sites. Salado

Table 4.3. Sierra Ancha Project Ceramics by Vessel Form and Type

Form\ Type*	Jar	Jar %	Bowl	Bowl %	Ladle	Ladle %	Other	Other %	Indet	Indet %	Total	% of total
Bidahochi Poly	1	0.03	0	0	0	0	0	0	0	0	1	0.03
Indet WMRW	49	1.25	297	7.60	0	0	0	0	103	2.63	449	11.48
Imitation WMRW	2	0.05	0	0	0	0	0	0	0	0	2	0.05
St Johns B/R	0	0	33	0.84	0	0	0	0	5	0.13	38	0.97
St Johns Poly	0	0	12	0.31	0	0	0	0	0	0	12	0.31
Pinedale B/R	3	0.08	17	0.43	0	0	0	0	1	0.03	21	0.54
Pinedale Poly	2	0.05	10	0.26	0	0	0	0	0	0	12	0.31
Cedar Crk Poly	0	0	24	0.61	0	0	0	0	0	0	24	0.61
Fourmile Poly	10	0.26	151	3.87	0	0	1	0.03	0	0	162	4.15
Showlow Poly	2	0.05	5	0.13	0	0	0	0	0	0	7	0.18
Indet. Salado Poly	4	0.10	8	0.20	0	0	0	0	5	0.13	17	0.43
Pinto B/R & Poly	0	0	25	0.64	0	0	0	0	9	0.23	34	0.87
Gila Poly	22	0.56	92	2.35	0	0	0	0	0	0	114	2.92
Tonto Poly	21	0.54	4	0.10	0	0	1	0.03	0	0	26	0.66
Pinnawa G/W	1	0.03	0	0	0	0	0	0	0	0	1	0.03
Kechipawan Poly	0	0	1	0.03	0	0	0	0	0	0	1	0.03
Indet. LC WW	3	0.08	4	0.10	0	0	0	0	4	0.10	11	0.28
Holbrook A B/W	0	0	1	0.03	0	0	0	0	0	0	1	0.03
Walnut B/W	0	0	4	0.10	0	0	0	0	0	0	4	0.10
Indet. Tus WW	0	0	2	0.05	0	0	0	0	6	0.15	8	0..20
Blk Mesa B/W	0	0	5	0.13	0	0	0	0	0	0	5	0.13
Shato B/W	0	0	1	0.03	0	0	0	0	0	0	1	0.03
Kayenta B/W	3	0.08	0	0	0	0	0	0	0	0	3	0.08
Indet. Cib WW	58	1.48	77	1.97	0	0	0	0	66	1.69	201	5.14
Kiatuthlanna B/W	0	0	2	0.05	0	0	0	0	0	0	2	0.05
Red Mesa B/W	0	0	2	0.05	0	0	0	0	0	0	2	0.05
Puerco B/W	1	0.03	12	0.31	0	0	0	0	0	0	13	0.33
Escavada B/W	1	0.03	3	0.08	0	0	0	0	0	0	4	0.10
Snowflake B/W	12	0.31	23	0.59	0	0	0	0	0	0	35	0.90
Reserve B/W	16	0.41	4	0.10	0	0	0	0	0	0	20	0.51
Tularosa B/W	7	0.18	10	0.26	0	0	0	0	0	0	17	0.43
Pinedale B/W	3	0.08	2	0.05	0	0	0	0	0	0	5	0.13
Subtotals	1556	39.80	941	24.07	8	0.20	13	0.33	1392	35.60	3910	100.00

Red Corrugated is classified as plain or decorated depending on the analyst (see Steen and others 1962:18, 61-62). The work by Crown (1994) for the Salado Polychromes (Roosevelt Red Ware), Zedeño (1994) for Cibola White Ware and Salado Red Corrugated, and Triadan (1997) for White Mountain Red Ware provide some interesting perspectives for the presence of these wares in the Sierra Ancha sites.

Roosevelt Red Ware (Salado Polychromes)

Roosevelt Red Ware, first defined by Gladwin and Gladwin (1930), has some of the most widely dispersed southwestern ceramic types. One type in particular is especially ubiquitous—Gila Polychrome. Studies by Crown (1994:30-31) confirm that Gila Polychrome was manufactured in many locales in the Southwest, primarily in the drainages and watersheds of the Salt and Gila rivers. What is

Table 4.3. Sierra Ancha Project Ceramics by Vessel Form and Type, cont'd

Form\ Type	Jar	Jar %	Bowl	Bowl %	Ladle	Ladle %	Other	Other %	Indet	Indet %	Total	% of total
Unk. Decorated	2	0.05	1	0.03	0	0	0	0	1	0.03	4	0.10
Unknown Plain	0	0	0	0	0	0	0	0	2	0.05	2	0.05
Brown Plain	665	17.01	30	0.77	6	0.15	8	0.20	689	17.62	1398	35.75
Verde Brown	256	6.55	0	0	0	0	3	0.08	116	2.97	375	9.59
Vosberg Plain	67	1.71	0	0	0	0	0	0	35	0.90	102	2.61
Tonto Red/ Plain	7	0.18	3	0.08	0	0	0	0	5	0.13	15	0.38
Salado Red Corrugated	290	7.42	58	1.48	2	0.05	0	0	240	6.14	590	15.09
Salado Red Smooth	27	0.69	10	0.26	0	0	0	0	100	2.56	137	3.50
Salado Red w/ White	6	0.15	1	0.03	0	0	0	0	2	0.05	9	0.23
Cibecue Plain	7	0.18	0	0	0	0	0	0	0	0	7	0.18
Cibicue Poly	7	0.18	7	0.18	0	0	0	0	0	0	14	0.36
Apache Plain	1	0.03	0	0	0	0	0	0	3	0.08	4	0.10
Subtotals	1556	39.80	941	24.07	8	0.20	13	0.33	1392	35.60	3910	100.00

*Note: Poly = polychrome; WMRW = White Mountain Red Ware; B/R = Black-on-red; Indet. = Indeterminate; G/W = Glaze-on-white; LCWW = Little Colorado White Ware; Tus WW = Tusayan White Ware; B/W = Black-on-white.

Table 4.4. Ceramic Groups and Characteristics for Dating Sierra Ancha Sites (see Ciolek-Torrello and Lange 1990:138-141)

a. Ceramic Groups for Decorated Ceramics

Ceramic Group	1	2	3
Period:	Pueblo II	Pueblo III	Pueblo IV
Dates:	AD 900 – 1100	AD 1100-1300	AD 1300-1400

Ceramic
Types
	Kiathuthlanna Black-on-White
	Red Mesa Black-on-White
	Puerco Black-on-White
	Kana-a Black-on-White
		Puerco Black-on-White
		Snowflake Black-on-White
		Reserve Black-on-White
		Tularosa Black-on-White
		Holbrook Black-on-White
		Flagstaff Black-on-White
		Pinto Black-on-Red &
		  Polychrome
		Wingate Black-on-Red &
		  Polychrome
		St. Johns Black-on-Red &
		  Polychrome
			Pinedale Black-on-White
			Gila Polychrome
			Tonto Polychrome
			Pinedale Black-on-Red &
			  Polychrome
			Cedar Creek Polychrome
			Fourmile Polychrome
			Showlow Polychrome
			Kinishba Polychrome
			Cibicue Polychrome

b. Additional Criteria

1) *Thin, polished brown ware was replaced by thick plain ware and corrugated ware by about AD 1200. Thin, polished brown ware should indicate Pueblo II period date.*

2) *Corrugated ware appears in the AD 1200s and becomes the dominant type of plain ware by AD 1300 (Pueblo IV).*

3) *White wares (including undecorated pieces) are more common in Pueblo II and Pueblo III times than black-on-red and polychrome types. The latter types replaced white wares in Pueblo IV. (Pinedale Black-on-White is the only Pueblo IV white ware.)*

4) *Mineral-painted white wares gradually replace carbon-painted white wares. High proportions of carbon-painted white wares are indicative of Pueblo II and Pueblo III (Pueblo III to a lesser degree).*

unusual is that this does not just mean at a few locales in the Tonto Basin, or on the southern Colorado Plateau, or in the Safford valley, but at locales across the Southwest. Crown (1994:30) discovered eleven geographically restricted sources that could be distinguished from the sample chosen for her study. She carefully points out, however, that the study cannot demonstrate that any of the pottery was specifically made at any of the sites from which her sample was drawn. She also demonstrates that Gila Polychrome bowls were widely exchanged, in spite of widespread production at numerous locations.

Another curiosity about Roosevelt Red Ware (Gila Polychrome, in particular) is that despite the compositional variability, implying multiple locations of production, there is a great uniformity in techniques and styles of decoration at the macroscopic level (Crown 1994:31). Studies by Zedeño (1994:19,95) indicate both local and non-local versions of Roosevelt Red Ware at both Chodistaas and Grasshopper pueblos. The sources of the non-local Roosevelt Red Ware seem to be on the Colorado Plateau to the north (Zedeño 1994:99). In the Tonto Basin, multiple in-basin sources have been posited for the Salado Polychromes found at the sites investigated by Arizona State University (Simon and others 1992:74). With such good petrographic information in areas to the east, northeast, and southwest of the Sierra Ancha, it might be possible to identify where the Roosevelt Red Ware found in middle Cherry Creek came from. There are clearly several possibilities.

Cibola White Ware

Zedeño's (1994) study emphasized Cibola White Ware, but also dealt with Roosevelt Red and White Mountain Red wares and Salado Red Corrugated. Her analysis involved ceramics from several sites: Chodistaas, Grasshopper

Pueblo, Grasshopper Spring, and P:14:197. In her summation, Zedeño states:

> …the compositional variation evident in these analyses indicates that (1) Cibola White Ware vessels from Chodistaas Pueblo represent at least four analytical sources; (2) two other contemporary sites, Grasshopper Spring and AZ P:14:197 (ASM), also contain white ware vessels that represent the same analytical sources as those from Chodistaas; (3) although a few vessels from Grasshopper Pueblo were chemically similar to at least one compositional group identified in the Chodistaas sample, the majority of Cibola White Ware vessels at Grasshopper (which have brown paste rather than white paste) represent a source that is completely different from those identified for the three earlier sites; only two brown paste Cibola jars were found in the Chodistaas assemblage. … Variation in paste composition of Cibola White Ware in the Grasshopper region occurs both spatially and temporally. Cibola White Ware vessel clays from late Pueblo III sites came from at least three chemically distinct, presumably non-local sources. Later, a shift to local manufacture of the ware is indicated by the use of local clays. This shift took place sometime during the Pueblo IV occupation of Grasshopper Pueblo (Zedeño 1994:76-77).

Cibola White Ware and White Mountain Red Ware are considered to be similar in paste composition and design style (Carlson 1970; Doyel 1984; Lightfoot and Jewett 1984; Martin and others 1961; Zedeño 1994:93). Light-paste White Mountain Red Ware [and by extension, Cibola White Ware] was probably manufactured from kaolinitic clays, and such deposits are located in Cretaceous shales along the Mogollon Rim (Moore 1968; Triadan

Table 4.5. Ceramics from the Upper and Lower Ruins, Tonto National Monument (from Steen and others, 1940)

Lower Ruin (N=2634)	Number	Percent of Total	Upper Ruin (N=11873)	Number	Percent of Unpainted	Percent of Total
Plainware	2241	85.1	*Unpainted*	8931		75.2
Tonto Red	2055	78.0	Tonto Red	7711	86.3	64.9
Salado Red Corrugated	132	5.0	Corrugated (Brown)	363	4.1	3.1
Gila Red	53	2.0	Salt Red	556	6.2	4.7
Corrugated (northern?)	1	0.04	Salt Smudged	198	2.2	1.7
			Gila Plain	22	0.2	0.2
Painted	154	5.8	Gila Red	5	0.06	0.04
Gila/Tonto Polychrome	132	5.0	Gila Smudged	55	0.6	0.5
Pinto Polychrome	5	0.2	Unknown	21	0.2	0.2
Roosevelt Black-on-White	3	0.1				
Pinedale Polychrome	8	0.3	*Painted*	2942	*Percent of Painted*	24.8
Fourmile Polychrome	5	0.2	Roosevelt Black-on-White	8	0.3	0.07
Salado White-on-red	1	0.04	Pinto Polychrome	6	0.2	0.05
			Gila Polychrome	2082	70.8	17.5
Not typed(?)	239	9.1	Salado Red Corrugated	736	25.0	6.2
			Salado White-on-Red	29	1.0	0.2
			Salado Scored	38	1.3	0.3
			San Carlos Red-on-Brown	3	0.1	0.03
			St Johns Polychrome	6	0.2	0.05
			Pinedale Black-on-red	6	0.2	0.05
			Pinedale Polychrome	2	0.07	0.02
			FourmilePolychrome	23	0.8	0.2
			Unknown Painted	3	0.1	0.03

Table 4.6. Proportions of Wares in the Eastern Tonto Basin (Heidke 1995) (N = 90,316)

Ceramic Type or Ware	Percent of Collection
Unslipped utility plain ware	51.7
Unslipped Tonto Basin Corrugated ware	8.6
Salado Red Corrugated	8.6
Cibola White Ware	8.1
Hohokam buff wares	4.7
+ three others with > 500 sherds	
Mogollon Brown Ware	0.8
Roosevelt Red Ware / Salado polychromes	0.7
White Mountain Red Ware	0.7
+ 22 other wares, each	< 0.5

1997:3). Clays found south of the Mogollon Rim are almost exclusively brown-firing or red-firing, and no extensive kaolinitic deposits are known (Triadan 1997:3). The known manufacturing loci of Cibola White Ware and White Mountain Red Ware overlap along the New Mexico-Arizona border, but Cibola White Ware was also produced in areas west of the Upper Little Colorado-Puerco rivers area, as far west as the Chevelon drainage (Zedeño 1994:93). Cibola White Ware required a control of firing technology to reduce the black (iron) paint without blackening the white background, a technology shared with Colorado Plateau ceramic traditions such as Little Colorado and Tusayan white wares (Zedeño 1994:98). This area of source clays and presumed manufacturing is approximately 34 km (21 mi) north of Grasshopper Pueblo, and twice as far (68 km [42 mi]) to the north-northeast from the Sierra Ancha sites along middle Cherry Creek. Triadan (1997:40) found that Cibola White Ware

Table 4.7. Comparison of Decorated Ceramic Percentages from Chodistaas, Grasshopper, and the Sierra Ancha Sites

Site\Ware	Cibola White Ware	Roosevelt Red Ware	White Mountain Red Ware	Other Decorated	Total (N)
Chodistaas Surface	88.0	3.0*	4.5	4.5	133[a]
Chodistaas Floor	48.4	35.1*	3.1	13.4	97[b]
Grasshopper Surface	21.1	16.0	63.7	6.4	418[c]
Sierra Ancha Sites	35.5	8.5	42.8	13.3	942[d]

* = essentially all Pinto Black-on-red or Pinto Polychrome.
a = rim sherds identified to individual vessels.
b = individual complete vessels.
c = rim sherds.
d = total of decorated sherds in Gila Pueblo Sierra Ancha collections (surface).

ceramics at Grasshopper and Chodistaas were imported from a different source or sources than White Mountain Red Ware.

Zedeño (1994:93) sees the shift toward local manufacture of Cibola White Ware as marking two important population trends in the transition period from late Pueblo III to Pueblo IV: (1) abandonment of several regions on the southern Colorado Plateau followed by southward migration, and (2) aggregation of ethnically diverse populations in large pueblos. The halt in Cibola White Ware production occurred when the regions where Cibola White Ware was produced were abandoned, and access to white-firing clays ended when the populations moved away from their former residences.

Thus, Zedeño (1994:92) characterizes the circulation of Cibola White Ware pots in the Transition Zone of east-central Arizona as a result of reciprocal exchange and long-distance relationships with communities on the southern rim of the Colorado Plateau. Two mechanisms account for the circulation (Zedeño1994:92): movement of pots and movement of people. Both mechanisms could account for the Cibola

White Ware ceramics present in the southeastern Sierra Ancha sites. However, there are subtle, but critical, issues of timing and chronology that must be pursued further in order to clarify the situation.

White Mountain Red Ware

White Mountain Red Ware seems to have continuity in manufacturing, spatially and temporally, in the Upper Little Colorado River area; the areas of the modern-day communities of Pinedale, Snowflake, St Johns, Springerville, and Zuñi (Bronitski 1986; Carlson 1970:39; Doyel 1984; Duff 2002; Martin and others 1961; Rugge and Doyel 1980; Triadan 1997:93). Temporally, the related types in this ware span from late Pueblo III into early Zuñi types (such as Heshota Polychrome)(Triadan 1997:93). The Pueblo IV White Mountain Red Ware distribution seems to involve networks that were not established until after AD 1300 (Zedeño 1994:94; Triadan 1997). Although non-local Cibola White Ware at Chodistaas dates to late Pueblo III, it and the PIV White

Mountain Red Ware are compositionally different, indicating different source areas (Zedeño 1994:94).

Triadan's (1997:40) analysis of White Mountain Red Ware from the Grasshopper region found four compositional groups, two that indicate imported White Mountain Red Ware, and two that represent local production. Again, no specific production sites were determined, but the non-local (to the region below the Mogollon Rim) White Mountain Red Ware was undoubtedly produced at multiple locations in the area noted above. Local copies also seem to have been produced at a number of locations.

A preliminary sort of the SAP White Mountain Red ware ceramics by the author, using macroscopic or lower-power microscopic examination, shows that they match better to the non-local varieties identified by Triadan (1997) rather thanto locally produced types in the Grasshopper area (Table 4.8). This indicates that these types in the Sierra Ancha sites were brought in or traded from sites above the Mogollon Rim and were not locally produced at Grasshopper or in Cherry Creek. Therefore, the White Mountain Red Ware ceramics present there must have come from the north-northeast from distances of 34 km to 145 km or greater.

Salado Red Corrugated

Like Roosevelt Red Ware, the locales of production for Salado Red Corrugated are enigmatic. It can be considered as a plain ware (Steen and others 1962:61-62), or as painted pottery (Steen and others 1962:18). Even the name has been considered to be problematical (Wood 1987:34), "as it appears to have been a product of the Salado/Mogollon frontier and points east, rather than an integral component of the Salado ceramic assemblage." In the Sierra Ancha, it is often the only pottery on a site, but away from the Sierra Ancha, it seems to have been used at many sites as a burial offering (Crown 1994:103, Wood 1987:34). The author has have observed its use as a cremation container in vandalized sites in the Cherry Creek and Q Ranch areas.

Wood (1987:35) identifies three varieties of Salado Red Corrugated, but it is not clear how these relate to compositional groups described by Simon and others (1992:71-72). Seemingly, these groups would best be seen as sub-varieties of Wood's Tonto variety. Wood

Table 4.8. Local vs. Non-local Ceramics in the SAP Collections

WARE	Bowl (non-local)*	Jar (non-local)	Bowl (gray)	Jar (gray)	Bowl (local)	Jar (local)
White Mountain Red Ware	348	58	70	2	44	7
Cibola White Ware	50	144	6	16	0	4
Totals	399	205	76	18	44	11

*"non-local" is a white-pasted ceramic implying source areas above the Mogollon Rim; "gray" has a darker gray paste; "local" is a brown-pasted ceramic implying local to the Grasshopper area (see Triadan 1997).

(1987:34) dates Salado Red to AD 1200-1350, while Steen and others (1962:61-62) place the date at AD 1150-1250. Steen and others (1962:62) characterize Salado Red Corrugated as "more typical of earlier periods in the Roosevelt Lake area" (as compared to the period of occupation of the Upper and Lower ruins). Simon and others (1992:62) used Salado Red Corrugated as one of three wares to study "Salado ceramic production." This implies production of Salado Red Corrugated is attributed to a cultural group identified as "Salado." They also acknowledge (citing Wood 1987) the greater time depth of Salado Red Corrugated than the Roosevelt Red Ware polychromes. This raises several questions: Is Salado Red Corrugated a good marker (given the discrepancy in timing) for the emergence of "Salado culture"? When does Salado begin—with a type like Salado Red Corrugated or with Pinto or Gila and Tonto polychromes? Are there overlaps in manufacturing areas for Salado Red Corrugated and Roosevelt Red Ware?

The studies reported by Simon and others (1992:71) indicate that within each of the ceramic groups they identified are utility wares, Salado Red Corrugated, and polychromes from various sites, that is, the same sets of clays are being used for different wares. Salado Red Corrugated vessels seem to be produced at several locations: the Livingston area, the Rock Island Mound, the Schoolhouse Mound, and the Cline Terrace Mound. The Schoolhouse Mound is also a major production site for the Roosevelt Red Ware polychromes in the Gila phase (Simon and others 1992:74).

At Chodistaas on the Grasshopper Plateau, Zedeño (1994:71) recognizes three distinct technological traditions in the corrugated and plain vessels: brown and gray corrugated, and red plain. Zedeño (1994:71) classifies Salado Red Corrugated as a slipped variant of brown corrugated. Paste chemistry and temper mineralogy indicate that the brown corrugated tradition, including Salado Red Corrugated, represents local manufacture. There are, however, multiple sources indicated for the corrugated wares, just as for the decorated Cibola White and White Mountain Red wares. And, there are locally available iron pigments that produce a raspberry red slip (Zedeño 1994:67-68). Northwest of Grasshopper, near Canyon Creek, is an area called the "Iron Mine." It has iron, hematite, and specular hematite that may be the source of the raspberry red slip.

The above factors and studies seem to present a strong case for local manufacture of Salado Red Corrugated in at least two general locations: the Tonto Basin and the Grasshopper region. Wood (1987:34) believes the type originated in the Sierra Ancha as well. Again, it is unclear if any of the varieties identified by Wood (1987:35) correspond to any of the compositional groups defined by Simon and others (1992) or Zedeño (1994). The red slip on Salado Red Corrugated varies a little from vessel to vessel, and can be fugitive. To the author, the Salado Red Corrugated slip is unlike the red slip of White Mountain Red Ware or Roosevelt Red Ware or Gila and Tonto Red. Crown (1994:187), however, believes there are similarities between the red-slip of the Salado polychromes and that of the Salado Red ceramics, but this has not been compositionally substantiated.

Some informal experiments have been done regarding the Salado Red Corrugated slip. Possible slip pigments from the cliff behind Hematite House, red and yellow limonite, were tested by Jackie Breheney and Allen Dart. Breheny mixed the pigments with other binders and clays, and used them pure as well (Breheney 1988). Dart (1988) decanted the slip solution several times to remove the larger grains. Both experiments had trouble getting the pure form of the slip to adhere. Dart's experiment unsuccessfully attempted to polish the slip, but wetting it more and floating it into the clay body permitted some polishing. The ceramics from both experiments (tiles in the case of Breheny; a bi-lobed vessel in Dart's case) were fired in open fires. Neither result matched the raspberry slip of Salado Red Corrugated.

Elson (1990) has proposed that argillite from the western Tonto Basin near Jake's Corner was the source of the Salado slips (polychromes and Salado Red). Experiments using this material were more successful in matching the color, but it is not clear if the chemical composition matches the Salado slips and may be difficult to determine, if the argillite was mixed with other binders. Preliminary XRF tests at the Arizona State Museum Conservation Lab (April 2003) on a few sherds of Salado Red reveal the presence of iron in the slip. Several pigments (unfired, however), including examples of argillite from around the state, were also tested, but did not match the compositional profile of the slip. Clearly, the composition and source of the Salado Red Corrugated red slip is unresolved.

SUMMARY

The ceramics found on sites in the southeastern Sierra Ancha reveal that most of the occupation there occurred between approximately AD 1100 and 1400. More specific chronological placements are considered on a site-by-site basis in later chapters. The wares present are dominated by those originating to the north and northeast of the middle Cherry Creek area. These wares include White Mountain Red Ware and Cibola White Ware. Utility wares are most likely locally produced, but this has not been demonstrated through compositional studies. Salado Red Corrugated is also typical of the assemblages, and it, too, is most likely locally produced. Notably absent in significant numbers are Roosevelt Red Ware types and Hohokam buffware types. Hohokam buffware types might be expected to date earlier than AD 1100; their absence indicates that the middle Cherry Creek was not settled by peoples bearing these pottery types, even when there are indications of buffwares in the Cholla Project sites in the Rock House and Campbell Creek areas to the northeast, as well as a significant occupation at Walnut Creek Village (Morris 1970), farther north along Cherry Creek and west of the Q Ranch. Buff ware is also, of course, present in significant quantities in Tonto Basin sites dating to the AD 750 to 1050 period (Elson and Gregory 1995).

Compositional studies (Crown 1994, Zedeño 1994, Triadan 1997, Simon and others 1992) indicate that Cibola White Ware, White Mountain Red Ware, Roosevelt Red Ware, and Salado Red Corrugated ceramics were produced at a number of locations. For Cibola White and White Mountain Red wares, the production locations are above the Mogollon Rim, although local copies (on different pastes) were made at multiple locations in the Grasshopper region. Roosevelt Red Ware and Salado Red Corrugated were also made at multiple locations in the Grasshopper region, in the Tonto Basin, and possibly in the Sierra Ancha. The potential of these sourcing studies to contribute to our understanding of population identities and movement, and exchange networks and patterns is just beginning to be tapped. How the southeastern Sierra Ancha sites fit into regional dynamics may not be totally clear; however, from the perspective of the ceramic assemblages, the orientation to the north and east is clear.

*This medallion was designed as the Gila Pueblo Archaeological Foundation logo by Harold Gladwin. It was inspired by a prehistoric ceramic design. This medallion appeared on publications, site forms, labels, and stationery. This medallion and other emblems from Medallion Paper #14 (Haury 1934) appear at the ends of some chapters in honor of Harold Gladwin and Emil Haury.

Chapter Five
Trees, Tree-Rings, and Chronology

Verifying the applicability of dendrochronology and the dating sequence established for the northern southwestern United States in June, 1929 (Haury 1986) was the principal reason for Gila Pueblo's interest in the Sierra Ancha cliff dwellings (Haury 1934:iii). The samples collected in the Sierra Ancha in 1929 and 1930 "exceeded all expectations"(Haury 1934:iii), and extended tree-ring dating into the area below the Mogollon Rim for the first time.

Haury told the author that the Gila Pueblo sampling emphasized primary beams. Unfortunately, provenience information for the samples taken was inconsistent. For example, although samples from GP C:1:25 (V:1:164) were provenienced by room, the samples from GP C:1:16 West, Central, and East (designated South, Middle, and North house groups by Haury and Gila Pueblo; V:1:132 [W/S], V:1:131 [C/M], and V:1:130 [E/N]) were only provenienced by "house group." Haury (1934:17) summarized the tree-ring dates and used these as the basis for establishing the beginning and duration of occupation in the southeastern Sierra Ancha cliff dwellings. He also reports the tree-ring dates for Canyon Creek Ruin and a nearby ruin in this table, and in the totals for the Gila Pueblo samples. Gila Pueblo recovered a total of 190 sections and cores (1-inch [2.5cm] diameter), and 94 specimens were dated (Haury 1934:17), a 49.5 percent success rate.

The samples were checked and redated by the UALTRR in 1966 and 1967, and Ban-nister and Robinson published the revised data in 1971. Unfortunately, 10 of the original samples are now missing, and confirmed dates were assigned to only 79 of these 180 samples. Dates from the 1934 publication and the subsequent revisions have been reported and used by a number of researchers to date and strengthen ceramic and regional chronologies (for example, Breternitz 1966; Ciolek-Torrello and Lange 1982, 1990). The SAP submitted 505 samples to the UALTRR. We hoped these samples would provide species identification to better understand wood use, match to earlier Gila Pueblo samples to provide more specific proveniences, and provide additional dates. Species identifications were made for all samples, 62 samples were matched to Gila Pueblo samples, and 38 samples provided new dates.

WOOD USE

The wood species selected or preferred and their structural functions are tabulated in Table 5.1 for the entire set of samples. The table includes both the samples collected by Gila Pueblo and those collected by the SAP, a total of 632 samples. Table 5.1 is a summary of wood-use in the cliff dwellings of the southeastern Sierra Ancha, representing nearly all wood present in the sites, not just the dated pieces. The goal for the SAP was to sample

Table 5.1. Wood Species and Structural Functions

Species/Function	Unknown	Ponderosa Pine	Douglas Fir	White Fir	Box Elder	Oak	Juniper	Populus	Sycamore	Agave	Yucca	Non-Conifer	Pinyon Pine	Pine ?	Total
Unknown	11	45	15	4			12	2			1	2		1	93
Primary		48	23	4	1		1	6	7			6			96
Secondary	1	48	29	15	2		2	24	11			10			142
Tertiary		2	8							2					12
Vertical support		8	1		1		5								15
Lintel	8	27	27	15	5	3	30	14	7	3		2			141
Window lintel			2												2
Door jamb		4	1												5
Roof auxiliary								2							2
Loose		12	16	3	3	1	5	4	1				1		46
General roof		12	1	2			1								16
Primary?	4	5	6				1	1				1			18
Secondary?	2	9	3	5		1	1	1				1			23
Vertical post?							1								1
Lintel?	1	6	1	1			2					1			12
Loose primary			1												1
Tertiary?		1	1												2
Jacal post		4	1					1							6
Door jamb?		1													1
Totals	27	231	135	49	12	5	61	55	26	5	1	23	1	1	632

all available wood for species identification and potential dates. However, some pieces of wood were not sampled because of their poor condition. Also, at the Devils Chasm Fortress (V:1:167), there are several stubs of secondary beams exposed only on the outside of a tall wall on the edge of a high cliff (see Fig. 5.1). There was no safe way to take samples from these beams. Thus, there is still some wood not sampled, but such pieces probably would produce only additional species identifications and no dates.

Ponderosa pine is the most commonly used species (36.6%), followed by Douglas fir (21.4%), and juniper and *Populus* (9.7 and 8.7%). Two varieties of wood require additional comments:

1) *Populus* can be either cottonwood or aspen when examined macroscopically (as was done for these samples), and,

2) White fir is also a category of two potential tree types—blue spruce and white fir (only a scanning electron microscope would be able to actually distinguish the two wood types, Jeffrey S. Dean, personal communication, January 2004).

In the case of the *Populus* species, cottonwood most likely comes from a lower elevation or riparian setting. The aspen is from a higher elevation setting, over 2134 m. In the instance of blue spruce and white fir, both are higher elevation species, growing at elevations above most of the cliff dwellings.

Primary beams make up 15.2 percent of the collection, secondary beams make up 22.5 percent, and door lintels make up another 22.3 percent. Other species and structural members are present in smaller numbers (see Table 5.1). Primary beams are most often ponderosa pine and Douglas fir, although lower elevation cliff dwellings, such as Hematite House (V:5:61), have cottonwood and sycamore primaries. Sec-

Figure 5.1 Beam ends on outside of wall, Devils Chasm Fortress (AZ V:1:167[ASM]) (2004-1733-image 1390)

ondary beams are dominantly ponderosa pine and Douglas fir, with cottonwood and sycamore again prevalent at lower elevation sites. Lintels show the most diverse use of species, with nearly equal amounts of ponderosa pine, Douglas fir, and juniper, and notable quantities of white fir, *Populus*, sycamore, and box elder as well. Site by site, wood species and function are presented in Table 5.2.

It is clear that the elevation of the cliff dwelling impacts wood use (Table 5.2). Martin McAllister, former Tonto National Forest archaeologist, stated to the author that he believed one of the functions of the cliff dwellings was harvesting wood for architectural use at lower elevation sites, for instance in the Tonto Basin. If that were the case, it would be expected that cliff dwellings at any elevation would be built with the same higher elevation species, unless there were strong directives about which species go to the Basin, and which were available for local building use. There is no evidence for such a power structure in the southeastern Sierra Ancha. The presence of higher elevation pines in the Tonto Basin may be due to two mechanisms. Trees may have been harvested and transported many kilometers from the higher elevations. Or, logs may have been brought into the basin by flood events on the Salt River as driftwood, as discovered for the Homol'ovi sites along the Little Colorado River (Adams and Hedberg 2002). Pines could enter the Salt River in its upper reaches or through tributaries such as Cherry and Canyon creeks. Chemical analyses may be able to pinpoint the source(s) of the wood (English and others 2001). Date clusters and ranges will help to determine harvested wood vs. driftwood.

Riparian species dominate the lower elevation sites (Table 5.2a-c), located in settings where the vegetation away from the drainages consists of saguaro and prickly pear cactus, mesquite, and a few junipers. As elevation increases, juniper and various pines come into increasingly frequent usage, but certain riparian species are still represented. With the exception of three of the cliff dwellings (V:1:162, 163, and 133), the main pine forest on the Sierra Ancha is higher than the cliff dwellings. However, riparian areas and small stands of conifers are available for construction materials and are not too far from any cliff dwelling. In the canyons, at elevations for the cliff dwellings (over 1220m), the canyon bottoms are rising such that the riparian area below any one cliff dwelling may be from only 6 to 60m away (vertically). Also, due to the differential sun exposure on opposite sides of the canyons, riparian-type species and small stands of juniper, pinyon and ponderosa pine or fir occur on the cooler, north facing side, at the same elevation as the cliff dwellings.

For example, in Pueblo Canyon, the three larger cliff dwellings are on the north side. Up canyon, several hundred meters, is a waterfall and riparian area where the canyon bottom rises up to meet the base of the waterfall. Directly opposite, on the south side, is a small stand of fir (many of which have died from the bark beetle infestation, 2002-2003) as well as other hardwood species. Such small stands of trees would not have supplied all of the construction needs of these villages, however. In Cold Spring Canyon at V:1:136, the riparian area is not far below, and relatively close, around the north canyon edge, is a small unnamed canyon between the main Cold Spring and Pueblo canyons. On the south, north facing, side of this canyon or notch is a stand of juniper and some ponderosa pine.

Wherever the cliff dwellings are located, some wood is located nearby (within several hundred meters), particularly for lintels and other smaller structural elements. However, much of the wood had to be found or harvested and carried from considerable and difficult distances (both horizontally and vertically), up to

Table 5.2. Wood Species and Structural Functions by Site

Site	Elevation	Function	Unknown	Ponderosa Pine	Douglas Fir	White Fir	Box Elder	Oak	Juniper	Populus	Sycamore	Agave	Yucca	Non-Conifer	Pinyon Pine	Pine ?	Total
a. V:5:61	3200 ft	Primary					1			1	2						4
		Secondary									9						9
		Lintel									5						5
		Subtotals					1			1	16						18
b. V:1:127	3960 ft	Unknown											1				1
c. V:1:135	4160 ft	Unknown		7	6				1					1			15
		Primary							1	1				6			8
		Secondary				5				7				10			22
		Lintel										1		1			2
		Loose				1			2	1							4
		Subtotals		7	6	6			4	9		1		18			51
d. V:1:201	4650 ft	Unknown							4								4
e. V:1:125	4770 ft	Unknown			1												1
		Loose														1	1
		Subtotals			1											1	2
f. V:1:136	4980 ft	Unknown		2	4				2	1							9
		Primary		5	3	2				4	5						19
		Lintel							6	2							8
		Roof Auxiliary								2							2
		Primary?								1							1
		Lintel?				1			1					1			3
		Subtotals		7	7	3			9	10	5			1			42
g. V:1:130	5200 ft	Unknown		3	1												4
		Primary		6	2												8
		Secondary		8	9	1	1		1								20
		Tertiary / Closing			3												3
		Vertical Support		3	1												4
		Lintel			2	3					2						7
		Vertical Support?		1													1
		Lintel?							1								1
		Subtotals		21	18	4	1		2		2						48

Table 5.2. Wood Species and Structural Functions by Site, cont'd

Site	Elevation	Function	Unknown	Ponderosa Pine	Douglas Fir	White Fir	Box Elder	Oak	Juniper	Populus	Sycamore	Agave	Yucca	Non-Conifer	Pinyon Pine	Pine ?	Total
h. V:1:131	5200 ft	Primary		12	7												19
		Secondary		11	1	1	1		1	2	1						18
		Tertiary / Closing			1												1
		Vertical Support		2			1		3								6
		Lintel		7	11	4	1	2		4		2					31
		Window Lintel			2												2
		Door Jamb		1	1												2
		Loose		3	2		1	1	1		1						9
		Primary?		1													1
		Secondary?			2												2
		Lintel?		1													1
		Tertiary?		1	1												2
		Subtotals		39	28	5	4	3	5	6	2	2					95
i. V:1:132	5200 ft	Unknown		5	1												6
		Primary		5	3	2											10
		Secondary		5	6	4				7	1						23
		Tertiary / Closing		1	4							2					7
		Vertical Support		2													2
		Lintel		11	10	8	4	1									34
		Loose		2					1								3
		General Roof		11					1		1						13
		Primary?			1												1
		Secondary?			1												1
		Lintel?			1												1
		Loose Primary			1												1
		Subtotals		42	28	14	4	2	2	7	2	2					102
j. V:1:134	5200 ft	Unknown		1													1
		Lintel		1					1								2
		Loose		2	4		2			2							10
		Subtotals		4	4		2		1	2							13
k. V:1:165	5200 ft	Unknown	3	5					4								12
		Lintel							6								6
		Subtotals	3	5					10								18

Table 5.2. Wood Species and Structural Functions by Site, cont'd

Site	Elevation	Function	Unknown	Ponderosa Pine	Douglas Fir	White Fir	Box Elder	Oak	Juniper	Populus	Sycamore	Agave	Yucca	Non-Conifer	Pinyon Pine	Pine ?	Total
l. V:1:168	5200 ft	Unknown				1											1
		Primary			2												2
		Lintel			2				2	2							6
		Primary?			1												1
		Secondary?		1										1			2
		Lintel?		1													1
		Subtotals		2	5	1			2	2				1			13
m. V:1:167	5240 ft	Unknown		2	4												6
		Primary			4												4
		Secondary		1	6					7							14
		Lintel		1	1				13	6				1			22
		Loose			1					1							2
		Primary?							1					1			2
		Lintel?			3												3
		Subtotals		4	19				14	14				2			53
n. V:1:174	5280 ft	Unknown				1											1
o. GP C:1:38	5860 ft	Unknown		3													3
p. GP C:1:47	5860 ft	Unknown		2													2
q. GP C:1:50	5860 ft	Unknown							1					1			2
r. V:1:164	6180 ft	Primary		7	1												8
		Secondary		12	2												14
		Vertical Support							2								2
		Lintel		1													1
		Door Jamb		1													1
		Loose		1					1								2
		Primary?		2													2
		Subtotals		24	3				3								30

Table 5.2. Wood Species and Structural Functions by Site, cont'd

Site	Elevation	Function	Unknown	Ponderosa Pine	Douglas Fir	White Fir	Box Elder	Oak	Juniper	Populus	Sycamore	Agave	Yucca	Non-Conifer	Pinyon Pine	Pine ?	Total
s. V:1:133	6800 ft	Unknown		2													2
		Lintel		2	1				1								4
		Loose		1													1
		General Roof		1		4											5
		Secondary?		2													2
		Subtotals		8	1	4			1								14
t. V:1:163	7120 ft	Unknown		2		1										1	4
		Secondary			1	3											4
		Door Jamb		2													2
		Loose			1												1
		Primary?		1													1
		Secondary?			1												1
		Lintel?		3													3
		Door Jamb?		1													1
		Subtotals		9	3	4										1	17
u. V:1:162	7180 ft	Unknown		1													1
		Primary		9													9
		Secondary		11	4	1				1							17
		Tertiary & Closing		1													1
		Vertical Support		1													1
		Lintel		3													3
		Loose		1	2												3
		Primary?		2													2
		Secondary?		5		5				2							12
		Jacal Post		4		2											6
		Subtotals		38	6	8				3							55
ALL SITES		TOTAL	27	231	135	49	12	5	61	55	26	5	1	23	1	1	632

1 km away, or possibly farther. As discovered at AZ V:1:136 (see Chap. 1, Fig. 1.6), transporting the larger beams would have required a work party of 4 to 6 people or more to carry and maneuver the beams through the canyons and across the slopes. Beams in the Sierra Ancha cliff dwellings seem to have been debarked and then hand carried to the sites. There is rarely bark present on the beams and no evidence of scarring and gouging that would have resulted from dragging or rolling the beams. Such scarring is evident, however, on beams at Canyon Creek Ruin (Haury 1934:55).

Estimates can be made for the total amount of wood required for the roofs of the Sierra Ancha cliff dwellings (Table 5.3), and the total amount of wood present for sampling by Gila Pueblo and the SAP can be documented. The numbers and proportions of dates obtained from the different types of structural elements can also be summarized. The following section will explore the chronological implications of the dates in more detail, but for the present discussion, it is important to point out that the cliff dwellings in the southeastern Sierra Ancha were generally constructed over a 50-year period, from AD 1280 to 1330, and mostly between AD 1300 and 1320. Thus, the numbers in Table 5.3 indicate a major impact on the forest and riparian areas during a relatively short time period, for construction as well as for firewood and other uses.

The data are generated from 19 cliff dwellings sampled by Gila Pueblo or the SAP; data for several other sites are too incomplete for consideration in this table. Construction materials would have required a large number of small-to-medium-sized trees, collected or harvested from dead-and-down, dead-and-standing, or living trees. Tertiary or closing material would have required collecting or cutting off additional limbs, branches, and split pieces, as well as cane or reed, grass tufts, and other materials. Estimates can be made that between 220 and 250 primary beams would have been needed for all of the roofs in the 19 sites, and that 150 to 170 of these beams are missing or have been missing certainly since before the Gila Pueblo sampling in 1929-30 (Table 5.3). Of these beams, only 67 (28.3%) are still present. For secondary beams, the numbers are even more alarming. Approximately 180 secondary beams are still present from a maximum estimate of 1855 beams (9.7 %).

The species (and their proportions) presented for primary beams are likely to be relatively accurate, however, the low percentage of secondaries still present could mean that the characterization of secondaries is somewhat less certain. The location of wood remaining in the sites was plotted. Both wood and wood with dates are fairly well distributed throughout or across sites (see SAP archives). Thus, all construction episodes should be represented in most cases. The amount of wood present varies from nearly totally intact (for example, V:1:162), to moderately intact (V:1:130-132), to almost or totally missing (V:1:174 and 188). There are several reasons why wood is missing from the cliff dwellings, and some interesting problems in interpreting how the wood became missing.

Initial construction in the cliff dwellings is expected to occur in the deepest, most protected, part of the overhang, and some overhangs are not very deep or sheltering. There are also situations (for example, V:1:136 and V:1:164) where rooms nearer the drip line may have been built first in order to hold up additional rooms built behind and above them. If additions were then made to the original construction, the new rooms would be farther toward the drip line at the front of the cavern or closer to the less well-protected ends of the cavern. These "outer" rooms, then, would be more susceptible to weathering and subsequent deterioration of their roofs and walls. The outer rooms would also be the easiest from

Table 5.3. Wood Present and Missing

SITE	PRIMARIES				SECONDARIES				TOTAL DATES*
	Present	Absent	Total	Dates	Present	Absent	Total	Dates	
V:1:130	7	5	12	5+2?	17	43-163?	60-180?	5	16
V:1:131	17	18-21?	35-38?	9+1?	13	217-332?	230-345?	2	21
V:1:132	7	15	22	6+2?	22	155?	177?	2	17
V:1:133	0	12-24?	12-24?	?	0	120?	120?	?	6
V:1:134	0	5	5	?	9	61?	70?	0	1
V:1:135	4	17?	21?	?	23	76?	99?	?	7
V:1:136	--	--	--	--	17	9	26	1?	1
V:1:162	11	0	11	10	26	14?	40?	2	13
V:1:163	1	1	2	0	4	1	5	2	4
V:1:164	4	5?	9?	4?	19	12?	31?	0	11
V:1:165	0**	11	11	3	1	83?	84?	0	3
V:1:167	4	23?	27?	4	11	130?	141?	1	10
V:1:168	2	4?	6?	3	2?	38?	40?	0	4
V:1:174	1	2?	3?	1	0	27?	27?	0	1
V:1:188	0	3?	3?	0	0	27?	27?	0	0
V:5:61	3	6?	9?	0	16	119?	135?	0	0
C:1:38	2	6?	8?	1	0	70?	70?	0	1
C:1:47	0	9?	9?	0	0	78?	78?	0	0
C:1:50	4	13?	17?	0	?	160?	160?	0	0
TOTALS	67	155-170?	222-237?	46#	180	1440-1675	1620-1855	15	116

*includes dates from vertical supports, lintels, door jambs, and tertiary or closing materials
**Gila Pueblo may have found as many as 5 primaries here in 1929-30
#Gila Pueblo may have gotten dates from 5 more beams that are primaries (so total would be 51)

which wood could be obtained for re-use—for construction or re-construction by the original inhabitants or later Apaches in the same or at nearby sites. Wood can also have been salvaged or roofs dismantled for firewood by the original residents, Apaches, cowboys, or campers and hikers. Salvage for firewood would have had the greatest impact on secondary and tertiary materials, with less impact on the primary beams. Forest fires are documented for the destruction of the roofs in V:1:163 in 1924 (see Gila Pueblo site form for C:1:14), and seems to be a possibility for the Devils Chasm Fortress (V:1:167) as well. In one case noted above, a Douglas fir log, presumably a primary beam, was removed by a California violin-maker (see Gila Pueblo site form for C:1:45). Finally, insects have taken and continue to take a toll on the remaining beams. Whatever the reason or reasons, a large number of beams are no longer present in most of the cliff dwellings.

How certain beams were removed can be puzzling. For secondary beams, often cantilevered near the cliff at one end, the beam can be lifted out of the socket in the front wall fairly easily. They can usually be removed without disturbing the plaster or any wall courses above the beam. However, for primary beams, the removal is more puzzling. Primary beans in these sites often span parallel to the cliff and are plastered into the side walls (Lange and others 1993). There are many instances where it is evident that the beam has shrunk, and this is expected to have occurred to the beams in nearly every roof. There are also many instances where the beam is no longer present, but the holes, plaster around the holes, and walls are still intact. Just how a beam could be slipped through the hole one direction or the other (due to shrinking) or just enough to free one end and then lift it up or down or move it side to side without disturbing the wall and plaster at the other end is a mystery. Only if the beam were cut or burned in half does it seem

possible to remove the beam without disturbing the plaster and the walls. However, cutting the beam in half negates its future use as a primary, or even a secondary, in another structure.

Dates for most sites are relatively few, so perhaps certain dates or date clusters are missing. With the existing dates and tree-ring information, there is no indication that a room or rooms were dismantled and the wood re-built into another room at the same or another site. There is, however, architectural evidence of the dismantling of rooms at several of the sites, so wood materials certainly could have been recycled to some extent. The sites in Pueblo Canyon (V:1:130-132), where the borrowing and re-use of wood between sites would be easiest to do, have relatively good and numerous dates. The dates are not distributed in a manner that would suggest dismantling and re-use from site to site.

However, there is another intriguing possibility that could explain the quantities of missing timbers. This possibility would also mean that certain aspects of tree-ring derived dates from sites in Cherry Creek would need to be carefully evaluated. It seems unlikely that so many primary beams, and even secondary beams, were removed for firewood—they are too large and too cumbersome to be efficient for camp and cooking fires. Several scenarios are possible if the beams were recycled for construction at some of the large pueblos that may have been built after the cliff dwellings were abandoned, or whose occupation outlasted that of the cliff dwellings. Based on the ceramics recovered, there are several sites built or occupied after the cliff dwellings had been abandoned. In particular, there are three, large pueblos: Granite Basin Pueblo (V:1:26), Pottery Point Pueblo (V:1:166), and V:1:177. There are approximately 250 rooms (combined) at these three sites.

There is not an abundance of wood available in the riparian community along Cherry

Creek. Much of the wood needed in these sites would have to be cut and transported from the top of the Sierra Ancha. Beams from the cliff dwellings would be already cut and lighter due to aging. And, they would essentially be the same distance away from the pueblos. For purposes of this argument, assume that it is possible to dismantle a roof without disturbing the walls or cutting the beams.

Thus, Scenario #1: The cliff dwellings were abandoned, and the beams from the cliff dwellings were salvaged and re-used in building or adding to surface pueblos in Cherry Creek by the residents of the large pueblos.

Scenario #2: As the cliff dwellings were abandoned, the residents of the cliff dwellings took their beams with them to build or add onto parts of the larger pueblos in Cherry Creek.

Implication #1: If beams or beam fragments are preserved in the sites noted, excavations may show higher proportions of higher elevation wood species than might be expected. Certain rooms or roomblocks may show almost exclusive use of the higher elevation species for the major primary and secondary roof components. It would also be interesting to find and sample driftwood piles in Cherry Creek, as was done at Homol'ovi (Adams and Hedberg 2002), to establish a baseline of species and to characterize the distribution of tree-ring dates from this type of source.

Implication #2: If beams have been recycled and datable materials are recovered, dates from the surface pueblos must be regarded carefully. Dates would be expected to match the dates from the cliff dwellings. The match could indicate contemporaneity of the cliff dwellings and the pueblos, or the re-use of older beams in later construction at the pueblos. Perhaps chemical sourcing studies of beams from the cliff dwellings and beams from the pueblos (see English and others 2001) would indicate the same source areas for the beams in each site type. If the source areas are different, the

expectation is that the sites are contemporaneous if the dates match. If the source areas are the same, and the dates match, they could be contemporaneous, or the beams may have been recycled.

CHRONOLOGY

It is fortunate that Gila Pueblo sampled when they did, and that the proportion of datable beams is relatively good. Of the original 180 samples taken from the Sierra Ancha area sites by Gila Pueblo, 79 were datable. And, among the 505 samples recovered by the SAP, 62 were matched to earlier Gila Pueblo samples. This means, though, that 118 Gila Pueblo samples were not matched, because the beams are now missing, or because it was impossible to conclusively match SAP to Gila Pueblo samples.

There were 443 SAP samples that did not match to Gila Pueblo samples. The SAP samples did provide 37 new dates, raising the total of dated samples for sites in the southeastern Sierra Ancha area to 116. The matched SAP and Gila Pueblo samples complemented each other well—in certain cases, one or the other provided better interior or outside dates.

In the final dataset, 46 of 67 (68.7%) of primaries still present in the sites were datable. Looking further at data in Table 5.3, the 67 primaries still present represent an estimate of 28.3 percent (67 of 237) primaries once there. And, 46 dated samples represents dates for only about 20 percent of primaries that were once there (46/222 = 20.7%; 46/237 = 19.4%). Finally, of the 116 total tree-ring dates from these sites, 46 (39.7%), are dates from primary beams.

For secondary beams, only 15 of 180 (8.3%) still present were datable. Again from Table 5.3, the 180 secondaries still present represent only about 9.7 percent (180/1855) of secondary beams ever there. The 15 dated secondary beams represent only about 1 percent of secondaries that were once there (15/1620 = 0.9%; 15/1855 = 0.8%). And finally, 15 (12.9%) of the total set of 116 tree-ring dates are from these beams. Other structural elements, including lintels, vertical supports, door jambs, and tertiary (closing) material, account for 47.4 percent of the dates (55/116).

Clearly, the Gila Pueblo emphasis on larger beams (primaries and vertical supports) to obtain dates is validated by the results from these samples. The more complete sampling by the SAP did provide more thorough data concerning species and wood use, better proveniences for the Gila Pueblo samples, and approximately 50 percent more tree-ring dates.

The best date ranges assignable to a particular sample are presented in Table 5.4. The date range for some samples is a combination of information from the earlier Gila Pueblo analysis, the Bannister and Robinson (1971) re-analysis, and the analysis of the SAP sample. The span of cutting dates, from AD 1274B to 1340rL, confirms the general date range first proposed by Gila Pueblo for the analysis and interpretation of their samples (Haury 1934:17). The tree-ring dates are discussed below on a site-by-site basis, in order to interpret the period(s) of construction at a site. Comments from Bannister and Robinson (1971) are used as the basis for many of these summaries. Architectural relationships and implications for site growth are considered in more detail in the following chapter on sites and architecture.

GP C:1:38

This site is a 6 room cliff dwelling in the cliff face above Granite Basin Pueblo (V:1:26), the largest pueblo and probably the latest occupied site in middle Cherry Creek. Wood is scarce at the site, and the single cutting date (1340rL)

recovered by Gila Pueblo "is toward the end of the range for the Sierra Ancha ruins"(Bannister and Robinson 1971:21).

V:1:130, GP C:1:16E/N

Bannister and Robinson (1971:17) felt that for the three house groups comprising GP C:1:16, "overall, construction falls between AD 1290 and 1320." One room in the east group (Room 7; Fig. III.26) has both the earliest and latest cutting dates, AD 1274B and 1324G, although the latest date is from a loose log, a possible lintel. Other cutting dates from the same room suggest a construction date in the very late AD 1290s (1287B, 1297B, 1299B). Dates from other rooms (unknown, and Rooms 2 and 3) are not cutting dates, but suggest construction in the mid to late decade after 1310 (1313vv), and in the 1320s (1320vv, 1321vv). Gila Pueblo Sample #346, attributed by Bannister and Robinson to the "north house group," is actually matched to a primary beam at V:1:131 (the middle or central house group), so the date should not be included with this group of rooms.

V:1:131, GP C:1:16 C/M

Dates presented in Bannister and Robinson (1971) have been somewhat revised. This is one of the two largest cliff dwellings in the southeastern Sierra Ancha, and seems to show roughly four clusters of dates. The earliest dates are AD 1284vv and 1287+G, from two different rooms; the latest are 1321v from one room. Rooms 8, 10, and 11 (Fig. III.27) seem to have been built in the mid to late AD 1290s (1284vv, 1291vv, 1293, 1294v, 1294+vv, 1297v). Rooms 3 and 20 may date to the early-middle 1310s (1312rL, 1312vv), and Room 5 to the late 1310s (1316vv). Room 15 has a cutting date (1319B) and some later non-cutting dates (1318v, 1319vv, 1320vv) that indicate probably

Table 5.4. Tree-Ring Dates from the Southeastern Sierra Ancha (TRL = UA Laboratory of Tree-Ring Research number; GPN = Gila Pueblo number; FLDNO = SAP Field Number; AZSITE = AZSITE number (AZ); GPSITE = Gila Pueblo Site Number (GP); PROV = Provenience; DATEIN = date of inside ring; DATEOUT = date of outside ring)

TRL	GPN	FLDNO	AZSITE	GPSITE	PROV	SPECIES	FUNCTION	DATEIN	DATEOUT	REMARKS
0	322		41018	C:1:38		Ponderosa pine	unknown	1281 p	1340 rL	incomplete
0	0	3-1	V:1:125		below	Pinyon pine		1790+/-p inc	1961 vv	
0	0	3-2	V:1:125		in cave	Pinyon pine		1691	1838B inc	
0	279		V:1:130	C:1:16E		Ponderosa pine	unknown	1234	1320 vv	
0	347		V:1:130	C:1:16E		Douglas fir	unknown	1242 np	1277 vv	
445	280	02-01	V:1:130	C:1:16E	Rm 2	Ponderosa pine	primary	1199 p	1313 vv	incomplete, erratic
446	282	02-02	V:1:130	C:1:16E	Rm 2	Ponderosa pine	primary	1233 fp	1321 vv	inc, doubles
448	283	03-01	V:1:130	C:1:16E	Rm 3	Douglas fir	primary	1203 np	1309 vv	incomplete
451	288	05-01	V:1:130	C:1:16E	Rm 5	Douglas fir	primary	1218 np	1313 ++vv	inc, ring count
453	0	06-01	V:1:130	C:1:16E	Rm 6	Douglas fir	lintel	1304 fp	1321 v	incomplete
464	0	07-10	V:1:130	C:1:16E	Rm 7	Douglas fir	secondary	1269 np	1297 B	complete
465	0	07-11	V:1:130	C:1:16E	Rm 7	Douglas fir	secondary	1252 p	1296 v	complete
466	0	07-12	V:1:130	C:1:16E	Rm 7	Douglas fir	secondary	1250 p	1274 B	complete
467	0	07-13	V:1:130	C:1:16E	Rm 7	Ponderosa pine	secondary	1259 p	1299 B	complete
468	0	07-14	V:1:130	C:1:16E	Rm 7	Ponderosa pine	secondary	1235 fp	1292 vv	inc, 1288 absent
476	284	07-22	V:1:130	C:1:16E	Rm 7	Ponderosa pine	lintel?	1241 fp	1324 G	complete
477	0	07-23	V:1:130	C:1:16E	Rm 7	Douglas fir	tertiary		1293	
479	286	07-25	V:1:130	C:1:16E	Rm 7	Douglas fir	tertiary	1247	1287 B	complete
485	0	08-01	V:1:130	C:1:16E	Rm 8	Ponderosa pine	primary	1164 np	1297 vv	incomplete, erratic
546	270		V:1:131	C:1:16C	?	Douglas fir	primary	1259 fp	1320 vv	
0	271		V:1:131	C:1:16C	?	Ponderosa pine	lintel	1239 p	1293 v	incomplete
487	0	01-02	V:1:131	C:1:16C	Rm 1	Douglas fir	lintel	1272 p	1321 v	complete?
488	0	01-03	V:1:131	C:1:16C	Rm 1	Douglas fir	lintel	1300 p	1321 v	comp, AVM489?
489	0	01-04	V:1:131	C:1:16C	Rm 1	Douglas fir	lintel	1296 fp	1321 v	comp, AVM488?
494	273	03-01	V:1:131	C:1:16C	Rm 3	Ponderosa pine	primary	1228	1312 vv	incomplete
499	275	05-02	V:1:131	C:1:16C	Rm 5	Ponderosa pine	primary	1246 np	1316 vv	inc, doubles
501	277	05-04	V:1:131	C:1:16C	Rm 5	Ponderosa pine	primary	1201 np	1304 np	incomplete
504	0	05-07	V:1:131	C:1:16C	Rm 5	White fir	lintel	1252 p	1287 +G	complete
512	0	08-01	V:1:131	C:1:16C	Rm 8	Douglas fir	primary	1227 p	1294 +vv	incomplete
527	0	09-05	V:1:131	C:1:16C	Rm 9	Douglas fir	door jamb	1250 fp	1268 vv	incomplete

Table 5.4. Tree-Ring Dates from the Southeastern Sierra Ancha, cont'd

TRL	GPN	FLDNO	AZSITE	GPSITE	PROV	SPECIES	FUNCTION	DATEIN	DATEOUT	REMARKS
283	0	10-03	V:1:131	C:1:16C	Rm 10	Ponderosa pine	lintel	1243 p	1291 vv	incomplete, erratic
529	272	10-05	V:1:131	C:1:16C	Rm 10	Ponderosa pine	lintel	1244 p	1297 v	erratic
286	0	11-03	V:1:131	C:1:16C	Rm 11	Ponderosa pine	primary	1245 fp	1294 v	complete
287	0	11-04	V:1:131	C:1:16C	Rm 11	White fir	secondary	1226 p	1284 vv	inc, 1263 absent
538	0	11-15	V:1:131	C:1:16C	Rm 11	Ponderosa pine	primary	1259	1293	
293	0	15-01	V:1:131	C:1:16C	Rm 15	Douglas fir	primary	1261 fp	1319 vv	inc, complacent?
294	0	15-02	V:1:131	C:1:16C	Rm 15	Douglas fir	primary	1231 Np	1318 v	complete, erratic
546	0	15-03	V:1:131	C:1:16C	Rm 15	Douglas fir	primary	1263 p	1319 B	complete
547	0	15-04	V:1:131	C:1:16C	Rm 15	Douglas fir	secondary	1259 fp	1320 vv	
295	346	20-01	V:1:131	C:1:16C	Rm 20	Douglas fir	loose log	1233 p	1312 rL	comp, same F4365?
0	244		V:1:132	C:1:16W	?	Ponderosa pine	unknown	1269 np	1307 vv	
0	246		V:1:132	C:1:16W	?	Ponderosa pine	unknown	1251 fp	1298 vv	
0	259		V:1:132	C:1:16W	?	Ponderosa pine	general roof	1265 fp	1285 v	incomp, roof plank
236	0	01-01	V:1:132	C:1:16W	Rm 1	Douglas fir	lintel	1284	1306	tentative, 23 rings
246	251	06-05	V:1:132	C:1:16W	Rm 6	White fir	primary	1277	1306	tentative
247	252	06-06	V:1:132	C:1:16W	Rm 6	Douglas fir	secondary	1210 p	1288 v	complete
577	0	06-19	V:1:132	C:1:16W	Rm 6	Douglas fir	secondary		1297	possible
578	0	06-20	V:1:132	C:1:16W	Rm 6	Douglas fir	tertiary	1232 fp	1303 B	complete
250	251	08-01	V:1:132	C:1:16W	Rm 8	Douglas fir	loose primary	1240 np	1287 vv	complete?
251	0	08-02	V:1:132	C:1:16W	Rm 8	Douglas fir	secondary	1255 p	1288 v	incomplete
253	251	08-04	V:1:132	C:1:16W	Rm 8	Douglas fir	primary	1243 p	1287 vv	incomplete
581	251	08-08	V:1:132	C:1:16W	Rm 8	Douglas fir	tertiary	1243 p	1287 vv	incomplete
586	248	10-01	V:1:132	C:1:16W	Rm 10	Douglas fir	primary	1262 np	1305 vv	incomplete
255	0	11-01	V:1:132	C:1:16W	Rm 11	Douglas fir	tertiary	1221 Fp	1287 vv	inc, see AVM257
257	0	11-03	V:1:132	C:1:16W	Rm 11	Douglas fir	tertiary	1221 Fp	1287 vv	inc, see AVM255
263	243	17-02	V:1:132	C:1:16W	Rm 17	Ponderosa pine	primary	1249 p	1305 vv	complacent
280	0	21-03	V:1:132	C:1:16W	Rm 21	Douglas fir	primary?	1227 p	1283 vv	incomplete
0	56		V:1:133	C:1:21		White fir	general roof		1291	loose log, gen roof
0	57		V:1:133	C:1:21		White fir	general roof	1238 p	1292 vv	incomplete
0	58		V:1:133	C:1:21		Ponderosa pine	general roof		1289	

Table 5.4. Tree-Ring Dates from the Southeastern Sierra Ancha, cont'd

TRL	GPN	FLDNO	AZSITE	GPSITE	PROV	SPECIES	FUNCTION	DATEIN	DATEOUT	REMARKS
0	60		V:1:133	C:1:21	Rm 2	Ponderosa pine	lintel		1300	
0	61		V:1:133	C:1:21	Rm 8?	Ponderosa pine	loose log		1298	
0	348		V:1:133	C:1:21		Ponderosa pine	unknown	1231 p	1320 rL	comp. same F-4362
613			V:1:134	C:1:23	downslope	Douglas fir	loose log	1242 p	1297 vv	incomplete
0	233		V:1:135	C:1:40	Rm 3?	Ponderosa pine	unknown	1306	1326 vv	incomplete
0	234		V:1:135	C:1:40	Rm 5?	Ponderosa pine	unknown	1292	1317 vv	incomplete
0	238		V:1:135	C:1:40	Rm 10?	Ponderosa pine	unknown	1265	1303 vv	inc. same as GP237
0	240		V:1:135	C:1:40	Rm 10?	Douglas fir	unknown	1195	1222 vv	incomplete
0	323		V:1:135	C:1:40		Douglas fir	unknown	1200 p	1304 r	comp. same as GP 241, F4360, F-4367
0	324		V:1:135	C:1:40		Douglas fir	unknown	1273 p	1304 r	complete
0	326		V:1:135	C:1:40		Douglas fir	unknown	1217 p	1304 cL	complete
357	0		V:1:136	C:1:36		Douglas fir	unknown	1252 p	1288 v	incomplete
0	80	01-01	V:1:162	C:1:8	Rm 1	Ponderosa pine	primary?	1233 p	1328 L	incomplete
0	340	01-02	V:1:162	C:1:8	Rm 1	Ponderosa pine	primary?	1221 p	1327 +L	incomplete
0	82	01-03	V:1:162	C:1:8	Rm 1	White fir	secondary?	1293 p	1327 rL	incomplete
0	85	02-01	V:1:162	C:1:8	Rm 1	Ponderosa pine	primary	1245	1327 rL	complete
0	84	02-02	V:1:162	C:1:8	Rm 2	Ponderosa pine	primary	1249 p	1327 rL	complete
0	86	02-03	V:1:162	C:1:8	Rm 2	Ponderosa pine	vert. support	1264	1328 rL	incomplete
0	79	02-19	V:1:162	C:1:8	Rm 2	White fir	loose log	1295 p	1327 L	complete
0	339	04-01	V:1:162	C:1:8	Rm 4	Ponderosa pine	primary	1255 p	1328 B	incomplete
0	87	04-02	V:1:162	C:1:8	Rm 4	Ponderosa pine	primary	1239 p	1327 B	complete
0	88	06-01	V:1:162	C:1:8	Rm 6	Ponderosa pine	primary	1243	1322 ++rB	complete
0	89	06-02	V:1:162	C:1:8	Rm 6	Ponderosa pine	primary	1262	1328 rB	incomplete
0	90	06-03	V:1:162	C:1:8	Rm 6	Ponderosa pine	primary	1245	1328 L	complete
0	91	06-04	V:1:162	C:1:8	Rm 6	Ponderosa pine	primary	1232	1327 v	incomplete
0	341	01-01	V:1:163	C:1:14	Rm 1	Ponderosa pine	lintel?		1064 vv	incomplete
0	71	01-04	V:1:163	C:1:14	Rm 1	White fir	secondary	1253 p	1312 cL	incomplete
0	70	01-10	V:1:163	C:1:14	Rm 1	Ponderosa pine	secondary?	1257 p	1311 rL	complete
617	74	03-01	V:1:163	C:1:14	Rm 3	Ponderosa pine	door jamb	1213	1295 B	comp. same GP75
0	96		V:1:164	C:1:25	Rm 4	Ponderosa pine	unknown	1191 p	1246 v	incomplete

Table 5.4. Tree-Ring Dates from the Southeastern Sierra Ancha, cont'd

TRL	GPN	FLDNO	AZSITE	GPSITE	PROV	SPECIES	FUNCTION	DATEIN	DATEOUT	REMARKS
0	100		V:1:164	C:1:25	Rm 1	Douglas fir	loose log	1183 p	1296 +v	incomplete
0	191		V:1:164	C:1:25	Rm 1	Douglas fir	unknown	1251	1310 v	complete
0	195		V:1:164	C:1:25	Rm 1	Ponderosa pine	unknown	1184	1266 vv	incomplete
0	196		V:1:164	C:1:25	Rm 1	Ponderosa pine	unknkown	1242	1295 vv	incomplete
0	202		V:1:164	C:1:25	beh. Rm1	Douglas fir	loose log	1072 fp	1317 vv	incomp, same as GP203 & 204
0	205		V:1:164	C:1:25	beh. Rm1	Ponderosa pine	loose log	1240	1305 v	complete
0	350		V:1:164	C:1:25		Ponderosa pine	unknown	1261 p	1316 L	complete
621	192	01-02	V:1:164	C:1:25	Rm 1	Ponderosa pine	primary	1263	1316 L	incomp. see GP192
633	0	01-14	V:1:164	C:1:25	Rm 1	Douglas fir	secondary	1268 p	1310 L	incomplete
642	99	03-02	V:1:164	C:1:25	Rm 3	Ponderosa pine	primary	1259	1299 rG	incomplete
0	228		V:1:165	C:1:30		Ponderosa pine	unknown	1267	1308 L	incomplete, loose
0	352		V:1:165	C:1:30		Ponderosa pine	unknown	1223 p	1300 v	inc, same F-4361
0	7202		V:1:165	C:1:30		Ponderosa pine	unknown	1261	1318 vv	inc, from C:1:30?
0	297		V:1:167	C:1:44		Douglas fir	unknown	1250	1323 rL	complete
0	298		V:1:167	C:1:44		Douglas fir	unknown	1261	1310 r	complete
0	301		V:1:167	C:1:44		Douglas fir	unknown	1280	1313 vv	complete
604	300	07-05	V:1:167	C:1:44	Rm 7	Douglas fir	primary	1240	1330 rB	complete
605	0	07-08	V:1:167	C:1:44	Rm 7	Douglas fir	secondary	1266	1312 v	incomplete
606	0	08-01	V:1:167	C:1:44	Rm 8	Douglas fir	primary	1207	1316 vv	incomplete
607	0	09-01	V:1:167	C:1:44	Rm 9	Douglas fir	primary	1249	1317 +vv	incomplete
608	295	10-01	V:1:167	C:1:44	Rm 10	Douglas fir	primary	1211	1313 r	complete
601	296	A-1	V:1:167	C:1:44	A	Douglas fir	primary?	1246	1330 vv	incomplete
602	0	A-2	V:1:167	C:1:44	A	Douglas fir	primary?	1238	1281 vv	incomplete
0	305	02-01	V:1:168	C:1:45	Rm 2	Douglas fir	primary	1249	1310 r	comp, see ?GP304
610	304	03-01	V:1:168	C:1:45	Rm 3	Douglas fir	primary	1228 p	1321 vv	incomplete
0	331	03-02	V:1:168	C:1:45	Rm 3	Douglas fir	primary?	1246 p	1322 rL	incomplete
611	0	03-03	V:1:168	C:1:45	Rm 3	Douglas fir	lintel	1249	1322 vv	incomplete
0	322		V:1:174	C:1:46		White fir	unknown	1216 p	1324 r	inc, same F-4366

construction in the early 1320s. Lintels with clustered non-cutting dates (1321v) indicate a similar early 1320s construction for Room 1. The lintels with one of the early dates (1287+G) is in a doorway between Rooms 3 and 5, both of which have primary beams with dates in the 1310s. This lintel is most likely a piece of old wood salvaged out of the forest.

V:1:132, GP C:1:16W/S

The SAP samples helped provide some revisions to the dates given in Bannister and Robinson (1971:17) for this site as well (GP C:1:16, South House Group). The dates include just one cutting date (AD 1303B), with the earliest non-cutting date at 1283vv, the latest at 1307vv. The dates appear to cluster into three groups. Rooms 8 and 11 (Fig. III.28) have non-cutting dates in the middle and late 1280s, indicating probable construction in the very late 1280s or early 1290s. Room 6 includes the cutting date, along with non-cutting dates of 1288v and 1297, and a tentative date of 1306. Construction of Room 6 most likely occurred in the middle of the first decade after 1300. Rooms 10 and 17 both have a non-cutting date of 1305vv, indicating probable construction late in the first decade of the 1300s. An unprovenienced, non-cutting date of AD 1307vv obtained by Gila Pueblo could indicate final construction or remodeling into the AD 1310s.

V:1:133, GP C:1:21

Just two dates were confirmed by the UALTRR – 1292vv and 1320rL. Other dates (Table 5.4) are attributed to Gila Pueblo, but these were not confirmed. The dates seem to suggest initial construction before AD 1300, with an addition about AD 1320. Unfortunately, the 1320 cutting date could not be better provenienced. This site is very exposed, despite being under an overhang (Fig. III.29), and has extremely high visitation. Both factors help explain the general lack of wood at the site.

V:1:134, GP C:1:23

The SAP sampled one loose log, recovered down slope from the site (Fig. III.14). It provided a non-cutting date of 1297vv. No other wood from the site provided dates, and this single date would indicate construction at this small site in the early AD 1300s.

V:1:135, GP C:1:40

Several cutting dates (1304cL, 1304r, 1304r) and a non-cutting date (1303vv) indicate that Room 10 (Fig. III.30) was built in or after AD 1304. Non-cutting, but considerably later dates from Rooms 3 and 5 (1326vv and 1317vv) suggest that these structures were added substantially after the original construction at the site.

V:1:136, GP C:1:36

For a site with several intact roofs, and many beams of usually datable species, (ponderosa pine and Douglas fir), disappointingly, there is a single, non-cutting date of AD 1288v from a primary beam. The date is from Room 1, a room that should have been built early in the construction sequence at this site (Fig. III.15a). Presumably, the four rooms in this same part of the site were built around or before AD 1300. Dating for the construction of three other rooms in another part of the cavern is uncertain.

V:1:162, GP C:1:8

This is one of the highest elevation cliff dwellings in the southeastern Sierra Ancha, and out of four first-story rooms, has three nearly or totally intact roofs (Fig. III.16). Thirteen dates were obtained from this site, almost exclusively from primary beams. The statement in Bannister and Robinson (1971:14) regarding the dating of this site ("the construction of C:1:8 (GP) is securely placed at AD 1327-28") can be modified due to better proveniencing of the samples. Each of the rooms with intact or nearly intact roofs has primary beams (or, in one case, a vertical support) with both 1327 and 1328 cutting dates. Thus, AD 1328 is a better date for the construction of this cliff dwelling.

V:1:163, GP C:1:14

This small cliff dwelling is another of the higher elevation sites. It consists of four rooms, with dates from two of the rooms. Bannister and Robinson (1971:15) state: "the seeming difference in construction between Room 1 and Room 2 is hard to understand, since the architectural data suggest construction at the same time" (Room 1 = 1295B; Room 2 = 1312cL). The SAP changed the numbering slightly for the rooms, revised the dating of one of these samples, and was able to provide better proveniences for the wood with dates. The AD 1312cL date is from a secondary beam in SAP Room 1 (Fig. III.17a). The AD 1295B date was revised to 1297vv and is from a doorjamb between SAP Rooms 3 and 4. The doorjambs are from the same log and were probably split pieces salvaged from a dead tree (old wood). Thus, it is likely that the entire cliff dwelling was built in or just after AD 1312.

V:1:164, GP C:1:25

Two rooms in this cliff dwelling each have half of an intact roof. Weathering (exposure relative to the drip line) has destroyed the rest of the roof in each case. The SAP tree-ring sampling provided additional cutting dates and revised some earlier dates. Beams from Room 1 (Fig. III.18a) contain a mixture of earlier,

non-cutting dates (1266vv, 1295vv, 1296+v) and later cutting dates (1310L and 1316L). Unfortunately, no dates were obtained from the roof remaining in Room 4. However, as at V:1:136, the construction of Room 1 was probably integral to the construction of the rooms above and behind it (Rooms 3 and 4). This cliff dwelling was probably constructed in 1316 or later.

V:1:165, GP C:1:30

None of the wood sampled by Gila Pueblo remained at the time of the SAP sampling, or perhaps it was impossible to match SAP samples to the earlier samples. Therefore, the dates obtained by Haury are the only available dates. The dates indicate at least two, and perhaps three, construction episodes. The 1300v and 1308L dates could be from two episodes, one in the early 1300s and another at 1308, or from a single event at or after 1308. The 1318vv date indicates a later construction event, but in the UALTRR notes, there is some question as to whether this sample is actually from this site. Although the date is reported here, Bannister and Robinson (1971:20) did not report it in their summary.

V:1:167, GP C:1:44

Just one SAP sample was matched to a Gila Pueblo sample, a primary beam in Room 10 with a cutting date of 1313. A primary beam in Room 7 (Fig. III.34) produced a cutting date of AD 1330rB. Although it seems most likely the site was built all at once, it is possible that initial construction was in the late 1310s or early 1320s, and Room 7 was a later in fill between Rooms 4 and 8. Two non-cutting dates, possibly from Room 15 in the lower "annex," are at opposite ends of the dates—the earliest and the latest—AD 1281vv and 1330vv. The lower rooms may have been constructed after AD

1330. This modifies the interpretation by Bannister and Robinson (1971:23) who concluded that "construction was irregular between AD 1310 and 1330."

V:1:168, GP C:1:45

This cliff dwelling seems to have been constructed in two stages. A date from a cluster of rooms at the down canyon end indicates construction there about AD 1310 (1310r). Room 3 (Fig. III.19) on the up-canyon end of the site has a cluster of cutting and non-cutting dates suggesting construction about AD 1322 or after (1321vv, 1322vv, 1322rL). The dates would seem to place the occupation of this site as contemporaneous with the Devils Chasm Fortress (V:1:167) located approximately a hundred meters or so farther up canyon.

V:1:174, GP C:1:46

This small site (Fig. III.21) has a single, cutting date of 1324r from an unprovenienced Gila Pueblo sample. A sample taken by SAP was not matched to the Gila Pueblo sample. Construction and occupation here seems to date to the mid- and late-1320s.

Other Sites

Other sites may have had wood for sampling, but provided no dates, so these sites and samples are not included in this discussion. However, the samples are recorded in the SAP archives.

SUMMARY

Tree-rings were a major factor in leading to the first formal archaeological study of these cliff dwellings (Haury 1934). Completing the sampling of all accessible wood, seeking additional dates, and providing more specific proveniences for the earlier samples was one of the principal goals of the SAP. The SAP recovered 505 samples, bringing the total of samples collected or documented from the sites to 623.

Dates were matched, revised, or obtained for 116 sets of samples, and largely confirmed the originally described occupation (Haury 1934). Primary and other large beams proved more capable of providing dates than other types of beams. Better proveniences permitted some reinterpretation and fine-tuning of the construction episodes and occupation. More detailed analyses of site growth will be considered in the following chapter.

Wood species used matched readily available resources, that is, differences in wood use were based upon general elevation and site setting. In most cases, wood had to be collected or harvested from difficult to traverse and distant areas (1 km or more away) relative to the dwellings it was used in. Bringing wood to the site locations involved challenging vertical as well as horizontal distances. The 30- to 50-year span of construction and occupation would have had a significant impact on the nearby wood resources. Trees were taken from riparian areas as well as from the general pine forest on the mountain. Primary and secondary beams alone probably required over 2000 trees for these sites (an average of 100 beams per site, and 15 to 20 beams per room). Only about twelve percent of these beams are still present in the sites, a significant loss of wood use information and potential tree-ring dates.

Chapter Six

Architecture of the Sierra Ancha Cliff Dwellings

Two of the more important aspects of cliff dwellings are standing architecture and other visible architectural features. The Sierra Ancha cliff dwellings share many architectural characteristics with sites in other areas of the southwestern U.S., and as a set, are internally consistent in architecture. Most architectural features in the cliff dwellings are probably also characteristic of the surface pueblos in this area, but exposure, weathering, and wall collapse have rendered most architectural details unidentifiable in the open, surface sites.

The following sections examine architectural elements and details of the southeastern Sierra Ancha cliff dwellings; the surface sites are not specifically addressed. Discussed below are construction materials and techniques; walls and site arrangements/configurations; architectural features such as doors, niches, vents, and roofing systems; and the process of building a cliff dwelling.

CONSTRUCTION MATERIALS

The construction materials that need to be collected to build a dwelling are stones, clay for mortar and plaster, water, wood, and other botanical materials such as reeds and grasses for roof closing materials, and flexible twigs, branches, and vines for roof and lintel ties. The source areas for the construction materials are considered, and some estimates for the quantities required are also given. Labor costs have not been estimated here,

but Craig and Clark (1994:188-196) did calculate material and labor estimates for structures in the Tonto Basin that would be applicable for sites in the southeastern Sierra Ancha as well.

Stone

Stone for construction was collected from most of the exposed geological units, focusing on what was nearest at hand. Stone was collected from the Troy Quartzite, the basalt and argillite that underlie it, and the Dripping Springs Quartzite (for more details, see Chapter 3). Most of the cliff dwellings are in shelters in the Troy Quartzite, caverns created at the contact between the Troy Quartzite and the underlying basalt and argillite layers, or in the Dripping Springs Quartzite. Thus, stone construction materials are available at the site or down slope (from the creation of the cavern), along the cliff at the same elevation, or from the loose rubble in a nearby fault or talus slope. The most common construction materials for the sites in the Troy Quartzite, or in the layers just below in the basalt and argillite, are Troy Quartzite and argillite, with lesser amounts of basalt and Mescal Limestone (the next lower geological unit). Sites in the Dripping Springs Quartzite are constructed nearly entirely of stones from that stratum (see Table 6.1).

All of these stone types are naturally tabular, or at least blocky, with flat facets. Compared to round cobbles or irregular pieces, assembling them into coursed and semi-coursed walls is relatively simple. Almost none of the stones were

Table 6.1. Raw Stone Materials for Sierra Ancha Cliff Dwelling Walls

a. Dominant Stone Types (34-100%)

SITE	ARGILLITE	BASALT	DRIPPING SPRINGS QUARTZITE	MESCAL LIMESTONE	TROY QUARTZITE	MISSING/ OTHER	TOTAL WALLS
V:1:124			2				2
V:1:126			2				2
V:1:127			5				5
V:1:129			1				1
V:1:130	21				8	2	31
V:1:131	12	2		1	38	8	61
V:1:132	32		3		10	8	53
V:1:133					19		19
V:1:134	8				8	1	17
V:1:135			23		2		25
V:1:136	2		8	1		3	14
V:1:144			15				15
V:1:145			17				17
V:1:162	1				9	3	13
V:1:163					9		9
V:1:164					9	1	10
V:1:165	6		8		11	2	27
V:1:167	5	5	1	8	30	1	50
V:1:168	6		1	1	4	1	12
V:1:170	2		31			1	34
V:1:174	8					1	9
V:1:188			5				5
V:1:201			5			2	7
V:5:61			20				20
Total	103	7	146	11	157	34	458

b. Second Most Common Stone Types (0-50%)

SITE	ARGILLITE	BASALT	DIABASE	DRIPPING SPRINGS QUARTZITE	MESCAL LIMESTONE	TROY QUARTZITE	MISSING/ OTHER/ "0"	TOTAL WALLS
V:1:124							2	2
V:1:126					1		1	2
V:1:127							5	5
V:1:129							1	1
V:1:130	5					23	3	31
V:1:131	24				10	12	15	61
V:1:132	10				1	25	17	53
V:1:133							19	19
V:1:134	6			1		4	6	17
V:1:135				1			24	25
V:1:136				2		3	9	14
V:1:144							15	15
V:1:145							17	17
V:1:162							13	13
V:1:163							9	9
V:1:164							10	10
V:1:165	11			4			12	27
V:1:167	21	8		1	1	12	7	50
V:1:168	3				1	7	1	12
V:1:170	3			2			29	34
V:1:174					1	5	3	9
V:1:188							5	5
V:1:201	4					1	2	7
V:5:61			4			1	15	20
Total	87	8	4	11	15	93	240	458

Table 6.1. Raw Stone Materials for Sierra Ancha Cliff Dwelling Walls, cont'd

c. Third Most Common Stone Types (0-33%)

SITE	ARGILLITE	BASALT	DRIPPING SPRINGS QUARTZITE	MESCAL LIMESTONE	TROY QUARTZITE	MISSING/ OTHER/ "0"	TOTAL WALLS
V:1:124						2	2
V:1:126						2	2
V:1:127						5	5
V:1:129						1	1
V:1:130	1			1		29	31
V:1:131	6			3	3	49	61
V:1:132	1	2		3		47	53
V:1:133						19	19
V:1:134						17	17
V:1:135						25	25
V:1:136				1		13	14
V:1:144						14	14
V:1:145						15	15
V:1:162						13	13
V:1:163						9	9
V:1:164						10	10
V:1:165						27	27
V:1:167	10	4		6	1	29	50
V:1:168	1	2				9	12
V:1:170						34	34
V:1:174					1	8	9
V:1:188						5	5
V:1:201						7	7
V:5:61				1	1	18	20
Total	19	8		15	6	407	455

d. Fourth Most Common Stone Types (0-10%)

SITE	ARGILLITE	BASALT	DIABASE	DRIPPING SPRINGS QUARTZITE	MESCAL LIMESTONE	TROY QUARTZITE	MISSING/ OTHER	TOTAL WALLS
V:1:124							2	2
V:1:126							2	2
V:1:127							5	5
V:1:129							1	1
V:1:130							31	31
V:1:131							61	61
V:1:132					1	1	51	53
V:1:133							19	19
V:1:134							17	17
V:1:135							25	25
V:1:136							14	14
V:1:144							15	15
V:1:145							17	17
V:1:162							13	13
V:1:163							9	9
V:1:164							10	10
V:1:165							27	27
V:1:167	1						49	50
V:1:168							12	12
V:1:170							34	34
V:1:174							9	9
V:1:188							5	5
V:1:201							7	7
V:5:61			1				19	20
Total	1		1		1	1	454	458

modified or shaped in any way. The stones occur naturally in convenient sizes, and are very hard, and are thus very difficult to shape or modify. Each room requires hundreds of stones and would require considerable time and effort to collect the necessary quantities. The immediate site area provided some proportion of the necessary stone, but certainly, a sizable number of the required stones, especially for the larger sites, would have been carried some distance.

Numbers of rocks per wall are difficult to determine. Walls are covered by plaster or are incomplete, the stones vary considerably in size, and the numbers depend upon the thickness, length, height, and the construction of the wall (see Wall Cross-Sections, below). However, examining some walls or wall portions where the rocks are visible, it is possible to create estimates for an entire wall and for the entire site. If 150 to 200 stones are required for most walls of typical height, length, width, and construction, the rocks needed for an entire site can be estimated (Table 6.2). With the four, roughly contemporaneous sites in Pueblo Canyon alone, from 25,000 to 34,000 stones would have been necessary to build these sites.

There are hints that the gathering of construction materials was an on-going process during construction, in contrast to collecting everything needed and then building from start to finish. One tall wall in particular shows the "junk drawer" phenomenon – if there is a drawer of miscellaneous items to be sorted, the tendency is to pick out the largest and larger items first, finally picking up and sorting the smaller pieces. So it goes with selecting building stones from a pile of raw material. The author noticed this in practice while building a room at Besh-ba-gowah in Globe. At V:1:131, the exterior front wall of Rooms 13 and 14 shows three separate episodes of collecting the wall stones for two full stories and a parapet at the top. Low on the wall are large, well-matched stones. Moving upward, the stones become smaller and less regular, then the pattern repeats two more times (Fig. 6.1). The transition from larger to smaller stones represents sorting

and selecting from the first pile. A new pile starts the selection process all over, first picking out the larger stones, then the smaller stones, until the pile is exhausted, or until new material is added to the pile.

Mortar and Plaster

In these dwellings, mortar and plaster are generally one and the same. The plaster on both interior and exterior wall surfaces is a coarse, rough coat or "brown coat," and is often thickly applied. On the exterior, it serves to protect the mortar joints from weathering and erosion. On the interior, it further seals gaps in and between walls, and creates an even (but not totally smooth) surface.

The mortar and plaster are similar in color from site to site and vary from a light, almost whitish tan to brown and golden brown. The similarity is due to the common use of the clay derived from diabase intrusions that occur throughout the mountain range. The plaster and mortar contain pebbles and small rocks that are natural in the clay deposits, but could also have been added to the mixture.

As noted in Chapter 3, at Canyon Creek Ruin, several pits were evident below the ruin and were presumed to be the source of the mortar and plaster there (Haury 1934:25, 32). The largest measured 14m in diameter and 1.5m deep (Haury 1934:32). This represents approximately 250 cu m of material from this one pit. No such features were noted near any of the Sierra Ancha cliff dwellings. Many segments of the Cherry Creek road traverse extensive exposures of the diabase clays, as the road climbs above the Ellison Ranch and works across the ridges and on past the major canyons. There are also exposures on the jeep trail that goes up from the Cherry Creek Road toward Pueblo and Cold Spring canyons.

These observations are not meant to indicate that these are the only places or the places where clay was collected for mortar and plaster. Rather, it is clear that this raw material is widely and abundantly available. And, even more than gathering the wall stones, considerable effort

Table 6.2. Estimates for Sierra Ancha Cliff Dwelling Wall Stones Needed (based on an estimate of 150-200 stones per wall)

SITE	Number of Walls	Low Count (x150)	High Count (x200)
V:1:124	2	300	400
V:1:126	3	450	600
V:1:127	8	1200	1600
V:1:129	1	150	200
V:1:130	32	4800	6400
V:1:131	59	8850	11800
V:1:132	61	9150	12200
V:1:133	26	3900	5200
V:1:134	16	2400	3200
V:1:135	23	3450	4600
V:1:136	7	1050	1400
V:1:144	20	3000	4000
V:1:145	25	3750	5000
V:1:162	10	1500	2000
V:1:163	8	1200	1600
V:1:164	9	1350	1800
V:1:165	29	4350	5800
V:1:167	38	5700	7600
V:1:168	8	1200	1600
V:1:170	39	5850	7800
V:1:174	11	1650	2200
V:1:188	5	750	1000
V:1:201	15	2250	3000
V:5:61	22	3300	4400
Totals	477	71550	95400

Figure.6.1. Wall Construction Process – Larger to Smaller Stones Repeated Three Times (2004-1733-image1689)

would have been required to dig out and transport the clay from the source areas to the cliff dwellings via baskets or hide bags. As with the stone, it appears that the clay was also not brought all at once to the site or from just one source. Different clay colors are often visible on a single wall, as on the exterior front walls of Rooms 7 - 10 at V:1:130 (Fig. 6.2). Some of the clay color differences could also be attributed to repairs after storms.

During the 1995 and 1996 documentation sessions, the recorders noted differences in the inclusions in the plaster. Architecture built during the earliest part of the construction tended to have more inclusions of charcoal and trash, whereas later construction showed "cleaner" mortar and plaster. The inclusions in the earlier construction indicate the use of materials from on and near the site that had become mixed with the trash and ash dumps from possible earlier occupations in the shelters. Later construction seemingly used materials gathered from farther away from the site that had not become mixed with trash deposits.

Although the plaster was smoothed, no final thin coat was applied. This is unlike the plaster in structures in the Homol'ovi pueblos near Winslow. Most structures there have at least a thin, fine plaster and some have a dozen or more replasterings with very thin layers. Occasionally, some surface texturing is visible in the Sierra Ancha plaster. Hand and finger impressions are often noticeable, and, like occasional knee prints in the lower portion of the wall, are unobliterated reminders of the process of applying and smoothing the plaster (Fig. 6.3a and b). In one small area of a wall in Room 8 in V:1:130, evidence of paddling the wall with a wooden slat was seen (Fig. 6.3c). And, in a more whimsical vein, three other treatments were noted, also in the sites in Pueblo Canyon. Also in Room 8 at V:1:130, on another wall, textile impressions are visible, but this also could be from when someone dressed in a cotton fabric accidentally brushed against wet plaster. In Room 20 at the Ring-Tail Ruin (V:1:132), using a pair of his or her fingers and

knuckles, a set of "deer tracks" was pressed into the upper portion of the left, interior wall (Fig. 6.3d). A corncob was rolled over the wet plaster high on the interior right wall of Room 6 at V:1:131 (Fig. 6.3e).

A few instances of painting were also noted, again, mostly in the cliff dwellings in Pueblo Canyon. The painting consists of white (kaolin?) clay used to create a band (flat or zigzag/serpentine) on one or more walls in a room. In one case, a couple of figures were also painted. The painted elements and rooms will be considered in more detail in the sections on site configuration and rock and wall art.

There are a couple of sites, such as Cooper Forks (V:1:135), where it is uncertain if the exterior surfaces of the outermost walls were ever plastered. Except for the regular, rectangular shape of the doorways, without plaster, the wall courses blend perfectly with the finely divided Dripping Springs Quartzite. This "camouflage" renders the site nearly invisible from a distance (Fig. 6. 4).

Water

Water was necessary for mixing mortar and plaster, as well as for other domestic uses during construction. Water resources in the area have been described in detail in Chapter 3. Many of the cliff dwellings were located where they are because of seeps in the same caverns or nearby along the cliff face. Unless quantities of water could be stored, however, some of the seeps may not have been capable of producing the volume of water necessary for construction. In that case, water would need to be hauled from whatever source was nearest and flowing—the canyon bottom, another seep, or from the main drainage, such as Cherry or Coon creeks.

Water could be hauled in tightly woven or pitch-covered baskets, in hide bags or animal bladders, or in ceramic vessels. If the distance to water were relatively far, this process, too, would have required considerable effort, planning, and coordination. Presently, there is no evidence at

Figure 6.2. Walls With Different Plaster Colors, Rooms 7-10, AZ V:1:130 (ASM) (2004-1733-image1675)

Figure 6.3c. Plaster Treatments – Paddling (2004-1733-image1681)

Figure 6.3a. Plaster Treatments – Finger Prints (2004-1733-image1682)

Figure 6.3d. Plaster Treatments – "Deer Prints" (2004-1733-image4032)

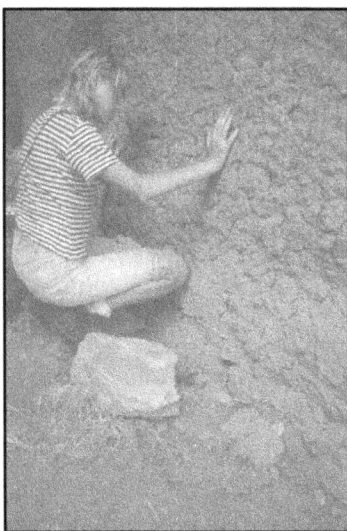

Figure 6.3b. Plaster Treatments – Knee Prints (2004-1733-image1720)

Figure 6.3e. Plaster Treatments -- Rolled Corn Cob (2004-1733-image1696)

Figure 6.4. Unplastered "Camouflage" Wall (2004-1733-image0323)

the Sierra Ancha cliff dwellings revealing where, how, or in what quantities water and clay were mixed for mortar and plaster.

Wood and Other Plant Materials

Wood was discussed in detail in Chapter 5. The trees and beams used, again, represent a serious investment in labor and effort to find, harvest, and transport them. Hundreds of trees were necessary for roofing. Details of roofing systems are examined in a later section in this chapter. Accessible wood materials, whether from the pine forest or riparian areas, were utilized. Thus, depending upon elevation and general location, commonly used wood included ponderosa pine, Douglas fir, juniper, box elder, sycamore, and *Populus* (either aspen or cottonwood). Smaller pieces of the same

species were necessary for door lintels, door-jambs, and for the tertiary component (see Lange and others 1993:487). The tertiary component, or closing materials, involved pieces of wood, split planks, and a host of other plant materials such as reeds and clumps of grass.

Door lintels were often tied together with vines, bear grass, or other flexible plants such as lemonade bush (*Rhus trilobata*). In just one site, V:1:162, is wood a major component of a wall, in this case a two story tall, jacal wall.

WALL CONSTRUCTION

The cliff dwellings in the southeastern Sierra Ancha consist of rooms defined by walls. Rooms may have been built singly or in groups, whereas walls seem to have been mostly built one at a time. The walls are not always seated on bedrock, but they are on firm, generally level, surfaces. The walls are built in fairly standard ways; however, there are some extremes. There are some very poor walls (Fig. 6.5a, Right wall, Rm 13, V:1:131), and some exceptionally well-made walls (Fig. 6.5b). Plaster covered a multitude of sins (such as poor coursing, poor placement of vertical joints, and so on) as well as some of the best craftsmanship.

There is a tendency for the basal courses to be larger stones, however, this may reflect the "junk drawer" phenomenon discussed above as much as attempting to create a true foundation. Walls are built of tabular and blocky stones, with occasional irregular spalls. Chinking stones often occur on just one face of the wall, and are relatively rare in these sites. Mortar and plaster can be thin, between courses and on wall surfaces, or extremely thick. The stones are often placed so as to create a faced or smooth wall to the exterior of the room (Fig. 6.6). Careful attention was paid to the placement of the stones, usually. Vertically aligned joints, which would create a weakness in the wall, are relatively rare. However, even, horizontal courses are also relatively rare.

The vast majority (50 percent) of walls are

a. Poorly Constructed   (2004-1733-image1690)

b. Well Constructed   (2004-1733-image1717)

Figure 6.5. Poorly and Well Constructed Walls

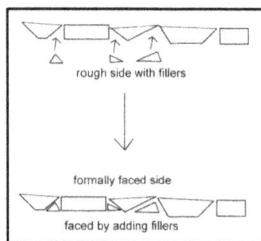

a. Diagram of wall facing (2004-1733-image3989)

b. Exterior smooth face, L Wall, Room 1, AZ V:1:167 (ASM) (2004-1733-image2000)

c. Interior rough face, L Wall, Room 1, AZ V:1:167 (ASM)(2004-1733-image0934)

Figure 6.6. Exterior vs. Interior Wall Surfaces

semi-coursed (Table 6.3, Fig. 6.7), with only about 20 percent fully coursed. A slightly higher percentage (24%) are indeterminate (for example, collapsed) or obscured by plaster. The tabular stones contribute to the ability of the masons to create relatively regular courses. Some walls are beautifully coursed (Fig. 6.6b), while others are moderately well coursed, and very few are poorly made. No matter the care or lack thereof in coursing, or the use of chinking to aid in the regularity of the courses or to create patterning, most wall surfaces were covered with plaster. The beauty or sloppiness of the masonry would not be visible.

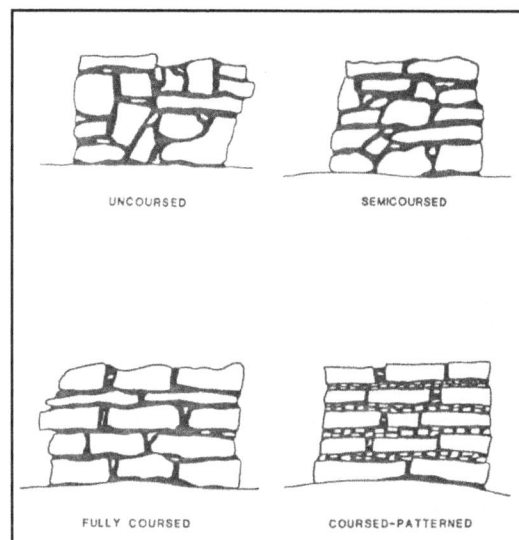

Figure 6.7. Types of Wall Coursing (from Metzger n.d.) (2004-1733-image3990)

Table 6.3. Sierra Ancha Cliff Dwelling Wall Coursing

	COURSING				TYPE			
SITE	Un-coursed	Semi-coursed	Fully Coursed	Coursed-Patterned	Vertical Slab	Obscured by Plaster	Indeterminate/Not Applicable	Total
V:1:124		2						2
V:1:126			2					2
V:1:127			1			2	2	5
V:1:129		1						1
V:1:130	1	13	9	1		3	4	31
V:1:131	3	20	20			8	10	61
V:1:132	2	25	9		1	4	12	53
V:1:133	2	7	5				5	19
V:1:134		6	2			5	4	17
V:1:135		20	3			2		25
V:1:136	1	6	2			3	2	14
V:1:144		8	4				3	15
V:1:145	2	5	8				2	17
V:1:162	3	7	1				2	13
V:1:163		8			1			9
V:1:164	2	4				2	2	10
V:1:165	3	20	2				2	27
V:1:167		28	14			5	3	50
V:1:168		8					4	12
V:1:170	1	20	6				7	34
V:1:174		3			1		5	9
V:1:188	1	4						5
V:1:201		2	2			1	2	7
V:5:61		12	4			2	2	20
Totals	21	229	94	1	3	37	73	458

Wall Types

Table 6.4 lists the types of walls by site, and the total number of wall surfaces recorded in these cliff dwellings (594 records). There are two basic wall types. One is the natural cliff, the other, a stone masonry wall. There are two, relatively infrequent exceptions to this. One site contains a two-story, jacal wall built of wood, irregular stones, and plaster. The second exception involves walls of mixed elements, that is, combinations of natural cliff and constructed stone masonry walls.

Stone Masonry

The wall can be put together with a mortar binder (wet-laid), the stones can be placed together without mortar (dry-laid), or some combination of the two (Fig. 6.8). Of the 458 walls documented 80 percent were wet-laid and 10 percent were dry-laid (Table 6.5). Many of the "dry-laid" walls are exterior walls and may have been wet-laid, but were stable enough that they are still standing even with the mortar eroded away. Other dry-laid walls are non-room walls, that is, walls that line the edge of the cliff or form barriers to support loose slopes below the main ruin (such as at V:1:134; Figs. 7.11 and III.14).

Jacal

As noted, there is a single instance of a two-story jacal wall in the Sierra Ancha cliff dwellings (V:1:162). It is a bit unusual for a jacal wall in that it also contains substantial numbers of rocks, not just wood and plaster members. Jacal walls are known from the Canyon Creek Ruin (V:2:1) and Red Rock House (P:14:14). At Canyon Creek Ruin, the wall is just a small screen forming the wall of a storage bin (Haury 1934:50 and Plate XXXIV). At Red Rock House there is a jacal wall that was added to subdivide an existing room (Reynolds 1981: 124). Jacal walls are much more common at Kiet Siel and Betatakin (Dean 1969:25), where they usually form the front wall of a habitation room.

Table 6.4. Sierra Ancha Cliff Dwelling Wall Types Recorded

WALLTYPE

SITE	Masonry	Cliff	Jacal	Mixed	Total
V:1:124	2				2
V:1:126	2				2
V:1:127	5	2			7
V:1:129	1				1
V:1:130	30	6		1	37
V:1:131	54	9		7	70
V:1:132	51	7		2	60
V:1:133	19	7			26
V:1:134	17	3			20
V:1:135	22	16		3	41
V:1:136	11	14		3	28
V:1:144	15	3			18
V:1:145	15			2	17
V:1:162	8	2	2	3	15
V:1:163	8	8		1	17
V:1:164	10	8			18
V:1:165	27	10			37
V:1:167	45	12		5	62
V:1:168	11	4		1	16
V:1:170	31	10		3	44
V:1:174	8	2		1	11
V:1:188	5	5			10
V:1:201	6	2		1	9
V:5:61	20	6			26
Totals	423	136	2	33	594

Table 6.5. Sierra Ancha Cliff Dwelling Wall Construction Methods

CONSTRUCTION TYPE

SITE	Wet-Laid	Dry-Laid	Dry-Laid Mudded	Combin-ation	Indeterminate/ Not Applicable	Total
V:1:124	1	1				2
V:1:126	2					2
V:1:127	4				1	5
V:1:129	1					1
V:1:130	28	2			1	31
V:1:131	55	1			5	61
V:1:132	50				3	53
V:1:133	16	1			2	19
V:1:134	13	4				17
V:1:135	25					25
V:1:136	13				1	14
V:1:144	12	1			2	15
V:1:145	13	2			2	17
V:1:162	10	1			2	13
V:1:163	9					9
V:1:164	10					10
V:1:165	22	3			2	27
V:1:167	43	2		1	4	50
V:1:168	7			1	4	12
V:1:170	1	28		2	3	34
V:1:174	4	1	2	1	1	9
V:1:188	3	1		1		5
V:1:201	6				1	7
V:5:61	18				2	20
Totals	366	48	2	6	36	458

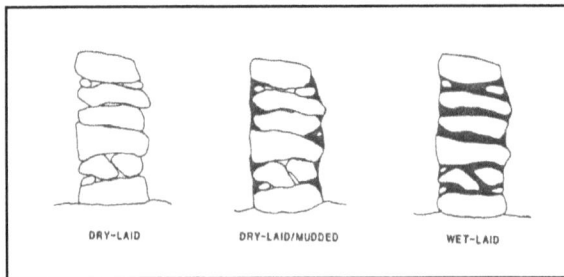

Figure 6.8. Types of Wall Construction (from Metzger n.d.) (2004-1733-image3991)

Wall Cross-Sections

Wall thickness was measured at or near the base of the wall, and at the top (both measurements whenever possible, Table 6.6). Walls average 35.6cm in thickness at the base, with a range from 12cm to 70cm (N = 312). Walls average 34.1cm at the top, with a range of 5cm to 82cm (N = 340). Two types of walls make up over 77 percent of the walls (Table 6.7). "Single stone" and "Double/single stone" walls occur in almost equal frequencies (see Fig. 6.9). A "double/single stone" wall has some courses that are one stone wide and some that are two stones wide. If two stones wide, the course usually consists of a larger and a smaller stone, alternating the placement of these stones on the exterior or interior of the wall as each new course is added. This allows for construction of a wider wall than a "single stone" wall, and yet ties the wall together so that there is no vertical seam within the wall. These wall construction patterns were relatively efficient in terms of quantities of stone needed, and were obviously successful in terms of stability and ability to carry the loads of the roof beams and roofs. Many of the walls are still standing, over 600 years later!

Even though the total numbers of the two wall types are nearly equal, at any one site, there is usually a clear preference for one wall type over the other (Table 6.7). Within one canyon (Pueblo Canyon, sites V:1:130-132 and 134), one site is dominated by one cross-section type, one by the other type, and two have nearly equal numbers of each type. The differences in wall cross-section may be related to raw materials available as well as to the experience and preferences of individual masons.

Wall Features

Documented wall features consist of doorways, niches, vents, and benches. Nearly 190 such features were recorded (Table 6.8). Doorways are by far the dominant type of wall feature; the others, combined, make up 41 percent of the wall features.

Doorways

Doorways were the principal means of ingress and egress for these structures. Hatches and ladders did exist (see below), with doorways providing access to both first and second story rooms. Most doorways are relatively small and are located in the center of a wall. There is usually a doorsill one to three courses high that must be stepped on or over when going through the door. The door lintel is usually composed of a wooden slat or slats, or bundle of smaller branches averaging 5 to 8cm in diameter.

Lintels and Walls Involved

There are usually 4 to 8 branches making up the lintel. Wooden lintels were necessitated because tabular stones long enough to span over the doorway were not readily available. Lintel ties (Fig. 6.10; CD04, CD05), made of flexible plant materials such as lemonade bush (*Rhus trilobata*) or grapevine, were commonly used to hold the bundle of lintels together (to keep them from rolling off the wall until the wall is built over the doorway and the lintels were capped in place). This is a widespread architectural trait in the US Southwest, and has been noted at the Tonto Cliff Dwellings, Canyon Creek Ruin and Red Rock House in the Grasshopper area, Kiet Siel in northern Arizona, Pueblo Bonito at Chaco Canyon, and at River House Ruin on the San Juan River in Utah (Fig. 6.11; CD06, CD07). Some of the Chacoan lintel ties are much more elaborate, and some researchers believe that these provide

Table 6.6. Sierra Ancha Cliff Dwelling Wall Thickness Data

a. Wall Bases

SITE	Average Width (cm)	Standard Deviation (N)	Minimum (cm)	Maximum (cm)
V:1:124	39.0	8.49 (2)	33.0	45.0
V:1:126	37.5	7.78 (2)	32.0	43.0
V:1:127	26.0	5.20 (3)	20.0	29.0
V:1:130	33.3	6.80 (26)	23.0	55.0
V:1:131	34.7	6.90 (41)	20.0	48.0
V:1:132	34.5	6.80 (38)	24.0	48.0
V:1:133	35.0	8.50 (16)	24.0	57.0
V:1:134	31.6	9.54 (7)	19.0	50.0
V:1:135	30.1	6.35 (22)	20.0	41.0
V:1:136	37.8	11.80 (9)	20.0	56.0
V:1:144	33.4	3.10 (10)	28.0	37.0
V:1:145	31.0	2.62 (10)	25.0	35.0
V:1:162	37.4	10.11 (11)	20.0	50.0
V:1:163	34.0	5.87 (5)	25.0	40.0
V:1:164	32.7	7.86 (6)	26.0	48.0
V:1:165	40.2	7.76 (14)	31.0	60.0
V:1:167	41.2	6.53 (33)	25.0	53.0
V:1:168	36.1	7.43 (7)	26.0	45.0
V:1:170	41.7	12.72 (18)	12.0	70.0
V:1:174	34.6	12.42 (8)	15.0	60.0
V:1:188	42.8	10.81 (4)	30.0	54.0
V:1:201	41.8	14.77 (5)	33.0	68.0
V:5:61	32.1	6.27 (15)	23.0	47.0
Totals	35.6	8.51 (312)	12.0	70.0

b. Wall Tops

SITE	Average Width (cm)	Standard Deviation (N)	Minimum (cm)	Maximum (cm)
V:1:124	31.0	9.90 (2)	24.0	38.0
V:1:126	33.5	4.95 (2)	30.0	37.0
V:1:127	22.3	4.04 (3)	18.0	26.0
V:1:129	35.0	. (1)	35.0	35.0
V:1:130	31.6	5.62 (24)	22.0	47.0
V:1:131	31.3	7.65 (45)	5.0	46.0
V:1:132	30.8	8.24 (42)	10.0	48.0
V:1:133	30.6	9.08 (16)	17.0	45.0
V:1:134	28.4	3.85 (11)	19.0	35.0
V:1:135	29.8	9.99 (25)	18.0	56.0
V:1:136	42.8	7.97 (9)	30.0	54.0
V:1:144	33.3	7.78 (10)	20.0	45.0
V:1:145	30.7	6.86 (9)	15.0	38.0
V:1:162	30.7	9.49 (10)	20.0	47.0
V:1:163	37.3	5.28 (7)	28.0	45.0
V:1:164	30.7	7.37 (6)	26.0	45.0
V:1:165	39.1	7.12 (20)	29.0	60.0
V:1:167	39.7	6.72 (33)	27.0	53.0
V:1:168	35.4	9.72 (8)	22.0	50.0
V:1:170	49.3	12.38 (23)	30.0	82.0
V:1:174	36.0	17.29 (7)	10.0	60.0
V:1:188	39.0	9.00 (5)	30.0	54.0
V:1:201	35.6	5.86 (5)	29.0	42.0
V:5:61	28.6	4.05 (17)	22.0	37.0
Totals	34.1	9.82 (340)	5.0	82.0

Table 6.7. Sierra Ancha Cliff Dwelling Wall Cross-Sections*

| | CROSS- | SECTION | TYPE | | |
SITE	Single Stone	Double/Single Stone	Double Stone	Indeterminate/ Not Applicable	Total
V:1:124	2				2
V:1:126	2				2
V:1:127	4			1	5
V:1:129	1				1
V:1:130	14	11		6	31
V:1:131	11	37		13	61
V:1:132	29	12	3	9	53
V:1:133	14	2		3	19
V:1:134	6	6		5	17
V:1:135	13	11	1		25
V:1:136	3	6	2	3	14
V:1:144	5	7	1	2	15
V:1:145	4	9		4	17
V:1:162		8		5	13
V:1:163	4	4		1	9
V:1:164	2	5		3	10
V:1:165	6	15	3	3	27
V:1:167	12	31	1	6	50
V:1:168	1	7		4	12
V:1:170	2	14	10	8	34
V:1:174	5	3		1	9
V:1:188	1	4			5
V:1:201	1	2	1	3	7
V:5:61	16			4	20
Totals	158	194	22	84	458

*For masonry walls only, walls that are cliff have been removed.

Table 6.8. Sierra Ancha Cliff Dwelling Wall Features Recorded

SITE	Bench	Door	Niche	Other	Vent	Total
V:1:124		1				1
V:1:126		1				1
V:1:127		1				1
V:1:130		5				5
V:1:131		16	4		5	25
V:1:132		18	5		1	24
V:1:133		2				2
V:1:134		3			3	6
V:1:135	2	8	4		10	24
V:1:136		6			3	9
V:1:144		3			1	4
V:1:162		5	2		1	8
V:1:164		4	1		1	6
V:1:165		7				7
V:1:167		13	7		11	31
V:1:168		2				2
V:1:170		7	2			9
V:1:188		5				5
V:1:201				1		1
V:5:61		4	5		8	17
Totals	2	112	30	1	44	189

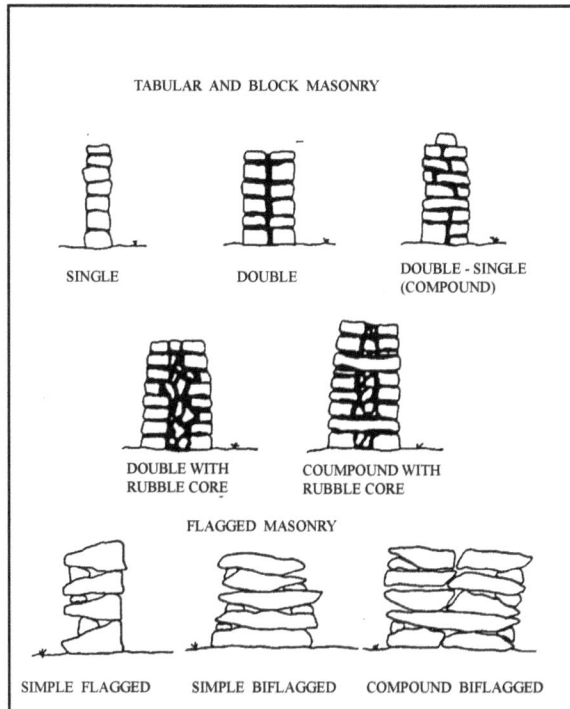

Figure 6.9. Types of Wall Cross-Sections (from Metzger n.d.) (2004-1733-image3992)

Figure 6.11. Other Lintel Ties: Pueblo Bonito, Chaco Canyon NM (2004-1733-image4033)

evidence of prefabrication of these structural elements (Windes and McKenna 2001:131-133). There is even an intriguing modern parallel with a baling wire tie at Jemez State Monument in New Mexico (CD08).

Doors occur with mostly Left, Front, or Right walls, with far fewer in Back walls (Table 6.9). The Back wall is commonly cliff. There are more doors in Front walls, aiding in the solution to one of the most serious engineering problems the builders faced—a primary beam over an open doorway. Because of the nature of the cliffs, beams are rarely seated in the cliff. Thus, the primary beams tend to run parallel to the cliff (from the Left to the Right wall, see Fig. 2.3 and Fig. 6.33), and would not bear down directly over a doorway in the front wall (see Roofs below for additional roofing details). The preference for door location reflects access around the site and into the rooms. Where there is space (for example, V:1:130-132 in Pueblo Canyon, Figs. III.26, III.27, and III.28), a large number of doors are in the Front walls. Where much of the site fills a narrow ledge (for example, V:1:167, the Devils Chasm Fortress, Fig. III.34), doors can only be in the Left and Right walls.

If a primary beam must be seated in a wall with an open doorway, several strategies are available for reducing the stress on the door lintels and transferring the load to the base of the wall. The first strategy is to lengthen the

Figure 6.10. Lintel Tie: AZ V:1:131(ASM) (diameter of lintel is approximately 7 cm) (2004-1733-image2016)

Table 6.9. Sierra Ancha Cliff Dwelling Doors in Walls

SITE	Back	Front	Left	Right	Total
V:1:124		1			1
V:1:126			1		1
V:1:127			1		1
V:1:130	2	3	1	1	7
V:1:131	3	4	4	5	16
V:1:132	1	6	6	8	21
V:1:133		1		1	2
V:1:134		1	2	2	5
V:1:135	1	6			7
V:1:136	2	3		1	6
V:1:144		2			2
V:1:162	1	2	1	1	5
V:1:163	1				1
V:1:164		2	1		3
V:1:165		5	2	1	8
V:1:167		1	5	9	15
V:1:168			2		2
V:1:170		4	2	1	7
V:1:188		3	1	1	5
V:5:61		2	2	1	5
Totals	11	46	31	32	120

lintels so that lines drawn from the center of the base of the primary beam to the corners at the base of the wall will pass over the ends of the lintels (see Fig. 6.12). Loads are transferred along the lintels, away from the door, then down through the wall (see Fig. 6.13). Secondly, a vertical support can be added in the middle of the room under the primary beam, reducing the loads carried by the walls under the beam (Fig. 6.14). Thirdly, the primary beam could be shifted toward the back of the room (Fig. 6.15), reducing the cantilever of the secondary beams if they are not supported at the back wall and removing the load of the primary from directly over the open door. Finally, two primary beams could be used (Fig. 6.16), reducing the load on each beam (and therefore reducing the stresses at the places in the wall where the beams are seated). Again, this moves the point(s) of maximum load away from the open doorway. That many walls with primary beams and open doorways in the same wall are still standing with only hints of stress loads and impending failures is witness to effective construction and use of the strategies just noted. Figure 6.17 shows the effects of poorly

overlapped vertical joints in a wall at V:1:131.

Door Shape and Dimensions

The vast majority of doors are rectangular or subrectangular (Table 6.10). As noted above, the Sierra Ancha cliff dwelling doors are built to this shape via stone masonry with stone sills and wooden lintels. The average height of a door opening is 0.99m (N = 85), and the average width is 0.58m (N = 99). One door with a width of 1.86m was removed from the calculations because it is an obvious outlier and anomaly. Statistical data for door dimensions are presented in Table 6.11.

Several doors were modified during the period of their use, effectively reducing the size of the opening. This process involved adding lower lintels to reduce the height of the opening (Fig. 6.18), or adding masonry to narrow the opening (Fig. 6.19), or adding masonry behind a wooden jamb to narrow the opening (Fig. 6.20).

An interesting characteristic is the addition of small lumps of stone and mortar to the lower

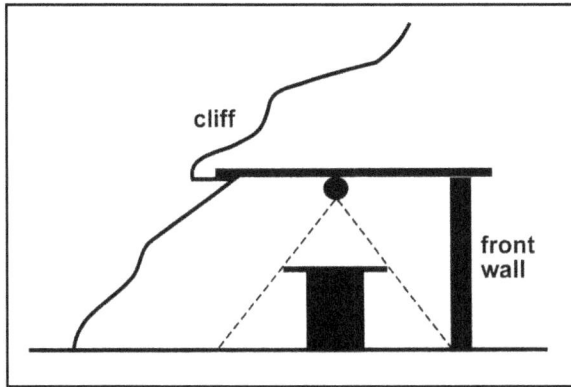

Figure 6.12. Transferring Roof Loads by Lengthening Lintels (2004-1733-image1891)

Figure 6.13. Stress of Roof Loads Shown in Cliff Dwelling Wall (2004-1733-image3281)

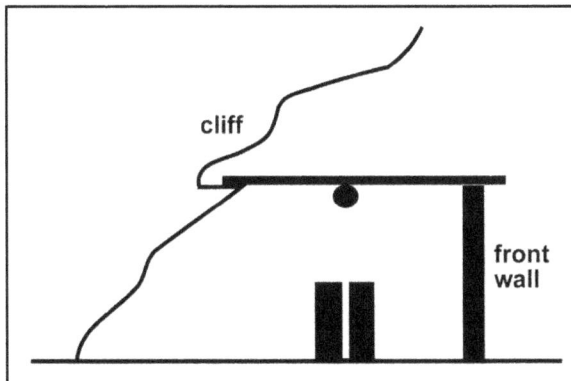

Figure 6.14. Adding Vertical Support Post to Reduce Roof Load on Walls (2004-1733-image1890)

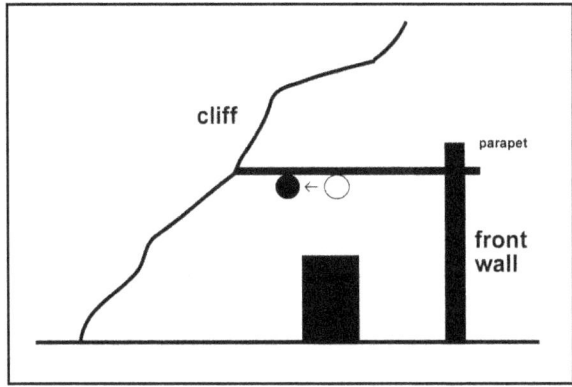

Figure 6.15. Shifting the Primary Beam Toward the Back of the Room to Reduce Load Above the Door (2004-1733-image1893)

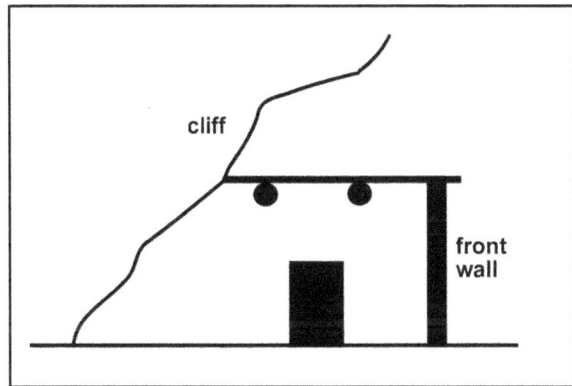

Figure 6.16. Using Two Primary Beams to Distribute the Roof Load (2004-1733-image1892)

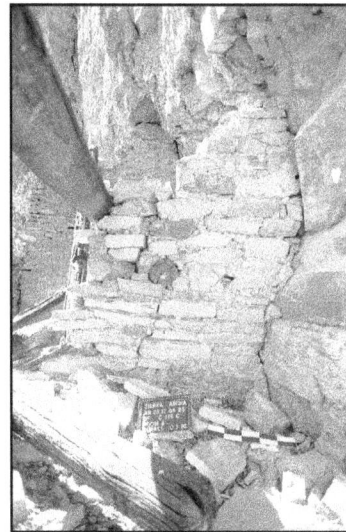

Figure 6.17. Partial Wall Failure Due to Poor Offset of Vertical Joints (AZ V:1:131[ASM]), Rm 3 (2004-1733-image2090)

Table 6.10. Sierra Ancha Cliff Dwelling Door Shapes

SITE	Rectangular	Sub-rectangular	True T-shaped	Filled T-shaped	Other	Total
V:1:124	1					1
V:1:126					1	1
V:1:127					1	1
V:1:130	1	2			2	5
V:1:131	12				4	16
V:1:132	14			1	1	16
V:1:133	2					2
V:1:134	1			1	1	3
V:1:135	7					7
V:1:136	5				1	6
V:1:144	2					2
V:1:162	3				2	5
V:1:163	1					1
V:1:164	2	1				3
V:1:165	5			1	1	7
V:1:167	9		1	1	3	14
V:1:168				2		2
V:1:170	3				4	7
V:1:188	5					5
V:5:61	2				2	4
Totals	75	3	1	6	23	108

Table 6.11. Sierra Ancha Cliff Dwelling Door Opening Data

a. Door Height

SITE	Average Height (m)	Standard Deviation (N)	Minimum (m)	Maximum (m)
V:1:130	0.88	0.14 (5)	0.69	1.07
V:1:131	0.93	0.24 (13)	0.48	1.41
V:1:132	1.02	0.21 (13)	0.77	1.56
V:1:133	1.24	0.36 (2)	0.99	1.50
V:1:134	1.06	0.37 (2)	1.02	1.10
V:1:135	0.97	0.12 (7)	0.85	1.18
V:1:136	1.02	0.18 (5)	0.70	1.17
V:1:144	0.98	0.02 (2)	0.97	1.00
V:1:162	0.93	0.10 (3)	0.83	1.02
V:1:163	0.85	. (1)	0.85	0.85
V:1:164	0.94	0.21 (2)	0.79	1.08
V:1:165	1.19	0.35 (2)	0.94	1.44
V:1:167	1.03	0.31 (10)	0.36	1.45
V:1:168	1.05	0.07 (2)	1.00	1.10
V:1:170	1.10	. (1)	1.10	1.10
V:1:188	0.99	0.41 (2)	0.70	1.28
V:5:61	0.92	0.16 (3)	0.81	1.10
Totals	0.99	0.21 (75)	0.36	1.56

b. Door Width

SITE	Average Width (m)	Standard Deviation (N)	Minimum (m)	Maximum (m)
V:1:124	0.51	. (1)	0.51	0.51
V:1:126	0.55	. (1)	0.55	0.55
V:1:127	0.50	. (1)	0.50	0.50
V:1:130	0.55	0.08 (4)	0.45	0.64
V:1:131	0.63	0.14 (14)	0.40	0.90
V:1:132	0.66	0.16 (13)	0.42	0.90
V:1:133	0.52	0.09 (2)	0.45	0.58
V:1:134	0.54	0.13 (2)	0.45	0.64
V:1:135	0.51	0.11 (7)	0.38	0.70
V:1:136	0.63	0.33 (5)	0.43	1.20
V:1:144	0.53	0.14 (2)	0.43	0.63
V:1:162	0.62	0.05 (4)	0.55	0.68
V:1:163	0.41	. (1)	0.41	0.41
V:1:164	0.61	0.13 (3)	0.50	0.75
V:1:165	0.52	0.03 (4)	0.49	0.56
V:1:167	0.57	0.13 (10)	0.39	0.88
V:1:168	0.50	0.01 (2)	0.50	0.51
V:1:170	0.56	0.24 (6)	0.36	1.00
V:1:188	0.65	0.19 (3)	0.50	0.86
V:5:61	0.51	0.02 (4)	0.48	0.53
Totals	0.58	0.15 (89)	0.36	1.20

Figure 6.18. Reducing Door Size by Lowering the Door Top (2004-1733-image1676)

Figure 6.19. Reducing Door Size by Narrowing the Door with Masonry (2004-1733-image0955)

Figure 6.20. Reducing Door Size by Narrowing the Door with Wood Slat and Masonry (2004-1733-image2114)

corners of the doorway. These lumps serve to narrow the doorway at the sill level, reducing the draft into the room and across the hearth. The lumps also provide somewhere to place your hands for support as you step through the doorway.

The lumps create a form of "T"-shaped doorway (Fig. 6.21). "T"-shaped doorways have been interpreted by some as symbols of clouds and rain (see Love 1975). The Sierra Ancha doorways, however, are not true "T" doors—they have been modified to look that way, rather than the masonry forming the "T" door shape as part of the wall construction. "T" doors made during the construction of the wall are common at Aztec, Mesa Verde, and Chaco Canyon (Fig. 6.22). "T"

Figure 6.21. Sierra Ancha "T-shaped" Door (2004-1733-image2006)

Figure 6.22. Chacoan "T-shaped" Door, Aztec Ruin NM (2004-1733-image2009)

doors also come in a variety of shapes and forms over the US Southwest and northern Mexico (CD09-11), and it is unclear if any or all of these forms have symbolic referents, or are purely functional in their design.

The variety of "T" shapes suggests that it is not likely that these doors represent a common ideological thread. Some may, but most treatments seem to be more oriented toward easing access through the door, providing surfaces to attach door closing materials (slabs, blankets, hides, or mats), and controlling floor-level airflow into the room (see also Lekson 1999:175-181).

Corner doorways are present in Chacoan sites such as Pueblo Bonito and the Aztec Ruins. Their function is to connect rooms that otherwise touch only at one corner. A single corner doorway is present in the Sierra Ancha cliff dwellings (V:1:131; at the LFX of Room 11). It differs from the Chacoan doorways in that it provided access from a room to the outside area, not into another room. It is otherwise a typical doorway, with a wooden lintel.

Most of the doors documented are open (78%, Table 6.12), and only approximately 15 percent were filled. A filled or partially filled door obviously changes access between the two connected structures or into a structure from the outside. The open or closed condition of doorways is used in Chapter 7, along with other characteristics and information, to discuss the growth or sequence of construction in the pueblos. Partially filled doors have the advantage of maintaining air circulation into rooms, even though access has been altered. Partially filled doors (as at V:1:124 and 126) also may be indicative of a "closing" of the structures with the idea of returning to re-occupy the room at a later point in time. The partial filling would make it easy to dismantle upon the return, and keep many creatures out in the meantime. Unfortunately, a large number of doors in the walls in the outer rooms of the cliff dwellings are no longer visible or obvious due to the collapse of the walls (Table 6.12). When the inhabitants walked away for what turned out to be the last time, were the outer doorways sealed or left open? For many of the outer walls and rooms, we may never know. However, in the available data, the overwhelming majority of exterior doors was left open. Following the same line of interpretation, this may indicate there were no plans to return when the occupants finally walked out.

Niches

A niche is a constructed opening in a wall that is not open through the wall, or a natural "hole" in the cliff. Thirty wall niches were documented in only 8 sites, clearly indicating that these are not common wall features (Table 6.8). One site has only one niche, and four sites have more than two. Multiple niches can occur in one wall or room, but there appears to be no patterning as to location in the site (center, ends, back or front rooms, first or second story). Five niches occur in the natural cliff, the remainder are constructed in the stone masonry walls.

Niches vary considerably in size (Table 6.13), particularly those taking advantage of the natural cliff. Average dimensions for the Sierra Ancha niches are 0.41 m high by 0.31 m wide, with ranges in height from 0.07 to 1.95 m, and width from 0.05 to 1.67 m (based on data from 27 of the 30 total niches).

Vents

A vent is a constructed opening that passes through a wall, with a presumed function of providing ventilation or light. Ventilation is the better option, as many of these features occur low on the walls (Table 6.14). Those that are higher may be also thought of as windows, in addition to providing ventilation. Metric data are available for 41 of the 44 vents recorded in the Sierra Ancha cliff dwellings. Vents average 0.19 m high (range 0.02 to 0.90 m) and 0.16 m wide (range 0.05 to 0.50 m). These features are also clearly not very common—they were documented at only 9 sites (Table 6.15).

Three sites have evidence for only one vent; four others have more than three vents. Multiple vents can also occur within one wall or room.

Table 6.12. Sierra Ancha Cliff Dwelling Door Filling

SITE	Number of Doors Present	Number of Doors Missing	Total Number of Doors	INTERIOR Open	Percent of Doors Present	Filled	Percent of Doors Present	Partially-Filled	Percent of Doors Present	EXTERIOR Open	Percent of Doors Present	Filled	Percent of Doors Present	Partially-Filled	Percent of Doors Present
V:1:126	1	0	1											1	100
V:1:127	1	2	3											1	100
V:1:130	6	7	13	5	83	1	17								
V:1:131	13	14	27	9	69			1	8	2	15	1	8		
V:1:132	18	5	23	8	44	3	17			7	39				
V:1:133	6	3	9	6	100										
V:1:134	5	2	7	1	20			1	20	3	60				
V:1:135	9	3	12	4	44					5	56				
V:1:136	6	3	9	3	50					2	33			1	17
V:1:144	3	7	10	3	100										
V:1:145	0	8	8												
V:1:162	4	2	6	1	25	2	50			1	25				
V:1:163	3	2	5	3	100										
V:1:164	4	2	6	2	50	1	25	1	25						
V:1:165	7	4	11	1	14	1	14			5	71				
V:1:167	12	7	19	8	67	2	17					2	17		
V:1:168	2	1	3							1	50			1	50
V:1:170	6	9	15	3	50					3	50				
V:1:174	2	4	6			1	50			1	50				
V:1:188	5	0	5	2	40	1	20			1	20	1	20		
V:5:61	4	4	8	3	75									1	25
C:1:38	2	4	6			1	50			1	50				
C:1:47	1	5	6							1	100				
C:1:50	3	4	7	1	33	2	67								
TOTALS	123	102	225	63	51	15	12	3	2	33	27	4	3	5	4

Table 6.13. Metric Data for Sierra Ancha Cliff Dwelling Niches

SITE	Number of Niches	Mean Height (m)	Minimum Height (m)	Maximum Height (m)	Mean Width (m)	Minimum Width (m)	Maximum Width (m)
V:1:131	4	0.40	0.12	0.79	0.40	0.12	0.70
V:1:132	4	0.63	0.07	1.95	0.20	0.05	0.48
V:1:135	3	1.45	0.95	1.80	0.57	0.40	0.80
V:1:162	1	0.35	0.35	0.35	0.40	0.40	0.40
V:1:164	1	0.40	0.40	0.40	0.24	0.24	0.24
V:1:167	7	0.14	0.12	0.18	0.12	0.07	0.24
V:1:170	2	0.16	0.15	0.17	1.04	0.40	1.67
V:5:61	5	0.14	0.11	0.20	0.14	0.11	0.20
Totals	27	0.46	0.07	1.95	0.39	0.05	1.67

Sooting:

Eight cliff dwellings have one or more rooms with vents and sooting on one or more walls (Table 6.16). Six sites have vents with no evidence of sooting. The greatest numbers of sites and rooms involve cases of sooting with no evidence of vents. This patterning suggests that rooms where there were domestic fires for cooking or warmth sometimes had vents, but usually did not. This relationship should be regarded carefully, however, because doorways also provide ventilation. Table 6.16 clearly shows that sooted rooms overwhelmingly also have doorways.

Fourteen sites had evidence of sooting on the masonry and cliff walls. Sooting can be difficult to discern due to water staining and mineral deposits on the walls that mimic smoke blackening. Presence of sooting in some rooms may be impossible to find because the walls have collapsed or all of the plaster has been eroded off. Plots of sooted walls on a site-by-site basis show

Table 6.14. Locations of Vents in Sierra Ancha Cliff Dwellings

SITE	Number of Vents	Bottom Courses	Bottom Half	Mid-Wall	Top Courses	Top Half
V:1:131	4		1		3	
V:1:132	1		1			
V:1:134	3		1			2
V:1:135	10		6	3	1	
V:1:136	3	3				
V:1:162	1	1				
V:1:164	1			1		
V:1:167	10	3	2	2	3	
V:5:61	8		4	2		2
Totals	41	7	15	8	7	4

Table 6.15. Metric Data for Sierra Ancha Cliff Dwelling Vents

SITE	Number of Vents	Mean Height (m)	Minimum Height (m)	Maximum Height (m)	Mean Width (m)	Minimum Width (m)	Maximum Width (m)
V:1:131	4	0.07	0.02	0.15	0.10	0.07	0.13
V:1:132	1	0.22	0.22	0.22	0.23	0.23	0.23
V:1:134	3	0.09	0.08	0.10	0.13	0.08	0.15
V:1:135	10	0.18	0.05	0.25	0.19	0.05	0.30
V:1:136	3	0.12	0.05	0.15	0.12	0.08	0.15
V:1:162	1	0.30	0.30	0.30	0.35	0.35	0.35
V:1:164	1	0.12	0.12	0.12	0.16	0.16	0.16
V:1:167	10	0.21	0.12	0.12	0.12	0.08	0.20
V:5:61	8	0.28	0.13	0.90	0.18	0.10	0.50
Totals	41	0.19	0.02	0.90	0.16	0.05	0.50

Table 6.16. Vents and Soot: Association of Vents and Sooting

SITE	Number of Rooms with Vents and Sooting	Number of Rooms with Vents and No Sooting	Number of Rooms with Sooting, but No Vents	Number of Rooms with Sooting and Doorways	Number of Rooms with Sooting and No Doorways
V:1:130				3	1
V:1:131	1	1	4	5	0
V:1:132	1		7	8	0
V:1:133				5	0
V:1:134	1	1		1	0
V:1:135	4	3	2	6	0
V:1:136		1	3	3	0
V:1:144	1		1	2	0
V:1:162	1		1	2*	0
V:1:164		1	2	2	0
V:1:167	2	2	3	5	0
V:5:61	2		2	4	0
TOTALS	13	9	25	46	1

*Note: one of these rooms probably has a door, but it is not certain.

some patterning to the sooting. Rooms with sooting tend to be first story rooms more than 3-to-1 (Table 6.17, number of first floor surfaces compared to number of second floor surfaces). Most sooted rooms are also in the first row of rooms built against the cliff, and at or near the center of the site (Tables 6.17 and 6.18; Fig. 6.23). If a room with sooted walls in the first story has a second story above, the walls in the second story are also often sooted (Table 6.19). However, there are examples of sooting in the first story and none in the second, as well as none in the first story and some in the second.

Not all walls show sooting, and in the larger sites there are often secondary clusters of rooms also showing sooting. The distribution of sooted-wall rooms, along with door or hatch information, may help define suites of rooms that may have belonged to one family group. Further, these characteristics may help define room function within the suite.

The differential sooting is also curious. As noted, the sooted rooms are often "deeper" in the site than other rooms. Such rooms tend to be storage rooms rather than habitation rooms (Adams 1983:51-54; Mindeleff 1989:103). Hearths are more likely to be in the habitation rooms—for cooking, warmth, and light, yet some of the rooms are incredibly blackened in the ceilings and from top to bottom on the walls. Is this because the rooms were formerly habitation rooms and their function has changed through the addition of rooms above or in front? Excavations that could search for sealed or dismantled hearths could help answer this question.

The extent of sooting also seems extreme relative to the need for heating or cooking in a climate that is relatively mild, where the inhabitants experienced substantial back radiation from the cliffs, and where a lot of cooking activities probably happened outdoors. If not, these inhabitants certainly suffered problems from breathing in the heavy smoke. There could be another reason for the sooting, however. If these "deeper" rooms are the principal storage areas in the sites, the author has heard that many foods keep better in cool,

dark spaces—such as the deeper rooms. The sooting, then, could result from purposeful smudging of the walls and room in order to darken it. The smudging may have also helped drive away or kill insect pests that may have worked their ways into the walls and ceilings. It might be possible to test residues from the walls and ceilings to see if the deposits come from firewood (pine, oak, or juniper probably) or from other plants that could indicate the more purposeful smudging (creosote bush, perhaps).

Sooting and Fire:

Walls at several of the sites show evidence of reddening of the plaster (Table 6.20), particularly in the area of the roofline—surrounding the primary and secondary beams or their sockets. The beams themselves are often charred. At least two sites (V:1:163 and 167) show evidence of roofs being burned out by forest fires sweeping up the slopes below the dwelling. Either sparks or the superheating effects of a large updraft could have started the roofs on fire. The Gila Pueblo site form for GP C:1:14 (V:1:163) specifically notes that a forest fire destroyed the roof. The Back wall of Room 1 shows evidence of fire, attesting to that event. Other reddening of the plaster indicates fires in some of the cliff dwelling rooms. Whether this burning was purposeful or accidental, or even if it occurred during the time the cliff dwelling was occupied, is unclear.

Steps

Steps are not common features, but do occur occasionally when there are ledges or other large differences in relative floor elevation. The step is usually created simply, by mounting a long tabular stone perpendicular to the surface of the wall (Fig. 6.24). A similar step was documented at the Upper Tonto Ruin (Steen 1962:9, Plate 3C). Two step-like stones occur high on the wall in V:1:131(Fig. 6.1: one is visible, the other is behind the tree). Their function is uncertain, but perhaps they were useful to hold scaffolding to provide a step on the outside of the wall for building the final courses or for hoisting room beams

Table 6.17. Location of Sooting in Sites – Horizontal, Front to Back Axis

SITE	Number of Rooms	Number of First Story Rooms	Number of Second Story Rooms	Number of Rooms with Soot	Percent of Rooms with Soot	Number of Rooms at Cliff	Number of First Floor Rooms at Cliff with Soot	Number of Built Wall Surfaces	Number of Built Wall Surfaces Missing	Number of Built Wall Surfaces with Soot	Number of Surfaces in Rooms at Cliff	Number of Surfaces at Cliff with Soot	Number of First Floor Surfaces with Soot	Number of Second Floor Surfaces with Soot
V:1:130	12	10	2	4	33	7	2	55	12	8	27	8	5	3
V:1:131	26	22	5	5	19	17	3	104	18	8	81	4	6	2
V:1:132	22	16	6	8	36	8	4	100	28	11	52	8	11	1
V:1:133	14	14	0	5	36	9	4	58	20	8	34	7	8	0
V:1:134	6	6	0	1	17	4	1	32	6	1	20	1	1	0
V:1:135	13	11	2	5	38	6	3	46	2	8	28	6	6	2
V:1:136	9	9	0	3	33	8	2	24	4	4	24	2	3	1
V:1:144	10	10	0	2	20	10	2	40	6	2	40	3	3	0
V:1:162	8	6	2	2	25	8	1	28	4	2	28	1	1	1
V:1:163	4	4	0	2	50	4	1	10	0	3	10	3	3	0
V:1:164	6	6	0	2	33	4	1	16	4	4	16	4	6	4
V:1:165	14	11	3	2	14	14	1	48	8	3	12	1	1	2
V:1:167	18	12	5	6	33	15	3	76	12	14	40	8	8	6
V:5:61	11	9	2	4	36	6	4	50	12	10	36	10	10	0
TOTALS	173	146	27	51	29	106	32	687	136	86	448	66	72	22

Table 6.18. Location of Sooting in Site – Horizontal, Left to Right Axis (Front to Back)*

SITE	Room Width of Site	From Left— Distance to First Sooted Room	From Left— Distance to Last Sooted Room	From Right— Distance to First Sooted Room	From Right— Distance to Last Sooted Room
V:1:130	8	5	6	1	2
V:1:131	14	1	10	3	12
V:1:132a	7	3	6	1	4
V:1:132b	5	0	1	2	4
V:1:133	9	4	7	1	4
V:1:134	3	1	1	1	1
V:1:135	10	1	10	0	9
V:1:136**	6	0	1	4	5
V:1:144	3	1	1	1	1
V:1:162**	3	2	2	0	0
V:1:163**	3	0	2	0	2
V:1:164**	5	0	2	2	4
V:1:165	8	1	1	6	6
V:1:167	5	1	3	1	3
V:5:61	6	1	5	0	4
TOTALS	Mean = 6.3	Mean = 1.4	Mean = 3.9	Mean = 1.5	Mean = 4.1

*Note: Distance of "0" means the room is on an outside end of the site; the greater the number over a value of "1," the more the room is away from one end or the other of the site. This measure was only done for sites and room clusters with two or more rooms. "From Left" can also be "From Front;" "From Right" can also be "From Back."

**Note: These four sites involve the Front to Back horizontal dimension, the others are all Left to Right. V:1:136 and V:1:164 also involve multiple levels in the vertical dimension, but these are not multiple stories.

Table 6.19. Location of Sooting in Sites—Vertical

SITE	first story only, no second story	first story soot, no second story soot	second story soot, no first story soot	first and second story soot
V:1:130				2
V:1:131	3	1	1	
V:1:132	4	2		1
V:1:133	5			
V:1:134	1			
V:1:135	4			1
V:1:136	3			
V:1:144	2			
V:1:162		1	1	
V:1:163	2			
V:1:164	2			
V:1:165				1
V:1:167	1		1	2
V:5:61	2	2		
TOTALS	29	6	3	7

Table 6.20. Locations of Fire Evidence in SAP Sites

SITE	Number of Structures with Evidence of Fire	First Floor Structures with Evidence of Fire	Second Floor Structures with Evidence of Fire
V:1:130	0	0	0
V:1:131	1	0	1
V:1:132	10	8	2
V:1:133	1	1	0
V:1:134	0	0	0
V:1:135	1	1	0
V:1:136	0	0	0
V:1:144	0	0	0
V:1:162	0	0	0
V:1:163	1	1	0
V:1:164	0	0	0
V:1:165	0	0	0
V:1:167	16	8	8
V:5:61	0	0	0
TOTALS	30	19	11

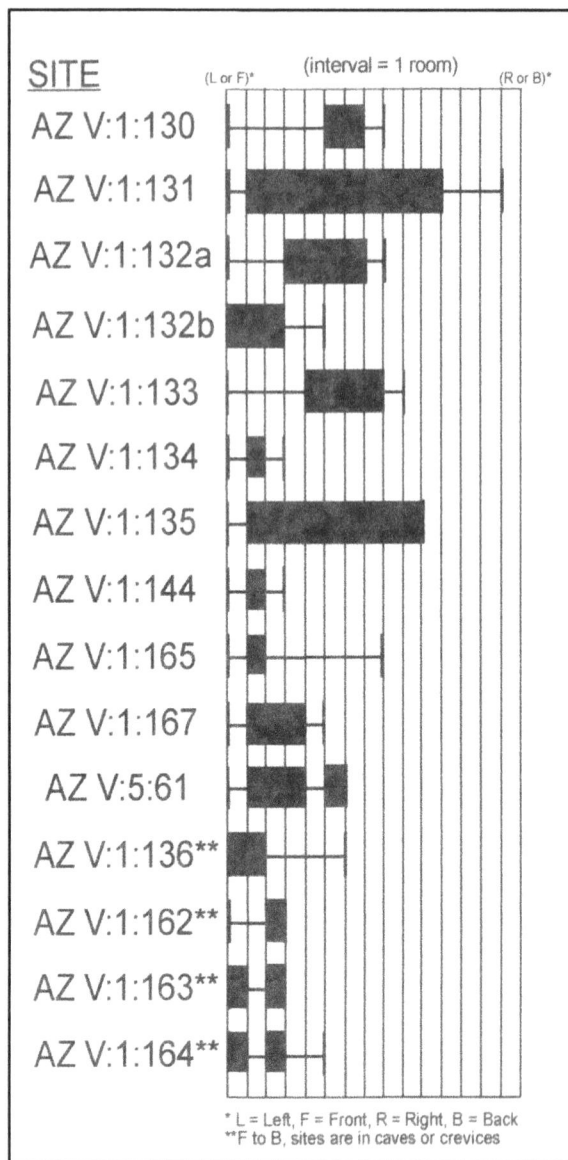

Figure 6.23. Locations of Sooted Rooms in SAP Sites (2004-1733-image3993)

*Figure 6.24. Wall Step on Exterior Wall ,
AZ V:1:168 (ASM) (2004-1733-image1400)*

often working together, provide access from one story to another or from one level to another, although ladders could also have been used independently from the hatches.

Hatches

Few hatches have survived in the Sierra Ancha cliff dwellings, although one could expect them to have been more numerous. Haury (1934:43) notes at Canyon Creek Ruin that "entrances occurred in all of the existing roofs." Those in the Canyon Creek Ruin showed uniformity in size and general manner of construction. The hatches at Canyon Creek Ruin range from 18 by 25 in (45.7 by 63.5 cm) to 21 by 23 in (53.3 by 58.4 cm), and are illustrated in Haury (1934: Plates XXXIa and b). One was rectangular and lined with upright stone slabs; the other was more

into the room. Somewhat similar stones, seemingly to aid in construction, are present on the exterior of several walls at Aztec Ruins National Monument (CD12), and on some kiva walls at Pueblo Bonito, Chaco Canyon (CD13).

OTHER ARCHITECTURAL FEATURES

Two other types of architectural features need to be discussed here—hatches and ladders. Both,

oval and lined with clay.

In the Sierra Ancha cliff dwellings, only six hatches are known. At V:1:136, the hatch is in a massive roof (0.56m thick) between a lower room that provides the access into the site and an upper room or workspace from which the rest of the site is accessed. There appears to have been no vertical slabs as part of the hatch, and there is no evidence of additional clay lining on the upper floor. The dimensions of the hatch are 54 by 66 cm, but beams in the roof actually narrow the hatch to only 38 by 66 cm (Fig. 6.25a). Three hatches are in V:1:162, where each of the standing roofs shows the presence of a hatch (Fig. 6.25b-d). These hatches measure 0.6 by 0.7m, 0.55 by 0.7 m, and 0.34 by 0.62 m. One hatch (Fig. 6.25d) has two wooden pegs on one side, and is similar to a hatch at Canyon Creek Ruin (Haury 1934:44). The pegs may serve to support a hatch cover. The other hatches are at V:1:135 and at V:5:61, and are similar in dimensions to those just listed.

b. Hatch, AZ V:1:162 (ASM), Roof of Room 2 (2004-1733-image2696)

c. Hatch, AZ V:1:162 (ASM), Roof of Room 4, Note small rod on right side (2004-1733-image2967)

a. Hatch, AZ V:1:136 (ASM), Roof of Room 1, Note extremely thick roof (2004-1733-image0487)

d. Hatch, AZ V:1:162 (ASM), Floor of Room 7, Note small pegs on far side (2004-1733-image2917)

Figure 6.25. Sierra Ancha Roof Hatches

Ladders

Gila Pueblo was fortunate to recover a ladder from V:1:162 (see Haury 1934:46 and Plate XXXII; ASM GP52795), and Haury also notes two others like it in the collections of the Arizona State Museum (ASM #23318 and 23319; from "northern Arizona," unfortunately, more specific histories and proveniences for these specimens are lacking). The ladder style is distinctive, consisting of two vertical poles (up to 3m long), a series of rungs (4 or 5 branches about [2.5cm in diameter), and two thinner, long branches that are tied to the main poles below each rung in order to hold the rung in place (Fig. 6.26). The long branches are also sometimes tied above the rungs as well. No ladders were found in the Canyon Creek Ruin, but Haury was certain they would be just like this Sierra Ancha ladder.

A similar ladder from southern Utah appeared on the cover of Arizona Highways magazine (September, 1987). And, a modern parallel, the author saw one at Picuris Pueblo in New Mexico made of wooden poles and rungs, and baling wire (CD14). Like many other architectural characteristics, this ladder form, too, has a wide distribution in the US Southwest.

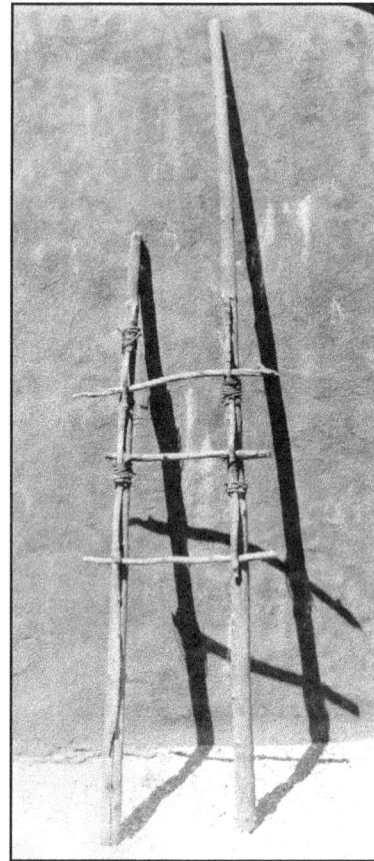

Figure 6.26. Prehistoric Ladder from GP C:1:8 (AZ V:1:162 [ASM]) (ASM Negative 71106)

SITE CONFIGURATION

The architecture built into an overhang primarily involves basic habitation and storage rooms, as best as can be determined without excavation and through comparisons with excavated sites in this same general region, such as Canyon Creek Ruin and the Upper and Lower Tonto ruins. There are apparently special rooms that may have functioned as religious or ceremonial chambers, but these are relatively rare. Also rare are specific architectural units that can be identified as granaries. Standard rooms are the vast majority of the Sierra Ancha architectural units, so the greater focus of the discussion concerning the arrangement of the architectural units is on these rooms. However, the special rooms and storage facilities are also noted below.

Room Construction

The caverns offer protection from the elements—perhaps most importantly, protecting the roofs, plaster and mortar, and therefore reducing the amount of repair required after storms. Thus, the initial construction is expected to have occurred in the deepest, most protected portion of each cavern (Graves 1982:121; Haury 1934:58; Pierson 1962:44). Also, constructing the initial room against the cliff provides two benefits not available to pueblos and rooms built out in the open. First, at least one wall of the room (the cliff) is solid and stable, providing strong support to any wall abutted to it. Second, use of the natural wall means that for each room built in the cavern, and added onto a previous room or also built against the cliff, one less wall needs to be constructed for each room. Cumulatively, this is a tremendous savings in effort (collecting, transporting, and constructing) and materials required (stone, clay, and water).

The relationships of walls to each other (including bonding or abutting), the tree-ring dates, and other details such as care in coursing, plaster color, and type of wall construction, also suggest that rooms or room clusters were often built separately, and were later joined together by other rooms. In all but one case (V:1:132), the rooms are built against the back of the cavern. As new rooms were added, they were built on either end of the original rooms, or in front of them (see also Graves 1982 for similar growth and construction at Canyon Creek Ruin; and Pierson 1962:44 for similar growth at the lower Tonto Ruin). Refer back to Figure 2.3 and Chapter 2 for the typical arrangement of a cliff dwelling room and the terminology applied for the walls and corners.

The preceding observations document construction tendencies when the caverns are large enough and deep enough to allow some choice as to where to begin construction. However, there are situations where the architecture fills all available space in a cavern or crevice (V:1:136, 162, and 163, for example) or along a ledge (V:1:167; Figs. III.15, III.16, III.17, and III.34, respectively). In these cases, construction location and sequence is obviously more constrained. Although many of the caverns and crevices in the three major canyons of the southeastern Sierra Ancha were occupied with cliff dwellings, not all were. This situation likely reflects subtle differences in amount of sun; presence, volume and reliability of seeps; and other factors.

As the sites grew larger, the rooms were built in less protected areas, even out beyond the drip line. While the sites are inhabited, any damage from storms can be repaired. After abandonment, however, the elements begin to erode plaster, mortar, and roofs, and to rot beams and

other organic materials. Roofs and walls, or parts of walls, eventually collapse. The sites in Pueblo Canyon show perfectly where the drip line is located (Fig. 6.27). For those rooms deeper in the cavern, the only factors that can affect them are water dripping from the cavern ceiling, rocks or slabs falling from the cavern ceiling, earthquakes, or malicious human activity.

Bonding and Abutting

Bonded or abutted corners often combine to reveal the relative construction sequence for walls and rooms. Unfortunately for this approach to understanding site growth, very few corners are bonded in the cliff dwellings of the southeastern Sierra Ancha. The low proportions of bonded corners appear to be true at other sites in the region, such as Canyon Creek Ruin (Fig. III.23) and the Upper and Lower Tonto ruins (Figs. III.24 and III.25).

At other sites, such as the nearby Grasshopper and farther away Homol'ovi pueblos, bonding and abutting relationships have allowed researchers to map and measure pueblo growth (Adams 2002; Ciolek-Torrello 1978; Riggs 2001; Wilcox 1982). The wall relationships specifically denote the growth of the village, however, understanding the social groups or organization responsible for the planning and construction involves the same relationships and a more extensive set of argu-

Figure 6.27. Dripline Effect on Architecture: Note How Walls at Shadowline are "Sheared Off," Marking the Dripline from the Cavern Roof, AZ V:1:132 (ASM) (2004-1733-image1265)

ments (Adams 2002:124-130).

In the Homol'ovi pueblos, construction and additions often involve spinal or ladder room blocks (Adams 2002:129). The walls within these room blocks show several interesting relationships. The "outer" corners that define the room block are usually bonded, whereas the interior cross-walls are abutted to the spinal walls. At Homol'ovi I, the same abutment relationship also applies to two stories, that is, the walls are abutted in the same relationship in the first and second story.

Besh-ba-gowah (Fig. 6.28) and Schoolhouse Mound (Fig. 6.29) show abutment relationships used in a different way. Most walls are abutted, but the cross-walls are occasionally offset from each other, rather than directly across against the main wall (in the Besh-ba-gowah figure, note rooms 40, 41, 48, and 46 across from rooms 64, 63, and 65, or rooms AA, BB, and 36 across from LL, KK, ZZ, and 39a). This serves to buttress the main wall and provide it more stability. This was perhaps a necessity in construction with mostly rounded cobbles that could lead to less stable walls.

Most of the cliff dwellings in the southeastern Sierra Ancha are not large enough, nor were they occupied long enough, to have experienced significant, planned growth, beyond their initial construction. Among 658 documented and defined corners (not including walls abutted to the cliff face), less than 5 percent are bonded (Table 6.21, Fig. 6.30). Of this same total, 38.8 percent are abutted, no cliff included, and 56.4 percent of corners do involve a cliff face.

Although most walls are abutted, the relationships of cross-walls to each other and of different stories vary from the relationships just noted at other sites. In the Sierra Ancha cliff dwellings, cross-walls tend to be directly across from each other, on either side of a main wall. When multiple stories are involved, the abutment is usually reversed from one story to the next (see Fig. 6.31a and b). That is, if the Left or Right wall abuts the Front wall in the lower story, the Front wall will abut the Left of Right

wall in the upper story (Fig. 6.32). This pattern has also been observed at Tonto National Monument (CD15), and at Honanki and Palatki near Sedona (CD16). This abutment pattern creates, in effect, a bonded architectural wall, but at a different scale than bonding two walls together course by course.

The predominance of abutted walls could be a common architectural practice learned from the construction of open pueblos. If the builders were concerned about the settling of walls after construction, abutted walls offer a degree of protection. Settling can occur due to either poor foundations or the effects of gravity on stone and mortar as the wall is built. The Sierra Ancha cliff dwellings are generally built on relatively level, firm surfaces, if not directly on the bedrock. If two walls were bonded at the corner, and settled differentially, the effect would be to weaken and pull apart both walls. If two abutted walls settle differentially and pull apart, the crack can be simply replastered, and there is no basic harm to the walls and structure. Pierson (1962:41) sees abutted walls as a structural liability. This seems to be an unfounded concern given the overwhelming percentage of abutted corners (Table 6.21).

Special Rooms

At Canyon Creek Ruin, one room (22B, see Fig. III.23) was identified as having potential ceremonial purposes. It was on the second story and was accessed through a doorway that one would enter by walking over the roof of a lower room. The room below, 22A, could only be accessed through a hatch in the floor of Room 22B. Room 22B had walls painted with red and yellow pigments and a stepped terrace design (Haury 1934:Plate XXXIII). Floor features included a hearth, deflector, and a flat-lying slab supported above the floor by small stones that Haury called an altar. On the slab, Haury found the following (see Haury 1934:53-54 for references to plates and figures illustrating some of these items): a small, unfired animal effigy; a cane arrow with a stone point; salt tied up in a piece of textile; a broken shell

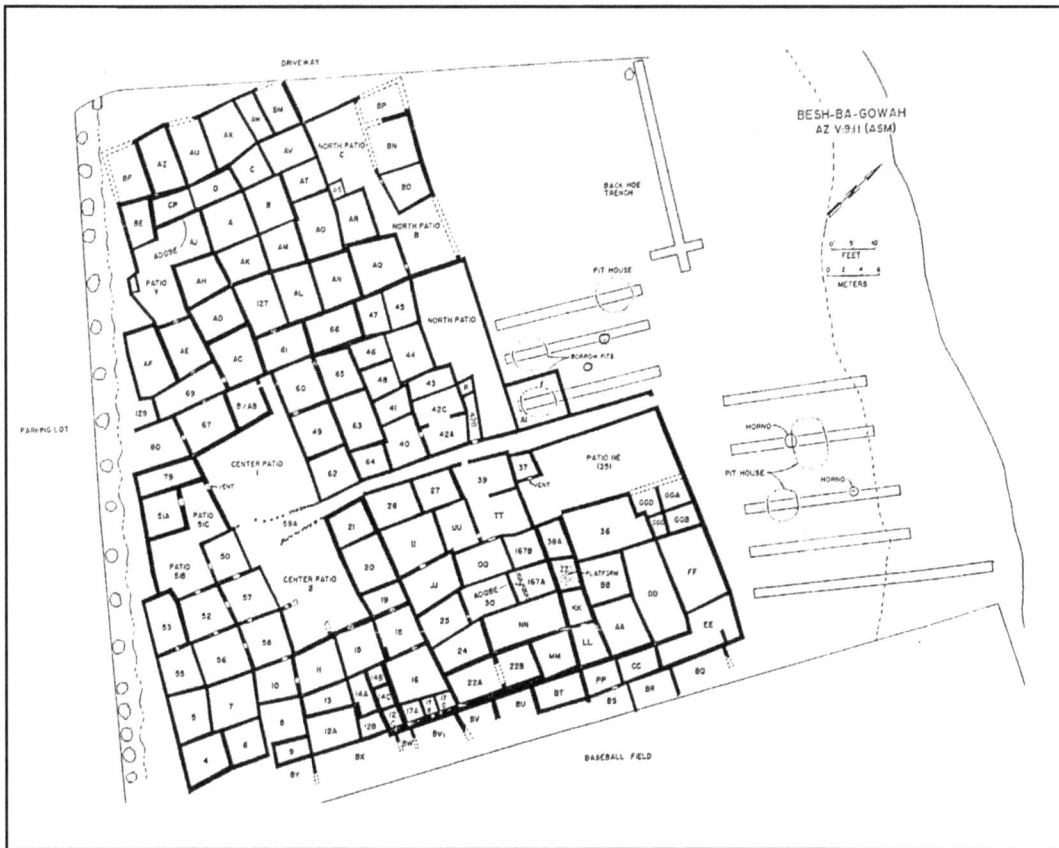

Figure 6.28. Besh-ba-Gowah Pueblo, Globe AZ (AZ V:9:11 [ASM]) (2004-1733-image3994)

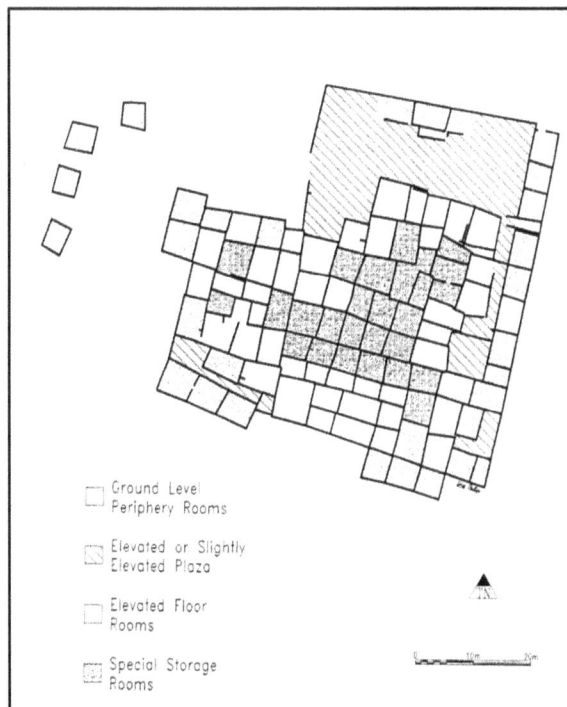

Figure 6.29. Plan Map of Schoolhouse Mound Pueblo, Tonto Basin (2004-1733-image3995)

Table 6.21. Bonding and Abutting Data For Sierra Ancha Cliff Dwellings

a. All Corners

Total corners documented including cliff:	940
Total corners identified as indeterminate:	282
Total corners defined:	658
Total corners defined not including cliff:	287
Total corners involving cliff:	371

b. Bonded Corners

Total bonded corners: 32

Percent of all defined corners (32/658):	4.9%
Percent of all defined corners without cliff (32/287):	11.1%

Percent of corners bonded at LBX (3/235):	1.3%*
Percent of corners bonded at LFX (13/235):	5.5%
Percent of corners bonded at RBX (6/235):	2.6%
Percent of corners bonded at RFX (10/235):	4.3%
Percent of all corners bonded (32/940):	3.4%

*Note: lower percents for LBX and RBX are because these corners usually abut a cliff face.

c. Cliff

Total corners with cliff: 371

Percent of all defined corners (371/658):	56.4%
Percent of all corners (371/940):	39.5%

Percent of cliffs at LBX (148/658):	22.5%
Percent of cliffs at LFX (38/658):	5.8%
Percent of cliffs at RBX (144/658):	21.9%
Percent of cliffs at RFX (41/658):	6.2%

Percent of cliff corners at LBX (148/371):	39.9%
Percent of cliff corners at LFX (38/371):	10.2%
Percent of cliff corners at RBX (144/371):	38.8%
Percent of cliff corners at RFX (44/371):	11.9%

d. Abutted Corners

Total abutted corners, not including cliff: 255

Percent of all defined corners (255/658):	38.8%

Percent abutted at LBX not including cliff (45/658):	6.8%
Percent abutted at LFX not including cliff (77/658):	11.7%
Percent abutted at RBX not including cliff (47/658):	7.1%
Percent abutted at RFX not including cliff (86/658):	13.1%

e. All Corners

Percent of corners that are LBX (abutted, bonded, no cliff)(87/940):	9.3%
Percent of corners that are LFX (abutted, bonded, no cliff)(197/940):	21.0%
Percent of corners that are RBX (abutted, bonded, no cliff)(91/940):	9.7%
Percent of corners that are RFX (abutted, bonded, no cliff)(194/940):	20.6%
Percent of corners that are defined or indeterminate, no cliff (569/940):	60.5%

a. Exterior Left Front Corner, Rm 3,
AZ V:1:168(ASM) (2004-1733-image1941)

b. Exterior Left Front Corner, Rm 2,
AZ V:1:170(ASM) (2004-1733-image2291)

Figure 6.30. Examples of Bonded Corners

a. Exterior Left Front Corner, Rm 3, from Left Side.
Left abuts Front in lower story
(2004-1733-image2004)

b. Exterior Left Front Corner, Rm 3, from Front.
Front abutted Left in upper story, but has fallen away
(2004-1733-image2003)

Figure 6.31. Alternation of Abutments from First to Second Stories, AZ V:5:61 (ASM)

Figure 6.32. Alternation of Abutments from First to Second Stories, AZ V:1:130 (ASM) (2004-1733-image1306)

pendant; fragments of a black-on-yellow bowl; and two clay legs from other effigies. Also in the room were antler arrow wrenches, parts of a textile bag, a broken jar with a yucca-fiber handle, and lots of yucca quids and hulls from walnuts and acorns. Haury (1934:54) notes that the items left on the altar are "suggestive of offerings made by the Zuñi as supplication for a successful hunt." There are other rooms at Canyon Creek Ruin that are also painted with multiple colors, including red, yellow, white, and blue pigments. There are no rooms known at this time in the Sierra Ancha cliff dwellings that are painted so elaborately or that have these sorts of floor features.

In the Sierra Ancha cliff dwellings, there are instances of rooms with painted elements—bands, and in one instance, figures—all done in white pigment. This decorative or symbolic treatment

is not present in all rooms at a site, and is concentrated in the Sierra Ancha in the pueblos on the north side of Pueblo Canyon. These are roughly contemporaneous sites (see Chapter 5) and not all that different in time from the construction and occupation of Canyon Creek Ruin. Two of the sites also represent the largest cliff dwellings in the Sierra Ancha. In the Pueblo Canyon sites, V:1:130 has 2 rooms with paint, V:1:131 has 6 rooms with paint, and V:1:132 has 5 rooms with painted elements on the stone masonry walls. Just one other site in the southeastern Sierra Ancha, V:1:167, was documented as having two rooms with painting. The relative proportions of painted to unpainted rooms suggests that the painting is likely to be more of a decorative preference. The proportion seems to be too large for these to all represent ceremonial rooms in the sense of a kiva. Wall painting is considered in more detail in Chapter 9.

Granaries

Granaries can be special structures or features within a room. Many storage rooms also served as granaries, undoubtedly, due to the paucity of obvious granary-type structures or features. Granary structures are often isolated architectural units along the canyon walls. This situation occurs in the US Southwest Four Corners area, as well as along Canyon Creek to the east. No structures like this are known in the Sierra Ancha canyons.

The only two structures in the Sierra Ancha that seem to be granaries are side-by-side in one site—Cooper Forks (V:1:135). They are at the back of an alcove and within a room (see Fig. III.30). There is a similar feature at Red Rock House, also at the back of an alcove and contained within a room (Reynolds 1981:137). The Sierra Ancha granary structures have rounded walls (as does the Red Rock House structure), and the walls are only about one-half as tall as the room walls. The Sierra Ancha granary structures are roofed similarly to the room roofs. Structures at V:1:131 may have also served as granaries

(Fig. III.27).

Granary-type features are known in the Tonto Basin (Lindauer 1992:38-39) and at Canyon Creek Ruin (Haury 1934:74, Plate L.b). These are circular features that occur in rooms and that are made of coarse-coiled basketry, plastered over with adobe. They appear to have been between 1 and 2m in diameter, and perhaps 0.75 to 1m tall. The top was sealed with a large stone or with basketry. Although these are specific structures dedicated to storage, they are not of the scale of the large granaries found in the Chihuahuan cliff dwellings such as Olla Cave (Blackiston 1905; Guevara Sánchez 1986:47). The size and shape is quite different, but the construction materials and techniques are similar.

There are other small features in the Sierra Ancha cliff dwellings that probably served as storage facilities. At the back of Room 11 in the Ring-Tail Ruin (V:1:132; Fig. III.28), a small gap in the cliff ended up behind the Back wall of the lower room (Room 10). The gap was not accessed from Room 10, but was roofed over and was presumably accessed from Room 11 and used as a small storage area.

ROOFING SYSTEMS

The original study of Sierra Ancha cliff dwelling roofs was published in 1993 (Lange and others 1993). The basic data and conclusions are included and reviewed here, in context with the other architectural data.

The roofing study was undertaken in order to better understand the engineering parameters behind choices made by the prehistoric builders concerning their roofing systems. The structural analysis examined the load-bearing capacities of different roofing systems and assessed those capacities relative to margins of safety based on modern structural standards. The modulus of rupture, that is, the point at which a beam fails, was used as the critical limit in this study.

Roofing systems that were theoretically possible given various combinations of beams,

supports, and cantilevered elements were examined first. The results were then compared to actual roofing situations in the cliff dwellings. The architectural documentation and tree-ring sampling made it possible to create a model room based on averaged dimensions of rooms, beams, and other roofing components in the Sierra Ancha cliff dwellings. Thus, the load bearing characteristics of various roofing systems could be compared by using standard parameters for beam spans, beam sizes, roof dimensions, and roof loads. Figure 6.33 shows a typical structure and the terminology applied to the various elements.

The architectural documentation and mapping recorded 262 rooms at 22 cliff dwellings. Of these total rooms, 158 were sufficiently intact to provide length and width measurements, and 53 rooms contained sufficient evidence to determine the type of roofing system, and often the numbers and sizes of the beams involved. Wall construction has been described above and was not further analyzed in this roofing study. Typically, the walls averaged about 35 cm wide, and were built of wet-laid, fairly regularly coursed, tabular stones, with single or double/single stones in cross-section (see Tables 6.3 – 6.7 and discus-

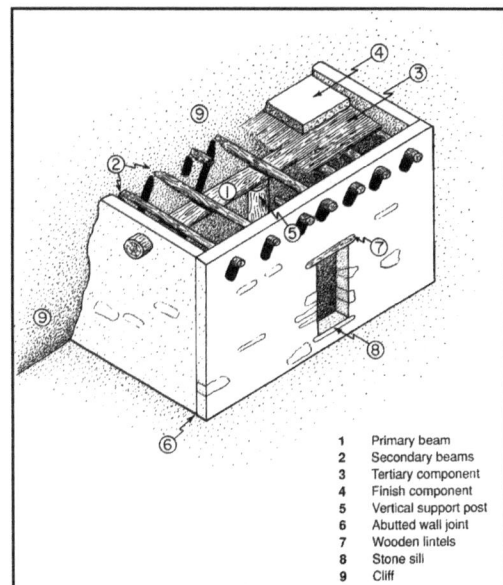

1	Primary beam
2	Secondary beams
3	Tertiary component
4	Finish component
5	Vertical support post
6	Abutted wall joint
7	Wooden lintels
8	Stone sill
9	Cliff

Figure 6.33. Typical Structure and Architectural Elements (2004-1733-image3996)

sion above for details). Walls were of varying length, but were about 2 m tall for a single story, and were plastered on both sides with a 3 to 5 cm thick, roughcast coat of plaster that was usually the same material as the mortar. No formal foundations are evident at the wall bases.

The model room (Fig. 6.34) was given the dimensions of 4 m long (from the Left to the Right walls) and 3 m wide (from the Front to the Back walls). Beams in the model room involved a single primary beam centered in the Left and Right walls, or two primary beams, spaced evenly between the Front and Back walls (Table 6.22). The diameter of the primary beam(s) used in the calculations was 19 cm (based on the average of 52 primary beams in the Sierra Ancha cliff dwellings, standard deviation is 4.3 cm). The primary beam(s) runs parallel to the cliff face. The primary beam(s) may or may not be supported by a vertical support post.

Secondary beams run perpendicular to the primary beams, and are therefore also perpendicular to the cliff. The secondary beams may or may not be supported at the cliff face. For the model room, the secondary beams were defined as 9 cm in diameter (based on 92 beams, standard deviation is 2.1 cm), and spaced 30 cm apart. There are therefore 12 secondary beams between the Left and Right walls in the model room. Wood species posited for the model room, and used to determine load-bearing values and properties, are the same as those typically used in the Sierra Ancha cliff dwellings.

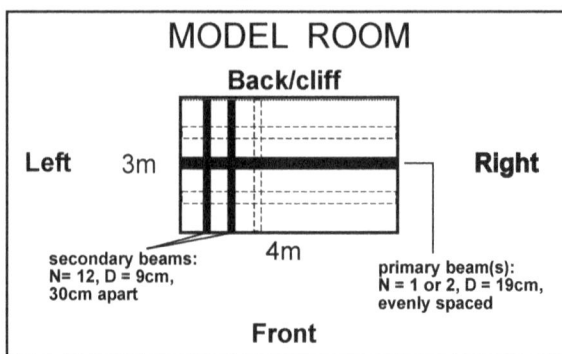

MODEL ROOM

Back/cliff

Left   3m   **Right**

secondary beams: 4m   primary beam(s):
N= 12, D = 9cm,   N = 1 or 2, D = 19cm,
30cm apart   evenly spaced

Front

Figure 6.34. A Model Room for Architectural Analysis: Elements and Their Dimensions (2004-1733-image3997)

Roof Components

Each room in a cliff dwelling has its own roof, although rooms were often contiguous with other rooms. The roof was flat, and served not only as the roof for the room below it, but also as a floor or work surface for the room or workspace above it. The roof loads are transmitted to the ground in three ways: through the masonry walls, a vertical support post under the primary beam, and the natural cliff. Transmitting the loads through the masonry walls is the most common condition, through the natural cliff, the rarest condition.

For the roofing study, four potential components were defined for each roof (Fig. 6.33). From the top surface to the bottom, these components are termed the finish, tertiary, secondary, and primary components. There are a few roofs (for example, Room 1, V:1:136) where, using this top down approach to the terminology, there is no primary component. However, this terminology does describe the majority of roof configurations.

The finish component is a clayey soil, sometimes including pebbles and tabular stones, that is applied wet so that it can be smoothed and will dry with a smooth, hard, even surface. The average thickness of the finish component in the Sierra Ancha cliff dwellings is 13 cm (Table 6.22). In addition to a compact work or floor surface, the finish component aids in distributing loads on that surface across the entire roof.

The tertiary component underlies the finish component. It averages 2 to 5 cm thick in these cliff dwellings, and serves to prevent materials making up the finish component from falling through the roof. For purposes of the model room, a weight equivalent to a 2.5 cm-thick layer of wooden planking is used. The tertiary component is often made up of several layers of a wide range and mixture of materials. Materials used in this layer include grass clumps, reeds, matting, wood planks and slats, small tree limbs and branches, agave stalks, and saguaro cactus ribs (Fig. 6.35a, b, c). Similar materials were used at the Tonto Ruins (Steen 1962:10-11).

The secondary component is below the tertiary component (Figs. 6.33 and 35) and generally includes a series of beams spaced relatively evenly apart that span the width of the room. The secondary beams are consistently supported at the Front wall and may be supported at the Back (cliff) wall. Figure 6.33 shows the secondary beams unsupported, or cantilevered, at the cliff wall. Remaining secondary beams or their sockets often show a pattern of alternating the beam orientation from butt to tip. This helps to level the roof, particularly if there are great differences in the diameters of the beam from butt to tip. Alternating butt-and-tip orientations for secondaries is also documented at the Upper Tonto Ruin (Steen 1962:9).

The primary component is the bottom component and involves one or more relatively large wooden beams spanning the length of the room. The primary beam(s) are perpendicular to the secondary beams, and in the case of the model room, are parallel to the cliff. Dean (1969:25) documents paired butt-to-tip primaries in Kayenta architecture. Butt-to-tip alternation was just noted for the secondary beams in the Sierra Ancha sites, but there is no evidence for the use of paired primaries in these sites.

One other element can be part of the roofing system—a vertical support post. Most vertical support posts are located under a primary beam at mid-span (12 of 17, Table 6.23; Fig. 6.36a and b). Their purpose was undoubtedly to shore up a sagging primary beam (or in anticipation of a sagging beam) and provide some peace of mind for the occupants. Occasionally, vertical support posts provided support at the end of a primary beam, where it needed to be supported at the cliff (CD17). Vertical support posts are also present at Canyon Creek Ruin, Tonto National Monument (Steen 1962), Montezuma Castle (Anderson 1988:159 and 174), and in the cliff dwellings in Chihuahua (Blackiston 1909:31).

Several of the vertical support posts show evidence of a grass-ring "pad" or cushion on top of the post (Fig. 6.36; CD17). The pad undoubtedly provided a better contact and seating for the

a. Pine planks, Roof of Rm 1, AZ V:1:136(ASM), a = secondary beams, b = tertiary materials (2004-1733-image4160)

b. Slats and Reeds, Roof of Rm 3, AZ V:1:135(ASM), a = primary beam, b = secondary beams, c = tertiary materials (2004-1733- image4161)

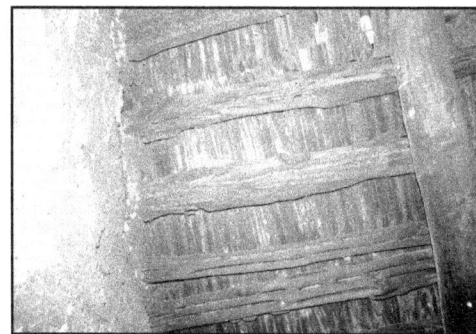

c. Saguaro ribs and stalks as secondary materials, Roof of Rm 3, AZ V:5:61 (ASM) (2004-1733image2050)

Figure 6.35. Typical and Atypical Sierra Ancha Secondary and Tertiary Roof Components

---

Table 6.22. Dead and Live Roof Loads

DEAD LOADS

Finish component – 13 cm of wet mud	2874 kg
Tertiary component – 2.5 cm thick pine slats	135 kg
Secondary component – 12 beams @ 9 cm D; 8.61 kg each	103 kg
Subtotal	3112 kg
Primary component – 1 or 2 primary beams, 19 cm D; 51 kg each Total (1)	3163 kg
Total (2)	3214 kg

LIVE LOADS

4 people, two metates, and miscellaneous items	444 kg
Difference between wet or dry beams and mud	500 kg

Table 6.23. Vertical Support Post Data

SITE	ROOM	Number Present	Orientation	Top Diameter (cm)	Bottom Diameter (cm)	Average Diameter (cm)	Location	Under	Species	Dates?
V:1:130	2	1	Top down	11	19	18	Midspan	Primary 1	Ponderosa	No
V:1:130	3	2	Top down	19	20	19	Midspan	Primary 1	Ponderosa	No
V:1:130	5	1	Bottom down	14	17	15	Midspan	Primary 1	Douglas Fir	No
V:1:130	7	1	Bottom down	16	14	15	Midspan	Primary 1	Ponderosa	No
V:1:131	8	1	Unknown				Unknown		Ponderosa	No
V:1:131	10A	1	Top down	20	20	20	Midspan	Primary 1	Ponderosa	No
V:1:131	11A	2	Top down	18	16	17	End		Juniper	No
V:1:131	15	1	Top down	11	22	18	Midspan	Primary 1	Juniper	No
V:1:131	17	1	Unknown				Unknown		Box elder	No
V:1:131	20	1	Unknown	17	17	17	Midspan	Primary 1	Unknown	No
V:1:132	17	2	Unknown	15	0	0	Midspan	Primary 1	Ponderosa	No
V:1:162	2	1	Bottom down	17	17	17	Midspan	Primary 1	Ponderosa	Yes
V:1:164	1	1	Unknown				Unknown		Juniper	No
V:1:164	4	1	Unknown	13	16	14	Midspan	Unknown	Juniper	No

a. Rm 7, AZ V:1:130 (ASM), mid-span vertical support post with grass ring pad (2004-1733-image1683)

b. Mid-span vertical support post, AZ V:1:130 (ASM), Rm 5 (2004-1733-image0140)

Figure 6.36. Vertical Support Posts and Grass Ring Pads

primary beam on top of the vertical support post. This architectural characteristic is illustrated in a diorama at Tuzigoot National Monument in the Verde Valley, suggesting it was found there, too.

Wood species were identified for 13 of the 17 vertical support posts recorded. The posts are mostly of two species (Ponderosa pine – 7 and juniper – 4; Table 6.23). There is also a tendency for the vertical support posts to be installed "top-down," that is, it is the base of the tree that is in contact with the primary beam; the top of the tree in contact with the floor (7 of 10 for which orientation could be determined; Table 6.23). This orientation for vertical support posts was also recorded at the Upper Tonto Ruin (Steen 1962:9). It may be that the vertical support posts in this orientation are less prone to splitting when the roof load is applied.

Finally, there can also be ties in the ceiling, probably fashioned of the same raw materials as the lintel ties, but also including yucca and sotol leaves. The ties do not seem to be braided rope or cordage. Such ties are not common features, and their need is unclear—during assembly the roofs would seem to be stable and not require the elements to be lashed together. One possible function, though, is to tie together the tertiary component materials and anchor them to beams in the primary or secondary components to prevent them from shifting during the application of the finish component. There are remnants of ties in the roof of Room 7 at V:1:130 and at Cooper Forks Ruin (V:1:135), and there are roof ties at Canyon Creek Ruin (Haury 1934:39; Reynolds 1981:207), Red Rock House (personal observation), and Montezuma Castle (Anderson 1988:160). Roofing ties are relatively more common in the roofs at Kiet Siel (personal observation), although Dean (1969) does not mention them.

Theoretical Roofing Systems

Two of the roofing components (primary and secondary) can vary in ways that significantly alter the load-bearing capacity of a roof. The primary beam(s) may or may not have a vertical support post, and secondary beams may or may not be cantilevered. The various values possible for the primary and secondary components can form a matrix defining the theoretically possible roofing systems (Table 6.24). There are five possible conditions for the primary component: 1) no primary component present, 2) a single primary beam with no vertical support, 3) a single primary beam with a vertical support post under it at mid-span, 4) two primary beams without vertical supports, and 5) two primary beams, each with a vertical support post at mid-span. Each of these conditions can be paired with one of three values for the secondary beams: 1) no cantilever, 2) a single cantilever, usually at the cliff face, and 3) a double cantilever.

Each cell of the matrix was designated with a capital letter. It is immediately obvious that there are four systems with problems, excluding them from further consideration (Roofing Systems B, C, F, and I; Figs. 6.37a-d). Roofing Systems B and C are not logically, theoretically, or practically possible—they have no primary beam, so cantilevering of the secondary beams is not possible. Roofing Systems F and I are practically impossible, although theoretically possible—they have double cantilevered secondaries sitting over a single primary—like a seesaw. Removing these four systems, then, leaves eleven roofing systems for consideration.

The possible theoretical roofing systems are shown in Figures 6.38a-k. Their load-carrying characteristics and capabilities are detailed next.

Structural Analyses of the Theoretical Roofing Systems

Structural analyses of the roofing systems involve the identification and calculation of forces acting on the roof. Forces acting on the roof are either dead loads or live loads (Table 6.22). The values assigned to the various components and loads are based on the model room. The dead loads are dictated by the numbers and dimensions of the roofing components (as specified by the model room). The live loads

Table 6.24. Matrix of Theoretically Possible Roofing Systems

	Type of secondary component cantilever		
Primary Component	None	Single	Double
No primary beam	A	B*	C*
One primary, unsupported	D	E	F*
One primary, supported	G	H	I*
Two primaries, unsupported	J	K	L
Two primaries, supported	M	N	O

*Practically, these are impossible roofing systems, see Figure 6.39.

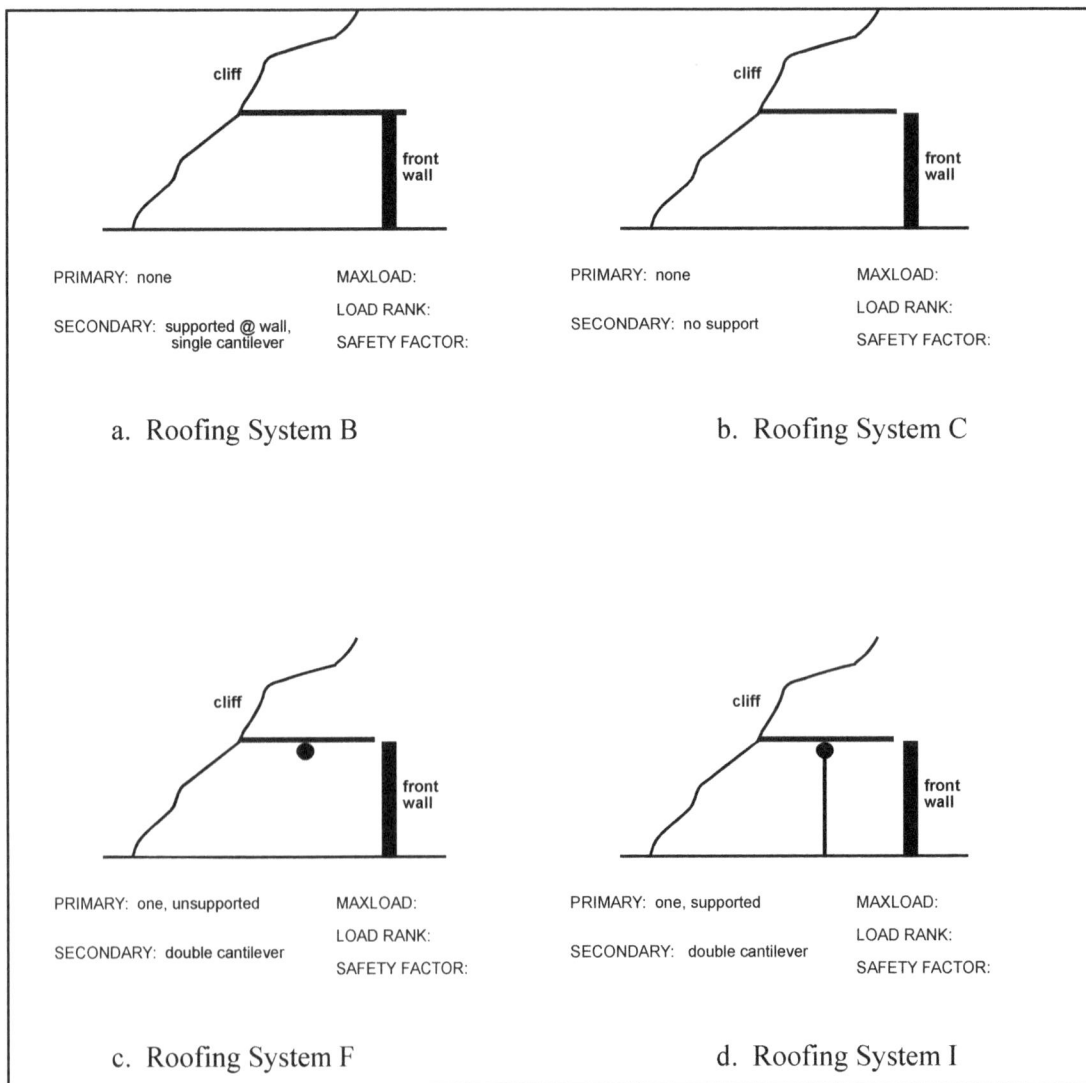

PRIMARY: none

SECONDARY: supported @ wall, single cantilever

MAXLOAD:
LOAD RANK:
SAFETY FACTOR:

a. Roofing System B

PRIMARY: none

SECONDARY: no support

MAXLOAD:
LOAD RANK:
SAFETY FACTOR:

b. Roofing System C

PRIMARY: one, unsupported

SECONDARY: double cantilever

MAXLOAD:
LOAD RANK:
SAFETY FACTOR:

c. Roofing System F

PRIMARY: one, supported

SECONDARY: double cantilever

MAXLOAD:
LOAD RANK:
SAFETY FACTOR:

d. Roofing System I

Figure 6.37. Impossible Roofing Systems (a - d), 2004-1733-image3998, 2004-1733-image3999), (2004-1733-image4000), (2004-1733-image4001

are more variable, and include forces such as wind, snow, people, and their possessions, tools, and stored materials.

Initially, live loads of 444 kg were estimated. The locations of the cliff dwellings minimize the effects of wind, water, and snow, so the load was based on the weight of two people, two large metates, and miscellaneous other objects. This combined weight was compared to the wet and dry figures for the roofing components, particularly for the wet vs. dry mud in the finish component. During construction, the live loads posited would not be present. However, various roof components would be wetter and heavier than they would be after they dry out. There is a 500 kg difference between the wet and dry dead loads. When "fresh," the beams contain significant moisture, contributing to heavier loads (and can lead to shrinkage later as the beams dry out). Thus, if the roof survives the application of wet materials during construction, it will be capable of supporting typical live loads after construction and drying.

As noted above, the modulus of rupture, the point of failure of a beam, was used to evaluate the strength of a roofing system, rather than other measures with arbitrarily established limits of "acceptable" deflection or loading. The modulus of rupture represents the unequivocal failure of the beam and thus, the entire roofing system. With the modulus of rupture, it is also possible to calculate a safety factor based on actual vs. required beam cross-sections (Lange and others 1993:492). A safety factor of 1.00 represents a match between the required and actual beam cross-sections. Values greater than 1.00 are margins of "over-design," values less than 1.00 indicate potential for structural failure.

The load-bearing capabilities of individual beams and each general roofing system were calculated. Some of the load factors are constant through all eleven systems. Secondary beams carry the same share of the total load, excluding the weight of the primary beam(s) in each system, that is, the area and load each secondary

supports is the same from system to system. This is true regardless of the type of cantilever. What does vary, dependent upon the type of cantilever, is the diameter of the secondary beam required to support a cantilevered load vs. the diameter required for an uncantilevered load.

In turn, the required diameter for a primary beam is also dependent upon any cantilever in the secondary component. When there are two primary beams and a single cantilever in the secondary beams, the area and load carried by each primary beam differs. Therefore, in the calculations, the required diameter for Primary 1 and 2 must be computed separately (see Roofing Systems K and N; Fig. 6.38 g and j, and Table 6.25). Primary 1 is the primary beam closest to the cantilevered ends; Primary 2 is the farthest away. When there are no cantilevers in the secondary component and double primary beams (Roofing Systems J and M), or when there are two cantilevers with two primary beams (Roofing Systems L and O), the primaries support the same proportion of the roofs. For these roofing systems, then, there is only one value calculated for the primary beams.

Observations on the Theoretical Roofing Systems
The theoretical roofing systems have a wide range of possible maximum loads (Table 6.25), ranging from 4822 kg to 104,259 kg (average is 27,400 kg; or an average of only 19,714 kg if the 104,259 kg load is excluded as an extreme outlier). With the dimensions of the components outlined for this study, it is clear that the size of the secondary beams is adequate for carrying the roof loads, regardless of any cantilevering. Interestingly, with the numbers, size, and spacing of the secondary beams as specified, the secondary component is capable of carrying a total roof load exceeding the load capacity of the primary beams in all but one roofing system (Roofing System O). Roofing Systems A, E, and H have the lowest load capabilities of any secondary components, but still have a safety factor of 5.36.

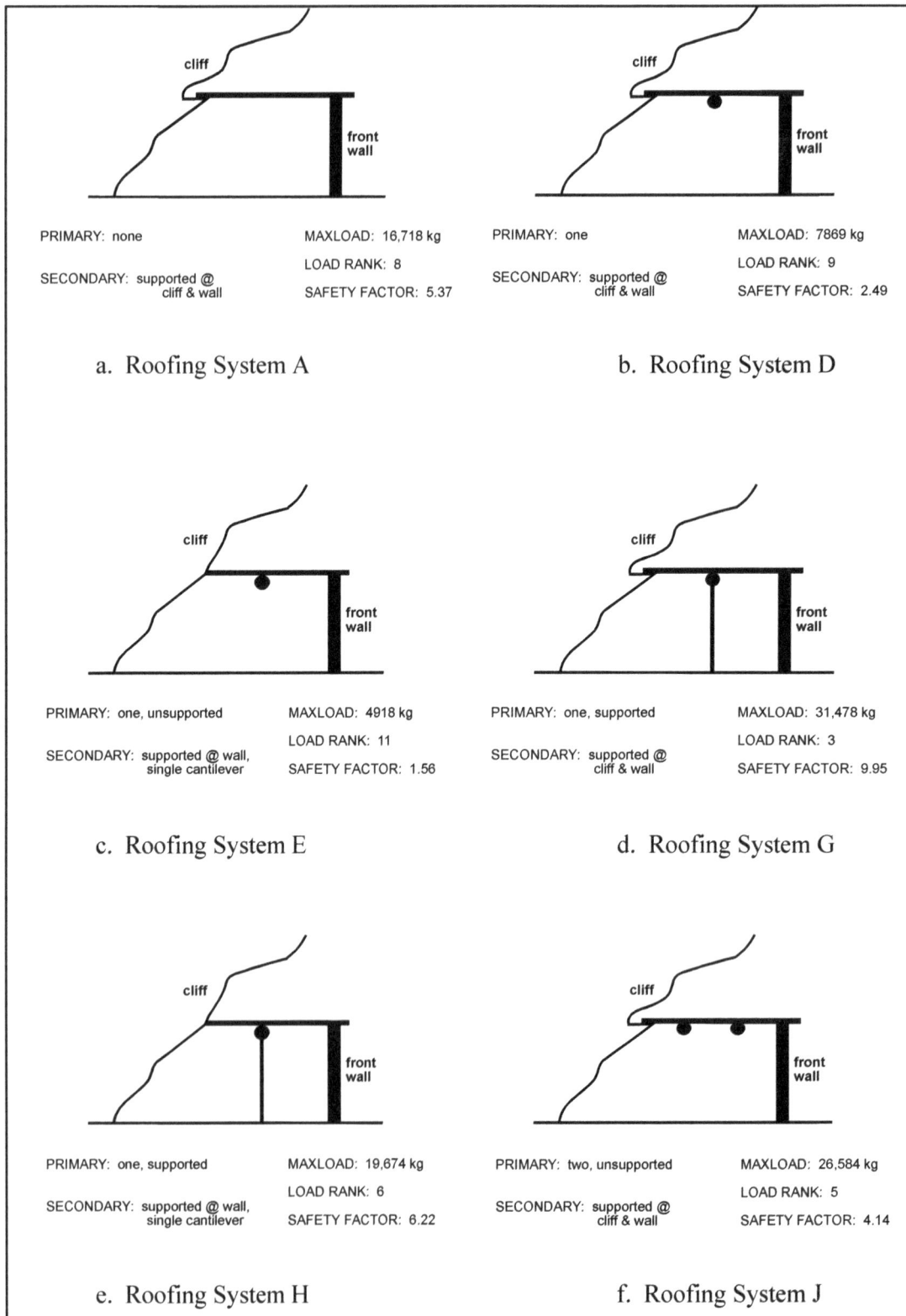

PRIMARY: none

SECONDARY: supported @
cliff & wall

MAXLOAD: 16,718 kg

LOAD RANK: 8

SAFETY FACTOR: 5.37

a. Roofing System A

PRIMARY: one

SECONDARY: supported @
cliff & wall

MAXLOAD: 7869 kg

LOAD RANK: 9

SAFETY FACTOR: 2.49

b. Roofing System D

PRIMARY: one, unsupported

SECONDARY: supported @ wall,
single cantilever

MAXLOAD: 4918 kg

LOAD RANK: 11

SAFETY FACTOR: 1.56

c. Roofing System E

PRIMARY: one, supported

SECONDARY: supported @
cliff & wall

MAXLOAD: 31,478 kg

LOAD RANK: 3

SAFETY FACTOR: 9.95

d. Roofing System G

PRIMARY: one, supported

SECONDARY: supported @ wall,
single cantilever

MAXLOAD: 19,674 kg

LOAD RANK: 6

SAFETY FACTOR: 6.22

e. Roofing System H

PRIMARY: two, unsupported

SECONDARY: supported @
cliff & wall

MAXLOAD: 26,584 kg

LOAD RANK: 5

SAFETY FACTOR: 4.14

f. Roofing System J

Figure 6.38. Theoretically Possible Roofing Systems (a – k), 2004-1733-image4002, 2004-1733-image4003, 2004-1733-image4004, 2004-1733-image4005, 2004-1733-image4006, 2004-1733-image4007, 2004-1733-image4008, 2004-1733-image4009, 2004-1733-image4010

PRIMARY: two, unsupported

SECONDARY: supported @ wall, single cantilever

MAXLOAD: 7340 kg

LOAD RANK: 10

SAFETY FACTOR: 2.28

g. Roofing System K

PRIMARY: two, unsupported

SECONDARY: double cantilever

MAXLOAD: 19,672 kg

LOAD RANK: 7

SAFETY FACTOR: 3.06

h. Roofing System L

PRIMARY: two, supported

SECONDARY: supported @ cliff & wall

MAXLOAD: 106,346 kg

LOAD RANK: 1

SAFETY FACTOR: 16.54

i. Roofing System M

PRIMARY: two, supported

SECONDARY: supported @ wall, single cantilever

MAXLOAD: 29,364 kg

LOAD RANK: 4

SAFETY FACTOR: 9.14

j. Roofing System N

PRIMARY: two, supported

SECONDARY: double cantilever

MAXLOAD: 37,557 kg

LOAD RANK: 2

SAFETY FACTOR: 12.24

k. Roofing System O

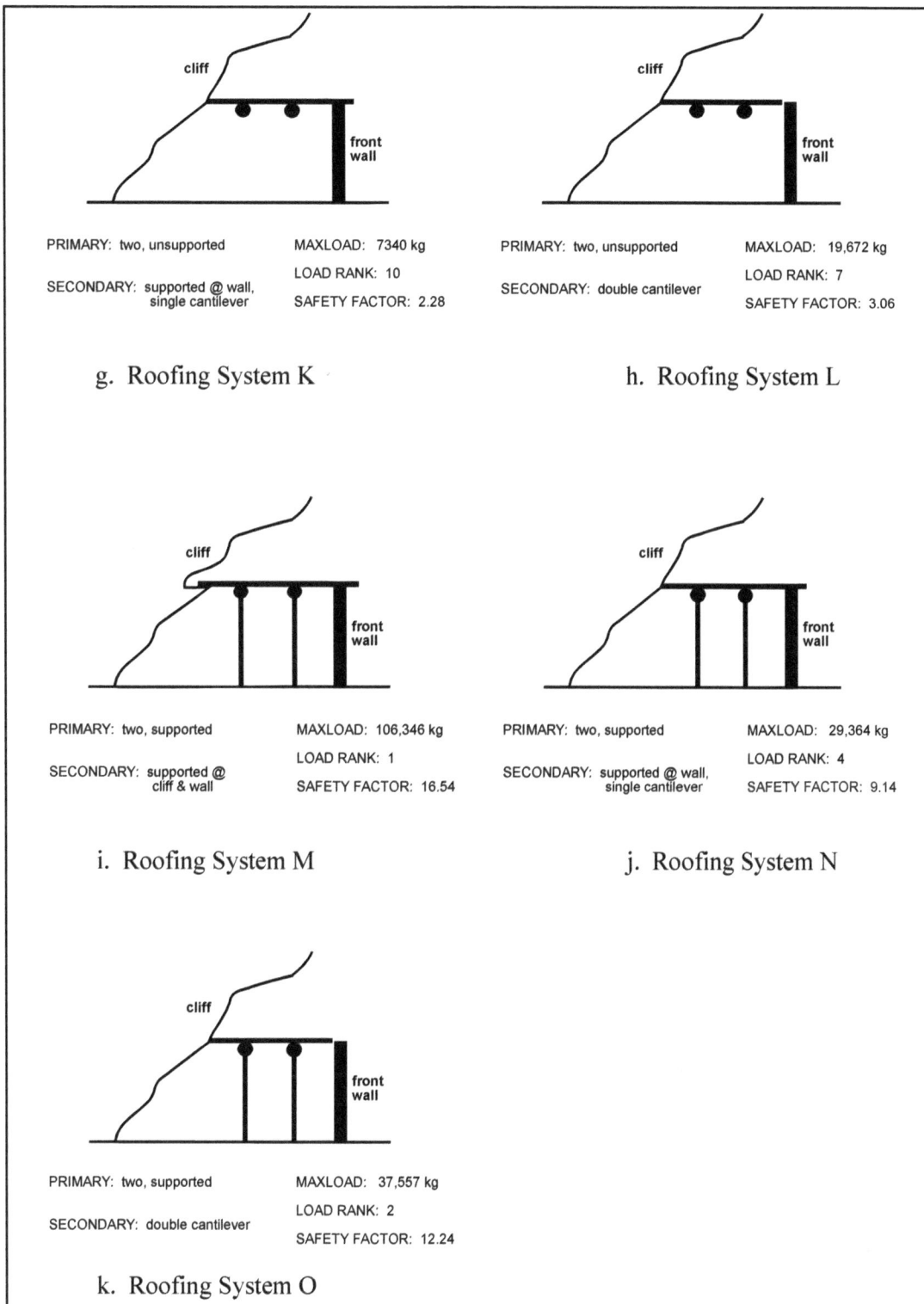

Figure 6.38. Theoretically Possible Roofing Systems (a – k), cont'd

Table 6.25. Load Capabilities of the Theoretical Roofing Systems

Roofing system	Type of beam	Area supported per beam (sq m)	Percent of total roof supported per beam	Load supported per beam (kg)	Safety factor	Minimum diameter for beam (cm)	Maximum load per beam (kg)	Maximum load per component (kg)	Maximum load for system (kg)	Rank by maximum load
A	Secondary	0.92	7.69	273.54	4.60	5.41	1,257	16,340	16,340	8
D	Secondary	0.92	7.69	273.54	18.41	3.41	5,036	65,468	–	
	Primary	7.50	62.50	2254.38	2.14	14.75	4,822	7,715	7,715	9
E	Secondary	0.92	7.69	273.54	4.60	5.41	1,257	16,340	–	
	Primary	12.00	100.00	3607.00	1.34	17.25	4,822	4,822	4,822	11
G	Secondary	0.92	7.69	273.54	18.41	3.41	5,036	65,468	–	
	Primary	7.50	62.50	2254.38	8.56	9.29	19,288	30,861	30,861	3
H	Secondary	0.92	7.69	273.54	4.60	5.41	1,257	65,468	–	
	Primary	12.00	100.00	3607.00	5.35	10.87	19,288	19,288	19,288	6
J	Secondary	0.92	7.69	273.54	51.70	2.42	14,143	183,859	–	
	Primary	4.44	37.00	1353.46	3.56	12.44	4,822	26,065	26,065	5
K	Secondary	0.92	7.69	273.54	10.34	4.13	2,829	36,777	–	
	Primary 1	8.04	67.00	2450.86	1.97	15.16	4,822	7,197	–	
	Primary 2	2.04	17.00	621.86	7.75	9.60	4,822	28,364	7,197	10
L	Secondary	0.92	7.69	273.54	10.34	4.13	2,829	36,777	–	
	Primary	6.00	50.00	1829.00	2.64	13.75	4,822	19,288	19,288	6
M	Secondary	0.92	7.69	273.54	51.70	2.42	14,143	183,859	–	
	Primary	4.44	37.00	1353.46	14.25	7.84	19,288	104,259	104,259	1
N	Secondary	0.92	7.69	273.54	10.34	4.13	2,829	36,777	–	
	Primary 1	8.04	67.00	2450.86	7.87	9.55	19,288	28,788	–	
	Primary 2	2.04	17.00	621.86	31.02	6.05	19,288	113,459	28,788	4
O	Secondary	0.92	7.69	273.54	10.34	4.13	2,829	36,777	–	
	Primary	6.00	50.00	1829.00	10.55	8.66	19,288	77,152	36,777	2

The dimensions, spans, and numbers of primary beams thus became the most critical in terms of being able to carry the roof loads. The primary beams in several systems (Roofing Systems D, E, and K) show low safety factors (less than 2.50). However, even with these low safety factors, the factors are still greater than 1.00 and the roofs are not expected to fail. Interestingly, each of these systems has single-cantilevered secondary components. Adding a vertical support post under the mid-point of a primary beam clearly allows the roofing system to carry a significantly greater load (compare Roofing Systems D and G). What is unclear is if the vertical support posts were part of the original roof design, or were added during construction, or at a later point in time, to improve the stability of the roof (for instance, if the primary beam began to sag). It seems that the ideal would be to avoid having a vertical support in the middle of the room—just something else to bump into. However, adding that post would clearly mean there was no danger of the roof collapsing under its own weight.

Comparing Actual Examples and the Model Roofing Systems

The 53 cases where the roofing system could be determined are not evenly distributed among the theoretically possible systems (Tables 6.26 and 6.27). Two systems dominate—Roofing Systems E and K. Both roofing systems are characterized by unsupported primary beam(s) with single cantilevers in the secondary component. The difference between Roofing Systems E and K is the presence of one (Roofing System E) or two (Roofing System K) primary beams. Interestingly, no examples of the top three load-bearing roofing systems were identified, and there are relatively few examples of the fourth through ninth ranked systems. The greatest numbers of roofs are in the tenth and eleventh ranked systems, Roofing Systems E and K.

The average room sizes for roofs assigned to these two systems are less than 2 sq m different from the model (13.72 sq m and 13.63 sq m compared to 12 sq m). The average beam spans are also similar to the model room: 4.19 m for the primary beam span, and 2.46 m for the secondary spans in Roofing System E; 3.70 m and 2.39 m, respectively, for the spans in Roofing System K.

In comparing actual roofs to their models, it became obvious that actual roofing systems are often hybrids between two or more of the theoretical roofing systems (Table 6.27). Structural analyses were not performed for these hybrids because of the large number of variations that would need to be investigated. In practice, the roofing components are often made up of a variety of materials, and have a variety of characteristics and dimensions: multiple materials in the tertiary component (see above), one or more species of wood for the primary and secondary beams, varying dimensions for the beam spans, irregular spacing of the secondary beams, and variable diameters for the beams. Depending upon the combination and different permutations of these factors, actual roofs may have been stronger or weaker than the model systems.

Several other general observations can be made. There is no evidence that larger rooms use "safer" roofing systems. There is no correlation between larger rooms and the use of vertical support posts, and no correlation between larger rooms and the use of an additional primary beam. Other comparisons of actual roofs to the model systems can be made on a case-by-case basis.

Roofing System A
Three examples of this roofing system were identified in the Sierra Ancha cliff dwellings (Fig. 6.38a). The average size of these rooms is about half the size of the model room (6.68 sq m; range is 5.2 to 9.2 sq m). The number of secondaries used is about half the number in the model room, which could be expected based on the smaller room size. However, the secondary beams in the actual roofs are approximately 2.5 times larger in diameter than the calculated required minimum diameter. It appears the builders were exceeding an already substantial safety factor calculated for the model system (5.37).

Table 6.26. Load Rank and Safety Factors for Roofing System Types

LOAD RANK	ROOF TYPE	SAFETY FACTOR	NUMBER OF CASES
1	M	16.54	0
2	O	12.24	0
3	G	9.95	0
4	N	9.14	2
5	J	4.14	2 (+3)
6	H	6.22	4
7	L	3.06	1
8	A	5.37	3
9	D	2.49	1
10	K	2.28	18
11	E	1.56	16

Table 6.27. Matrix of Actual Roofing Systems (53 cases)

	Type of secondary beam cantilever			
Primary component condition	None	Hybrid	Single	Double
No primary beam	3	--	0*	0*
Single primary beam, unsupported	1	--	16	0*
Single primary beam, supported	0	--	4	0*
Double primary beam, unsupported	2	3†	18	1
Double primary beam, hybrid	3‡	--	--	--
Double primary beam, supported	0§	--	2§	0

*Impossible roofing systems; see Table 6.18.

†A hybrid, J/K; about half of the secondaries are cantilevered (single), and about half are not.

‡A hybrid, J/M; only one of the two primaries has a vertical support.

§There may be one example of Roofing System M, and there is also an odd example of Roofing System N which has not been included: one of the primary beams has two vertical support posts.

Roofing System D

One example of this system was identified (Fig. 6.38b), and it is over twice the size of the model room (24.5 sq m). The diameter of the primary beam is unknown, and the secondary beams are three times larger than the required minimum. However, there are half the number of secondaries compared to the model system.

This raises the possibility that this room could have had an additional primary, and is therefore not an example of Roofing System D, but of Roofing System J. Calculations were done for the actual example of this roofing system. The secondaries do have a safety factor of 1.57, and the minimum required diameter for these beams is only 9.46 cm. A single primary beam would need to be at least 19.21 cm in diameter, within the range of primary beams and the model room as well. This roof was supportable with this roofing system, so it remains classified here.

Roofing System E

Sixteen examples of Roofing System E (Fig. 6.38c) were noted. Half of these rooms are larger than the model, half are smaller. The average size is only slightly larger (13.7 sq m) than the model.

For the rooms the same size or smaller than the model, the dimensions of the primary beam are known for five cases. In these five instances, the primary beams are larger (20 to 26 cm) than the dimensions in the model. The number of secondary beams is the same as or greater than the model, and the diameters are the same or slightly smaller. However, the diameter is still 1.2 to 1.5 times the required minimum. In general, these differences would create a roof with even greater safety factors than in the model system.

In the larger rooms, the numbers and diameters of secondary beams are again similar to the model or greater in size and number. The primary beams (3 cases) are the same diameter as specified in the model, or larger (4 cases). Again, these differences should create a roof with equivalent or greater safety factors than the model.

Roofing System G

Although Roofing System G (Fig. 6.38d) is one of the strongest theoretically and practically possible roofing systems, no examples were identified in the Sierra Ancha cliff dwellings.

Roofing System H

Four examples of this roofing system were noted (Fig. 6.38e), three of which are much larger (17 to 18 sq m) than the model room. In the only example of this roofing system where the number of secondary beams can be determined, there were more beams than in the model. Interestingly, the greater number of secondaries occurs in the one room that is about the same size as the model. Although primary beams spans are 0.5 to 0.9 m longer than in the model, three of the four examples have primary beams larger (20 to 24 cm) than the model. These diameters are about twice the minimum required diameter. The actual cases of this roofing system show the builders tending toward increasing the safety factors of the roof components.

Roofing System J

Two examples of this roofing system were identified (Fig. 6.38f). The average size of the rooms is the same as the model. No evidence remains for the number and sizes of the secondary beams or for the size of the primary beam. Thus, there is no way to judge the practical application of this roofing system against the theoretically derived safety factors.

Roofing System J/K

This is a hybrid system because about one-half of the secondary beams are supported. Three examples of this type of roofing system were found, with average room sizes smaller than the model. Beam dimensions are discernible for only one of the rooms. The primary beams are smaller (12 and 13 cm) than those in the model, but these diameters approximate the minimum required.

The secondaries are the same size as in the model, a diameter that is two to four times greater than the required minimum, and are more numerous (15). Thus, the secondary beams clearly exceed the safety factors calculated for Roofing Systems J or K. This configuration for the primaries is borderline, and could fail in a room the size of the model room. The actual example, however, shows reduced total loads, due to shorter spans for the primary beams and a smaller total roof area (8.84 sq m).

Roofing System K

Roofing System K (Fig. 6.38g) is the most common system identified in the Sierra Ancha cliff dwellings; there are 18 examples. The average size is a bit larger (13.6 sq m) than the model room, with, again, half of the rooms larger, and half smaller.

Rooms the same size or smaller have fewer secondaries than the model room, but they are larger in diameter. For primary beams for which there are data, three are smaller than the model (13 to 18 cm), and two are much larger (25 to 27 cm). In these five cases, the spans of the primary beams are shorter than in the model. It seems that the safety factors of the model roof are being met, if not exceeded, in these actual cases.

There are no good data for the number or sizes of secondaries in the larger-than-average rooms. One room seems to have fewer secondaries than the model. Data for the primary beams (5) shows that all are larger (20 to 25 cm) than those in the model room. These diameters represent values 1.3 to 1.6 times larger than the minimum required diameter. Due to the missing information on the secondary component, however, actual cases cannot be fully evaluated with respect to the model system.

Roofing System L

There is one example of Roofing System L (Fig. 6.38h). The room is about one-half the size (6.89 sq m) of the model room, with possibly fewer secondaries but of the same size as in the model. The primaries do match the required minimum diameter for the area of the model roof. Thus, with the match to certain elements of the model roof, and reduced load of the actual roof, this actual case seems to have matched or exceeded the modeled safety factors.

Roofing System J/M

Roofing System J/M is another hybrid (see Fig. 6.38i for Roofing System M). In the actual cases (3), only one of the two primary beams has a vertical support post. Two of the rooms are larger than the model (14.6 to 18.4 sq m), and the average of the actual cases is larger as well (14.8 sq m). In the two larger rooms, the average primary beam diameters are 1.8 to 2.8 times larger than the calculated minimum required. One of the larger rooms also has more secondaries (15), and they are larger than the minimum required (4.5 times larger). Load capacities for Roofing Systems J and M are, respectively, the fifth and first rated. Roofing System M also has the highest calculated safety factor. With a required minimum diameter of only 2.4 cm for the secondary beams, it is apparent that the actual roofs would clearly exceed the required minima and be capable of carrying heavy loads.

Roofing System N

Just two cases of this roofing system (Fig. 6.38j) were documented in the Sierra Ancha. The two rooms are similar in size (15.7 and 15.8 sq m), and are larger than the model room. One room might have had fewer secondaries than the model, and there is no information available on their diameters. The primary beams in this room average slightly larger (20 cm) than the model room. This diameter is 2 to 3 times the minimum required (in a room only 1.3 times larger than the model). The span of the primary beams in this room is only ten percent longer than the beams posited for the model room. The second room has more (15) and larger (10 cm) secondary beams. The primaries are slightly smaller (18 cm). The model for this roofing system has large safety factors, and again, the builders have matched or exceeded the required minima.

Roofing System O

There are no examples of this roofing system (Fig. 6.38k) in the Sierra Ancha cliff dwellings. Although there are double cantilevers on the secondary beams, with the two supported primary beams, this roofing system has the second highest load rank and a high safety factor (12.24). Clearly, the builders opted not to have cantilevers whenever possible, and preferred not to use supported primary beams (Tables 6.23 and 6.27).

Roofing Systems Summary

Based on data and observations from the cliff dwellings in the Sierra Ancha, a matrix of theoretically possible roofing systems was created. Structural analyses were done on those theoretical roofing systems in order to compare their load-bearing capacities and evaluate their structural integrity.

The theoretically possible roofing systems were then compared to actual cases from the cliff dwellings. Several interesting insights were immediately apparent. Minimum diameters required for roof beams were calculated for the theoretical systems. In the actual roofs, modifications increasing the safety factors were often made—spacing between secondary beams was reduced, the size of the secondary beams was increased, and the size of the primary beam was increased.

For the Sierra Ancha roofs, secondary beams range between 7 and 11 cm in diameter, while primary beams range from 12 to 23 cm in diameter. These beam dimensions and a fairly standard spacing of the beams provided a sound roof structure with sufficient margins of safety. The beam sizes found in the cliff dwellings may reflect natural growth patterns in the wood species used, but could also reflect building traditions that established that a primary beam should be "about this big," and a secondary beam "about that big." This "standardization" could have been imposed when harvesting timbers for the roof because:1) selection of appropriately sized trees would reduce the amount of chopping and

trimming required, 2) the amount of labor and energy required to transport larger beams may have been excessive, and 3) experience may have shown that the weight of substantially larger beams could cause structural problems in the supporting masonry walls.

The builders of these cliff dwellings seem to have had a clear concept of the materials, the dimensions of these materials, and the means of putting the materials together required to make a structure and its roof. Deviations, short cuts, or scrimping on the basic pattern or components were certainly quickly, and in no uncertain terms, shown to be catastrophic. The builders favored two roofing systems (E and K), involving single or double primary beams without vertical support posts. For freestanding architectural units, or any of the cliff dwelling rooms not abutting the cliff, cantilevering of the secondary beams would not have been a problem, if they were cut to the proper length. These roofs would have been capable of carrying even greater loads—compare the maximum loads for Roofing System E to D and Roofing System K to J. The roofing systems used most frequently (E and K) are not the most structurally sound. In the theoretical systems, they are ranked last in terms of the loads they can carry, and they have the lowest values for safety factors. The margins of safety were certainly adequate, however, and the structures and roofs are clearly capable of carrying the loads placed on them. The builders of these structures and roofs obviously did not excessively overbuild, nor did they underbuild.

BUILDING A CLIFF DWELLING

Building a cliff dwelling or any other set of structures may be the result of a population moving into a new area, or existing groups changing the pattern and locations of settlements in their landscape. Triadan and Zedeño (2004:95) observe that the decision-making process as reflected in the pattern of settlements and facilities is a compromise between geographical and political choices. Risk, danger, economic gain, and political power all influence settlement choices. Prior knowledge, or that acquired early on in a new landscape, allows groups to weigh the potential and limitations of new settlement locations against the possible social or political risks and gains. It may take many years, even generations, before an area is actually colonized, or particular locations in the landscape are utilized.

The process of building a cliff dwelling in the Sierra Ancha starts with the need or decision on someone's part to build in these types of remote locations. Perhaps the canyons had been visited on a hunting trip or just out of curiosity. Coupled with the need for constructing in a remote location are the negative and positive factors of building and living in such locations. The presence of water and the varieties and general locations of building materials have been discussed in greater detail in earlier chapters. Water is available at seeps, springs, or in the canyon bottoms. The water sources can be right in or immediately adjacent to particular cliff dwellings. Building materials are available from in the caverns, nearby, and at various distances. The negative factors related to water and building materials may be that water flow in the nearest source(s) is irregular or unreliable, and that the cost in time or effort of finding, preparing, and hauling building materials may be too great. Positive factors include the presence of water and at least as easy access to building materials in comparison to building in other locations.

Solar and Temperature Considerations

Cliff dwellings, because they tend to be constructed in locations that face directions in the quadrant from east to south (see Fig. 7.5), are frequently thought of as optimal locations for passive solar heating, particularly during the winter months. Adams (1979) and Christenson (1991) have compiled temperature data for other locations, and also point out that villages and fields are often located where they are in order to avoid cold air drainage. The SAP cliff dwelling

site locations also clearly support this idea. The cliff dwellings are at high elevations with respect to the major stream course, in this case

Cherry Creek. This avoids the cold air drainage, from either the top of the Sierra Ancha or coming down from the Mogollon Rim, that settles in the lower elevations in the valley. During the course of the SAP, experiential as well as numerical data were acquired that support the ideas of passive solar heating and avoiding cold air drainage, but with an interesting twist. The SAP cliff dwelling locations moderate seasonal temperatures, making summer or winter occupation equally comfortable.

Figures 6.39-6.45 show various combinations of night and daytime temperatures; minimum, mean, and maximum temperatures by location; and a detail of December temperatures over a three-day period. The records are from the period of December 1995 to October 1996 and represent four recording locations (also see Chapter 2). The lowest elevation recorder was hidden in the branches of a juniper tree on a ridge top on the south side of Pueblo Canyon, about 1160m elevation, and approximately 140m above Cherry Creek. This location is susceptible to cold air drainage coming down Pueblo Canyon from the top of the Sierra Ancha, as well as cold air coming down Cherry Creek from the north (Fig. 6.39). Another recorder was located on the north side of Pueblo Canyon about 1585m elevation, a short distance away from a cliff dwelling (Fig. 6.40). This recorder is susceptible to cold air drainage from higher elevations in the canyon; is in a sunny location most of the day, although it was hidden in the branches of pinyon tree; and can be affected by back radiation from the cliff at night. The third recorder was placed in a cliff dwelling room, tucked above a secondary beam in the nearly intact roof (V:1:130, Rm 7; Fig. 6.41), and the external channel was activated to attach a cable and sensor that was placed in a joint in the interior surface of the Front wall of the room (Fig. 6.42). When the sun is shining, the exterior of this wall receives direct sunlight for varying periods of time each day. Tem-

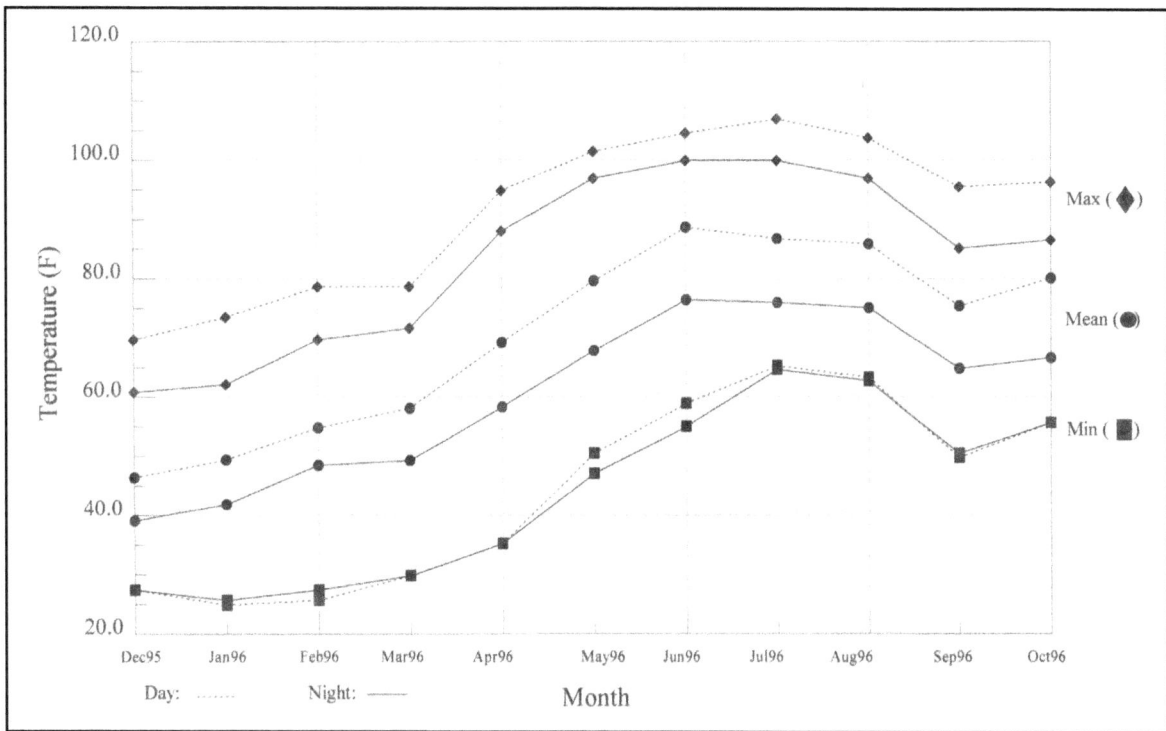

Figure 6.39. Daytime and Nighttime Mean, Maximum, and Minimum Temperatures at 3800 ft Elevation (2004-1733-image4013)

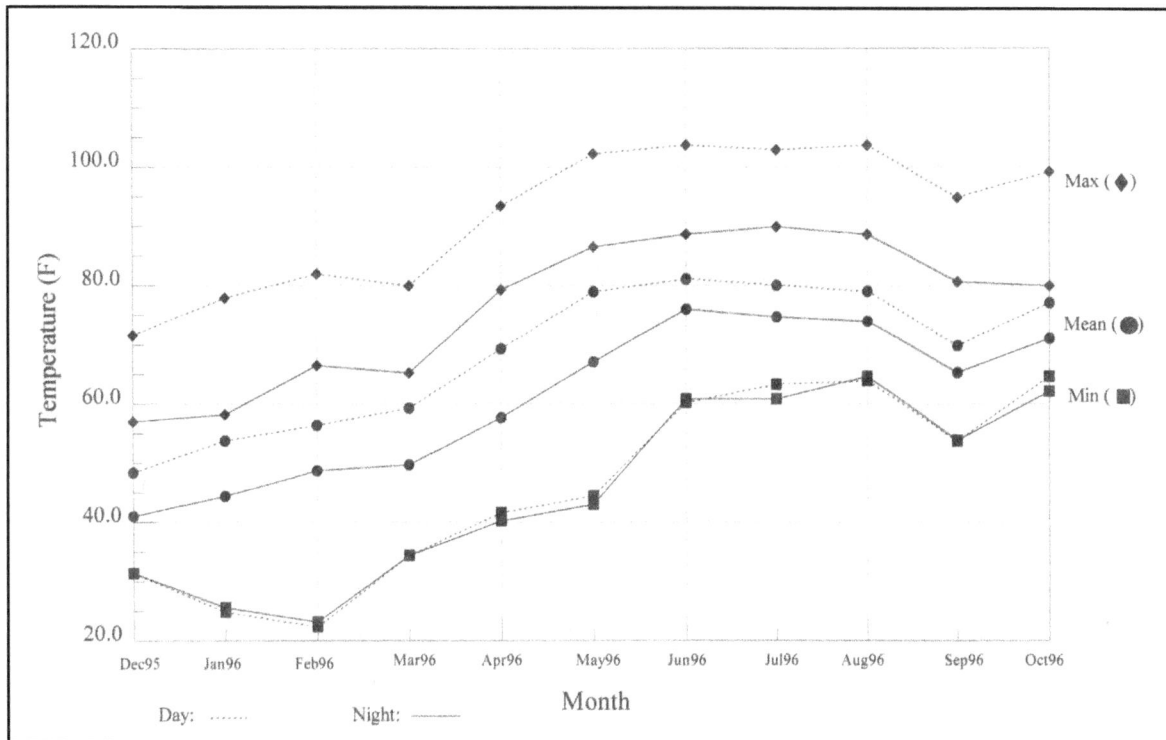

Figure 6.40. Daytime and Nighttime Mean, Maximum, and Minimum Temperatures in Open Canyon at 5200 ft Elevation (2004-1733-image4014)

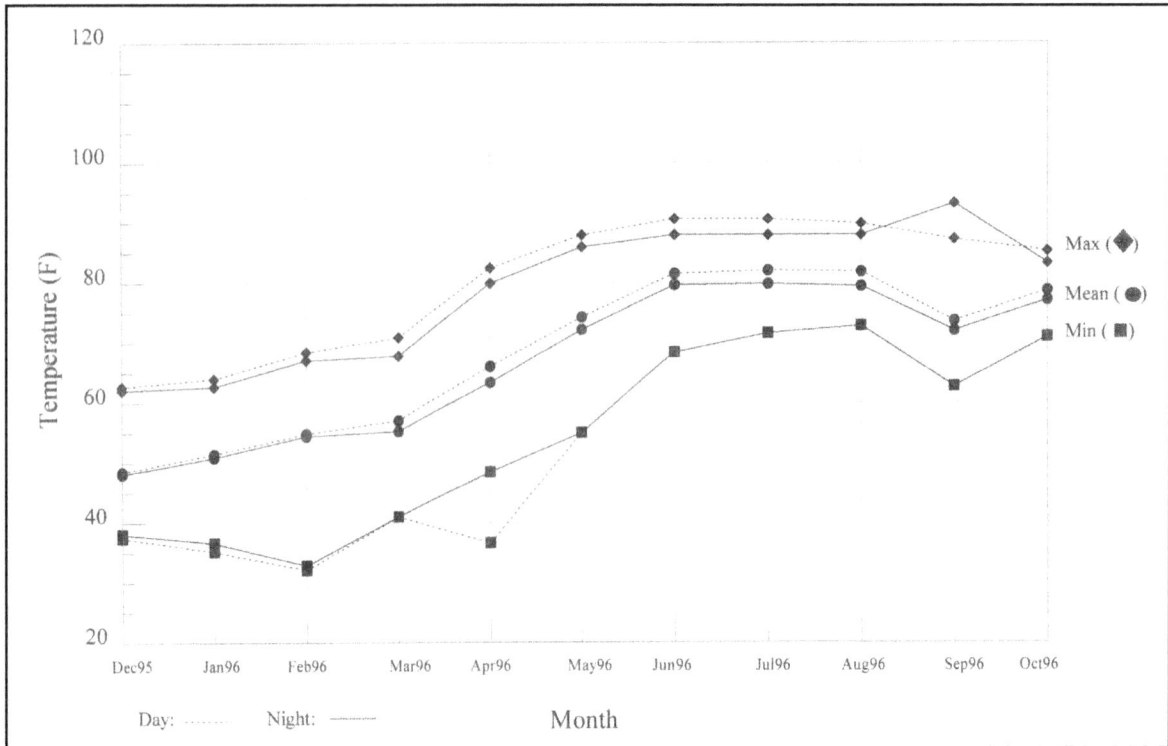

Figure 6.41. Daytime and Nighttime Mean, Maximum, and Minimum Temperatures, Interior of Cliff Dwelling Room, ca. 5200 ft Elevation (2004-1733-image4015)

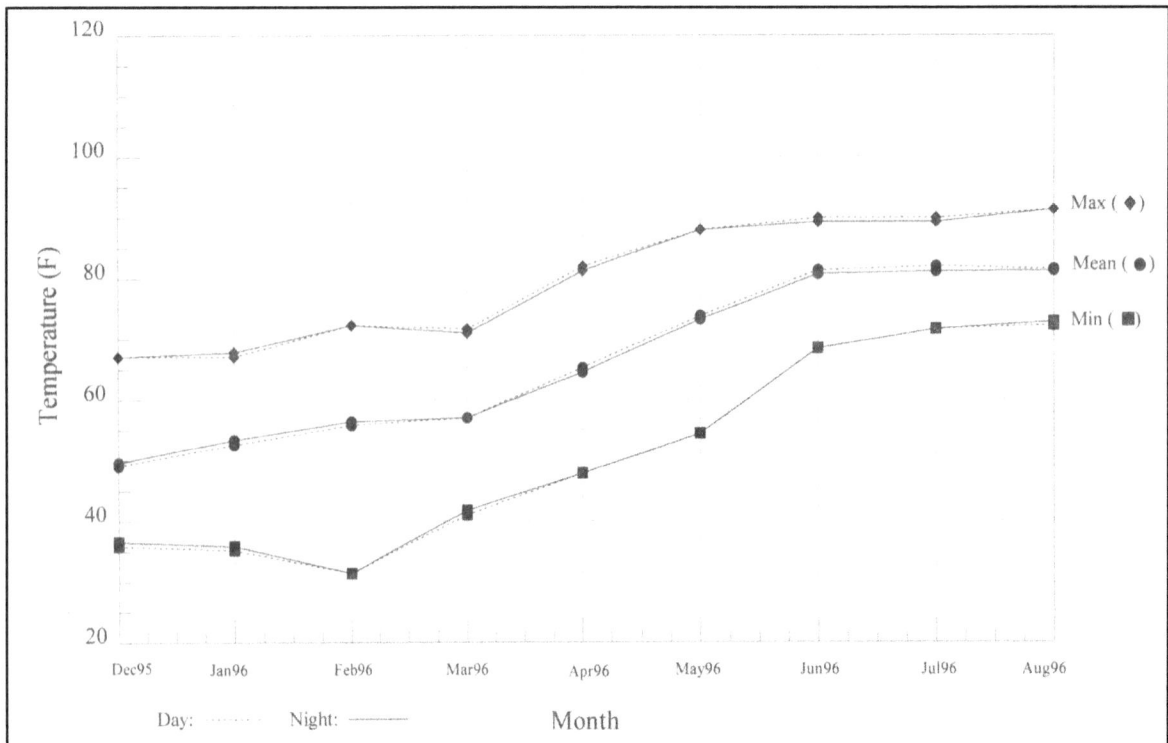

Figure 6.42. Daytime and Nighttime Mean, Maximum, and Minimum Temperatures, Interior of Cliff Dwelling Wall Surface, ca. 5200 ft Elevation (2004-1733-image4016)

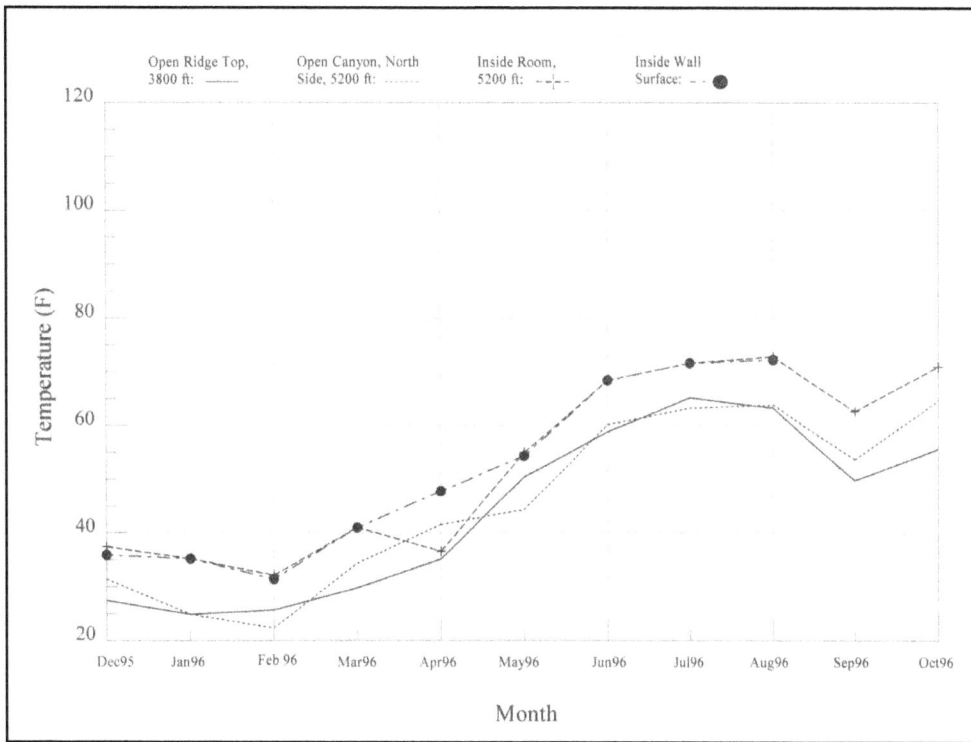

Figure 6.43. Comparing Minimum Daytime Temperatures (2004-1733-image4017)

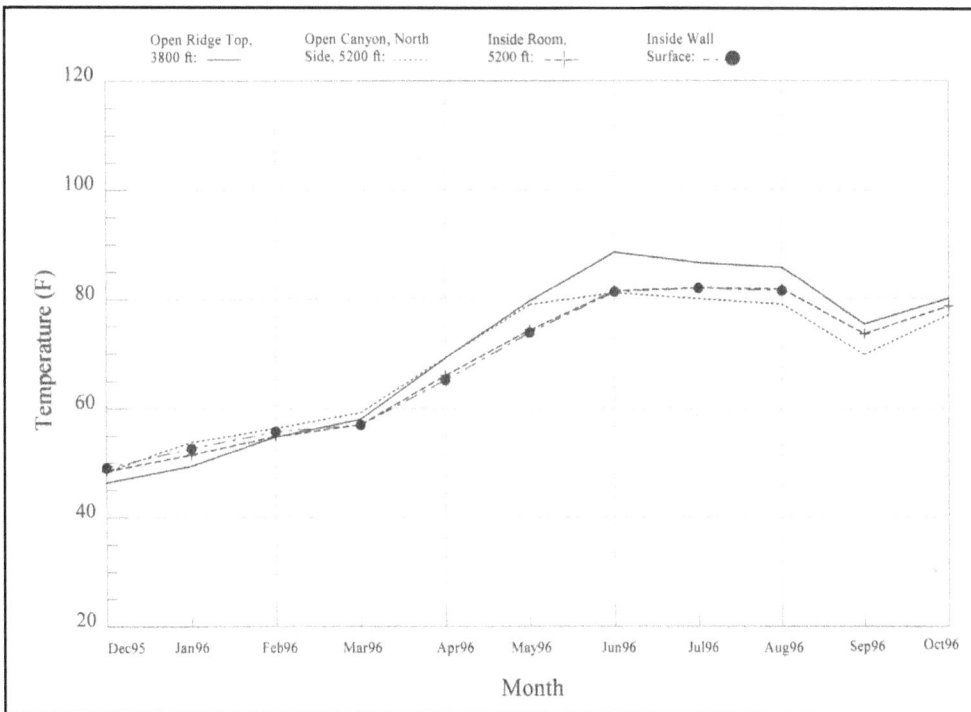

Figure 6.44. Comparing Mean Daytime Temperatures (2004-1733-image4018)

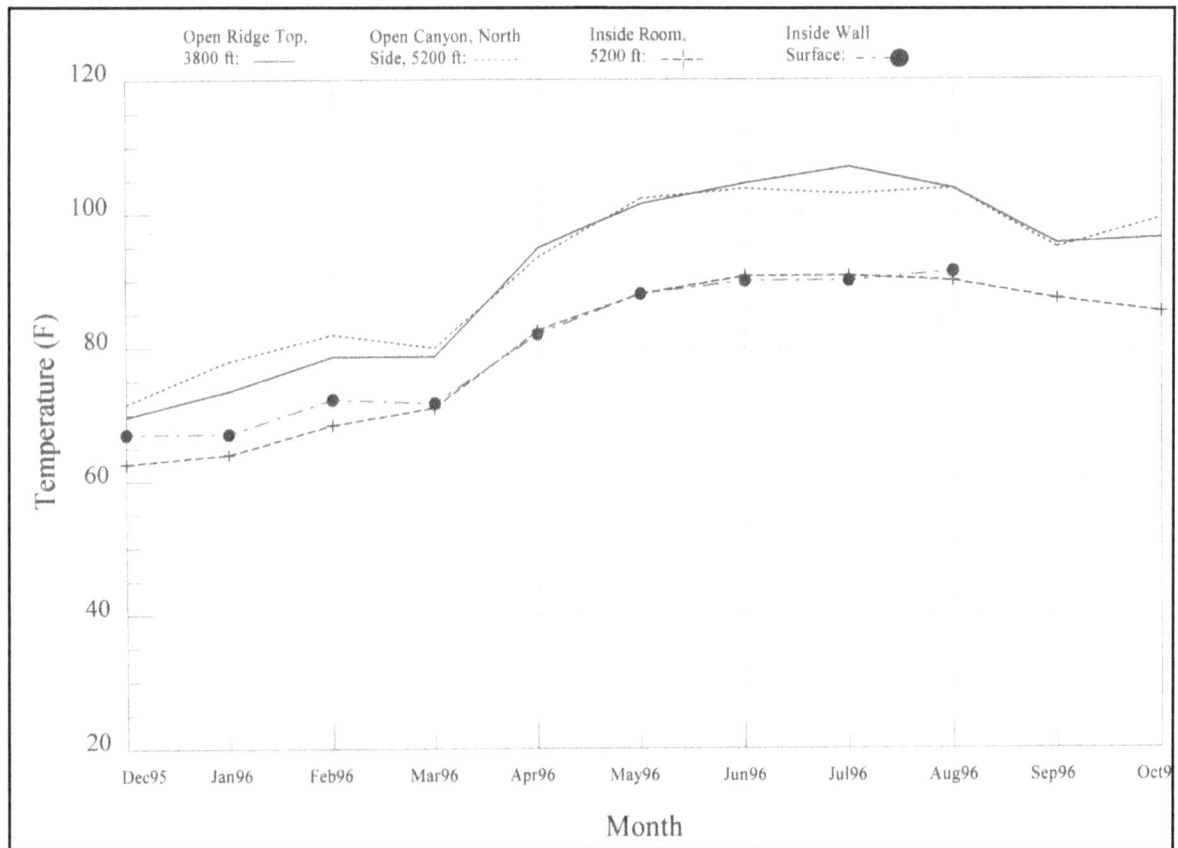

Figure 6.45. Comparing Maximum Daytime Temperatures (2004-1733-image4019)

perature in the room is affected by heat that is transferred through the wall, long after the sun has passed, and by back radiation from the cliff that affects the setting of the entire site (see Fig. 6.43). Temperatures could be further regulated or manipulated by the number of people in the room, blocking the door with a hide, mat, or blanket, or by building a fire in the room.

Cliff dwelling locations, then, when they are built in south- to east-facing locations, are taking advantage of a number of factors related to the sun and general temperatures. Location in higher elevation cliffs allow the cliff dwellings in the southeastern Sierra Ancha to receive earlier morning sun than locations at lower elevations (see Fig. 6.47). This is possible because the hills and ridges on the east side of Cherry Creek are lower than the elevations of the cliff dwellings. Early morning sun would be particularly beneficial in the winter, making the cliff dwellings

warm up earlier than lower elevation settings. Other site types also take advantage of their elevation or location to receive early morning sun. On the west side of Cherry Creek, sites on high ridges or hilltops receive early sun in the same way the cliff dwellings do. Pottery Point is on the east side of Cherry Creek, but is in a perfect location to receive sunlight one-half hour earlier than nearby flats and ridges due to a fortuitous gap in the ridges to the east that allows the sun to pass through.

The cliffs the dwellings are built in cause different effects related to the sun and temperature depending upon the season. During the summer, the sun is high in the sky. Generally, because the cliff dwellings are toward the backs of the rockshelters, this means that the cliff dwellings are in the shade most of the day, with direct sun usually only early in the morning and late in the afternoon. Thus, the cliff dwellings are relatively

Figure 6.46. Early Sun on Pueblo Canyon (2004-1733-image1128)

cool in the summer (see Figs. 6.39-6.45). Conversely, during the winter, the sun angle is low, and the cliff dwellings (or parts of each one) can be in full sun for most of the day. Additionally, the sun on the bare cliffs around the cliff dwellings heats those cliffs. The huge heat reservoir created by the cliffs radiates heat back out at night, keeping the area around the cliff dwellings warmer than they would otherwise be due to their elevation.

Clearly, the cliffs are also heated up during the summer. However, the relative temperature in the cliff dwellings is cooler and stays cooler than the daytime temperatures outside of the caverns; and the temperatures are cooler or the same as outside temperatures at night. The relatively cooler temperatures result from the shading of the cliff dwelling walls and cavern interior during the day, the elevation (1585m compared to 1160m or lower), and cooler night air draining off even higher elevations into the canyons. Cloudy

days reduce the extreme high temperatures, but the basic relationships of inside and outside temperatures remain the same.

During the colder months, the effects are opposite, but again result in comfortable relative temperatures. The winter relative temperature in the cliff dwellings is as warm or warmer than areas outside the cavern during the day, and the temperatures generally stay warmer than areas outside of the cavern at night. The relatively warmer temperatures result from sun penetrating into the cavern and warming the cavern and wall surfaces during the day, warmer temperatures from outer wall surfaces bleeding through to warm the rooms later at night, and warming of the cliffs in the canyon during the day and back radiation at night, making the area around the cliff dwellings warmer as well. Cloudy days more severely impact the relative temperatures during the colder months. Interior temperatures fall rapidly to match the general outside temperatures and could be uncomfortably cool to cold if storms persisted for several days (see Fig. 6.47). These lower temperatures, however, can be easily countered by wearing more clothing or using blankets, sealing up rooms (body heat), and lighting small fires.

Thus, despite the obvious passive solar advantages of cliff dwellings, the locations chosen were based on a more complex set of considerations. In terms of temperature, it is not just that the cliff dwellings take advantage of winter-time passive solar heating, but that throughout the year, the many attributes of the sites and their locations moderate the relative temperatures to make them comfortable places of residence. Other site locations can often match one or more of the cliff dwelling location attributes, but rarely as many positive factors as the cliff dwelling locations offer.

Building the Cliff Dwelling

At some point, it would require convincing other friends and family members that such an undertaking was necessary or a good idea. As the occupation of the canyons began, all of the caverns were seemingly unoccupied, and there would be no direct competition for building locations. However, once the first cliff dwellings were established, later arriving groups would have to consider and negotiate with those already in place to determine acceptable places to build in the same or nearby canyons. As is typically documented in ethnographies of US southwestern pueblo groups, actual construction could have involved various combinations of immediate family members, relatives, and friends (Hill 1982:73-74; Mindeleff 1989:101; Titiev 1992:197). However, there was usually a clear division of labor according to gender

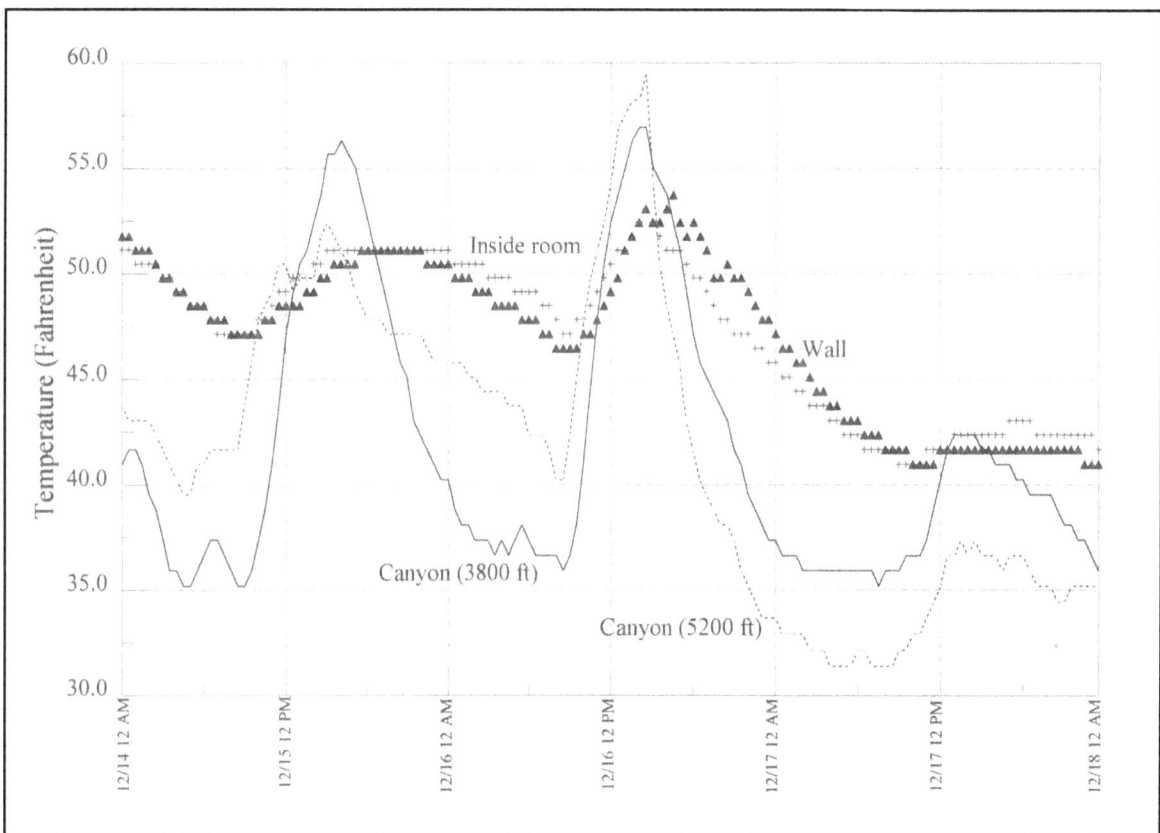

Figure 6.47. Details of Temperatures from December 14 to 18, 1995 (2004-1733-image4020)

(Hill 1982:73-74; Mindeleff 1989:101; Titiev 1992:16). Men were responsible for constructing the walls and for harvesting, preparing, and installing the roofing materials. Women attended to the plastering of the walls.

Once the decision was made to build in the canyon, and the location decided upon, it would require some scouting around to locate all of the necessary materials. If there was no pressure to build quickly, the process of scouting and collecting could take several years. Materials would be stockpiled, until some critical mass is reached and construction actually begins. Hill (1982:74) notes that "plans for building were begun six months or a year in advance of actual construction" at Santa Clara Pueblo in New Mexico. Graves (1982) interprets dates from the Canyon Creek Ruin as stockpiling of beams (particularly secondary beams) from as early as A.D. 1301, certainly by 1310. The stockpiling peaked in 1316 to 1325 with actual construction beginning in 1326. The Canyon Creek case, however, may be an unusually long period of stockpiling and anticipation of construction. At Betatakin, Dean (1969:77) reported stockpiling of beams for 3 to 6 years, but noted minimal stockpiling at Kiet Siel (Dean 1969:144).

The initial burst of construction would involve wall building and require stone, clay, and water. Wooden elements could be gathered later, or as construction is underway. The advantage to gathering wood earlier and stockpiling it is that it would dry out and be somewhat lighter and stronger. The danger might be that the wood could become infested with insects. Reynolds (1981:40) was told by builders at Taos Pueblo in New Mexico that "primary beams must be dry or cure at least one year prior to their use in room construction; otherwise they sag, eventually ruining the roof."

There are mixed messages, however, about when and why the cutting and curing activities occur. Graves notes that secondary beams were cut and stockpiled, in some cases decades before their actual use. However, "primary beams were cut for use" (Graves 1982:125). The

primaries at Canyon Creek Ruin seem to have been used within a year or two of their cutting, attributable to general planning and organizing for construction, and/or for the need to dry the beams. Reynolds (1981:40) was told that the tree-cutting activity "usually takes place in the Fall after the sap has stopped running, which allows the bark to be peeled off more easily in the Spring." However, Ken Gates, who led the author to many of the sites in the Sierra Ancha and who had homesteaded in Alaska and built his own cabin, said it was best to cut trees in the spring when the sap was running, making it easier to peel the bark. Perhaps both situations are true, and the actual time of cutting is more dependent upon how it fits with a group's other seasonal activities that need to be done (hunting and farming, for example).

The preponderance of abutted corners creates a small problem in interpreting the order of wall construction. Bonded corners clearly indicate the simultaneous construction of two walls. Abutted corners indicate walls were built "separately," however, for any one structure, this would necessarily mean essentially at the same time in order to complete the structure. However, which wall is built first? In the first story rooms, the common pattern is for the Left and Right walls to be abutted to the Front wall (see Figs. 2.3 and 6.31). The Front wall is often contiguous across several rooms, so is this the wall built first to define the depth of the room (the distance from the Front to the Back wall)? Or, are the side walls built first (Left and Right walls) to define the width of the room, perhaps based on the length of an already cut primary beam? The beams, primaries or secondaries, seem to fit the dimensions of the room; they rarely protrude into the next room or beyond the wall to the exterior. The only obvious exception to this is the outer wall of the Devils Chasm Fortress (V:1:167), where the beams noticeably extend beyond the wall (Fig. 5.1). The Sierra Ancha situation is in obvious contrast to roofs at Kiet Siel (Dean 1969), where roof beams frequently protrude beyond the surface of the wall.

The room dimensions could be established using a string or a small beam already cut to a desired length used as a template. Either template could be used both in defining the dimensions of the room, as well as indicating the length of beams needed to roof it. Pre-cut beams would heavily dictate the dimensions of the room. It would be difficult to resize a large pre-cut primary beam by trimming off a few centimeters or more. It would be easier to design the room to be larger.

Even if a wall was not built until later, its location can be indicated by drawing a line on the ground or dry-laying a course or two of stone masonry in the desired location. This could be done for all walls of the structure so that size or alignment could be adjusted before the room is actually built. The rough layout of a room could also be critical to define that room relative to existing or other planned rooms; a room constructed totally by itself is probably a relatively rare occurrence. For the remainder of this discussion, the room under construction is being built against the cliff (that is, the Back wall is cliff), and the primary beam runs parallel to the cliff.

For the actual construction of the walls, the author believes that the Left and Right walls are built first. Doing the construction in this order simplifies three concerns. First, there would be no Front wall blocking light while constructing the Left and Right walls (the walls that connect the Front and Back [cliff] walls). Second, it would be easier to pass or carry materials (stone, mortar and plaster) into the room if there were no Front wall. Otherwise, materials would need to be passed through a doorway or over the Front wall. These side walls could have been built from the outside, however; if no existing room blocked the way. The third concern may be the most critical. It would be much easier to lift the primary beam into place in the Left and Right walls if the Front wall were not in the way, or the beam had to be lifted over it. It would also be dangerous to try to roll a beam into place by sliding or rolling the primary up two or more beams leaned against the Front wall. The Front wall would probably not

support such an operation.

As soon as the primary beam is in place, the next priority would be to build the Front wall, so that the secondary beams can be seated. The walls can then be completed before the roof is fully closed in. The assembly of the roof involves a completely different set of materials and source area than the walls. Not until the finish component is there a return to the previously used water and clay resources that are needed to complete the final floor or roof surface.

As the materials are added to the roof, it would quickly become obvious if a vertical support post was needed. If the primary beam were too small or too green, it could begin to sag. The vertical support post more than doubles the load capacity of the roof and would virtually guarantee its stability (see the earlier discussion above).

Another concern in the roof is the cantilevering of the secondary beams. If the secondary beams cannot be supported at the cliff, there are a couple of ways of minimizing their tendency to tip. If enough weight were concentrated on the cliff side of a single primary beam, the roof could flip up, like a seesaw. One way of minimizing this was discussed above: by shifting the primary beam toward the back of the room, the length of the lever pivoting over the primary beam is shortened, requiring a greater load to lift the edge of the roof at the Front wall. Moving the primary beam to the back also removes the direct load from above any doorways in the Left and Right walls. The other means of solving the cantilever problem puts a common architectural feature in a different light. Parapets are common upper story structures and are often thought of as low walls to make the edge more visible and to keep children from falling off. They may have served another important function, however. Adding several courses above the secondary beam ends along the Front wall creates an effective counterbalance to any loads on the cantilevered side of the primary beam. Combining these strategies seems to have created a successful solution to the problem posed by cantilevered secondary beams. Without these adjustments in the roof, it could have been dangerous to walk on the floor or roof on the cliff side of the primary beam.

When the roof adobe is dry, the room is done. In a cliff dwelling, generally well protected from the elements, there may be only occasional repair work needed. After extreme storms, there can be drips from the cavern ceiling that could be caught in pots or might require some repair to the plaster and mortar if it is not captured or diverted. An occasional storm may blow into the cavern, requiring some repair of plaster on the exterior walls. Any rooms out beyond the drip line of the cavern would suffer more serious damage and therefore require more extensive repairs. In general, though, the structure just completed is going to last for a number of years, even centuries.

Chapter Seven
Site Descriptions

Providing better locational information for sites originally recorded by Gila Pueblo in the southeastern Sierra Ancha and middle Cherry Creek valley areas was one of the emphases of the SAP. In particular, work focused on relocating the many cliff dwellings that had been originally recorded in 1929-30 by Dewey Peterson and Emil Haury (see Chapters 1 and 2). All but two of the Gila Pueblo cave or cliff dwelling sites were rediscovered. Some of the surface pueblos and compounds were refound, but it was often unclear which site was which. Many other Gila Pueblo sites were recorded in the "C:1" area, but the focus of the SAP was not on re-finding all of these sites.

Better locations and descriptions of the sites are critical for understanding settlement patterns in this area, as well as for management purposes. As noted in Chapter 2, maps published by Gila Pueblo (Haury 1934:2; and re-used by Bannister and Robinson 1971:7) were not totally accurate. An unknown individual attempted to plot the Gila Pueblo sites on a 15-minute USGS map in the ASM Archives. Haury (10/29/69) noted on this map that the Gila Pueblo site "locations are *not* accurate" (emphasis his) and it was also evident that many of the sites were misplotted.

Sites in the southeastern Sierra Ancha and middle Cherry Creek areas have been recorded by four projects: Wesley Wells (1971), the Cholla Project (Teague and Mayro 1979; see also Chapter 1), Gila Pueblo, and the SAP.

Wells (1971) surveyed along lower Cherry Creek as a student project. The Cholla Project powerline survey recorded sites potentially impacted by the construction of towers and access roads. The Gila Pueblo survey focused on cliff dwellings and larger pueblos, and is now represented in the data set by sites relocated by the SAP. The Gila Pueblo site descriptions and collections were valuable for ceramic analysis and a basic understanding of settlement and chronology. However, Gila Pueblo sites not confidently matched or relocated will not be included in this chapter because their true locations are unknown. "New" sites recorded by the SAP may represent some of the unmatched Gila Pueblo sites, but also includes sites not recorded by Gila Pueblo. Gila Pueblo did not record rock art or artifact scatters, and did not record some cliff dwellings (for example, V:1:126, 127, and 129), perhaps because they were very small (1 to 3 rooms), and contained no wood. The sites recorded by Wells and the Cholla Project have been discussed in other reports or papers, and will not be discussed further in this chapter. They will be part of the overall examination of settlement and culture history in the final chapter of this report.

THE SAP SITES

The SAP recorded or re-recorded 151 sites in the middle Cherry Creek area, including areas to the west along Coon Creek, on top of the Sierra Ancha in Workman Creek, above Pueblo and Cold Spring canyons, and east along Mustang Ridge (Table 7.1). Most of the sites date to PIII, PIII/IV, or PIV, based on the ceramics present and tree-ring dates in the case of the cliff dwellings (see Chapters 5 and 7; Fig. 10.6). The number of sites, although not all contemporaneous, indicate an intensive use of the middle Cherry Creek valley in the AD 1200s and 1300s.

No sites with noticeable quantities of Hohokam buffware were recorded in middle Cherry Creek, although such sites are present in lower Cherry Creek (Wells 1971) and upper Cherry Creek (Morris 1970). Buff ware sherds were noted at four sites (V:1:204, 227, 232, and 242), and Gila Pueblo recovered just one sherd from their survey (see Chapter 4). Also, no sites with apparent pit house depressions were recorded in middle Cherry Creek, but again, such features have been recorded or excavated in lower and upper Cherry Creek.

Many of the sites are located at lower elevations along the west side of Cherry Creek. This is an area of at least two distinct terraces too high to receive overbank flooding from Cherry Creek. However, there are usually extensive slopes to the west that would provide runoff across these terraces. The terraces are cut by other drainages that could be diverted upslope in order to provide additional runoff across the slopes and terraces. These slopes also receive earlier morning sun (due to lower ridges on the east side of Cherry Creek) and the sun also stays on the slopes longer (due to lower ridges that are not like the massive canyons farther upstream that tend to cast shadows over the lower ridges by mid to late afternoon).

The number of checkdams and isolated walls or borders, small pueblos, and compounds that occur on these same slopes and terraces attest to the importance of these settings for agricultural production. The floodplain of Cherry Creek proper is too rocky in most areas and the flows can be devastating, making the main channel of Cherry Creek extremely risky for farming. The small pueblos and compounds (small and large) seem to represent farmsteads located near the probable field areas.

Artifact scatters appear to be under-represented, but they were recorded incidentally as well as during the formal survey. It may just be that most sites in this area do involve some sort of structural elements or features. Artifact scatters are not very numerous (N = 10), and seem to mostly date to the PIII period (Table 7.2). Isolated walls and checkdams are also not numerous (N = 13; Table 7.4). They cannot be assigned to any time period due to the lack of diagnostic artifacts. Surface pueblos are the most numerous site type, with 66 sites divided into three classes (Table 7.1). Of the surface pueblos, the smallest class size (1 to 3 rooms) is the most numerous (N = 45). The small surface pueblos date to PIII, PIII/IV, and PIV, and represent temporarily occupied field houses in most cases. Many of these sites have three-walled structures, where only parts of three walls were stone masonry. The rest of the three walls and the fourth wall were presumably brush or jacal construction. Medium-sized pueblos (4 to 8 rooms) are the next most numerous of the surface pueblos (N = 12; Table 7.1). They seem to date to PIII/IV and PIV, with an emphasis on PIV (Table 7.7). Larger pueblos (more than 9 rooms; N = 9) are dated to PIII and PIII/IV (Table 7.9). These are located in Coon Creek and at generally low elevations in Cherry Creek.

Compounds (N = 27) also date to PIII and PIII/IV and were divided into small compounds (N = 9) with less than 10 rooms and under 400 sq m in size, large compounds with less than 10 rooms (N = 6) and larger than 400 sq m, and large compounds with 10 or more rooms (N = 4) and larger than 400 sq m. The Granite Basin Pueblo (V:1:26) is included

Table 7.1. The SAP Sites

Site type	N	Percent of Sites	DATE			ELEVATION*			LOCATION				
			PIII	PIII/IV	PIV	Low	Middle	High	West	East	Granite Basin	Coon Creek	Interior
Artifact Scatter	10	6.6	4		1	5	4	1	5	1	2	2	
Isolated Walls & Checkdams	13	8.6				10	3		10	3			
Field Houses, 1-3 Rooms	45	29.8	4	6	5	36	9		26	12	4	3	
Medium-sized Surface Pueblos, 4-8 Rooms	12	7.9		3	6	7	4	1	7	3	1	1	
Large Surface Pueblos, 9 or more Rooms	9	6.0	4	5		5	4		5	1		3	
Compounds	27	17.9	11	14	2	20	6	1	16	5	1	5	
Small Cliff Dwellings, 1-8 Rooms	15	9.9				1	11	3	12	3			
Large Cliff Dwellings, 9 or More Rooms	13	8.6				1	11	1	5	5		2	1
Historic	2	1.3					2		1			1	
Apache**	1	0.7					1					1	
Rock Art	4	2.6				3	1		3	1			
Totals	151	100	23	28	14	88	56	7	90	34	8	18	1

*Elevation ranges: 2500-3999 ft = low elevation; 4000-5999 ft = middle elevation; over 6000 ft = high elevation
**There are two additional sites with Apache sherds, but these are classified according to their prehistoric components.

with the large compounds and is one of only two compounds that appear to have an exclusively PIV occupation (Table 7.11). Another group of sites (N = 12) was considered as a cluster, many of them focused on the Cherry Creek Mound Site (Table 7.11). Most all of the sites in the compound cluster are dated to PIII or PIII/IV. The small compounds occur in Coon Creek and west of Cherry Creek and represent small family farmsteads with 2 to 9 rooms and low compound walls enclosing small courtyards. Much of the construction of the rooms was probably brush or jacal. Wall fall does not indicate enough stone to have been full-height stone masonry walls. The configuration of compounds in Middle Cherry Creek is as variable as the arrangements of rooms and roomblocks in pueblos.

"Compounds" have been identified as "multiroomed units in which the arrangement of structures is non-contiguous and dispersed...following the spatial rules of earlier pithouse settlements in that the rooms

are arranged to face a common courtyard" (Clark 2004:176). The difference is that the rooms are surrounded or joined by walls (see also Clark 1995a:Fig.9.9; Germick and Crary 1990; Jacobs 1994; Lindauer 1997; Oliver and Jacobs 1997; and Wood 2000). Such a definition leaves out other site configurations that are also recognized as compounds. In this report, "compound" is also used to describe sites with contiguous rooms and roomblocks that are surrounded or joined by a wall. The courtyard space defined by the outer wall is at least three times the area of an individual room. Not all compound walls are fully closed, that is, there can be gaps or the complete absence of walls on one or more sides.

There were 28 cliff dwellings documented by the SAP (Table 7.1). These were divided into small cliff dwellings (1 to 8 rooms); N = 15) and large cliff dwellings (9 or more rooms; N = 13). Of the small cliff dwellings, all but three are west of Cherry Creek, with dates from AD1292 to 1345 (Table 7.16). Among the large cliff dwellings, five are west of Cherry Creek, five are east of Cherry Creek, two occur in the Coon Creek drainage, and one is located high in the interior of the Sierra Ancha. Dates for the large cliff dwellings range from 1287 to 1340 (Table 7.20).

The remaining sites in the SAP dataset include historic (N = 2), Apache (N = 1), and rock art (N = 4) sites. Additional historic sites could be recorded, but these were not a focus of this project and are thus under-reported. The discussion now turns to the distribution of these sites through time and the implications of the dynamic settlement systems evident in middle Cherry Creek, particularly during the late prehistoric period of occupation.

Artifact Scatters

Artifact scatters are relatively rare, constituting 6.7 percent of the SAP sites (Table 7.1). Compare this to 52.2 percent in the Homol'ovi area (Lange 1998:16), 1.9 percent in the Wupatki area (Anderson 1990:2-4), and 25.3 percent along the Cholla Project powerline corridors in the Sierra Ancha area (Young and McFadden Peak USGS quadrangles (Ciolek-Torrello and Lange 1979:151-152). Nine of the ten artifact scatters involve ceramics and eight involve flaked stone; five of ten have ground stone present (Table 7.2). Half of the scatters are at low elevations (760 to1220m [2500 to 3999ft]); only one is at high elevation (over 1830m [6000ft]; Table 7.1). Most are on the west side of Cherry Creek, and most are relatively near sites with structures, indicating they may be activity areas associated with these sites.

Of the five artifact scatters that could be dated, four appear to have strong PIII components, and one is dated as PIV (see Table 4.4 for dating criteria and period dates). Ceramics were collected from only two of the sites (Table 7.3). The low numbers of artifact scatters may reflect reality or may be a function of the relatively low

extent and intensity of archaeological surveys in the middle Cherry Creek area. The distribution of artifact scatters relative to the entire set of sites is shown in Figure 7.1.

Isolated Walls and Checkdams

A slightly higher percentage of sites (8.7 percent) involve isolated walls or checkdams. Their distribution is shown in Figure 7.1. Lack of diagnostic artifacts made it impossible to date any of these sites. Ten of the thirteen sites occur at low elevations, and ten occur west of Cherry Creek. Most are concentrated along the terraces on gentle slopes where they would help distribute run-off and help control the erosion and accumulation of sediments in presumed agricultural areas. Eight of the sites are checkdams and are assumed to be mostly prehistoric (Table 7.4). Of the remaining sites, consisting of isolated walls, three may be historic. These are dry-laid walls, usually two to three courses of tabular or irregular stones, walling off small seep areas in the canyons. The checkdams are more commonly made of one or two courses of rounded cobbles. There are also checkdams and border-type walls associated with some habitation sites. The distribution of these features indicate agriculture was pursued on low terraces along Cherry Creek, on the ridges and slopes above Cherry Creek, and in swales and saddles where soil accumulated at higher elevations. Occasionally, agriculture seemed to have been practiced right next to the habitation sites.

Surface Pueblos and Compounds

Surface pueblos and compounds are different varieties of habitation sites. Surface pueblos tend to be grouped rooms, with no discernible interior plazas and no surrounding walls. Compounds consist of a few to many rooms and the rooms are attached to or surrounded

Table 7.2. SAP Sites – Data for Artifact Scatters (N = 10)

Site Number	Site Type	Date	Comments	Elevation (ft)	Size (m²)	Location*
V:1:128	Sherds & lithics	PII/III?	ridge top; middle elevation**	4600	2800	West
V:1:161	Sherds and ground stone	PIII	saddle; high elevation	6320	100	West
V:1:173	Sherds	?	ridge top; middle elevation	4840	200	West
V:1:194	Sherds & lithics	PIII	saddle; middle elevation	5580	2500	Coon Creek
V:1:196	Sherds & lithics	?	flat on slope; middle elevation	5210	600	Coon Creek
V:1:214	Sherds, lithics, & ground stone	?	low elevation	3810	1200(?)	Granite Basin
V:1:216	Sherds, lithics, ground stone & grinding slick	PIV	low/middle elevation	4080	3500(?)	Granite Basin
V:1:217	Sherds, lithics, & ground stone	PIII?	low elevation	3000	3900	West
V:1:221	Lithics & ground stone	?	low elevation	2845	2500(?)	West
V:1:224	Sherds & lithics	?	low elevation	3000	36000	East

*Location: West or East = west or east of Cherry Creek, otherwise general location is specified
**Elevation ranges: 2500-3999 ft = low elevation; 4000-5999 ft = middle elevation; over 6000 ft = high elevation
(?) indicates site sizes estimated from maps; not recorded in field

Table 7.3. Ceramics at Artifact Scatters*

Ceramic Type\Site**	161	173	Total
WMRW† – St. Johns Black-on-red	/1		/1
CWW†– Reserve Black-on-white	/1		/1
MBW†-- Brown Plain	/2	/6	/8
MBW†-- Tonto Red or Plain	/1		/1
Alameda Brown Ware -- Verde Brown	/2		/2
TOTALS	/7	/6	/13

*Counts in the format "16/12" mean 16 sherds from Gila Pueblo collections, 12 sherds
  from SAP collections; "/12" means only sherds from the SAP collections; "16/" means
  only sherds from the Gila Pueblo collections.
**All sites are preceded by "AZ V:1:" and are all Arizona State Museum site numbers.
†Abbreviations for ceramic wares: WMRW = White Mountain Red Ware; CWW =
  Cibola White Ware; MBW = Mogollon Brown Ware.

Table 7.4. SAP Sites -- Data for Isolated Walls and Checkdams (N = 13)

Site Number	Site Type	Date	Comments	Elevation (ft)	Size (m²)	Location*
V:1:149	Checkdams	?	mouth of Cold Spring Canyon; low elevation**	3240	2500	West
V:1:175	Isolated Wall	?	could be historic; middle elevation	5280	25	West
V:1:176	Isolated Wall	?	walls off a seep near a mine cairn, probably historic; middle elevation	5280	12	West
V:1:179	Isolated Wall	?	walls off a seep, probably historic; middle elevation	4400	25	East
V:1:206	Isolated Walls	?	lining a ditch?, most likely prehistoric; low elevation	3125	24	West
V:1:225	Checkdams	?	low elevation	2920	2619	East
V:1:237	Isolated walls	?	could be a structure or two, or checkdams/borders, low elevation	3040	400	East
V:1:244	Checkdams	?	checkdams/borders; low elevation	2845	1350	West
V:1:245	Checkdam	?	checkdam; low elevation	2880	800	West
V:1:251	Checkdams	?	multiple dams/terraces; low elevation	3220	2400	West
V:1:254	Checkdams	?	multiple dams/terraces; low elevation	3080	160	West
V:1:255	Checkdams	?	multiple dams/terraces; low elevation	3285	700	West
V:1:257	Checkdams	?	checkdams/borders; low elevation	3200	1000	West

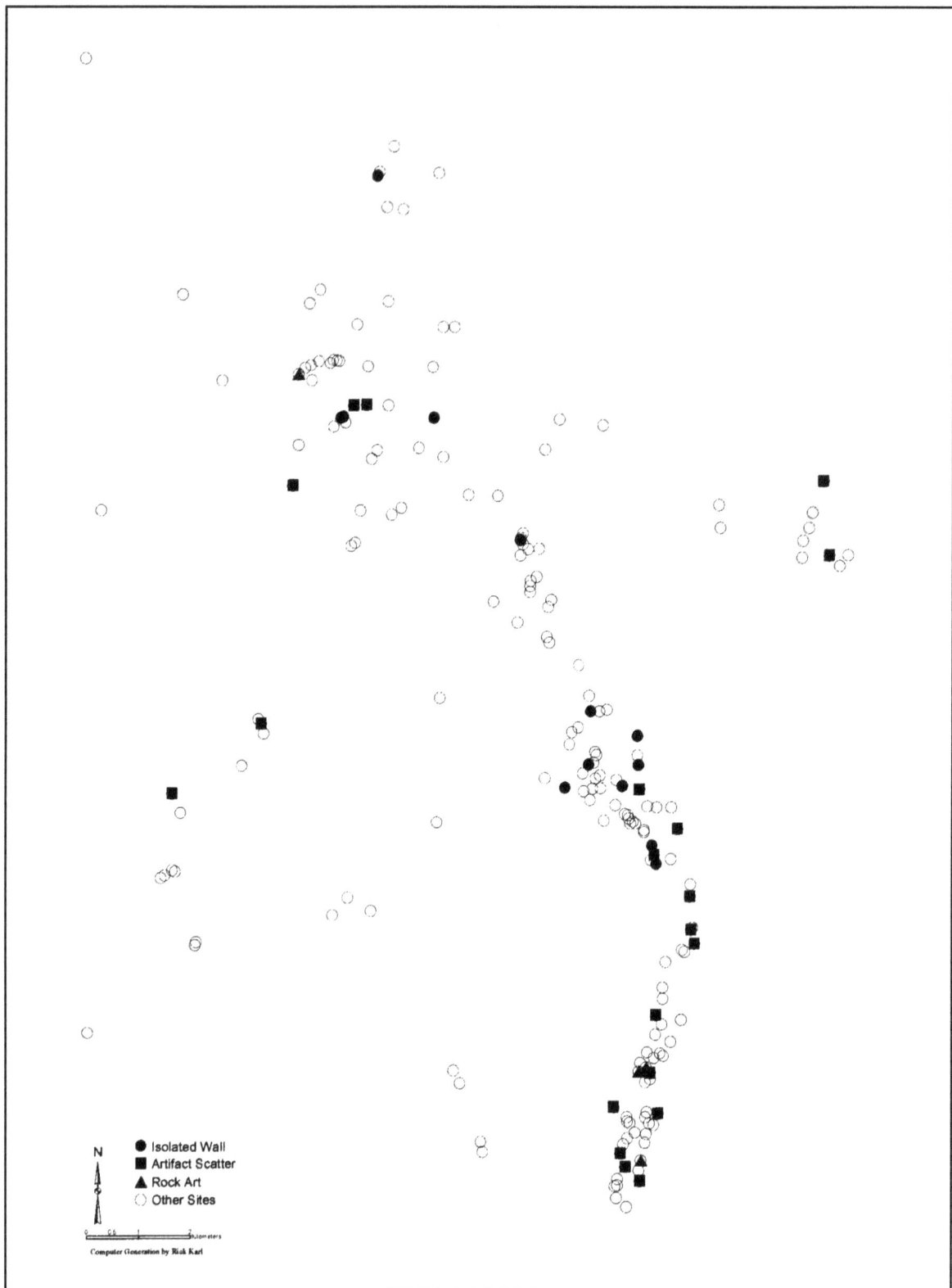

Figure 7.1.   Distribution of Isolated Walls and Checkdams, Artifact Scatters, Rock Art and Other Sites (2004-1733-image4021)

by a wall. Excavations in the Tonto Basin showed some of these perimeter walls to be one-and-a-half meters to two meters tall (Elson 1994:209-210). These projected wall heights are similar to standing, seemingly intact, walls at some of the open sites in Cherry Creek—Ken Gates Compound (V:1:200), the Horse Camp Compound (V:1:172), and the Bronco Canyon Fortress (V:1:192). Some sites are indicated by only a course or two of cobbles or tabular stones, and have no indications of wall fall. Excavations on the Cholla Project on similar sites (for example, V:5:14) in the Coon Creek area showed that such structures are often shallow and that the cobble wall outlines were the supports for vertical posts that formed the walls. Interior large postholes indicated that the structures were roofed (Gregory 1982:48-54). Thus, much of these structures was constructed with perishable materials, so only the outlines of the walls remain. Each of these site types and appropriate sub-types is considered in more detail below.

Field Houses, 1-3 Rooms
Sites in this category are the most numerous of the 11 site types used here (N = 45; 30% of the total sites). Their location on terraces and slopes near drainages and other sites with checkdams and borders suggests that these may be mostly field houses related to the tending of agricultural plots. Their distribution relative to all sites is shown in Figure 7.2. Only 15 of the sites had sufficient diagnostics to assign temporal placements: 4 PIII, 6 PIII/IV, and 5 PIV. Most of these sites (N = 36) are at low elevations, none are at high elevations (Table 7.1). Twenty-six sites are west of Cherry Creek; twelve are on the east side. Seven others are scattered in the Granite Basin and Coon Creek areas.

At least 9 of these sites seem to have 3-sided structures (Table 7.5). Such structures have sometimes been called "carports," and

are known in the general Q Ranch area and north to the Mogollon Rim as identified by the Cholla Project (Quads P:6 and V:1; Teague and Mayro 1979:Volume 2:Site Descriptions). Figures III.1a-q show examples of these sites. It is clear that many of these small sites contain isolated walls, borders, or checkdams, as noted above. Ceramics collected from the small surface pueblos are listed in Table 7.6.

Medium-sized Surface Pueblos, 4-8 Rooms
Just 12 sites (8%) belong to this category. Interestingly, it is the only site type dominated by the PIV period (Table 7.1). Nine sites were assigned dates—three are PIII/IV, six are PIV. Seven of the sites are at low elevations; four are in the middle elevations. Seven are west of Cherry Creek; three are to the east. Two of the sites west of Cherry Creek are in the interior of the Sierra Ancha, not on the face overlooking Cherry Creek. Several of the sites, regardless of whatever their actual elevation is in the low or middle ranges, are on high points within the surrounding topography (Table 7.7). The distribution of this site type is plotted in Figure 7.2. Ceramics collected at medium-sized surface pueblos are summarized in Table 7.8.

Cow Dung Pueblo (V:1:139) consists of a cluster of rooms including a very large room or a very small courtyard (Fig. III.2a). There are also isolated walls and a 3-sided structure at this site. The site is on the point of a ridge 320 ft (97.5 m) above Cherry Creek. It is assigned to the PIII/IV period.

Laughing Rock Pueblo (V:1:143) is exposed on the top of a knoll. It has tall walls that are visible at some times, and that blend into the hillside at others. Many walls are intact, that is, at full height, because there is no rubble fallen from them. It is curious, then, that no beam holes are evident. Were the beams just set on the tops of the walls and oriented just one way (like the roofs at Cuarenta Casas, Chihuahua, Mexico [Guevara Sánchez 1986]),

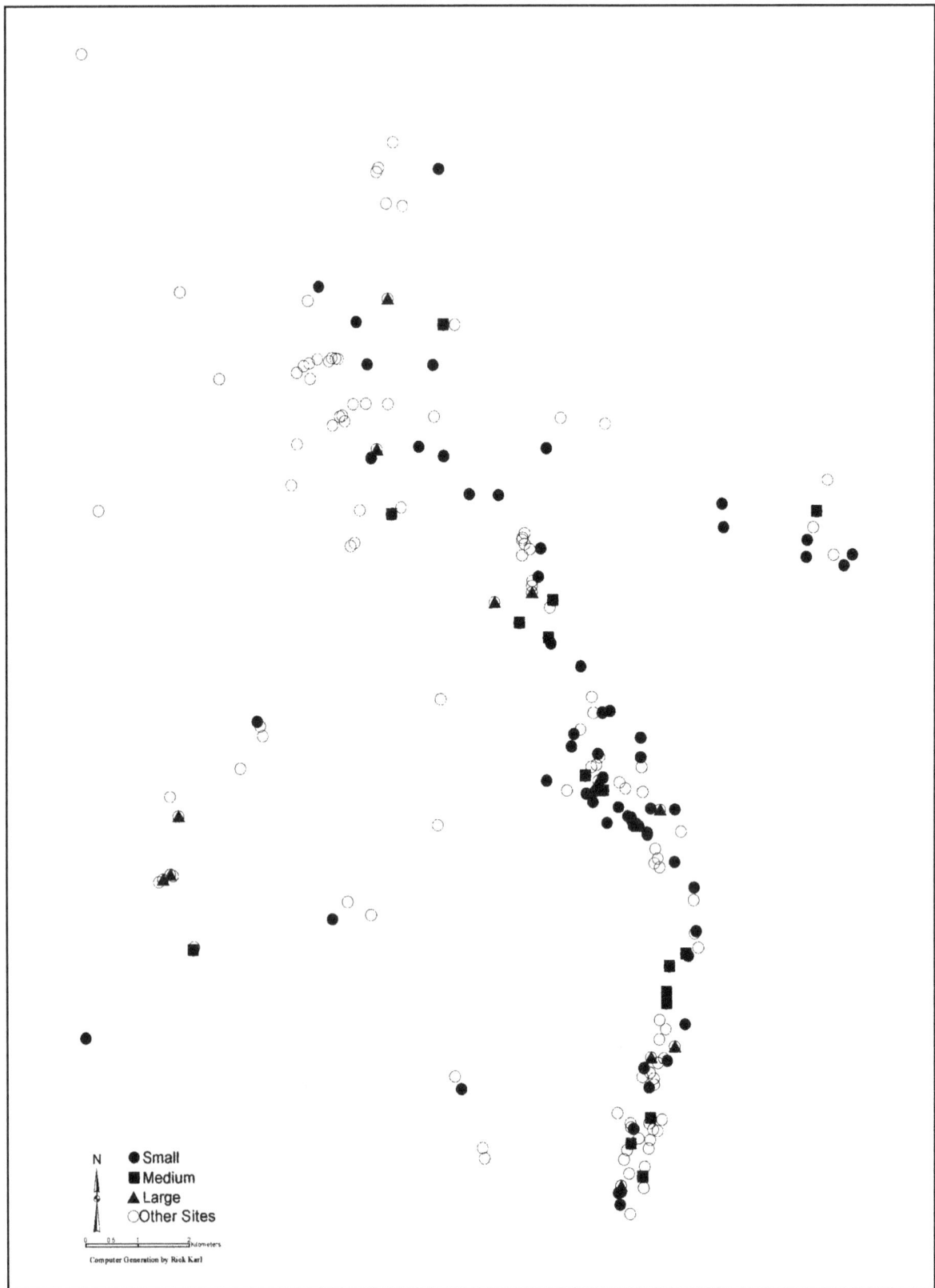

Figure 7.2.   Distributions of Pueblos and Other Sites (2004-1733-image4022)

Table 7.5. SAP Sites -- Data for Field Houses, 1 – 3 Rooms (N = 45)

Site Number	Site Type	Date	Comments	Elevation (ft)	Location*
V:1:137	Field House	?	2 separate rooms; could be PIII?; middle elevation**	4680	West
V:1:138	Field House	PIV	2 separate rooms; low elevation	3240	West
V:1:141	Field House	PIII/IV	2 contiguous rooms; low elevation	3090	East
V:1:142	Field House	?	3 possible, almost contiguous, rooms; low elevation	3410	East
V:1:146	Field House	?	2 separated rooms; middle elevation	4880	East
V:1:147	Field House	PIV	1 room; low elevation	2920	East
V:1:148	Field House	?	single room with ephemeral wall alignments; low elevation	3200	East
V:1:150	Field House	PIII?	1-3 rooms, plus additional walls/borders; low elevation	2960	West
V:1:151	Field House	?	1 room; low elevation	3120	West
V:1:153	Field House	?	1 room; low elevation	3080	West
V:1:154	Field House	?	1 room; low elevation	3120	West
V:1:156	Field House	?	2-3 rooms; low elevation	2980	West
V:1:157	Field House	?	1 room, maybe 3-sided; middle elevation	4376	Coon Creek
V:1:178	Field House	PIII	3, maybe 4 rooms, plus checkdams; middle elevation	4020	West
V:1:180	Field House	PIV	2-3 rooms, eroding out of road cut; middle elevation	4120	West
V:1:181	Field House	?	1, maybe 2 rooms; middle elevation	4010	West
V:1:189	Field House	?	1 room; low elevation	3115	West
V:1:193	Field House	?	1 room, maybe 3-sided; middle elevation	5580	Coon Creek
V:1:199	Field House	?	3 rooms: 2 contiguous, 1 isolated; middle elevation	4980	West
V:1:204	Field House	?	1 room; low elevation	3080	West
V:1:209	Field House	?	2, maybe 3 rooms plus checkdam; low elevation	2920	West
V:1:210	Field House	?	2 isolated structures; probably PIV; low elevation	3720	Granite Basin
V:1:211	Field House	?	1 room, 3-sided plus retaining wall; probably PIV; low elev	3720	Granite Basin
V:1:212	Field House	?	1 room ; probably PIV; low elevation	3720	Granite Basin
V:1:213	Field House	?	1 room?; probably PIV; low elevation	3820	Granite Basin
V:1:219	Field House	?	2 contiguous, 3-sided rooms; low elevation	2920	West
V:1:220	Field House	PIII/IV	2 nearly contiguous rooms plus checkdam; low elevation	2880	West
V:1:223	Field House	PIII/IV	1 room plus checkdams; low elevation	2880	West
V:1:229	Field House	PIII/IV	2 possible rooms; low elevation	2960	West
V:1:230	Field House	PIII/IV	2 isolated rooms, 1 maybe 3-sided; low elevation	3020	East
V:1:235	Field House	PIV	1 room, maybe 3-sided; low elevation	3060	East
V:1:236	Field House	?	1 room, maybe 3-sided; low elevation	3040	East
V:1:239	Field House	?	1 possible room; low elevation	3240	East
V:1:240	Field House	?	possible structures; middle elevation	4156	East
V:1:241	Field House	?	1 room; low elevation	3125	West
V:1:243	Field House	?	1 room, 3-sided; low elevation	3202	West
V:1:246	Field House	?	1 room, maybe 3-sided plus checkdam; low elevation	2880	West
V:1:247	Field House	PII/III?	possible pit houses; low elevation	3045	West
V:1:248	Field House	?	2-3 rooms plus checkdams; low elevation	2920	West
V:1:249	Field House	?	2-3 structures plus walls and checkdams; low elevation	2920	West
V:1:250	Field House	?	2 rooms, 3-sided?; plus isolated walls/checkdams; low elev	2920	West
V:1:252	Field House	PIII?	1 room; low elev; relatively high up slope, away from creek	3480	West
V:1:255	Field House	PIV	1 room plus checkdams downslope; ridge top; low elevation	3285	East
V:1:256	Field House	PIII/IV?	1 room; ridge top; low elevation	3260	East
V:5:62	Field House	?	1 room; low elevation	3200	Coon Creek

*Location: West or East = west or east of Cherry Creek, otherwise general location is specified
**Elevation ranges: 2500-3999 ft = low elevation; 4000-5999 ft = middle elevation; over 6000 ft = high elevation

Table 7.6. Ceramics at Field Houses*

Ceramic Type\Site**	137	138	141	142	147	150	157	178	180	181	229	Total
WMRW†– Indeterminate		/1	/4		/1	/15					/4	/25
WMRW† – St. Johns Blk-on-red						/4						/4
WMRW† -- St. Johns Polychrome								/1				/1
WMRW† -- Fourmile Polychrome		/1			/7							/8
Roosevelt Red Ware –Gila Poly					/1				/4			/5
Roosevelt Red Ware –Tonto Poly					/3							/3
CWW†– Indeterminate		/1	/2			/3					/3	/9
MBW†-- Brown Plain	/5		/6	/13	/21	/22	/3	/1	/15	/3		/89
MBW†-- Salado Red Corrugated		/2			/2	/3						/7
MBW† -- Salado Red Smooth						/1						/1
Apache – Apache Plain					/2							/2
TOTALS	/5	/5	/12	/13	/37	/48	/3	/2	/19	/3	/7	/154

*Counts in the format "16/12" mean 16 sherds from Gila Pueblo collections, 12 sherds from SAP collections; "/12" means only
  sherds from the SAP collections; "16/" means only sherds from the Gila Pueblo collections.
**All sites are preceded by "AZ V:1:" and are all Arizona State Museum site numbers.
†Abbreviations for ceramic wares: WMRW = White Mountain Red Ware; CWW = Cibola White Ware; MBW = Mogollon Brown Ware.

Table 7.7. SAP Sites -- Data for Medium-sized Surface Pueblos, 4 - 8 Rooms   (N = 12)

Site Number	Site Type	Date	Comments	Elevation (ft)	Location*
V:1:139	Medium pueblo	PIII/IV	4 rooms or 3 around a small compound; low elevation**	3520	West
V:1:143	Medium pueblo	PIII/IV?	7 rooms; on high point; middle elevation	4313	East
V:1:152	Medium pueblo	PIV	5 rooms; low elevation	3040	West
V:1:159	Medium pueblo	PIV?	6-8 rooms; interior mountain; high elevation	6305	West
V:1:182	Medium pueblo	?	6? rooms; interior mountain; middle elevation	5720	West
V:1:215	Medium pueblo	PIV	4-5 rooms; low elevation	3965	Granite Basin
V:1:231	Medium pueblo	PIV	4-5 rooms plus isolated walls; low elevation	3020	East
V:1:232	Medium pueblo	PIV	4 rooms; on high point; low elevation	3545	West
V:1:233	Medium pueblo	PIV	6-8 rooms, may be small compound; low elevation	3100	East
V:1:253	Medium pueblo	PIII/IV	4 rooms; low elevation	3120	West
V:1:259	Medium pueblo	?	5 rooms; on high point; middle elevation	4557	West
V:5:163	Medium pueblo	?	4-5 rooms; middle elev; on side of knoll with other site on top	4560	Coon Creek

*Location: West or East = west or east of Cherry Creek, otherwise general location is specified
**Elevation ranges: 2500-3999 ft = low elevation; 4000-5999 ft = middle elevation; over 6000 ft = high elevation

Table 7.8. Ceramics at Medium-sized Surface Pueblos*

Ceramic Type\Site**	139	143	152	159	Total
WMRW†– Indeterminate	/2	/2	/27		/31
WMRW† -- Fourmile Polychrome			/2		/2
CWW†– Indeterminate				/1	/1
CWW†– Escavada Black-on-white				/1	/1
CWW†– Pinedale Black-on-white				/1	/1
MBW†-- Brown Plain	/12	/1	/32	/36	/81
MBW†-- Salado Red Corrugated				/30	/30
Alameda Brown Ware -Verde Brown				/32	/32
TOTALS	/14	/3	/61	/101	/179

*Counts in the format "16/12" mean 16 sherds from Gila Pueblo collections, 12 sherds from SAP
  collections; "/12" means only sherds from the SAP collections; "16/" means only sherds from
  the Gila Pueblo collections.
**All sites are preceded by "AZ V:1:" and are all Arizona State Museum site numbers.
†Abbreviations for ceramic wares: WMRW = White Mountain Red Ware; CWW = Cibola White
  Ware; MBW = Mogollon Brown Ware.

or were these rooms never roofed? The site is assigned a PIII/IV date and it is located close to a large cliff dwelling, Cooper Forks Ruin (V:1:135), on the east side of Cherry Creek. It has a commanding view up Cherry Creek toward the Elephant Rock Fortress and V:1:163, and into Pueblo and Cold Spring canyons (V:1:130-132,134, and 136).

Following concepts of construction discussed in Chapter 6, it appears that the architectural unit containing Rooms 1-5 was constructed all at once (Fig. III.2b). This is based on the abutting and bonding relationships of the walls. Room 7 was constructed as a separate unit at an unknown time relative to the other rooms.

V:1:152 (Fig. III.2c) is a cluster of rooms on the edge of a terrace on the west side of Cherry Creek. The site seems to contain several of the 3-sided structures discussed above. Diagnostic ceramics indicate a PIV date for the site. It is approximately 0.75 mi (1.2 km) from Pottery Point, and could be a farmstead related to that pueblo.

The Limestone Pueblo (V:1:159) is one of the sites on the "interior" of the mountain range, and occurs at a high elevation. It is on a ridge top and is surrounded by even higher elevations. It is assigned a tentative PIV date.

The site appears to be a cluster of contiguous rooms, and may actually contain more than 8 rooms. Walls and corners are quite indistinct. To the east of the room cluster is a low wall built on the edge of a limestone ledge (Fig. III.2d).

Vic's Villa (V:1:233) is a medium-sized surface pueblo on the east side of Cherry Creek. It may have been larger than eight rooms and could be a compound. Some of the site may have been lost off the north side of the terrace (an almost straight drop of over 20m down to Cherry Creek). Parts of the site on the east side may be buried by colluvium from the erosion of upslope sediments. It has also been assigned a PIV date (Fig. III.2e).

Although it may not be a true compound, this site may be part of the cluster of sites centered on the Cherry Creek Mound Site (V:1:191). One other site, V:1:203, is also not a true compound like the others, it is more a mass of rooms. It and the other sites in the cluster are discussed below under "Compounds."

The Devils Chasm Lookout (V:1:259) consists of probably 5 rooms and once had massive stone masonry walls (Fig. III.2f). Although it is at a middle elevation, it is on a very high point with sheer cliffs on three sides overlooking the fork in Devils Chasm. The absence of diagnostic ceramics make it impossible to assign a date to this site. By working up the ridge above the site to the west, it might be possible to access the cliff dwellings in the south fork of Devils Chasm.

Large Surface Pueblos, 9 or More Rooms
Large surface pueblos, stone masonry habitation sites with 9 or more rooms, are not very common (N = 9; Table 7.1). Most of the sites have 20 or more rooms, only two have close to the minimum required for this site type. Four of these larger pueblos are dated to PIII, five to PIII/IV. Five are at low elevations; four are at middle elevations. Five of the sites are west of Cherry Creek, one is to the east, and three are in the Coon Creek area (Fig. 7.2). The three sites in Coon Creek represent 3 of the 4 large pueblos dating to PIII (Table 7.9). Several of the large sites are illustrated in Figures III.3a-c. Ceramics collected from the large surface pueblos are listed in Table 7.10.

Pottery Point Pueblo (V:1:166) has at least 23 rooms; others may have slumped off the top due to erosion of the topographic feature on which it is built on (Fig. III.3a). The pueblo is a mass of rooms, with some depth evident in the vandal holes. Most of the walls are constructed of rounded river cobbles, but a few walls show the use of caliche blocks, cut out of an exposure below the site. The site has good views up and down stream. It is assigned a PIII/IV date, but it is undoubtedly one of the last sites occupied in the area immediately along middle and lower Cherry Creek. There is an abundance of Fourmile Polychrome and other late White Mountain Red Ware sherds at this site. Due to a gap in the ridges to the east of the site, and its location on a high point (Fig. 7.3), Pottery Point Pueblo is also one of the first locations along the east side of Cherry Creek to receive early morning sun.

Across from Pottery Point Pueblo are slopes and terraces that also receive early morning sun (even before Pottery Point), and that receive a tremendous amount of run-off from the slopes above—leading up to the watershed between Cherry and Coon creeks. Many of the smaller surface pueblos (many with borders and check-dams) and sites with checkdams and borders are in this area along the west side of Cherry Creek. These sites appear to occur at the edges of the first and second terraces above Cherry Creek, and overlooking now deeply dissected washes that cut through the terraces and drain into Cherry Creek.

"The-Women-Must-Have-Carried-The-Water" Site (V:1:169) is located on a high ridge point south of Cold Spring Canyon, but it is

Table 7.9. SAP Sites -- Data for Large Surface Pueblos, More Than 8 Rooms   (N = 9)

Site Number	Site Type	Date	Comments	Elevation (ft)	Location*
V:1:140	Large pueblo	PIII	12 rooms + cist; low elevation; on narrow ridge and point**	3800	West
V:1:155	Large pueblo	PIII/IV	~17 rooms; on narrow ridge; low elevation	3080	West
V:1:166	Large pueblo	PIII/IV	23 rooms; on a high point; low elevation	3040	East
V:1:169	Large pueblo	PIII/IV	8-10? rooms; on high ridge; middle elevation	4600	West
V:1:177	Large pueblo	PIII/IV	30-50 rooms; on a high point; low elevation	3990	West
V:1:185	Large pueblo	PIII	60-80 rooms; on a low ridge; middle elevation	4725	Coon Creek
V:1:186	Large pueblo	PIII?	20-30 rooms; middle elevation	4680	Coon Creek
V:1:195	Large pueblo	PIII	30-50 rooms, maybe compound; middle elevation	5010	Coon Creek
V:1:203	Large pueblo	PII-IV	20+ rooms; may be a compound; low elevation	3140	West

*Location: West or East = west or east of Cherry Creek, otherwise general location is specified
**Elevation ranges: 2500-3999 ft = low elevation; 4000-5999 ft = middle elevation; over 6000 ft = high elevation

Table 7.10. Ceramics at Large Surface Pueblos*

Ceramic Type\Site**	140	155	166	169	177	185	186	195	203	Total
WMRW†– Indeterminate		/11	/64	/4	/13	/3	/1	/2	/4	/102
WMRW† – St. Johns Black-on-red		/1	/5		/2					/8
WMRW† -- St. Johns Polychrome			/1	/1					/3	/5
WMRW† -- Pinedale Black-on-red			/6		/2					/8
WMRW† -- Pinedale Polychrome			/6							/6
WMRW† --Cedar Creek Polychrome			/3		/1					/4
WMRW† -- Fourmile Polychrome			/55	/1	/12				/2	/70
RRW† – Indeterminate type		/2	/7						/3	/12
RRW† – Pinto Black-on-red/ Polychrome			/10		/3				/1	/14
RRW† – Gila Polychrome			/37						/1	/38
RRW† – Tonto Polychrome			/19							/19
LCWW†– Indeterminate		/2	/2	/3						/7
LCWW†– Holbrook A Black-on-white			/1							/1
CWW†– Indeterminate		/17	/29	/10	/5	/8			/2	/71
CWW†– Kiathuthlanna Black-on-white									/1	/1
CWW†– Puerco Black-on-white			/2			/2			/1	/5
CWW†– Escavada Black-on-white				/2						/2
CWW†– Snowflake Black-on-white			/6	/2		/3		/2	/2	/15
CWW†– Reserve Black-on-white			/8		/2					/10
CWW†– Tularosa Black-on-white				/1	/1				/2	/4
CWW†– Pinedale Black-on-white			/2							/2
TWW† -- Black Mesa Black-on-white									/5	/5
MBW†-- Brown Plain	/34	/154	/214	/47	/10	/23	/4	/1		/487
MBW†-- Unknown Plain			/2							/2
MBW†-- Salado Red Corrugated	/15	/44	/68	/2	/11	/9	/1	/1		/151
MBW† -- Salado Red Smooth		/6	/89	/1	/4					/100
MBW† -- Salado Red with white			/2		/1					/3
MBW†-- Tonto Red or Plain		/1	/6						/1	/8
MBW† -- Unknown Decorated			/1							/1
MBW† -- Cibecue Polychrome			/1							/1
Alameda Brown Ware -- Verde Brown	/28	/25	/82	/9						/144
TOTALS	/77	/263	/728	/83	/67	/48	/6	/6	/28	/1306

*Counts in the format "16/12" mean 16 sherds from Gila Pueblo collections, 12 sherds from SAP collections; "/12" means only sherds from the SAP collections; "16/" means only sherds from the Gila Pueblo collections.
**All sites are preceded by "AZ V:1:" and are all Arizona State Museum site numbers.
†Abbreviations for ceramic wares: WMRW = White Mountain Red Ware; RRW = Roosevelt Red Ware; LCWW = Little Colorado White Ware; CWW = Cibola White Ware; TWW = Tusayan White Ware; MBW = Mogollon Brown Ware.

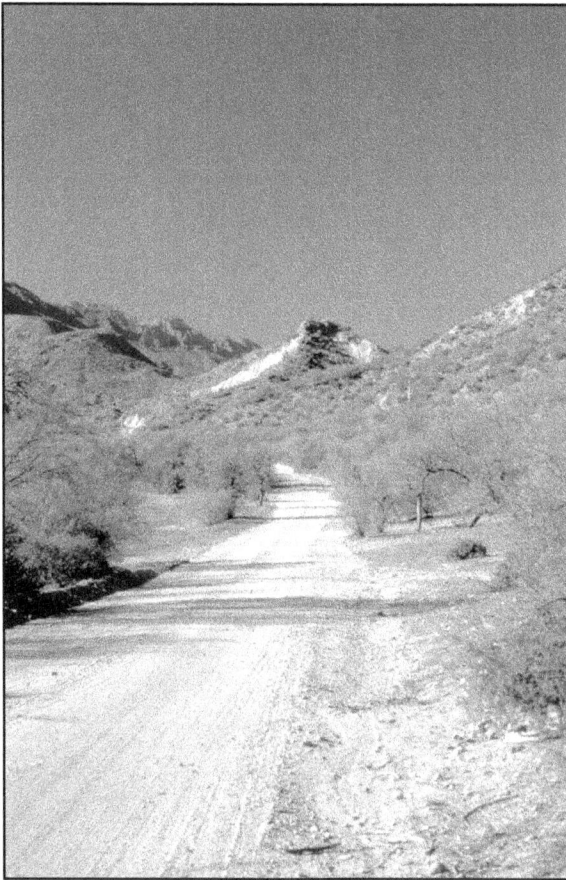

*Figure 7.3 Location of Pottery Point Pueblo
(AZ V:1:166[ASM]) (2004-1733-image1352)*

still technically at a middle elevation (Table 7.9). It is named from a comment scrawled by Dewey Peterson on the Gila Pueblo site form (GP C:1:52). There are seeps nearby, and certainly there is water in Cold Spring Canyon. It is built on a diabase clay exposure and has been heavily impacted by a mining road. The present map shows a long wall, another wall that could be part of a compound, and just two structures (Fig. III.3b). It was originally recorded as being 8 to10 rooms, thus the site is included here. Diagnostic ceramics indicate a PIII/IV temporal assignment for this site.

V:1:177 is at a low elevation, but it is on a high topographic feature that positions it higher than any of the immediately surrounding area, and gives the site tremendous views both up and down the Cherry Creek valley. This particular location must have been consciously selected, because there are two lower saddles on the same ridge (closer to Cherry Creek) where the site could have been built. The site has 30 to 50 rooms with some depth (indicated by vandalism holes; Fig. III.3c). There is a low wall defining the edge of the ridge top on the west side of the pueblo, and facing the area of the gentlest slope to the top. To the east of the pueblo is a small swale filled with diabase clay soils. Heavy vandalism activity and large stone slabs may indicate this was the cemetery area. Diagnostic ceramics indicate a PIII/IV occupation for this site. Along with Granite Basin Pueblo, the cliff dwellings above Granite Basin, and Pottery Point Pueblo, the author believes this is one of the latest sites occupied in the Cherry Creek valley due to the abundance of late White Mountain Red Ware polychrome sherds at these sites. Although it is far above Cherry Creek in terms water, there are indications of a seep in the saddle area west of the site.

Compounds

Other than the small surface pueblos, this is the most numerous site type (Table 7.1). Most of the compounds are at low elevations and are west of Cherry Creek (Fig. 7.4). There is considerable variation in the dimensions, number of rooms, and configuration of the compounds (Table 7.11). Many of the compounds are illustrated here, to show this diversity (Figs. III.4a-e). For this discussion, the compounds are divided into subgroups based on overall dimensions. A small compound is 15 to 20 m on a side, regardless of the number of rooms. A total of 400 sq m was used as the cut-off between large and small compounds, an intuitively derived figure for the smaller compounds (20 X 20m) that also has validity in actual dimensions (Table 7.11). No "small" compound is larger than 400 sq m, and no "large" compound is less than 600 sq m. A

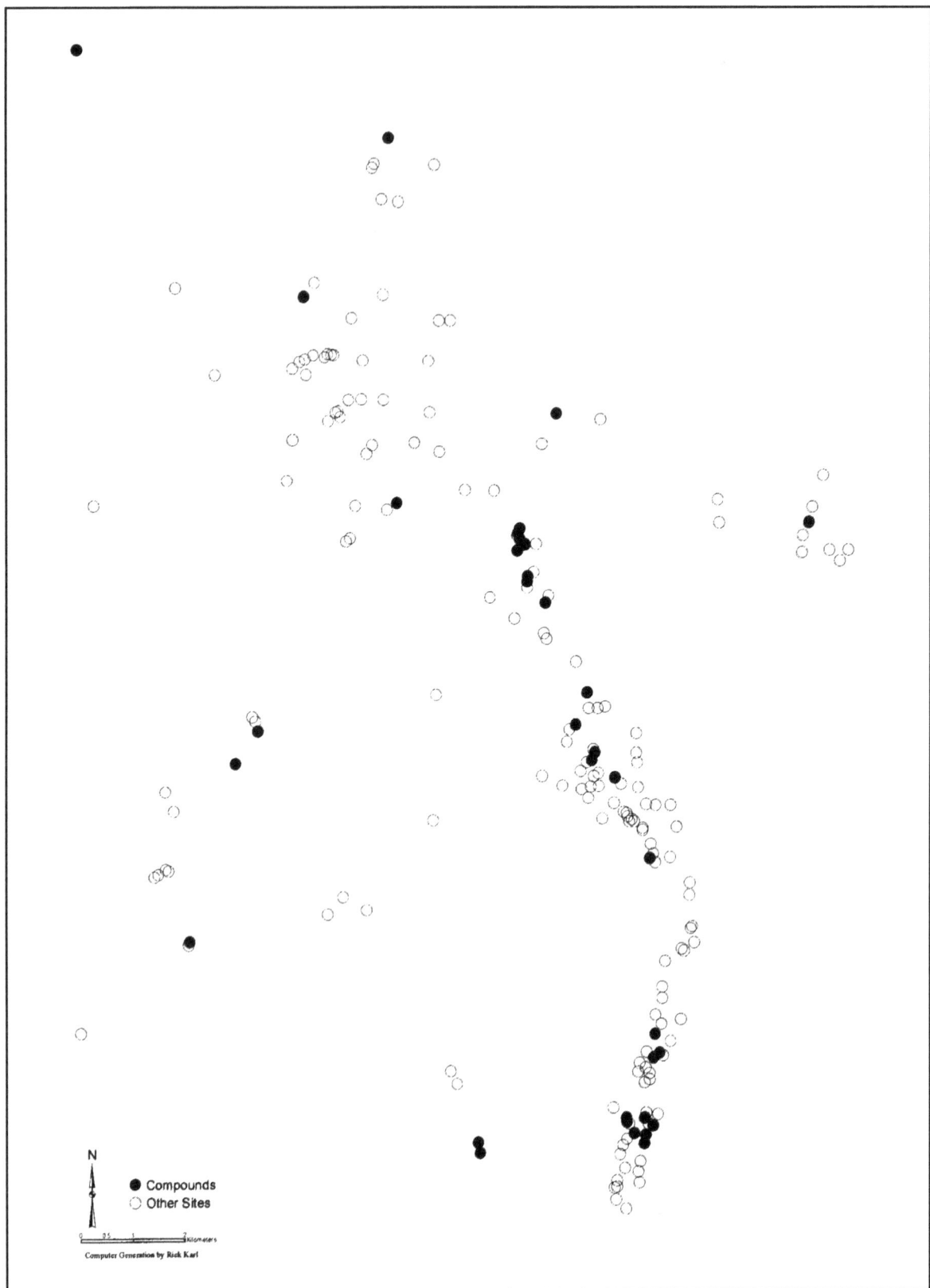

Figure 7.4. Distributions of Compounds and Other Sites (2004-1733-image 4023)

Table 7.11. Data for Compounds of Varying Sizes (N = 27)

a. Small Compounds (less than 10 Rooms and less than 400 sq m) N = 9

Site Number	Alignment*	Size (sq m)	Date**	Number of Rooms	Location†	Elevation (ft)
V:1:160‡			PIII	4+?	West	7160
V:1:183			PIII	4-6	Coon Creek	4810
V:1:184			PIII	4?	Coon Creek	5560
V:1:200‡	15	270	PIII/IV	2	West	5480
V:1:205			PIII/IV	2+	West	3120
V:1:228‡	342	216	PIII/IV	6+?	West	2960
V:1:242			PIII/IV	4+	West	3010
V:5:63‡	79	308	PIII	3+?	Coon Creek	3160
V:5:64‡	22	340	PIII	7	Coon Creek	3180

b. Large Compounds (less than 10 Rooms and more than 400 sq m) N = 6

Site Number	Alignment*	Size (sq m)	Date**	Number of Rooms	Location†	Elevation (ft)
V:1:172‡	349	672	PIII/IV	6+?	East	4940
V:1:192‡	41	1008	PIII/IV	6	East	4630
V:1:218‡	346	625	PIII/IV	3	West	3880
V:1:226			PIII	2+	East	2960
V:1:238			PIII/IV	?	East	3040
V:5:164‡	10	832	PIII	4	West	2710

c. Large Compounds (10 or more Rooms and more than 400 sq m) N = 4

Site Number	Alignment*	Size (sq m)	Date**	Number of Rooms	Location†	Elevation (ft)
V:1:26	26	7280	PIV	150-200	Granite Basin	3880
V:1:222‡	345	1404	PIII	10	West	2940
V:1:227‡	344	770	PIII	19	West	3000
V:5:162			PIII	30-50	Coon Creek	4611

* Alignment is the alignment of the long walls of the compound relative to true north.
** Dates are as follows: PIII = AD 900-1100; PIII/IV = 1100- 1300; and PIV = 1300-1400.
† Location is east or west of Cherry Creek, or in another sub-locality.
‡ Indicates that there is a formal map and the site will be discussed individually.
‡ Indicates that there is a formal map and the site will be discussed individually.

d. Compound Cluster N = 12 (4 are not true compounds, but are counted as part of the cluster; 2 of these are classified as pueblos, 2 are unknown)

Site Number	Direction from Mound	Distance from Mound	Site Type	Alignment*	Size (sq m)	Date**	Number of Rooms	Location†	Elevation (ft)
V:1:191‡ (Mound)	--	--	compound		1786	PIII/IV	4	West	3130
V:1:203	south	~100m	pueblo			PII-IV	20+	West	3130
V:1:233	south		pueblo			PIV	6-8	East	3100
V:1:234‡	south		compound	344	2112	PIII/IV	15+	East	3100
V:1:231	south		unknown				4-5+?	East	3020
V:1:230	south	~1120m	unknown			PIII/IV	2+	East	3020
V:1:202	north	~150m	compound	3	2064	PIII/IV	10?	West	3130
V:1:258A‡	north	~600m	compound	85	352	PIII	10+	West	3180
V:1:258B‡	north		compound	2	228	PIII/IV	10+	West	3180
V:1:190‡	north		compound	348	1960	PIII	10+	West	3130
V:1:207‡	north		compound	347	924	PIII	11+	West	3130
V:1:208‡	north	~1000m	compound	330	360	PIV	4+	West	3120

* Alignment is the alignment of the long walls of the compound relative to true north.
** Dates are as follows: PIII = AD 900-1100; PIII/IV = 1100- 1300; and PIV = 1300-1400.
† Location is east or west of Cherry Creek, or in another sub-locality.
‡ Indicates that there is a formal map and the site will be discussed individually.

large compound is often 30 to 40 m on a side. Compounds can be compared on combinations of the variables used throughout this discussion (date, elevation, and location) and those just mentioned above (Table 7.12a-d).

Alignments of the long axes of the compounds were also measured and tabulated (Table 7.11). There appear to be rather random alignments as well as a cluster of alignments in the range of 340 to 350 degrees true north. Rather than a specific alignment based on the cardinal directions, this seems to reflect the alignment of Cherry Creek. Cherry Creek runs at an approximate angle of 330 degrees true north. Thus, it appears that there was a preference to aligning the compounds parallel to the stream course.

Table 7.12a shows that only a couple of compounds, large or small, date to the PIV period. Small and large compounds are evenly divided between PIII and PIII/IV. Many more compounds occur at low or middle elevations, rather than on high topographic features (Table 7.12b). Compounds with 10 or more rooms occur almost exclusively at low elevations, and most of these date to PIII (Table 7.12c1). For compounds with less than 10 rooms, the high or middle elevation compounds are split evenly between PIII and PIII/IV (Table 7.12c2). However, again, the most are at low elevations, with slightly more assigned to PIII/IV than PIII. Looking at the number of rooms compared to overall compound size, it is clear that those compounds with 10 or more rooms are almost exclusively large compounds in terms of dimensions. Those with less than 10 rooms tend to be the small compounds (Table 7.12d), but some large compounds also contain relatively few rooms. Whether this is indicative of anticipated growth at the compound that never happened or just the way the residents bounded out their community space is uncertain.

As noted, the compounds will be considered in groups based on overall dimensions (small and large) and with respect to one cluster of compounds that appears to be focused on a small platform mound. Small and large compounds contain rooms inside them, as well as "outside," that is, the rooms are attached to the compound wall, but "outside" of the rectangle formed by the compound walls, rather than inside. There is a tendency for rooms to be along the east and west sides of the compounds, but this situation is not absolute (Table 7.13).

Small compounds (Table 7.11a):
There are nine compounds classified as "small" based on their overall dimensions (less than 400 sq m), and that are not included in the cluster of compounds to be discussed below. Nine of the small compounds have less than 10 rooms, only two have 10 or more rooms (Table 7.11a and d [V:1:258A and B; discussed with the compound cluster]). Table 7.14 lists the ceramics collected from small compounds.

Four of the small compounds with less than 10 rooms are in the Coon Creek drainage and all are dated to PIII (Table 7.11a). Of the other small compounds, all are on the west side of Cherry Creek, one dates to PIII, and the others are dated to PIII/IV.

The Elephant Rock Fortress (V:1:160) is an anomaly among the small compounds. It is the highest non-cliff dwelling site recorded by the project and it sits on an isolated pedestal off of McFadden Horse Mountain. It has several levels of surrounding walls and perhaps four rooms on the highest level (Fig. III.4a). Only undecorated, heavy plain ware was found at the site, and it seems to be prehistoric. The site can be seen from several sites in the middle Cherry Creek valley, and it can see a vast area, including Castle Peak and Gunsight Butte on the Q Ranch block and Blue House Mountain and Chediski Peak on the Grasshopper block.

Ken Gates' Compound (V:1:200) is on a high knoll on a ridge that extends northeastward from the north side of Pueblo Canyon. Its inac-

Table 7.12. Data Comparisons for Compounds

a. Compound Size and Date

Size\Date	PIII	PIII/IV	PIV	Total
Large	7	7	1	15
Small	6	5	1	12
Total	13	12	2	27

b. Compound Elevation and Date

Elevation\Date	PIII	PIII/IV	PIV	Total
High elevation; points or ridges	2	3	0	5
Low/middle elevation	11	9	2	22
Total	13	12	2	27

c. Compound Size, Elevation, and Date

1) 10 Rooms or More

Elevation\Date	PIII	PIII/IV	PIV	Total
High	1	0	0	1
Low	5	3	1	9
Total	6	3	1	10

2) Less Than 10 Rooms

Elevation\Date	PIII	PIII/IV	PIV	Total
High/middle	3	3	0	6
Low	4	6	1	11
Total	7	9	1	17

d. Number of Rooms and Compound Size

Rooms\Size	Large compound	Small compound	Uncertain	Total
10 Rooms or More	7	2	0	9
Less Than 10 Rooms	7	10	1	18
Total	14	12	1	27

cessibility is confirmed by several full height, standing walls, not knocked down by people or cattle. A high wall surrounds the north and east sides; a lower wall is on the west side, at the edge of a sharp drop-off (Fig. III.4b). There are two rooms in the compound, joined at one corner, and each has an east-facing door. From this site, like many others on high, prominent features, one can see an impressive number of other sites: V:1:143, 144, 145, 160, 162, 163, maybe 166, 169, 172, 177, the cluster around 191, and 240.

V:1:228 is on the west side of Cherry Creek at a low elevation and the site has at least six rooms (Fig. III.4c). There are some "random" walls to the north of the principal room cluster. The presence of late Roosevelt Red Ware sherds indicates a PIV date for the site, although there are earlier black-on-white sherds as well.

Frisco Flat (V:1:242) was not formally mapped, but deserves a quick note. The site consists of three small compounds, 50m or less apart, and each seemingly with less than

Table 7.13. Data for Compounds – Room locations (N = 27)

a. Small Compounds (less than 10 Rooms) N = 9

Site Number	Attached to Compound Wall	Center	North	South	East	West	Random
V:1:160*	x						x
V:1:183	x						
V:1:184	x		x			x	
V:1:200*		x					
V:1:205	x		x			x	
V:1:228*	x			x		x	
V:1:242	x			x			x
V:5:63*	x			x	x	x	
V:5:64*	x		x		x		
Totals	8	1	3	3	2	4	2

b. Large Compounds (less than 10 Rooms) N = 6

Site Number	Attached to Compound Wall	Center	North	South	East	West	Random
V:1:172*	x						x
V:1:192*	x	x		x			
V:1:218*	x	x					
V:1:226	x			x			
V:1:238							
V:5:164*	x		x		x		
Totals	5	2	1	2	1	0	1

c. Large Compounds (10 or more Rooms) N = 4

Site Number	Attached to Compound Wall	Center	North	South	East	West	Random
V:1:26	x					x	
V:1:222*	x		x	x	x		
V:1:227*	x	x			x	x	
V:5:162	x		x		x		
Totals	4	1	2	1	3	2	0

d. Compound Cluster N = 12 (4 are not true compounds, but are counted as part of the cluster; 2 of these are classified as pueblos, 2 are unknown)

Site Number	Attached to Compound Wall	Center	North	South	East	West	Random
V:1:191* (Mound)	x	x			x		
V:1:203							
V:1:233							
V:1:234*	x			x	x		
V:1:231							
V:1:230							
V:1:202	x		x				
V:1:258A*	x						x
V:1:258B*	x	x			x	x	
V:1:190*	x	x			x		
V:1:207*	x				x	x	
V:1:208*	x					x	
Totals	8	3	1	1	5	3	1
Grand Totals	25	7	7	7	11	9	4

* Indicates that there is a formal map and the site will be discussed individually.

Table 7.14. Ceramics at Small Compounds*

Ceramic Type\Site**	160	200	205	5:63	5:64	Total
WMRW†– Indeterminate				/1	/2	/3
WMRW† – St. Johns Black-on-red					/1	/1
CWW†– Indeterminate			/1	/1	/9	/11
CWW†– Escavada Black-on-white					/1	/1
CWW†– Snowflake Black-on-white					/1	/1
CWW†– Tularosa Black-on-white					/1	/1
MBW†-- Brown Plain	/4	/1				/5
MBW†-- Salado Red Corrugated	/7			/6		/13
MBW† -- Vosberg Series -Vosberg Plain	/3					/3
MBW†-- Tonto Red or Plain	/2					/2
TOTALS	/16	/1	/1	/8	/15	/41

*Counts in the format "16/12" mean 16 sherds from Gila Pueblo collections, 12 sherds from SAP collections;
 "/12" means only sherds from the SAP collections; "16/" means only sherds from the Gila Pueblo collections.
**All sites are preceded by "AZ V:1:"; except for the last two sites, they are AZ V:5:63 and 64 (ASM). All
 are Arizona State Museum site numbers.
†Abbreviations for ceramic wares: WMRW = White Mountain Red Ware; CWW = Cibola White Ware;
 MBW = Mogollon Brown Ware.

six rooms. The site has been disturbed by cattle and ranching activities, and parts are buried by colluvium from the steep slope to the west.

V:5:63 and 64 (Fig. III.4d and e) are both in the Coon Creek drainage, and are on small ridge tops that run east from a larger ridge to the west. Both are located on the west side of Coon Creek, downstream from Hematite House (V:5:61), and both seem to date to PIII, earlier than the cliff dwelling. Both sites show the typical configuration of rooms along the east and west sides of the compound, with some rooms "inside" the compound, and others "outside."

Large compounds with less than 10 rooms (Table 7.11b):

Table 7.15 summarizes ceramics collected from the large compounds. Horse Camp Compound (V:1:172) is on a high knoll on the north side of Horse Camp Canyon. It is in the vicinity of V:1:171, 144, and 145, all cliff dwellings on the east side of Cherry Creek. The site consists of three to four rooms in two sections (Fig. III.5a). Some walls stand over 1.5m tall. This site, too, maintains intervisibility with a number of

other sites on high, prominent features. Like many of the others, Horse Camp Compound is dated to PIII/IV. There is a possible slab cist at the site.

The Bronco Canyon Fortress (V:1:192) is another site with tall remnant walls on a high ridge. The ridge runs west from Hog Mountain, on the east side of Cherry Creek. A high wall surrounds the south and east sides; the west side is a sharp drop-off (Fig. III.5b). Six rooms are enclosed within the main part of the site; two isolated rooms and a slab-lined cist occur downslope to the southwest. This site also dates to PIII/IV, and has good views downstream to Pottery Point, the Cherry Creek Mound complex, and into the major canyons on the west side of Cherry Creek.

The Devils Chasm Compound (V:1:218) is on a saddle on the ridge at the fork in Devils Chasm. It is below the Devils Chasm Lookout (V:1:259). The compound fills the extent of the saddle and contains at least three rooms (Fig. III.5c). Several metates are present at the site, one in the site, the others down slope to the north on a lower terrace. Ceramics present

Table 7.15. Ceramics at Large Compounds*

Ceramic Type\Site**	<10 rooms 172	<10 rooms 192	<10 rooms 218	<10 rooms 226	<10 rooms 238	<10 rooms Total	>10 rooms 26	>10 rooms 222	>10 rooms 5:162	>10 rooms Total
WMRW†– Indeterminate	/8	/1	/2	/5	/2	/18	/196	/3		/199
WMRW† – St. Johns Black-on-red					/1	/1	/3			/3
WMRW† – St. Johns Polychrome							/2			/2
WMRW† – Pinedale Black-on-red							/6			/6
WMRW† – Cedar Creek Polychrome							/17			/17
WMRW† – Fourmile Polychrome							/38			/38
WMRW† -- Show low Polychrome					/1	/1	/3			/3
RRW† -- Indeterminate Roosevelt Red Ware							/2			/2
RRW† -- Pinto Black-on-red/Polychrome							/1			/1
RRW† – Gila Polychrome	/3					/3	/53			/53
RRW† – Tonto Polychrome							/1			/1
LCWW†– Indeterminate				/2	/1	/3				
LCWW†– Walnut Black-on-white					/1	/1				
CWW†– Indeterminate			/1	/6	/10	/17	/22	/5	/1	/28
CWW†– Red Mesa Black-on-white				/1		/1				
CWW†– Snowflake Black-on-white	/2			/1		/3	/2			/2
CWW†– Reserve Black-on-white							/2			/2
CWW†– Tularosa Black-on-white				/3	/1	/4		/1		/1
CWW†– Pinedale Black-on-white							/1			/1
JYW† – Bidahochi Polychrome							/1			/1
MBW†-- Brown Plain	/4		/5	/1	/1	/11	/1	/1		/2
MBW†-- Salado Red Corrugated	/2		/1			/3	/59		/3	/62
MBW†-- Salado Red Smooth							/1			/1
MBW†-- Tonto Red or Plain					/1	/1				
MBW†-- Cibecue Polychrome							/13			/13
WMRW†– Imitation WMRW							/2			/2
Vosberg Series – Vosberg Plain							/59			/59
ABW†– Verde Brown								/1		/1
TOTALS	/19	/1	/9	/19	/19	/67	/487	/11	/4	/502

*Counts in the format "16/12" mean 16 sherds from Gila Pueblo collections, 12 sherds from SAP collections; "/12" means only sherds from the SAP collections; "16/" means only sherds from the Gila Pueblo collections.
**All sites are preceded by "AZ V:1:" and are all Arizona State Museum site numbers.
†Abbreviations for ceramic wares: WMRW = White Mountain Red Ware; RRW = Roosevelt Red Ware; LCWW = Little Colorado White Ware; CWW = Cibola White Ware; JYW = Jeddito Yellow Ware; MBW = Mogollon Brown Ware; ABW = Alameda Brown Ware.

indicate a PIII/IV date for the site.

V:1:226 and 238 were not formally mapped. Both are badly disturbed by ranching, road, fencing, and/or leveling activities. Both are on the east side of Cherry Creek, and appear to have been sizable compounds. One is dated to PIII, the other to PIII/IV (Table 7.11b).

The Cherry Creek Corral Site (V:5:164) has also been disturbed by a fence and a road (Fig. III.5d). The site seems to date to PIII and seems to be a typical compound with rooms both inside and outside the compound wall alignment. There are indications of at least four rooms at the site. There is a large terrace area to the south of this site.

Large compounds with 10 or more rooms (Table 7.11c):

There are four sites in this category. These sites are undoubtedly similar in function to the medium-sized and large pueblos, but their configuration is different. The medium-sized and large pueblos also date more to PIII/IV and PIV; the large compounds date to PIII, with one exception—the PIV-period Granite Basin Pueblo. Table 7.15 also summarizes ceramics collected from these compounds.

Granite Basin Pueblo (V:1:26) is the largest site in the Cherry Creek valley, containing perhaps as many as 200 rooms. It is on the east side of Cherry Creek, near Sombrero Peak.

As a result of a pot-hunting case, some of the vandal holes were backfilled (Breternitz 1987), and a basic site map was generated (Fig III.6a). Granite Basin Pueblo consists of a mass of rooms along the west side of the site, on the edge of a steep slope down to a drainage and spring. On the east side seem to be compound walls. Room blocks seem to fill into the plaza areas, as well as divide the site into two or three plazas. The site is situated where it could be easily located from afar (due to the prominence of Sombrero Peak), and at an important point where it is possible to traverse from Cherry Creek to Canyon Creek below the escarpment of Mustang Ridge.

Avery's Nap Site (V:1:222), named after one of the young Earthwatch volunteer's afternoon siesta, is a large compound on the west side of Cherry Creek. It is down stream from Pottery Point, and contains relatively few rooms for its overall size (Fig. III.6b). Avery's Nap shows the common arrangement of rooms attached to a compound wall, with some inside the compound, others outside.

The Steel Arrow Site (V:1:227) is upstream from Pottery Point and is across Cherry Creek on the west side. The site is divided into two courtyards with rooms along the east and west compound walls in the southern portion of the site (Fig. III.6c). It is on a large terrace overlooking Cherry Creek. Like Avery's Nap, the Steel Arrow Site seems to date to PIII.

V:5:162 was recorded by Gila Pueblo as GP C:1:61. It is on top of a high knoll on the west side of Coon Creek on the south face of the Sierra Ancha. The site has been vandalized, revealing some rooms inside and outside attached to the compound wall. The site is probably smaller than the Gila Pueblo estimate of 75 rooms, but could contain 30 to 50 rooms. Based on the absence of polychrome pottery, the site is assigned a PIII date. The site has not been formally mapped.

The Compound Cluster (Table 7.11d):

The definition of this cluster is somewhat arbitrary, but it seems to define a coherent group of sites. These sites occur both up- and down-stream within approximately 1000 m from a particular compound that appears to have a platform mound—the Cherry Creek Mound Site (V:1:191). Vandalism in the raised feature indicates rooms or cells (Craig and others 1992; Lindauer 1992). If it is not actually a platform mound, then the amount of rubble and mound height would indicate a compact, two-story structure of six to eight rooms (in itself an unusual architectural pattern compared to the other sites in this area). If these are not habitation and storage structures, then the room count for this large compound is quite low—only four rooms can be defined from the surface elsewhere in the compound (Fig. III.7a). There has also been vandalism, perhaps machine trenching, both inside and outside of the east compound wall. Diagnostic ceramics are very sparse at this site, but indicate a PIII/IV temporal placement.

Five sites in the cluster are located downstream. All but one of the sites to the south are located on the east side of Cherry Creek. Two sites are more pueblos than compounds, one is a compound, and two are so heavily disturbed that it is impossible to determine exactly what site type is involved (Table 7.11d). The one pueblo on the west side (V:1:203) is only approximately 100m south of the Cherry Creek Mound site, and could have a compound wall. It seems to be a mass of rooms, many more than at the other sites in this cluster. V:1:203 has not been formally mapped.

All of the sites to the south have a temporal assignment to the PIII/IV period, except for one of the pueblos (Vic's Villa, V:1:233; Fig. III.2e), which was given a PIV date. Sparse diagnostic ceramics make these dates somewhat tentative (Table 7.16). There is every possibility that all of these sites were

Ceramic Type\Site**	191	203	202	258	190	207	Total
WMRW†– Indeterminate	/6	/4	/4	/4	/5	/4	/27
WMRW† – St. Johns Black-on-red	/3	/3		/4	/5		/15
WMRW† – St. Johns Polychrome					/1		/1
WMRW† – Pinedale Black-on-red				/1			/1
WMRW† – Cedar Creek Polychrome					/1		/1
WMRW† – Fourmile Polychrome	/2	/2	/2				/6
RRW† -- Indeterminate Roosevelt Red Ware		/3	/2				/5
RRW† -- Pinto Black-on-red/Polychrome		/1	/2		/5	/1	/9
RRW† – Gila Polychrome		/1					/1
LCWW†– Indeterminate				/1			/1
LCWW†– Black Mesa Black-on-white		/5					/5
LCWW†– Walnut Black-on-white				/3			/3
CWW†– Indeterminate	/7	/2	/10	/18	/6	/6	/49
CWW†– Kiatuthlanna Black-on-white		/1		/1			/2
CWW†– Puerco Black-on-white	/6	/1		/2			/9
CWW†– Red Mesa Black-on-white				/1			/1
CWW†– Snowflake Black-on-white	/2	/2		/7	/2	/1	/14
CWW†– Reserve Black-on-white	/1			/1	/1	/4	/7
CWW†– Tularosa Black-on-white	/1	/2	/2	/1			/6
TWW† – Indeterminate Tusayan White Ware					/2		/2
TWW† – Shato Black-on-white	/1						/1
TWW† – Kayenta Black-on-white						/3	/3
MBW†-- Brown Plain	/13		/3	/5	/10	/3	/34
MBW†-- Salado Red Corrugated	/2		/1	/2		/1	/6
MBW†-- Tonto Red or Plain		/1					/1
ABW†– Verde Brown					/1		/1
TOTALS	/44	/28	/26	/52	/38	/23	/211

*Counts in the format "16/12" mean 16 sherds from Gila Pueblo collections, 12 sherds from SAP collections;
   "/12" means only sherds from the SAP collections; "16/" means only sherds from the Gila Pueblo collections.
**All sites are preceded by "AZ V:1:" and are all Arizona State Museum site numbers.
†Abbreviations for ceramic wares: WMRW = White Mountain Red Ware; RRW = Roosevelt Red Ware;
   LCWW = Little Colorado White Ware; CWW = Cibola White Ware; TWW = Tusayan White Ware;
   MBW = Mogollon Brown Ware; ABW = Alameda Brown Ware.

contemporaneous. Near Vic's Villa, on the east side essentially across from the Cherry Creek Mound, is Vince's Villa (V:1:234). It has been heavily disturbed by blading for erosion control (Fig. III.7b).

Six compounds are located upstream from the Cherry Creek Mound site. All are on the west side of Cherry Creek, like the mound site (Table 7.11d). Of these six sites, all are com-

pounds; three date to PIII, two date to PIII/IV, and one dates to PIV. These temporal classifications could indicate that not all of these compounds are contemporaneous. However, relatively sparse ceramics suggest that one or two sherds could significantly alter the temporal placements (see ceramics tables in this chapter). The total number of sherds collected ranges from 23 to 52; up to half of each collection can be diagnostic ceramic types, that is between 7 and 24 sherds). Architecturally and spatially, the temporal placements of two pairs of sites can also be called into question. The compounds of Cherie's Compounds (V:1:258, designated A and B, but with dates of PIII and PIII/IV) are contiguous (Fig. III.7c), suggesting they could have been built and occupied simultaneously. The orientations of their long axes, however, is almost 90-degrees different, and one compound may have continued to be occupied after the other was abandoned.

The Big Buzz Compound (V:1:207) and Leslie Pueblo (V:1:208) present a slightly different problem. The sites are approximately 30 to 50 m apart, one (Big Buzz) on a slightly higher terrace south of the other. There is a formally constructed, stone-lined stairway cut into the terrace (Figs. III.7d and e). This certainly implies some connection and contemporaneity to these sites, even though one is dated PIII, the other PIV.

With the exception of the PIV-dated site (which contains 4-plus rooms), all of the sites have 10 or more rooms. Five of these sites are illustrated in Figure III.7b-f. The River Bend Compound (V:1:190) lies between Cherie's Compounds and Big Buzz. River Bend is dated to PIII and contains 10 or more rooms. The arrangement of the rooms inside the compound almost divides it into quarters (Fig. III.7f).

How this site cluster interacted with the other contemporaneous sites in the middle Cherry Creek valley is uncertain. The cluster of compounds focused on a platform mound is typical of the Early Classic Roosevelt Phase in the Tonto Basin, AD 1250/1275 to 1325/1350 (Gregory 1995). And, it is located at the point where Cherry Creek flows out of a narrower stream course into a wider floodplain with broad terraces. Does this cluster represent a transplanted population from the Tonto Basin looking for ideal agricultural land and production? If so, what did the residents of Cherry

Creek do? Did they build and occupy the more traditional looking Western Pueblo-type pueblos? Were they the builders of the cliff dwellings? Does this cluster drop out after the Gila and Fourmile polychrome pottery types arrive, leaving a few small sites, the large pueblos and compounds (Granite Basin Pueblo, Pottery Point, and V:1:177), and Cooper Forks and the other cliff dwellings along Mustang Ridge as the only occupied sites in the Cherry Creek valley? Interestingly, all but one of these sites are east of Cherry Creek. Are the compounds a different population from the builders of the pueblos and cliff dwellings, or is this one population with slightly different preferences for settlement types and structures? Answers to these questions may someday be obtained through careful excavations, tree-ring dates, and new ceramic seriations.

Cliff Dwellings

These sites are the focus of this study. With the exceptions of one cliff dwelling and one cave site recorded by Gila Pueblo, SAP relocated and documented all of the other Gila Pueblo cliff dwelling sites, as well as additional cliff dwellings not recorded by Gila Pueblo. It would be surprising to learn of others in the middle Cherry Creek area.

To have cliff dwellings, there must be cliffs. However, cliffs do not always mean there are cliff dwellings. Facing, overhang depth and height, presence or absence of seeps, elevation, and ease or difficulty of access all factor into whether or not a cliff dwelling was built in a particular cliff. With two exceptions in the Sierra Ancha cliff dwellings, the preferred cliff sites face in a southerly to easterly direction (Fig. 7.5).

The architectural characteristics of cliff dwellings in the Sierra Ancha were examined in detail in Chapter 6. Chronological aspects of the sites were defined in the chapters on

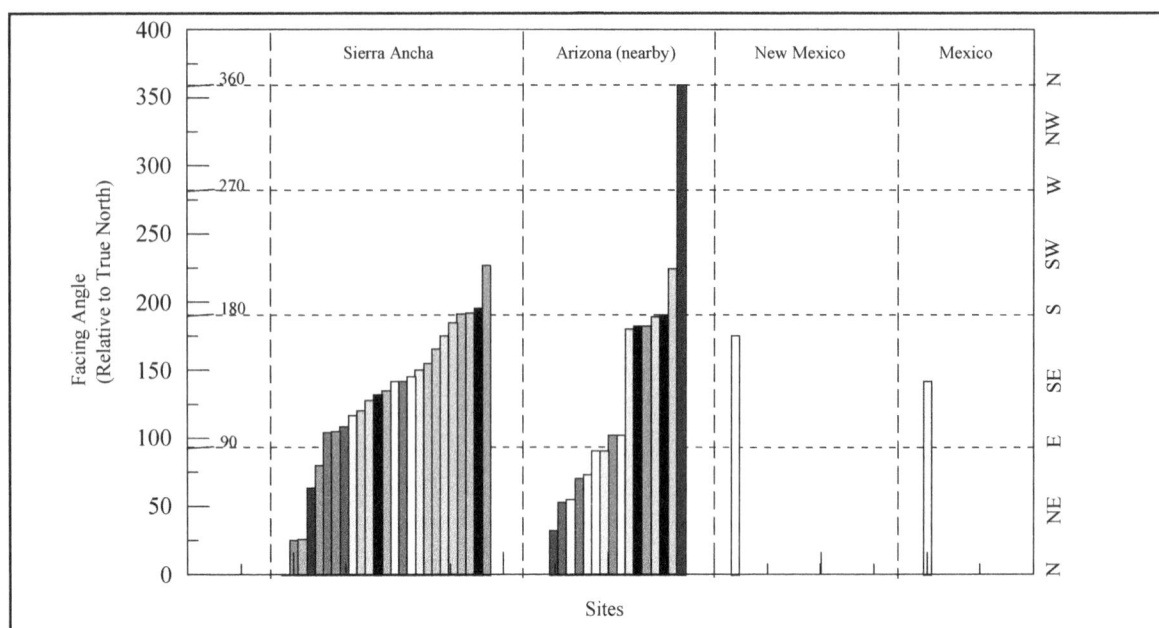

Figure 7.5. Facing Angles for Cliff Dwellings (2004-1733-image4024)

ceramics (Chapter 4) and wood studies (Chapter 5). Tables 7.17, 7.19, and 7.21 summarize chronological, photographic, and architectural data available for all Sierra Ancha cliff dwellings. These characteristics and data are now examined on a case-by-case basis, with a particular focus on examining the growth and development of each site.

For the following discussions, the growth of each site can be considered to have occurred in phases. Describing the phases of growth and construction involves several assumptions (see also Riggs 2001:119).

> (1) The construction of particular rooms or walls in one phase may not have happened all at the same time. Episodes of construction that are not dependent upon another will be called sub-phases. For example, Phase 1a may involve the construction of a group of rooms. The construction of an isolated room would be termed Phase 1b. The construction of the isolated room may or may not have happened at the same time as the construction of the room cluster. However,

it would have to be built before another phase of construction can occur—such as the joining of the original cluster of rooms and the isolated room by filling in the gap with one or more rooms. Thus, the isolated room is assigned to Phase 1.

> (2) Following from the preceding, all construction in one phase must be completed before a new phase can begin. Then the process of assumptions and construction starts again.

Occupation spans for the cliff dwellings are depicted in Figure 7.6. The span was calculated in the following manner: for the beginning of the occupation, "B" or "L" qualified dates were specified as the beginning date, unless there were others later but close in time. For example, if there were dates of AD 1288B, 1289B, and 1290B (especially all from one room or roof), then the beginning date was selected to be 1290. For beginning dates, those dates qualified with "v," or "vv" were moved 4 years later for a "v" date and 6 later for a "vv" date. For example, if the earliest date was

1287vv, the occupation was said to begin in 1293. These date assignments are only guesses, but seem possible given the condition of the roof beams. These roof beams are in generally good condition and were not dragged and scarred or shaped in any way—processes that could potentially remove a large number of tree-rings (see also Graves 1982:112-114).

For the end of occupation, a date 5 years after a "B" or "L" date was determined; similarly, dates 5 years after the assigned start dates for "v" and "vv" dates were specified. This procedure was intended to indicate an occupation of at least 5 to 6 years after the last indication of construction at a site. This may underestimate the length of occupation at a site, but in the Sierra Ancha cliff dwellings, the occupations are not expected to be more than 10 to 30 years in total. This relatively short duration of occupation is supported by the general tree-ring dates across the sites and by associated ceramics cross-dated by tree-rings from elsewhere.

Initial construction dates begin in the late AD 1280s and continue through the early AD 1300s (up to 1320) for some sites (N = 84 dates, Table 5.4), compared to 32 dates after AD 1320, 16 of which are from two sites (neither of which has dates before AD 1320).

Small Cliff Dwellings (N = 15)
Five of the small cliff dwelling sites have no ceramics and no tree-ring dates, so chronological placement is problematical (sites V:1:124, 126, 127, 188, and 210). However, they are expected to date in the same general time period as the other cliff dwellings (Tables 7.17 and 7.21), based on similarities of building materials and technologies. All but one of these five sites (V:1:188) is west of Cherry Creek. Photographic documentation for all SAP sites, emphasizing the cliff dwellings, is summarized in Table 7.18 (for details see SAP archives).

Three of the small cliff dwellings (124, 126, and 127) are in Pueblo Canyon at the

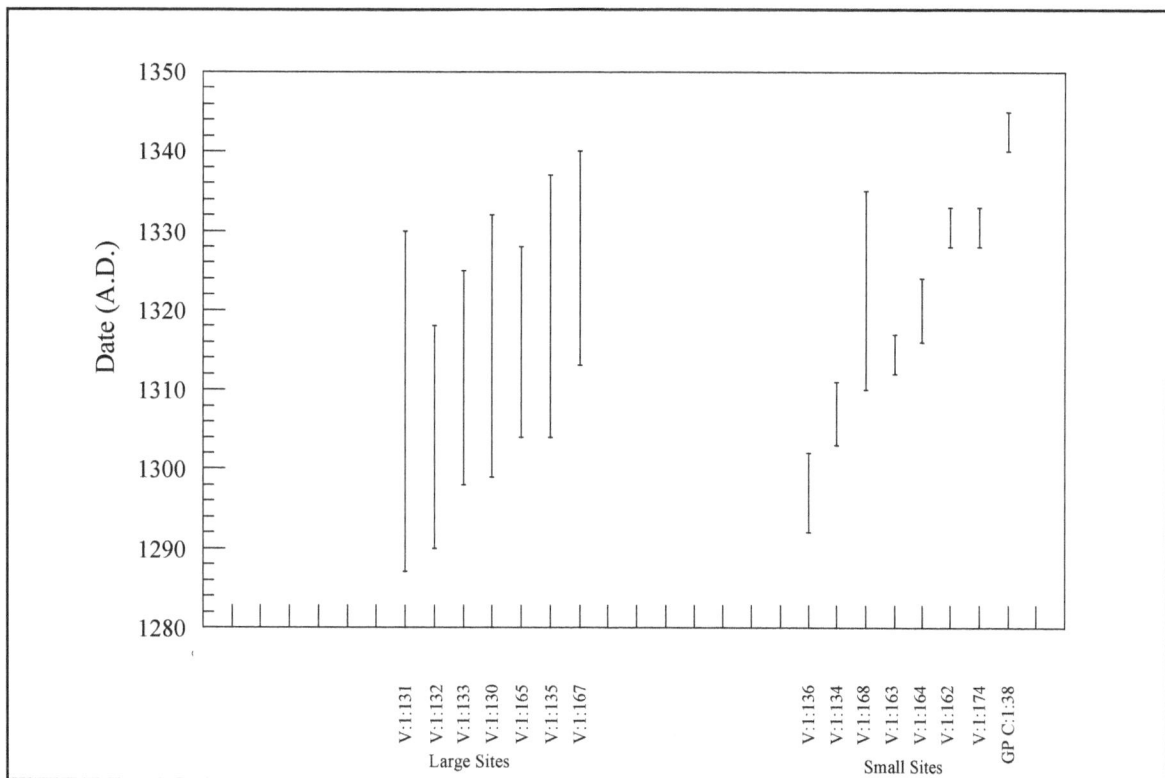

Figure 7.6. Cliff Dwelling Estimated Occupation Spans (2004-1733-image4025)

Table 7.17. SAP Sites -- Data for Small Cliff Dwellings, 1 – 8 Rooms   (N = 15)

Site Number	Site Type	Date of Occupation*	Comments	Elevation (ft)	Location**
V:1:124	Small cliff dwelling	?	1 room; in small cavern; middle elevation†	4760	West
V:1:126	Small cliff dwelling	?	1 room; middle elevation	4760	West
V:1:127	Small cliff dwelling	?	2 rooms; middle elevation	4760	West
V:1:129	Small cliff dwelling	PIII	1 room; low elevation	3960	West
V:1:134	Small cliff dwelling	PIII	6 rooms; middle elevation	5200	West
V:1:136	Small cliff dwelling	1292-1302	7 rooms; middle elevation	5000	West
V:1:162	Small cliff dwelling	1328-1333	8 rooms; high elevation	7180	West
V:1:163	Small cliff dwelling	1312-1317	4 rooms; high elevation	7120	West
V:1:164	Small cliff dwelling	1316-1324	6 rooms; high elevation	6180	West
V:1:168	Small cliff dwelling	1310-1335	4 rooms; middle elevation	5200	West
V:1:171	Small cliff dwelling	PIII?	3 rooms; middle elevation; in small canyon	4400	East
V:1:174	Small cliff dwelling	1328-1345	6 rooms; middle elevation	5280	West
V:1:188	Small cliff dwelling	?	4 rooms; middle elevation; on face of high knoll	5000	East
V:1:201	Small cliff dwelling	?	6 rooms; middle elevation	4650	West
C:1:38	Small cliff dwelling	1340-1345	6 rooms; middle elevation; in high cliff	5800	East

*Date: if PIII or PIV, etc, this is based on ceramics; if actual numbers, for example 1304-1320, this is the estimated occupation span based on tree-ring dates (see Chapter 5).
**Location: West or East = west or east of Cherry Creek, otherwise general location is specified.
†Elevation ranges: 2500-3999 ft = low elevation; 4000-5999 ft = middle elevation; over 6000 ft = high elevation.

Table 7.18. Photographic Documentation for SAP Sites

SITE*	1995 & 1996 Black and white	1995 & 1996 Color Slide	1995 & 1996 Total
V:1:124	5	1	6
V:1:125	1	2	3
V:1:126	5	2	7
V:1:127	11	2	13
V:1:130	168	146	314
V:1:131	139	74	213
V:1:132	213	83	296
V:1:133	42	41	83
V:1:134	42	17	59
V:1:135	142	97	239
V:1:136	167	82	249
V:1:144	70	46	116
V:1:145	39	19	58
V:1:162	170	68	238
V:1:163	30	28	58
V:1:164	32	10	42
V:1:165	95	39	134
V:1:167	62	61	123
V:1:168	18	14	32
V:1:170	31	38	69
V:1:174	18	19	37
V:1:188	36	24	60
V:1:201	14	15	29
V:1:210	5	3	8
V:5:61	87	5	92
TOTALS	1642	936	2578

*All sites are ASM Site numbers, preceded by "AZ" and followed by "(ASM)."

Table 7.19. Architectural Documentation for SAP Cliff Dwellings (numbers of forms)

SITE*	General Structure	Wall Recording	Wall Features	Roof Data	Wall Condition
V:1:124	1	4	1		2
V:1:125					
V:1:126	1	4	1		3
V:1:127	3	11	1		5
V:1:129	1	1			1
V:1:130	15	56	2	9	47
V:1:131	32	113	6	11	91
V:1:132	25	100	6	13	83
V:1:133	12	43	3	1	24
V:1:134	6	29	2	2	16
V:1:135	14	54	6	3	33
V:1:136	9	34	2	4	13
V:1:144	11	27	2	4	15
V:1:145	7	17		1	10
V:1:162	9	25	1	3	19
V:1:163	6	23	1	1	15
V:1:164	7	22	1	3	16
V:1:165	13	48	2		32
V:1:167	19	79	6	4	63
V:1:168	5	21	1	2	
V:1:170	14	50	3		32
V:1:174	5	15			9
V:1:188	4	15	2		9
V:1:201	3	14	1		7
V:5:61	10	35	3	5	22
TOTALS	232	840	53	66	567

*All sites are ASM Site numbers, preceded by "AZ" and followed by "(ASM)."

Table 7.20. Ceramics at Small Cliff Dwellings*

Ceramic Type\Site**	129	134	136	162	163	164	168	171	174	Total
WMRW†– Indeterminate			/1		/1					/2
WMRW† – St. Johns Black-on-red			/1							/1
RRW† – Pinto Black-on-red Polychrome	/1									/1
RRW† – Gila Polychrome							/1			/1
RRW† – Tonto Polychrome							/3			/3
CWW†– Indeterminate	/4									/4
CWW†– Puerco Black-on-white						1/				1/
CWW†– Snowflake Black-on-white						1/				1/
CWW†– Reserve Black-on-white						2/				2/
MBW† -- Brown Plain	/14	/3	/5		/43	/74	/5		/2	/146
MBW† -- Salado Red Corrugated			/1	/9	/7	/22	/7	/3		/49
MBW† -- Salado Red Smooth			/1				/3		/2	/6
MBW† -- Vosberg Series -Vosberg Plain							/1			/1
Alameda Brown Ware-- Verde Brown	/27			/95		/10	/7			/139
Zuni -- Pinnawa Glaze-on-white							/1			/1
Zuni -- Kechipawan Polychrome							/1			/1
TOTALS	/46	/3	/9	/104	/51	10/106	/29	/3	/4	10/355

*Counts in the format "16/12" mean 16 sherds from Gila Pueblo collections, 12 sherds from SAP collections; "/12" means only sherds from the SAP collections; "16/" means only sherds from the Gila Pueblo collections.
**All sites are preceded by "AZ V:1:" and are all Arizona State Museum site numbers.
†Abbreviations for ceramic wares: WMRW = White Mountain Red Ware; RRW = Roosevelt Red Ware; CWW = Cibola White Ware; MBW = Mogollon Brown Ware.

Figure 7.7. Small Cliff Dwellings – AZ V:1:124 (ASM) (2004-1733-image0967)

Figure 7.8. Small Cliff Dwellings – AZ V:1:126 and AZ V:1:127 (ASM) (2004-1733-image1994)

a: Site Photograph (2004-1733-image0271)

Figure 7.9. Small Cliff Dwellings – AZ V:1:188 (ASM)

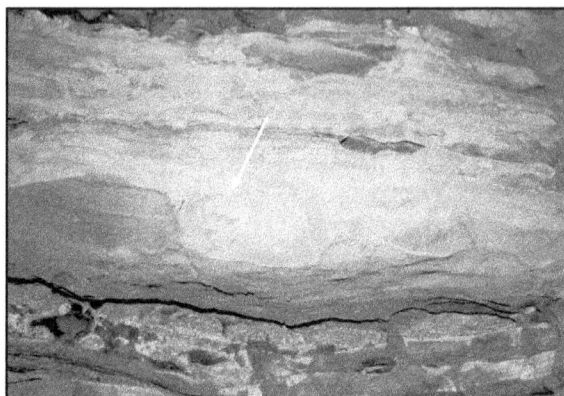

b: Rock Art on Cliff (2004-1733-image2511)

same elevation and at an elevation lower than the principal sites there (Figs. 7.7, 7.8, III.8, III.9, and III.10). Due to limited overhangs, they have not been as well protected, and are thus represented by only low wall stubs.

The Quail Spring Pasture Cliff Dwelling (V:1:188) fills a small cave high on the south face of a knoll with a great view over Cherry Creek to the south. It consists of four rooms (Fig. III.11). Rooms 1 and 2 were probably built first, with Room 3 added at some point later. The relative dating of Room 4 is uncertain. There is a rock art in the back of the cavern (Fig. 7.9b). The rock art consists of red lines, and may pre-date the cliff dwelling (see Chapter 9).

V:1:201 was recorded by Gila Pueblo as

GP C:1:34 and is in the north fork of Devils Chasm. The site consists of six rooms in three closely spaced areas at the base of a south-facing cliff (Figs. 7.10 and III.12). The rooms are well up from the bottom of the canyon, but not as high as the sites in the south fork.

The remaining small cliff dwelling sites have ceramics, tree-ring dates, or both to indicate their chronological position (Table 7.17). The Cold Spring Cave site (V:1:129) consists of a single room with an additional wall in front of a small niche (CD18 and Fig. III.13). It is well below the elevations of the other three sites in Cold Spring Canyon, but is above the FS 203 road. Ceramics indicate a late PIII or PIII/IV date for the site, probably pre-AD1300 (Table 7.20).

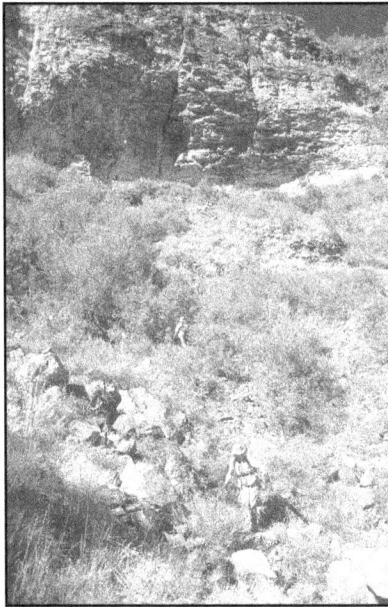

Figure 7.10. Small Cliff Dwellings – AZ V:1:201(ASM): Site Photograph (2004-1733-image0723)

a. View from across canyon (2004-1733-image1724)

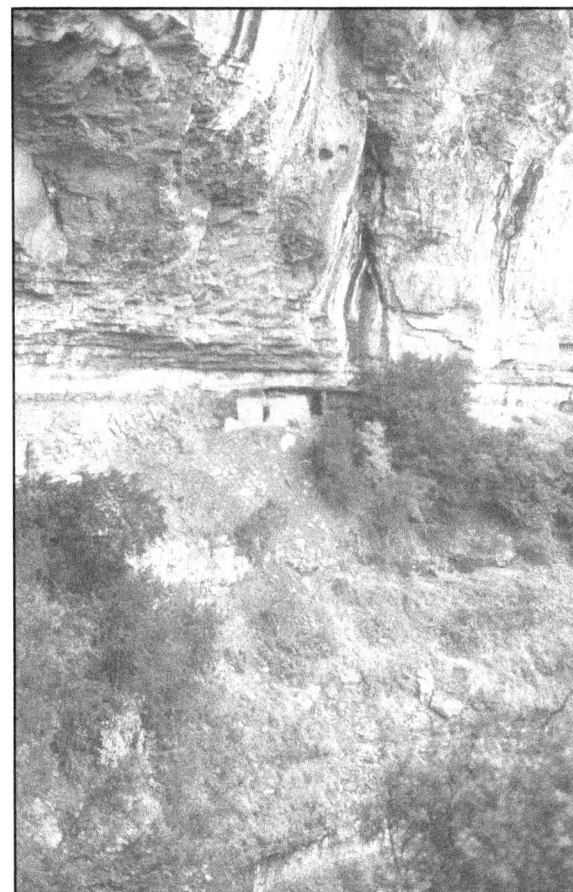

b. View from within cavern (2004-1733-image1179)
Figure 7.11. Small Cliff Dwellings --
AZ V:1:134 (ASM)

V:1:134:

The Uranium Mine site (V:1:134) is one of two north-facing cliff dwellings documented in the southeastern Sierra Ancha (Figs. 7.11 and III.14). The few ceramics recovered are not particularly helpful (Table 7.20), and there are two poor tree-ring dates from the site, indicating probable occupation in the AD 1290s or early 1300s. There is a good seep in this cavern, farther to the left in the cavern than Rooms 1 and 2.

A possible construction sequence for the Uranium Mine site is as follows: In Phase 1a, Room 4 is built, then Room 5 (based on relative roof height). Phase 1b involves the construction of the isolated Rooms 1 and 2, but the timing relative to Rooms 4 and 5 is unknown. Phase 1c involves another isolated room, Room 6. Finally, as Phase 2, Room 3 was added onto Room 4. Rooms 3, 4, and 5 all have doorways in the Front walls. A doorway between Rooms 4 and 5 was almost completely filled, changing the relationship and access between these two rooms.

V:1:136:

V:1:136 has one of the more interesting layouts (Fig.III.15). It is L-shaped. with openings in two different cliff faces, but only one is an access (Fig. 7.12 a-d). V:1:136 also consists of multiple levels and several intact roofs. The site is at the lowest elevation of the major sites in Cold Spring Canyon, occurring in the Mescal Limestone formation. Sparse ceramics and unspecific tree-ring dates (Tables 7.17, 7.20, and 5.4) lead to an estimated occupation span from AD 1292 to 1302. V:1:136 is one of the most intensively photographically documented sites (Table 7.18). Most of the wood in V:1:136 is hardwood, so no dates are available despite the intact roofs. Thus, it is impossible to provide any finer absolute or relative dating for the construction here.

The construction sequence for V:1:136 is divided into two major parts. In the lower part of the cave, Rooms 1 and 2 had to be built before Rooms 3 and 4. This first group of rooms (1 through 4) was probably necessary before Rooms 5 through 7 could be constructed.

V:1:162:

V:1:162 is one of the two small cliff dwellings that occurs at a high elevation (Table 7.17), and it is another of the most thoroughly photographically documented sites (Table 7.18). The ceramics recovered are not informative chronologically (Table 7.20), but there is a good series of tree-ring dates from the site (Table 5.4). Tightly clustered dates of AD 1326 to 1328 from different rooms and different structural elements indicate construction and the beginning of occupation in 1327 and 1328.

The site consists of eight architectural spaces, but probably only 5 actual rooms (Figs. 7.13 and III.16). The jacal wall between Rooms 2 and 6 is two stories tall, thus, Rooms 2, 3, and 6 were probably built at the same time. The tree-ring dates suggest that Room 2 could have been built in 1327 and Room 6 in 1328; however, the roof of Room 2 is above that of Room 6, suggesting that construction began in 1328 and the roof of Room 2 followed the roof of Room 6. Room 3 was probably done at the same time due to the tall jacal wall. Room 7

is an architectural space, but it seems to have never been walled-in as a formal room. At some point later, Rooms 1 and 4 were added. Even though a building sequence is posited, the tree-ring dates suggest that the site was built all within a short interval of time.

V:1:163:

V:1:163 consists of six architectural spaces, not all of which may have been formally roofed as rooms (CD19 and Fig. III.17a). It is one of three small cliff dwellings at an elevation above 1830m. Room 4, at the back of the cavern, has a natural roof; spaces 2 and 3 are more like hallways or passageways. Ceramics indicate a general PIII/IV date for the site (Table 7.20), while tree-ring dates suggest construction of Room 4 could have occurred as early as AD 1295 and the construction of Room 1 in AD1312 or later. The general occupation of the site is projected to be from AD 1312 to 1317. Of architectural interest at the site is the use of split logs (in at least once case from the same tree) to form doorjambs. This is not a common feature in the Sierra Ancha cliff dwellings.

Construction at the site seems to have built Room 4 in Phase 1, Rooms 1 and 2 in Phase 2, and Rooms 5 and 6 in Phase 3. Based on site size, this may have happened rapidly at about 1312, or may be split into two more distinct episodes as noted above.

V:1:164:

V:1:164 is high in Cold Spring Canyon, the third small cliff dwelling at over 1830m. The site contains six rooms (Figs. 7.14 and III.18), and was so remote and rarely visited that an original Gila Pueblo site tag was found in the site (Fig. 7.15). Just two of the original site tags were found, the other was also in Cold Spring Canyon, at V:1:174. Both Gila Pueblo tags were collected by SAP and are the only stamped Gila Pueblo tags in the ASM collections. The low visitation meant that a large

a. Site Setting (2004-1733-image1735)

b. Entry Point Into Site (2004-1733-image1738)

c. Overlook Room (2004-1733-image1737)

d. Overlook Detail (2004-1733-image1736)

Figure 7.12. Small Cliff Dwellings – AZ V:1:136 (ASM)

a. View from below (2004-1733-image1797)

Figure 7.13. Small Cliff Dwellings – AZ V:1:162 (ASM)

b. In cavern (2004-1733-image1801)

quantity of macrobotanical and perishable materials was present on the surface. Some of these materials were collected and are discussed in the following chapter.

Several tree-ring dates are available from the site (Table 5.4). The tree-ring dates combined with architectural evidence suggest construction in or after AD 1316. Ceramics indicate a potentially earlier date (Table 7.20). Rooms 1 and 2 (Phase 1) probably had to be built before any of the other rooms could be constructed. Phase 2 added Room 3, Phase 3a added Room 4, and Phase 3b created Room 6. The size of the site suggests this all happened rather rapidly.

V:1:168:

V:1:168 is a five-room cliff dwelling in Devils Chasm, down canyon, but at the same elevation, from the larger Devils Chasm Fortress (V:1:167). The site has less overhang than many of the other cliff dwellings, so many of the walls are no longer intact. The site is divided into two clusters of rooms (Figs. 7.16 and III.19), Rooms 1, 2 and 5, and Rooms 3 and 4. Tree-ring dates suggest the Rooms 1, 2 and 5 cluster may be earlier, circa AD 1310, and the Rooms 3 and 4 cluster later, after 1322 (Table 5.4). The site has been vandalized: Room 2 has been dug into, part of the top of the Front wall of Room 3 was pushed over, and the presence of late Roosevelt Red Ware ceramics (Table 7.20) may indicate a burial was disturbed. These ceramics also support the later period of occupation.

Architecturally, several details can be noted. Room 2 appears to have been a storage room, with a slab-lined cist in the room. There is a stone step on the exterior Left wall of Room 3 (Fig. 6.24), a feature that is relatively rare in the Sierra Ancha cliff dwellings. The doorway in the Left wall of Room 3 was modified, adding fill to one side to reduce the size of the opening, then adding lumps of adobe and stone

to create a T-shaped doorway (see Chapter 6 for further discussion of doorways).

Construction is divided into two main phases. Phase 1a involves the construction of Room 5, Phase 1b the construction of Room 3. Phase 2a is the addition of Room 1 to the right of Room 5. Finally, Phase 2b is the addition of Room 4 to Room 3.

The Hole-in-the-Wall Ruin:

The Hole-in-the-Wall Ruin (V:1:171) is named for a "window" in the cliff wall near the site (Figs. 7.17 and III.20). The site is at a lower elevation than many of the cliff dwellings, and is on the east side of Cherry Creek in Horse Camp Canyon. There are no tree-ring dates from the site, and ceramics collected are minimally diagnostic, implying a general PIII/IV time frame (Tables 7.17 and 7.20). At the time the site was mapped, two quartzite metates were still present in the site.

The Hole-in-the-Wall Ruin consists of three rooms, with a filled doorway between Rooms 2 and 3. Architectural relationships of the walls, and the continuous Front wall across all three rooms, suggest the rooms were all constructed at the same time.

V:1:174:

V:1:174 was recorded by Gila Pueblo as C:1:46, and is the second Sierra Ancha cliff dwelling where a Gila Pueblo site tag was recovered. V:1:174 is in Cold Spring Canyon, on the same, north side, but in between V:1:136 and 164 in terms of elevation. The site consists of three main rooms, a front terrace wall, and three more ephemeral spaces (CD20 and Fig. III.21). Part of the Front wall of Room 1 incorporated a large, immovable boulder. There is a seep area to the right of the three main rooms, but it does not have much of a flow rate.

One Gila Pueblo wood sample provided an incomplete tree-ring date of 1324 (Table 5.4). Ceramics are not any more diagnostic than

Figure 7.14. Small Cliff Dwellings – AZ V:1:164 (ASM) (2004-1733-image1327)

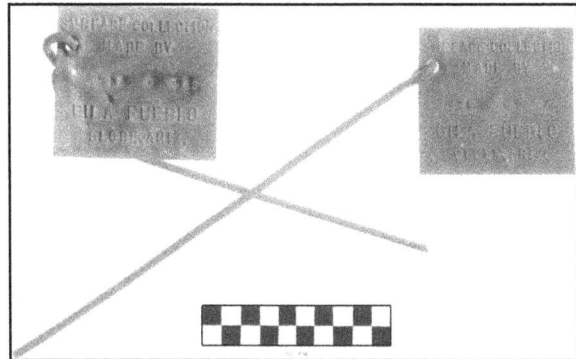

Figure 7.15. Gila Pueblo Site Tags from GP C:1:25 (AZ V:1:164 [ASM]) and GP C:1:46 (AZ V:1:174 [ASM]) (2004-1733-image4135)

Figure 7.16. Small Cliff Dwellings – AZ V:1:168 (ASM) (2004-1733-image1941)

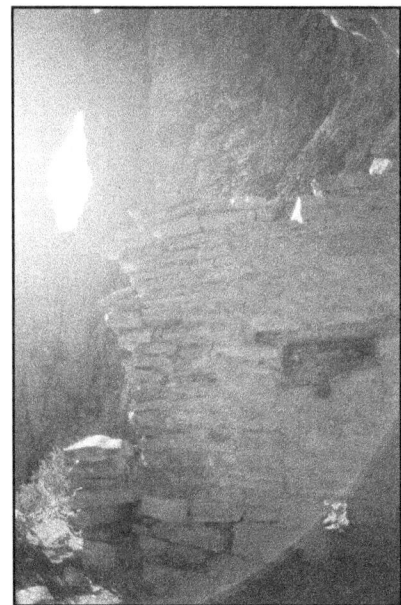

Figure 7.17. Small Cliff Dwellings – AZ V:1:171 (ASM) (2004-1733-image1843)

a general PIII/IV date. Two nearly complete and one less complete plain ware vessels were salvaged from pothunter's backdirt (CD21-24). One is a Salado Red Corrugated jar; the other two are brown plain. The Salado Red jar seems to have patterned fire-clouding, a more typical Hohokam trait often seen on Gila Red vessels (Haury 1945).

As in many of the sites, the remaining visible doorway was sealed (between Rooms 1 and 3). Whether this is simply an indication of a change in relationship or access between the rooms, or was a final act when departing the site (for the last time, or until the next planned visit), is unclear.

GP C:1:38:

GP C:1:38 is the smallest of three cliff dwellings recorded by Gila Pueblo between Sombrero Peak and Canyon Creek. GP C:1:38 is on a narrow ledge, with an interesting architectural feature. The Front wall of Room 2 is supported by a juniper log, which bridges a gap in the cliff (Figs. 7.18 and III.22). There is a somewhat similar site, La Cueva del Puente, in the Cuarenta Casas area in Mexico (Guevara Sanchez 1986:61-62). At GP C:1:38, there are six rooms, most of which are not intact due to exposure on the cliff face.

Ceramics collected by Gila Pueblo (Ciolek-Torrello and Lange 1990:140) and observed downslope during the documentation in 1996 indicate a predominance of Fourmile Polychrome pottery. The ceramics indicate that the occupation of the site is on the late end of the occupation in the middle Cherry Creek/southeastern Sierra Ancha area, probably after AD 1320. The later occupation is confirmed by two tree-ring dates obtained by Gila Pueblo—AD 1339 and 1340 (Table 5.4).

Figure 7.18. Small Cliff Dwellings – GP C:1:38 (SAP C32-31)

Large Cliff Dwellings (N=13)

All of the large cliff dwellings (that is, cliff dwellings with nine or more rooms) have either tree-ring dates, ceramics, or both. The extent of photographic and architectural documentation is detailed in Tables 7.18 and 7.19.

Five of the large cliff dwellings are west of Cherry Creek, another five are on the east side, two are in the Coon Creek drainage, and one is in the interior of the Sierra Ancha (Table 7.21). The site in the interior is the only large cliff dwelling at an elevation over 1830m. Two of the large cliff dwellings east of Cherry Creek are sites recorded by Gila Pueblo on the White Mountain Apache Indian Reservation.

V:1:130, 131, and 132:

V:1:130, 131, and the Ringtail Ruin (132) are all on the north side of Pueblo Canyon at the same elevation, with 60 to 80 m between the sites (Fig. 7.19). All three groups of rooms were originally recorded as a single site (C:1:16) by Gila Pueblo. The Gila Pueblo ceramic collections are summarized under V:1:132 (Table 7.22), because they were not differentiated by room cluster. Gila Pueblo records refer to the "north," "middle," and "south" "house group," SAP records refer to them as west (= south), central, and east (=north). Individually, two of the sites (V:1:131 and 132) are the largest cliff dwellings in the southeastern Sierra Ancha/ middle Cherry Creek area (Table 7.21). Only the Canyon Creek Ruin is substantially larger (Fig. III.23). The Upper and Lower Tonto ruins (Figs. III.24 and III.25) are approximately the same size.

Diagnostic ceramics are remarkably absent at these sites, even in the Gila Pueblo collections (Table 7.22). Gila Pueblo recovered mostly Snowflake and Reserve black-on-white and other indeterminate Cibola White Ware sherds. Fortunately, each site produced numerous tree-ring dates (Table 5.4), and SAP sampling was able to match many of the Gila Pueblo samples, providing more specific room by room proveniences (see Chapter 5 for further discussion and details).

V:1:130 is the smallest of these three sites, with 13 rooms (Figs. 7.20 and III.26). Tree-ring dates and wall-and-corner relationships indicate at least three principal phases of construction. Relative roof heights from room to room were noted where possible, but do not always seem to logically conform to the posited construction sequence.

The first phase would have involved the

Table 7.21. SAP Sites -- Data for Large Cliff Dwellings, 9 or More Rooms   (N = 13)

Site Number	Site Type	Date*	Comments	Elevation (ft)	Location**
V:1:130	Large cliff dwelling	1299-1332	12 rooms; middle elevation†	5200	West
V:1:131	Large cliff dwelling	1287-1330	28 rooms; middle elevation	5200	West
V:1:132	Large cliff dwelling	1290-1318	24 rooms; middle elevation	5200	West
V:1:133	Large cliff dwelling	1298-1325	14 rooms; high elevation	6800	Interior
V:1:135	Large cliff dwelling	1304-1337	13 rooms; middle elevation; high cliff	4160	East
V:1:144	Large cliff dwelling	PIII/IV	11 rooms; middle elevation; small canyon	4400	East
V:1:145	Large cliff dwelling	PIV	15-20 rooms; middle elevation; small canyon	4260	East
V:1:165	Large cliff dwelling	1304-1328	12+ rooms; middle elevation; high cliff	5200	West
V:1:167	Large cliff dwelling	1313-1340	18 rooms; middle elevation	5240	West
V:1:170	Large cliff dwelling	PIII	20+ rooms; middle elevation	4760	Coon Creek
V:5:61	Large cliff dwelling	PIV	11 rooms; low elevation	3200	Coon Creek
C:1:50	Large cliff dwelling	PIV	14 rooms; middle elevation; on high cliff	5800	East
C:1:47	Large cliff dwelling	PIV	9 rooms; middle elevation; on high cliff	5800	East

*Date: if PIII or PIV, etc, this is based on ceramics; if actual numbers, for example 1304-1320, this is the estimated occupation span based on tree-ring dates (see Chapter 5).
**Location: West or East = west or east of Cherry Creek, otherwise general location is specified.
†Elevation ranges: 2500-3999 ft = low elevation; 4000-5999 ft = middle elevation; over 6000 ft = high elevation.

Table 7.22. Ceramics at Large Cliff Dwellings*

Ceramic Type\Site**	130	131	132	133	135	144	145	167	170	5:61	Total
WMRW†– Indeterminate				1/	/15	/13	/1		/8	/9	/46
WMRW† – St. Johns Black-on-red					/1	/3	/1		/2		/7
WMRW† -- St. Johns Polychrome					/2	/1					/3
WMRW† -- Pinedale Black-on-red					/1	/4	/1				/6
WMRW† -- Pinedale Polychrome					2/1	/3		2/2	1/		5/6
WMRW† --Cedar Creek Polychrome					/1			1/		/1	½
WMRW† -- Fourmile Polychrome					6/16	/13	/3	2/3		/5	8/40
WMRW† -- Show low Polychrome						/1	/1			/1	/3
RRW† – Indeterminate type						/1		2/			2/1
RRW†- Pinto Black-on-red/ Polychrome					1/1	/3			/3	/3	1/10
RRW† – Gila Polychrome			/1			/2		21/9	3/	/2	21/14
CWW†– Indeterminate			9/	2/1	½	/6		1/	/2	/2	13/13
CWW†– Snowflake Black-on-white			4/	1/		/2					5/2
CWW†– Reserve Black-on-white			6/	2/							8/
CWW†– Tularosa Black-on-white			1/			/3					1/3
CWW†– Pinedale Black-on-white						/1					/1
MBW†-- Brown Plain	/1				/248	/74	/17	/4	/107	/15	/466
MBW†-- Salado Red Corrugated			/1		/135	/44		/8	/74	/5	/267
MBW† -- Salado Red Smooth			/1		/22	/1		/2	/2		/28
MBW† -- Salado Red with white						/2		/1	/3		/6
MBW† -- Vosberg Series-Vosberg Plain								/1	/38		/39
MBW†-- Tonto Red or Plain					/1					/2	/3
MBW† -- Unknown Decorated					/1						/1
MBW† -- Cibecue Plain					/7						/7
Alameda Brown Ware - Verde Brown	/1				/18	/26	/6			/5	/56
Apache – Apache Plain					2/						2/
TOTALS	/1	/1	20/3	6/1	10/474	/203	/30	29/30	4/239	/50	69/1032

*Counts in the format "16/12" mean 16 sherds from Gila Pueblo collections, 12 sherds from SAP collections; "/12" means only sherds from the SAP collections; "16/" means only sherds from the Gila Pueblo collections. Gila Pueblo collections from GP C:1:16 are all tabulated under "AZ V:1:132 (ASM)."
**All sites are preceded by "AZ V:1:" and are all Arizona State Museum site numbers; except for the last site, it is AZ V:5:61 (ASM).
†Abbreviations for ceramic wares: WMRW = White Mountain Red Ware; RRW = Roosevelt Red Ware; CWW = Cibola White Ware; MBW = Mogollon Brown Ware.

construction of Rooms 7, 8, 10, and 11, probably in 1299 or 1300. A date of 1324, from a loose, possible lintel, is not considered; the wood may not even be from these rooms. Phase 2a adds Rooms 1 and 2 to the left of the original rooms. Phase 2b adds Rooms 6 and 9 in front of the original rooms. Phase 2 probably dates after 1321. Phase 3a involved the construction of Rooms 4 and 5. Phase 3b adds Rooms 12 and 13, on opposite ends of the site. These rooms could have been added at any point after Phase 2 construction was completed. Finally, in Phase 4, Room 3 is filled in between room groups 1/2 and 4/5. Room 3 has an early appearing date on a primary beam (1309), but it is qualified as "vv." Potentially a large number of rings are missing, as this construction appears to have occurred after 1321. The span of occupation at V:1:130 is estimated to be approximately 1299 to 1332 (Tables 5.4 and 7.21).

This interpretation of construction phases and sequences is not as detailed as that done by Punzmann (1986:114-123), nor have the assumptions and logical progressions been as explicitly stated. However, there is independently achieved agreement in the overall span of construction and occupation at V:1:130, with the exception of Room 10. The author interprets Rooms 10 and 11 as part of the initial construction, Punzmann believes Room 10 to be much later in the occupation.

Several architectural details of interest are present in V:1:130. Rooms 1, 2, and 3 are not built against the cliff—there is a small crawl space behind. Perhaps this is simply an unusable low space, a damp area due to small seeps in the cliff, or perhaps, it served as a storage area behind these rooms. The last possibility is given some credence because there appears to have been a 1 to 2m wide corridor between the Left wall of Room 1 (now totally demolished) and the Right wall of Room 13. However, the dampness of this area behind the walls would make this a less than ideal storage area. The

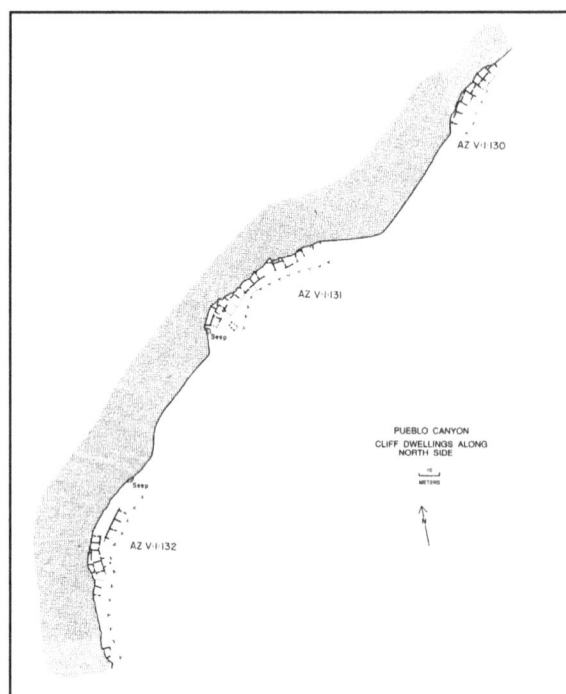

Figure 7.19. Large Cliff Dwellings: Relative Locations of AZ V:1:132, 131, and 130 (ASM) (2004-1733-image4026)

first and second stories in the Rooms 7/8/10/11 cluster clearly show the alteration of abutment relationships between the stories. Multiple plaster colors in the front walls of Rooms 8 and 11 indicate the potential for different plaster and mortar sources. Unfortunately, the Front wall of Room 11 fell or was pushed over sometime before November 2000.

Other architectural details involve a "coat hanger," a grass ring on a vertical support post, sherds used as chinking in a wall, and wall painting. The "coat hanger" is a large sliver of wood split off of a log and stuck in the plaster and wall joints high in the Left wall of Room 11. The grass ring is a pad on the top of a vertical support post to seat a primary beam in Room 7 (see Chapter 6, Fig. 6.36a). Two sherds, which seem to be Salado Red Corrugated, were used as chinking in the stone masonry courses in the Back wall of Room 4. Given the abundance of broken pottery available for such uses, this is the only occurrence noted for this type of use.

a. Site from across canyon (2004-1733-image1679)

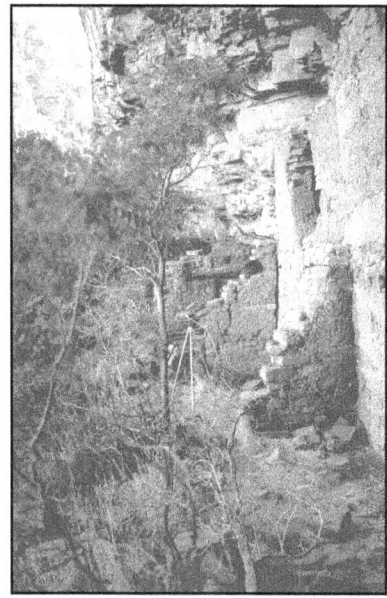

b. General site photograph (2004-1733-image1680)

Figure 7.20. Large Cliff Dwellings – AZ V:1:130 (ASM)

Finally, there is evidence of wall painting (zig-zag lines) in Rooms 2 (Left wall) and 3 (Left and Back walls). Wall painting is discussed further in Chapter 9. There do not appear to be any pictographs in this room cluster, unlike the abundant figures in V:1:131 and the Ringtail Ruin.

V:1:131 is the largest cliff dwelling in the southeastern Sierra Ancha, consisting of 28 rooms (Figs. 7.21 and III.27, Table 7.21). Consequently, the site has a large number of tree-ring dates, (Tables 5.4 and 7.21), and an estimated occupation span of 1287 to 1330. These dates place the central group (V:1:131) earlier than the east group (V:1:130), but with the occupation lasting to about the same point in time.

Relative roof heights and tree-ring dates are more consistent here, and lead to a possible construction sequence involving three principal phases. Phase 1a is the construction of one room near the center of the site (Room 17), and a room at the left end (Room 20). Phase 1b is the construction of Room 1 at the right end of the site. Phase 1b may actually be

late in the construction sequence, with dates on three lintels of "1321v." Phase 2a involves Rooms 10, 11, 13, and 15. Architecturally, this makes sense, largely based on the "continuous" Front wall across these rooms. However, tree-ring dates suggest Rooms 10 and 11 were built after 1297, and Room 15 in or after 1319. Rooms 5, 8, 2, 3, 6, 9, and 4 are all assigned to Phase 2b. Architectural clues (for example, Room 8) suggest this construction may have occurred more at the same time as Rooms 10 and 11, but the tree-ring dates (for Rooms 3 and 5) indicate potential contemporaneity with the later part of Phase 2a, after 1316. Phase 2c is the addition of Rooms 22 and 24 "behind" and abutted to Room 20.

Rooms 18, 19, 21, 23, 25, 27, and 28 are all added as part of Phase 3a. One date from a loose log suggests the construction may have occurred about 1322. Phase 3b is the addition of Room 12.

The portion of the site from Room 2 to Room 17 is particularly complex. It seems that Room 17 is earlier than Room 15. There then appears to be two areas with continuous Front

Figure 7.21. Large Cliff Dwellings – Site Location of AZ V:1:131(ASM) (2004-1733-image1303)

walls. One area is the Front wall from Room 2 to Room 8. The other is from Room 10 to Room 15. The latter case appears to be continuous, but there are at least two seams that hint at a lack of actual continuity (but expert masonry to blend the segments to make them appear to be continuous). The first seam is at the juncture between Rooms 13 and 15. The second seam is between Rooms 11 and 13 (Fig. 7.22a), and is the result of filling what appears to be a corner doorway (Fig. 7.22b).

Rooms 10 and 11 are unusual in other ways. Room 11 has painted lines on the walls, in addition to the corner doorway. Room 11's two primary beams ran perpendicular to the cliff, supported on vertical posts at the cliff. Room 10 also has two primary beams, running parallel to the cliff, with one beam having a vertical support at mid-span. There is no wall (a Right wall of Room 11 or Left wall of Room 10) between the rooms. There is some cliff rubble (large blocks) in the rooms, but no evidence of wall fall or wall rubble, unless the rooms are

fairly deep. Based on the room on either side, this could have been a two-story wall, if it ever existed. Also curious is how a continuous roof would have been constructed, given one set of primaries parallel to the cliff, the other perpendicular. It seems most likely that there was at least a one-story wall between Rooms 10 and 11, but it has been totally demolished.

This proposed sequence again parallels that of Punzmann (1986:103-114), with slight variations in which rooms are considered to be the earliest rooms.

The following summarizes some architectural details at V:1:131. There are numerous examples of pictographs at V:1:131, and some walls with lines or figures (discussed in detail in Chapter 9). On a high parapet wall (Right wall of Room 6), there is a rare occurrence of plaster texturing by rolling a corncob over the wet plaster (Fig. 6.3e). There is a lot of wood present at the site, principally primary beams, but only one intact roof. Room 22 was probably a storage room due to its low ceiling, but is a

a. Seam in Exterior Front Wall of Rooms 11 and 13 (2004-1733-image0059)

b. Interior, corner door/ "fireplace," Room 11 (2004-1733-image0054)

Figure 7.22. AZ V:1:131 (ASM) – Wall Details

good example of beams, planks, and ties in a roof. Room 15 contains the largest diameter primary beam in the southeastern Sierra Ancha. Harvesting and transporting this massive beam would have been quite an undertaking. Finally, Room 26 may not truly be a room (Fig. III.27). It is set out from the cliff and the rest of the site, and may only have Left and Right walls. Room 26 is just above a notch that permits access to lower areas in the canyon. Exploration of this notch discovered no additional masonry architecture, but this room could have served as an entry corridor into the site when accessed from below.

The Ringtail Ruin (V:1:132) is the second largest cliff dwelling in the southeastern Sierra Ancha (Figs. 7.23 and III.28), and is the farthest up-canyon of the three principal cliff dwellings in Pueblo Canyon (Fig. 7.19). This site also has a number of tree-ring dates from Gila Pueblo and SAP sampling (Table 5.4), but like the other sites in Pueblo Canyon, there is a noticeable lack of diagnostic ceramics

in either the Gila Pueblo or SAP collections (Table 7.22). The Ringtail Ruin has been given an occupation span of 1290 to 1318 (Table 7.21). Thus, it was almost as early as V:1:131, but seems to have been abandoned, or at least new construction ceased, much earlier than at V:1:131 or V:1:130.

The cavern containing the Ringtail Ruin may be the best cliff dwelling location in Pueblo Canyon, and even in the general southeastern Sierra Ancha area. The cavern is large and deep, offering maximal protection, yet the winter sun still penetrates deeply into the cavern. Rooms 1 through 5 and 23 took advantage of a natural shelf, but are the only rooms in any cliff dwelling in this area that are substantially off the back wall of the cavern. There are numerous seeps in the ceiling that may have contributed to the positioning of the rooms (to avoid constant drips and ultimately the destruction of roofs, mortar, and plaster), but the open space also provides a shaded, comfortable work area. The most reliable seep found in the southeast-

a. View of site from above, left to right: AZ V:1:132, 131, and 130 (arrows) (ASM) (2004-1733-image1288)

b. View of site from across canyon
(2004-1733-image1702)

c. General site photograph (2004-1733-image1713)

Figure 7.23. Large Cliff Dwellings – AZ V:1:132 (ASM)

ern Sierra Ancha or middle Cherry Creek area is at the right end of this cavern. All of these factors combine to create an ideal setting for a cliff dwelling. It seems obvious why it was among the first locations to be built in. It is a mystery why it was not occupied longer, or at least as long as the nearby cliff dwellings in Pueblo Canyon.

Four principal phases are posited for the construction of the Ringtail Ruin. The sequence of construction is based on available tree-ring dates, bonding and abutting wall relationships, and relative roof heights. Phase 1 is divided into four sub-parts. Phase 1a involves the construction of the room cluster that is set out from the back of the cavern—Rooms 23, 1, 2, 3, and 5. The only tree-ring date associated with this cluster is 1306, from a lintel in Room 1. Phase 1b adds Room 4, and completes this room cluster. Phase 1c concerns Rooms 8, 6, and 24 near the center of the site, and involves some of the earliest construction at Ringtail Ruin. Several dates of "1287vv" are derived from primary, secondary, and tertiary roofing components in Room 8. The roofs of Rooms 6 and 8 are at the same height, so Room 6 was built at the same time as Room 8. Phase 1d is the construction of Room 22, an isolated room at the left end of the site. No specific date is known for the construction of this room.

Phase 2 involves Rooms 17, 18, and 19, and has a single tree-ring date of "1305vv" from a primary beam in Room 17. Phase 2 construction is thus potentially contemporaneous with Phase 1a construction.

Phase 3 has two parts: Phase 3a is the construction of Rooms 10, 13, 15, 14, and 11; Phase 3b is the addition of Rooms 20 and 21. The Room 10/13/15/14/11 cluster fills the gap between two presumably prior clusters—Rooms 8/6/24 (Phase 1c) and Rooms 17/18/19 (Phase 2). A primary beam in Room 10 provides the only tree-ring date for this cluster (1305vv), indicating the construction

of this cluster may be essentially contemporaneous with the construction of the Room 17/18/19 cluster in Phase 2. Wall relationships also suggest this entire group (Rooms 10, 13, 15, 14, 17, 18, and 19) may have all been built at the same time. Rooms 20/21 are added onto the Room 17/18/19 cluster (Phase 2). A possible primary beam from Room 21 has an early appearing date of "1283vv." Room 24 (Phase 1c) was demolished sometime between 1930 and 1981, only a few stones remain at the RBX. A Gila Pueblo photograph (ASM 71112) shows Room 24 still standing, with a doorway in the Front wall.

Phase 4 is the construction of two rooms (Rooms 12 and 16) in front of rooms constructed in Phases 2 and 3a. No tree-ring dates are possible from these rooms as there was no wood present, so the dating of Phase 4 is unknown.

Once again, the basic outline of construction just presented is matched by the sequence proposed by Punzmann (1986:92-103). Some differences exist in the identifications of the core units, resulting in a slightly different sequence. And, as before, Punzmann's use of dates, including some tentative ones, permits some possible refinement of the construction sequences that were not considered here.

Architecturally, there are several interesting features of the Ringtail Ruin (Fig. III.28). The group of rooms set out from the back of the cavern (Rooms 1-5 and 23) is worth noting again. There is an isolated single room (Room 22) on the up-canyon end of the site, just as at the Uranium Mine site (V:1:134) directly across the canyon. There are pictographs on the cliff wall, particularly behind Rooms 6, 8, and 24. There is also room painting in Room 6. Both types of painted figures and elements are discussed below in Chapter 9. Two shells, probably prehistoric, were found in an unmortared joint in the exterior Front wall of Room 6 (CD25, CD26). The Ringtail Ruin is also where someone added a unique touch to the wet plaster, using his or her knuckles to simulate deer prints (Fig. 6.3d).

The area between Rooms 5 and 12 is also puzzling. In Room 5 is a deposit that appears to be quite deep (perhaps exposed in a vandalism hole). And, some holes in the Front wall of Room 8 may be vents for Room 8, however, due to their size, could also be sockets for primary beams for a room in front of and below Room 8. If this is the case, there may be several rooms in front of Rooms 10 and 12 and between Rooms 8, 10, and 5. These rooms are no longer visible if they do or did exist, however. They may have been removed by a vandalism hole, or were perhaps dismantled prehistorically.

Workman Creek Ruin (V:1:133):

The Workman Creek Ruin is the highest elevation site among the large cliff dwellings. The site is in a southwest-facing alcove in a cliff above the Workman Creek falls with a beautiful view out over the interior of the Sierra Ancha. V:1:133 consists of approximately 14 rooms (Figs. 7.24 and III.29), most of which are demolished due to heavy visitation and not much of a protective overhang.

Walls do not stand tall enough to document relative roof heights, so architecturally, the construction sequence relies on wall and corner relationships. There are a few tree-ring dates for the Workman Creek Ruin (Tables 5.4 and 7.21), indicating a general occupation from approximately 1298 to 1325. Unfortunately, the best cutting date (1320rL) is on an unprovenienced Ponderosa pine log. The other dates are "vv" or not annotated, and range from 1289 to 1300. Ceramics recovered or noted at the site are largely Cibola White Ware (Table 7.22), with types that reinforce the pre-polychrome pottery date (that is, pre-1320).

Two principal phases can be proposed for the construction of V:1:133. Each principal phase has two sub-phases. Phase 1a involves

Figure 7.24. Large Cliff Dwellings –
AZ V:1:133 (ASM) (2004-1733-image1722)

the construction of Rooms 1 through 6, which probably occurred around 1296 to 1300. Phase 1b is the construction of Room 9 at the left end of the site (Fig. III.29). Phase 2a adds Room 8; Phase 2b completes the site with the addition of Rooms 11 to 14 in front of Room 1 to 6. The space marked Room 10 may just be a retaining wall, not a true room.

Interesting architectural features include large, pine-plank door lintels (Front wall of Room 3 and Right wall of Room 4) and the plastering on several walls. Some of the plaster in the Workman Creek Ruin is a distinctive yellow/gold color. It seems to have been applied over earlier sooted plaster (for example, on the Right wall of Room 4), or over mortar containing ash and charcoal (for example, the Left wall of Room 2). Room 2's Left wall also shows an interesting use of "chinking" rocks pressed into the roughcast plaster (Fig. 7.25).

Cooper Forks Ruin (V:1:135):

Cooper Forks Ruin is an interesting site with 13 rooms tucked into 5 large niches in the cliff face (Figs. 7.26 and III.30). The site is on the east side of Cherry Creek and is visible from down stream along the creek. It blends well into the cliff, the masonry courses mimicking the natural stratigraphy in the Dripping Springs Quartzite cliff. From a distance, only the rect-

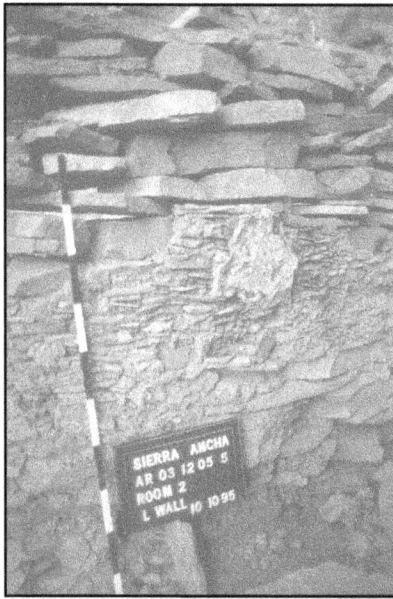

Figure 7.25. Large Cliff Dwellings –
AZ V:1:133 (ASM): Chinking and Plaster Detail,
Room 2 Left Wall (2004-1733-image0744)

Figure 7.26. Large Cliff Dwellings –
AZ V:1:135 (ASM) (2004-1733-image1382)

angular doorways give the site away; perhaps the exterior walls were never plastered.

A few tree-ring dates are available from the site, indicating an occupation span from 1304 to 1337 (Tables 5.4 and 7.21). Despite being at a relatively low elevation and farther removed from higher altitudes pines, the wood assemblage shows quantities of Ponderosa pine, Douglas fir, and white fir. The occupation, toward the later end of dates in the southeastern Sierra Ancha/middle Cherry Creek area, is confirmed by the dominance of Fourmile Polychrome pottery collected from the site (Table 7.22).

Relative roof heights can be used with wall and corner relationships to architecturally define the construction sequence at Cooper Forks Ruin. Four principal phases of construction are defined. Phases 1a and 1b are the building of Room 10 and the suite of Rooms 3, 4, 5, and 11, respectively, rooms that had to be constructed before other rooms were built. However, the timing of construction of Room 10 compared to the Rooms 3/4/5/11 suite may

be quite different. Possible dates from Room 10 indicate its construction may have occurred in the early 1300s (1303vv, 122vv). Dates from Room 3 suggest construction after 1326 (1326vv). The roof of Room 3 was recorded as being higher than that of Room 5; and the roof of Room 5 was recorded as higher than the roof of Room 11. These roof relationships would seem to indicate that Room 11 was built before Room 5, and Room 5 was built before Rooms 3 and 4. However, the corner relationships indicate the reverse, that Room 5 was abutted to Room 3 and Room 11 was abutted to Room 5. The primary beams for Room 11 are missing, but their sockets in the Left wall of Room 11 pass entirely through the wall. One possibility that could make Room 11 later than Room 5 is that these primary beam sockets were created by removing rocks from the wall after Room 5 had been constructed. It is difficult to decide one way or another in this situation. Phase 1c is the construction of Room 9 in another niche; Phase 1d is the construction of Room 1 in yet another niche at the left end of the site. Not enough architectural evidence remains to determine where Room 13 fits in the construction sequence.

Phase 2 involves the addition of one room in each of four sub-phases. Phase 2a is the addition of Room 5 in the middle of the site; Phase 2b is the addition of Room 2 at the left end; Phase 2c is the addition of Room 8 in front of Room 9; and Phase 2d is the addition of Room 12 in front of Room 10. No dates are available from any of the Phase 2 rooms. Phase 3 involves the addition of Room 6 behind Room 11. Phase 4 is the addition of Room 7, filling in an area in the middle of the site, and completing the growth sequence at Cooper Forks Ruin.

This site receives heavy visitation as evidenced by considerable modern trash. There is a nearly intact roof in Room 3, showing the use of cane (Phragmites australis) as closing material (Fig. 6.35b). The roof of Room 5 is also nearly intact, with a hatchway in the right front corner. Several metate fragments were noted outside of Rooms 3 and 5.

There is a small natural passageway in the cliff between Room 9 and the cavern area above it—where Room 10 is located. The passageway is somewhat above the roof level of Room 9, more at the floor level of Room 10. Access between the two niches may have been possible without a ladder, or with only a short ladder necessary. At the back of Room 3 are the only formal architectural units identifiable as granaries in the middle Cherry Creek cliff dwellings—Rooms 3a and 3b (Fig. III.30). Both were roofed separately and below the ceiling level of Room 3. They were undoubtedly accessed through hatches in the roofs, as there are no doorways in the walls of these structures.

Six Caves Ruin (V:1:144):

Six Caves Ruin is another cliff dwelling at a relatively low elevation on the east side of Cherry Creek (Table 7.21). The site is in a side canyon SAP named Buster Canyon (in memory of Travis "Buster" Ellison). There are no tree-ring dates from Six Caves Ruin, but the ceramics suggest a PIII/IV date, with occupation extending beyond AD 1320 (because of the abundance of Fourmile Polychrome pottery).

As the name implies, the site consists of rooms built into six separate caverns. In total, there are 11 rooms; the most in any one cavern is 3 rooms (Figs. 7.27 and III.31). There is a long retaining wall in front of the caverns, particularly in front of Cavern B and Caverns D through F.

The site is poorly preserved due to the minimal overhang in most of the caves. Little artifactual material remains in the sites, most of the ceramics were recovered from downslope. Six Caves Ruin by itself is not overly impressive, but the presence of architecture here indicates the inclination of the prehistoric peoples in this area to put architecture into nearly every inhabitable spot during the late 1200s and early 1300s.

Cock's Comb Ridge Site (V:1:145):

The Cock's Comb Ridge Site is directly across a small canyon from Six Caves Ruin, on the east side of Cherry Creek. The acoustics of this small canyon are remarkable. During mapping from the ridge top above Six Caves, no radios were required as the crew conducted the mapping with a theodolite and electronic distance meter, even though the distance was over 200m. Communication was possible in normal speaking voices.

Not many rooms are standing or even definable due to the lack of protective overhangs, but there appear to be 15 to 20 rooms. More remarkable are the terraces built on the steep slope to create additional work and living areas (Figs. 7.28 and III.32).

Features of interest include a large wall between two of the "combs" at the ridge top. There is a slab-lined cist on one of the lower terraces, and there are several pieces of ground stone at the site. The positioning of walls and rooms above a steep chute at the south end of the ridge is also noteworthy. Ceramics are dominated by plain Mogollon brown ware, but the presence of Fourmile polychrome

Figure 7.27. Large Cliff Dwellings – AZ V:1:144 (ASM) (2004-1733-image0846)

Figure 7.28. Large Cliff Dwellings – AZ V:1:145 (ASM) (2004-1733-image0846)

suggests a PIV (post-1320) date for the site (Table 7.22).

V:1:165:

V:1:165 was recorded by Gila Pueblo as C:1:30. This cliff dwelling is in a cliff high above Cherry Creek on the west side. It is one of the longest hikes (psychologically as much as any-thing) because the trail starts at Cherry Creek, the ascent is continual, and the cliff dwelling is in view almost the entire time. V:1:165 has at least 12 rooms, and includes some multiple story structures among the rooms along the cliff (Figs. 7.29 and III.33). There is a long retaining wall that once ran in front of most of the rooms. There are no ceramics from the site in either the Gila Pueblo or SAP collections, but brown and

Salado Red corrugated sherds were noted at the site, implying a PIII/IV occupation. However, Gila Pueblo did recover several datable wood samples (Table 5.4). The tree-ring dates were interpreted to show an occupation from 1304 to 1328. Unfortunately, none of the dates are assignable to a specific room.

Architecturally, three principal phases in the growth of the village can be detected. Phase 1a involves Rooms 5, 6, and 7 in the center of the site (Fig. III.33). Phase 1b denotes the construction of Rooms 1a and 1b at the far left end of the site, and Room 12 at the far right end. Phase 1c is the addition of a two-story unit (Rooms 9a and 9b) to the right of the Phase 1a cluster. Phase 2a is the addition of Rooms 10 and 11 to the right of Room 9a; the addition of Room 8 between Room 9a and the Room 5/6/7 cluster; and the addition of Rooms 3 and 4 to the left of the Room 5/6/7 cluster. Phase 3 completes the construction with Room 2.

V:1:165 has tremendous views up and down Cherry Creek and across the Q Ranch block toward Canyon Creek. The site is also near a saddle on this high ridge that provides access toward Coon Creek to the west.

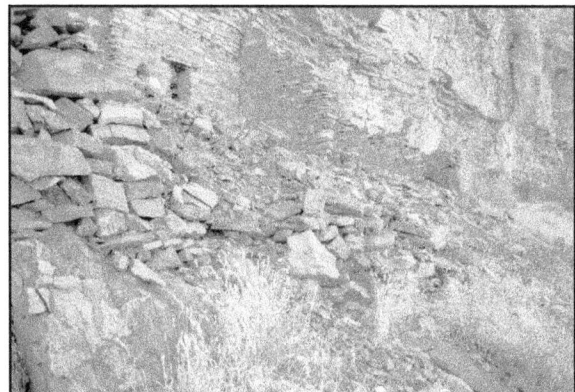

Figure 7.29. Large Cliff Dwellings – AZ V:1:165 (ASM) (2004-1733-image2027)

Devils Chasm Fortress (V:1:167)

The Devils Chasm Fortress is one of the most spectacular sites in one of the most spectacular canyons in the southeastern Sierra Ancha. At first glance, it appears to be massive, but the main (upper) part of the site contains just 11 rooms on the ledge (Figs. 7.30 and III.34). Another 8 rooms are on another ledge below the main part of the site. The upper part of the ruin has mostly intact walls, but no completely intact roofs. It appears fires, probably forest fires sweeping up the slope below, have burned out many of the roofs. The lower portion of the site is 11m below the upper ruin and is almost totally demolished due to the lack of a protective overhang.

A recent (April 2000) forest fire burned trees and brush on parts of the slope below the site, while other parts were unscathed. This fire did no further damage to Devils Chasm Fortress or the other cliff dwelling in this part of Devils Chasm, V:1:168, located closer to the mouth of the canyon at the same elevation.

Gila Pueblo recovered a number of tree-ring samples and dates from the site; SAP sampling acquired some additional dates and provided more specific proveniences for the Gila Pueblo samples (Table 5.4). The general span of occupation can be listed as AD1313 to 1340, adding the Devils Chasm Fortress to the list of sites occupied after AD1330 in the middle Cherry Creek area.

The construction sequences for the upper and lower portions of the site were probably similar. Both are long rows of rooms, each block probably built in succession from one end to the other. Dates for the lower portion come from Room 15, in the middle of the roomblock, and suggest this roomblock is late, after AD1330 (1330vv). Dates from the upper portion suggest Rooms 10 and 11 were the earliest (1313r, Room 10, primary beam). This is logical, beginning the construction at the far end of the ledge and working back

a. *View from below (2004-1733-image1397)*

b. *View along cliff (2004-1733-image1389)*

Figure 7.30. Large Cliff Dwellings – AZ V:1:167 (ASM)

toward the up-canyon end and access point. Otherwise, it would be difficult to transport construction materials through or over rooms built first and closer to the access point. A date on a primary beam from Room 7 (1330rB)

c. View from above (2004-1733-image1821)

Figure 7.30. Large Cliff Dwellings –
AZ V:1:167 (ASM), cont'd

supports this interpretation, and shows that the Room 8/9/10/11 cluster was the earliest, with the rest of the rooms added to the upper ruin in AD1330 or after.

Ceramics in both the Gila Pueblo and SAP collections support this general dating (Table 7.22). Both collections are dominated by Gila Polychrome pottery, with lesser, but equal, amounts of Pinedale and Fourmile polychrome pottery. The abundance of Gila Polychrome could be related to a disturbed burial in Room 7 or 8 (see Chapter 4 for a discussion of ceramic wares and contexts).

There is a seep in the cliff outside the entry wall, up-canyon from the main ruin. It has never had a steady flow or much volume in SAP visits to the ruin. More reliable water would be in the bottom of the canyon, a 30 to 60 minute roundtrip down and back up a loose talus slope. There is a cave in a cliff below the cliff dwelling, about halfway up from the canyon bottom, that hikers pass as they scramble up the notch. Nothing prehistoric was found near the opening of the cave, and serious cavers have explored the cave extensively and reported nothing. The cave apparently goes quite deep into the mountain.

Nordhoff-Hope Site (V:1:170)

The Nordhoff-Hope Site is at a relatively low elevation in the Coon Creek drainage. It is on the east side of Coon Creek, in a cliff with the typical southern exposure. At least 20 rooms and spaces are mostly contiguous along the base of the cliff, with a possible workspace enclosed by a low wall (Figs. 7.31 and III.35). Room 6 is up in the cliff in a crevice about 3 to 4 m above the bottom of the cliff. Rooms 15, 16, and 17 are in a "balcony" alcove even higher in the cliff and above the main block of rooms. Rooms 1 and 2 are isolated from the main part of the site to the down canyon side of the main cluster of rooms.

No tree-ring dates are available for the Nordhoff-Hope site. Ceramics collected by Gila Pueblo and SAP indicate a PIII/IV date (Table 7.22). There are both Pinto and Gila polychrome sherds, as well as St. Johns Black-on-red and Pinedale Polychrome. There is a large quantity of Salado Red Corrugated pottery.

Construction sequences are only discernible for the separate room clusters. How they relate to each other temporally is unknown. At the right end of the site, Room 1 was built before Room 2. In the upper balcony area, Room 17 had to be constructed before Rooms 15 and 16. In the core area of the site, the sequence is more complex due to the number and positions of the rooms. Rooms 12 and 14 were built first, followed by Rooms 11 and 8, and finally, the addition of Rooms 13, 10, and 9 completed construction in this cluster of rooms. Rooms 7, 5, 4, and 3 were probably built before Rooms 11 and 8, if the wall relationships between Rooms 7, 8, and 9 have been properly interpreted.

This site certainly has a commanding view down Coon Creek and over toward the Coon Creek Butte area. One can easily see the cliff area where Hematite House (V:5:61) is located downstream. The "balcony" rooms are an inter-

*a. View from Upper Room cluster
(2004-1733-image0075)*

Figure 7.31. Large Cliff Dwellings – AZ V:1:170 (ASM)

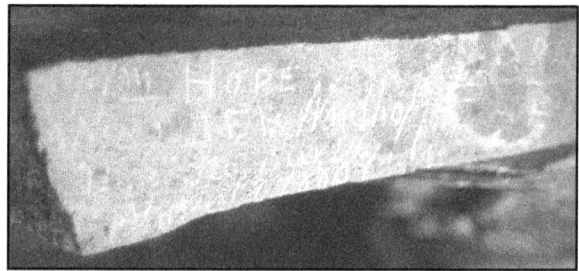

*b. 1880 Nordhoff-Hope Inscription in Room 6
(2004-1733-image1426)*

esting use of space in the cliff and the Front wall of Room 17 is truly massive. Another remarkable aspect of Room 17 is some modern rock art on the back cliff wall. Executed in charcoal is a short sequence of "hunter-aims at-deer" and "deer-gores-hunter." Another historic memento, considerably older, is the source of the name for this site. By scratching on a rock in the cliff wall/ceiling of Room 6, Mssrs. Walter Nordhoff and William Hope signed in as visitors to the site in November 1880 (Fig. 7.31b). They were conducting a reconnaissance for the USGS for gold and other minerals in Gila County (see Chapter 1).

Hematite House (V:5:61)

Hematite House is lower on Coon Creek than the Nordhoff-Hope Site just discussed; in fact, it is the lowest elevation cliff dwelling in the study area. It is one of two north facing cliff dwellings—the other is V:1:134 in Pueblo Canyon. The north facing aspect is particularly useful in the summer. The site is in the environment where mesquite, prickly pear cactus, and saguaros grow, that is, it is hot. Visits during the summer feel like walking into an air-conditioned room. During the winter, if it was cold in the cavern, it is a short walk down and across Coon Creek to the sunny slopes and terraces

on the other side.

The site consists of 11 rooms in a small cavern up a short slope from Coon Creek (Figs. 7.32 and III.36). Coon Creek is essentially perennial in this part of the drainage. The site is named for the powdery, red and yellow mineral bands in the Dripping Springs Quartzite. However, it is a misnomer—the bands are limonite, not hematite. Attempts to create pottery slips using these materials were not successful (see Chapter 4).

There are no tree-ring dates from Hematite House, because the wood used is all riparian hardwoods and non-conifers—sycamore and box elder. Even saguaro ribs were used in the roofing (Room 3; Fig. 6.35c). The roof of Room 3 is almost totally intact, and the roof of Room 7 was somewhat complete when the author first saw the site in the mid- to late-1970s. By the early 1980s, the roof of Room 7 no longer existed.

Ceramics, though, are plentiful, and suggest a PIV (post-1320) date for the site. White Mountain Red Ware dominates the assemblage (Table 7.22), with Fourmile Polychrome the most common identifiable type. Pinto Black-on-red or Polychrome and Gila Polychrome are both present, as well as Brown plain and Salado Red Corrugated.

Figure 7.32. Large Cliff Dwellings – Hematite House (AZ V:5:61 [ASM]) (2004-1733-image1851)

Without tree-ring dates, the construction sequence relies totally on wall-and-corner relationships and relative roof heights. Construction at Hematite House can be accounted for in three phases. Phase 1a is the construction of Rooms 3 and 7 (3 before 7) in the core of the site. Phase 1b is the construction of Room 9 and the right end of the site. Phase 2a adds Room 11 between the original room cluster (3/7) and Room 9. Phase 2b involves the addition of Rooms 1 and 2 to the left of Room 3. Finally, Rooms 10, 5, and 6 are added in front of Rooms 2, 3, and 7 in Phase 3.

GP C:1:47 and GP C:1:50:

Two more large cliff dwellings were recorded by Gila Pueblo. They are on the White Mountain Apache Indian Reservation east of Cherry Creek. Gila Pueblo obtained two tree-ring samples from each site, but none of the samples dated. Many ceramics were noted on the slopes below each site during the mapping and documentation. The dominant pottery type is Fourmile Polychrome, securely giving these cliff dwellings a PIV and post-1320 date.

GP C:1:47 consists of 9 rooms arranged around a semi-circular cavern with a steep slope below (Figs. 7.33 and III.37). Two retaining walls help to stabilize the areas where the rooms were built. At least one cluster of rooms (Rooms 6, 7, 8, and 9) involves two stories. There is a small seep in the back of the cavern. It was moist, but not producing much water during the SAP visit in October 1996. From the left side of the cavern, a ledge goes to the west and provides access to GP C:1:50. Part of the ledge has a low cobble wall along the edge.

GP C:1:50 has 15 architectural spaces, of which 14 are rooms. Room 12 is a small, walled-off niche in the cliff (Figs. 7.34 and III.38). The rooms are tightly packed into a deep notch in the cliff. At least three of the rooms involve multiple stories. The wall between Room 5/7 and 9A/10A is massive, as is the wall that forms the Front wall to Rooms 5 and 9A. Rooms 5 and 7 may be the result of subdividing a once larger room. Similarly,

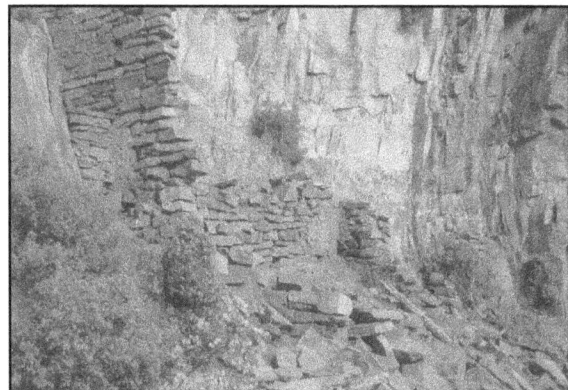

Figure 7.33. Large Cliff Dwellings – GP C:1:47 (SAP C39-19)

Rooms 9A and 10A could have originally been one space. There are pictographs on the cliff wall at GP C:1:50 (Fig. 7.35). The pictographs are more like those at Canyon Creek Ruin rather than like the pictographs in Pueblo Canyon (see Chapter 9).

Other Sites

The "other sites" category contains seven sites that do not fit within the site types discussed above. The category is a mixture of Apache, historic, and rock art sites (Table 7.23).

Apache Sites (N = 1)
Only one site was identified as a purely Apache site (V:1:158). It is a large feature with a mound of thermally cracked rocks—an agave-roasting pit. It is in a saddle, on a ridge near the Nordhoff-Hope Site, roughly at the watershed between Coon and Cherry creeks. V:1:158 is similar to a site component recorded by the Cholla Project, on the highest ridges east of Cherry Creek ("Room-block C," V:1:4 ; Reid 1982c:22-25). There are two sites discussed above that have Apache sherds (V:1:135 and 147). However, these sites were not classified as primarily Apache sites.

Historic Sites (N = 2)
Two sites were recorded as historic. One, V:1:125, is in the middle elevations of Pueblo Canyon and was initially thought to be prehistoric. V:1:125 is in a cave approximately 4m up a small cliff. A pinyon pine beam runs parallel to the mouth of the cave and had a fragment of yellow nylon rope tied around it. Certainly, the rope was modern, but the beam could have been prehistoric. An aluminum extension-ladder barely enabled access into the cave. A sample from the beam in the cave produced a date of "1838B inc." A sample from a loose log below the cave dated "1961 vv inc." Thus, this site is certainly historic.

Figure 7.34. Large Cliff Dwellings – GP C:1:50 (SAP C34-38)

Figure 7.35. Large Cliff Dwellings – GP C:1:50 Pictographs (SAP C36-2)

V:1:187 is an historic cabin, probably constructed of rocks from the rubble of a nearby pueblo (V:1:186). There is an irregularity in one wall that could have been a fireplace, and another wall that could be part of a porch. There are two wooden posts in the structure. The cabin was recorded, but no further information about the site was sought.

There are many other historic structures that could be recorded, but these were not the focus of this project. Sites that could be recorded as separate sites, or additional temporal components of previously recorded prehistoric sites, include: the foundations of Slim Ellison's cabin in Devils Chasm, portions of the Ellison Ranch on Cherry Creek, the uranium mine and associated line shack on the south

Table 7.23. SAP Sites -- Data for Other Sites (N = 7)

Site Number	Site Type	Date	Comments	Elevation (ft)	Location*
V:1:158	Apache**	Historic	large roasting pit in saddle; middle elevation†	4830	Coon Creek
V:1:125	Historic	Historic	cave with modern beam and rope; middle elevation	4770	West
V:1:187	Historic	Historic	cabin; middle elevation	4685	Coon Creek
V:1:260	Rock art	PIII/IV?	pictographs on isolated panel; middle elevation	5200	West
V:5:160	Rock art	Archaic?	petroglyphs; low elevation	2750	West
V:5:161	Rock art	Archaic?	petroglyphs; low elevation	2750	West
V:5:250	Rock art	?	petroglyphs; low elevation	2760	East

*Location: West or East = west or east of Cherry Creek, otherwise general location is specified.
**There are other sites with Apache sherds, but they have not been classified as "Apache sites": V:1:135 and V:1:147.
†Elevation ranges: 2500-3999 ft = low elevation; 4000-5999 ft = middle elevation; over 6000 ft = high elevation.

side of Pueblo Canyon, a cabin and corrals in Horse Camp Canyon, and an irrigation canal on the east side of Cherry Creek at the first crossing.

Rock Art (N = 4)

Although there is rock art in the form of pictographs at several of the sites, in particular at two of the cliff dwellings in Pueblo Canyon, the rock art sites noted here are exclusively rock art. Rock art and room painting are discussed in detail in Chapter 9; only summaries are presented here. V:1:260 is also in Pueblo Canyon, on the north side between the Ringtail Ruin and the waterfall. The site is all pictographs, in white, and has over 30 individual elements. The elements are similar to those in the nearby cliff dwellings and are thus attributed to a similar PIII/IV time period.

Two sites are close to each other on the west side of Cherry Creek, a few hundred meters above the first crossing (FS 203 road over Cherry Creek). V:5:160 and 161 contain deeply engraved, heavily patinated geometric patterns that are generally attributed to the Archaic period (Figs. 9.1 and 9.2). The fourth site, the Bob Conforti Site (V:5:250), is below the first crossing and on the east side of Cherry

Creek. It is at the base of a cliff that is above a very loose slope above Cherry Creek. The elements at V:5:250 seem to be more similar to typical Hohokam and other southern desert petroglyphs (Fig. 9.4).

As noted at the beginning of this chapter, there are reports of more rock art in the Cherry Creek drainage (Cummings 1930:42), but the SAP has not systematically surveyed the middle and lower Cherry Creek areas. Additional rock art is expected to be below the second crossing (at the Ellison Ranch). Rock surfaces and types above the second crossing are generally not appropriate for petroglyphs, whereas the cliffs and boulders below the second crossing are.

Other rock art sites recorded or visited during the course of the SAP are in Chalk Creek and Coon Creek. The glyphs in Chalk Creek (Fig. 9.5) are in a side drainage, near its confluence with the Salt River. The Coon Creek petroglyphs (Fig. 9.6) are on boulders on the east side of the creek, near an old Civilian Conservation Corps camp area downstream from the FS 203 road crossing. Both of these sites contain petroglyphs that are in the Hohokam style. Neither of these rock art sites has been assigned an ASM site number.

Chapter Eight
Other Material Culture and Other Materials

In addition to the ceramic, photographic, architectural, and environmental data and materials collected by the SAP, a number of other materials and data were collected. No formal collecting or sampling strategy was followed to obtain these materials. They were most often incidental to the collection of other information or artifacts. The purpose of this chapter is to summarize and discuss the other materials collected by the SAP. The other data to be considered here are flaked stone, ground stone, pot plugs, steatite objects, shell, human bone, macrobotanical remains, and textiles.

FLAKED STONE

Flaked stone tools and debris were collected at 20 sites. In some cases, the collection involved a single tool, such as a drill or projectile point; in other cases, a number of artifacts were recovered. Collections by SAP were not systematic and were not large enough from most sites to pursue issues of reduction technology or activities represented at a site. Nor were the collections from individual sites large enough to permit statistical manipulations of the data. However, the raw materials are representative of materials available and used in the Cherry Creek drainage, and are typical of materials used elsewhere in the Tonto-Roosevelt-Q Ranch areas (see assemblage descriptions in Reid 1982c).

A total of 426 flaked-stone artifacts was collected (Table 8.1). Complete flakes are the most numerous artifact type, constituting over 35 percent of the assemblage. Combined, the artifact types representing debris from the reduction of materials to make tools (complete, broken, and split flakes, flake fragments, and debris) constitute over 83 percent of the collection. Tools, including edge-damaged and retouched pieces, projectile points, drills, bifaces, and wedges, constitute over 5 percent. Cores represent just fewer than 4 percent of the assemblage, while manufacturing tools (peckingstones, hammerstones, and hammerstone spalls) are 1.4 percent of the collection. The SAP projectile points are illustrated in Figure 8.1.

As is typical of other Tonto-Roosevelt-Q Ranch area assemblages (Reid 1982c), the majority of tools are made of finer-grained materials such as chert and silicified limestone (Table 8.1). Thus, the majority of debris from making these tools consists of the same materials. The chert in particular, is a distinctive white color that occurs in the limestone strata along Cherry Creek and as eroded gravels in the stream channels. Two pieces of obsidian were collected, but their source area is unknown. Strong possibilities include the sources near Superior in the Superstition Mountains (so-called "Apache Tears") or in the White Mountains and other ranges to the east in western New Mexico. The manufacturing tools are of coarser, tougher materials (quartzite).

GROUND STONE

Ground stone was noted at 52 of the SAP sites. In addition, one isolated trough metate was recorded in the general area of the compounds across from

Table 8.1. SAP Flaked Stone: Artifact Types and Material Types

Material: Artifact Type:	chert	silicified limestone	quartzite	igneous	rhyolite	obsidian	fine-grained sandstone	Total
edge-damaged piece	1							1
retouched piece	7	1			1			9
projectile point	4			1				5
biface	6							6
drill	1							1
wedge	2							2
complete flake	60	60	17	3	9		1	150
broken flake	36	27	7	1	11			82
split flake	11	7	5	1	5			29
flake fragment	45	23	5	1	9			83
debris	13	14	2		2			31
fire-cracked rock	2	2						4
core	5	6		1	2	2		16
peckingstone		1	2					3
hammerstone			2					2
other/tested piece		1						1
hammerstone spall		1						1
Total	193	143	40	8	39	2	1	426

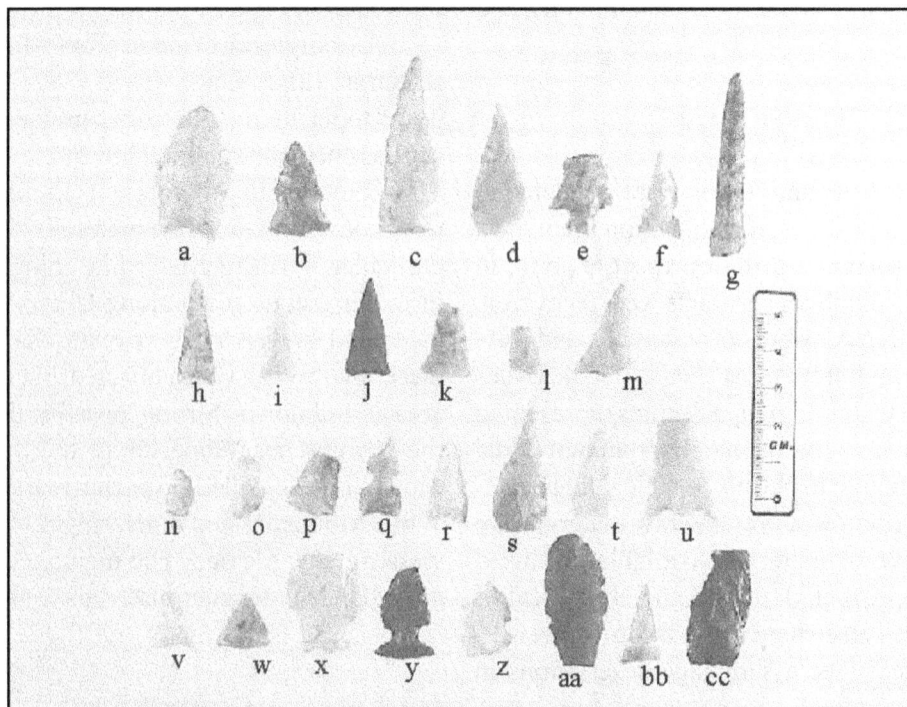

Figure 8.1. SAP Projectile Points: a = IN 134, b = IN 143, c = IN 69, d = IN 227, e = IN 450, f = IN 228, g = IN 241, h = IN 4, i = IN 134, j = IN 9, k = IN 232, l = IN 455, m = IN 451, n = IN 230, o = IN 527, p = IN 535, q = IN 566, r = IN 577, s = IN 571, t = IN 580, u = IN 550, v = IN 558, w = In 558, x = 524, y = 541, z = 541, aa = IN 539, bb = IN 520, cc = IN 175 (2004-1733-image3976)

Pottery Point Pueblo (V:1:166; Fig. 8.2). Only a ground stone bowl from V:1:209—the Stone Bowl Site—was collected (Fig. 8.3).

One-third to one-half of the sites in each site type were noted with ground stone present (Table 8.2). Unfortunately, the recording of the ground stone is uneven. Unspecified generic ground stone was noted as present at 16 sites. Metates were often fragmentary, with at least 24 unclassified metates present at 12 sites. Slab or flat metates were rare, with just two noted at two sites. Trough metates are the dominant metate type, with at least 29 recorded from 16 sites. Notes for at least 29 manos (type not specified) were made at another 16 sites. Four unifacial, loaf-shaped manos were recorded at three sites. Two sites were recorded as having abundant ground stone. Pottery Point Pueblo (V:1:166) had numerous pieces of ground stone in vandalized rooms at the time it was recorded. Similarly, large piles of ground stone, particularly manos, were present in vandalized areas at Granite Basin Pueblo (V:1:26).

The majority of ground stone, both metates and manos, was made of white or light-gray quartzite. Interestingly, there are no basalt or other igneous materials represented. This may be because the local igneous materials are fine-grained. Thus, the material provides no natural grip or bite as grinding implements. The quartzite used appears to be from the Troy Quartzite formation. It can be easily obtained as rounded cobbles from the Cherry Creek streambed or from the bottoms of the major side canyons.

POT PLUGS

Eight plugs or plug fragments were recovered from three sites (Table 8.3). Haury (1934:128) discusses similar "jar plugs" from Canyon Creek Ruin under "Objects of Unfired Clay." Intrigued by his comment that the impressions showed that the cobs were usually without kernels, the pot plugs from the SAP sites were closely examined.

Of the eight plugs from the SAP sites, four have no impressions of corn (cobs or kernels), one has impressions of corn with kernels, two have impressions of cobs with no kernels, and one has impressions of cobs with kernels and cobs without kernels. This variation raises several questions.

■ Is corn being stored on the cob in sealed jars, or is corn also being stored in other ways, on the cob as well as shelled?

■ Are some varieties of corn being stored on the cob in jars, while others are not?

■ Are cobs without kernels really being stored, or is this just a final covering layer before the plug is put into the mouth and neck of the jar?

■ If the cobs are just a covering layer, is it corn or are there other materials stored in the jars?

■ For the plugs lacking corn impressions, does this just indicate that corn was stored in the jar, but was covered with something that did not leave clear impressions (for example, with leaves or loose dirt)?

Most of the plugs show a smooth, concave edge, indicating the plug was packed into the neck of the jar when wet (Fig. 8.4). Curiously, some are complete or nearly complete. Does this mean that the plugs were so hard and tight (and below the curve of the jar neck) that the only way to get at the contents was to break the pot? Or, perhaps the pots were never reclaimed by their original packers—the pots were broken by collapsing walls, roofs, and cavern ceilings or by later visitors (prehistoric, protohistoric, historic, or some combination thereof) who smashed the pots to see what was inside.

Table 8.2. Ground Stone Present at SAP Sites

SITE TYPES	SITES	GENERIC GROUND STONE	METATE(S)	SLAB METATE(S)	TROUGH METATE(S)	MANO(S)	UNIFACIAL MANO(S)	AXE	OTHER/ NOTES
Alignments and Checkdams (5 of 10 sites)	V:1:225	xx							
	V:1:237	xx							
	V:1:244	xx							
	V:1:251			1					
	V:1:254		1*						
Field Houses (16 of 45 sites)	V:1:138		1*			1*			
	V:1:141		1*			1*			
	V:1:142		1*						
	V:1:147		1						
	V:1:178				1				
	V:1:181				1				
	V:1:199					1			stone bowl
	V:1:209	xx	1			1			
	V:1:220	xx				1			
	V:1:223		1						
	V:1:230	xx							
	V:1:241					2			
	V:1:247	xx							
	V:1:248		2			2			
	V:1:249	xx	6*			1			
	V:1:250	xx							
Medium-sized Pueblos (4 of 12 sites)	V:1:215		1			1			
	V:1:231	xx							
	V:1:232					1			
	V:1:233		2						
Large Pueblos (3 of 9 sites)	V:1:166	xx							abundant; in rooms
	V:1:177				2		2		
	V:1:203	xx							

* Note: indicates a fragmentary artifact

Table 8.2. Ground Stone Present at SAP Sites, cont'd

SITE TYPES	SITES	GENERIC GROUND STONE	METATE(S)	SLAB METATE(S)	TROUGH METATE(S)	MANO(S)	UNIFACIAL MANO(S)	AXE	OTHER/NOTES
Compounds (17 of 27 sites)	V:1:160				1				
	V:1:183				1				
	V:1:184				1*		1		
	V:1:205				2				
	V:5:64					1			
	V:1:192				2*	1			
	V:1:218		4*						
	V:1:226				2				
	V:1:26								abundant; vandalized
	V:1:222	xx				5		1	
	V:1:227	xx							
	V:1:234	xx							
	V:1:202	xx							
	V:1:258		3*						
	V:1:190	xx							
	V:1:207	xx							
	V:1:208	xx							
Small Cliff Dwellings (3 of 15 sites)	V:1:171				2				
	V:1:188				1*				
	GP C:1:38			1	1		1		
Large Cliff Dwellings (4 of 13 sites)	V:1:135				3				
	V:1:167				2	2			
	GP C:1:50				5	6			abundant
	GP C:1:47				2	2			
TOTALS		16	24	2	29	29	4	1	1

* Note: indicates a fragmentary artifact

Figure 8.2. Isolated Trough Metate
(2004-1733-image1947)

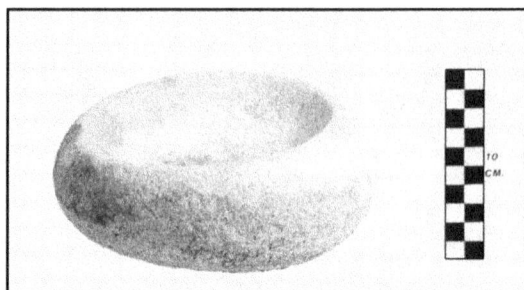

Figure 8.3. Stone Bowl from AZ V:1:209 (ASM),
IN 547 (2004-1733-image3828)

Table 8.3. Pot Plugs from SAP Sites

Site	Inventory Number	Room	Comments
V:1:131	212	8A	impressions of leaves & twigs, no corn
V:1:131	213	10	2 pieces, one with corn with kernels on the cob; the other has no impressions of kernels or cobs
V:1:132	513	20	artifact in computer inventory, not in box inventory; missing?
V:1:162	121	6	impressions of cobs, some with kernels on some with kernels off
V:1:164	280	7	cob impressions, without kernels on
V:1:164	583	5	3 plugs: a) no cobs or kernels; b) no cobs or kernels – complete; c) cobs without kernels

Figure 8.4. SAP Pot Plugs: a = IN 213, b-c = IN 212
(2004-1733-image3715)

STEATITE

Steatite, or soapstone, is a naturally occurring mineral in the Sierra Ancha area. Its composition relative to serpentine and asbestos, and use in the Q Ranch area sites, has been documented (Lange1982b, 1989). Much of the steatite there was related to what was assumed to be Hohokam exploitation of this resource (primarily for the manufacture of small, disc beads). Hohokam artisans often used steatite to create other objects such as carved and polished bowls (Gladwin and others 1937). However, there are other steatite objects that can be attributed to other groups in this same region. There are small animal effigies occasionally, and there are numerous loaf-shaped objects that are assumed to be arrowshaft straighteners (Cosgrove 1951). Several fragments of arrowshaft straighteners were found at the SAP sites (Fig. 8.5). The presence of steatite shaft straighteners does not appear to be related to an increase in hunting. In most cases, for instance at Grasshopper Pueblo (Reid and Whittlesey 1999:106), small game increases in faunal assemblages over time as large game decreases. Small game, such as rabbit, is generally not hunted with bows and arrows. So, if these objects are in fact related to arrow making or maintenance, they are expected to be related to and indicative of warfare (see Lange 1992:331). Others are known from many other PIII/IV sites in the region {for example, Tonto National Monument (Pierson [1962:51; identified as schist, but certainly steatite], the Vosberg area (Cartledge [1976]), Kinishba (Cummings [1940]), Casa Grande (Fewkes [1912]), Grasshopper (seen by the author), Q Ranch (Chris Lange, personal communication), several Miami Wash sites (Doyel [1978]), and Canyon Creek Ruin (Haury [1934:120])}. Cosner (1951) wrote an early description of the use of such artifacts for straightening arrows. These objects, often,

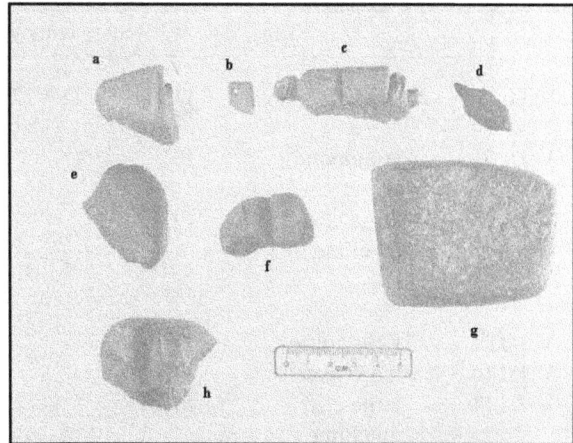

Figure 8.5. SAP Steatite Objects: a = IN 1, shaft straightener; b = IN 286, serpentine or turquoise pendant; c = IN 133, steatite zoomorph; d = IN 133, steatite zoomorph; e = IN 407, shaft straightener; f = IN 274, shaft straightener; g = IN 283, "mano;" h = IN 592, shaft straightener (2004-1733-image3977)

but not always steatite, seem to make a sudden appearance in the late 1200s and early 1300s.

Worked steatite was noted or recovered from 13 SAP sites (Table 8.4, Fig. 8.5). Steatite is available as large or small nodules, loose or in exposed bands and layers in the Sierra Ancha and east of the Sierra Ancha around Rock House on the Q Ranch block. Steatite, as well as serpentine, is occasionally found in the gravels in the Cherry Creek streambed. There are also exposures near the top of the Mescal Limestone, as the trail/old jeep road nears the old line shack area and turns in to Pueblo Canyon. This is a relatively low quality steatite, however. There is better quality steatite exposed in the roadbed and the slopes above and below the road just before reaching the Workman Creek falls in the interior of the Sierra Ancha. There are undoubtedly other exposures in the Sierra Ancha that could have been exploited as well.

SHELL

Among the shell artifacts recovered by the SAP were two particularly interesting pieces. They were found together in an open mortar joint in

Table 8.4. SAP Sites with Worked Steatite Present (N = 13)

SITE	SITE TYPE	DATE	INVENTORY NUMBER	ARTIFACT TYPE
V:1:26	compound	PIV	133*	one small, flat carved piece; one large carved piece—figurine?
V:1:135	large cliff dwelling	PIV	15 20	2 small rounded pebbles with facets and abrasions evident fire-cracked pebble, smooth with abrasions
V:1:137	field house	?	276	small, worked, shaped(?) pebble
V:1:140	large pueblo	PIII	405	tabular pebble with work striations
V:1:144	large cliff dwelling	PIII/IV	274*	small, grooved pebble, not a classic shaft straightener
V:1:145	large cliff dwelling	PIV	421	large tabular piece with worked facets
V:1:147	field house	PIV	286* 287	serpentine pendant fragment small, round pebble, smooth with work striations
V:1:152	medium-sized pueblo	PIV	183	small, rounded pebble, no clear work striations
V:1:159	medium-sized pueblo	PIV?	407*	shaped object, flat facet, fire cracked, groove, probably a shaft straightener
V:1:169	large pueblo	PIII/IV	278	9 pieces; 3 are tabular with work facets, others smooth and rounded; 1 has a groove from and abrader or shaft straightener
V:1:186	large pueblo	PIII?	458	smooth, flat pebble, no clear work striations
V:1:190	compound	PIII	592*	shaft straightener, fire-cracked
V:5:61	large cliff dwelling	PIV	1*	shaft straightener on small pebble
Isolate			283*	large, shaped block with hole bored in one end; some notches in edges, hafting grooves?

*Note: artifact(s) illustrated in Figure 8.5.

the exterior Front wall of Room 6 at the Ringtail Ruin (V:1:132; CD25-26). Thus, they appear to be offerings for the structure or the site. Both pieces have been shaped and are nearly complete. One is perforated, while the perforated area of the other may have broken off. These shells may have been pendants or ear ornaments. Both pieces are somewhat discolored, due to smoke or exposure. The shells were examined by Arthur Vokes of the Arizona State Museum. Although they are a bit anomalous, there is no reason to believe they are not prehistoric. Both are freshwater, nacreous shells, but are more massive than usually associated with the local species (*Anodonta californiensis*). Vokes noted there are more massive varieties in the Rio Grande drainage in New Mexico, but that without the hinge area, a more specific identification is impossible (see SAP archives).

Other shell collected included fragments of bracelets and other worked pieces (Table 8.5, Fig. 8.6). The species present are virtually identical to those at Canyon Creek Ruin (Haury 1934:128). Many of the SAP shell artifacts are of species and objects typical of Hohokam shell assemblages (Haury 1976:305-321). They were probably obtained through trade with Hohokam populations in the Tonto Basin or with indigenous Tonto Basin populations who acquired the shell objects from the Hohokam of the Tonto or Phoenix basins.

HUMAN BONE

Several human bones were collected by SAP. The reason the bone was evident on the surface was due to vandalism and the disturbance of burials. Human remains were collected from three sites—two cliff dwellings (the Devils Chasm Fortress [V:1:167] and Hematite House [V:5:61]) and one surface pueblo (Pottery Point Pueblo [V:1:166]). The human remains were collected to prevent them from being collected illegally or destroyed by humans or natural processes.

From Hematite House and Pottery Point are isolated skeletal elements. From Hematite House (IN 7), there is a proximal phalange (finger) from a young adult. At Pottery Point (IN 584), three pieces were found—a maxilla, a parietal, and a portion of a femur—all from young adults.

The human remains from the Devils Chasm Fortress came from Rooms 1, 3, and 7. There is a hole in Room 7 that clearly is a vandal hole and probably was the location of the burial. Many skeletal elements had been removed, or are still

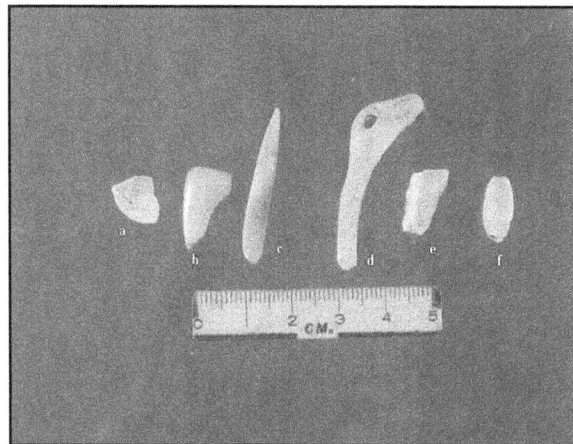

Figure 8.6. SAP Shell Artifacts: a = IN 288, b = IN 285, c = IN 279, d = IN 277, Glycymeris bracelet fragment; e = IN 277, Glycymeris; f = IN 135, Olivella bead (2004-1733-image3975)

buried in the room. Two pelvis bones were determined to be from the same approximately 45 to 49 year old female, who had carried a child or given birth at some point in her life. There were also skull fragments and three rib fragments, some of which show evidence of post-mortem burning. There was a forest fire that destroyed much of the roofing in this site, and could have impacted loose or unburied bones on the floors as the roofing material collapsed. It is likely that all of the bones come from a single individual, but this is not certain at this time.

Table 8.5. Freshwater and Marine Shell from SAP Sites

Site	Inventory Number	Genus/Species	Artifact type
V:1:26	135	Olivella	shell bead
V:1:132	613	Anodonta californiensis?	pendants?
V:1:135	285	Conus	worked shell/tinkler fragment
V:1:144	277	Glycymeris	bracelet fragments; perforated umbo
V:1:144	279	Glycymeris?	reworked bracelet fragment, into awl or punch
V:1:144	288	Glycymeris (juvenile)	possible bead

Human burials were found downslope at Canyon Creek Ruin (Haury 1934:144), interred into a formal terrace. No such features are evident in the Sierra Ancha cliff dwellings, so the locations of most burials associated with these sites is unknown.

MACROBOTANICAL REMAINS

As is typical in dry, protected sites, preservation of perishable materials is enhanced. SAP did not formally sample these materials, but a number of them were often seen on the surface. These were collected because they were fragile (for example, textiles) and likely to be collected by visitors or further disturbed and destroyed by rodents and insects. The types of plant remains recovered are listed by site in Table 8.6.

Abundant corncobs were also recovered by SAP from many of the sites. Other cobs, collected by USFS personnel, were also turned over to the project. Lisa Huckell examined the materials and identified taxa and plant parts represented in the macrobotanical materials (Appendix IV).

Some of the artifacts are summarized here. Several knots and knotted bundles of agave/yucca fibers were recovered (Fig. 8.7; knots of cleaned [e] and incompletely cleaned [d] agave fiber). One knotted piece may show evidence of direct fire being used to process the fibers (Fig. 8.7c). Also from agave/yucca fibers are sandal fragments (Fig. 8.8), comparable to "finely-woven" sandals at the Lower Tonto Ruin (Pierson 1962:55; Plate 13 D and E). A nearly complete sandal was collected from the Ringtail Ruin (V:1:132; Fig. 8.9). It is very similar to the coarser weave sandals depicted by Pierson (1962:55; Plate 13 A, B, and C), also from the Lower Tonto Ruin. The final example of artifacts from agave and yucca is a ready-made needle and thread (Fig. 8.10). This clever artifact was made from an agave leaf, with the terminal point intact, by twisting the fibers together after the tissue was removed. Similar artifacts are referred to at the Lower Tonto Ruin (Pierson 1962:59).

University of Arizona Agricultural Experimental Station botanist J.J. Thornber identified *Apocynum* fiber as a major component of the fiber-based artifacts at Canyon Creek Ruin (Haury 1934:86, 101-102). Huckell (Appendix IV) identified no *Apocynum*-based artifacts in the SAP collections; however, Teague identified at least one textile as *Apocynum* fiber (Appendix V).

Figure 8.11 shows some typical roofing materials from the tertiary and finish components (see the discussion of roof components in Chapter 6). This particular set of materials is from V:1:164, one of the higher elevation cliff dwellings. The materials include entire clumps of grass, sticks and stalks, and finally the clay that sealed it all and formed the roof or floor.

Other plant parts were modified or combined to form tools and other artifacts. Figure 8.12 shows possible weaving tools. A "fire hearth" and small bow, possibly a child's toy, are shown in Figure 8.13. The length of the bow is approximately 30cm. Bohrer (1962:82, Plate 1 d, e, and f) illustrates similar "fire hearths" from Tonto National Monument. Two are agave stalks, and one is saguaro rib. The SAP specimen was identified by Lisa Huckell as an agave or beargrass (*Nolina*) stalk. Bohrer (1962:86; Plate 3a) illustrates a small bow, but it is much longer, approximately 45 cm.

Figure 8.14 shows the same small SAP bow (Fig. 8.14a), and a fragment of a cane arrow with a hafted hard wood foreshaft (Fig. 8.14b). Bohrer (1962:84-85) discusses the bows and arrows found at Tonto National Monument. In the Tonto cliff dwellings, the arrows were constructed in identical fashion, and some are complete enough to show that no stone point was hafted to the foreshaft. Citing ethnographic records, Bohrer believes such arrows were used for hunting small game. The Tonto arrows were commonly painted; the fragment of an arrow from the SAP cliff dwelling shows no evidence of painting. Figure 8.14a(c) is another stick with attached ties. Its function is uncertain; it could be part of another small bow.

Table 8.6. Macrobotanical Remains at SAP Sites

MATERIAL TYPE	SITE	INVENTORY NUMBERS	MATERIAL TYPE	SITE	INVENTORY NUMBERS
General botanical	GP C:1:16	478, 483, 485	Roofing Material	AZ V:1:135	31, 56
	AZ V:1:26	138			
	AZ V:1:130	205, 206	Pot Plugs	AZ V:1:131	212, 213
	AZ V:1:131	88, 101, 207, 588		AZ V:1:132	513
	AZ V:1:132	76, 81, 82, 83, 100, 102, 202		AZ V:1:162	121
	AZ V:1:133	90, 477		AZ V:1:164	280, 583
	AZ V:1:134	94, 96, 211, 476, 479, 480, 612			
	AZ V:1:135	43, 45, 46, 47, 48, 49, 50, 51, 52, 53, 54, 55, 139, 292, 293, 294	Ties	AZ V:1:131	72
				AZ V:1:134	67
				AZ V:1:168	115
	AZ V:1:136	104, 300			
	AZ V:1:144	168, 203, 204, 208, 209, 210	Matting	AZ V:1:131	73
	AZ V:1:162	118, 119			
	AZ V:1:164	125, 126, 296, 297, 298, 299, 376, 388, 389, 390, 392, 393, 394, 396, 397	Sandal	AZ V:1:132	89
				AZ V:1:144	508
				AZ V:1:164	295
	AZ V:1:167	91, 106, 114, 493		AZ V:5:61	545
	AZ V:1:168	366, 368, 369, 370, 371, 372, 373, 377, 391, 424, 426, 481	Cotton fabric	AZ V:1:131	99
	AZ V:1:170	142		AZ V:1:132	84, 97, 98
	AZ V:2:1	498		AZ V:1:134	95
	AZ V:2:79	496, 497		AZ V:1:164	375
	AZ V:5:61	103, 387			
			Quids	AZ V:1:134	93, 489
Thread/Cordage	AZ V:1:134	62, 384, 486, 487		AZ V:1:135	291
	AZ V:1:167	491		AZ V:1:167	492
	AZ V:1:168	382, 383, 385, 425		AZ V:1:168	367, 378, 428
	AZ V:5:61	8, 594		AZ V:2:79	495
				AZ V:5:61	488, 546
Corn cobs	GP C:1:16	475			
	AZ V:1:133	500	Bulk Cotton	AZ V:1:134	482
	AZ V:1:134	92, 499		AZ V:1:144	365
	AZ V:1:162	123		AZ V:1:168	386
	AZ V:1:164	374, 395		AZ V:5:61	512
	AZ V:1:167	490			
	AZ V:1:168	381, 429	Wood sample	AZ V:1:132	86, 87
	AZ V:1:188	459		AZ V:1:145	398, 399
	AZ V:2:79	494			

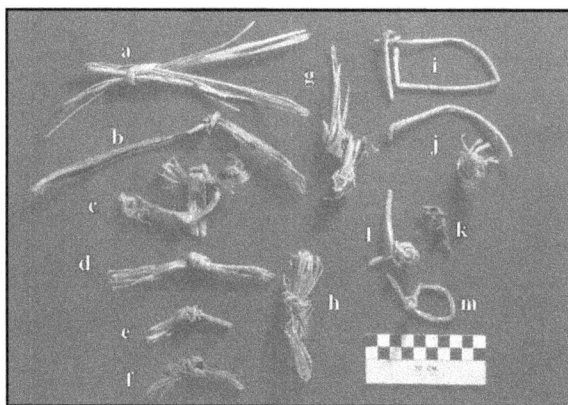

Figure 8.7. SAP Macrobotanical Materials – Knots: a = IN 125, b-c = IN 67, d = IN 448, e = IN 142, f = IN 387, g = IN 392, h = IN 204, i = IN 205, j = IN 115, k = IN 126, l = IN 206, m = IN 448 (2004-1733-image3734)

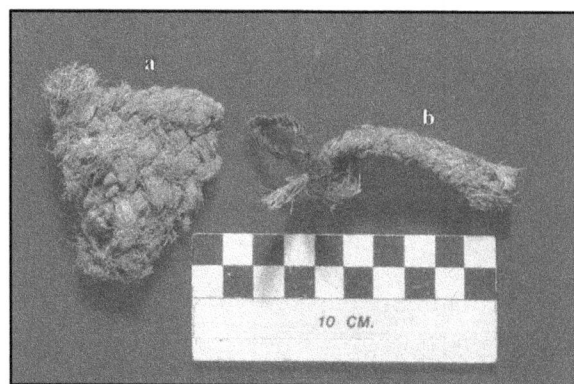

Figure 8.8. SAP Macrobotanical Materials – Sandal Fragments: a = IN 73, b = IN 295 (2004-1733-image3726)

Figure 8.9. SAP Macrobotanical Materials – Sandal:
IN 89, from AZ V:1:132 (ASM)
a. Top view (2004-1733-image3721)

Figure 8.9. SAP Macrobotanical Materials – Sandal:
IN 89, from AZ V:1:132 (ASM)
b. Bottom view (2004-1733-image3722)

Figure 8.10. SAP Macrobotanical Materials
– Agave Needle-and-Thread:
IN 125 (2004-1733-image2039)

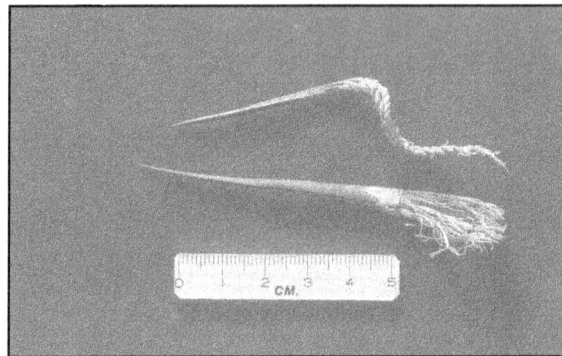

Figure 8.11. SAP Macrobotanical Materials – Roofing Materials, Adobe pieces = IN 56, remainder = IN 299
(2004-1733-image4138)

TEXTILES

Cordage and textiles from the SAP sites were examined by Lynn Teague. Her full report is given in Appendix V; a brief summary is presented here. Textiles and cordage were recovered from five sites, Teague's analysis concerns materials from just three of the sites: V:1:131, V:1:134, and V:1:136.

Several masses of fiber and textiles destroyed by rodents were recovered (for example, Fig. 8.15). The fibers are consistent with the typical aboriginal cotton, *Gossypium hirsutum*. Cordage is also present at many sites (Fig. 8.16). It is made of leaf and stem fibers from plants such as yucca, agave, milkweed, and Indian hemp or *Apocynum*. These fibers were sought for cordage because of their strength. One fragment was identified as *Apocynum*, relatively rare in the SAP collections, but abundant at Canyon Creek Ruin (Haury 1934:86, 101-102). Some of the cordage was dyed orange or red (Fig. 8.16).

Seven separate pieces of cloth seem to be represented in the SAP collections, but they are so fragmentary that their original use or function is uncertain. Teague found the SAP fabrics to be broadly similar to those of other traditions below the Mogollon Rim and above the Mexican border (Appendix V). The SAP fabrics are not dissimilar to other US Southwestern traditions—Anasazi, Hohokam, Salado, and Sinagua, but there are differences. This SAP sample shows only woven cotton fibers, and only plainweave structures (Fig. 8.17 and CD27). Yarns tend to be fine, and the absolute frequencies of warps and wefts are low. Finally, the SAP assemblage lacks strongly warp-dominant fabrics typical of some sites in the area north of Mexico and south of the Mogollon Rim. Additional textiles that might someday be collected from the SAP sites would help to better characterize this assemblage, and determine if these perceived differences with the other traditions are real.

Figure 8.12. SAP Macrobotanical Materials – Weaving Tools: a = IN 293, b = IN 390 (2004-1733-image4142)

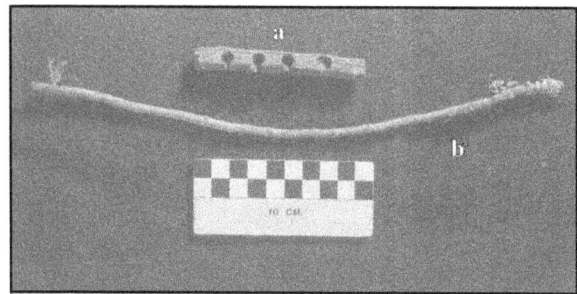

Figure 8.13. SAP Macrobotanical Materials – Miniature Bow and Fire Hearth: a = IN 366, b = IN 126 (2004-1733-image3717)

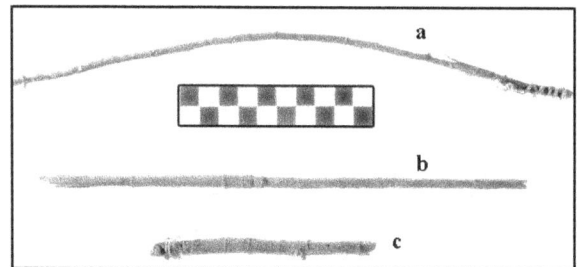

Figure 8.14. SAP Macrobotanical Materials – Bow and Arrow Foreshaft
a. Miniature Bow and Arrow Shafts: [a = IN 126, b = IN299, c = IN 62] (2004-1733-image4143)

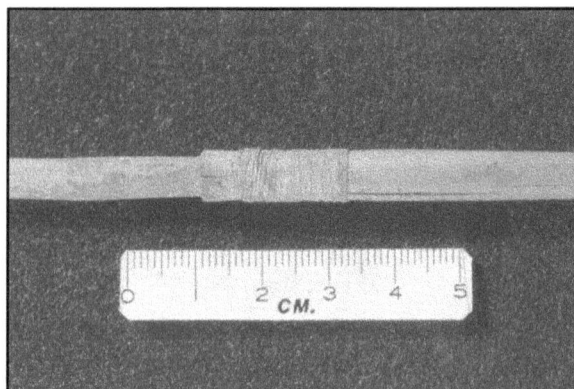

Figure 8.14. SAP Macrobotanical Materials – Bow and Arrow Foreshaft b. Detail – Arrow Foreshaft, IN 299 (2004-1733-image3712)

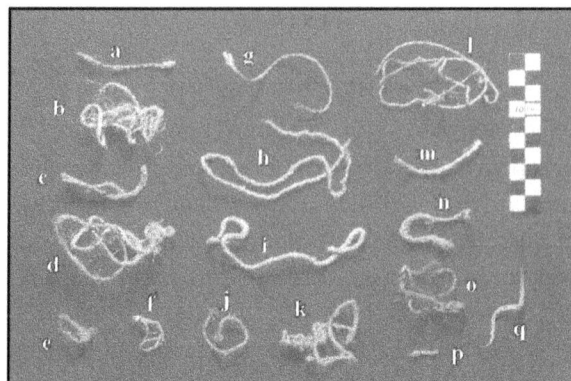

Figure 8.16. SAP Cordage: a-b = IN 424, c = IN 95, d-e = IN 425, f = IN 91, g = IN 294, h = IN 486?(C:1:23), i-k = IN 211, l = IN 377, m = IN 96, n = C:1:23 L4, o = IN 8, p = IN C:1:44 L1, q = IN 125 (2004-1733-image3740)

Figure 8.15. SAP Textiles – Cotton and Textile Mass Disturbed by Rodents, IN 91 (2004-1733-image3741)

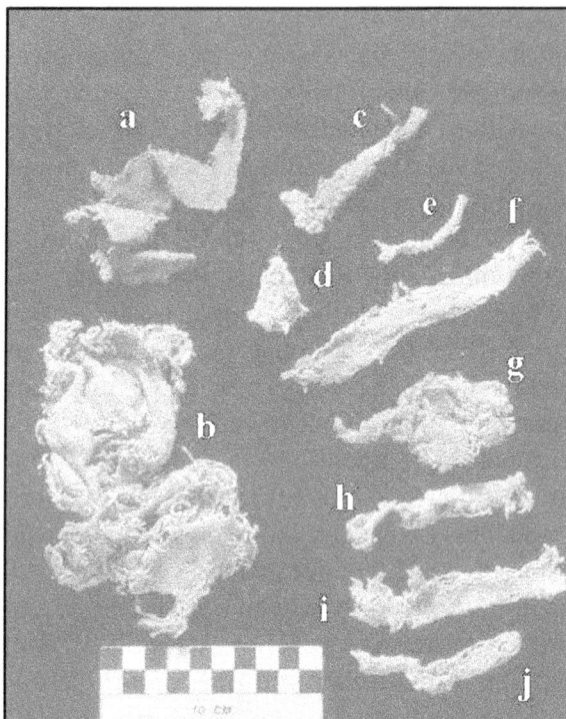

Figure 8.17. SAP Textiles -- Miscellaneous Textiles: a = IN 202, b = C:1:23, c = IN 84, d = IN 211, e = IN 54, f-j = IN 95 (2004-1733-image3720)

Chapter Nine

Rock Art and Wall Painting in the Southeastern Sierra Ancha

Christine H. Virden-Lange

INTRODUCTION

The Sierra Ancha mountain range cuts a swath across central Arizona, stretching from the Mogollon Rim on the north to the Salt River on the south, and from Tonto Creek on the west to Cherry Creek on the east. For thousands of years, people have had knowledge of this mountain range and of Cherry Creek, huddled in the shadow of the Sierra Ancha. We know this because of the images on stone that they left behind them—both petroglyphs and pictographs.

Petroglyphs, most of which are deeply pecked, wide, and patinated over by time, are found along the edges of Cherry Creek. The older, heavily patinated petroglyphs of abstracts, including grids, rakes, ladders and atlatls, can probably be attributed to the Western Archaic Tradition (Schaafsma 1980:34-43; Thiel 1995:63) with later contributions from culture groups such as the Hohokam and the Mogollon. Pictographs in red, white, black, and yellow pigments can be found in the shelter of the cliff dwellings, particularly in Pueblo Canyon. Pictograph styles include the Mogollon Red (Schaafsma 1980:187) and Canyon Creek Polychrome Pictograph (Weaver 1991a:4) traditions, however, these styles do not fully describe the pictographs in Pueblo Canyon.

The purpose of this chapter is to discuss the petroglyphs and pictographs found in sites in the southeastern Sierra Ancha. To identify the pictographs in Pueblo Canyon, the Pueblo Canyon Style is defined in this chapter. Wall painting, mostly limited to Pueblo Canyon, is also discussed in this chapter.

BACKGROUND HISTORY

The history of the research in the Sierra Ancha is discussed in Chapter 1. Regarding research on rock art in the region, however, very little has been done. Byron Cummings (1930:42, 1931-1936) mentions the presence of rock art along Cherry Creek, south of the Ellison Ranch, as well as Haury (1934), who did basic documentation of the rock art at Canyon Creek Ruin and in the Sierra Ancha. No formal survey has been undertaken to find and document these sites.

The SAP has provided an opportunity to better document and research the rock art located at Pueblo Canyon and along Cherry Creek. Over the years, many volunteers from Earthwatch, the Arizona Archaeological Society, the Arizona Archaeological and Historical Society, friends, and spouses have assisted in the process. Rock art in the southeastern Sierra Ancha has been documented photographically, and two of the sites have been recorded in detail.

In years past, the study and documentation of rock art has taken a back seat to other archaeological interests such as habitation sites or architectural features. Professional archaeologists are becoming more aware of the value of rock art in the archaeological record and its contributions to the understanding of cultures and changes through time. For example, Wallace and others have noted a similarity between isolated Hohokam/Gila style rock art elements and design elements on Hohokam ceramics (Wallace, Heidke and Doelle 1995:601). And, at Homol'ovi, the arrival of the katsina cult is clearly evident in the rock art (Cole 1992) as well as in architectural and ceramic remains.

ROCK ART TECHNOLOGY AND TERMINOLOGY

Two types of rock art occur in the vicinity of the eastern flank of the southern Sierra Ancha – petroglyphs and pictographs. Petroglyphs occur in the lower elevations along Cherry Creek, whereas the pictographs and wall painting occur in the higher elevations in the rockshelters and within the cliff dwellings themselves.

Petroglyphs

Petroglyphs (Figs. 9.1 and 9.2) are created by removing the outer cortex of a boulder or rock face in a controlled manner in order to reveal the interior matrix of the rock face (Cole 1992:7; Schaafsma 1980:1). The interior is usually a different color, and thus enhances the design that is created. Occasionally, softer sedimentary or volcanic rocks were used as well, and the elements could be cut or incised into the soft matrix (Thiel 1995:5).

Several methods can be used to create petroglyphs. A direct percussion method (use of a pecking rock) or indirect method of percussion (using an intermediate tool such as a chisel) can be used to chip off the cortex. Incising or scratching can be done on the softer rock surfaces using a stone flake or other hard substance such as a deer antler or bone. Grind-

Figure 9.1. Archaic Rock Art in Cherry Creek (AZ V:1:161 [ASM]) (2004-1733-image4118)

ing the surface with another rock can create a petroglyph by abrasion. Over time, rock varnish acts to coat the exterior of a boulder or rock face, and over long periods of time, can re-cover the petroglyph.

The petroglyphs along Cherry Creek are made using the direct percussion method. Utilizing nearly vertical rock faces as a canvas upon which to work, designs and motifs were created over the centuries. These panels are south or west facing (toward the creek) and were created on the darker portions of the stone in order to have a more dramatic effect. Rock varnish is already covering some of the older elements, making them essentially the same color as the original rock. Relative dating of some of the glyphs is possible, based on more recently added elements having less re-patination.

Figure 9.3. Pictographs in Pueblo Canyon (AZ V:1:260 [ASM]) – Pueblo Canyon Style (2004-1733-image3837)

Figure 9.2. Archaic Rock Art in Cherry Creek (AZ V:1:160 [ASM]) (2004-1733-image1596)

Pictographs

Pictographs are paintings on the rock surface (Fig. 9.3 and CD28). They can be monochrome, bichrome, or polychrome. Common pigments used for pictographs include red ochre, hematite or iron oxide for the red paint; any chalky rock, ash from a wood fire, or kaolin clay for white; charcoal for black; limonite for yellow; malachite or copper-rich rocks for green; and azurite for blue. The pigment was prepared by pounding or grinding it to a fine powder. A binder needs to be added to carry the pigment. Substances used as binding agents have included animal fat, water, blood, or eggs (Sanger and Meighan 1990:26). The use of a binder improves the consistency of the pigment

and can also aid in its preservation. Various techniques have been used to apply the paint, including fingers, hands, and brushes, and even blowing paint through a tube or by mouth. Most of the pictographs were made by simply putting pigment on a finger tip, using the finger as the drawing tool. In a few instances where white pigment was used, it appears as if the artist used a brush of some sort. Brushes could be made from yucca, agave, sotol or hair (either human or animal). Negative handprints are present, and were made by blowing paint with the mouth or through a tube to spray white paint over the hand, leaving a negative print.

It appears that the notion of using contrasting colors to enhance the paintings was utilized in this medium as well as in the creation of the petroglyphs. The basalt, argillite, and quartzite formations at the elevations of the cliff dwellings are not conducive to petroglyphs—they are extremely hard and would be difficult to peck or scrape to create images. Pigments or paints were chosen that created the best contrast on the rock surface. An example of a pictograph created with red pigment is shown in CD28.

Terminology

Interpreting the designs or elements in rock art

can be problematic. However, a term needs to be applied to an element to identify it for discussion and recording purposes, and that term needs to be something that can be readily understood. Thus, terminology has developed over time as a means of describing the iconography depicted on rock faces.

Rock art symbols have been categorized by researchers as being abstract or representational, geometric, human-like (anthropomorphic) or animal-like (zoomorphic) as they appear on the rock surface (Thiel 1995:3). Anthropomorphs and zoomorphs are also called "life-forms." Thus, those are the categories or terms assigned to the elements for this report. Meaning, of course, is subjective at best – one person's "squiggle" is another's "snake". Rather than trying to interpret what the element is intended to represent (for example, a snake), a descriptive term is applied instead – squiggle. Table 9.1 presents a list of selected rock art terms and definitions used in this report.

It is not known what function petroglyphs and pictographs served, however it is not unusual to find them along waterways such as creeks and rivers or next to seeps (Schaafsma 1980:45; Schoonover 2003:47; Schoonover and Virden 1999:231), which could imply their association with water or trails. Interpretations have been suggested for many of the elements, which may represent a wide range of things, including doodling, ritual and ceremonial markings, trail markers, and the recording of events (Schoonover 2003:12). Perhaps some of the motifs serve as maps, with individual elements representing topographical features and spatial orientation (Dockal and Smith 2005:420). Other designs could represent boundary markers or territorial markers as a signal to passers-by (Schoonover and Virden 1999:247; Thiel 1995:54); still other motifs could be personal identifiers to let people know who had been there. Perhaps they are portraying a ceremony of some sort, while others may be clan symbols (Colwell-Chanthaphonh 2003:18).

Dating Techniques

Absolute dating techniques for rock art are in the experimental stage. Just a few of the techniques will be mentioned here, including cation ratios, accelerator mass spectrometry, lead dating and microlaminations (see also Thiel 1995:44-51). Ronald Dorn has been experimenting with different techniques involving samples of rock varnish to deter-

Table 9.1. List of selected terms and definitions (adapted from Thiel 1995:3)

Term	Definition
Abstract element	Not recognizable as having a pictorial representation
Anthropomorph	A human-like figure
Element	An image or design created by painting, pecking, or incising
Geometric element	An element created by using geometric shapes such as circles, rectangles, triangles, and squares
Representational element	One that represents animals, plants, humans, geographical features, or astronomical events
Zoomorphic element	An animal-like figure

mine the minimum age for the rock art using cation-ratio dating "...to establish a relative sequence of ages in a given area, that can be calibrated by numerical dating methods such as radiocarbon" (Dorn 1983:49-73). He also has used accelerator mass spectrometry to date organic matter collected from underneath the varnish, encapsulated after the varnish started to grow (Patterson 1992: xi). Dorn has discovered it is possible, but unusual, for rock varnish to form within 100 years given the right conditions (Dorn 2005:9). More recently, however, Dorn has acknowledged that there is no single method that is widely accepted. He suggests "two relatively inexpensive strategies that have been replicated by a variety of laboratories which are "lead dating" and "microlaminations," both of which use properties of rock coatings (varnish/patina) that have formed over the top of the petroglyph (Dorn 2005:9). "Microlaminations... is a strategy that looks at the nature of layers formed in the rock coatings on the petroglyphs" (Dorn 2005:9). In order to obtain a sample for analysis by any of these methods, a specimen of the glyph must be removed. Absolute dates can be obtained for some pictographs and room wall paintings based on tree-ring dating of ceiling beams, radiocarbon or archeomagnetic dating of hearths associated with those rooms, and potential radiocarbon dating of organically-based pigments (Thiel 1995:50).

Another method that can useful in dating petroglyphs is called lichenometry (Burton 1988:273). It is a method that can provide estimations of the age of lichen patches on rock, which then might provide end bracket dates when lichen grows over petroglyph elements. In some cases, a site will contain glyphs that are superimposed over another glyph, therefore it can be inferred that the glyphs covering the others are not as old as the ones underneath. In other instances, at a particular site the glyphs

may be higher up the face of the rock wall than others that are lower on the wall nearer the present ground surface, indicating that the higher glyphs are probably older than the lower glyphs in age, as the present ground surface can be lower due to causes such as flooding and erosion (Schoonover 2003:11). Relative dates can sometimes be assigned to petroglyphs and pictographs that may be associated with habitation sites. Datable ceramics can provide a temporal placement for the rock art; however, such dates should be applied cautiously, because the ceramics may have come from an earlier or later occupation and not be related to all of the rock art. Researchers continue to experiment with ways to date pictographs, but unfortunately, many techniques involve destructive methods to extract paint or other components (Urban 2004:3). Destruction of all or parts of the rock art clearly is not an ideal situation for getting chronological information.

ROCK ART AND WALL PAINTING OF THE SOUTHEASTERN SIERRA ANCHA

In the southeastern Sierra Ancha, the petroglyphs seem to occur mainly in open areas, such as on boulders and rock outcrops along Cherry Creek. There are no examples of this art form occurring in Pueblo Canyon or any of the other cliff dwelling locations, or in the cliff dwellings at Canyon Creek (Haury 1934:140). The location along Cherry Creek can be considered a public area that is unrestricted for viewing, and thus can be viewed by anyone. On the other hand, the pictographs in the southeastern Sierra Ancha occur at the cliff dwellings. Thus, only the residents and their visitors to the cliff dwellings would have knowledge of the pictographs. Some of these paintings appear to have restricted viewing within the cliff dwelling.

Recording and Analysis

The Sierra Ancha and nearby areas have not been systematically surveyed for rock art, thus the number of rock art sites is unknown. Several petroglyph sites along Cherry Creek do have site numbers assigned to them and, though not formally recorded, have been partially photographically documented as part of the SAP. These include V:5:160, V:5:161, and V:5:250 which consist of multiple panels of sometimes deeply pecked and heavily patinated petroglyphs. Pictographs are known from several of the cliff dwellings, including V:1:130, V:1:131, and V:1:132 in Pueblo Canyon. There are also pictographs at GP C:1:50 and V:1:188. Haury (1934) also noted pictographs at GP C:1:67, but this small cliff dwelling has not been relocated.

In 1984, pictographs in Pueblo Canyon in the three pueblo room blocks were formally documented. A long string was attached to the ceiling with masking tape above the pictograph locations. Then, 1.5- to 2m-long strings 50 centimeters apart were hung from this long string to make a grid. A sketch map (close to scale) was drawn of each panel, using the grid as a reference. Each grid was labeled alphabetically (A, B, C, and so on), and recording and photography was done in reference to each grid. Scale drawings were made if possible. When drawings were not made to scale, measurements were given of the elements. The declination and inclinations were recorded for each panel as well. Colors of pigments were noted on the drawings, using a Munsell color chart to identify the variable colors of the red paint used. The white paint was consistent and was not keyed with the Munsell color charts. Since the initial recording, digital photographs have been taken (2004) and are archived with the other SAP materials.

Element count sheets used on this record-ing project were created by Jane Kolber (2004: I). Kolber's form is similar to forms developed by other researchers (Ferg 1979; Thiel 1995; Wallace 1989) in attempts to standardize element categories for comparisons among sites. There will certainly be some variation of elements from one site to the next, but it is important to recognize similarities in order to determine cultural affiliation based on style. Illustrations of the elements are beneficial for synthesizing the data. Table 9.2 lists and illustrates the rock art elements found in the southeastern Sierra Ancha.

A few notes regarding recording conventions followed in this study are necessary. When counting elements, occurrences of each discrete pictograph are counted. For example, a chain of circles or a line of dots is considered to be one element or pictograph, although it is made up of many individual circles that are connected or individual dots. However, when counting the short, vertical lines, each line was counted as one element.

In the instances where the rock art had been previously documented, records were organized by site, room, and panel for tabulation. In the cases where the rock art was not already documented, available photographs were examined to identify the elements involved. To provide comparisons to other rock art summaries (for example, Thiel 1995), the elements were tabulated (see Table 9.3) by categories such as anthropomorph (anything human-like, including hand prints), zoomorphic (anything representing an animal or quadruped, bird, or insect) and geometric (lines, circles, rakes). The medium used to create the pictographs was noted as well. The historic and modern graffiti was counted also – historic was classified by associated dates as anything prior to 1950, while modern was classified as post-1950. The medium used was also identified for the graffiti.

Table 9.2. Rock Art Elements in the Southeastern Sierra Ancha

a. Dot	b. Row of Dots	c. Outlined Circle	d. Solid Circle	e. Connected Circles	f. Fringed Circle	g. Rayed Circle	h. Tailed Circle
i. Appendaged Circle	j. Circle Cluster	k. Dotted Pattern	l. Semi-circle	m. Semi-circle with Dot	n. Appendaged Semi-circle	o. Oval	p. Straight Line
q. Curved Line	r. Concentric Arcs	s. Angle	t. Chevron	u. S-Curve	v. S-Curve with Angles	w. Zigzag	x. Diagonal
y. Parallel Lines	z. Cross	aa. Negative Cross	bb. Asterisk	cc. Dotted Line	dd. T Shape	ee. Squiggle	ff. Squiggle-horned
gg. Squiggle with Outlined Circle	hh. Complex Abstract Design	ii. Attached Squared Spirals/ Spirals	jj. Rake	kk. One-pole Ladder	ll. Two-pole Ladder	mm. Solid Rectangle	nn. Appendaged Rectangle
oo. Rectangular Design—Closed	pp. Triangle	qq. Amorphic Shape	rr. Unidentified Shape	ss. Unidentified Painting	tt. Human-like/ Anthropomorph	uu. Human-like/ Anthro with Head Ornament	vv. Human-like/ Anthro – incomplete
ww. Human-like/ Anthro–attached	xx. Human-like/ Anthro – round belly	yy. Stick Figure	zz. Quadruped	aaa. Insect-like Figure	bbb. Reptile-like Figure	ccc. Life-form/ Biomorph	ddd. Life-form/ Biomorph – splayed legged
eee. Life-form/ Biomorph – incomplete	fff. Hand Print	ggg. Negative Handprint	hhh. Inverted Basket Shape	iii. Bisected Circles	jjj. Atlatl	kkk. Footprints	lll. Concentric Circles

Table 9.3. Distribution, Element Count, and Medium Used in Pueblo Canyon Pictographs

SITE*	ROOM	Anthropomorph	Zoomorph	Geometric	Historic	Modern	Total	Medium**
V:1:260	outside	15	2	21	0	0	38	W
V:1:132	6,8	11	1	155	43	4	214	W, R, O, B, C, CH
V:1:132	9,10	1	0	74	0	0	75	W, R, Y, B
V:1:132	10/11	0	1	18			19	W, R
V:1:131	2	3	0	32	0	0	35	W, R
V:1:131	3/4	0	0	4	0	0	4	W, R
V:1:131	5/6	3	0	47	1	4	55	W, R, O, S, C, Pn
V:1:131	7	0	0	36	0	2	38	W, R, P, S
V:1:131	8A	2	3	62	1	4	72	W, R, CH
V:1:131	10	7	1	45	13	43	109	W, R, CH, C, P
V:1:131	11	8	2	108	11	3	132	W, R, CH, P
V:1:131	13	0	0	15	0	0	15	R
V:1:131	14	6	0	31	0	0	37	W, R
V:1:131	21,22	2	0	4	0	0	6	W, R
V:1:130	2	0	0	1	0	0	1	W
V:1:130	10	0	0	1	0	0	1	W
V:1:130	13	1	0	0	0	0	1	W
V:1:130	outside	0	0	0	5	13	18	P, C, CH
TOTAL		59	10	654	74	73	870	

Notes: *All sites are "AZ V:1:xxx(ASM)".
        **Medium: W = white paint; R = red paint; Y = yellow paint; B = black paint; O = orange paint; C = charcoal; CH = white chalk; P = pencil; Pn = pen; S = scratching.

Table 9.4. Distribution of Room Wall Painting and Rock Art by Site

SITE	ROOM	WALL PAINTING	ROCK ART	LOCATION
V:1:167	4	X		Devils Chasm
	6	X		
	11		X	
	15		X	
	16		X	
V:1:168	3		X	Devils Chasm
	4		X	
V:1:260			X	Pueblo Canyon
V:1:132	6	X		Pueblo Canyon
	7	X	X	
	8	X		
	9	X	X	
	10	X		
	19		X	
	24		X	
V:1:131	2		X	Pueblo Canyon
	3/4	?	?	
	5/6	X	X	
	7A		X	
	7B		X	
	8	?	?	
	10A	X	X	
	10B		X	
	11B	X	X	
	14	X	X	
	21		X	
	22		X	
V:1:130	2	X		Pueblo Canyon
	3	X		
	10		X	
	13		X	
V:1:188	2		X	Quail Spring Pasture
GP C:1:50	10A		X	Mustang Ridge
	10B		X	
	11		X	
GP C:1:67			X	Aztec Peak area
V:2:1	16B	X	X	Canyon Creek Ruin
V:5:160			X	Cherry Creek
V:5:161			X	Cherry Creek
V:5:250			X	Cherry Creek
Chalk Creek			X	
Coon Creek			X	
Cueva de las Ventanas		X		Chihuahua, Mexico

Distribution of Rock Art by Site

The distribution of rock art by site is presented in Table 9.4. As noted above, the rock art elements along Cherry Creek are petroglyphs while the elements associated with the cliff dwellings are in the form of pictographs. In Table 9.4, wall painting refers to any lines or figures painted on the interior, stone-masonry walls, while rock art refers to any petroglyphs or pictographs on rock surfaces.

Not all rooms within sites contain walls with wall painting, and wall painting seems to be restricted to several rooms within each site. Eight rooms listed have both pictographs (rock art) and wall painting, while most of the rooms have either wall painting or pictographs, but not both. Sites V:5:160, V:5:161, and V:5:250, Chalk Creek, and Coon Creek are petroglyphs only.

Petroglyphs

The geology along middle Cherry Creek below the second road crossing is more conducive for petroglyphs than the geology above the crossing. V:5:160 and V:5:161 are two sites in close proximity to one another, located on the west side of Cherry Creek, just above the first crossing, while V:5:250 (the "Bob Conforti Site") is located at the base of a cliff located on the east side of Cherry Creek below the first crossing. The first two petroglyph sites have multiple panels (Figs. 9.1 and 9.2) that have elements including squiggles, curvilinear motifs, rows of parallel lines that are framed, connected diamonds, animal and human footprints, rows of parallel squiggles, rows of dots, meandering lines of dots, lizards, holes in the rock that have been outlined, and elements recognized by some researchers as atlatls (Schaafsma 1980). Some of the designs are pecked in clean and heavy lines, which have been patinated over until they are nearly the same color as the natural rock. Some of these glyphs have been super-imposed by glyphs that are less patinated.

The third petroglyph site, V:5:250, has elements that or more typical of the Gila style used by the Hohokam (Fig. 9.4). Other known petroglyph sites with Gila style elements are at Chalk Creek (in a side drainage near its confluence with the Salt River; Fig. 9.5) and Coon Creek (on boulders on the east side of the creek; Fig. 9.6). The petroglyphs at Chalk Creek include squiggles, a scroll, crosses, an outlined cross, concentric circle, centipedes and meanders. All of these elements are spaced close together on the darker varnished area of the rock face. At Coon Creek, the petroglyphs are on a rock outcrop and include lizards, a spiral, and quadrupeds of a sheep/goat type of animal.

Western Archaic Petroglyph Style and the
Abstract Style:

The older elements at V:5:160-161 can be classified as belonging to the Abstract Style of the Western Archaic Tradition (Schaasfma1980:36; Thiel 1995:63) in which most of the elements bear no resemblance to any real life image. Motifs of life forms are lacking and the elements are mainly geometrical. Both the boulder or rock face and the glyph are similar in color, due to re-patination of the rock over time. The elements are pecked using direct percussion in lines that are wider and deeper than those made by later cultures. The elements appear to be both abstract and curvilinear, sometimes in an elaborate design, and include chevrons, circles, cupules, curves, grids, rakes, sectioned rectangles, curvilinear margined grids, curve-backed rakes, geometric figures, snakes, spirals, squiggles, T-shapes, unidentified pecking, U-shapes and zigzags (singular or in sets) (Schoonover 2003:14; Thiel 1995:64). The realistic elements have been identified as atlatls and footprints. The motifs often follow the shape and surface of the rock face,

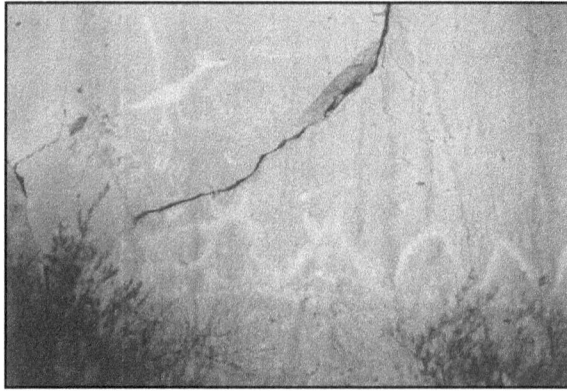

Figure 9.4. Petroglyphs on Cherry Creek – Gila Style (AZ V:5:250 [ASM]) (2004-1733-image4125)

Figure 9.6. Petroglyphs on Coon Creek – Gila Style (2004-1733-image4120)

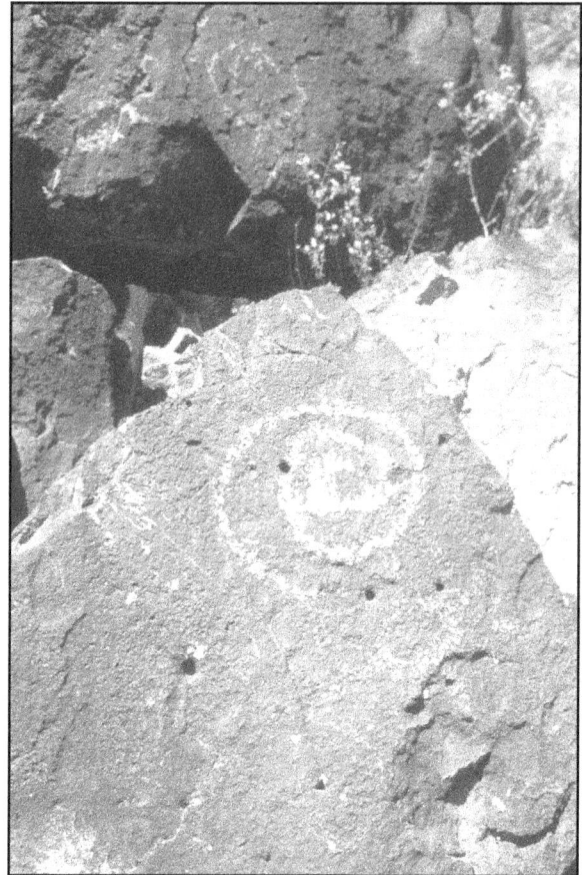

Figure 9.5. Petroglyphs on Chalk Creek – Gila Style (2004-1733-image4123)

integrating cracks, holes and depressions into their designs (this occurs at V:5:161). This style of rock art is considered the oldest and is attributed to the hunter-gatherers of the Greater Southwest somewhere between BC 5500 to AD 100 (Thiel 1995:62) and may have continued into the Hohokam Colonial period or as late as AD 800 (Fig. 9.7). Their nomadic existence would bring them to a particular geographic or ecologically rich area. Cherry Creek would have been a welcome spot to get water and a variety of wild plants and animals for food. It would not be unusual for a nomadic group to re-visit an area on their seasonal rounds and each time leave their mark on the boulders of Cherry Creek. Although evidence for Archaic occupation is sparse, a few sites have been reported with possible Archaic affiliations to

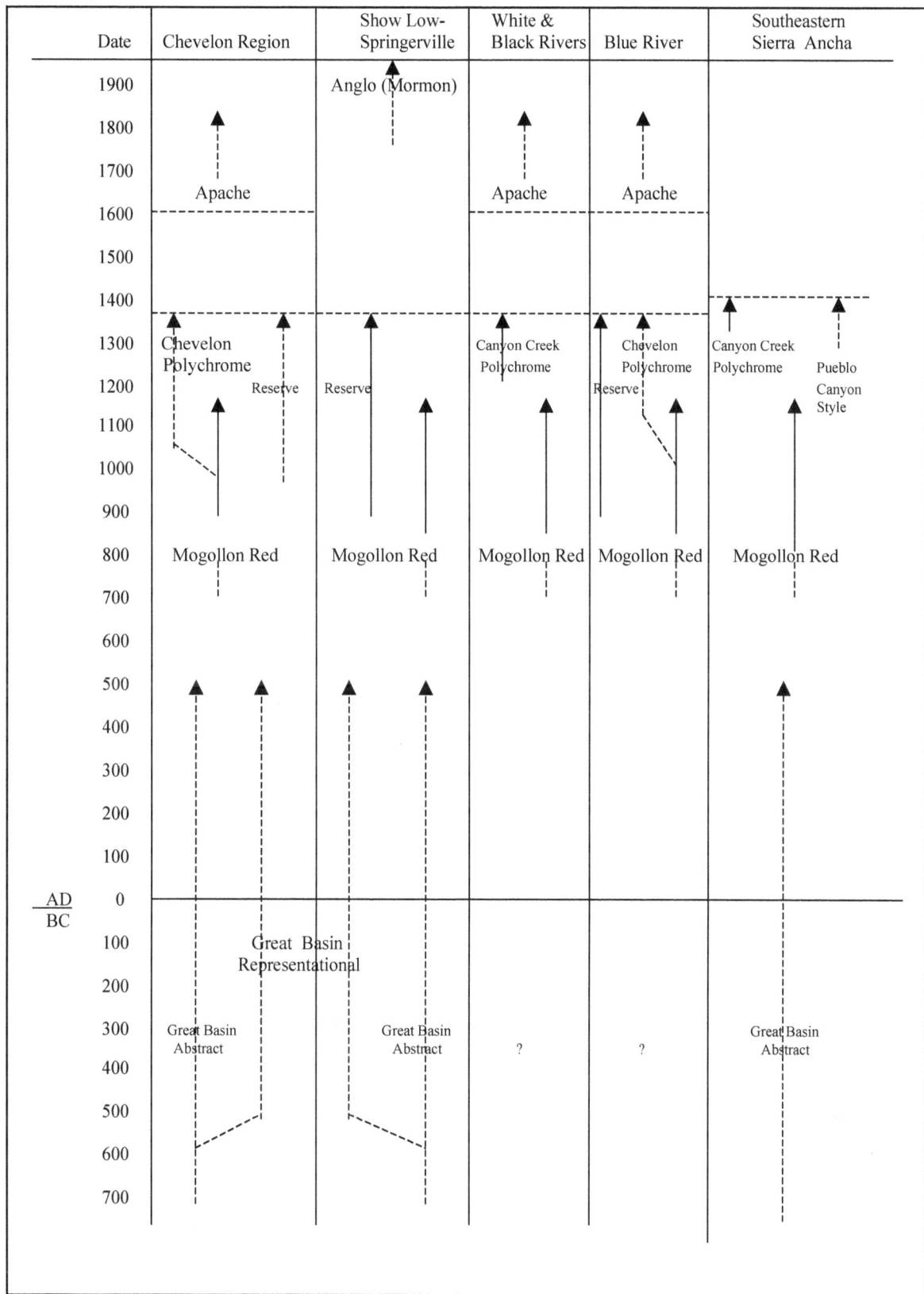

Figure 9.7. Rock Art Chronologies (adapted from Weaver 1991a:10)

the northeast of Cherry Creek in the Vosberg Valley (Reid 1982b:125). Thus, the older rock art elements confirm the movement of the Archaic people through the southeastern Sierra Ancha.

Although there are regional differences, for the most part a similarity in the execution of the designs as well as the design elements themselves is seen. Whether found in the Growler Mountains in Yuma County (AZ), San Diego Mountain and Carrizozo in south-central New Mexico, (Schaasfma 1980:44) or along Cherry Creek in Gila County (AZ) an observer would note designs such as single zigzags, pairs or sets of parallel zigzags, wavy lines, concentric circles, varied grid patterns, circles with dots, rakes and "nets", atlatls, rows of circles, one-pole ladders, and sawtooth elements. Regional differences may be seen in the composition or arrangement of the elements; however, Cherry Creek has many similarities with the site near Carrizozo, New Mexico. For example, both sites are unusual in that they have a large number of imposing rectilinear designs as well as repetitive designs such as sets of parallel wavy lines, triangles/diamonds and circles.

Petroglyph elements can be seen on rock faces along both sides of Cherry Creek. For the most part, rocks that were already dark with patina were chosen as the canvas upon which to create the artistic expressions of those people that came this way. The stark contrast between the darker cortex and lighter interior rock matrix was obviously important. Some of the elements are randomly placed, while others appear to be grouped and related to each other in some fashion.

Representational Style:
Another category of rock art is called representational. The representational style is usually composed of life forms such as anthropomorphs with large hands and feet, supernatural beings,

lizards, snakes, insects, birds, quadrupeds, and plants. Although the subjects represent real objects such as people or animals, they appear to be more stylized, rather than naturalistic. They may represent what is found in the natural environment of a particular area (Schaafsma 1980).

Petroglyphs assigned to the Gila Petroglyph Style of the Hohokam culture group (Schaasfma 1980:83-98) are created in the more natural representational-style, as well as in the geometrical abstract-style discussed above, and are present along Cherry Creek. Petroglyphs at Chalk Creek and Coon Creek, noted above, also represent Hohokam or Gila style. Images of the Gila style include reptiles, birds, insects, anthropomorphs, quadrupeds, curvilinear elements, circles, spirals, scrolls, sunbursts, bull's-eyes, circles attached by lines, meandering lines and outlined crosses (Schaasfma 1980:83; Thiel 1995:73).

The Gila rock art style has components similar to the Mogollon petroglyphs referred to as the Reserve Style (Schaasfma 1992:57-60). Elements represented in the Reserve Style, and post-dating AD 1000 (Fig. 9.7), include stick figures that are not static and are expressive, with hands and feet often exaggerated; life-forms (zoomorphs) including lizards, snakes small animals, birds, quadrupeds; animal tracks, with bear tracks being very important; abstract elements sunbursts, spirals, concentric circles and spoked-cirles, wavy lines, dot rows, rakes and barred elements, with the outlined cross appearing frequently (Schaasfma 1992:59). Schaasfma speculates the content and style of the Reserve Style of petroglyphs is possibly a Mogollon style with Anasazi influence, which also co-occurred with changes in the architecture (from pit houses to surface structures) and ceramics (the addition of black-on-white ceramics after AD 1000).

Elements pecked by the later groups were also created using the direct percussion method, but the depths of the glyphs are shallower than those created by the Archaic people. There are also differences in widths between the earlier and later glyphs. The later glyphs are lighter and do not have the degree of patination that the earlier elements display. Sometimes representatives of both the older and newer styles appear in the same panel or series of elements. The abstract style seems to pre-date the representational style (Schaasfma 1980:45). Table 9.5 presents a list of petroglyph elements found in the Cherry Creek area. This list includes both Archaic and later prehistoric figures. Element counts and summaries are not presented for the petroglyphs at these sites because the sites and elements have not been formally recorded.

Some of the petroglyph elements are seen in the pictographs at Pueblo Canyon and at Canyon Creek Ruin, indicating that some of the petroglyphs may have been created by the same people. Petroglyphs recorded in the nearby Apache-Sitgreaves National Forest to the east of the Sierra Ancha have been identified as belonging to the Great Basin Abstract and Representational style, then the later Reserve style. The pictographs are assigned to Mogollon Red as well as Canyon Creek and Chevelon Polychrome Pictograph styles (Weaver 1991a:9). These petroglyphs are associated with Mogollon habitation sites dating from A.D. 1000 to 1150 with polished plain brown ware, Cibola white ware, and corrugated brown ware (Fig.

9.7; Weaver 1991a:9). Apache Pictograph and Anglo (Mormon) Petroglyph styles have also been recorded in the region (Weaver 1991a:9), but are not known in the southeastern Sierra Ancha.

Cherry Creek Pictographs
Table 9.6 presents a list of elements and symbols used for the element counts that were recorded in Pueblo Canyon. A total of 59 different combinations of colors and elements were recorded during the sessions. Some of the elements were complete, while others appeared to be remnants of elements that had weathered or faded away, leaving only a trace of what had once been, and not enough of the original to determine what had been there.

Tables 9.7 and 9.8 present the distribution and count of the elements by color at Pueblo Canyon and V:1:260, located just to the west of pueblo group V:1:132 and probably associated with that pueblo group. The paint colors include white (kaolin clay?), red (hematite), and yellow (limonite) and black (charcoal?). Samples have not been taken, thus the composition of the colors is speculative. The majority of the elements are identified as geometrics (N=654) (lines, concentric circles, crosses), followed by anthropomorphs (N=59) and zoomorphs (N=10)(see Table 9.3). Rooms 6/8 in V:1:132 (West group) contain the majority of the pictographs in this group (N=214). Rooms 5/6

Table 9.5. Petroglyph Elements in the Cherry Creek Area

Anthropomorphs	One-pole ladders
Atlatls	Rakes
Bubbles	Rayed figure
Concentric circles	Rows of dots
Crosses	Snakes
Dot within a circle	Sunburst
Horizontal and vertical parallel squiggles	Various grid patterns
Horned serpent	Vertical parallel lines
Human foot prints	Water birds
Lizards	Zoomorphs

Table 9.6. Distribution of Elements by Color at Pueblo Canyon (AZ V:1:130, AZ V:1:131, AZ V:1:132, and AZ V:1:260 [ASM])

ELEMENT	RED	WHITE	BLACK	YELLOW	TOTAL COLORS/ ELEMENT
Curved line	x		x		2
Straight line			x		1
Semi-circle			x		1
Appendaged semi-circle	x				1
Appendaged circle		x			1
Parallel lines	x	x	x		3
Dotted lines	x	x			2
Solid rectangle	x	x			2
Appendaged rectangle		x			1
Amorphic shape	x	x			2
Unidentified painting	x				1
Rows of dots	x	x			2
Bubble insect	x				1
Solid circle	x				
Squiggle with tail	x				1
Chevron	x				1
One-pole ladder	x	x			2
Two-pole ladder		x			1
Dotted pattern	x	x			2
Vertical parallel squiggles	x	x	x		3
Horned squiggles		x			1
Cross	x				1
Negative cross	x	x			2
Room line		x			1
Rake	x	x			2
S-curve		x			1
Zigzag		x		x	2
Negative hand print		x			1
Positive hand print		x			1
Tapestry design		x			1
Lizard		x			1
Quadruped		x			1
Connected circles		x			1
Anthropomorph	x	x			2
Curvilinear abstract	x	x			2
Square spirals		x			1
Rayed circle		x			1
Rayed stick figures		x			1
Solid vertical oval		x			1
Snake		x			1
Concentric arc with rays		x			1
Bio-morph		x			1
Insect-like figure		x			1
TOTAL ELEMENTS/COLOR	20	33	5	1	59

in V:1:131 (Central group) contained the most pictographs for the Central group (N=55; Table 9.3). While only three pictographs were associated with the rooms at V:1:130 (East group), 18 historic or modern elements occurred outside of the rooms. There were occurrences of historic (N=74) and modern (N=73) graffiti throughout the three room groups (see Table 9.11). In the West group, the majority of the historic and modern graffiti occurred in Room 5/6, which is where the majority of the prehistoric pictographs occur. In the Central group, most of the historic and modern graffiti occurs in Rooms 10 and 11, which is where the bulk of the prehistoric pictographs occur as well. For the East group, most of the historic and modern graffiti occurs just outside the room block, as do the prehistoric pictographs at this locus. Apparently, certain rock faces were more inviting for painting and writing upon.

The pictographs at Pueblo Canyon are located on the rock surface in the deepest part of the cavern at the back of the cliff dwellings, which is also where the pueblos were built (Figs. III.26, III.27, and III.28) as well as at V:1:260. The pictographs at the pueblos occur either on the rear wall of the room (which is the cliff face) or, where there is a second story, they are near the roofline. Others appear as if the artist was standing on a roof or ladder in order to paint high on the rock surface. There are no petroglyphs in Pueblo Canyon as the rock is too hard to be pecked. Approximately 481 discreet red pictographs were recorded, representing 20 different elements (see Tables 9.7 and 9.9 for the distribution). Also recorded were 19 pictographs in black paint (representing 5 elements), and one in yellow ochre. There were 264 total white pictographs recorded at Pueblo Canyon, representing 33 elements.

In total, there were 786 pictographs representing 59 different elements created using 4 different colors of pigment. Although there are more occurrences of red pictographs, there are fewer types of elements represented as the individual elements used were repeated over and over again. Thus, although there were fewer occurrences of white pictographs, the diversity of elements increased. There were several occurrences of white paint super-positioned over red paint, with only one of red over white (but in this case, the red used was different from the earlier red paint and elements). Some of the pictographs appear to be randomly spaced, while others appear to be grouped and may compose a scene, ritual or ceremonial event (Thiel 1995:54). The following discusses in more detail the various pictographs and possible chronology.

The pictographs in Pueblo Canyon appear to have been made by two different groups of people based on the style of the elements, the colors of paint used, and super-positioning. The older pictographs are of red paint. Some of the red paint is a lighter red to orange. The figures appear to have been created using fingertips or sticks to apply the paint onto the rock surface. The elements are, for the most part, geometric and repetitive, except for one stick figure anthropomorph. Also included are what appear to be randomly placed groups of vertical parallel lines and lines or rows of dots, some of which meander into curvilinear designs. The dots in each row are proportionately similar in size (finger tip point) and are replicated within a group of rows. They are symmetrical and patterned, especially the meandering curvilinear motifs.

The difference in placement and execution between elements looks as if more than one person created the pictographs and at different times. One of the designs looks as if it was applied with a stick and follows the outline of the rock (V:1:131, Room 2; CD31). Another pattern is then painted within this outline, with the whole resembling a woven net. The individual lines in the groups of parallel lines are all about the same length and width, while

Table 9.7. Distribution of Elements by Site, Room, and Color (AZ V:1:260 and AZ V:1:131 [ASM])

SITE*	260		131 2		131 3		131 4		131 5/6		131 7		131 8A		131 10		131 11		131 13		131 14	
ROOM / Element	N	C**	N	C**	N	C**	N	C**	N	C**	N	C**	N	C**	N	C**	N	C**	N	C**	N	C**
Dot/Dots	2	W	6	R													46, 2	R, W				
Row of Dots																					1	W
Outlined Circle			1	R																		
Solid Circle																						
Connected Circles													1, 1	R, W								
Fringed Circle																					1	W
Rayed Circle													1	W								
Tailed Circle			1	R									1	W								
Appendaged Circle															1	W						
Circle Cluster																						
Dotted Pattern																						
Semi-Circle																						
Semi-circle with Dot													1	R							1	R
Appendaged Semi-circle			1	R																		
Oval	1	W															1	W				
Straight Line	2	W											1	R								
Curved Line													1	R			3	R				
Concentric Arcs													2	R	2	W						
Angle																						
Chevron																						
S-Curve	1	W													1	W	1	R				
S-Curve with Angles									2	R							2	R				
Zigzag	1	W																				
Diagonal	3	W											1	R								
Parallel Lines			3	R	3	W	10	R	17, 7	R, W	17, 2	R, W	22	R	17, 9	R, W	35	R	14	R	17	R
Cross											1	R	1	R	2	R					3	R
Negative Cross															6	W					2	W
Asterisk																						
Dotted Line																						
T-Shape																	3	W				
Squiggle	3	W	16	R					11	R			4	R	1	R	2	W				
Squiggle-horned																					1	W
Squiggle with Outlined Circle																	1	W				
Complex Abstract			2	R													2	W			2	W
Attached Squared Spirals	1	W																				
Rake									1	W			1	W								
One-pole Ladder											1	W	2	W	1	W					1	R
Two-pole Ladder																	1	W			1	W

*All sites are "AZ V:1:xxx (ASM)" **C = color: B = black; R = red; W = white; Y = yellow.

Table 9.7. Distribution of Elements by Site, Room, and Color (AZ V:1:260 and AZ V:1:131 [ASM]), cont'd

SITE*	260		131		131		131		131		131		131		131		131		131		131	
ROOM			2		3		4		5/6		7		8A		10		11		13		14	
Element	N	C**	N	C**	N	C**	N	C**	N	C**	N	C**	N	C**	N	C**	N	C**	N	C**	N	C**
Solid Rectangle	1	W																				
Appendaged Rectangle	1	W																				
Rectangular Design—Closed															1	R						
Triangle	1	W																				
Amorphic Shape	3	W							1	W			2 6	R W	1	W	1 6	W R			2	R
Unidentified Shape	1	W															1	W			2	R
Unidentified Painting			2 1	R W					2	R	3 3	R W	5	R	2	R						
Human-like/ Anthropomorph	5	W													1	W	1	W			3	W
									3	W												
Human-like/ Anth with Head Ornament	1	W													1	W	1	W			1	W
Human-like/ Anth incomplete	3	W	1	W																		
Human-like/ Anth attached																					2	W
Human-like/ Anth round belly	1	W																				
Stick Figure																						
Quadruped	2	W											2	W	1	W	2	W				
Insect-like Figure													1	W								
Reptile-like Figure																						
Life-Form/ Biomorph	1	W													1	W						
Life-Form/ Biomorph—Splayed-legged													1	W	2	W					1	W
Life-Form/ Biomorph—incomplete															2	W						
Hand Print																						
Negative Hand Print	1	W	1	W									1	W			2 1	W R				
Inverted Basket Shape																						
SUB-TOTALS	34	W	4 32	W R	3	W	10	R	12 32	W R	6 21	W R	17 10	W R	29 23	W R	20 94	W R	15	R	15 26	W R
TOTAL	34		36		3		10		44		27		57		52		113		15		41	

*All sites are "AZ V:1:xxx (ASM)"   **C = color: B = black; R = red; W = white; Y = yellow.

Table 9.8. Pictographs at AZ V:1:131 (ASM)

ROOM	ELEMENTS AND COMMENTS
2	large, red abstract: curvilinear meanders and straight grid lines framed in a red outline that traces the edge of the rock panel; groups of parallel vertical squiggles (red); group of vertical dotted lines with a horizontal zigzag base; curvilinear meanders of red dots, partial white lifeform superimposed over red squiggles; negative white handprint; incomplete anthropomorph
3	short, white parallel lines
4	short, red parallel lines
5/6	short, red parallel lines; 3 anthropomorphs with head ornaments; numerous parallel red squiggles; white appendaged curvilinear shape; white rake-like object; group of anthropomorphs with head ornaments
7	red cross over white paint; also white elements over red; majority of elements in red paint; white, thick one-pole ladder
8A	most are geometrical or abstract; many are ambiguous; snake with wide body and sun occur in white paint on downward facing surfaces; white figures are superimposed over red painted elements; chain of 4 white circles; vertical red zigzag; negative handprint in white; one pole ladder and quadruped in white; chain of 3 circles with half circle on top and tail below the third circle in red
10	most in white, but numerous vertical parallel lines in red; several lifeforms: anthropomorphs, a quadruped, and several partial lifeforms; 2 crosses in red paint (thin lines) and 6 crosses in white (thick lines); negative cross; possible one-pole ladder; white handprint over white squiggles; two concentric arcs in white, one rayed; historic graffiti
11	mostly geometric or abstract; greatest number of elements; red vertical parallel lines and zigzags; 2 white negative handprints; white anthropomorph; red element like an inverted basket; white dots; paired left and right negative hands in white; insect or reptile element in white; 2-pole ladder; possible lizard, and large-body anthropomorph; anthropomorph with head ornament; historic graffiti
13/14	partial one-pole ladder ; groups of red lines; red rakes; several crosses in red and white; paired anthropomorphs (white); horned squiggle (white); red thick lines over the white squiggle; fringed circle inside a larger shape (white); small anthropomorphs (white); one-pole ladder with solid circle of paint above the bottom rung
21-22	2 negative handprints (white), one may have 6 fingers; asterisk or star (white); 3 red parallel lines

each of the dots in a group is about the same diameter. The spacing is close between the lines or the dots so that it appears each group of elements was created with some purpose in mind such as counting, although the groups are randomly placed on the rock face.

Seven elements are executed in red paint, including an appended semi-circle, a bubble insect, cross, solid circle, squiggle with tail and a curved line. None of these elements are present in white paint (see Tables 9.7 and 9.9). An unidentified element resembling an upside down basket painted in red is replicated in several instances. Eight element types are represented in both red and white paint (anthropomorph, parallel lines, dotted lines, amorphic shape, rows of dots, one-pole ladder, dotted pattern, vertical parallel squiggle, negative cross, curvilinear abstract). Twenty-four element types are represented in white paint only (appendaged circle, appendaged rectangle, two-pole ladder, horned squiggle, rake, s-curve, zigzag, negative and positive hand prints, solid rectangle, tapestry design, lizard, quadruped, connected circles, square spirals, rayed circle, rayed stick figures, solid vertical oval, snake, concentric arcs with rays, biomorph and insect-like figure). Many of the red-painted figures are faint and difficult to see as time and weathering are taking their toll. Others have been painted over by white-painted elements.

The remaining pictographs include five different elements in black (curved line, straight line, semi-circle, parallel lines, and a set of vertical parallel squiggles), and a single occurrence of yellow pigment that was smeared on the wall, in no identifiable shape. Only two elements, parallel lines and vertical parallel squiggles, occurred in red, white, and black paint.

Mogollon Red Pictographs:

The red-painted pictographs can be attributed to the Mogollon Red pictograph style. Schaafsma (1980:187) describes it as small elements painted in red. Mogollon Red is the predominant type of rock painting in the Mogollon highlands, wherever pictographs have been documented. The sites extend from the San Francisco drainage and along the Gila River in New Mexico, into eastern and central Arizona to the Mogollon Rim and below. Schaafsma (1980:191) suggests that it was an enduring style that lasted from about AD 500 to 1250

(see Fig. 9.7), although Martin (1979) suggests dates from 500 BC to AD 1400 (Thiel 1995:86). According to Schaafsma (1980:1919) it may possibly date early in the Mogollon sequence, having derived from the earlier polychromes of the Western Archaic tradition. Steen (1962:4) proposed that sometime after AD 1100, Native Americans migrated from the Gila Valley (which extends northward along the Gila River from Duncan, by the New Mexico border) to settle in the Tonto Basin. If this did occur, it could account for the appearance of Mogollon Red pictographs in the southeastern Sierra Ancha, prior to the establishment of the cliff dwellings at Pueblo Canyon.

More recent fieldwork in east-central Arizona has generated new information on the Mogollon rock art in this region. In addition to the Mogollon Red pictograph style, other styles include the Mogollon Chevelon Polychrome pictograph style (Weaver 1991a,b,c) dating from AD 1100 to 1350; the Mogollon Jornada petroglyph and pictograph styles (New Mexico and southeastern Arizona) dating from AD 1000 to 1450 (Schaafsma 1980:199-242—also known as the Mimbres style); and lastly, the Mogollon Reserve style of petroglyphs found in central-eastern Arizona (Weaver 1991a, b) dating from AD 1000 to 1400 (Fig. 9.7). Table 9.12 presents a distribution of the different Mogollon styles of rock art and how Pueblo Canyon relates to these styles. It appears as if the pictographs in Pueblo Canyon share many commonalities with Mogollon Red, Mogollon Chevelon Polychrome and the Mogollon Reserve style of rock art.

It appears that the red-painted pictographs pre-date not only the white pictographs, but perhaps the cliff dwellings themselves. This speculation is based on multiple occurrences of white pictographs super-positioned over the red elements (CD29-30), with only two occurrences of red over white (found in Rooms 7 and 14 in V:1:131). However, in the cases where

Table 9.9. Distribution of Elements by Site, Room, and Color (AZ V:1:132 and AZ V:1:188 [ASM], and GP C:1:67)

SITE* ROOM Element (N C**)	132 6/7	132 8/9	132 10	132 24	132 24 out	188 2	GP C: 1:6 7?	Total from Table 9.7	TOT (N)	AL† (C**)
Dot/Dots	1 W		2 W, 1 R	12 W				15 W	17,46	W,R
Row of Dots	3 W, 3 R	11 W, 1 R	1 R					14 W	16,11	W,R
Outlined Circle								5 R	5	W
Solid Circle					2 W			4 W	3	R
Connected Circles					2 R		2 W	2 R	1,1	R,W
Fringed Circle									1	W
Rayed Circle									1	W
Tailed Circle									1,1	R,W
Appendaged Circle									1	W
Circle Cluster				4 W				4 W	4	W
Dotted Pattern	1 W		1 R		1 R			2,1 R,W	2,1	R,W
Semi-Circle	2 R			2,1 B,W	1 R			2,3,1 B,R,W	2,3,1	B,R,W
Semi-circle with Dot									1	R
Appendaged Semi-circle									2	R
Oval									2	W
Straight Line	1 W	1,1 B,W						2,1 W,B	4,1	W,B
Curved Line	2 W			4 W				7 W	7,4	W,R
Concentric Arcs					1 W				2	W
Angle		1 W						1 W	1,2	W,R
Chevron		2 R						2 R	2	R
S-Curve									1,1	R,W
S-Curve with Angles									4,1	R,W
Zigzag		1 Y, 8 W	8 R, 8 W	1 R				1,1 Y,R	1,1,2	W,Y,R
Diagonal				4,11 R,W	1 R			4,19 R,W	4,22	R,W
Parallel Lines	6,20 B,R; 4 W	10 B, 21 R		69 R, 14 W	29 R			16,147 B,R; 26 W	16,299,47	B,R,W
Cross								2 W	2,4	W,R
Negative Cross							2 W	2 W	8,3	W,R
Asterisk										
Dotted Line									3	W
T-Shape								1 W	1	W
Squiggle	1 W	1 W, 2 R	1 W		4 R	13 R	3 W	5,19 W,R	10,55	W,R
Squiggle-horned									1	W
Squiggle with Outlined Circle									1	W
Complex Abstract		2 R			6 W			2,6 R,W	4,10	R,W
Attached Squared Spirals									1	W
Rake								1 R	2,2	W,R
One-pole Ladder	1 W	1 R						1,1 W,R	6,2	W,R
Two-pole Ladder									1	W

*All sites are "AZ V:1:xxx (ASM)". **C = color. B = black; R = red; W = white; Y = yellow. † = Total for Tables 9.7 and 9.9.

Table 9.9. Distribution of Elements by Site, Room, and Color (AZ V:1:132 and AZ V:1:188 [ASM], and GP C:1:67), cont'd

SITE* / ROOM — Element	132 6/7	132 8/9	132 10	132 24	132 24 out	188 2	GP C: 1:67 ?	Total from Table 9.7	TOT	AL†
Solid Rectangle				3 R				3 R	1,3	W,R
Appendaged Rectangle									1	W
Rectangular Design—Closed		2 W					1 W	3 W	3,1	W,R
Triangle									1	W
Amorphic Shape				1 R	3 R / 1 W			4 R / 1 W	6 / 7	R / W
Unidentified Shape		1 R / 1 W						1 R / 1 W	9 / 9	R / W
Unidentified Painting	1 R / 1 W			1 R / 2 W / 1 W	1 R / 2 W			3 R / 3 W / 3 W	19 / 7 / 13	R / W / W
Human-like/Anthropomorph										
Human w/ Head Ornament									6	W
Human-like/Anth incomplete	1 W				1 W			2 W	5	W
Human-like/Anth attached									2	W
Human-like/Anthro—round belly									1	W
Stick Figure				1 R				1 R	1	R
Quadruped									7	W
Insect-like Figure	1 W			1 W				2 W	2	W
Reptile-like Figure	2 W			2 W				5 W	6	W
Life-Form/Biomorph			1 W					1 W	1	W
Life-Form/Biomorph—Splayed-legged									2	W
Life-Form/Bio-morph incomplete									4	W
Hand Print										
Negative Hand Print	2 W	1 W						3 W	2 / 7	W / R
Inverted Basket Shape									1	R
SUB-TOTAL	21 W / 26 R / 6 B	26 W / 30 R / 11 B / 1 Y	12 W / 10 R	52 W / 83 R / 2 B	13 W / 39 R	0 W / 13 R	8 W	132 W / 201 R / 19 B / 1 Y	272 W / 494 R / 19 B / 1 Y	W / R / B / Y
TOTAL	53	68	22	137	53	13	8	353	786	

*All sites are "AZ V:1:xxx (ASM)".   **C = color: B = black; R = red; W = white; Y = yellow.   † = Total for Tables 9.7 and 9.9.

red-painted elements superimpose white ones, the red elements are the wider line-style similar to the white-painted elements. It is possible that an earlier group of people who created the Mogollon Red pictographs had utilized the cavern at one time, but their remains are hidden beneath the cliff dwellings of Pueblo Canyon.

White-painted Pictographs:

It is more difficult to assign a style to the white-painted pictographs, although according to Schaasfma (1980:190), white paint can also be used for the Mogollon Red pictograph style. There are similarities in some elements, such as the use of dots and repeated vertical lines, appearance of one-pole ladders, vertical parallel squiggles and negative crosses. However, there are many more elements in white pigment that are not found painted in red pigment in the southeastern Sierra Ancha (see Tables 9.7 and 9.9). These include a 2-pole ladder, a rake, zigzag, handprints, lizards, quadrupeds, connected circles, insect-like figures, many anthropomorphs, and the addition of ceramic and textile designs. Also, there are stylistic differences in the execution of the anthropomorphs. The ceramic or textile designs are unlike the Mogollon Red style and unlike anything else in the southeastern Sierra Ancha as well. Therefore, it is proposed that this style of pictographs be called the "Pueblo Canyon style" (Table 9.12). Temporally, the style probably coincides with the occupation of the cliff dwellings (Fig. 9.7).

The paint may be a combination of kaolin clay with a fixative, or may have derived from chalk from Chalk Creek. It appears that the same pigment was used to paint the pictographs on the cliff as well as inside the rooms on some of the plastered walls. Some of the white pictographs are superimposed over the red, however, most elements were painted in open space on the cliff face. A few of the white elements are also located behind walls or beams in a room, indicating that the room was built after the elements were painted on the cliff face (walls: V:1:131, Rooms 5/6 and 8A, and V:1:132, Rooms 6/7; beams: V:1:131, Room 11).

Although some of the elements are similar to the red, such as white parallel lines and white dotted lines, the execution and style of the elements is different, with wider and more robust lines in white. These differences may show not only a different group of people, but perhaps also a later point in time. For the most part, the pictographs have been executed using fingers and sticks, and in some instances brush strokes are seen. Positive handprints were created by painting the palm and fingers of the hand, then pressing it on the rock face. The negative handprints were created by placing the palm of the hand upon the rock face, then blowing paint all over the area of the hand, thus producing a negative image on the rock face.

Some of the elements are similar to designs found on decorated ceramics and textiles. For example, the interlocking squared scroll motif that is found in Room 7 at V:1:132 (West Group) is similar to the interlocking squared scroll motif seen on cotton textiles recovered from the Tonto Ruin (Steen and others 1962:56,139). Pendant triangles are another motif that is found on the textiles, as well as zigzags. Steen and others (1962:139) believe that some of the weaving "in southern and central Arizona in late Pueblo III and IV contained many features not typical of Pueblo II Anasazi work (as seen in the earlier weavings)… and that they probably represent ideas brought to the Tonto area from the Salado homeland along the Little Colorado and …reflect influences from northern Mexico which reached the Southwest either by way of the Hohokam or the Mogollon of southwestern New Mexico." After examining the textiles from the Sierra Ancha, Teague (Appendix V) feels that although there are slight differences, the assemblage is similar

ROOM	ELEMENTS AND COMMENTS
	Table 9.10. Pictographs at AZ V:1:132 (ASM)
6/7	heavily impacted by historic graffiti; about half of the elements are in red paint, half in white; one line of black dots; red are geometrical or abstract; lifeforms in white; negative handprint; several partial elements (lifeforms in white); 6 black vertical parallel lines; red vertical lines and dots; possible lizard in white
8/9	rows of white dots; straight and curved heavy lines in Rm 8 that continue behind a wall; red parallel squiggles; white snake; white negative handprint; white geometric blanket or textile design with rectangular, interlocking frets; bird-like or plant-like red stick figures; block of white dots (8 rows and 6 columns); anthropomorph in white; patch of polychrome, red and yellow, but unclear if this is a unified element or two separate painting events
10	most are abstract or geometrical; lifeform of lizard in white; groups of horizontal and vertical lines in white; patch of short red lines
24	most pictographs at this site; impacted by historic graffiti; short, red parallel lines dominant; short lines also in white; semi-circles and circles in white; stick figure in red; anthropomorph and insect-like figures in white; rake in white; many indistinct shapes and overpainting in white

in appearance to traditions in the region below the Mogollon Rim and north of Mexico, and it is not much different from other assemblages reported from Mogollon and Salado sites in the area. It appears that there is an amalgamation of Hohokam, Mogollon and Anasazi traits that occurs in the Tonto region, which may have spread to other areas as well.

Polychrome Style:
A few sites in east central Arizona have pictographs that have been produced using more than one color within a design, and have been identified as a "polychrome style." While Mogollon Red pictographs appear usually as isolated elements that are randomly placed on the rock surface, the elements and figures associated with the polychrome motifs appear to be grouped more as if to show an association with a larger, central figure such as a shield or blanket/textile design.

Two polychrome styles have been defined (Weaver 1991 a, b, c). The Mogollon Chevelon Polychrome Pictograph style (Weaver 1991a, 1999b, 1999c: Figure 3.18) is found at only a few sites in central eastern Arizona. This style includes elements that are categorized as simple geometrics, animal figures (zoomorphs) and human figures (anthropomorphs) (Thiel 1999:86). A general list of elements associated with this pictograph style is given in Table 9.12.

Although there are four pigment colors identified for the pictographs in Pueblo Canyon, they are not integrated into a single design or composition, thus are not categorized as "polychromes." However, there are a few identified as such in the southeastern Sierra Ancha area. Polychrome and possible bi-chrome pictographs are present at Canyon Creek Ruin, GP C:1:50, and Red Rock House. The designs incorporated include possible shields as well as textile or blanket designs.

Canyon Creek Polychrome Pictograph style is attributed to the area near Canyon Creek Ruin during the Pueblo IV period (Fig. 9.7; Haury 1934:142; Weaver 1991a, b, c). Elements in the Canyon Creek style are representational and abstract and are either circular or rectangular in form with designs composed of shields or

Table 9.11. List of Names, Dates, and Sayings Recorded at Pueblo Canyon

a. Historic Names, Dates, and Places

Helen Peterson	Aug. 11, 1920
Andy	1920
Andy	April 15, 1921
	1921
Arley	Aug. 27 Mesa 1914
	5-Jun-48
Bertha Murphy	Aug. 11, 1920
V.J. Marlar	4,15,1921
G.W. Edwards	April 15, 1921
Andy Gleser	Aug. 11, 1920
Grace Wyeth	1921
Jr.	June 13, 1913 Phoenix
	Spring 1922
Henry Ellison	March 3, 1931
Richard Mayne	
Travis Ellison	
Buck McFarland	
Leona Lee	11 1920
P.G. Reddington	6/18/1920
A.T. Potter	June 19, 1919
P.P. Peterson	
W.H. Goddard	
Joyce (Trylok)	6/5/1948
rh	Young Globe, Az
Herman	1949
Dorothy Hacker	10.26.20
H.E. Hooker	
Dean Hunt Mesa	Age 16, May 1972
Kelly Benham Mesa	Age 14, April 19, 1982

b. Sayings

O what a hell of a trail up hear (sic)

When the Golden Sun is setting
Your mind is
While of others you are thinking
Will you still think of me?

Roses are Red
Violets are Blue

c. Other Names and Dates

| David Porter   Age 7, August 22, 1964 |
| Leslie Porter   Age 8, August 22, 1964 |
| David Porter, again, Age 15, April 29, 1972 |
| Zinnia Dodsen – One of the fire and feather members |
| Age 11, 1955 |
| May -66 |
| Andy Gleser |
| Dewey Peterson   Dick Mayere |
| Hark |
| Ileen Curnulf |
| Clarice Lewis   1977 was here |
| Kelly |
| David |
| Bill M. |
| Wardy |
| Syl Peter |
| ERSEW |
| Amrleyn rley Aug. 29 |
| Leonard |
| Michael |
| Dick Mayere |
| EPR RSG   Mar -77 |
| Edward Ellison – Young Az |
| Ole |
| Harold Smit |
| Bob D |
| Buster Ellison |
| Buck McFarlane |
| Harry Ellison |
| George Lamb |
| ERN |
| Marston Richards |
| Ely Cline   1967 |
| Jul 7 '53 |
| GWALD |
| Ray Adams |
| Phil, Dana Oc63 |

Dr. Byron Cummings
Steve Kuykendall
Linda DeYoung 1958 Yac

blanket/textile designs. Life forms are similar to those that are typically found throughout the region in contemporaneous sites; however, the presence of hand prints, while found also at Pueblo Canyon, are more commonly associated with the earlier Basketmaker-period sites in northern Arizona. Colors of pigments used include red, white, yellow, light blue-green (turquoise), brown, and black, with white commonly used as a field upon which other designs are drawn (Haury 1934:140). Other colors possibly present include tan and dark green or blue.

The pictographs at Canyon Creek ruin are very striking, with several different motifs present incorporating both representational and abstract elements. Of particular interest is a combination of vibrant pigments that are integrated into two blanket designs or textile compositions that occur beside each other under an overhang (Fig. 9.8). The two rectangular pictographs have a white background outlined in a red sawtooth design, the whole of which is then framed in blue-green (turquoise?). Within this larger framework are other designs in red and blue-green, including rectangles with sawtooth fringe, columns of red ticks, as well as a row of small, red rectangles that extend horizontally along the top and base of the interior of the design. These beautiful pictographs were included in Haury's (1934) publication; however, a problem should be noted. The colors on the frontispiece design (which depict the polychrome pictograph just described) are not correct. What is depicted on the frontispiece as yellow in fact should be a reddish color, while the brown depicted is a deeper red; and the green should be a light, turquoise blue-green color – only the white is accurate. The rendition of the design elements in the pictograph is accurate.

Another prominent pictograph at Canyon Creek ruin is a sunburst motif or shield, consisting of four red concentric circles with white in between the red (Fig. 9.9). The center is solid white. The outside is fringed with triangles, with the points facing outwards. Red is used from 12 o'clock (the top of the design) to four o'clock (lower right area of the design), while white pigment is used from four o'clock around the remainder of the exterior to 12 o'clock. This pictograph is placed just below the ceiling on the rock surface. Haury (1934; Plate LXXXII) also suggests the color brown is used in this pictograph, in addition to the red and white.

Several pictographs, including polychromes, are present at Red Rock House, located north of Canyon Creek Ruin. One of the largest is a polychrome composition that was created using white, yellow, turquoise green and red paint. It is a horizontal, rectangular design that is framed and fringed, probably representing a textile or blanket design (Fig. 9.10). There are three or four smaller designs that are framed within the larger rectangle, painted in white with white and red fringe extending vertically from the bottom of the designs. The other linear designs on the interior are not discernible, but have yellow as well as turquoise green pigment visible. To the left of this motif, on the same panel, is a horizontal and slightly rectangular white shape. It also appears to be fringed with red paint along the top and left side edges. Adjacent to this motif is a white zoomorphic figure that appears to be the profile of a bird. A vertical, linear motif is contiguous to the bird, and appears to have two parallel dark red or black lines that are infilled with white pigment. A white line near the bottom of this figure extends to the right, where it becomes the base of three concentric arcs or a rainbow. There are other figures to the right of the rainbow, but they are too indistinct to determine what they may be. To the right, nearby, is a linear configuration of white dots that appears to be a group of three or four crosses created from dots. To the right of this figure is a white square or box that is slightly irregular in shape,

Table 9.12. Distribution of Mogollon Elements by Style (adapted from Thiel 1995:89,93)

DESCRIPTION	MOGOLLON RED	MOGOLLON CHEVELON POLYCHROME	MOGOLLON JORNADA	MOGOLLON RESERVE	PUEBLO CANYON
Static stick figures	X				X
Stick figure				X	X
Hourglass figures	X				
Humans with horned headdresses	X				X
Figures with headdresses					
Figures with headdresses and clothing or body paint		X			
Figure with exaggerated hands		X			
Figure with exaggerated hands/feet					X
Masks			X		
Faces			X		
Human footprints				X	
Animal tracks				X	
Hand prints					X
Bird tracks	X				
Birds	X	X			
Flying birds			X		
Coyotes/dogs			X	X	
Fringed-wing birds				X	
Fish	X				
Insects		X			
Snakes		X			X
Toads/frogs		X		X	
Lizards		X		X	X
Mountain lions				X	
Mountain sheep			X	X	
Quadrupeds	X				X
Zigzags	X				X
Circles		X			X
Concentric circles	X	X		X	
Connected circles/bubbles					X
Spirals				X	
Ovals	X				
Sunbursts	X			X	X
Parallel waves	X				X
Wavy lines				X	X
Diamond chains	X				
One-pole ladders	X	X			X
Two-pole ladders					X
Short line series	X				X
Lines (parallel or zigzag)		X			X
Lines (curved or straight)					X
Rainbow figures		X			
Multiple crescents		X			
Dot patterns		X			X
Cloud terraces			X		
Blanket designs			X		X
Rainbow arches			X		
Concentric arcs with rays					X
Semi-circle					X
Appendaged semi-circle					X
Appendaged circle					X
Interlocking frets				X	
Squared spiral					X
Grids				X	
Barred elements				X	
Cross					X

Table 9.12. Distribution of Mogollon Elements by Style (adapted from Thiel 1995:89,93), cont'd

DESCRIPTION	MOGOLLON RED	MOGOLLON CHEVELON POLYCHROME	MOGOLLON JORNADA	MOGOLLON RESERVE	PUEBLO CANYON
Negative cross					X
Outlined crosses				X	
Rake					X
Chevron					X
Horned squiggle					X
Solid rectangle					X
Appendaged rectangle					X
Squiggle with tail					X
Bubble insect					X
Insect-like figure					X
Room lines					X

which has a white dot in the center. It is similar in style to the figures painted at GP C:1:67 (see below). On a panel directly below the rainbow is a group of three filled white ovals, which are indistinct. The oval on the left appears to have at least one appendage, and maybe two, near the top as if they were arms. The oval in the center has a white horizontal line beneath it. The oval on the right is nearly indistinguishable, but appears to also have a horizontal line beneath it.

V:1:260:

Pictographs of white paint are located at V:1:260. The site is in a small alcove along the path that goes from the waterfall at the head of the canyon to V:1:132 in Pueblo Canyon. An element count was done from the drawings for V:1:260 (see Table 9.7). Similar elements were recorded at V:1:260 as were found at the three cliff dwellings in Pueblo Canyon. Element style and type of white paint were also the same, thus V:1:260 is interpreted as being contemporaneous with the cliff dwellings (see Chapter 5).

V:1:260 consists of approximately 34 elements, represented by both geometric and representational styles (Figs. 9.11-14). No historic or modern graffiti was present at this site, and only white paint was used. About 40 percent of the elements are anthropomorphic designs and are possibly arranged in several horizontal rows within this panel. Several of the figures appear to have headdresses as well as something in their hands (such as wands). Their bodies are solid, elongated and mostly thick. Several individuals have upraised arms and splayed legs, without having fingers and toes. However, there is one large, thick-bodied individual with arms lowered, splayed legs, with splayed fingers and toes, similar to petroglyph figures of the Reserve Style seen near Tularosa Creek (Schaafsma 1992:56). There is also a rayed stick figure as well as one that has a rounded belly. Two quadrupeds of unknown species are represented in this group, and there are several smears of amorphic shapes also present.

The remaining elements are geometric, and include zigzags, diagonal lines, squiggles, solid and appendaged rectangles, vertical lines, appendaged and attached squared spirals, and finger-tip dots. The squared spiral is placed horizontally on the wall, and from a distance is similar to the head of a Tlaloc figure (see Schaafsma 1992:64), which is a Mexican rain deity and is replicated in the Jornada Style petroglyphs of southern New Mexico. It also

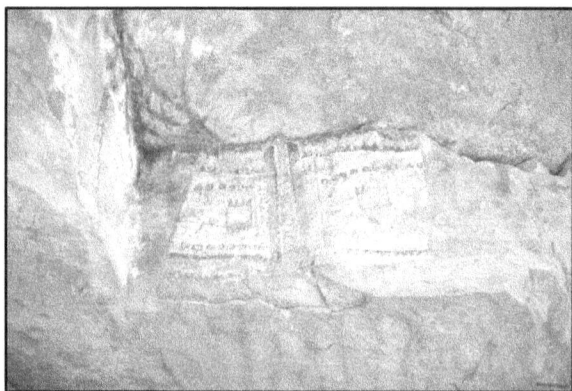

Figure 9.8. Textile or Blanket Design, Canyon Creek Polychrome Style, Canyon Creek Ruin (AZ V:2:1 [ASM]) (2004-1733-image4126)

Figure 9.11. Pictographs at AZ V:1:260 (ASM) – Pueblo Canyon Style   (2004-1733-image3839)

Figure 9.9. Sunburst or Shield Design, Canyon Creek Polychrome Style, Canyon Creek Ruin (AZ V:2:1 [ASM]) (2004-1733-image4127)

Figure 9.12. Pictographs at AZ V:1:260 (ASM) – Pueblo Canyon Style   (2004-1733-image4133)

Figure 9.10. Pictograph at Red Rock House   (2004-1733-image4129)

Figure 9.13. Pictographs at AZ V:1:260 (ASM) – Pueblo Canyon Style   (2004-1733-image3833)

Figure 9.14. Line Drawing of Pictographs at AZ V:1:260 (ASM) – Pueblo Canyon Style (length of panel is approximately 2m; all figures are white paint) (2004-1733-image4164)

is similar in style to decorative elements found on ceramics and textiles, but is different from the other designs found in the Sierra Ancha cliff dwellings.

Several of the figures are incomplete, thus it is not known what elements they may have represented. Some of the elements appear to be grouped, such as two figures near the top in Figure 9.3, both with outstretched arms. To the right of this are a few more anthropomorphs; one appears to be incomplete with just legs and splayed toes, while the one immediately to the right appears to be more complete, with splayed fingers and toes. Others appear to be randomly drawn. Although located on the only pathway to the waterfall, the location is somewhat secluded and was hidden behind brush. This location away from the main pueblo suggests it may have been used for ritual or ceremonial purposes, to the exclusion of other inhabitants of Pueblo Canyon.

V:1:130— East Group:

A single pictograph was associated with the East group—a negative hand print in white paint of a left hand. The pictograph is near Room 1 (see Fig. III.26). Handprints are known from Basketmaker (Anasazi) sites north of this region, and are still important to the modern Pueblo Indians today (Schaafsma 1980:119). They are reportedly left at sacred places where

someone has prayed, in order for the supernatural beings to recognize the person who left the prayer (Schaafsma 1980:119; 1992:9). It is not known why there was a dearth of pictographs at this locus. There is wall painting in two rooms in this group (see below).

V:1:131— Central Group:

Thirteen rooms in the Central Group had pictographs associated with them (Tables 9.7 and 9.8). The following discusses the elements and color of paint of the pictographs associated with each of the rooms (see Fig. III.27). Room 2 has 36 pictographs, with the majority (N=32) produced in red paint. The red elements appear to be more abstract, while the white-painted elements are more anthropomorphic, including a negative handprint.

Rooms 3/4 and 5/6 all have groups of the short parallel lines, however, in Room 3 they are in white paint, while Rooms 4 and 5/6 have them in red paint. The pictographs in Rooms 5/6 were recorded as a single unit, thus could not be separated out for analysis. The majority of the elements (Tables 9.7 and 9.8) are abstract or geometric. Room 7 has a single occurrence of a red cross on top of white paint, which is unusual at this site. The red cross is painted in thicker lines, similar in style to the figures painted in white. There is also an occurrence of white super-positioned over red. Once again, the majority of the elements are in red paint.

Room 8A has a very diverse set of element types (Tables 9.7 and 9.8), some of which are grouped on rock faces that are labeled as different panels. Some of the motifs are ambiguous, while others are recognizable. Several elements appear on faces of the cliff rock that face downward (Fig. 9.15).

Room 10 also has a very diverse array of elements (Tables 9.7 and 9.8). The wall dividing Rooms 10 and 11 is partially intact. The majority of the pictographs are created in white paint; however, vertical parallel lines in

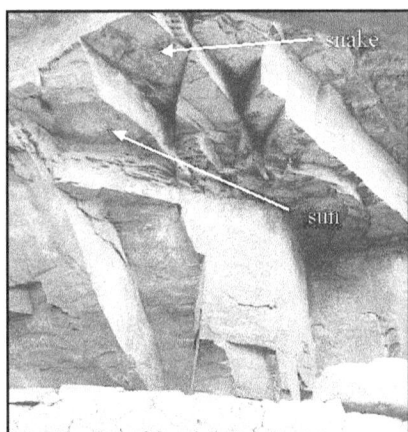

Figure 9.15. Pictographs at AZ V:1:131 (ASM) – White, Rm 8A, Sun and Snake and Others (2004-1733-image3931)

red paint have the highest frequency. There are several lifeforms in white, including anthropomorphs, a quadruped, and several partial lifeforms. Once again, historic graffiti obscures many of the elements on the rock face.

Room 11 (Tables 9.7 and 9.8) has the largest number of pictographs, mostly geometric or abstract. There are more occurrences of red than white, mainly due to the repetition of the vertical parallel lines and zigzags. Again, historic graffiti covers some of the pictographs.

Rooms 13 and 14 were recorded together as one is above the other, forming a two-story suite. Room 13, the lower room, has a partial one-pole ladder as well as a group of the red short, parallel lines with indeterminate smears. Room 14 (Tables 9.7 and 9.8) has several groups of the red lines, a rake in red, and several crosses in red and white. Only six pictographs, representing three element types, were recorded for Rooms 21 and 22. The two rooms were recorded as a single unit.

V:1:132— West Group:
This cliff dwelling contains many pictographs and also contains abundant historic and modern graffiti (Tables 9.9 and 9.10). Six rooms, including Rooms 6, 7, 8, 9, 10, and 24, were recorded with rock art in the West group (see

Fig.III.28). Pictographs also occur in an area outside of Room 24 and were recorded as well. Rooms 6/7 and 8/9 are two-story rooms, and each pair was recorded as a single unit.

In the Rooms 6/7 unit (Tables 9.9 and 9.10) 53 pictographs representing 19 different elements were recorded. Room 6 has been heavily impacted by graffiti that frequently obscures the pictographs. About half of the pictographs are in red paint (N=26), with a line of dots in black (N=6) and the remainder in white (N=21). The red pictographs are represented in abstract or geometrical elements, while the white pictographs have several life forms represented as well as the abstract elements.

Although they were recorded as a unit, the rock art in Rooms 8 and 9 is different, based on the composition of the elements and the paint used (Tables 9.9 and 9.10). The back walls of the rooms are rock, with several panels of pictographs (Figs. 9.16 and 9.17). Near the floor level of Room 9 is a vertical column of red dots and lines, with a smear of yellow ochre above the red lines. This use of polychrome motifs is unusual in the Pueblo Canyon cliff dwellings.

Room 10 is composed of three small panels, with a total of 22 pictographs (Tables 9.9 and 9.10). The majority are abstract or geometrical elements. Room 24 has the most pictographs of any of the other rooms at this site, with a diverse set of elements associated. Unfortunately, historic and modern day graffiti have impacted the pictographs. The short, red parallel lines of the Mogollon Red style again dominate the assemblage.

V:1:188:
The pictographs are on the cliff face at the back of the small cave containing this cliff dwelling. The elements consist of 13 squiggles of varying lengths and orientations in red paint (Table 9.9). Stylistically, they can be classified as Mogollon Red pictographs. The pictographs at V:1:188

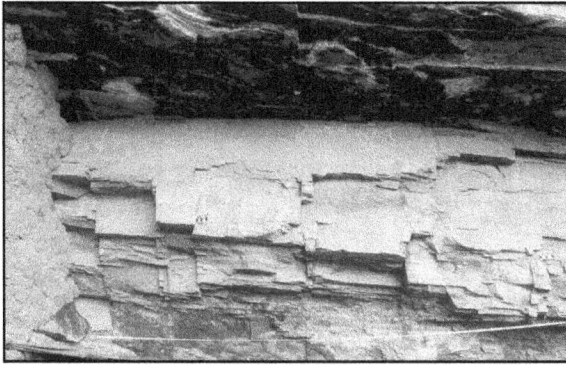

Figure 9.16. Pictographs at AZ V:1:132 (ASM) –
Rooms 8/9, Textile Designs   (2004-1733-image3852)

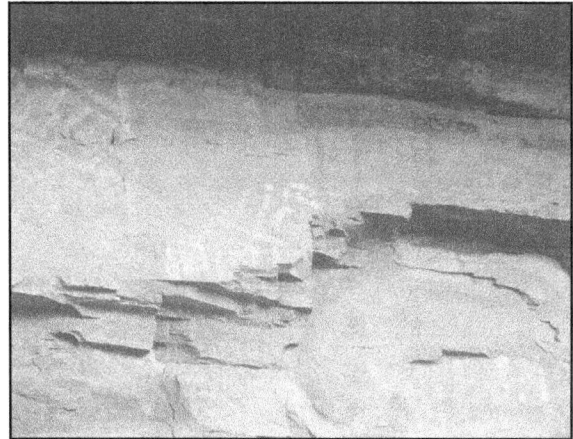

Figure 9.17. Pictographs at AZ V:1:132 (ASM)
– Pueblo Canyon Style, Rm 8/9, Panels S-W
(2004-1733-image3845)

have not been formally recorded.

GP C:1:67:

The pictographs at this site were photographed by Gila Pueblo (ASM Negatives 71164, 71165, and 71166), however, the cliff dwelling has not been relocated by the SAP. The pictographs are painted in white, and appear to be on the back wall (rock surface) in the interior of the cliff dwelling. The elements consist of three sets of vertical, rectangular motifs (Figs. 9.18 and 19; see also Haury 1934: Fig. 26g) that are slightly irregular. The set of rectangles or boxes on the left are connected, with the upper box containing a white cross in the center while the lower box is empty. The set of rectangles in the center are not joined; the upper box is empty while the lower box contains a small circle that is centrally located. The set of rectangles on the right consists of three smaller boxes approximately the same overall length as the two sets to the left. The upper box contains a white cross, which is centrally located, similar to that in the far left box; while the two lower boxes are empty. Above the motifs, situated almost halfway between the left and center designs, a single solid circle was painted. In addition to this set of motifs, a group of squiggles was documented, apparently on a different panel. This panel consists of three white

vertical squiggles, two long and one short, and a number of red squiggles on the same and an adjacent panel (Table 9.9).

GP C:1:50:

Figure 7.35 illustrates the pictographs at this site, the only site in the southeastern Sierra Ancha area with polychrome pictographs. The author has not seen these pictographs, and the lighting and glare in the available photography make it difficult to discern the form and colors of the pictograph elements. The pictographs are located behind the rooms on the rock face at the back of the cliff dwelling. There are three, large bichrome (and possibly polychrome) pictographs, as well as several smaller red elements. Although each of the pictographs is painted on a separate panel, they appear to be grouped in the upper region of the cliff face, just below the overhang. The natural folds and irregularities of the rock have been incorporated into the designs as well as utilized to provide a division between the designs, visually and spatially.

The first large pictograph is a sub-rectangular bichrome motif with a red-painted outline and an interior design of possibly yellow pigment. The design is indeterminate due to glare in the photograph and weathering. Above and

Figure 9.18. Pictographs at GP C:1:67 (2004-1733-image4130)

Figure 9.19. Pictographs at GP C:1:67 – Pueblo Canyon Style, squiggles (2004-1733-image4131)

left of this large design is a small, indeterminate shape in red paint. The second large pictograph, located to the right of the first large pictograph, is a horizontal rectangle outlined in dark red. The base of the rectangle has a line break due to irregularities in the rock face. The interior design is abstract and may represent the design of a ceramic or textile motif. It may be a polychrome composition; however, only two colors are discernible—red and yellow. It may have had a white background, but, again, due to the glare in the photograph, it is difficult to determine. The design in this second large pictograph appears to be quartered, with red, saw-tooth elements, but other elements are indistinguishable. Other similar abstract wall paintings are found in Rooms 8/9 of V:1:132 in Pueblo Canyon, Spruce Tree House in Mesa Verde National Park (Schaafsma 1980:142), Palatki near Sedona, and Betatakin in Navajo National Monument.

Above and to the right of the second pictograph, on a small ledge under the overhang, is a small, oval, red pictograph. Farther to the right, on another small panel, is a small, red, diamond-shaped element, with a solid, dark red, cigar-shape over the left side of the diamond. Farther above and to the right is a small red figure that may represent an anthropomorph with raised arms. Immediately below this figure, on the same panel, is a large circular, shield pictograph. This pictograph consists of three concentric circles of dark blue or green on a white background. The two inner circles have a saw-tooth motif, with the tips pointed inward to the center. The inner circles also appear to have either red or yellow pigment (or both) adjacent to the saw-tooth elements to further enhance them. Shield-type pictographs are also seen at other cliff dwelling sites such as Room 8A at V:1:131 in Pueblo Canyon and at Canyon Creek Ruin (Fig. 9.20).

Wall Painting

The pictographs in the southeastern Sierra Ancha are mostly in the cliff dwellings in

Figure 9.20. Pictographs at Canyon Creek Ruin, Canyon Creek Polychrome Style, shield (2004-1733-image4128)

Pueblo Canyon, but do occur in other cliff dwellings as well. However, not only are there pictographs, but some of the rooms contain painting on the interior walls. Table 9.4 shows the spatial distribution of the various cliff dwellings and rooms that contain wall painting, and cliff walls that contain pictographs upon them. There are 15 room walls with wall painting, including both masonry and natural cliff walls. The painting, which is done in white paint only, usually is about a meter above the floor surface, or midway up the wall and approximately 5 to 8cm in width. The chemical composition of the paint is unknown, however it appears to be the same as that used for the pictographs. The preservation of the wall paintings is in jeopardy. The paint is beginning to disappear off the plastered walls due to

weathering and loss of the plaster, and some of the walls are collapsing. The wall painting in southeastern Sierra Ancha cliff dwellings is summarized in Table 9.13.

Wall painting occurs at V:1:130, V:1:131, V:1:132, all in Pueblo Canyon, and at V:1:167 in Devils Chasm. The design of the wall painting is variable from room to room. In some rooms it is a white line running horizontally along one or two walls (Fig. 9.21). In other cases, it is a zigzag design. More rarely, the painting involves an element other than a line, such as a circle or figure. For instance, in Room 5 of the Central group (V:1:131), what may be a male and female anthropomorph are near a doorway and appear to be walking (Fig. 9.22). These two figures are similar to those seen in the pictographs. One of the figures is depicted in Haury's report (1934:Fig. 26f), but is incorrectly shown as being painted in black.

Although no formal kivas are found at the cliff dwellings in the southeastern Sierra Ancha, perhaps the rooms with wall painting held a similar function for ceremonial and ritual activities. For example, Red Bow Cliff Dwelling in the Point of Pines region contains a ceremonial room, Room 4, which is thought to perhaps take the place of a formal kiva (Gifford1980:30). Gifford speculated that the inhabitants of this cliff dwelling, as well as Tule Tubs Cave (which also has stylistically similar pictographs), may have utilized kivas at other sites in the Point of Pines area while maintaining a smaller domestic offertory within the cliff dwelling. Rooms with painting on the walls were also reported from nearby Canyon Creek Ruin (Haury 1934:140). However, in the room illustrated by Haury (1934:PlateXXXIII), the painting is red and yellow, and is solid from the floor up to about half the height of the wall, instead of a line or zigzag. The wall painting also has steps or terraces along the top edge. This occurs in a room (22B) that Haury believed had an altar, and paraphernalia he interpreted as

Table 9.13. Wall Painting at Southeastern Sierra Ancha Sites

SITE	ROOM	LOCATION
AZ V:1:130 (ASM)	2	left wall, white line, horizontal then curves upward
(Pueblo Canyon)	3	back wall, white, thick (5 cm) wavy (zigzag) line
AZ V:1:131 (ASM)	2	left wall, white line, zigzag
(Pueblo Canyon)	3	back and left walls, white
	5	left wall, white, figures left of door, zigzag line to right of door (see Fig. 9.24)
	6	left wall, white, at center bottom
	10A	notes unclear – small patch of paint or line on Front or Right wall
	11A	notes unclear – probably small patch of paint from a line
	11B	notes unclear – probably small patch of paint from a line
	14	notes unclear as to wall, probably small paint patch
AZ V:1:132 (ASM)	6/7	back and front walls, white, horizontal lines; up 80 cm on back wall, 52 cm on front wall
(Pueblo Canyon)	8/9	back and left, white; line on back wall is continuation of line from Rm 6, on left wall, white patch in middle of plastered area
	10	left wall, white, painted over soot-blackened plaster, 2 circles?
AZ V:1:167 (ASM)	4	anthropomorph (head, shoulders, one arm) low on Right wall near RFX
(Devils Chasm)	6	notes unclear – probably small patch of paint from a line

Figure 9.21. Wall Painting, Pueblo Canyon (AZ V:1:132 [ASM]), Rm 6, horizontal line (2004-1733-image3861)

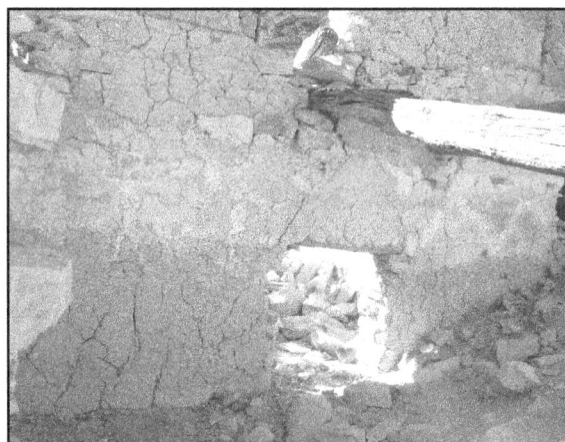

Figure 9.22. Wall Painting, Pueblo Canyon (AZ V:1:131 [ASM]), Room 5, Figures and Zigzag Line (2004-1733-image4132)

offerings related to hunting (see also Chapter 6). Perhaps the rooms with painted walls in Pueblo Canyon served a similar purpose, thus solidifying rituals and ceremonies within these residential units.

Graffiti and Historic Inscriptions

The hike up to Pueblo Canyon is not overly difficult, but can be challenging. Some visitors to the cliff dwellings have felt compelled to leave their marks on the rock walls, just as people did a thousand years ago. Unfortunately, not only did they write on the walls of the archaeological sites, but in some cases wrote over the prehistoric pictographs. Some signatures and dates are now themselves historic in nature. The earliest recorded dates are those of "Jr. June 13, 1913 Phoenix" and "Arley Aug. 27 Mesa 1914". Other names and dates are listed in Table 9.11. Victor Ackland (see Chapter 1) proclaimed "Oh, What a hell of a climb up hear (sic)." Others waxed poetic with "Roses are Red, Violets are Blue."

Several people returned as evidenced by multiple signatures, including Dewey Peterson (the cowboy who first brought Haury into the area), Helen Peterson and Andy Gleser. David Porter came up at the age of 7 on August 22, 1964 and returned at the age of 15 on April 29, 1972. Local visitors also came to visit from nearby Young and Globe. Charcoal, chalk, pens, pencils and scratching were used to write on the rock faces in Pueblo Canyon.

DISCUSSION

The distribution of Mogollon Red pictographs has changed little over the years since Schaafsma (1980:184) first proposed her map. Since 1980, however, several projects have recorded Mogollon Red pictographs that will fill in the gaps. Weaver (1991a:10) compiled a style chronology while working on several sites in the Apache-Sitgreaves National Forest that expands the boundary of Mogollon Red pictographs and Reserve style petroglyphs farther west, and that is useful in discussion of the pictographs in the southeastern Sierra Ancha (see Fig. 9.7). Other sites with Mogollon Red pictographs include several in the Apache-Sitgreaves National Forest (Weaver 1991:9) at Mormon Crossing, Chevelon Crossing, Pigeon Creek, and Fools Hollow Lake, and Tule Tubs Cave near Point of Pines (Gifford 1980:11).

Several pictographs were recorded at Tule Tubs Cave, which has two Mogollon-Pueblo occupations (an earlier AD 900 to 1150 occupation known as the Nantack and Reserve phases, and a later Canyon Creek Phase, dating from AD 1325 to 1400). The figures were painted on the natural rock wall at the back of the sites, in red or black paint. At Tule Tubs Cave, motifs include a rake, anthropomorphs, crescents and circles, one-pole ladders, and lizards. One set of anthropomorphs include both a male and female figure, with the female having the hour-glass body that has been associated with Mogollon Red style of pictographs (Burton 1988:36, 37; Jernigan 1992:62). The male figure may have a headdress. Both figures display splayed appendages, although the female does not appear to have any toes. The female is slightly smaller, and is painted above and almost behind the male. A long squiggle or snake separates the two. Similarities with Pueblo Canyon pictographs are seen in the rake, in one of the styles of lizards, and in one style of anthropomorph (several different styles are present) in that the legs are straight out from the body at right angles. However, the pictographs at Tule Tubs Cave are painted in red or black (the rake), instead of being painted in white. Also, the bodies of the anthropomorphs are not as thick and robust as those at Pueblo Canyon.

The example from Mexico is included as a comparison because it is painted on a room wall with wide, white lines, similar to many of the pictographs in Pueblo Canyon. It is a pictograph of a lizard, painted in white, on the interior wall of a room at the site of Cueva de las Ventanas located in Chihuahua, Mexico (Sanchez 1986:48, 49). The lizard, approximately 30cm long, is painted vertically on the plastered wall, with the head up and the tail pointed down towards the floor, and is about midway up the wall. The legs of the lizard extend perpendicular to the body, with the lower portion of the legs extending downward in a 90-degree angle, which makes this segment parallel to the main body. The tail extends below where the legs connect to the body, but does not go beyond the ends of the legs. Another figure is adjacent to the lizard on the plastered wall, but it is unidentifiable. Pictographs and petroglyphs of similar lizards are found in the southeastern Sierra Ancha along Cherry Creek and at Pueblo Canyon. It is intriguing that not only are there similarities in architecture (see Chapter 7) with northern Mexico, but in the wall painting and pictographs as well.

Pictographs painted on the cliff walls at GP C:1:50 have not been formally recorded; however, they are more similar in style to those recorded at Canyon Creek Ruin (see above). The pictographs recorded at Canyon Creek Ruin (V:2:1), are different from those at Pueblo Canyon in composition and motifs as well as in colors used in their design. These have been designated as the Canyon Creek Polychrome Pictograph Style (Weaver 1991a:4) and have been assigned to the Pueblo IV time period (Haury 1934:142). In addition to the polychrome pictographs is a large spiral in white, located on the cliff wall in Room 16B. Handprints, both negative and positive in white and red paint, are also present. Haury (1934:140) suggested they were like those found at Basketmaker sites and are similar to those found in Pueblo Canyon. The handprints are scattered in small groups along the cliff in the recess occupied by Canyon Creek Ruin, which is different from the scattered distribution of the handprints found in Pueblo Canyon that occur either as single units or, occasionally, in pairs. There are some similarities in representations of anthropomorphs to those from southeastern Arizona (Jernigan 1992:55), although the torso is more similar to that depicted in a rock shelter on Cibecue Creek (Reid and Whittlesey 1999:43).

Some elements may be representations of pottery or textile designs. For example, one white pictograph at V:1:260 is rectangular and appears as if someone were attempting to draw the rectangular interlocking scroll motif found in V:1:132 (Fig. 9.16). However, it is incomplete and the lines do not connect quite the way they do at V:1:132.

CONCLUSION

Throughout time, people have sought different ways to express themselves. Many objects are created with decorative aspects, and some have symbolic significance attached to them. For many perishable objects including basketry and textiles, it is unknown to us how they were decorated except, for the most part, those items recovered from dry cave sites. Fortunately, decorated items such as ceramics are still occasionally found, presenting an opportunity to view the artistry and creativity of those that made the items (Reid and Whittlesey 1999:133). Pictographs and petroglyphs are another such medium in which this creativity is still observable. The reasons for their creation are not known, only that they were used as a form of self-expression and communication, and were an integral part of functioning dynamic cultures. Many Native American groups, such as the Hopi, have an oral tradition that associates many of the petroglyphs with their migration stories. Clans can track their ancestors to specific areas with associated rock art whether it is found up north at Homol'ovi or in the southern part of the state along the San Pedro River (Bernardini 2005; Colwell-Chanthaphonh 2003:18). In this way, the symbols left on stone are a communication link from the ancestors to the present day Native Americans. Furthermore, although archaeologists are unable to determine the function of each rock art site, studying the placement, kinds of elements present, and a comparison with motifs on other forms of medium such as ceramics, textiles and basketry can allude to possibilities by incorporating these other means of communication.

The preservation of rock art is important as a part of our cultural heritage for future generations to observe and enjoy, thus these archaeological resources are protected by federal (in this case) and State laws. However, natural processes such as wind, rain, extreme temperatures, plant growth and the decomposition of organic paints all lead to the eventual deterioration and loss of pictographs and petroglyphs (Weaver 1993:28). Humans occasionally also contribute to the destruction of images left on stone by removing the art, as well as defacing boulders and cliff faces with graffiti, thus making it even more imperative to record sites.

The presence of rock art elements (including both petroglyphs and pictographs) similar to what is found in the Hohokam and Mogollon cultures as well as earlier Archaic motifs, suggests that this area was not static, but was a crossroads for thousands of years. The diversity of rock art supports the mixture of ceramics recovered from both culture groups and also includes material culture from the Tonto Basin and the northern regions, thus providing clues to the aboriginal land use in this region from a more holistic view. Additionally, the textile assemblage suggests it is most similar to that of Mogollon and Sinagua textile traditions (see Teague this volume).

The rock art in the southeastern Sierra Ancha is unique and wonderful for many reasons. It is a testimony to those who have passed this way maybe once or many times. It is unique and thought provoking, representing symbolic thinking that took place either as a response to a ritual, or as a reaction to an environmental or historical event. Some of the petroglyph elements along Cherry Creek are similar to those found elsewhere, perhaps providing a symbolic link of sorts to anyone who passed that way, a sign that says this is a familiar spot. On the other hand, while there are similarities, there are also differences in some of the motifs and representations of the Pueblo Canyon Style pictographs, which are different from those seen elsewhere. The paintings on the interior room walls in the cliff dwellings and some of the white-painted pictographs are found in areas where access might be restricted; in other words, not in a public place, but in a private space reserved for only a few to see. We do not know for sure who these people were that passed this way, but it is up to us to respect what they did, and preserve it for others to wonder at and enjoy in the future.

Chapter 10
Regional Culture History and the Southeastern Sierra Ancha

Richard C. Lange and Richard S. Ciolek-Torrello

The Sierra Ancha is unparalleled in its rich, colorful, and sometimes bloody past. It may have been occupied as early as 10,000 BC by Paleoindian hunters and collectors, who were followed by peoples archaeologists call Archaic, Hohokam, Salado, Mogollon, Western Pueblo, Anasazi, and Anchan. In the protohistoric period and historic times, Western Apache, Yavapai, and Euro-american groups occupied the area. This general pattern of history is similar to other areas in central Arizona, such as the Verde Valley (Fish and Fish 1977; Pilles 1976; Van West and Altschul 1994; Whittlesey and others 1998), the Tonto Basin (Macnider and Effland 1989), and the upper Salt River drainage (Ciolek-Torrello and Lange 1979; Ferguson and Lomaomvaya 1999; Haury 1932; Reid 1989; Reid and Whittlesey 1999).

Despite its rich past, relatively little archaeological research has been conducted in the Sierra Ancha, and much of what is interpreted about this region is based on what is known from adjacent areas where more work has been done. To the west and southwest is the much better known area of Tonto Basin, to the north is the Payson Basin, and to the east are the Vosberg, Q Ranch, and Grasshopper regions (Figs. 1.1, 10.1, and 10.2; Table 10.1). At various times in the past, the prehistory of parts of the Sierra Ancha appears to have been more closely tied to the cultures and historical events of Tonto Basin, whereas at other times the Sierra Ancha was more closely related to the Payson, Vosberg, Q Ranch, and Grasshopper areas.

Even if the archaeology of the area was better known, the culture history of the Sierra Ancha could not be considered in isolation. As previously noted (see Chapters 1 and 4), the Sierra Ancha lies at, between, or within the boundaries of the Hohokam and Salado cultures of the Tonto and Phoenix Basins, the Anasazi of the Colorado Plateau, and the Mogollon of east-central Arizona. At various times in the past, the Sierra Ancha was a frontier region for some of these cultures, while during other times it was an area of cultural mixing, with fluid boundaries that shifted over time. As a result, mixed archaeological assemblages in the Sierra Ancha are common, with mixtures of architectural styles and ceramic wares. Sorting out cultural relationships and developing a chronological framework for the Sierra Ancha is made even more difficult by the paucity of diagnostic materials such as decorated or trade ceramics (Ciolek-Torrello 1987; Wood 1986). Some investigators have emphasized the area's intermediate location and cultural mixing in addressing its culture history. Others, however, argue that the Sierra Ancha was inhabited by a localized, indigenous people — the Anchan culture or Central Arizona Tradition (Wood 1987; Elson 1992a) — who interacted to varying degrees with surrounding groups.

Regardless of viewpoint, to discuss the culture history of the Sierra Ancha it is neces-

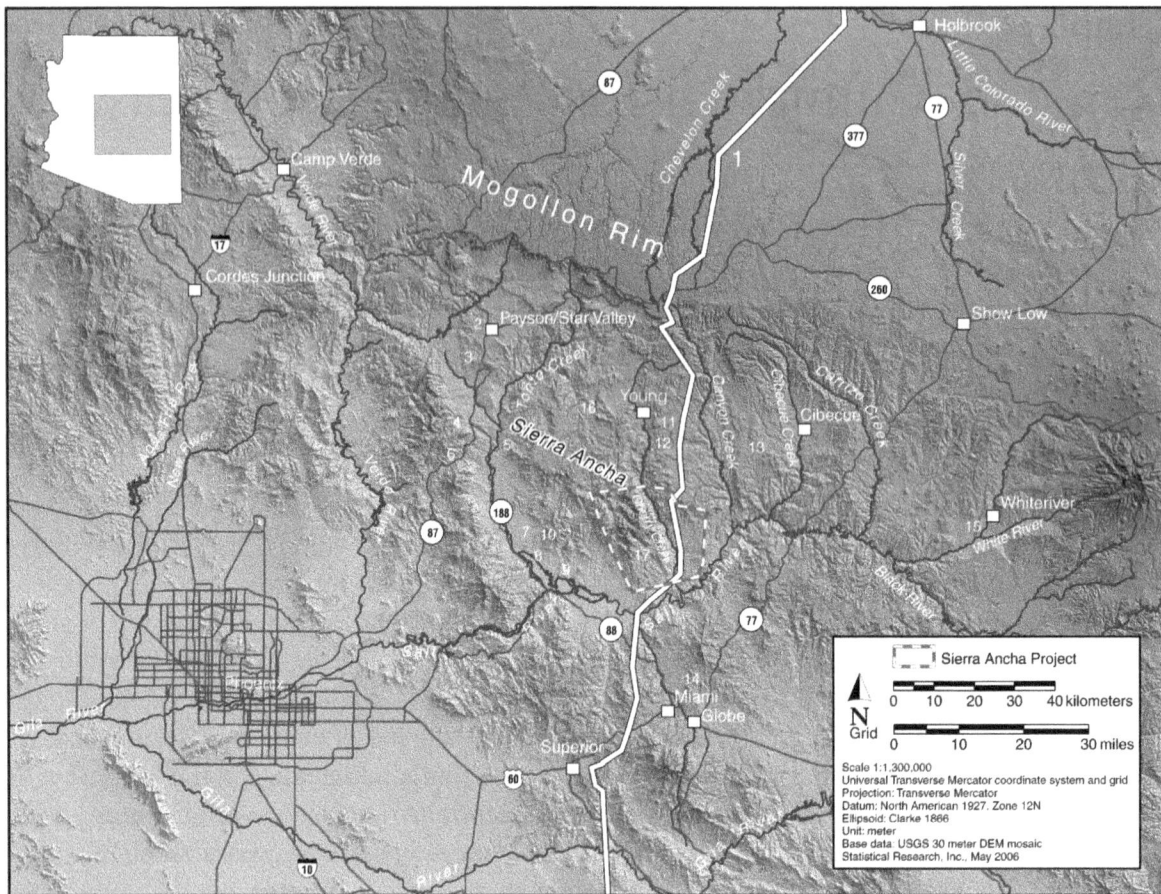

Figure 10.1. Regional Map Showing Archaeological Projects: 1) APS, 2) Payson/Star Valley, 3) Ox-bow Hill, 4) Rye Creek, 5) State Route 188/Cottonwood Creek, 6) Mazatzal Piedmont, 7) FLEX Tonto Basin, 8) Tonto Creek, 9) Roosevelt Archaeological Project, 10) Other Tonto Projects, 11) Vosberg Field School, 12) Q Ranch Field School, 13) Grasshopper Field School, 14) Miami Wash, 15) Canyon Day Wastewater, 16) Sierra Ancha Overviews and Surveys, 17) Sierra Ancha Project (for project information, see Table 10.1) This figure is the sole property of Statistical Research, Inc., and may not be reproduced without its permission.

sary to review that of the surrounding areas. The culture histories of the different traditions that impinged on the Sierra Ancha, however, are described by widely divergent chronological frameworks. For example, Mogollon and Anasazi chronologies are often framed in periods such as Pueblo I, II, III, and so on, whereas Hohokam and Salado sequences are based on the Phoenix Basin chronology of Colonial, Sedentary, and Classic periods. The chronologies for these adjacent areas are summarized in Figure 10.3, showing the approximate temporal equivalencies for the various periods, phases,

and sequences of the different regional chronologies. It is not the intent of this report to construct a separate chronological framework for the Sierra Ancha. Given the cultural and historical variability within the Sierra Ancha, a single chronological framework for the Sierra Ancha is probably not possible. Furthermore, the focus is on the southeastern Sierra Ancha and middle Cherry Creek area (Figs. 1.1, 10.1, 10.2).

The intent is to place the southeastern Sierra Ancha and middle Cherry Creek areas into a regional perspective. This review begins

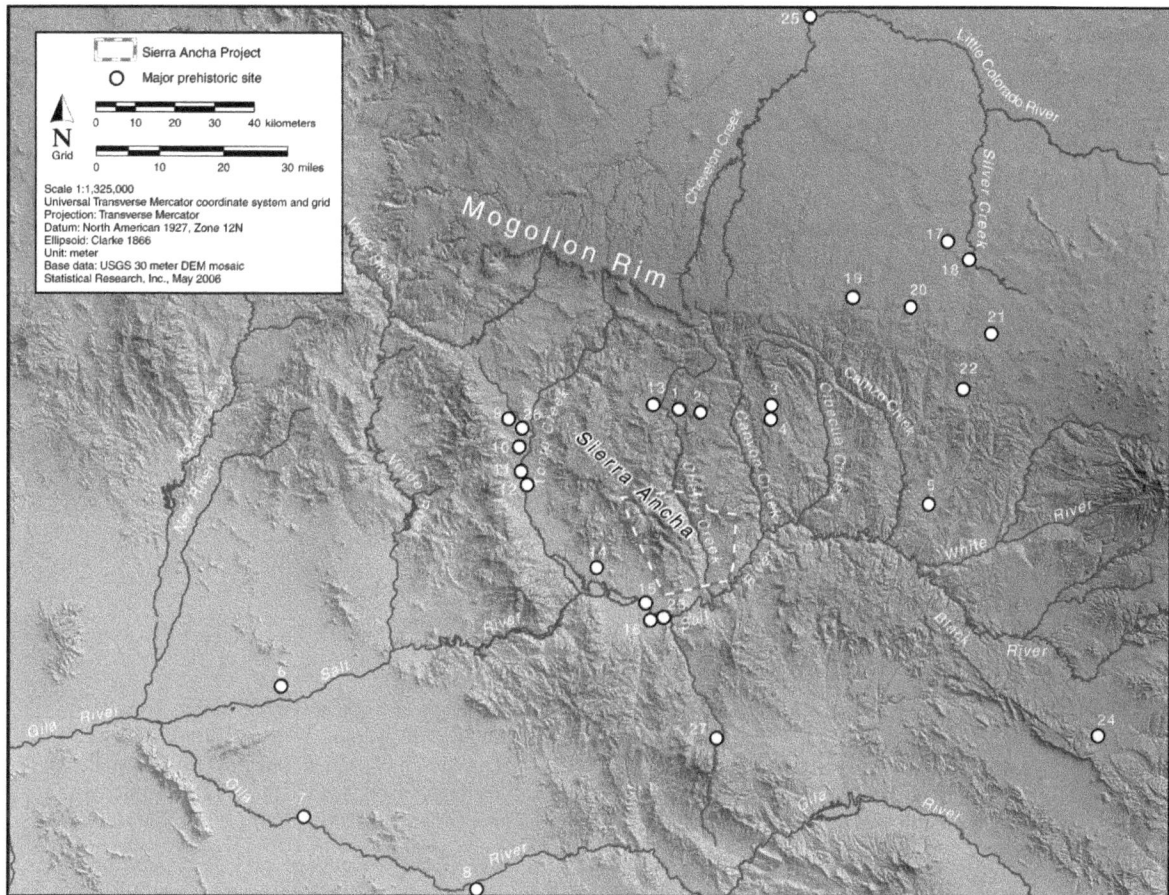

Figure 10.2. Regional Map Showing Important Archaeological Sites: 1) Vosberg, 2) Q Ranch, 3) Chodistaas, 4) Grasshopper, 5) Kinishba, 6) Pueblo Grande, 7) Snaketown, 8) Casa Grande, 9) Deer Creek Village, 10) Ushklish, 11) Boatyard, 12) Heron Hatch, 13) Antler Ruin, 14) Tuzigoot-on-Salome, 15) Eagle Ridge, 16) Hedge Apple, 17) Fourmile Ruin, 18) Shumway Ruin, 19) Bailey Ruin, 20) Pinedale Ruin, 21) Showlow Ruin, 22) Tundastusa, 23) Meddler Complex, 24) Point of Pines, 25) Chevelon Pueblo, 26) Rye Creek Ruin, 27) Gila Pueblo and Besh-ba-gowah (for site information, see Table 10.2) This figure is the sole property of Statistical Research, Inc., and may not be reproduced without its permission.

to the north and east and proceeds counter-clockwise, concluding in the Middle Cherry Creek area. In turn, areas considered are: Silver Creek, Grasshopper, Upper Cherry Creek, the Payson-Star Valley areas, Tonto Basin, Globe-Miami, Lower Cherry Creek, and finally Middle Cherry Creek.

SILVER CREEK

Silver Creek is the most remote area from the

Sierra Ancha and the only area on the Colorado Plateau considered in this review (Figs. 1.1, 10.1, 10.2). This area is included because of its role in the production of Cibola White and White Mountain Red wares that commonly occurred in the late archaeological assemblages in middle Cherry Creek.

The Silver Creek area runs from the Bailey Ruin near Cottonwood Wash on the west, to Fourmile Ruin near Snowflake on the north, to Showlow and the Showlow Ruin on the east (Kaldahl and others 2004: 85). In their discus-

Table 10.1. Project Information and References for Projects Shown in Figure 10.1

Project	Institution/Agency/Organization	References
1. Az Public Service Cholla-Saguaro Transmission Line	Arizona State Museum	Reid (1982a); Teague and Mayro (1979)
2. Payson/Star Valley	Arizona State University	Redman (1993)
3. Oxbow Hill	Arizona State Museum	Huckell (1978)
4. Rye Creek	Desert Archaeology, Inc.	Elson and Craig (1992)
5. State Route 188 – Cottonwood Creek	Statistical Research, Inc.	Klucas and Ciolek-Torrello (2005)
6. Mazatzal Piedmont	Museum of Northern Arizona	Ciolek-Torrello (1987)
7. FLEX Tonto Basin	Arizona State University	
8. Tonto Creek Arch'l Project	Desert Archaeology, Inc.	Clark and Vint (2000)
9. Roosevelt Archaeological Project	Arizona State University; Desert Archaeology, Inc.; Statistical Research, Inc.; and SWCA	Ahlstrom and others (1991); Ciolek-Torrello, Shelley, Altschul and Welch (1990); Ciolek-Torrello, Shelley, and Benaron (1994); Doelle, Wallace, Elson, and Craig (1992); Elson, Stark, and Gregory (1995); Oliver (1997); Rice (1998a)
10. Other Roosevelt/Tonto Basin Projects	Gila Pueblo; Tonto National Forest Surveys; National Park Service; Archaeological Consulting Services—SR88	Haury (1932); Germick and Crary (1989, 1990); Wood and McAllister (1984); Tagg (1985); Steen and others (1962)
11. Vosberg Field School	Arizona State University Archaeological Field School	Cartledge (1976, 1977); Dittert (nd), Morris (1969, 1970)
12. Q Ranch Field School	Arizona Archaeological Society	Dart (1997); Riggs (2005)
13. Grasshopper Field School	University of Arizona Archaeological Field School	Reid and Whittlesey (1999)
14. Miami Wash Project	Arizona State Museum	Doyel (1978)
15. Canyon Day Wastewater Project	Museum of Northern Arizona	Halbirt and Dosh (1986)
16. Sierra Ancha Overviews and Surveys	Statistical Research, Inc.; Archaeological Consulting Services; Archaeological Research Services	Ciolek-Torrello (1999); Effland and MacNider (1991); Curtis (1990)
17. Sierra Ancha Project	Arizona State Museum	this volume and Lange (2005)

Table 10.2. Site Numbers and References for Sites Shown in Figure 10.2

Site Name	Site Number	Reference(s)
1. Vosberg	many	Cartledge (1976, 1977), Dittert (nd); Morris (1969, 1970)
2. Q Ranch	AZ P:13:13(ASM)	Dart (1997); Riggs (2005)
3. Chodistaas	AZ P:14:24 (ASM)	Montgomery (1992); Reid and Whittlesey (1999)
4. Grasshopper	AZ P:14:1 (ASM)	Reid and Whittlesey (1999)
5. Kinishba	AZ V:4:1 (ASM)	Cummings (1940)
6. Pueblo Grande	AZ U:9:1 (ASM)	
7. Snaketown	AZ U:13:1 (ASM)	Haury (1976)
8. Casa Grande	AZ AA:2:51 (ASM)	
9. Deer Creek Village	AZ O:15:52 (ASM)	Elson and Craig (1992)
10. Ushklish	AZ O:15:31 (ASM)	Haas (1971)
11. Boatyard	AZ U:3:286 (ASM)	Huckell and Vint (2000)
12. Heron Hatch	AZ U:3:224 (ASM)	Clark and Vint (2000)
13. Antler Ruin	AZ P:13:2 (ASM)	Harrill (1967); Troncone and others (1993)
14. Tuzigoot-on-Salome	AZ U:8:28 (ASM)	Ciolek-Torrello (1999); Germick and Crary (1989)
15. Eagle Ridge	AZ V:5:104 (ASM)	Elson and Lindeman (1994)
16. Hedge Apple	AZ V:5:189 (ASM)	Swartz and Randolph (1994)
17. Fourmile Ruin	AZ P:12:4 (ASM)	Kaldahl, Van Keuren and Mills (2004); Mills, Herr, and Van Keuren (1999)
18. Shumway Ruin	AZ P:12:6 (ASM)	Kaldahl, Van Keuren and Mills (2004); Mills, Herr, and Van Keuren (1999)
19. Bailey Ruin	AZ P:11:1 (ASM)	Kaldahl, Van Keuren and Mills (2004); Mills, Herr, and Van Keuren (1999)
20. Pinedale	AZ P:12:2 (ASM)	Kaldahl, Van Keuren and Mills (2004); Mills, Herr, and Van Keuren (1999)
21. Showlow Ruin	AZ P:12:3 (ASM)	Kaldahl, Van Keuren and Mills (2004); Mills, Herr, and Van Keuren (1999)
22. Tundastusa	AZ P:16:7 (ASM)	Kaldahl, Van Keuren and Mills (2004); Mills, Herr, and Van Keuren (1999)
23. Meddler Complex	AZ V:5:4 (ASM)	Elson, Stark, and Gregory (1995)
24. Point of Pines	AZ W:10:50 (ASM)	Haury (1989)
25. Chevelon Pueblo	AZ P:2:11 (ASM)	Adams (2002)
26. Rye Creek Ruin	NA9584	
27. Gila Pueblo and Besh-ba-gowah	AZ V:9:52 and AZ V:9:11 (ASM)	Haury (1988) and Hohmann (1990)

sion, Kaldahl and others (2004) also include the site Tundastusa below the Rim (Fig. 10.2). The Silver Creek area is different from other areas discussed in *The Protohistoric Pueblo World* volume (Adams and Duff 2004) in that the relatively few PIV villages there never formed a settlement cluster in the sense that they were a socially and politically interacting cluster of villages with an intersettlement social identity (Kaldahl and others 2004: 85). And, there are relatively few Late PIII and PIV sites in the Silver Creek area (see below). In contrast, there are "literally dozens of sites that date to the Pueblo IV period" in areas below the Mogollon Rim (Kaldahl and others 2004: 87).

Newcomb (1999) uses a number of models, parameters, and assumptions to investigate the paleodemography and settlement of the Silver Creek area. The models show a population peak in the period from AD 1000 to 1100 (Newcomb 1999:46). The peak in population is shown to result from an influx of people in that period, natural population growth alone could not account for the increase (Newcomb 1999:49). Until the late 1200s, the Silver Creek area population was living in dispersed settlements with usually less than 10 rooms (Mills 1999:505).

"By about AD 1290, most residents of the Silver Creek area lived in six large pueblos: Bailey, Fourmile, Pinedale, Showlow, Shumway, and Tundastusa"(Kaldahl and others 2004:86), spaced 12 to 20 km apart (Kaldahl and others 2004:86-87). They further divide the Pueblo IV period into two sub-periods: an earlier period, AD 1275 to 1325; and a later period, AD 1325 to 1390. The earlier part of the Pueblo IV period has sites dispersed throughout the drainage, near permanent streams or springs, with an estimated total of 1000 rooms (Kaldahl and others 2004:87). Plazas in these sites are relatively small and are generally fully enclosed. Archaeological evidence indicates that there was a reorganization of population about AD 1325. New construction is evident at Pinedale, Showlow, and Fourmile.

In the later period, Bailey Ruin is no longer occupied, and the remaining settlements are restricted to streams. With the new construction just noted, the estimated total number of rooms is 1500. Large plazas are added to the sites, but were often only partially enclosed (Kaldahl and others 2004:86-87).

Recent studies support the view of the Silver Creek area as the production locus for Cibola White, White Mountain Red, and even some Roosevelt Red wares (Crown 1994; Triadan 1997; Zedeño 1994), including the examples of these wares found in the Sierra Ancha (see Chapter 4). Cibola White Ware and White Mountain Red Ware production was dependent upon the kaolinitic Cretaceous clays that outcrop near the Rim in the upper Silver Creek area (Mills, Herr, Stinson, and Triadan 1999:296). Chemical analyses of ceramic pastes indicate that Cibola White Ware and White Mountain Red Ware from the Silver Creek area were produced by the same potters, using the same paste recipes (Mills, Herr, Stinson, and Triadan 1999:309). Roosevelt Red Ware, however, may have been made by a different group of potters and was made in a number of different locales, including the Tonto and Phoenix Basins (Crown 1994).

The Pinedale style, common on Cibola White Ware and early White Mountain Red Ware vessels, was relatively short-lived. The Pinedale-style appears in the 1270s and 1280s on Cibola White Ware types and after AD 1285 (Zedeño 1994) on Roosevelt Red Ware. This style is applied throughout eastern Arizona and western New Mexico before 1300, and it appears on the three principal wares in the Silver Creek area—Cibola White Ware, Roosevelt Red Ware, and White Mountain Red Ware (Kaldahl and others 2004:88). By AD 1330, the Pinedale style gave way to diverse design schemes on decorated pottery. Also at this time, Cibola White Ware ceased to be produced in the Mogollon Rim area, and was replaced by the decorated pottery of choice—White Mountain Red Ware. White Mountain Red Ware, however, appears later in the Silver Creek area than the upper Little Colorado River valley to the east (Kaldahl and others 2004:88). Fourmile-style first appears in White Mountain Red Ware vessels in the upper Little Colorado. It represents a dramatic shift in styles, and "marks the cessation of cross-ware stylistic homogeneity"(Kaldahl and others 2004:89). Also, for the first time in the early Pueblo IV assemblages, there are "classic, high-fired White Mountain Red Ware, and low-fired copies"(Kaldahl and others 2004:89).

Taken together, Crown's (1994), Triadan's (1997), and Zedeño's (1994) interpretations suggest that Roosevelt Red Ware was initially produced by potters who migrated into the Silver Creek area (circa AD 1280). The migration processes continued and Silver Creek residents then moved below the Rim after AD 1325-1330 (Mills 1999:508; Mills, Herr, Stinson, and Triadan 1999:311). Further, the ceramic sourcing studies indicate that there were two migrations into the Grasshopper area from Silver Creek—one in the 1280s, the other after 1325 (Mills 1999:508; see also below). Migration into the Silver Creek area occurred over a long period of time, however, it was not just a migration to the area, but also through it.

Clearly, people were moving out of the Silver Creek area during and after the late AD 1200s. The area was not abandoned at this time, however, nor was this emigration a large population loss. Newcomb's (1999:48) models indicate that possibly a net loss of less than 250 people left Silver Creek in the century from AD 1275 to 1375. Populations in Silver Creek were aggregating during this period, even as population was declining (Mills 1999:508). And, as will be noted below, Grasshopper may

not have been the only area Silver Creek people moved to—Cherry Creek and Tonto Basin are also possibilities.

GRASSHOPPER

Human occupation in the Grasshopper area, located near the western end of the Mogollon Highlands, begins in the Late Archaic (Figs. 1.1, 10.1 – 10.3). Throughout the occupation of this region, the principal people there are considered to have been Mogollon, a cultural group that pursued a mixed hunting, collecting, and farming strategy, less reliant on corn than their Anasazi or Hohokam neighbors (Reid and Whittlesey 1999:15). Reid and Whittlesey (1999) divide the prehistoric chronology into three periods: the Early Pit House Period (AD 100-600), the Late Pit House Period (AD 600-1150), and the Mogollon Pueblo Period (AD 1150-1400).

The Early Pit House Period is similar to the Late Archaic lifestyle, with the addition of plain brown pottery (Reid and Whittlesey 1999:14). Early in the period, residential structures were round, later they became rectangular. Some villages have a "great kiva," a large, circular pit-type structure, presumed to be used for community gatherings and ceremonies. The settlement and land-use pattern involved a small, seasonally mobile population pursuing hunting, collecting, and farming. The location of villages on ridges and hilltops could signal some concern for defense (Reid and Whittlesey 1999:14; Tuggle and Reid 2001).

The Late Pit House Period involves population growth, with people living in settlements that tended to cluster around a village with a great kiva (Reid and Whittlesey 1999:15). Villages at this time tended to be located on valley floors, closer to agricultural plots. A pattern that was to continue for centuries also appears to have been established during this period. The

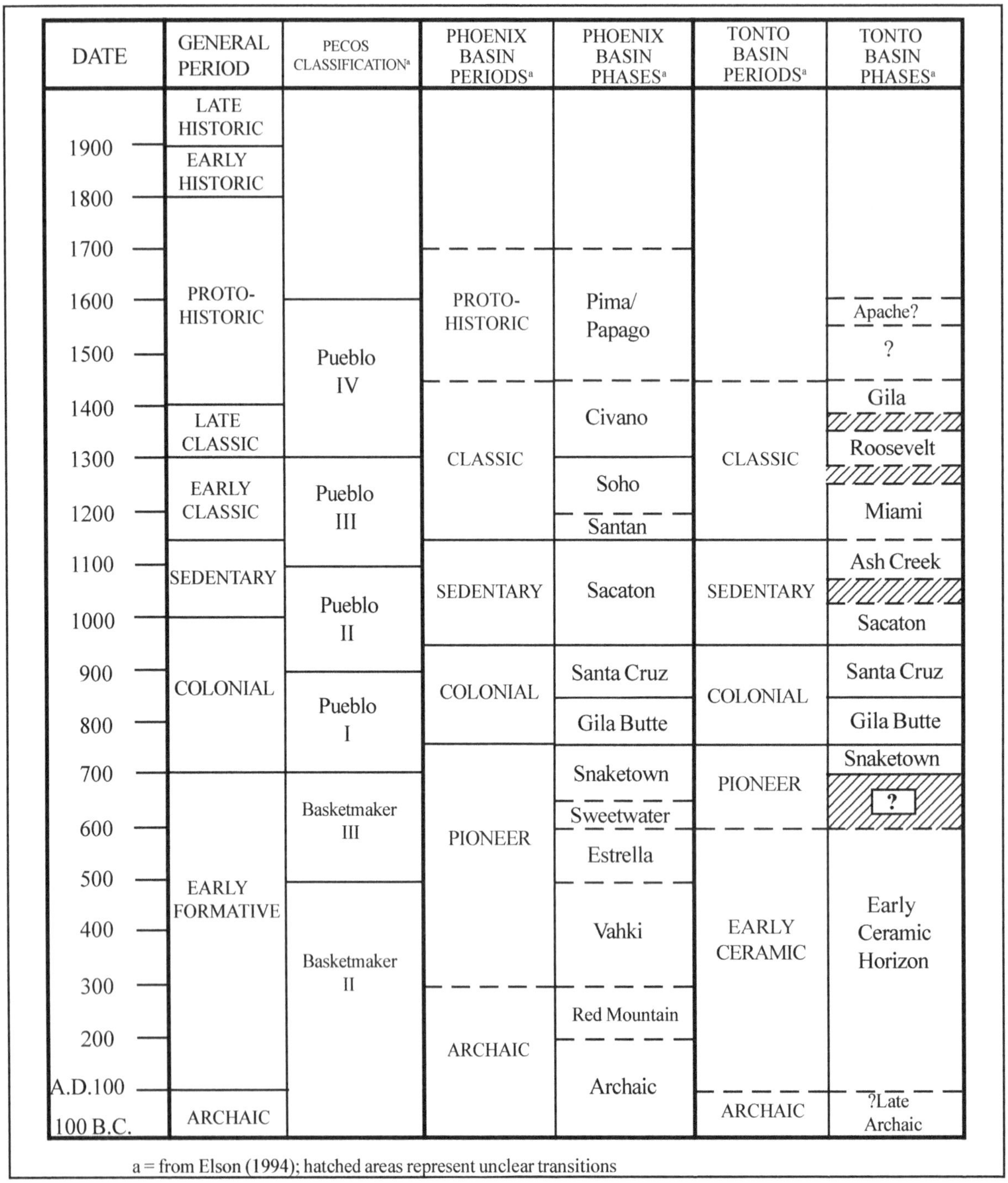

DATE	GENERAL PERIOD	PECOS CLASSIFICATION[a]	PHOENIX BASIN PERIODS[a]	PHOENIX BASIN PHASES[a]	TONTO BASIN PERIODS[a]	TONTO BASIN PHASES[a]
1900	LATE HISTORIC					
	EARLY HISTORIC					
1800						
1700	PROTO-HISTORIC		PROTO-HISTORIC	Pima/ Papago		Apache?
1600						
1500		Pueblo IV				?
1400	LATE CLASSIC			Civano		Gila
1300			CLASSIC		CLASSIC	Roosevelt
1200	EARLY CLASSIC	Pueblo III		Soho		Miami
				Santan		
1100	SEDENTARY		SEDENTARY	Sacaton	SEDENTARY	Ash Creek
1000		Pueblo II				Sacaton
900	COLONIAL		COLONIAL	Santa Cruz	COLONIAL	Santa Cruz
800		Pueblo I		Gila Butte		Gila Butte
700	EARLY FORMATIVE	Basketmaker III	PIONEER	Snaketown	PIONEER	Snaketown
				Sweetwater		?
600				Estrella		
500						Early Ceramic Horizon
400		Basketmaker II		Vahki	EARLY CERAMIC	
300						
200			ARCHAIC	Red Mountain		
A.D.100				Archaic		
100 B.C.	ARCHAIC				ARCHAIC	?Late Archaic

a = from Elson (1994); hatched areas represent unclear transitions

Figure 10.3. Regional Chronologies

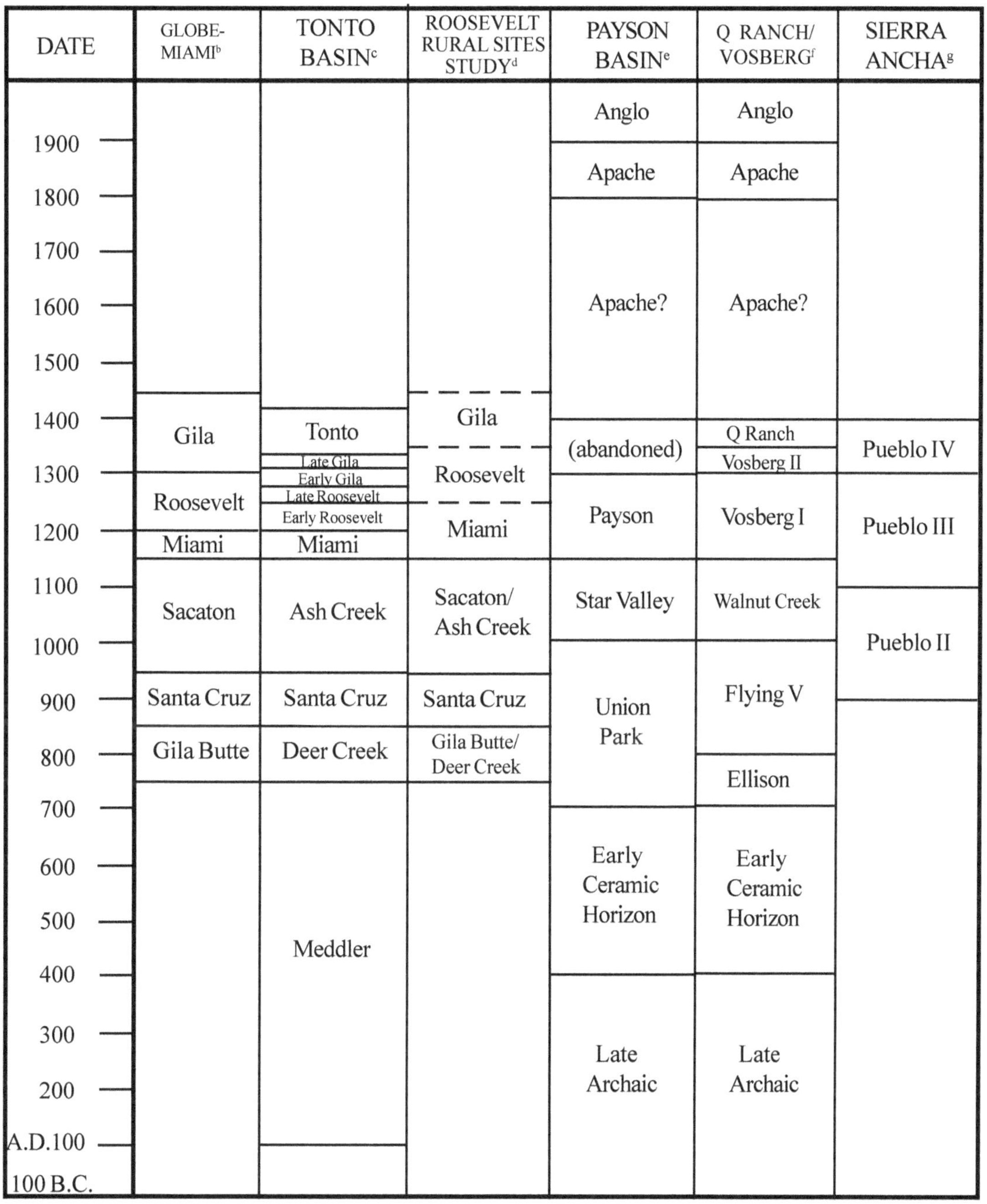

DATE	GLOBE-MIAMI[b]	TONTO BASIN[c]	ROOSEVELT RURAL SITES STUDY[d]	PAYSON BASIN[e]	Q RANCH/VOSBERG[f]	SIERRA ANCHA[g]
1900				Anglo	Anglo	
1800				Apache	Apache	
1700						
1600				Apache?	Apache?	
1500						
1400	Gila	Tonto	Gila	(abandoned)	Q Ranch	Pueblo IV
1300		Late Gila / Early Gila	Roosevelt		Vosberg II	
	Roosevelt	Late Roosevelt / Early Roosevelt		Payson	Vosberg I	Pueblo III
1200	Miami	Miami	Miami			
1100	Sacaton	Ash Creek	Sacaton/ Ash Creek	Star Valley	Walnut Creek	
1000						Pueblo II
900	Santa Cruz	Santa Cruz	Santa Cruz	Union Park	Flying V	
800	Gila Butte	Deer Creek	Gila Butte/ Deer Creek		Ellison	
700						
600				Early Ceramic Horizon	Early Ceramic Horizon	
500		Meddler				
400						
300				Late Archaic	Late Archaic	
200						
A.D.100						
100 B.C.						

b = Doyel 1976; c = Wood 1992; d = Ciolek-Torrello and others 1994; e = Redman 1993; f = Ciolek-Torrello 1999; g = Ciolek-Torrello and Lange 1990

Figure 10.3. Regional Chronologies, cont'd

Bear Village in the Forestdale Valley is among the first settlements in the region to evidence the co-residence of Anasazi and Mogollon peoples in the same area, and even in the same village (Reid and Whittlesey 1999:31).

The Mogollon Pueblo Period is marked by the appearance of above-ground pueblo architecture. Larger aggregated settlements appear late in the Grasshopper area, much later than other Mogollon areas. For example, large settlements of over 50 rooms appear in the Point of Pines area in the mid-1200s, but not at Grasshopper until after 1300 (Reid and Whittlesey 1999:17). Population growth during the Pueblo period was greatly augmented by immigration into the Grasshopper area. Much of the migration at the end of the thirteenth century was probably spurred by the Great Drought, with people coming from both the north and south in search of better-watered farmland (Dean and Robinson 1972; Reid 1989; Reid and Whittlesey 1999:18-19). Rapid population growth from this immigration undoubtedly contributed to the construction of large nucleated settlements at Grasshopper. Reid and Whittlesey (1999:19) also feel that the earlier pattern of aggregation in neighboring areas encouraged aggregation in the Grasshopper area to counter real or perceived threats. The drought eased in the early fourteenth century, as people in the area grouped together and were joined by more immigrants. In the 1200s, the number of rooms in the area is estimated to have been around 200. Between 1300 and 1330, the number of rooms increased dramatically to around 2000 (Reid and Whittlesey 1999:19; see also Triadan and Zedeño 2004:98). The pattern of ethnic co-residence continued into the late 1200s. At this time, Anasazi people may have settled along side local residents at Chodistaas, the largest thirteenth century settlement in the Grasshopper area. Anasazi may also have established the settlement of Grasshopper Springs, a con-temporary settlement to Chodistaas (Reid and Whittlesey 1999:41,44).

As noted above, the population leaving the Silver Creek area was relatively small, whereas population increase in the Grasshopper area was quite large. Some of the later thirteenth and early fourteenth century immigrants to the Grasshopper area may have come from Silver Creek, but must have come from other areas as well.

Ceramically, locally produced brown plain wares were made throughout the prehistoric occupation of the Grasshopper area, and brown corrugated wares were made locally during the Mogollon Pueblo period. Decorated types were mostly derived from areas to the north and east. These imported types principally include Cibola White Ware (Mills, Herr, and Van Keuren 1999; Triadan 1997; and Zedeño 1994) and White Mountain Red Ware, both made in the Silver Creek and Upper Little Colorado areas (Duff 2002). There were also locally made versions of White Mountain Red Ware, particularly of the type called Fourmile Polychrome. Roosevelt Red wares and Salado Red Corrugated were also imported from Tonto Basin, the Sierra Ancha, and other areas during the thirteenth and fourteenth centuries. Locally produced versions of these wares were also made. Of the surrounding areas being considered here, the ceramic assemblages of sites in the Grasshopper area are most similar to the fourteenth century assemblages in middle Cherry Creek and the southeastern Sierra Ancha (see also Ciolek-Torrello and Lange 1990).

Triadan and Zedeño (2004) provide the most recent synthesis of settlement in the Grasshopper region and surrounding areas, although their focus is on the fourteenth century when occupation of the region was most intense and widely distributed. Triadan and Zedeño (2004:99) believe that the dynamics of landscape knowledge, social networks, and topography combined to influence greatly the formation and structure of settlements in the different sub-regions of the Mogollon Highlands. Geographic barriers had an especially important influence on the structure of settlements in areas such as Grasshopper, which were isolated from some adjacent regions by the barriers. The western highlands are separated into several blocks by a series of creeks running through deep and narrow canyons (see Chapter 3). Triadan and Zedeño (2004:97) note that travel laterally (east-west) across the region is very difficult, but travel is more feasible along the numerous north-south trending drainages. There is no doubt that traversing the mountains from Tonto Creek to Cibecue Creek is difficult, but the distinction between north-south and east-west travel may be too strongly stated. For example, it is relatively easy to traverse the mountains east-west between Cherry and Canyon creeks following the Salt River. It is also possible to traverse the high ridges and mountains comprising the Grasshopper and Q Ranch blocks following subsidiary drainages. Travel between the Mogollon Highlands and Colorado Plateau was also possible following the canyons that drained the Mogollon Rim. By contrast, traveling north or south along any of the major streams such as Coon, Cherry, or Canyon creeks was hindered by box canyons and meandering stream courses.

Triadan and Zedeño (2004:105) also note that the cores of the settlement clusters in the Grasshopper and neighboring Q Ranch regions are several large surface pueblos, the largest being located on alluvium in situations with the greatest agricultural potential. They also observe that these clusters typically have smaller, isolated pueblos on their northern and eastern peripheries, and cliff dwellings on their southern edges. They interpret these satellite settlements as representing "strategic patterns involving boundary monitoring and defense"(Triadan and Zedeño 2004:105). As part of this pattern and focusing on the south-

and "outward"-facing locations of cliff dwellings in Cherry and Canyon creeks, Triadan and Zedeño (2004:100-103) suggest that these settlements occurred at the boundaries between the Mogollon and Salado culture areas. They suggest that cliff dwellings controlled access from Tonto Basin to the Sierra Ancha, Q Ranch, and Grasshopper areas and provided the first line of defense for the highland regions.

Although the cliff dwellings of Cherry and Canyon creeks do face south and away from the settlements of the Grasshopper and Q Ranch areas, noncultural factors also must be considered in the placement of these settlements, and the notion that they served as outposts or defensive locations protecting the Grasshopper region must be questioned. Cliff dwellings occur along the southern rim of these areas precisely because this is where suitable locations for building cliff dwellings are most common. It is the southern margins of the highlands below the Mogollon Rim that have been subject to the greatest amount of erosion, creating many cliffs with natural caves and overhangs. Such suitable locations for building cliff dwellings are rare along the northern rim of the highlands. As discussed in Chapter 6, cliff dwellings also tend to face southward for a number of reasons other than the fact that they orient "outward" from Grasshopper and face the Tonto Basin. Furthermore, most cliff dwellings in Cherry Creek predate the fourteenth century (see Chapter 5) and were abandoned by the time the large settlement clusters were forming in the Q Ranch and Grasshopper areas. Most of the Sierra Ancha cliff dwellings, as well as those in Horse and Willow canyons farther north on the Q Ranch plateau, occur in cliffs on eastward-draining canyons, facing the Grasshopper plateau, not exactly a posture for the best defense of the Grasshopper area.

Finally, what are the true implications of "controlling access"(Triadan and Zedeño 2004:100)? Controlling access could mean anything from just watching to more formal monitoring of the landscape, to forcibly responding to intruders, to raising the alarm to obtain help from the core communities. Many of the cliff dwellings are in canyons that could not be considered to be practical travel corridors and are so far up the canyons from potential travel routes that, at best, they could only monitor the landscape from a distance.

It is clear that many cliff dwellings as well as sites situated on isolated buttes in the Cherry Creek area and on the west side of Canyon Creek were defensive in character. What is not clear, however, is who these sites were defending. The age and orientation of many of these sites do not fit Triadan and Zedeño's model of defensive outposts of Grasshopper. Their model, however, may be more appropriate for the tight cluster of cliff dwellings along the east side of Canyon Creek and Oak Creek to the south and west of Grasshopper (see also Tuggle and Reid 2001). The latter do in fact face outwards from the Grasshopper area and were contemporary with the large settlement clusters. Curiously, if the Canyon and Oak creek cliff dwellings were defensive outposts, their placement would indicate more concern with the Q Ranch area, which based on ceramics and architecture was the most culturally similar area to Grasshopper.

Upper Cherry Creek: Pleasant Valley, Vosberg, Q Ranch, and Rock House Areas

Ciolek-Torrello (1999) has previously contrasted lower and upper Cherry Creek, with lower Cherry Creek beginning about the Ellison Ranch, where the creek first breaks out of its narrow canyon into a broader floodplain. For this report, Cherry Creek is divided into three portions—upper, middle, and lower. Upper Cherry Creek includes the Pleasant Valley, Vosberg, Q Ranch, and Rock House areas (Figs.

1.1, 10.1, 10.2). Today, Pleasant Valley, despite being the most urbanized area in the Sierra Ancha, is not well known archaeologically. Vosberg, a small upland valley formed by the headwaters of Walnut Creek, was the location of the Arizona State University Archaeological Field School for several years during the late 1960s and early 1970s (see Chapter 1), the Rock House area was investigated as part of the Cholla Project, and Q Ranch has been investigated recently by the Arizona Archaeological Society (also see Chapter 1). China Spring Creek marks the southern boundary of the Upper Cherry Creek area. From this point south to Bull Canyon is the Middle Cherry Creek area, which was the focus of the Sierra Ancha Project (SAP) (see below).

Archaic Period (up to circa AD 400)

Archaic-style projectile points similar to those in the Petrified Forest area (Tagg 1994; Wendorf 1953) have been found in the Vosberg valley (Chenhall 1972; Ciolek-Torrello 1999). Otherwise, evidence of Archaic-period occupation or use of these upland woodlands and basins is scanty (Macnider and Effland 1989:138; Whittlesey 1982a:125). Aceramic sites may be potentially confused with pre-ceramic sites (Wood 1976), but if some are pre-ceramic, there are then greater indications of Archaic period use in upper Cherry Creek and near Pleasant Valley (Leonard 1996). The upper Cherry Creek area was probably used intermittently as a resource zone for hunting, lithic procurement, and limited collecting activities (Whittlesey 1982a:125).

Early Ceramic Horizon (AD 400-700)

Sites dating to this period are better known and documented in Tonto Basin (Ciolek-Torrello 1999:38-39; Elson and Lindeman 1994; Huckell and Vint 2000). However, occupation during this period is also suspected in the Payson, Q Ranch, and Vosberg areas. This period represents a time of fully agricultural settlements. Formal courtyard groups typical of later Hohokam sites are not known from this period. Instead, small circular and bean-shaped houses seem to be arranged in loose clusters, with parallel, usually east-facing, entryways. The house clusters are often associated with a large, communal pit structure. The settlements produced a varied inventory of ceramic vessels, but it is not yet known when pottery first appeared in the Tonto Basin or Upper Cherry Creek.

Pit House Period

The Vosberg area is the best-known area within Upper Cherry Creek during this period. Vosberg is similar to other areas, such as Payson-Star Valley, with a mixture of Hohokam and indigenous architectural styles. However, when Vosberg is contrasted with the Tonto Basin, Vosberg has less formal household arrangements, lower frequencies of Hohokam material culture items, inhumations, and a primary cremation pattern (Elson 1992a; Gregory 1995). The Salt River arm of the Tonto Basin reflects a more complete suite of typical Hohokam architectural and artifactual elements—houses-in-pits in formal courtyard groups, Hohokam Buff Ware ceramics (including flare-rimmed bowls), and elements of Hohokam ritual systems such as secondary cremations, palettes, and censers.

Vosberg is important as an example of settlement in Upper Cherry Creek as a whole. The earliest settlements in Vosberg date to periods corresponding to the Hohokam Colonial and Sedentary periods. Settlements at this time are small and few in numbers. They typically contain 5 to 8 pit houses, similar to the smaller contemporary settlements in Tonto Basin. These settlements are clustered in small

upland basins associated with pinyon-juniper woodland in Vosberg (Cartledge 1976), Pleasant Valley (Leonard 1996; Troncone and others 1993), and in Rock House and Campbell creeks (Ciolek-Torrello and Lange 1979). At Walnut Creek village, in the earliest phase (Ellison phase, AD 700-800, see Fig. 10.3), pit houses are oval or sub-rectangular with east-facing entries. This arrangement reflects a similar organizational pattern as seen in Mogollon houses and settlements in the early Pit House period (Gregory 1995). Later in the Pre-classic, houses occur in one of two forms—those like Hohokam houses-in-pits, and those like Mogollon types (Morris 1970). Clusters of both types of houses are oriented toward a central plaza (Macnider and Effland 1989:138).

Chenhall (1976) identifies three ceramic wares or types that characterize the Early Pit House or Colonial period: local, indigenous, diabase-tempered plain wares; a local variety of Hohokam buff ware; and early Anasazi white wares. The Anasazi white wares are predominantly Cibola White Ware, with lesser amounts of Tusayan White Ware, and even lesser quantities of Little Colorado White Ware. These general proportions of white wares from above the Rim are maintained in the assemblages throughout Cherry Creek and throughout the periods of occupation there (see also Whittlesey 1982a:126-131).

Morris (1970) interpreted the mixed architectural and artifactual assemblages at Walnut Creek village as indicative of co-residence of Hohokam and Anasazi groups. Initially, Wood (1980:106) generally agreed with this interpretation, but suggested that the immigrant Hohokam were interacting with a Mogollon, not Anasazi, population. Wood (1987) later revised this view, and proposed the "Anchan culture" as an indigenous group, isolated in the Sierra Ancha, that became involved in trading with Mogollon groups to the east, Anasazi groups to the north, and Hohokam groups to the south and west. In exchange for ceramics from these areas, the Anchans are believed to have provided steatite, hematite, and argillite (see also Lange 1982b, 1989).

Sedentary Period (AD 1000 – 1150)

In Vosberg, as in other areas in the region, the Sedentary period marks evidence of the first stage of expansion of settlement and diversification of agricultural strategies (Ciolek-Torrello, Whittlesey, and Welch 1994). Small hamlets and farmsteads, probably seasonally occupied, occur in areas previously unoccupied. V:1:11 was a large site (1.3 sq km) defined in the APS/SRP powerline corridor near Campbell Creek. Smaller concentrations of artifacts within the site boundaries were defined as clusters. Ultimately, 112 clusters were defined (Lange 1982c:105). Some of the clusters date to the Sedentary period, as indicated by the presence of Sacaton Red-on-buff pottery (Lange 1982c:114-118). Burned daub on the surface indicated the presence of jacal structures at many of the clusters. The clusters in this site further illustrate the nature of Sedentary period dispersed small settlements and special activity sites in the general Q Ranch area. It was in these clusters and other sites in the area that the statistical correlation between Hohokam pottery and the presence of steatite manufacturing debris was determined (Lange 1982b, 1989).

Early Classic Period   (AD 1150-1300)

In the Vosberg area, occupation continues, although changes are evident in architecture, settlement patterns, social organization, and ceramics. Whittlesey (1982a:134) has called this the "Cobble Structure Period" to indicate a time when surface architecture was more common, contrasted with earlier subterranean pit houses, but before true stone-masonry pueblos

appeared.

Houses of this period were combinations of stone and jacal walls. They are rectangular, with stacked cobble foundations excavated slightly into the ground. They were often 3-sided, with the fourth wall presumed to be totally jacal. Similar constructions occur above the Mogollon Rim from Chavez Pass to Silver Creek, and in the cliff dwellings of the Kayenta country in northeastern Arizona (Dean 1969). The rooms occur as contiguous, linear blocks, or as isolates in multi-roomed sites. Plazas or open spaces between room-blocks are known, and the rooms are often contained within walled compounds (Cartledge 1976, 1977; Chenhall 1972; Ciolek-Torrello 1999:50; Whittlesey 1982a:134). Settlements usually consisted of less than 20 rooms. V:1:31 in the Campbell Creek area of the Q Ranch block is a good example of this type of site (Reid, Tuggle, and Klie 1982: Fig. 4.5). The site consists of rooms made of rounded diabase cobble and boulder walls and enclosed by a compound wall. A late Sedentary period occupation may be present at this site as well.

Permanent features for water control and soil retention for agriculture first appear during this period. The features include such constructions as checkdams, diversion walls, and linear borders (Rodgers 1970). Such agricultural features typify the attempts to bring new areas into production.

The ceramic assemblages begin to shift noticeably during this period. There is a decrease in Hohokam buff ware, and a rise in locally produced plain ware (including Salado Red Corrugated) and in decorated wares from the north and east (Ciolek-Torrello 1999:47; Whittlesey 1982a:136-139). Salado Red Corrugated pottery is seen as one of the hallmarks of Wood's (1987) local Anchan culture.

In the late 13th century, much of the population in the Pleasant Valley, Vosberg, Q Ranch, and Rock House areas began to aggregate into large settlements that were organized into more complex settlement systems. In addition to the aggregated villages, defensively situated hilltop settlements were established (Ciolek-Torrello 1979, 1999:50; Wood 1987). These sites, on high, prominent features, may have linked the entire region in a complex line-of-sight communications network (but see Lange 2001 for cautions about such interpretations). Fortified sites were established on Gunsight Butte (V:1:74), Castle Peak (V:1:34), "L" Ridge (V:1:76), and Double Buttes (V:1:72) in the Rock House area (Reid, Tuggle, and Klie 1982: Figs. 4.8, 4.38, and 4.36 illustrate the last three sites in this list).

At the same time, cliff dwellings were built in rock shelters and canyons. Gunsight Butte, Castle Peak, and Double Buttes all have structures in shelters on the sides of the buttes. Cliff dwellings were also built in two drainages leading toward Canyon Creek on the east side of the Q Ranch block—V:1:49 and V:2:64 (Reid, Tuggle, and Klie 1982:Figs 4.23-27 and 4.41-42). Architecturally, they are identical to the numerous cliff dwellings in middle Cherry Creek and to Canyon Creek (Graves 1982; Haury 1934; Reynolds 1981) and Red Rock House (Reynolds 1981) on the Grasshopper block.

Late Classic Period (AD 1300-1400)

This is the time of the Vosberg II phase in the Vosberg area and the Q Ranch phase in the Q Ranch area. It is a time of abandonment of some neighboring areas such as Payson-Star Valley and a period of further reorganization in Tonto Basin, following the demise of the Roosevelt phase platform mound system. Throughout central Arizona, small settlements and larger settlement clusters were replaced by a much more nucleated settlement system involving a smaller number of very large settlements (Ciolek-Torrello 1999:54; Ciolek-Torrello and Lange 1979; Reid 1989).

In upper Cherry Creek, at Pleasant Valley and Vosberg, small early Classic period settlements were common. Most of these sites were abandoned, however, by the early 14th century, and local population aggregated into a few large sites—the Antler Ruin, Q Ranch Pueblo, Asbestos Spring Pueblo, and Rock House Pueblo. The Antler Ruin (P:13:2) in Pleasant Valley may have 200 rooms (Harrill 1967; Troncone and others 1993), but was probably a much smaller 40- to 50-room pueblo (Ciolek-Torrello 1999:57). Q Ranch Pueblo (P:13:13) is near Vosberg and is in an upland basin similar to the locations of the Antler Ruin, Grasshopper, and Kinishba. It may contain as many as 320 rooms (Dart 1997; Reid, Tuggle, and Klie 1982:Fig. 4.6), and like Grasshopper (Reid and Whittlesey 1999:113) and Kinishba, consists of two principal masses of rooms divided by a drainage. Asbestos Springs Pueblo (V:1:32; Reid, Tuggle, and Klie 1982:Fig. 4.6) is much smaller, containing approximately 20 rooms, but represents the aggregation of the formerly dispersed population in the Lacey Forks Canyon area. Similarly, Rock House Pueblo (V:1:33; Reid, Tuggle, and Klie 1982:Fig. 4.7) is the settlement where population from the Rock House Creek area came together. It also has about 20 rooms. The hilltop, fortified sites (Gunsight Butte, Castle Peak, and Double Buttes) and cliff dwellings to the east of Rock House were still occupied well into the late Classic period and probably expanded in size during this time.

The end of the Classic period was marked by even greater and more widespread abandonments than those that characterized its onset. By the end of the 14th century, or certainly by the early decades of the 15th century, the entire Upper Cherry Creek area was completely abandoned.

PAYSON-STAR VALLEY

The Payson-Star Valley area is an upland basin located in the headwaters of Tonto Creek below the Mogollon Rim and to the northwest of the Sierra Ancha (Figs. 1.1, 10.1, 10.2). The area was investigated by the Arizona State University Archaeological Field School first through a series of surveys and then through excavations of sites for federal land exchanges. The present outline for a chronology is derived from Redman's synthesis of this work (1993:39) and is given for comparison in Figure 10.3.

Before AD 800, there was only sparse evidence of human settlement in the Payson-Star Valley area. The area, however, was used lightly and sporadically throughout Paleoindian and Archaic times (Huckell 1978; Redman 1993:40-41). The Union Park phase marks the first recognizable settlement. Around AD 850, a set of archaeological remains similar to the Hohokam were found: Santa Cruz and Sacaton Red-on-buff and Gila plain ceramics, slate palettes, worked shell, and houses-in-pits. It is uncertain if these remains represent actual Hohokam colonization of the area, or trade contacts being established between the Hohokam and indigenous Payson groups.

Major population growth occurred in the Star Valley (AD 1000 to 1150) and Payson (AD 1150 to 1300) phases, dramatically changing the nature of settlement (Redman 1993:42). In fact, the overwhelming majority of sites presently known in the Payson area (approximately 95 percent) date to these two phases. The Star Valley phase is basically a continuation of Union Park phase patterns, with the addition of more numerous and more permanent household-sized settlements with surface architecture. The Payson phase shows further aggregation of population into large villages with compounds (50 to 100 rooms) and smaller hamlets with 6 to 40 rooms. Small, household-sized settlements still continue as well, and

there appears to have been an emphasis on run-off-control agriculture during the Payson phase (Redman 1993:39). Recent work in the area east of Payson may indicate a slightly different pattern of population growth, however (Herr 2004, 2006). Population appears to peak in the AD 1000 to 1150 period, and then drop off in the AD 1150 to 1300 period.

After 1300, the Payson-Star Valley area returns to the earlier condition of sparse population. Apparently, the area was once again used as a resource zone for people living elsewhere. Redman (1993) suggests that the Payson-Star Valley area is one of the areas that could have provided new immigrants into Tonto Basin during the fourteenth century.

Over 98 percent of the ceramics recovered from sites in the area during all time periods were plain wares (Redman 1993:122). Chemical and petrographic analyses indicate these were mostly produced locally, while none of the decorated wares were local. Hohokam buffwares, when present, date to AD 600 to 1000, and have a limited distribution (Redman 1993:129). Cibola White Ware, Little Colorado White Ware, and Mogollon plain ware are all present, but in very small quantities. The Payson area was largely abandoned before Roosevelt Red Ware or White Mountain Red Ware types became common in the larger region.

TONTO BASIN

The culture history of the Tonto Basin can be divided several ways. Rice (1998b:11) suggests it can be divided into two principal epochs—the earlier Hohokam phases (Gila Butte, Santa Cruz, and Sacaton) and the later Salado phases (Roosevelt, Gila)(Fig. 10.3). Lengyel and Deaver (2005) suggest a third division—the Archaic-Early Formative—and combine the Hohokam phases under the rubric of the Formative period and the Salado phases under the Classic period.

Haury's (1932) description of Roosevelt 9:6 was one of the few reports available for many years on the Hohokam Colonial period, basing the definition of an important Hohokam period on a site outside of the Phoenix Basin. Tonto Basin has also been regarded as the homeland of the Salado (Haury 1945:210; Rice 1998b:11). In the last decade a large quantity of new data has been gathered to address the Salado issue.

Following a series of small testing and data recovery projects sponsored by the Arizona Department of Transportation (ADOT) and sporadic efforts by Gila Pueblo and independent researchers, the Roosevelt Archaeological Project (RAP) was the first major excavation project conducted in Tonto Basin (Figs. 1.1 and 10.1). Sponsored by the Bureau of Reclamation, RAP was in the field from 1989 to 1993 and was associated with planned modifications to the Theodore Roosevelt Dam. The project consisted of four separate studies, conducted by four different contractors, and was designed to address a wide range of issues involving the nature of the prehistoric Hohokam and Salado occupations in Tonto Basin. As a result of this work, Tonto Basin has become one of the largest, most intensively studied areas in the US Southwest. The Arizona State University team assumed the overall lead for synthesizing the entire project (Rice 1998a) and was responsible for the Roosevelt Platform Mound Study (Rice 1990). This study concentrated on Classic period sites in the lower Tonto Basin from the northern edge of Roosevelt Lake to its southeastern perimeter. Desert Archaeology Inc. of Tucson conducted the Roosevelt Community Development Study (Doelle, Wallace, Elson, and Craig 1992; Elson, Stark, and Gregory 1995), focusing on sites representing a broad range of time periods in the upper Salt River arm of Tonto Basin. Statistical Research Inc. of Tucson was responsible for the Roosevelt Rural Sites Study, and focused on groups of small sites surrounding Roosevelt Lake (Ciolek-Torrello, Shelley, Altschul, and Welch 1990). SWCA Environmental Consultants of Tucson was also contracted to do a survey of the bajada areas around the expected reservoir pool (Ahlstrom and others 1991). Tonto National Forest archaeologist J. Scott Wood played a major role in the project, focusing research and choosing sites for excavation and areas for survey (Rice 1998a:2-3).

Perhaps it was unrealistic to expect the RAP to answer the wide range of research issues outlined for the project; but regrettably, the studies have certainly not provided any real consensus of interpretation about what happened prehistorically in Tonto Basin. The patterns of site types and their distribution and timing have become clearer. What is not clear, and mired in debate, are the interpretations of what these patterns mean, how they became that way, and why they changed. In recent years, several large data recovery projects sponsored by ADOT along State Routes 87, 88, and 188 have provided more data, filling in many of the gaps of the RAP. This summary will review the patterns observed through time and the interpretations that have been proposed, using data from these new studies as appropriate.

Paleoindian and Archaic Periods (10,000 BC to AD 100)

Direct evidence of Paleoindian and Early Archaic occupations is lacking to the extent that these periods are not even represented in most local chronologies (see Fig. 10.3). There are a few projectile points in the area that suggest that these populations were in the Tonto Basin from time to time (Huckell 1978, 1982). The lack of evidence may be attributed to low visibility of a low-level occupation, limited survey coverage, inundation of likely site locations by Roosevelt Lake, or deep burial under later sediments.

The Middle Archaic is better documented, for instance, on the eastern slope of the Mazatzal Mountains in the upper Tonto Basin (Ciolek-Torrello 1987; Huckell 1973, 1998a,b) and near Black Mesa in the eastern Tonto Basin (Reid 1982c). Ciolek-Torrello (1987:348-350) defined the Corral Creek phase for the middle Archaic in the upper Tonto Basin (5000 to 1500 BC). Settlement in this phase is represented by small, short-term campsites and resource procurement and processing sites. Sites are known mostly in the uplands, but the Boatyard Site is on the floodplain of Tonto Creek, with a wood charcoal date of 2900 to 2500 BC (Huckell and Vint 2000).

The Late Archaic is also known as the Early Agricultural Period (1000 BC to AD 100) (Ciolek-Torrello 1999:38) and is not well represented in the Tonto Basin archaeological record. The Boatyard Site again provides evidence of settlement in this period (Huckell and Vint 2000). Features at the Boatyard Site at this time include a possible structure and extramural cooking pits.

Early Ceramic Horizon (AD 100-600)

The Early Ceramic Horizon is the period of the first fully agricultural settlements in the Tonto Basin (Elson and Lindeman 1994). The Eagle Ridge site has structures with formal architecture, a variety of ceramic vessel forms, and evidence of domesticated plants. The Eagle Ridge site has similarities to Mogollon sites of the same time period, with small, circular or bean-shaped pit houses arranged in loose clusters with parallel, usually east-facing, entry ways (Burton 1991; Ciolek-Torrello 1998, 1999:38; Deaver and Ciolek-Torrello 1995; Gregory 1995:251; Sayles 1945).

Preclassic Period (AD 600-1150)

After AD 700, areas below the Mogollon Rim came under the influence of the Hohokam regional system (see Wilcox 1979). In the Tonto Basin, the Hohokam influences may have arrived via actual Hohokam peoples from the Phoenix Basin. The Hohokam were targeting riverine areas for floodwater and irrigation farming, and areas with desired wild desert resources. The floodplains and lower terraces of the Salt River arm of the Tonto Basin may have been settled by Hohokam looking for these types of settings. The lower Tonto Basin Hohokam settlements have typical Hohokam architecture (including houses-in-pits arranged in courtyard groups), abundant Hohokam buff ware ceramics, and elements of Hohokam ritual such as secondary cremations, palettes, and ceramics (Ciolek-Torrello 1999:39; Craig and Clark 1994). Thus, the Preclassic Period is described with the Hohokam chronology (see Fig. 10.3).

Pioneer Period (AD 600? to 750)
Archaeological remains of this period are not well documented, however, the occupation seems to be more widespread than the earlier pre-ceramic occupations. Settlements of the Pioneer period were insubstantial and transitory (Doyel 1985). Snaketown phase remains were found at Deer Creek Village in the upper Tonto Basin (Elson and Craig 1992), but no associated houses were found. Late Pioneer period remains were also found at the Heron Hatch Site, but no houses or features were definitely associated with this period there, either (Clark and Vint 2000). Sites with later Colonial and Sedentary period occupations may be obscuring earlier Pioneer period occupations.

Colonial Period (AD 750-1000)
The Colonial period marks an increase in settlement intensity in Tonto Basin and surrounding areas due to actual movements of Hohokam peoples from the Phoenix Basin (Clark and Huckell 1998:162). Still, the small hamlets

and farmsteads were few in number and were widely scattered. Given the long duration and relatively low number of sites, very few were occupied at any one time. The settlements were located on lower terraces overlooking the floodplains of major drainages—taking advantage of the possibility of floodwater farming in the floodplains and irrigation on the streamside terraces (Ciolek-Torrello and others 1990:20-21; Wood and McAllister 1984). It is expected that the early Colonial period residents were pursuing a mixed subsistence strategy of horticulture, wild plant gathering, and hunting, a good approach given the highly variable climatic conditions of this time (Ciolek-Torrello 1999:40).

Gila Butte phase sites are the best known of the early Tonto Basin occupations. Sites with primarily Gila Butte phase occupations include Deer Creek (Swartz 1992) and Ushklish (Haas 1971) in the upper Tonto Basin, Heron Hatch and the Boatyard Site along upper Tonto Creek, and the Hedge Apple Site near Meddler Point on the Salt River arm (Swartz and Randolph 1994). Gregory (1995:149-151) believes that house arrangements at Deer Creek and Ushklish reflect a continuation of Early Formative period, Mogollon-like patterns that seem to be the organizational pattern adopted by indigenous populations. This pattern was subsequently modified into courtyard arrangements through interactions with the Hohokam migrants into the Tonto Basin.

The Santa Cruz phase is characterized by the development of large, permanent settlements. Again, the actual density and distribution of sites is often obscured, because some Santa Cruz phase components are buried under later occupations (Effland and Macnider 1991:36). The settlement systems involved a more diversified set of sites—resource procurement loci, field houses, small seasonal farmsteads, farming settlements with evidence of more permanent occupations, and larger primary villages (Ciolek-Torrello 1999:41). The larger villages, such as the Santa Cruz phase occupation at Meddler Point, shows the same formal arrangement of courtyard groups, middens, and plazas as found in the Phoenix Basin. However, there are still differences—some villages, such as Roosevelt 9:6, Ushklish, and Deer Creek, lack the formal courtyard groups and shifting locations of house clusters associated with the re-use of courtyard areas at contemporary Phoenix Basin sites. Also, large communal houses at settlements in the upper Tonto Basin contrast with the courtyard groups in the Phoenix and lower Tonto basins.

Until recently, the Gladwinian model (Gladwin 1957; Gladwin and Gladwin 1934, 1935) of Hohokam expansion into the Tonto Basin and other areas below the Mogollon Rim had been the primary interpretive model employed by archaeologists to explain the development of Formative culture (sedentary farming) in Tonto Basin. This model was based in part on the work done by Haury (1932) at Roosevelt 9:6. According to the Gladwinian model, the first farmers in Tonto Basin were colonists from the Phoenix Basin who settled in the Colonial period near the large floodplain at the confluence of the Salt River and Tonto Creek. However, the discovery of older agricultural settlements lacking obvious Hohokam traits in other parts of Tonto Basin led to an alternative view (Elson, Gregory, and Stark 1995). This view was confirmed by the discovery of the Early Formative period agricultural settlement at Eagle Ridge, with closer affinities to the Mogollon Forestdale Branch. In the alternative model, the Colonial period Hohokam migrants encountered an indigenous farming population with whom they interacted, producing a distinctive Tonto Basin tradition that maintained connections with the Hohokam to varying degrees (Elson 1992a; Elson, Gregory, and Stark 1995; Gregory 1995; Wood 1992). Although the Eagle Ridge site is located on the Salt Arm, these indigenous farmers appear to have been more established in the upper Tonto Basin at sites such as Deer Creek and the Ushklish Ruin. Thus, the Hohokam migrants were discouraged or prevented from settling in the upper basin areas where prime agricultural areas were already occupied. Instead, they moved into a relatively sparsely occupied area in the lower basin, where expanses of arable land were favorable to the irrigation farming strategies with which they were most familiar (Ciolek-Torrello 1999:43).

Sedentary Period (AD 1000 to 1150)
The Sedentary period in Tonto Basin has been divided into the Sacaton and Ash Creek phases in the currently accepted chronology (Elson 1996), although recent ADOT-sponsored research on a number of sites spanning the Sedentary and early Classic period suggests little evidence for a distinct Ash Creek phase (Lengyel and Deaver 2005). Many see the Sedentary period as a time of "experimentation" in agricultural exploitation and residence in the uplands—the bajada and piedmont zones—surrounding the basin (Ciolek-Torrello, Whittlesey, and Welch 1994; Clark and Vint 2000; Germick and Crary 1989:14; Wood and McAllister 1984:282). Sacaton phase settlements in the bajada and piedmont zones were forerunners of a later, more intensive Classic period occupation of the uplands. In some upland areas, Sacaton phase settlements were replaced by larger early Classic period habitations, as in the bajada above the Armer Ranch area and in the Cholla and Grapevine areas along the eastern slopes of the Mazatzal Mountains (Ciolek-Torrello, Shelley, and Benaron 1994). Not all upland areas farmed later in the Classic period, however, show evidence of use during the Sacaton phase. For example, in the Porter Springs-Tonto National Monument area, 74 Classic period sites have been identified by survey, but there is no evidence for a Sacaton

phase occupation there (Ciolek-Torrello, Shelley, and Benaron 1994; Tagg 1985).

The Sedentary period is a time when significant differences in archaeological interpretations first become apparent. The fact of expansion into upland areas is generally agreed upon, but the nature and scale of the occupation remain controversial (Ciolek-Torrello and others 1990:10-11). The debate can be highlighted as follows.

• The Gladwins (Gladwin and Gladwin 1930, 1934, 1935) believed the Tonto Basin and Globe-Miami areas were abandoned by the Hohokam in the Sedentary period, and remained unoccupied until the Salado arrived around AD 1100 (see also Steen and others 1962). This occupational hiatus is not supportable (Ciolek-Torrello 1999:44). An earlier review of previous investigations in the area (Ciolek-Torrello, Shelley, and Benaron 1994) suggested that small Sedentary period farmsteads are the most numerous and widespread site types in the region, although these appear to be mostly seasonal settlements.

• Wood (1985b:246) believes that the majority of Preclassic period occupation in the region dates to the Sedentary period. Wood and McAllister (1984:282) believe in a high degree of settlement permanence and elaboration at this time, as well as a great increase in population. They suggest changes in agricultural practices associated with population growth were a reflection of changes in political, economic, and settlement structures. They argue that the floodplains became filled with colonists and their descendants, and that villages grew into economic and administrative centers. This situation led to the primary floodplain resource zones becoming restricted, forcing the use of non-irrigation strategies in upland settings.

This position does not appear to be supportable either. Although Sedentary period settlements are abundant throughout Tonto Basin, these settlements are very small; large Sedentary period villages have not been found. Furthermore, models of agricultural productivity based on paleoclimatic reconstructions and soils data (Van West and Altschul 1994) indicate these population estimates are too large for the carrying capacity of the agricultural systems predicted for this time period. Doelle's (1995) reconstruction of population also indicates much lower population totals throughout Tonto Basin history than Wood and McAllister (1984; Wood 1989) have stated.

• Ciolek-Torrello (1999:43-45, 1994:631; see also Doyel 1978:207; and Germick and Crary 1990:9) believes that the Sedentary period settlements are, to the contrary, less substantial than similar Colonial period settlements or contemporary settlements in the Phoenix Basin. The presence of large, informal pit houses, and a lack of formal hearths, burials, nonutilitarian artifacts, and evidence for subsistence diversification instead suggest a shift from the short-term sedentism of the Colonial period to recurrent seasonal occupations. Support for this interpretation is also found in the shapes of the houses. In the worldwide ethnographic literature, sedentary populations tend to build square or rectangular houses, more mobile populations tend to build round or oval houses (Ciolek-Torrello 1998, 1999:45; Elson 1992a; Gilman 1987; Flannery 1972). Among excavated houses in the Tonto Basin (Ciolek-Torrello 1994:633), 70 percent of 37 Sacaton phase pit houses were round, oval, or asymmetrical in shape. Only 12 percent of Colonial period houses were of these shapes. Additionally, only 78 percent of the Sacaton phase houses contained

hearths or fire pits, whereas 92 percent of the Colonial period houses contained such features. Courtyard groups, the hallmark of Preclassic Hohokam domestic architectural organization, are also not common in the Tonto Basin Sacaton phase settlements (although Eagle Ridge. Locus A, is an exception [Elson and Lindemann 1994]). Recent research along the Tonto Creek arm of the lower Tonto Basin reveals more permanent Sedentary period settlements. These settlements, however, are small, single-family farmsteads, not the villages and administrative centers Wood and McAllister (1984) suggest (Ciolek-Torrello and Klucas 2005; see Clark 2004 for another alternative).

Based on paleoenvironmental reconstructions by Van West and Altschul (1994), Ciolek-Torrello, Whittlesey, and Welch (1994) argue that unusually salutary climatic conditions in the Sedentary period spurred expansion of settlement into areas previously too unpredictable to exploit more than intermittently. It was not that the riverine fields improved greatly because of the climatic conditions, but that the reliability of different agricultural strategies or systems was improved. These more stable conditions and greater productivity would have encouraged population growth, which in turn would have led to the expansion of settlement into upland bajada and piedmont areas that Wood and McAllister (1984) observed. Ciolek-Torrello, Whittlesey, and Welch (1994:449) propose that late Preclassic subsistence land uses are best described by a mixed economy, rancheria model (Welch 1994).

• Rice (1998c:51) has questioned some of the data, in particular the soils map, upon which the Van West and Altschul (1994) reconstructions were based. Further, Rice and Oliver's (1998:86) perspective is that Sedentary period use of the uplands was very limited and "probably no more than a few small scattered hamlets or very small villages at any one time." In reviewing the "mixed rancheria subsistence strategy" posited by the Statistical Research team (Welch 1994:79-80; Welch and Ciolek-Torrello 1994:44; Ciolek-Torrello, Whittlesey, and Welch 1994:440-441), Rice and Oliver (1998:96-100) note that the implications of the model include population estimates too low to form the complex organization posited by his earlier work (Rice 1990). They also believe the Tonto Basin data do not show a delayed focus on agriculture, as indicated by the rancheria model. Rice and Oliver (1998:100) believe the Tonto Basin subsistence system did not change in the ways the rancheria model predicts. They conclude that the rancheria hypothesis is not supported by the Roosevelt project's data.

Haury's (1932) research at Roosevelt 9:6 was the basis for positing an actual migration of Phoenix Basin Hohokam into Tonto Basin. This view has been modified, and currently is mostly limited to settlements in the lower Tonto Basin (Elson 1992a). In the upper Tonto Basin, Payson, and Vosberg areas, the similarities in material culture are attributed to Hohokam-like traits exhibited by local indigenous populations who participated, to varying degrees, in the Preclassic period Hohokam regional exchange system, rather than direct acculturation from co-resident migrants (Gregory 1995; Redman and Hohmann 1986). Both the indigenous populations and Hohokam migrants in Tonto Basin and the surrounding region maintained close ties with the core area, as indicated by the imported buff ware ceramics; however, evidence for participation in cremation ritual, Hohokam ceremonial paraphernalia, and ball courts are rare or notably absent (Ciolek-Tor-

rello 1998; Elson, Gregory, and Stark 1995). Some have maintained that the lack of ball courts was due to low levels of investigation and Roosevelt Lake covering the sites with ball courts (Wood 1985b). Although this view may have been tenable 20 years ago, it no longer is, as the intensive investigations sponsored by the Bureau of Reclamation and ADOT in the past two decades have failed to uncover any evidence of ballcourts. Others believe that low population densities obviated the need for integrative features like ball courts (Elson, Gregory, and Stark 1995). The authors here would argue that the greater abundance of Hohokam Buff Ware pottery; secondary cremation burials; Hohokam shell artifacts, censers, and palettes; Hohokam-style houses-in-pits; and house arrangements involving courtyard groups indicates that some Hohokam migrants were actually present in the lower Tonto Basin and in some surrounding upland areas. In the case of the Vosberg and Q Ranch areas, the Hohokam interest in the uplands seems to be in acquiring and processing steatite and serpentine (Lange 1982b, 1989). For the most part, however, Tonto Basin appears to have been outside of the Hohokam regional system that focused on the use of ballcourts (Abbott 2000; Wilcox 1979; Wilcox and Sternberg 1983).

Lower frequencies of Sacaton Red-on-buff pottery in late Sedentary period contexts, the replacement of cremation with inhumation ritual, and the absence of later Classic period Hohokam Buff Ware ceramics seem to indicate a reduction in contact with the Phoenix Basin. At the same time, the appearance of Cibola White Ware ceramics and changes in architecture signal a shift in exchange and contact to the Little Colorado River and White Mountain areas, or even an influx of people from these areas. These changes have been the primary rationale for defining the Ash Creek phase in the latter part of the Sedentary period in the Tonto Basin (Elson 1996; see Fig. 10.3). The

Ash Creek phase marks the first disjuncture with the Hohokam sequence since the Snaketown phase. A recent review of the chronological markers of Sedentary and Classic period occupations in Tonto Basin, however, does not support the definition of a discrete Ash Creek phase. Assemblages assigned to early Sedentary period and Ash Creek phases were not temporally discrete (Lengyel and Deaver 2005). Furthermore, there is no evidence for an increase in Cibola White Ware in the late Sedentary period. While Hohokam Buff Ware does indeed drop out of archaeological assemblages at the end of the Sedentary period, white ware frequencies remain relatively constant.

Late in the Sedentary period, the Hohokam cultural and political system underwent a major restructuring, including abandonment of many outlying areas such as the Salt-Gila confluence and the Agua Fria, New River, and lower Verde valleys, which had been major components of the Preclassic period Hohokam regional system (Ciolek-Torrello 1999; 2003). Within the Phoenix Basin proper, changes in canal systems were associated with abandonment of some settlements and establishment of new and larger settlements in the Scottsdale and Mesa areas. Such restructuring and abandonment did not occur in Tonto Basin, where more continuity in settlement location and distribution was evident between the Sedentary and Classic periods (Ciolek-Torrello 1999:47). Many of the early Classic period settlements are superimposed over older Sedentary period settlements (Clark and Vint 2000; Doyel 1978; Rice 1985), and the internal structure of large sites such as Meddler Point continued unchanged (Gregory 1995:168).

Early Classic Period (AD 1150-1350)

Around AD 1100 to 1150, the end of the Sedentary period, substantial changes occurred in the Phoenix Basin and across the entire region below the Mogollon Rim, as the Preclassic Hohokam regional exchange system collapsed. The Ash Creek (Sedentary period) and Miami (Classic period) phases have been suggested as transitional phases in the Tonto Basin (Elson 1999:50; see also Ciolek-Torrello, Whittlesey, and Deaver 1994). The first phase is believed to represent the gradual decline of Hohokam populations and Hohokam influences on material culture and architecture, although as noted above recent research does not support this phase distinction. The Miami phase notes the initial development of the Salado culture that characterizes the region in the Classic period. The latter portion of the early Classic period in the Tonto Basin is called the Roosevelt phase (Ciolek-Torrello, Whittlesey, and Deaver 1994; Doyel 1976; Elson 1996).

Understanding of the Miami phase in the Tonto Basin is still rudimentary and is still not accepted by all investigators, but the Roosevelt phase is currently the best known of any period of time in regional prehistory. Agricultural and settlement diversification were expanded to their practical limits in the early Classic period. Wood and McAllister (1984:282-283) see the Roosevelt phase as a time when previously seasonal upland farmsteads became full-time residences. This was the time of maximal distribution of small settlements throughout the riverine and upland zones (Ciolek-Torrello 1987; Curtis 1990; Germick and Crary 1989, 1990). Rice and Oliver (1998:86) believe that the upland population reached its maximum in the Roosevelt phase (Fig. 10.4).

The explanations for expansion into upland areas are opposed in a sort of push-pull relationship. On the one hand, expansion has been attributed to steady population growth in the valley bottoms and resulting need to use all available farmland with the inevitable effects of degrading the local environment (see Ciolek-Torrello and others 1990:20-21 and Wood and McAllister 1984 for more detailed

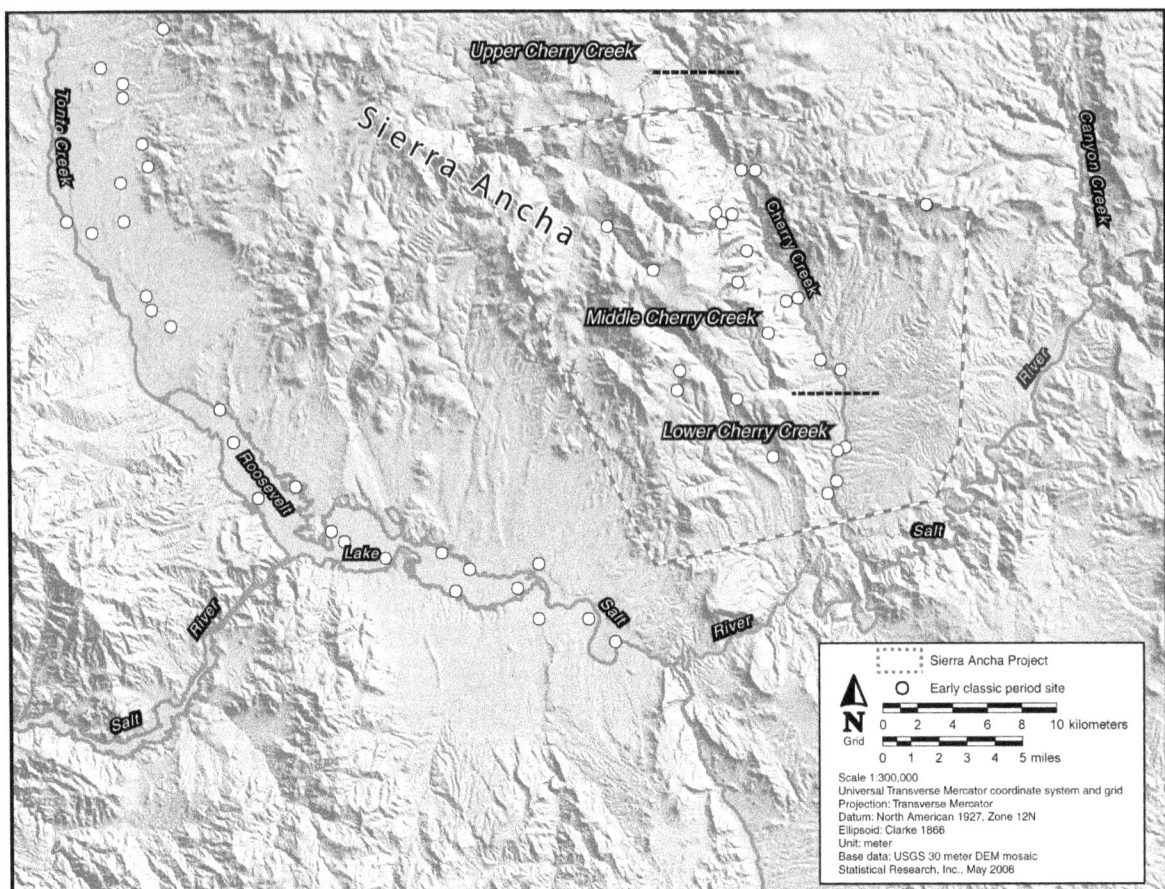

Figure 10.4. Early Classic Period Distribution of Sites in Tonto Basin and Cherry Creek. This figure is the sole property of Statistical Research, Inc., and may not be reproduced without its permission.

discussion of this model). On the other hand, the usually dry and unpredictable uplands may have become attractive due to good climatic conditions that characterized the period from the end of the Sacaton phase through the Miami phase (Rose 1994; Van West and Altschul 1994). These good conditions made it possible to exploit normally marginal upland areas, albeit for short periods of time. Although early Classic period farmsteads in the uplands were somewhat larger and evidenced more intensive occupations than their predecessors, they appear to have been short-term occupations that probably did not exceed ten years, a span that probably coincided with short periods of optimal climatic conditions. Also, as of yet, the large Sacaton and Miami phase populations,

administrative centers, and intensive and large-scale agricultural systems posited by Wood and McAllister's (1984) reconstruction have not been found (Ciolek-Torrello 1999:52).

During the early Classic period, the small sites of the bajada and piedmont zones consisted of two or three detached, low-walled masonry and adobe structures that were more oval than rectangular. Interestingly, they lack compound walls and more rectangular structures that are important components of Doyel's (1976) definition of the Miami phase. Less is known about large riverine settlements in the Miami phase. Most were covered by or incorporated into later Roosevelt phase settlements. It is possible that the complex settlement hierarchy proposed for the Gila phase (Wood

1989; Wood and McAllister 1984:285) began as early as the Miami phase. Several groups of settlements, made up of farmsteads, hamlets, and villages, are found along the lower terraces of the floodplain, on higher terraces, and also along the line of springs at the edge of the upper bajada. Ciolek-Torrello, Whittlesey, and Welch (1994) view the expansion into upland areas as an opportunistic endeavor to extend the mixed-economy rancheria strategy into upland areas where temporary conditions permitted its application and success for short periods of time. Thus, the expansion represents the spread of an existing land-use system in order to reduce risk, rather than being the evidence of a new and more complex system. Higher than normal precipitation, making riverine systems vulnerable to flood-damage, may have made the exploitation of upland areas attractive. The expansion into the uplands was, therefore, not a product of new agricultural innovation developed as a result of population pressure (Wood and McAllister 1984), nor is it a product of entrepreneurial activities of an incipient elite (Minnis and Rice 1990; Rice 1990).

In the Roosevelt phase, population expanded rapidly into piedmont and mountain zones in the Sierra Ancha, and into small upland basins and valleys and along drainages such as Salome, Cellar, Oak, and Greenback creeks. These upland settlements were small-scale replicas of the valley communities. The upland settings allowed the immigrants to pursue a variety of farming strategies, including dry and floodwater farming, and small-scale irrigation using springs and the small creeks draining the mountain slopes.

A new and unusual aspect of the Classic period settlement system was the location of many sites on hilltops or in cliff faces and caves. These new site locations are coupled with a pattern of aggregating into increasingly larger settlements (Ciolek-Torrello 1999:53). In the latter decades of the Roosevelt phase, Tonto Basin was distinguished from surrounding areas by the appearance of platform mounds, a new feature added to the existing pattern of walled compounds. Platform mounds are thought to be associated with an attempt to organize or integrate the communities of the Tonto Basin into a more coherent socioeconomic system similar to contemporary communities in the Phoenix Basin (Ciolek-Torrello 1999:53). Conflict may have also become more prevalent during the course of the Classic period. Gregory (1995:182) notes that nearly every Roosevelt phase house examined by Desert Archaeology in their Roosevelt Community Development Studies had been burned. Rice (1998d:239) notes that the percentage of burned rooms increases from 36 percent in the Roosevelt phase to 82 percent in the Gila phase.

The early Classic period is also characterized by what appears to have been a new wave of immigration into lower Tonto Basin, this time of puebloan people (Whittlesey and Ciolek-Torrello 1992; Whittlesey and Reid 1982). This migration is seen as part of a much larger phenomenon, as thousands of drought-stricken Anasazi farmers abandoned the Four Corners and shifted southwards into the better-watered regions around the Mogollon Rim and in the Little Colorado and Rio Grande river valleys (Ciolek-Torrello, Whittlesey, and Welch 1994; Reid 1989; Van West and Altschul 1994). While the Gladwins' original model of a Salado intrusion into Tonto Basin has been rejected, new evidence derived from the Reclamation- and ADOT-sponsored projects provides evidence for a revised view of the impact of Classic period migration into the region (Clark 2001).

The precise origin of these immigrants is unknown; it is not clear whether they were Anasazi or Western Pueblo people who had been dislocated by the Anasazi from the Mogollon Rim. Their presence, however, is signaled by the appearance of new architectural forms and pottery types. Clark (2001) proposes the presence of puebloan enclaves in local Classic period communities. These enclaves were distinguished from indigenous settlements by differences in the organization of domestic space and technological styles exhibited in house construction and utilitarian ceramic production. Specifically, the enclaves were characterized by the construction of room blocks and the use of corrugated pottery.

In contrast to the Gladwinian migration model in which the puebloan groups took control of Tonto Basin, Clark (2001) suggests that this migration was limited and resulted in co-residence of migrant and indigenous groups within the same communities. Furthermore, Clark believes that the migrants were at a distinct disadvantage with respect to land ownership and familiarity with canal irrigation. He suggests that several of these immigrant groups turned to alternative ways of obtaining food by producing pots and other commodities for exchange with their indigenous neighbors.

Platform mounds, which do not have the same developmental history as those in the Phoenix Basin, were first constructed in Tonto Basin shortly after the initial influx of immigrants. One of the functions of these public structures may have been to integrate the ethnically diverse residents of these communities (Ciolek-Torrello, Whittlesey, and Welch 1994; Clark 2001; Whittlesey and Ciolek-Torrello 1992).

Late Classic Period (AD 1350-1450)

The late Classic period in the Tonto Basin is represented by the Gila phase, a time of further reorganization that involved the demise of the Roosevelt phase platform mound system. Platform mound-centered settlements were replaced by a more aggregated system with a smaller number of highly nucleated communities (Fig. 10.5). Wood (1992) revised earlier views (1986, 1989) to see the period AD 1350 to 1450 as a time of cultural retrenchment and decreasing complexity from the Roosevelt phase peak in cultural development and complexity. The Roosevelt phase development of a basin-wide platform mound system in the riverine zone was replaced by a Gila phase lower-order settlement system with roomblocks. Most platform mounds were abandoned, although a few, such as at Cline Terrace, may have continued to be used throughout the fourteenth century.

This Gila phase reorganization also entailed large-scale abandonments of most of the settlements in the piedmont and mountain zones and of many of the sites on the valley floor as well. Only the upland areas with the most stable resources continued to be occupied (Germick and Crary 1989:15-16; Wood and McAllister 1984:287). The large roomblock complex of Tuzigoot-on-Salome was one of the few large settlements that persisted in the western Sierra Ancha piedmont in the Gila phase.

By the mid-1300s, most late Roosevelt phase site complexes were abandoned and were replaced with a basin-wide aggregation into as few as eleven larger and more nucleated settlements (Fig. 10.5; see also Ciolek-Torrello and others 1994:Fig. 15.6; Wood 1992). In the upper Salt Arm—the best studied part of Tonto Basin—the Meddler complex and several smaller platform mound settlements were abandoned and replaced by the Schoolhouse Ruin, a large complex of elevated rooms surrounding single-story storage rooms. The larger Armer Ruin complex, at the southwestern foot of the Sierra Ancha, appears to have exhibited more continuity, although it has not been as well studied as the Meddler area. The Armer Ruin complex appears to have been abandoned by the Gila Phase, based on the near absence of Gila Polychrome pottery (Germick and Crary 1998). The Tonto Cliff Dwellings, on

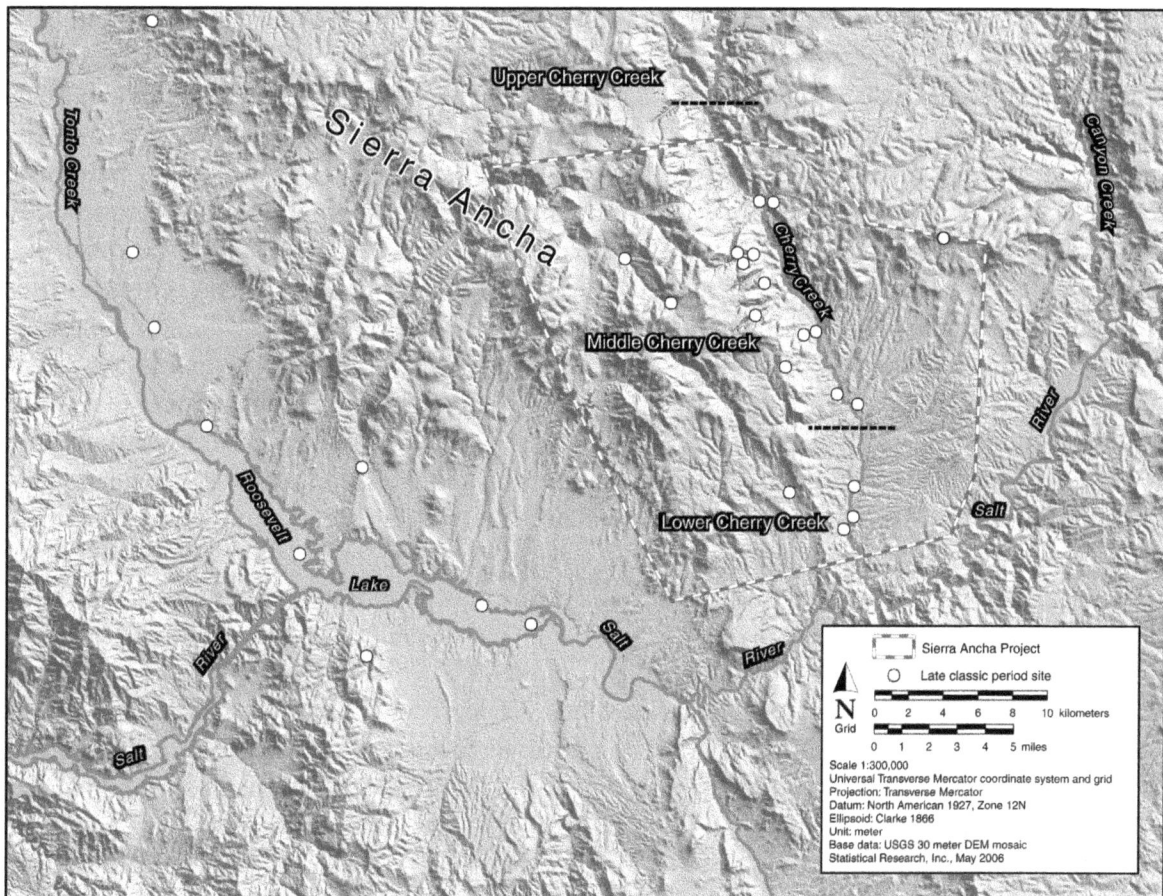

Figure 10.5. Late Classic Period Distribution of Sites in Tonto Basin and Cherry Creek. This figure is the sole property of Statistical Research, Inc., and may not be reproduced without its permission.

the southeastern slopes of the Mazatzal Mountains represent the most unusual Gila phase settlements in Tonto Basin and may reflect the persistence of a strong puebloan influence at this time. The late Classic period ended with the complete depopulation of the area, and with that, the end of any recognizable Salado cultural tradition in the Tonto Basin.

The ASU team has taken a very different view of the Gila phase, and even modified that view over time. Contrary to the pattern of reorganization just described, the ASU team has argued that platform mound construction continued unabated through the Gila phase. As an example, Lindauer (1996:381) believes Schoolhouse Point represents a form of plat-

form mound construction despite differing views from other researchers (Craig and Clark 1994; Whittlesey and Ciolek-Torrello 1992; Wood 1992).

Rice (1990), following the lead of Gerald (1976), proposed the Salado horizon was a regional-level association of complex social groups among the Classic period Hohokam (AD 1100-1450). Rooms built on top of the platform mounds were seen as elite residences and evidence that the Classic period Hohokam were organized into competing chiefdoms (Rice 1998b:14). Gila polychrome pottery was used as a symbol of wealth and importance. However, Rice (1998b:14) now acknowledges a "critical problem" with this view—there is no evidence that Gila polychrome was limited to an elite and use-wear studies indicate that many of these vessels were employed in practical, utilitarian uses.

Rice (1998b:27) interprets dates from the ASU investigations as establishing that populations in the Tonto Basin were building public centers with unusually large rooms that were surrounded by walled compounds by the early 13th century. Rice (1998b:29) further notes that the phase chronology he uses differs from that used by Ciolek-Torrello and others (1994:600-602), Whittlesey (1994:401), and Wood (1992). Rice finds no support in absolute dates for the distinctions the other researchers make between early and late Gila phase or between the different styles of Gila Polychrome (Whittlesey 1994:401-402). Thus, Gila phase platform mounds and Gila phase room blocks are treated as contemporaneous settlement types in a single settlement system (Rice 1998b:30).

Rice (1990) had proposed in the Platform Mound Study research design that Classic period settlements in different locations were specialized with respect to subsistence. Upland settlements were positioned to follow a subsistence strategy of both agriculture and harvesting of natural plant foods. Platform mound communities managed the redistribution of subsistence products among the settlements in various zones. However, Rice and Oliver (1998:94) rejected these views because no category of data showed the expected differences between upland and lowland settlements. Thus, the platform mound settlements did not manage the redistribution of subsistence resources between upland and lowland communities. An unexpected finding (Rice 1998d:231) was that relationships between settlements were often highly competitive—for land, trade contacts, and ultimately for occupancy of the Tonto Basin.

This competition is manifested in what

Rice sees as two distinct settlement patterns established by the 13th century (Rice 1998d:234). One pattern involved platform mounds as settlement centers, as well as other public architecture that links this pattern to similar contemporaneous developments in the Hohokam Phoenix Basin. The other pattern involved large primary communities with surrounding clusters of small, dispersed settlements, similar to settlements in various areas around Tonto Basin, especially to the east. The platform mound-based communities persisted in the Tonto arm of the basin, notably the Cline Terrace community, whereas, in the Salt arm, elements of both strategies combined into a new pattern involving the large primary villages as well as the architecture of platform mounds.

Clearly, there are significant differences in interpretations of the culture history of the Tonto Basin. The relationships of upland and lowland sites, the reasons for expansion into new areas, the relationships of platform mound and "puebloan" sites, and even the ultimate end of the Gila phase and the abandonment of the basin are highly controversial. Where there does seem to be consensus is that migrant populations are no longer the sole agents for changes and events in the Tonto Basin. There appears to have always been an indigenous population that interacted to varying degrees, first with Hohokam immigrants and later with puebloan immigrants. Interactions between the indigenous population and puebloan groups led to the Tonto Basin version of the region-wide Salado phenomenon. The replacement of most platform mounds by a smaller number of large pueblos, as well as the construction of Tonto Cliff Dwellings, suggests an increase in puebloan influence in the Gila phase. The abundance of White Mountain Red Ware ceramics in upper Salt Arm settlements during the Gila phase also indicates increased interaction with puebloan groups. Furthermore, contrary to some previous overviews of Tonto Basin pre-history, there appear to be no significant gaps in occupation from the Early Ceramic Horizon to the abandonment after AD 1400. Tonto Basin population peaked in the Roosevelt phase, at a level that is now thought to be no more than 3500 to 5000 people at any one time (Doelle 1995). Finally, the entire socioeconomic and political system seems to have been at a much lower level of organization than some initially believed. There is no evidence for a manage-rial elite deriving their power from control of the best farmland and the redistribution of subsistence resources, ceramics, or other exotic materials.

GLOBE-MIAMI

The Globe-Miami area is southeast of the Tonto Basin (Figs. 1.1, 10.1 and 10.2), 24 to 32 km up Pinal Creek (Rice 1998d:239-241). Little or no real evidence of Pre-ceramic or Pioneer period occupation exists in the Globe-Miami area (Doyel 1978:191). The first evidence of sedentary populations occurs in the Colonial period (AD 500-900), with greater emphasis in the later Santa Cruz phase. As in the Tonto Basin and elsewhere at this time, this occupa-tion is indicated by the presence of Hohokam buff ware ceramics, and was seen as an attempt to transplant the Hohokam life-style into areas to the north and east of the Phoenix core (Doyel 1978:192). Sacaton phase, Sedentary period, occupation is clearly indicated, but was lim-ited to small, seasonal sites near drainages. Doyel (1978:194) defined a Miami phase, a mixed cultural pattern, with elements of the prior Hohokam occupation and the addition of numerous puebloan traits. There is good evidence for intensified occupation of the Globe-Miami area, and a shift to intrusive ceramics from the east, north, and southeast. There is little evidence, however, to suggest that the Miami phase represented the appear-ance of a new cultural group in the area (Doyel 1978:194-195).

In the Roosevelt phase, numerous small settlements were located along terraces above the valley floor and prime agricultural areas. In contrast, Gila phase pueblos were built in clusters of three to four room blocks located on high, neighboring, easily defended hilltops (Doyel 1978; Rice 1998d:239). The Gila phase pueblos were large "Salado" villages with 50 to 250 rooms, but lacked the platform mound architecture so characteristic of the Tonto Basin. Salado polychromes were the dominant decorated pottery types, although White Moun-tain Red Ware ceramics were abundant at many sites. As is typical in Gila phase structures in the Tonto Basin, burning also occurred at Gila Pueblo (McKusick 1992). By the late AD 1300s, this area, too, was abandoned.

LOWER CHERRY CREEK

Lower Cherry Creek has been defined as the area of the drainage below the Badlands and Pringle Wash noted on the USGS 15-minute McFadden Peak and Rockinstraw quadrangles south to the confluence of Cherry Creek and the Salt River (Figs. 1.1 and 10.4). A single, somewhat intensive survey project was done on lower Cherry Creek as a student paper at Arizona State University (Wells 1971). His survey was limited to the riparian area and nearest terrace and ridge areas on each side of the creek. A small segment of the APS and SRP powerlines (see Chapter 1) crosses the northern edge of lower Cherry Creek (Fig. 10.1). The powerline survey recorded several compounds (Reid 1982a; Teague and Mayro 1979), but no mitigation work was done. The SAP mapped and further documented several of these sites, and assigned a site number to a petroglyph panel in this same area.

Lower Cherry Creek would appear to be the area along Cherry Creek with the greatest predictability and potential for agricultural intensification. In this area is the largest and longest-lived community in Cherry Creek. On a smaller scale, lower Cherry Creek best mimics the characteristics of the Tonto Basin when compared to the other parts of Cherry Creek.

Based on the concentration and types of lithic tools and debris (and the absence of ceramics and visible architecture), AZ V:5:61 (ASU) is believed to represent a pre-ceramic, Archaic period occupation. Wells (1971) defined two ceramic groups, the earliest corresponds to the Hohokam Colonial period. In the Colonial period, small habitation sites are distributed on stream-side terraces in a pattern like the Tonto Basin. These are small settlements, probably farmsteads and small hamlets, with 5 to 8 pit houses. The residents of these settlements could have farmed the broad area of alluvium above the confluence of Cherry Creek and the Salt River.

During the Early Classic period, there is a shift in settlement types and locations documented by Wells' (1971) survey. Initially, there are two classes of sites that occur on ridge tops or slopes back from the stream edge. The larger sites are compounds with less than 20 rooms, the smaller sites consist of 3 or 4 low-walled structures of stacked cobbles. Later, settlements shift back to the terraces along the stream course and are more concentrated near two large areas of bottomland. The northern portion of lower Cherry Creek is abandoned at this time. There are 14 sites dated to the late Preclassic period, each averaging approximately 20 rooms. A possible prehistoric canal is located on the east side of Cherry Creek across from the Dagger Ranch. Apparently this part of Cherry Creek was experiencing the same type of reorganization into small irrigation communities as in the Tonto Basin.

The Late Classic in lower Cherry Creek reveals further changes in settlement (Figs. 10.4 and 10.5). Many sites are abandoned, just as in the western Sierra Ancha piedmont. A couple of large sites persisted and sites were built in new locations, for instance, on high topographic features. The move to defensive locations near the confluence of Cherry Creek and the Salt River is typical of sites at this time throughout Cherry Creek. Just two large sites remain occupied, located across from each other near the Dagger Ranch. Lower Cherry Creek appears to have been abandoned by AD 1375 to 1400, and remained unoccupied until the arrival of Apachean groups.

MIDDLE CHERRY CREEK AND THE SOUTHEASTERN SIERRA ANCHA

The preceding discussion of regional culture history provides a context and framework for interpreting the cultural events that occurred in the middle Cherry Creek area. The interpretations are somewhat tenuous, however, because there are no datasets derived from excavations in the middle Cherry Creek area. There are a limited number of absolute dates from cliff dwellings, occupied only in the later prehistoric periods. In contrast, survey coverage in middle Cherry Creek is better than in many of the surrounding areas, but is still not as complete as it could be. The Middle Cherry Creek data are summarized here, primarily using the Puebloan chronological framework.

Paleoindian, Archaic, and Early Ceramic Horizon Periods

The regional discussion indicates sparse use of the broader region of Central Arizona during the PaleoIndian and Early Archaic periods, with increasing evidence of occupation in the Middle and Late Archaic periods and the Early Ceramic Horizon. Throughout the centuries represented by these early periods, individuals or small groups of people also must have passed through, camped, or lived in the middle stretch of the Cherry Creek valley. Little or no evidence, however, exists for occupation or activities associated with these early periods. One reason for this lack of evidence may relate to the low surface visibility of occupations dating to these early periods. Deeply incised, heavily patinated petroglyphs are the most compelling evidence of Archaic period people in middle Cherry Creek (see Chapter 9). In addition, evidence for Middle Archaic period occupation has been identified in excavations of rockshelters in the Black Mesa area, located a short distance to the west of middle Cherry Creek (Gregory 1982), and Archaic period projectile points were found in a survey block near the northern edge of the middle Cherry Creek area (Ciolek-Torrello and Riggs 1999).

Preclassic Period: Colonial and Sedentary or Pueblo I through Pueblo III Periods

As with the earliest potential periods of occupation, the Colonial or Pueblo I (PI) and Pueblo II (PII) periods also seem to be times of low-level and ephemeral use of middle Cherry Creek. This pattern is similar to the mountain areas to the east and north of middle Cherry Creek, but stands in contrast to the Tonto Basin and lower Cherry Creek areas where small Colonial period settlements were common in riverine areas. In the Gila Pueblo collections (Ciolek-Torrello and Lange 1990:136-138) and the SAP collections from middle Cherry Creek sites (Chapter 4, Table 4.4), there are small quantities of the ceramic types that date to the Colonial or PI and PII periods. The paucity of these remains may be related to the limited potential for constructing pit houses in middle Cherry Creek, and the difficulty of floodplain and floodwater farming in this part of the creek due to limited alluvium. Such farming was the mainstay of

Colonial period subsistence (Welch 1994). It is not until the Sedentary or PIII period, that is, until approximately AD 1100, that ceramics recovered from the sites indicate a significant presence in middle Cherry Creek.

It is clear that occupation began earlier in the lower Cherry Creek area. Earlier occupation is also true for Upper Cherry Creek in the vicinities of Walnut and Campbell creeks. Ceramics and architecture indicate that Hohokam migration or at least Hohokam influence was important in the earlier occupations in both areas. In contrast, evidence of Hohokam influence is absent in the archaeological record of middle Cherry Creek.

Early Classic Period: Roosevelt Phase or Late Pueblo III

The situation changed dramatically in the 13th century. In the late AD 1200s (Roosevelt phase or late PIII), there was a substantial population in the middle Cherry Creek area (Fig. 10.4). These demographic changes were associated with two important changes in settlement. These changes were precursors to similar changes in the adjoining Q Ranch and Grasshopper regions to the north and east (see also Mehalic 2002). One change was the beginning of a trend toward aggregation of population into large nucleated settlements. The other was the construction of settlements in canyons and other protected locations.

On the south face of the Sierra Ancha around Coon Creek Butte was a community of at least 15 pueblos together containing over 400 rooms, and ranging in size from 6 to over 70 rooms (Ciolek-Torrello and Lange 1982:110, 115-116). Site configurations consisted mainly of room blocks with attached compound walls, more in the style of settlements in the Grasshopper and Q Ranch areas than the more open compounds found in contemporary settlements in Tonto Basin (see Clark 2001 for a discussion of these architectural differences).

In contrast to the Coon Creek Butte area, two distinct communities that, interestingly, were more similar to contemporaneous settlements in the Tonto Basin were present in the lower elevation areas in middle Cherry Creek. The Ellison Ranch community was located just below the point where Cherry Creek leaves the steep and narrow canyons between the Sierra Ancha and Q Ranch blocks and flows through a broader part of the valley, with more extensive terraces that are more amenable to farming. This community consisted of as many as 11 residential compounds focused around a small platform mound.

Another community was present many kilometers downstream from Ellison Ranch and west of the later Pottery Point pueblo. The architectural layouts of the compounds within these communities are different from the more pueblo-like settlements in the Coon Creek area. These compounds, although large in area (greater than 400 sq m), contain a few, mostly non-contiguous rooms rather than the compact roomblocks characteristic of Coon Creek (see Chapter 7). These two communities are similar, if not identical, to Roosevelt phase villages in Tonto Basin such as the Meddler Point group (see Elson, Gregory, and Stark 1995). Perhaps the large area in the compounds was in anticipation of additional population that never arrived or reflected the more outdoor oriented living arrangements of Sonoran Desert groups.

In addition to these two communities, a large number of cliff dwellings ranging in size from single rooms to the 70 nearly contemporaneous rooms in Pueblo Canyon were present on the southeastern flanks of the Sierra Ancha and in the narrow canyons above the Ellison Ranch community. Pueblos of various sizes were also situated on high, often isolated topographic features that provided tremendous vantage points for observation into the side canyons where cliff dwellings were built, up

and down Cherry Creek, and of areas to the north and east. Despite the caveats previously expressed (Lange 2001), a case could be made that these sites provided an observational network to protect and inform the cliff dwelling residents of movements of other people across the surrounding landscape. The Elephant Rock Fortress, high and at the north end of middle Cherry Creek, has views down Cherry Creek as well as to sites to the north and east, including Gunsight Butte, Castle Peak, and Double Buttes on the Q Ranch block, and views even farther east to the Grasshopper area. As Wilcox and others (2001a, b) have suggested from their work in the Perry Mesa and Verde Valley areas, a premium appears to have been placed in locating outposts in relatively inaccessible and highly intervisible locations.

Despite the great diversity in architectural style, settlement size, and location, the settlements of this time period shared a common ceramic assemblage. The decorated ceramics in this assemblage consisted largely of PIII white wares—mostly Cibola White Ware with smaller numbers of Little Colorado and Tusayan White wares—and early types of Roosevelt Red and White Mountain Red wares.

Two major problems remain in the settlement reconstruction for this time period—problems that can only be resolved by obtaining absolute dates and better ceramic assemblage data from excavations in the Coon Creek pueblos and middle Cherry Creek compounds. The first problem involves the precise timing for the construction and abandonment of the pueblos in the Coon Creek Butte area and the compounds along Cherry Creek. The second problem involves the temporal and functional relationships between these sites and the cliff dwellings in middle Cherry Creek.

Tree-rings indicate construction dates for the cliff dwellings with a precision that is not possible for the other types of sites. These dates indicate that construction of many of the cliff dwellings in middle Cherry Creek began in the AD 1280s and 1290s and most were probably abandoned by the early decades of the 14th century (see Chapters 5 and 7). Although the cliff dwellings had ceramic assemblages similar to the pueblos and compounds, suggesting relative contemporaneity (see Dean 1969:198), the precise temporal relationships between these three types of sites is not known. This is an important issue as Clark (2001) and Gregory (1995), among others, have argued that similar architectural differences between contemporary sites in the Meddler Community reflect the presence of ethnically diverse, co-resident groups. Who were the builders of the compounds, pueblos, and cliff dwellings? Do the compounds, surface pueblos, and cliff dwellings represent (1) contemporaneous settlements of ethnically distinct, but co-resident populations; (2) contemporaneous occupations by the same people; or (3) sequential occupations by the same people?

If the cliff dwellings, pueblos, and compounds were contemporaneous, at least in the last two decades of the 1200s (and possibly the first two or three decades of the 1300s), then perhaps they represent two different groups of people. In this scenario as different groups, they co-existed in nearly the same environment but in very different types of settlements. They probably employed different subsistence strategies—the residents of compounds in the valley bottom had access to irrigable farmland, whereas the residents of cliff dwellings and pueblos had access to narrow canyons and spring-fed mountain slopes. At present, there is no evidence for open belligerence between these groups, but the size, numbers, and locations of the cliff dwellings and associated fortresses suggest an uneasiness or wariness between these neighbors. A number of scholars have suggested that conflict was common in the adjacent Tonto Basin and Grasshopper regions during the Roosevelt Phase/Pueblo III period (Oliver 2001; Shelley

and Ciolek-Torrello 1994; Tuggle and Reid 2001; Turner and Turner 1999).

In this first scenario, the compounds in Middle Cherry Creek would represent the culmination of the growth and development of an indigenous population with close ties to Tonto Basin that had settled in lower Cherry Creek during the Colonial period, if not earlier. Like their neighbors in Tonto Basin, this group exploited farmland with a reliable and controllable water supply. The compounds in middle Cherry Creek were located in the best settings for irrigation farming in the valley. The cliff dwellings and pueblos may have been built by an immigrant population who established enclaves on the periphery of the settlements of the valley bottom farmers, taking the marginal farmlands in the uplands. If these different types of settlements were contemporary, the cliff dwellers may have been:

(a) residents of the Coon Creek Butte area who "fell back" to the canyons as the irrigation farmers from the Tonto Basin expanded into Middle Cherry Creek;

(b) new immigrants from the Colorado Plateau or Mogollon Rim who were part of the mass southward movement to the better watered regions of east-central Arizona at the end of the 13th century. In middle Cherry Creek they encountered a resident population farming the valley bottom. The newcomers were either forced into the more marginal canyons and upland areas because they could not access the valley bottoms or they were hostile to the farmers. Eventually, they drove the Tonto Basin population out of Cherry Creek.

In the second scenario, the compounds, pueblos, and cliff dwellings were contemporaneous and occupied by the same people. If this is the case, then this population was conducting an interesting experiment in living in different environmental settings, organizing villages in different ways, and exploiting different resources and subsistence strategies. However, such a pattern is not known from adjacent regions and seems unlikely.

Given the temporal ambiguities, it is also possible that the compounds were abandoned before the initial construction of the cliff dwellings and the two types of settlements were not absolutely contemporaneous. In this third scenario, settlement of Cherry Creek was initially part of the development of Salado culture in Tonto Basin, and the abandonment of the Ellison Ranch community and other compounds in lower and middle Cherry Creeks was part of the restructuring of Tonto Basin settlement at the end of the Roosevelt phase. Construction of the cliff dwellings, in turn, can be seen as part of the great wave of immigration of people from the Colorado Plateau to the better-watered regions below the Mogollon Rim. The departure of the Saladoan people from Cherry Creek would have left a vacuum into which these new immigrants moved. The cliff dwellings of middle Cherry Creek may have been constructed at what would have been the frontier of this southward movement at the end of the 13th century. The residents of the cliff dwellings chose this defensive posture against the potential return to the area by the Tonto Basin population that was previously there. Perhaps the Tonto Basin population in the compounds, as noted above under the first scenario as well, had been driven out by force by the eventual residents of the cliff dwellings.

Late Classic Period: Gila Phase or Pueblo IV (AD 1350-1450)

As in the Tonto Basin, the Late Classic period in middle Cherry Creek was characterized by a process of abandonment and continued aggregation of population into fewer, larger, more nucleated settlements (Fig. 10.5). By the early AD 1300s, only five sites, including two cliff dwellings, with a total of 100 rooms or less remained in the Coon Creek Butte area. Many of the cliff dwellings in middle Cherry Creek were also abandoned, as were the Ellison Ranch community and the other middle Cherry Creek compounds. As noted earlier in this chapter, most of the settlements in lower Cherry Creek had also been abandoned by this time. Much of the population from these areas appears to have shifted eastwards into the neighboring Granite Basin area.

Pueblo IV sites in the Cherry Creek area are distinguished by a ceramic assemblage that includes, but is not restricted to, many ceramic types dating after AD 1320. The diagnostic ceramics in this assemblage include Pinedale Black-on-white, late White Mountain Red Ware types such as Pinedale Black-on-red and Polychrome and Fourmile Polychrome, Gila and Tonto polychromes, and other types of polychromes (see Table 4.4). The number of sites with substantial numbers of these ceramics is quite small (N = 5; Table 10.3b and c). Five large compounds contained representatives of this Pueblo IV assemblage (Table 10.3a), but less than 10 sherds each. Perhaps these ceramics represent a later reoccupation of these compounds rather than continued occupation. Ten cliff dwellings have post-AD 1320 tree-ring dates (see Tables 5.4 and 10.3d). These sites are located all over the middle Cherry Creek area—on top of the Sierra Ancha and east and west of Cherry Creek (Fig. 10.6). Only four cliff dwellings have post-AD 1325 dates—one on top, one in Devils Chasm west of Cherry Creek, and two east of Cherry Creek. Just two cliff dwellings have dates after AD 1330—one in Devils Chasm west of Cherry Creek, and the other along Mustang Ridge east of Cherry Creek at the foot of the Q Ranch Plateau. No tree-ring dates were obtained from the other two cliff dwellings along Mustang Ridge, but these sites do have

Table 10.3. SAP Sites with Late Pottery (post-1320) or Late Tree-Ring Dates

a. Sites With Small Amounts of Late Pottery (N=13), Less Than or Equal to 10 Sherds*

Site Type	Site
small surface pueblo	AZ V:1:138
small surface pueblo	AZ V:1:180
medium surface pueblo	AZ V:1:152
large surface pueblo	AZ V:1:169
large compound	AZ V:1:172
large compound	AZ V:1:191
large compound	AZ V:1:202
large compound	AZ V:1:203
large compound	AZ V:1:238
small cliff dwelling	AZ V:1:168†
large cliff dwelling	AZ V:1:132
large cliff dwelling	AZ V:1:145
large cliff dwelling	AZ V:5:61

b. Sites With More Late Pottery (N=5), Between 10 and 20 Sherds

Site Type	Site
small surface pueblo	AZ V:1:147
large surface pueblo	AZ V:1:177**
large cliff dwelling	AZ V:1:135†
large cliff dwelling	AZ V:1:144
large cliff dwelling	AZ V:1:167†

c. Sites With Abundant Late Pottery (N=5), More Than 20 Sherds

Site Type	Site
large surface pueblo	AZ V:1:26
large surface pueblo	AZ V:1:166
small cliff dwelling	C:1:38†
large cliff dwelling	C:1:47
large cliff dwelling	C:1:50

d. Sites With Late Tree-Ring Dates (after AD 1320) (N=9)

Site Type	Site	Where		Post-1320 Dates
lrg cd	AZ V:1:131	Pueblo Canyon	W/Ch Crk	1320vv, 1321vv, 1320vv
lrg cd	AZ V:1:133	Workman Creek	W/Ch Crk	1320rL
lrg cd	AZ V:1:130	Pueblo Canyon	W/Ch Crk	1320vv, 1321vv, 1321v, 1324G
lrg cd	AZ V:1:135†	Cooper Forks	E/Ch Crk	1326vv
lrg cd	AZ V:1:167†	Devils Chasm	W/Ch Crk	1323rL, 1330rB, 1330vv
sml cd	AZ V:1:168†	Devils Chasm	W/Ch Crk	1321vv, 1322rL, 1322vv
sml cd	AZ V:1:162††	Center Mtn	W/Ch Crk	1328L, 1327+L, 1327rL, 1328rL, 1322++rB
sml cd	AZ V:1:174	Cold Spring Canyon	W/Ch Crk	1324rV
sml cd	C:1:38†	Mustang Ridge	E/Ch Crk	1340rL

* Types involved are: Fourmile Polychrome, Showlow Polychrome, Gila Polychrome and Tonto Polychrome.
** This site could be included with the sites with large amounts of late pottery.
†Sites with late pottery & late tree-ring dates. If not marked in this manner, sites have one or the other, not both.
††There are additional dates, in the same 1327-1328 range, not enough space to list all.

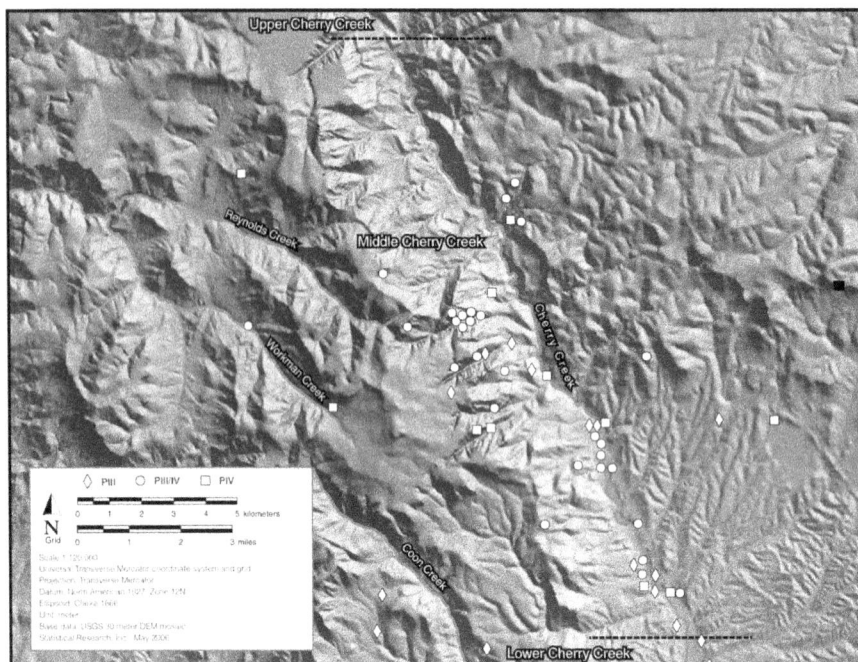

a. Middle Cherry Creek. This figure is the sole property of Statistical Research, Inc., and may not be reproduced without its permission.

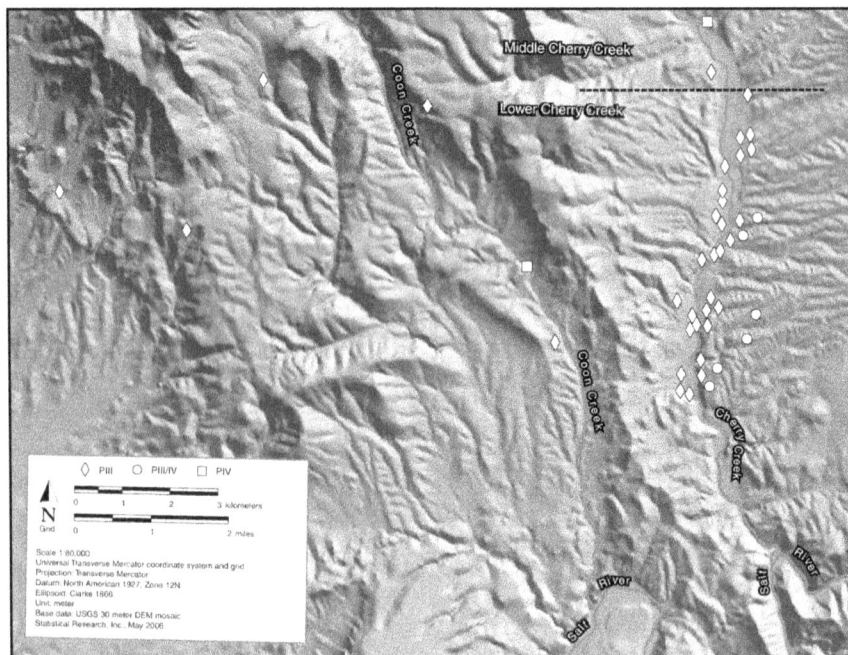

b. Lower Cherry Creek. This figure is the sole property of Statistical Research, Inc., and may not be reproduced without its permission.

Figure 10.6. Pueblo III, Pueblo III/IV, and Pueblo IV Period Sites in Middle and Lower Cherry Creek.

abundant Pueblo IV pottery (Table 10.3c). By AD 1330, it is possible that the only sites still occupied in the middle Cherry Creek area were the cliff dwellings along Mustang Ridge, Granite Basin Pueblo, Pottery Point Pueblo, V:1:177 above the Ellison Ranch, and the Devils Chasm Fortress (V:1:167) in Devils Chasm west of Cherry Creek (Fig. 10.7). By the end of the 1300s, all of middle Cherry Creek seems to be abandoned. There are no tree-ring dates and no ceramic types indicating occupation beyond the late AD1300s.

Despite the abandonment of numerous settlements, there was a small overall increase in the number of occupied rooms along middle Cherry Creek, primarily at V:1:177, a large fortified pueblo with about 30 rooms situated on an isolated knoll overlooking the old Ellison Ranch community, and the smaller Pottery Point Pueblo, situated on another isolated knoll overlooking the Cherry Creek valley. In addition, the early 14th century witnessed a tremendous population expansion in the Granite Basin area, a large desert basin located a short distance to the east of Cherry Creek. Granite Basin Pueblo, V:1:26, dominated the entire southeastern Sierra Ancha and Cherry Creek area. Similar in layout and construction to the large, contemporary Mogollon pueblos, this site contained about 150 rooms arranged into several large, multi-story room blocks surrounding a plaza (Ciolek-Torrello and Lange 1982:110, 126). Population from the Coon Creek Butte and lower Cherry Creek areas, as well as abandoned settlements in middle Cherry Creek, may have fueled the growth of this large settlement. Some of the population from the lower and middle Cherry Creek areas also could have moved to the eastern Tonto Basin, becoming the pueblo enclaves found in the Meddler Point community (Elson, Gregory, and Stark 1995:452-453), especially the later settlement at Schoolhouse Point.

The paucity of Pueblo IV ceramics in the large compounds in middle Cherry Creek suggests that they were abandoned by this time. It is possible that a few of the compounds persisted into the Late Classic period. As in the case of the cliff dwellings, where Pueblo IV ceramics were not always found in sites with late tree-ring dates (Ciolek-Torrello and Lange 1990:146-147), the absence of Pueblo IV ceramics does not necessarily signify the absence of occupation after roughly AD 1325. The lack of later diagnostic ceramics and compound-style architecture, however, suggest that the compounds and the platform mound at Ellison Ranch were probably abandoned before AD 1330. With their abandonment, the Cherry Creek-Granite Basin area came to resemble contemporary settlements of the Q Ranch and Grasshopper areas, in the remaining architectural forms and in the dominance of White Mountain Red Ware among decorated ceramics.

This pattern of abandonment suggests that the 14th century occupation of the area was characterized by a gradual shift in population from the Coon Creek and western side of the Cherry Creek drainage to the east side and Granite Basin. As this population shifted eastwards, the focal point of settlement changed from the Ellison Ranch community on the west side of Cherry Creek to the Granite Basin Pueblo. This eastward shift in settlement in Cherry Creek was matched by a westward shift in Tonto Basin, as much of the Meddler Point community (except for the Schoolhouse Point site) and the Armer Ranch community were abandoned. This left a void in what had been almost a continuous distribution of settlement along the south face of the Sierra Ancha in the preceding period.

One cliff dwelling is an exception to the pattern of abandonment along the southern face of the Sierra Ancha. Hematite House (V:5:61), is a PIV site located in the low cliffs along Coon Creek. No tree-ring dates were

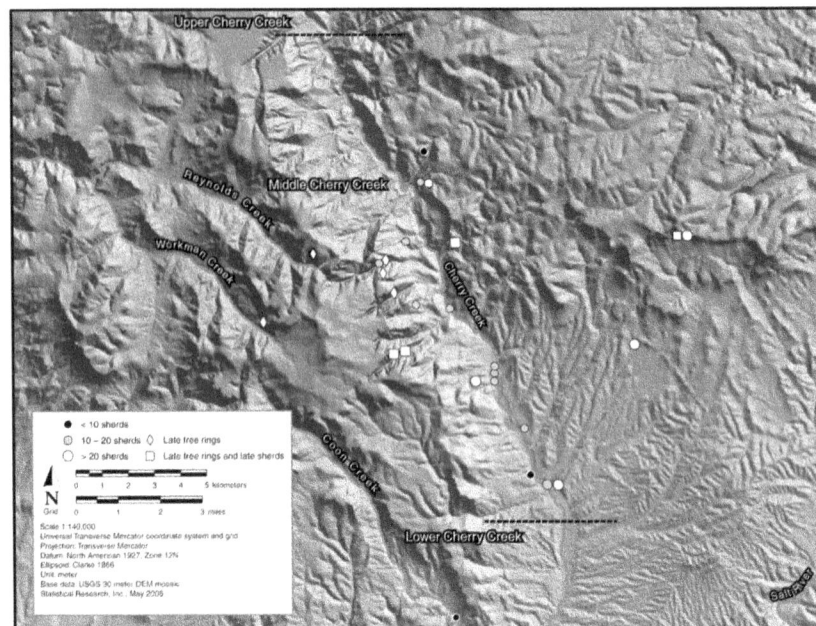

Figure 10.7. Latest Sites in Cherry Creek. This figure is the sole property of Statistical Research, Inc., and may not be reproduced without its permission.

obtained from this site, but the site is among those with PIV pottery (Table 10.3a). Although low numbers of late sherds are reported in the table, large numbers of late White Mountain Red Ware sherds (for example, Fourmile Polychrome) were observed on the slope below the cliff dwelling. Assuming this site was indeed occupied at least in the 1320s and 1330s, it is practically alone on the south face of the Sierra Ancha, between the Tonto Basin and middle Cherry Creek. Hematite House was one of only two cliff dwellings that faced northwards in the entire SAP sample. This context and its low-lying location did not permit monitoring of the surrounding landscape. It would have been relatively easy, however, to reach higher areas above the site that do provide views of the surrounding areas. Was Hematite House the farthest outpost of the now Mogollon-affiliated Pueblo IV population in Cherry Creek, situated at Coon Creek to warn them of incursions from Tonto Basin? Or, were the residents of Hematite House intent on exploiting the reliable water supply provided by Coon Creek to farm nearby plots of land? In this circumstance, was

it necessary for them to hide their homes under a low-lying cliff because of their extremely vulnerable position between the Tonto Basin Salado and the Western Pueblo populations of Cherry Creek and Granite Basin?

Conclusion

The region of east-central Arizona is a culturally diverse and rich area that has undergone mixed levels of archaeological research over the decades. Intensive excavations and surveys have occurred in some areas, while other areas are virtually unknown. The earliest periods of human occupation are represented in the region, but are poorly known, mostly due to the low visibility of such remains. Complicating the interpretations of regional cultural history is the transitional nature of archaeologically defined cultures in the region. The region is intermediate between the Hohokam and Salado cultures of the Tonto and Phoenix basins, the Anasazi of the Colorado Plateau, and the Mogollon and Western Pueblo of the mountains of east-central Arizona (see Chapter 1). The striking environmental diversity of the region is matched by the rich variety of cultural remains.

The cultural and environmental diversity meet in middle Cherry Creek and the southeastern Sierra Ancha in spectacular fashion. Archaeologists were first drawn to the southeastern Sierra Ancha to further define the geographical extent of various archaeological cultures, and to determine if tree-ring dating could be expanded into new areas (Gladwin and Gladwin 1934, 1935; Haury 1934). This dataset from the 1930s was critical for first attempts to characterize the relationships of groups in central Arizona through time (Ciolek-Torrello and Lange 1979, 1990; Reid 1982a). The SAP was an opportunity to acquire additional, detailed data from a particular site type without excavation, before the data were lost or destroyed by natural or human agents. The goals were to locate and document the cliff dwellings in Middle Cherry Creek and nearby areas. A rich dataset of photography, maps, measurements, notes, and artifacts was collected by the SAP, and has been discussed in this report.

Through the earlier research and the SAP, it became clear that although the southeastern Sierra Ancha was not a central place in the cultural dynamics of the area. However, changes in more central places, such as the Tonto Basin or Grasshopper, were quickly reflected in the settlements in Middle Cherry Creek. As in much of central Arizona, influences seem to come first from one direction and then another. Changes in settlement and artifact assemblages are probably due as much to population movements as to trade and exchange. Particularly in the late AD 1200s and early 1300s, changes in settlement and material culture were rapid and significant.

In middle Cherry Creek, Archaic period populations are primarily evident through the rock art they created. Deeply incised and heavily patinated petroglyphs along Cherry Creek and Mogollon Red-style pictographs in various rockshelters are the principal indicators of these peoples in this area (see Chapter 9). Archaic period peoples may have been the first to inhabit the rockshelters and caves in middle Cherry Creek, but any evidence of structures seems to have been erased or covered by the late 13th century occupants. In addition to the rock art, charcoal in the plaster of the first rooms built in the late AD 1200s (see Chapter 6) may also indicate an earlier occupation in the rockshelters. The charcoal may be chance inclusions from the earlier occupation while mixing mortar and plaster for the later occupation.

Through the Sedentary Period and into the Roosevelt phase (see Fig. 10.3), the culture history of middle Cherry Creek most closely resembles that of the Tonto Basin to the south and west. During the Colonial and early Sedentary periods, the Hohokam Regional System expanded throughout central Arizona, bringing with it certain characteristics of architectural village organization, buff ware ceramics and other items of Hohokam material culture, and distinctive mortuary patterns (Wilcox 1979). Interestingly, although Hohokam peoples or their influences are seen in upper and lower Cherry Creek, they seem not to have been present in middle Cherry Creek. Late in the Sedentary Period (circa AD 1150), Hohokam presence and influence declined, and was replaced by something different in the Tonto Basin. Jacal and cobble-and-adobe-walled surface rooms within walled compounds replaced pit houses and courtyard groups. Tonto Corrugated, Salado Red Corrugated, Pinto Polychrome, and various White Mountain Red Ware types replaced Hohokam ceramics. Inhumation replaced cremation as a treatment for the dead.

In the Early Classic period (Roosevelt phase), lower and middle Cherry Creek both took on characteristics of the Tonto Basin settlements, having smaller versions of communities with residential compounds and roomblocks clustered around platform mounds. Platform mounds are seen as a means of integrating the communities in the Tonto Basin and outlying areas. One small platform mound, the Cherry Creek Mound Site (V:1:191), is the only platform mound known in the Cherry Creek drainage (see Chapter 7). In contrast, upper Cherry Creek and the mountain areas of the Sierra Ancha (Pleasant Valley) take on many of the characteristics of the Q Ranch and Grasshopper areas to the east (Ciolek-Torrello and Lange 1979).

An interesting change in settlement occurred in middle Cherry Creek. Cliff dwellings and hilltop sites proliferated in the late 13th and early 14th centuries. Most of these sites were abandoned by the AD 1330s (Chapter 7; Ciolek-Torrello and Lange 1990; Haury 1934). Although similar trends are evident in the Tonto Basin, the concentration of cliff dwellings in the southeastern Sierra Ancha, Coon Creek, Middle Cherry Creek, and Mustang Ridge areas does not occur anywhere else in the Sierra Ancha or the Mazatzal Mountains on the west side of Tonto Basin (except for the Tonto Cliff Dwellings). Only along Canyon Creek is there a similar concentration of cliff dwellings, but these seem to be later in time (see also Mehalic 2002).

By the Late Classic Gila phase, the Cherry Creek drainage as a whole and the eastern Tonto Basin undergo similar transformations. The earlier Roosevelt phase site complexes are mostly abandoned, replaced by larger, more nucleated settlements (Ciolek-Torrello and others 1994), such as the Pottery Point and Granite Basin pueblos. In the Tonto Basin and Cherry Creek areas, this represents a complete breakdown in the continuity of residential patterns that had characterized previous changes in settlement. However, the pattern of courtyard groups and compounds did continue in the Phoenix Basin.

By the mid-14th century, relatively few sites are occupied in Cherry Creek, and the focus of the community has shifted to Granite Basin Pueblo. The period of settlement reorganization and aggregation was followed by the complete abandonment of the entire region between the Mogollon Rim and the Salt River. Abandonment of the remaining pueblos and cliff dwellings in the southeastern Sierra Ancha and Middle Cherry Creek may have begun as early as AD 1350.

The demise of the platform mound communities, the abandonment of large areas of the landscape, the aggregation of the remaining population at the beginning of the Gila phase, and the eventual abandonment of the entire region defy simple explanations. Interpretations of these events have ranged from a focus on social factors to environmental conditions, to some combination of the two.

Interpretations based on social forces see the population movements from the Four Corners and Upper Little Colorado River areas to better-watered regions below the Mogollon Rim as a major contributing factor. The movements were evidently spurred by the Great Drought and resulted in the establishment of enclaves of immigrant social groups in the existing settlements and communities in the Grasshopper, Sierra Ancha and Tonto Basin areas.

The immigrant enclaves are indicated by the presence of small, scattered room blocks, as opposed to the more typical compound architecture, distinctive aspects of material culture, and possibly different subsistence practices. Initially, the assimilation of the immigrants seems to have been peaceful. By the end of the Roosevelt phase (ca. AD 1300 to 1350), however, there may be evidence for widespread conflict in the Tonto Basin (Turner, Regan, and Irish 1994; Rice 1985; Wood 1989:19-20) and other areas below the Mogollon Rim (Reid 1989). Reid (1989) notes the catastrophic burning of the three villages that preceded the construction of Grasshopper Pueblo. Burning is also known from Gila Pueblo in Globe (McKusick 1992), Kinishba (Cummings 1940), and Point of Pines (Haury 1958). However, burning has also been interpreted as a result of ritual activities rather than conflict, for instance at Chodistaas Pueblo (Montgomery 1992; Montgomery and Reid 1990). Conflict is evident in Tonto Basin during the Roosevelt (PIII) and Gila (PIV) phases, in the form of bodies with indications of wounds and traumatic fractures, and some of these found unburied on room floors (Oliver 2001; Turner and Turner 1999).

Perhaps the social system failed to integrate the diverse and densely settled inhabitants of the region, and eventually, the forces of conflict and competition prevailed. A more complex sociopolitical organization than the already rejected Roosevelt phase platform mound system does not appear to have developed to integrate the larger Gila phase settlements. Instead, the response of the communities in the Tonto Basin and elsewhere in this part of east-central Arizona appears to have been, first, to aggregate into fewer communities, and then to abandon the area altogether.

Alternatively, some researchers (Gregory 1995:183; Van West and Altschul 1994) have provided data and interpretations that suggest that the scale of changes seen in the Gila phase indicates catastrophic events, possibly related to environmental factors. The AD 1330s, roughly the time of the Roosevelt-Gila phase transition (Ciolek-Torrello, Whittlesey, and Deaver 1994; Elson 1996), began a period of severe drought and reduced productivity lasting over 20 years. These long-term drought conditions may have exceeded the ability of the platform mound system to cope. Farmers on the bajada and piedmont areas would have been the most vulnerable to these adverse conditions. These

conditions may have favored intensification in riverine areas of Tonto Basin, especially along the Salt River arm.

Paleoclimatic reconstructions indicate dramatic increases in stream flow in the late fourteenth and early fifteenth centuries, implying floods of unprecedented severity. The floods were then followed by a decade of severe drought. Massive flooding would have devastated the irrigation systems upon which the riverine populations were dependent, by destroying headgates and entrenching river channels (Ciolek-Torrello and others 1994). The ensuing drought would have limited the possibilities of using farming strategies less prone to flooding.

The combination of social, economic, and environmental problems would have been catastrophic for the large, nucleated Gila phase populations and undoubtedly hastened their demise. Perhaps some of these populations were among those that joined with growing communities at Homol'ovi, Hopi, or Zuñi, or those who established large, short-lived settlements in the upper Gila River Valley. Nonetheless, the complete abandonment of the region resulting from the failure to develop a new social order remains an incompletely understood issue.

Settlement in the southeastern Sierra Ancha had its own special characteristics of spectacular cliff dwellings and other defensively situated sites. Settlement there also reflected trends evident in the wider region, but the dynamics and identities of populations moving into and out of Cherry Creek are still hazy. The impact of the social and environmental problems, which afflicted Tonto Basin, on the smaller and more agriculturally diverse settlements in the Sierra Ancha also remains unclear. Further survey, testing, and excavation in middle Cherry Creek and surrounding regions will someday help to understand the complicated changes that occurred in this area.

Appendix I
Work Plans: Proposed and Actual
(1981, 1995, 1996)

Table I.1. Research Plan and Actual Activities, June 5-26, 1981

DATE	PLANNED	ACTUAL
June 5, Fri	Drive up, set up camp along Cherry Creek	Drove up, set up camp along Cherry Creek
June 6, Sat	Up Cooper Forks, map C:1:40, back to base camp	Up Cooper Forks, mapped C:1:40, mapped and did photography, back to camp at 7:45 pm
June 7, Sun	Up south side of Pueblo Canyon, survey and map C:1:23	Sorted camp & notes, plotted C:1:40. Up Pueblo at 5:15pm, made camp at 7pm
June 8, Mon	Continue survey in Pueblo, around to C:1:16	Up to "A" cave (SA2), Recorded sites SA 2,3,4, &5 on the north side of Pueblo, spotted these from further up canyon
June 9, Tue	Begin mapping at C:1:16, survey back to base camp	Up to bends in Pueblo, up notch above the "chute", crawled into C:1:23, saw C:1:16 across the canyon, back to base camp 5:30 pm
June 10, Wed	Up into Cold Spring Canyon, north side, C:1:25, C:1:36, C:1:46), survey and map	Up Pueblo to retrieve RCL's pack, out to Rock House Gas, called ASM; up to Rattlesnake Crossing (flat between Pueblo and Cold Spring), made trail camp
June 11, Thu	Continue survey in Cold Spring	To C:1:36 in Cold Spring, mapped and did photos, camped in Rm 6
June 12, Fri	Continue survey in Cold Spring, back to base camp early afternoon	Finished mapping C:1:36, scouted around Cold Spring, back down to base camp
June 13, Sat	Into Cold Spring, back to base camp	In camp, plotted sites; Bill Deaver & others arrived 3 pm; looked for C:1:43 unsuccessfully
June 14, Sun	In Cold Spring, or survey along Cherry Creek in cliff face between Cold Spring and Devils Chasm, out to Lake Roosevelt area, evening back to base camp	Left at 7:30 am, to C:1:23; RCL and WLD found C:1:16 trail. To C:1:36 for photos and to check measurements
June 15, Mon	In Cold Spring, C:1:52, survey of upper Cold Spring and upper Pueblo	To Pueblo Canyon stream to recover; left at 3 pm for Cold Spring, hiked up until 7 pm and made trail camp
June 16, Tue	Survey of upper Cold Spring and upper Pueblo	Surveyed in Cold Spring, up to water fall, back to previous trail camp
June 17, Wed	Survey of upper Cold Spring and upper Pueblo	Back to base camp, saw helicopter; up to C:1:23 (Pueblo); made trail camp
June 18, Thu	Survey of upper Cold Spring and upper Pueblo; return to base camp	Around to C:1:16, worked on East group; camped in West group
June 19, Fri	In base camp, possible trip out to Lake Roosevelt area or Globe; PM: return to base camp	Finished mapping on C:1:16E, down to base camp, out to Rock House Gas, back in to camp at 11 pm
June 20, Sat	Return to Pueblo, finish C:1:16 mapping	With RC-T and others, to C:1:16 (Pueblo)
June 21, Sun	In Pueblo or along Cherry Creek; return to base camp	Recovering at Pueblo Canyon stream, to Ellison's, talked with Buster and Nathan, to Rock House and back to base camp
June 22, Mon	In Devils Chasm or Dripping Springs Canyon	Tried jeep road up south side of Devils, part way in and stuck in brush, back to camp
June 23, Tue	In Devils Chasm, possible return to base camp	Up to C:1:16, worked on notes on C:1:16E
June 24, Wed	In Devils Chasm	Did notes on C:1:16 East & Central
June 25, Thu	In Devils Chasm, return to base camp	Mapped C:1:16 C; thunderstorm, down to camp, broke camp, over to Lone Pine Divide
June 26, Fri	Pack up, possible short trip to pueblos in Coon Creek Butte/Moody point area; return to Tucson	Took photos from east side of Cherry Creek, drove up Bull Canyon road part way, back to Tonto Basin and Tucson, 11 pm

---

Table I.2. Research Plan and Actual Activities, October, 1995, First Earthwatch Season

DATE	PLANNED	ACTUAL
Sept 30, Sat	In camp; set-up	In camp; set-up
Oct 1, Sun	Earthwatchers & other volunteers arrive; orientation; EVENING: Rich Lange, Orientation and Project History	Earthwatchers & other volunteers arrive; orientation
Oct 2, Mon	All to Hematite House – A* & P** EVENING: Richard Ciolek-Torrello, Regional History: Archaeology and Prehistory	Hematite House – A & P
Oct 3, Tue	C:1:16W – A; C:1:16C – P	C:1:16W -- A; C:1:16C – P
Oct 4, Wed	C:1:16W - A, C:1:44 – A; C:1:16C – P EVENING: Barbara Murphy, Beam Replacement in Cold Spring Canyon	C:1:44 – A; C:1:16W – A. P; C:1:16C – P; C:1:16E – P
Oct 5, Thu	C:1:23 – A; C:1:16E – A; C:1:16E – P; C:1:23 – P EVENING: Bonnie Pitblado, Tree-ring Dating	C:1:16E – P; C:1:34 – A,P
Oct 6, Fri	C:2:4 – A,P EVENING: Rich Lange, Weekly Wrap-up	C:2:4 – A, P
Oct 7, Sat	Globe: laundry, Tonto NM, Besh-ba-gowah	Globe as planned
Oct 8, Sun	In camp EVENING: Rich Lange, Orientation and Project History for new volunteers	In camp; over the weekend, it got unusually hot for October, and continued into the next week
Oct 9, Mon	C:1:21 – A, P	C:1:36 – A; C:1:16W – A; C:1:21 – A, P
Oct 10, Tue	C:1:25 – A, P; SA 4, 5, 7 – A, P EVENING: Rich Lange, Environment and Signalling/Intervisibility	C:1:23 – A; C:1:16W – A; C:1:16C – P; C:1:16E – P; C:1:21 – A, P
Oct 11, Wed	C:1:30 – A, P	C:1:30 – A, P (very hot, hard hike)
Oct 12, Thu	C:1:53 – A, P	SA 80 – P
Oct 13, Fri	new (?) & Bronco Canyon EVENING: Rich Lange, Weekly Wrap-up	C:1:16W – A; C:1:53 – A, P
Oct 14, Sat	Team I leaves, Team II arrives	transition of teams; food and water runs

*Note: A = architectural documentation
**Note: P = photography

Table I.2. Research Plan and Actual Activities, October, 1995, First Earthwatch Season, cont'd

DATE	PLANNED	ACTUAL
Oct 15, Sun	Out to camp; orientation EVENING: Rich Lange, Orientation and Project History	in camp; orientation
Oct 16, Mon	C:1:40 – A, P EVENING: Stephanie Whittlesey, Regional History: Archaeology and Prehistory	C:1:40 – A, P
Oct 17, Tue	Cock's Comb Ridge – A; Hole-in-the-Wall – P	C:1:16C – A; C:1:16E – A
Oct 18, Wed	Hole-in-the-Wall – A; Cock's Comb Ridge – P EVENING: Barbara Murphy, Beam Replacement in Cold Spring Canyon	C:1:16C – A; C:1:16E – A; C:1:40 – A
Oct 19, Thu	C:1:8 – A, P	C:1:14 – A, P
Oct 20, Fri	C:1:14 – A, P EVENING: Rich Lange, Weekly Wrap-up	C:1:8 – A, P
Oct 21, Sat	Globe: laundry, Tonto NM, Besh-ba-gowah	Globe as planned
Oct 22, Sun	In camp EVENING: Rich Lange, Orientation and Project History for new volunteers	In camp
Oct 23, Mon	C:1:16C – A; C:1:16W – P	C:1:36 – A, P; C:1:16E – P; C:1:40 – A
Oct 24, Tue	C:1:16C – A; C:1:16W – P; C:1:25? EVENING: Bonnie Pitblado, Tree-ring Dating	C:1:16W – P; C:1:16C – A; C:1:16E – P
Oct 25, Wed	C:1:45 – A; C:1:44 & 45 – P EVENING: Rich Lange, Environment and Signalling/Intervisibility	C:1:44 – A; C:1:23 – P; C:1:16W – P; C:1:16C – A; SA 7 – A, P
Oct 26, Thu	C:1:46 – A; C:1:36/58 – P EVENING: Bonnie P and Barbara M, Archaeological artifacts—ceramics, lithics, and other things	C:1:44 – A
Oct 27, Fri	C:1:36/58 – A; C:1:46 – P EVENING: Rich Lange, Weekly Wrap-up	C:1:44 – A, C:1:45 – A; SA 31 – A, P
Oct 28, Sat	Team II back to Globe; begin breakdown of camp	
Oct 29, Sun	Camp breakdown	

*Note: A = architectural documentation
**Note: P = photography

Table I.3. Research Plan and Actual Activities, October, 1996, Second Earthwatch Season

DATE	PLANNED	ACTUAL
Sept 28, Sat	Camp to be set-up by Amaterra	Camp set up by Amaterra; RCL there
Sept 29, Sun	Camp to be set-up by Amaterra	Camp set up by Amaterra
Oct 3, Thu	RCL, RC-T arrives late evening	RCL, RC-T arrives; A little excitement on the way up. Axle on Bonnie and RA's trailer broke. Spent a couple of hours in Winkelman getting it repaired.
Oct 4, Fri	RCL & RC-T Setting up camp, digging outhouses, etc	RCL & RC-T Setting up camp, digging outhouses
Oct 5, Sat	RCL & RC-T Setting up camp; food and water runs	RCL & RC-T Setting up camp; food and water runs
Oct 6, Sun	RCL & RC-T; crew arrives at camp; set up personal tents, orientation; RCL leaves	RCL & RC-T; volunteers arrive, orientation; RCL back to Tucson
Oct 7, Mon	RC-T Survey	RC-T Survey:
Oct 8, Tue	RC-T Survey	RC-T Survey:
Oct 9, Wed	RC-T Survey	RC-T Survey:
Oct 10, Thu	RC-T Survey	RC-T Survey:
Oct 11, Fri	RC-T Survey	RC-T Survey:
Oct 12, Sat	RC-T leaves; RCL returns Crew into Globe; laundry, Tonto NM, etc	RC-T leaves; RCL returns Crew to Globe; Elaine Hughes & Robert Crowell arrive
Oct 13, Sun	RCL; up Pueblo Canyon with Elaine and Robert to move dataloggers	RCL; moved dataloggers in Pueblo Canyon; C:1:16C – A*
Oct 14, Mon	RCL: SA 2, 4, 5 – A*, P** Survey	RCL: SA 2, 4, 5 – A, P Survey: K. Grimm & K. Fite
Oct 15, Tue	RCL: SA 7, up to Murphy/Halde Ranch, Aztec Peak area Survey	RCL: up to Aztec Peak, C:1:21 – A Survey: K. Fite
Oct 16, Wed	RCL: C:1:25; out to Reynolds Creek? Survey	RCL: C:1:21 – A; C:1:25 – A, P
Oct 17, Thu	RCL: out to Reynolds Creek, C:1:14, back to base camp	RCL: C:1:14 – P, back to camp Survey: K. Fite
Oct 18, Fri	RCL: in camp, organizing Survey	RCL: SA 31 – A
Oct 19, Sat	RCL to Globe Transition from Team I to II	RCL to Globe, new volunteers

*Note: A = architectural documentation
**Note: P = photography

Table I.3. Research Plan and Actual Activities, October, 1996, Second Earthwatch Season, cont'd

DATE	PLANNED	ACTUAL
Oct 20, Sun	RCL: with volunteers, tour to Besh-ba-gowah, out to camp, orientation	RCL: tour, and out to camp, orientation; over this weekend, weather changed dramatically—it was unseasonably hot, now unseasonably cold with some rain. Snowed while we were on Mustang Ridge! Got last parts for shower.
Oct 21, Mon	RCL: C:1:46; John Welch arrives in camp Survey	RCL: C:1:46 – A, P; John Welch arrives Survey: K. Grimm
Oct 22, Tue	RCL: with JW, Mustang Ridge on FAIR; C:1:38, 47, & 50 Survey	RCL: with JW, crew to Mustang Ridge, C:1:38 – A; C:1:47 –A Survey: K. Grimm
Oct 23, Wed	RCL: Mustang Ridge	RCL: C:1:38 – A, P; C:1:47 – A
Oct 24, Thu	RCL: Mustang Ridge	RCL: C:1:50 – A, P; C:1:47 – A
Oct 25, Fri	RCL: Hole-in-the-Wall	RCL: C:1:50 – A, P; C:1:47 – P Survey: C. Freeman
Oct 26, Sat	RCL: crew to Globe, RCL leaves	RCL leaves, crew to Globe
Oct 27, Sun	RC-T back, orientation; in camp Or recreational hike?	RC-T: returns, in camp
Oct 28, Mon	RC-T Survey	RC-T Survey: RC-T & B. Deaver
Oct 29, Tue	RC-T Survey	RC-T Survey: RC-T, K. Grimm, B. Deaver
Oct 30, Wed	RC-T Survey	RC-T Survey: RC-T, K. Grimm, B. Deaver
Oct 31, Thu	RC-T Survey	RC-T Survey: RC-T, B. Deaver
Nov 1, Fri	RC-T Survey	RC-T, RCL returns; Kimberly Grimm's WEDDING! Survey: RC-T, B. Deaver
Nov 2, Sat	RCL, RC-T Volunteers to Globe, begin taking camp down	RCL, RC-T Finally took a shower in the propane-fired hot water! Taking camp down, volunteers to Globe
Nov 3, Sun	RCL, RC-T Taking camp down	RCL, RC-T Taking camp down
Nov 9, Sat	Amaterra takes camp down, RCL back up	RCL back up, Amaterra taking camp down
Nov 10, Sun	Camp taken down and leave	Camp taken down, All done!

*Note: A = architectural documentation
**Note: P = photography

Site Data and Site Number Concordances

a. Site Data and Site Number Concordances

ASM Site Number (AZ V:1:x)	Gila Pueblo Site Number (GP C:1:x)	SAP Site Number (SA–x)	Tonto National Forest Site Number (AR-03-12-05-x)	Site Name	Site Type	Elevation (Gila Pueblo) (ft)	Elevation (SAP) (ft)	Site Size (number of rooms)
	1		51			5600		
	2							
	3		37			5800		10
	4		48			4300		6
	5		40			6600		8
	6					4700		8
	7		49			5000		40
	9		44			4600		6
	11					4900		12
	12		42			5900		60
	13		45			5100		12
	17		38			5400		
	18		50			5200		22
	19		47			5100		
	20		7					
	22		41			5340		1
	24		4					
	26		63					100
	27							
	29							
	32		39			5000		100
	33		41			2800		
	35		65			4200		
	39					4900		10
	41		315			3200		11
	42		61			4300		7
	43		32			3900		8
	48		59			3000		50
	49		53			3200		30
	51					3000		50
	54		52			3300		40
	56		56			3200		60
	57		57			3160		25
	59		34			4400		16
	60		31			3515		38
	62		30					10
	63		16					8
	65					5000		
	66		38			5000		8

b. Site Data and Site Number Concordances, cont'd

ASM Site Number (AZ V:1:x)	Gila Pueblo Site Number (GP C:1:x)	SAP Site Number (SA –x)	Tonto National Forest Site Number (AR-03-12-05-x)	Site Name	Site Type	Elevation (Gila Pueblo) (ft)	Elevation (SAP) (ft)	Site Size (number of rooms)
26	67	144	2		large compound	6700	3820	5
124	68	2	1		small cliff dwelling	5000	4760	5
125		3			historic		4770	16
126	C:2:12	4	8		small cliff dwelling		4760	8
127	C:5:15	5	212		small cliff dwelling		4600	100
128	C:5:17	6	214		artifact scatter			2
129	28	7			small cliff dwelling	3900	3960	1
130	16E	139	25		large cliff dwelling	4400	5200	2
131	16C	138	25		large cliff dwelling	4400	5200	2
132	16W	140	25		large cliff dwelling	4400	5200	12
133	21	141	5	Ring-Tail Ruin	large cliff dwelling	6300	6800	25
134	23	142	27	Workman Creek Cliff Dwelling	small cliff dwelling	4900	5200	28
135	40	150	71	Mine Shaft Cliff Dwelling	large cliff dwelling	4800	4260	14
136	36	148	28	Cooper Forks Cliff Dwelling	small cliff dwelling	5800	4840	6
136	58	1	30		small cliff dwelling		4840	18
137		8			field house		4680	9
138		9		Ken's Site	field house		3240	1
139		10		Cow Dung Site	medium surface pueblo		3520	2
140		11		Madsen Pueblo	large surface pueblo		3800	2
141		12		Flying H Gate Site	field house		3090	4
142		13		3 Junipers Site	field house		3410	12
143		14		Laughing Rock Pueblo	medium surface pueblo		4313	2
144		15		Six Caves Ruin	large cliff dwelling		4400	3
145		16		Cock's Comb Site	large cliff dwelling		4260	7
146		17		Line Shack Site	field house		4880	11
147		18		Pottery Point #1	field house		2920	15
148		19		Pottery Point #2	field house		3200	1
149		20			isolated wall/checkdam		3240	1
150		21			field house		2960	1
151		22			field house		3120	3
152		23			medium surface pueblo		3040	1
153		24			field house		3080	5
154		25			field house		3120	1
155		26		Knife Ridge Site	large surface pueblo		3080	1
156		27			field house		2980	12
157		29			field house		4376	2
158		30			Apache		4830	2

c. Site Data and Site Number Concordances, cont'd

ASM Site Number (AZ V:1:x)	Gila Pueblo Site Number (GP C:1:x)	SAP Site Number (SA –x)	Tonto National Forest Site Number (AR-03-12-05-x)	Site Name	Site Type	Elevation (Gila Pueblo) (ft)	Elevation (SAP) (ft)	Site Size (number of rooms)
159		32		Limestone Pueblos	medium surface pueblo		6305	9
160		33		Elephant Rock Fortress	small compound		7160	
161		36			artifact scatter		6320	
162	8	136	26		small cliff dwelling	4600	7180	8
163	14	137	24		small cliff dwelling	7000	7120	4
164	25	143	31	Upper Cold Spring Cliff Dwelling	small cliff dwelling		6180	6
165	30	145	21		large cliff dwelling	4000	5200	8
166	31	146	40	Pottery Point Pueblo	large surface pueblo	3000	3040	22
167	44	151	16		large cliff dwelling	5700	5240	17
168	45	152	35		small cliff dwelling	4900	5200	5
169	52	153	34		large surface pueblo	5500	4600	10
170	C:2:4	28	36	Upper Coon Creek Cliff Dwelling	large cliff dwelling	4900	4760	22
171		37		Hole-in-the-Rock Ruin	small cliff dwelling		4400	2
172		41		Horse Camp Compound	large compound		4940	8
173		45			artifact scatter		4840	
174	46	46	29		small cliff dwelling	5000	5280	6
175		47			isolated wall/checkdam		5280	
176		48			isolated wall/checkdam		5280	1
177	37	149	60		large surface pueblo	4600	3990	50
178		49			field house		4020	3
179		38			isolated wall/checkdam		4400	
180		39			field house		4120	
181		40			field house		4010	5
182		50		Isolated Metate Site	medium surface pueblo		5720	2
183	15	54	43		small compound	4800	4810	6
184		55			small compound		5560	3
185	64	56	32		large surface pueblo	4600	4725	80
186		57			large surface pueblo		4680	30
187		58			historic		4685	
188	53	61	64	Quail Spring Cliff Dwelling	small cliff dwelling	3500	5000	4
189		62			field house		3115	
190		76		River Bend Compound	large compound		3130	
191		64		Cherry Creek Mound Site	large compound		3130	20
192	55	65	54	Bronco Canyon Lookout	large compound	4100	4630	8
193		66			field house		5580	1
194		67			artifact scatter		5580	
195	10	68	46		large surface pueblo	5000	5010	50
196		69			artifact scatter		5210	
199		134		Brushy Ridge Site	field house		4980	3
200		135		Ken Gates Compound	small compound		5480	2
201	34	147			small cliff dwelling	5800	4640	6
202		71			large compound		3130	

d. Site Data and Site Number Concordances, cont'd

ASM Site Number (AZ V:1:x)	Gila Pueblo Site Number (GP C:1:x)	SAP Site Number (SA –x)	Tonto National Forest Site Number (AR-03-12-05-x)	Site Name	Site Type	Elevation (Gila Pueblo) (ft)	Elevation (SAP) (ft)	Site Size (number of rooms)
203		72			large surface pueblo		3130	
204		73			field house		3060	1
205		74			small compound		3120	1
206		75			isolated wall/checkdam			
207		156		Big Buzz Compound	large compound		3125	12
208		77		Leslie Pueblo	large compound		3130	6
209		78		Stone Bowl Site	field house		3120	2
210		79		Quail Run Site	field house		2920	1
211		88		Horny Toad Site	field house		2920	2
212		80		Juniper Flat Site	field house		3720	2
213		81			field house		3720	1
214		82		Rabbit Rock Site	artifact scatter		3720	
215		83		Seis Damas Site	medium surface pueblo		3810	4
216		84		Devils Claw Site	artifact scatter		3965	
217		85			artifact scatter		4080	
218		86		Devils Chasm Compound	large compound		2970	3
219		87		Kovacic Site	field house		3880	2
220		154			field house		2920	2
221		89			artifact scatter		2880	
222		90		Avery's Nap Site	large compound		2845	10
223		91		Creek Overlook Site	field house		2940	1
224		92		Lithic Point Site	artifact scatter		2880	
225		93		Slim Pickins Site	isolated wall/checkdam		3000	5
226		94		Easy Pickins Site	large compound		2920	5
227		95		Steel Arrow Site	large compound		2960	20
228		96		Wounded Bum Site	small compound		3000	7
229		101		Raindrop Site	field house		2960	2
230		102			field house		2960	2
231		103		Honeymooner's Site	medium surface pueblo		3020	2
232		104		Vic's Villa	medium surface pueblo		3020	4
233		105		Vince's Villa	medium surface pueblo		3545	5
234		106			large compound		3100	10
235		108			large compound		3060	15
236		109			field house		3040	1
237		110			isolated wall/checkdam		3040	1
238		111			large compound		3040	1
239		112			field house		3240	
240		113			field house		4156	1
241		114			field house		3215	1
242		115		Frisco Flat Site	small compound		3010	6

e. Site Data and Site Number Concordances, cont'd

ASM Site Number (AZ V:1:x)	Gila Pueblo Site Number (GP C:1:x)	SAP Site Number (SA –x)	Tonto National Forest Site Number (AR-03-12-05-x)	Site Name	Elevation (Gila Pueblo) (ft)	Elevation (SAP) (ft)	Site Type	Site Size (number of rooms)
243		118		Poquito Pueblo		3202	field house	1
244		119				2845	isolated wall/checkdam	
245		120				2880	isolated wall/checkdam	
246		121				2880	field house	1
247		122				3045	field house	3
248		123				2920	field house	3
249		124				2920	field house	3
250		125				3240	isolated wall/checkdam	2
251		126				3480	field house	1
252		127				3120	medium surface pueblo	4
253		128				3080	isolated wall/checkdam	1
254		129				3285	isolated wall/checkdam	1
255		131					isolated wall/checkdam & field house	
256		131				3260	field house	1
257		132				3200	isolated wall/checkdam	
258		133		Cherie's Compound		3180	large compound	5
259		155		Devils Chasm Lookout		4557	medium surface pueblo	
260		157					rock art	
V:5:61		31	60	Hematite House		3200	large cliff dwelling	11
V:5:62		42				3380	field house	1
V:5:63		43				3160	small compound	5
V:5:64		44				3180	small compound	11
V:5:160		34				2750	rock art	
V:5:161		35				2750	rock art	
V:5:162	61	59	33		4620	4611	large compound	50
V:5:163		60				4560	medium surface pueblo	5
V:5:164		70		Cherry Creek Corral Site		2710	large compound	4
V:5:250		158				2760	rock art	
	38					5800	small cliff dwelling	
	47					5800	large cliff dwelling	6
	50					5800	large cliff dwelling	20

Appendix III
Site Maps from SAP Sites and Other Sites in the Vicinity of the Southeastern Sierra Ancha*

(*Note: all figures in Appendix III are included on the accompanying CD)

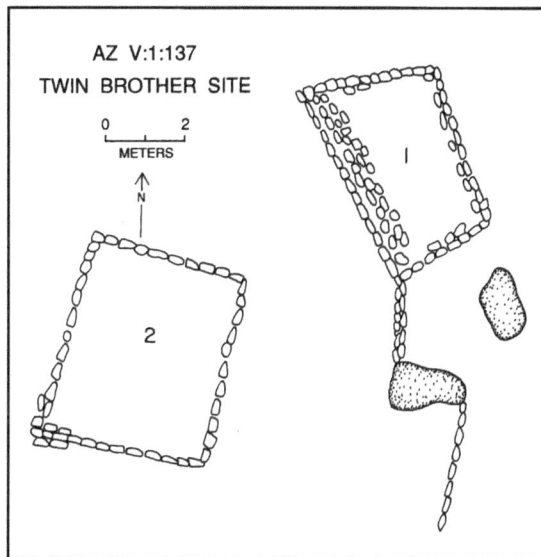

Figure III.1a. Field House: AZ V:1:137 (ASM)
(2004-1733-image4038)

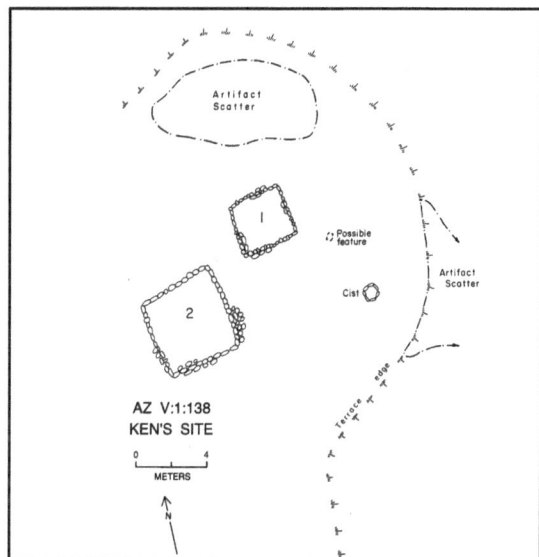

Figure III.1b. Field House: AZ V:1:138 (ASM)
(2004-1733-image4039)

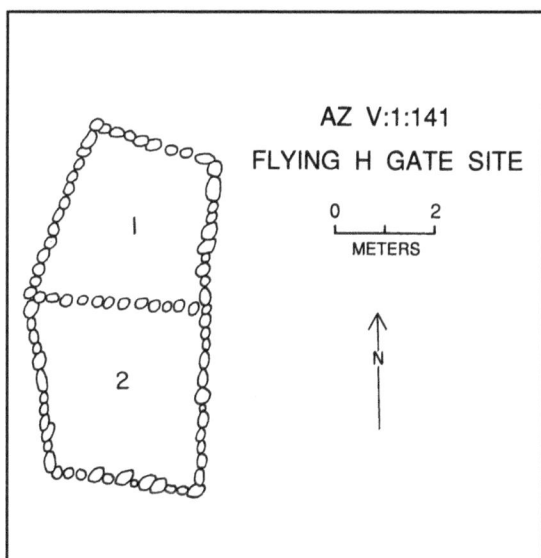

Figure III.1c. Field House: AZ V:1:141 (ASM)
(2004-1733-image4040)

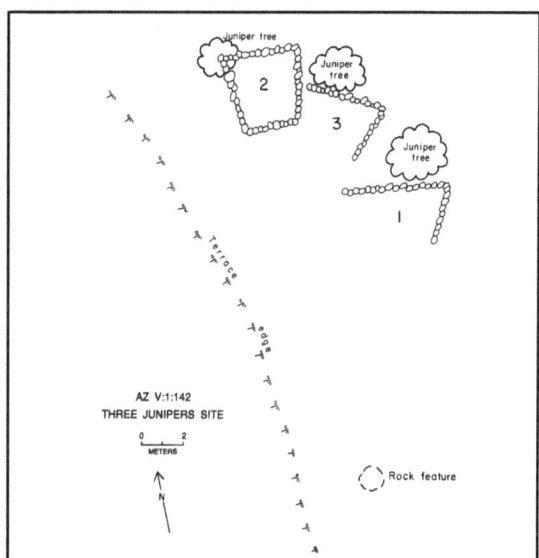

Figure III.1d. Field House: AZ V:1:142 (ASM)
(2004-1733-image4041)

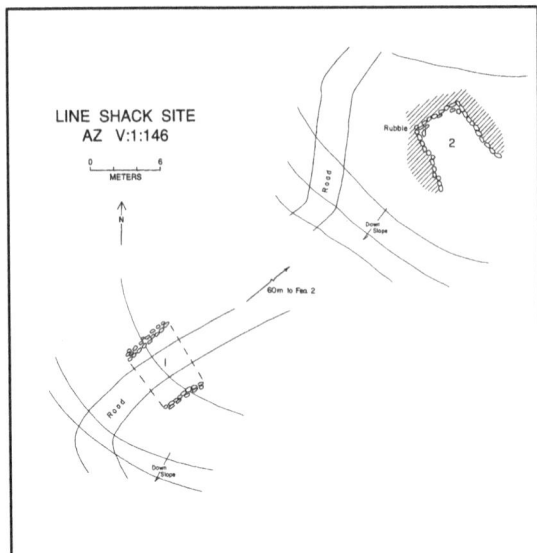

Figure III.1e. Field House: AZ V:1:146 (ASM)
(2004-1733-image4042)

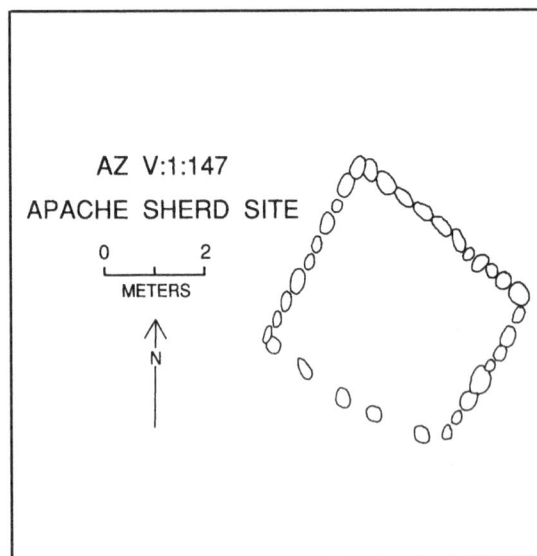

Figure III.1f. Field House: AZ V:1:147 (ASM)
(2004-1733-image4043)

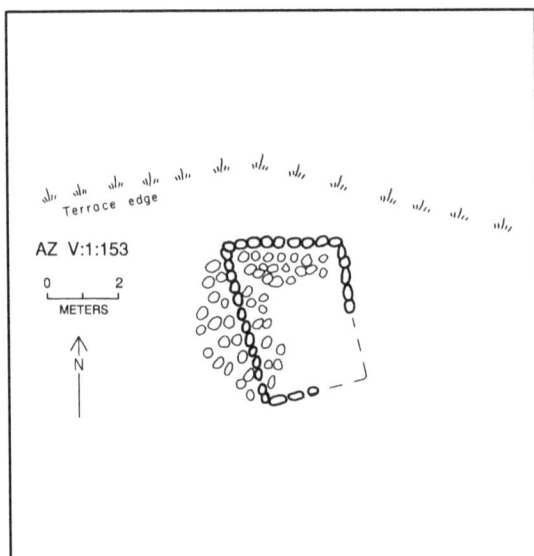

Figure III.1g. Field House: AZ V:1:153 (ASM)
(2004-1733-image4044)

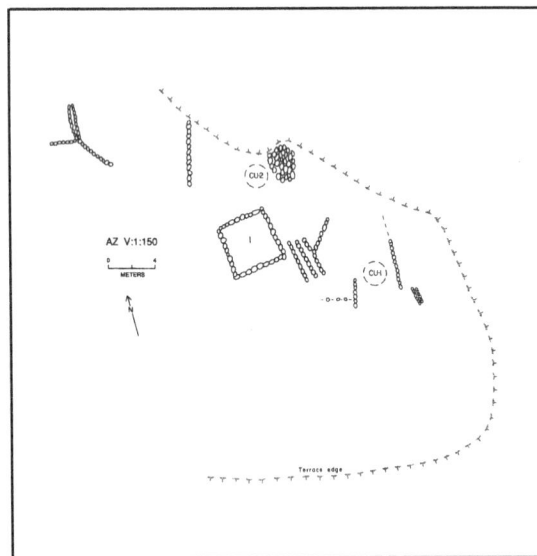

Figure III.1h. Field House: AZ V:1:150 (ASM)
(2004-1733-image4045)

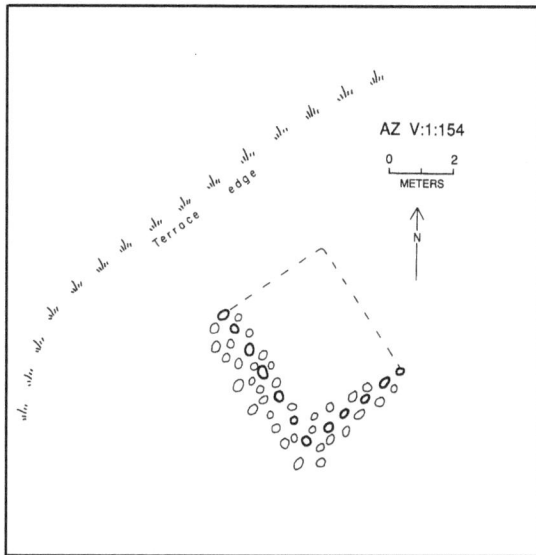

Figure III.1i. Field House: AZ V:1:154 (ASM) (2004-1733-image4046)

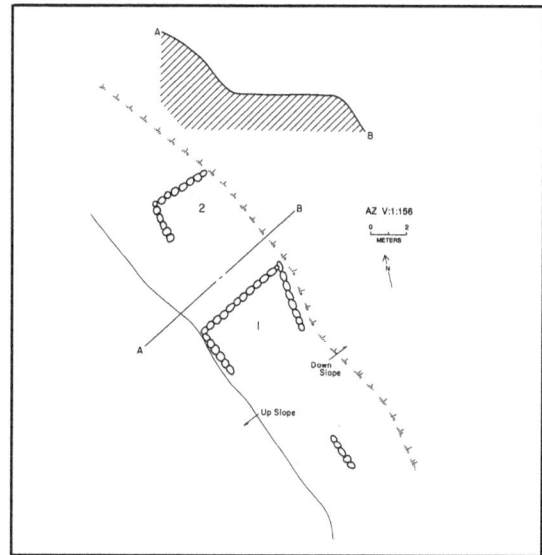

Figure III.1j. Field House: AZ V:1:156 (ASM) (2004-1733-image4047)

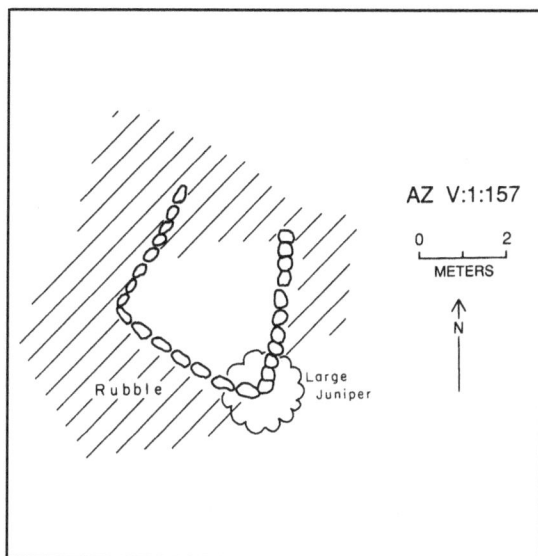

Figure III.1k. Field House: AZ V:1:157 (ASM) (2004-1733-image4048)

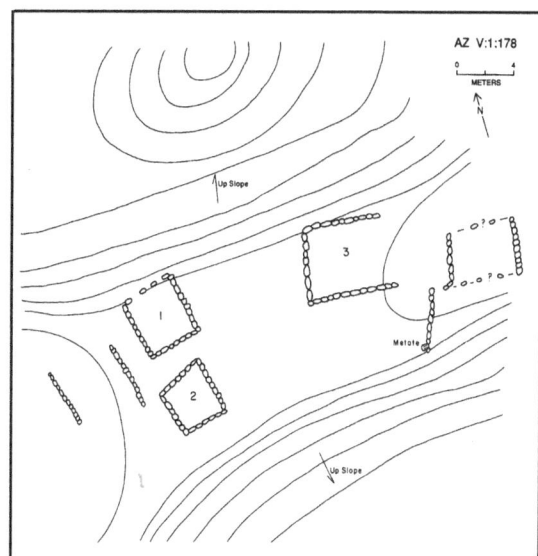

Figure III.1l. Field House: AZ V:1:178 (ASM) (2004-1733-image4049)

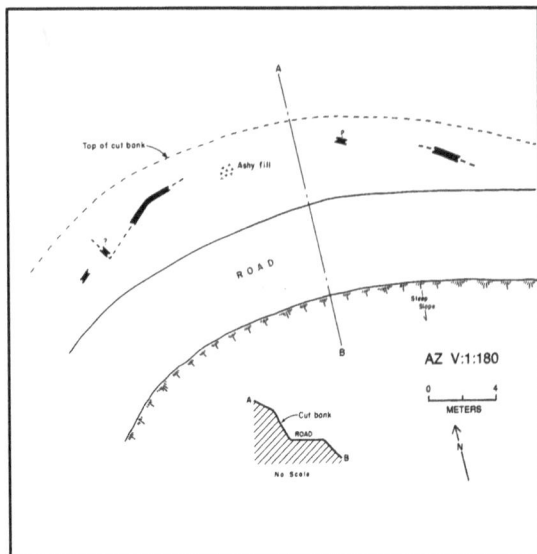

Figure III.1m. Field House: AZ V:1:180 (ASM)
(2004-1733-image4050)

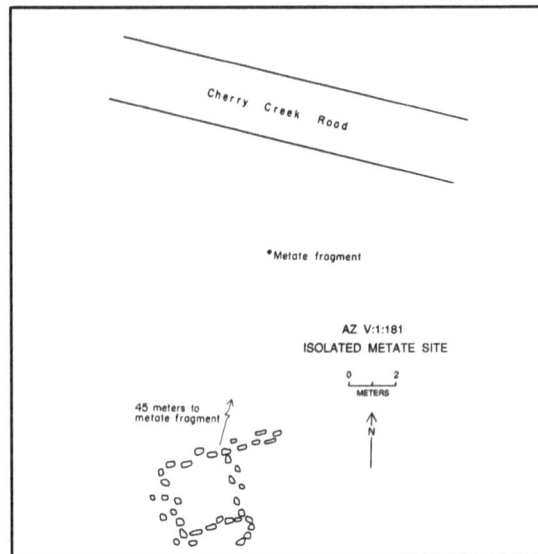

Figure III.1n. Field House: AZ V:1:181 (ASM)
(2004-1733-image4051)

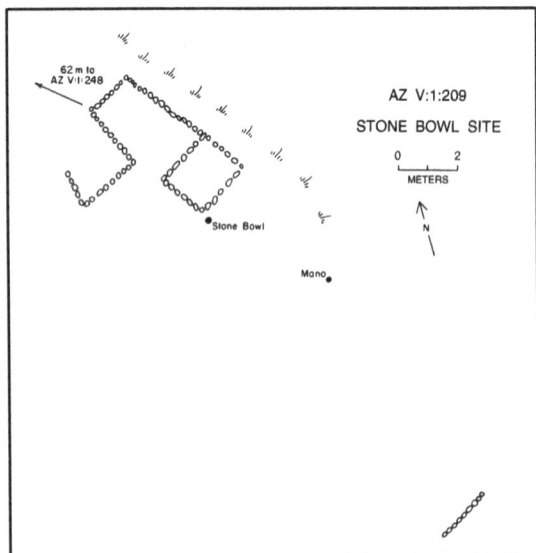

Figure III.1o. Field House: AZ V:1:209 (ASM)
(2004-1733-image4052)

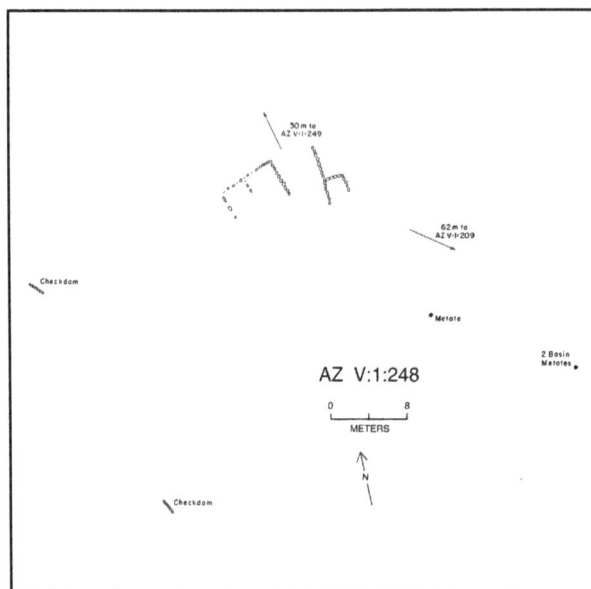

Figure III.1p. Field House: AZ V:1:248 (ASM)
(2004-1733-image4053)

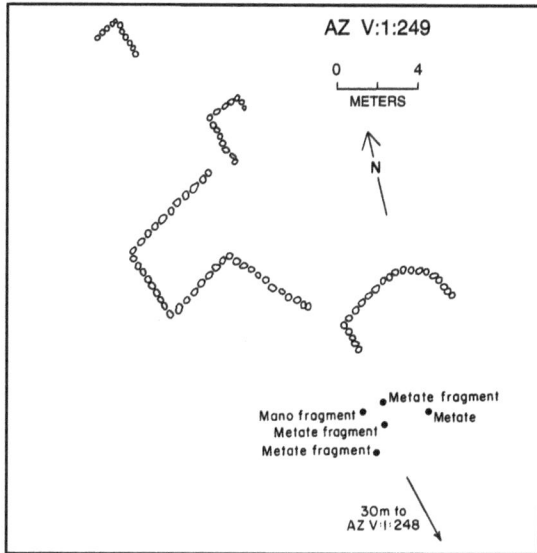

Figure III.1q. Field House: AZ V:1:249 (ASM)
(2004-1733-image4054)

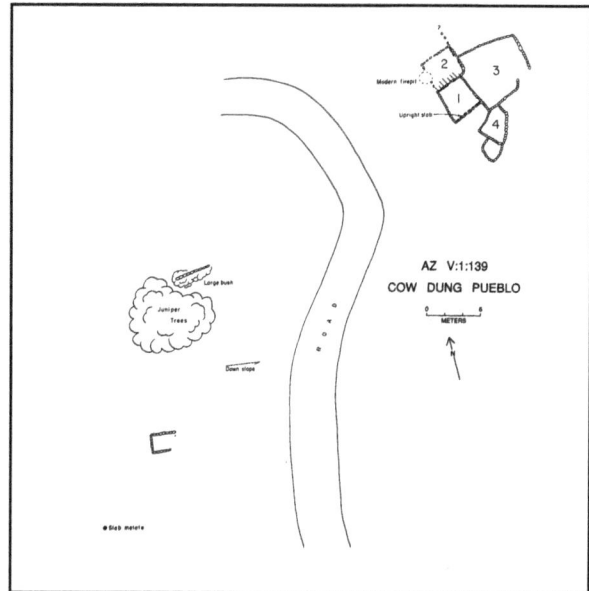

Figure III.2a. Medium-sized Surface Pueblo:
AZ V:1:139 (ASM) ((2004-1733-image4055)

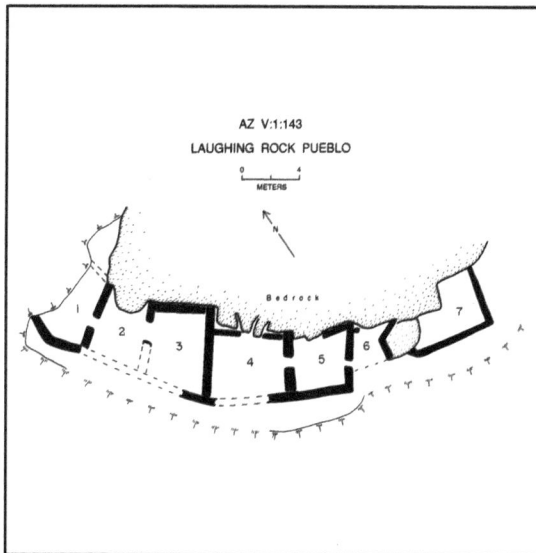

Figure III.2b. Medium-sized Surface Pueblo:
AZ V:1:143 (ASM) (2004-1733-image4056)

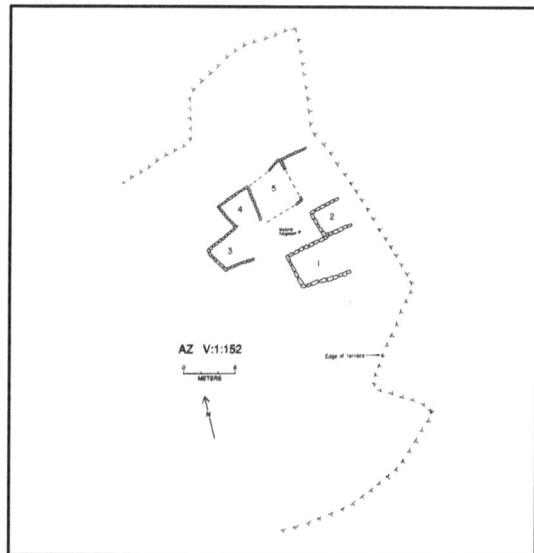

Figure III.2c. Medium-sized Surface Pueblo:
AZ V:1:152 (ASM) (2004-1733-image4057)

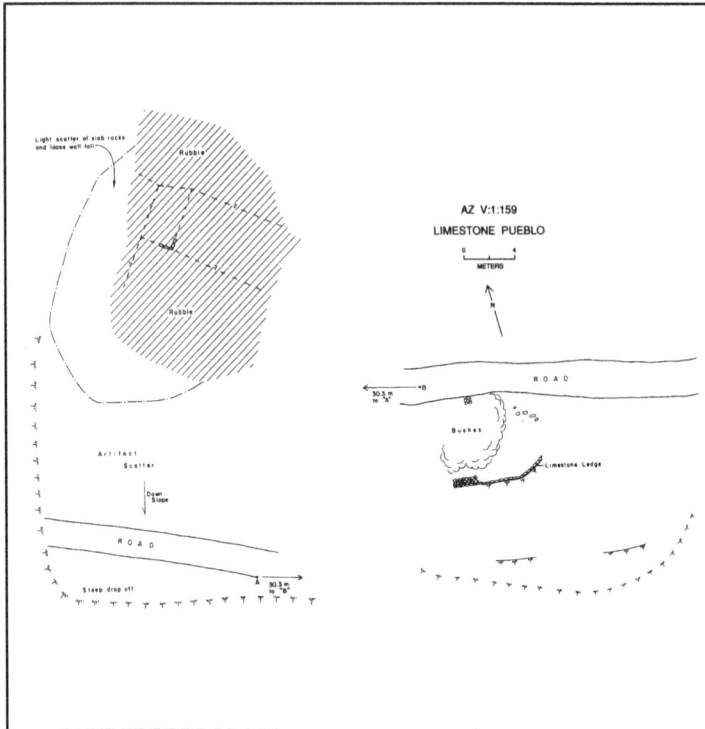

Figure III.2d. Medium-sized Surface Pueblo: AZ V:1:159 (ASM) (2004-1733-image4058)

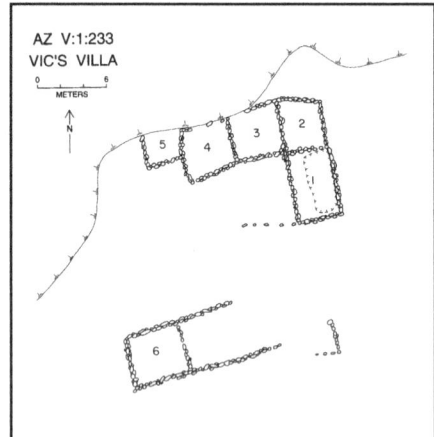

Figure III.2e. Medium-sized Surface Pueblo: AZ V:1:233 (ASM) (2004-1733-image4059)

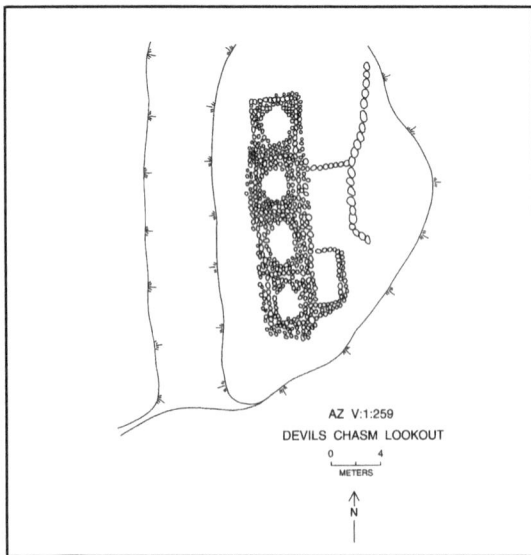

Figure III.2f. Medium-sized Surface Pueblo: AZ V:1:259 (ASM) (2004-1733-image4060)

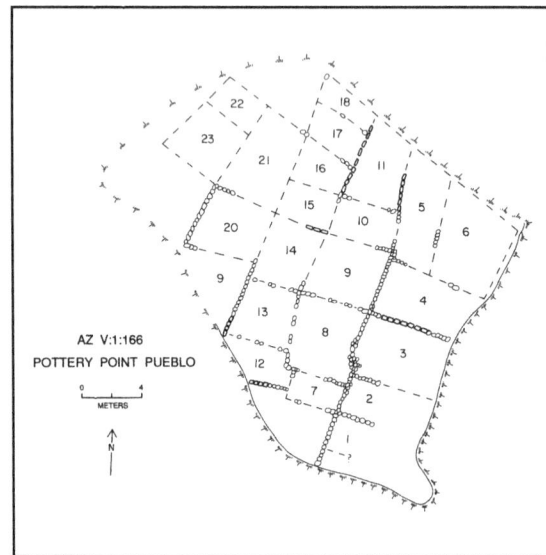

Figure III.3a. Large Surface Pueblo: AZ V:1:166 (ASM) (2004-1733-image4061)

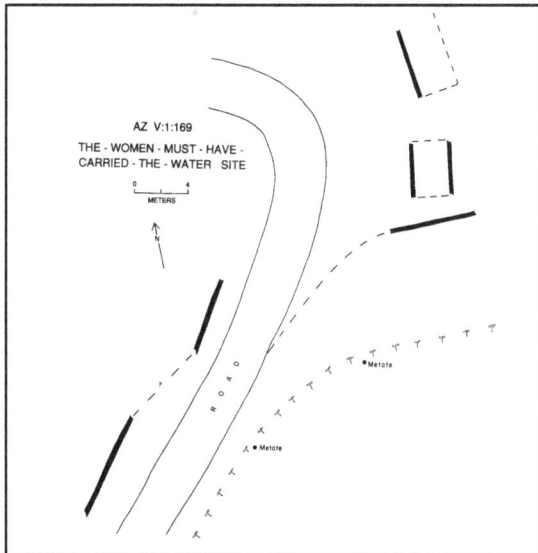

Figure III.3b. Large Surface Pueblo:
AZ V:1:169 (ASM) (2004-1733-image4062)

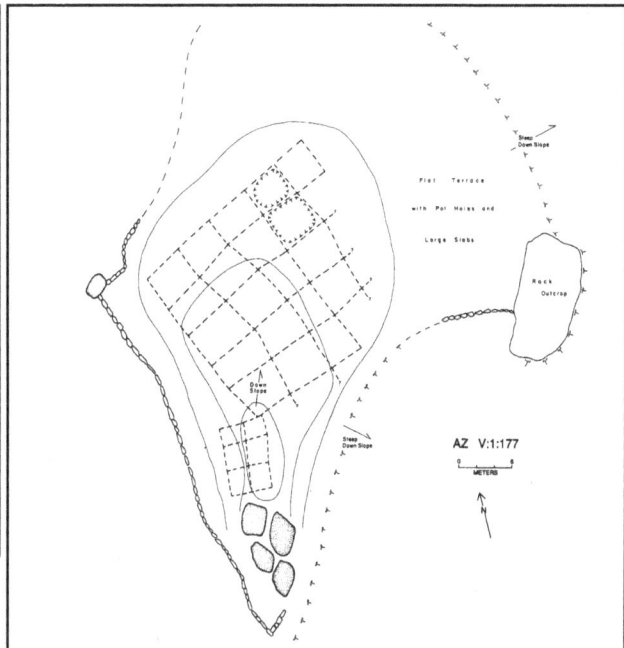

Figure III.3c. Large Surface Pueblo:
AZ V:1:177 (ASM) (2004-1733-image4063)

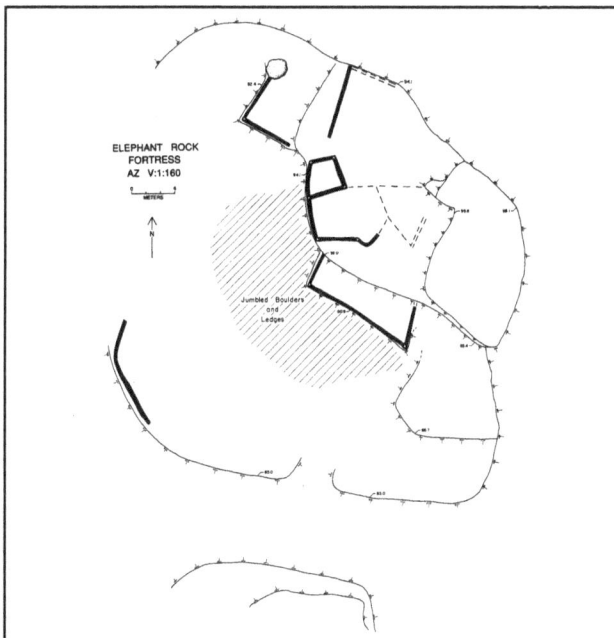

Figure III.4a. Compounds: AZ V:1:160 (ASM)
(2004-1733-image4064)

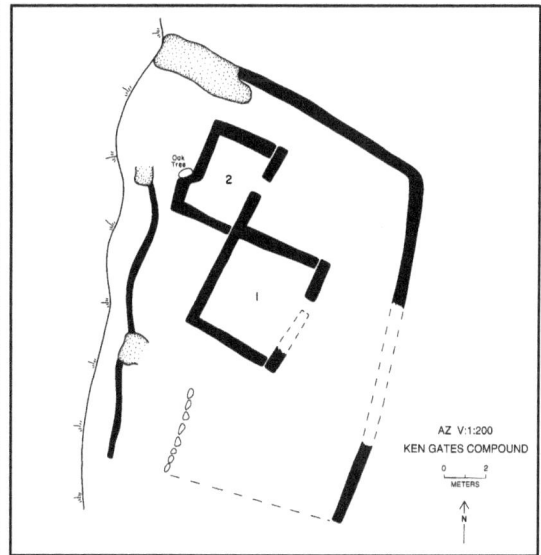

Figure III.4b. Compounds: AZ V:1:200 (ASM)
(2004-1733-image4065)

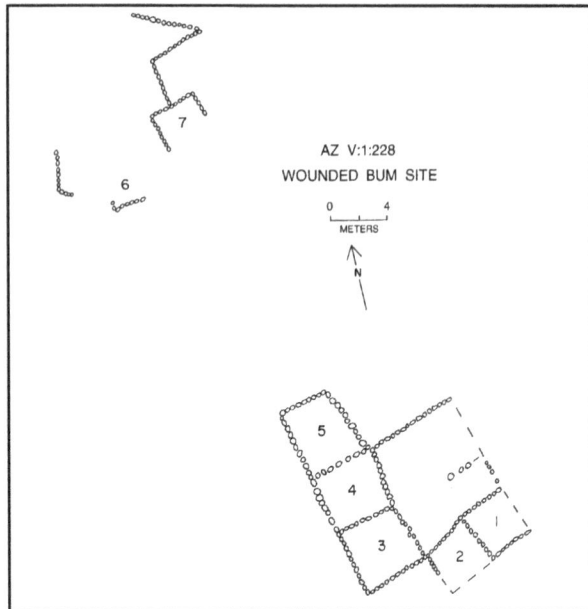

*Figure III.4c. Compounds: AZ V:1:228 (ASM)
(2004-1733-image4066)*

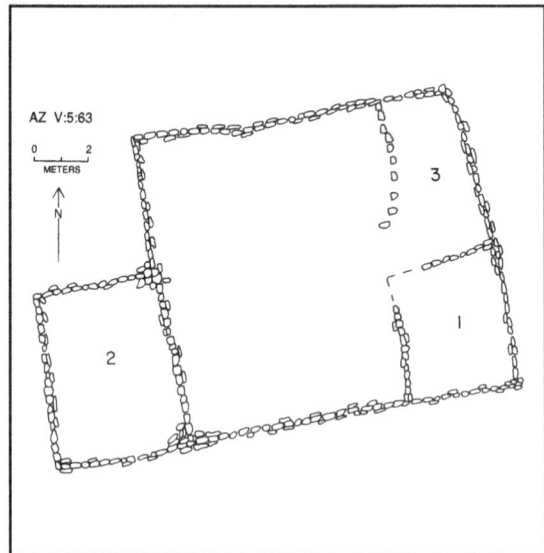

*Figure III.4d. Compounds: AZ V:5:63 (ASM)
(2004-1733-image4067)*

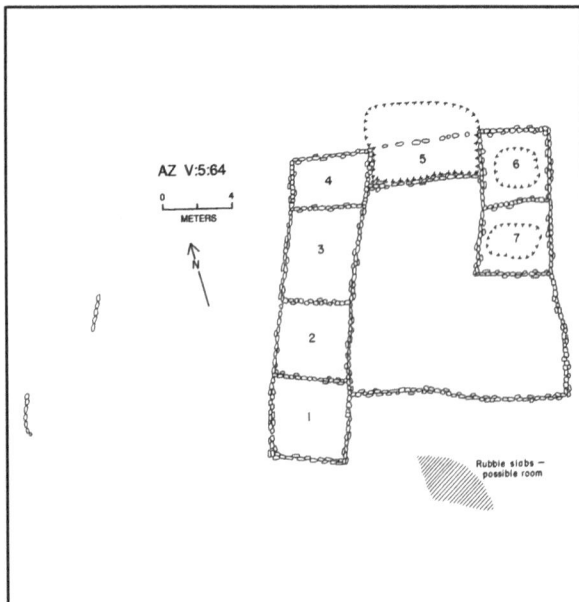

*Figure III.4e. Compounds: AZ V:5:64 (ASM)
(2004-1733-image4068)*

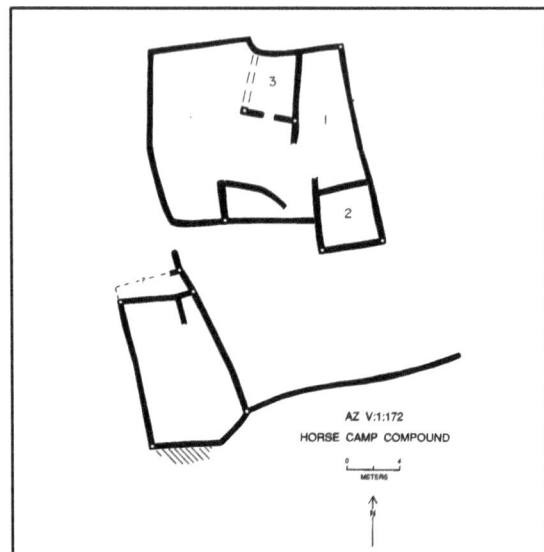

*Figure III.5a. Compounds: AZ V:1:172 (ASM)
(2004-1733-image4069)*

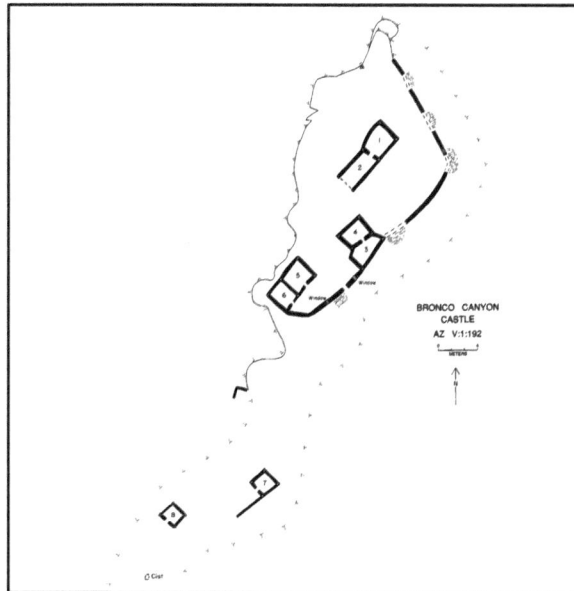

Figure III.5b. Compounds: AZ V:1:192 (ASM)
(2004-1733-image4070)

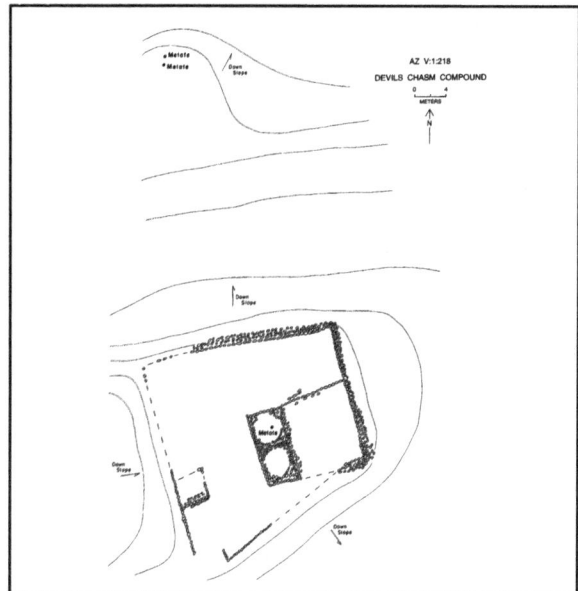

Figure III.5c. Compounds: AZ V:1:218 (ASM)
(2004-1733-image4071)

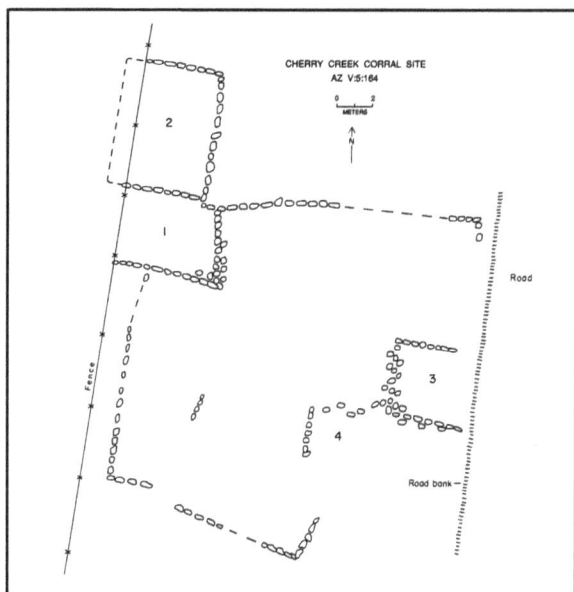

Figure III.5d. Compounds: AZ V:5:164 (ASM)
(2004-1733-image4072)

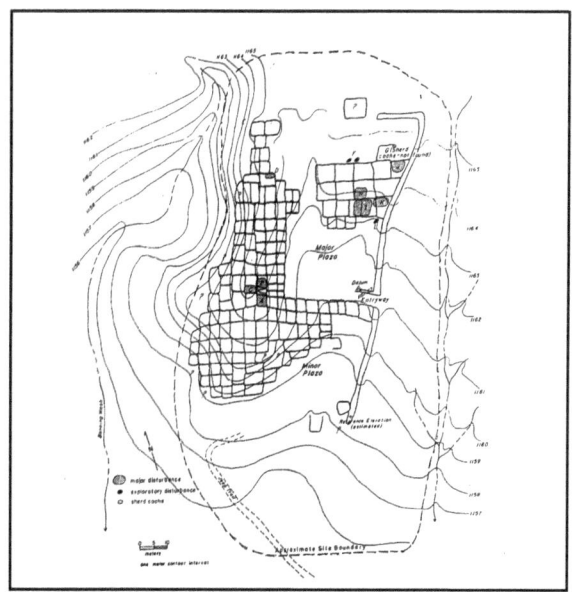

Figure III.6a. Granite Basin Ruin
(AZ V:1:26 [ASM]) (2004-1733-image4073)

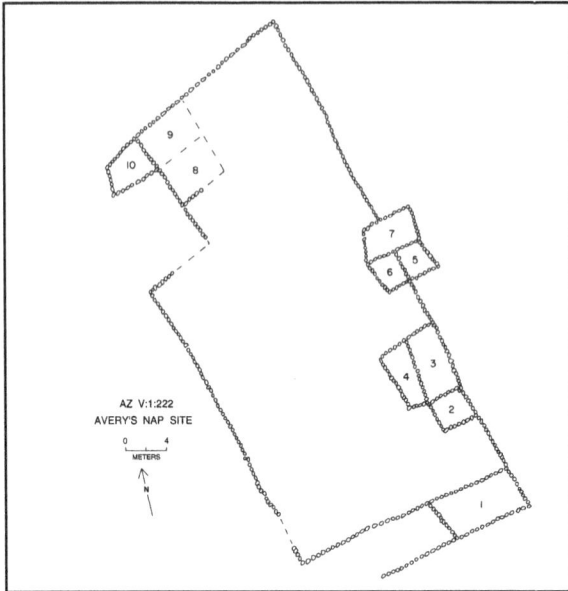

Figure III.6b. Compounds: AZ V:1:222 (ASM)
(2004-1733-image4074)

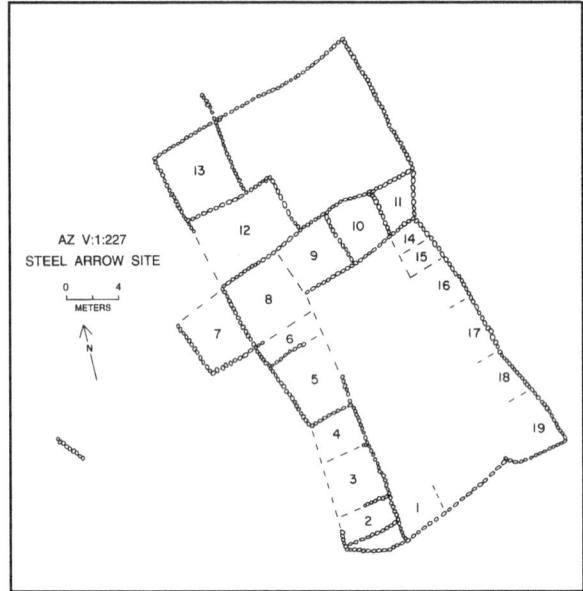

Figure III.6c. Compounds: AZ V:1:227 (ASM)
(2004-1733-image4075)

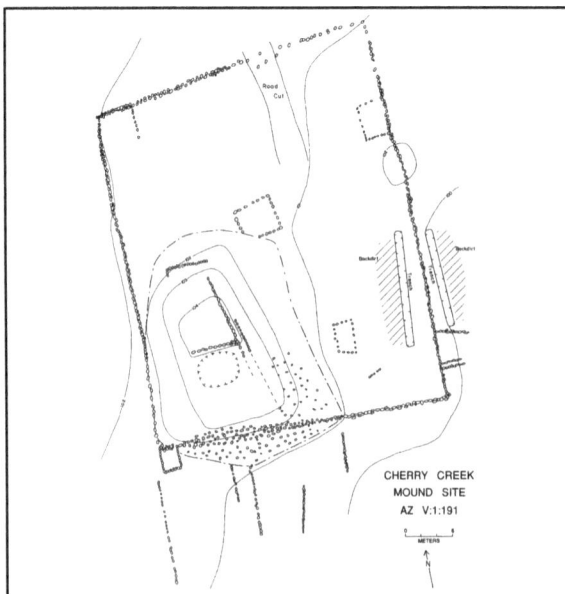

Figure III.7a. Compounds: AZ V:1:191 (ASM)
(2004-1733-image4076)

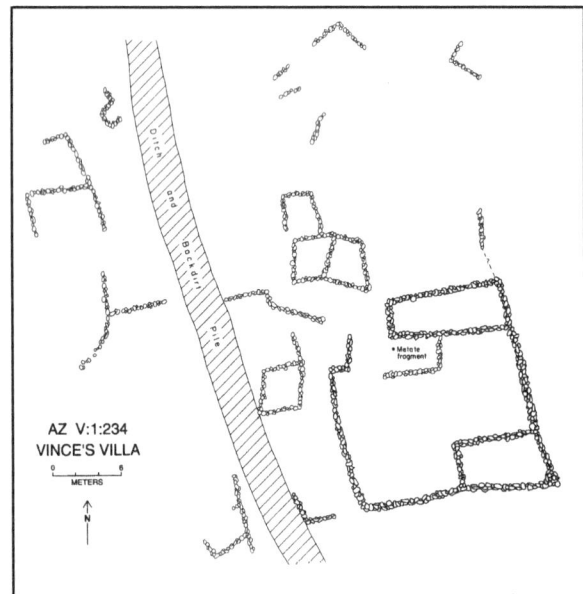

Figure III.7b. Compounds: AZ V:1:234 (ASM)
(2004-1733-image4077)

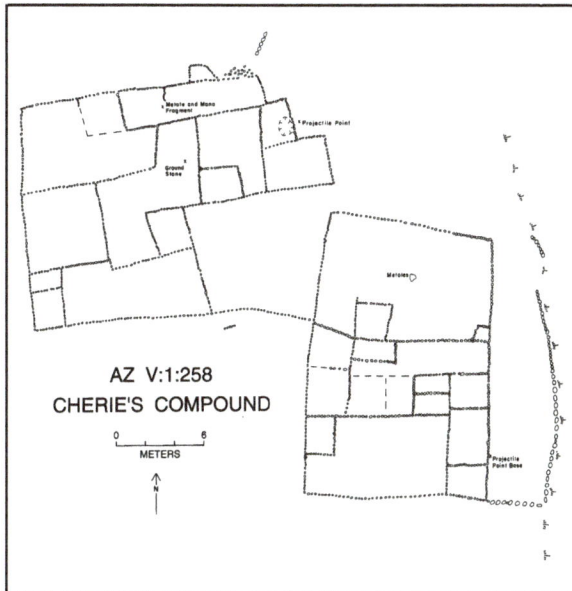

Figure III.7c. Compounds: AZ V:1:258 (ASM)
(2004-1733-image4078)

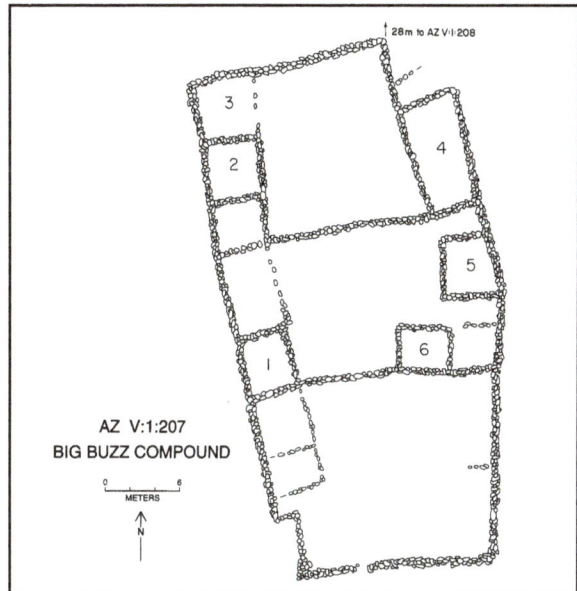

Figure III.7d. Compounds: AZ V:1:207 (ASM)
(2004-1733-image4079)

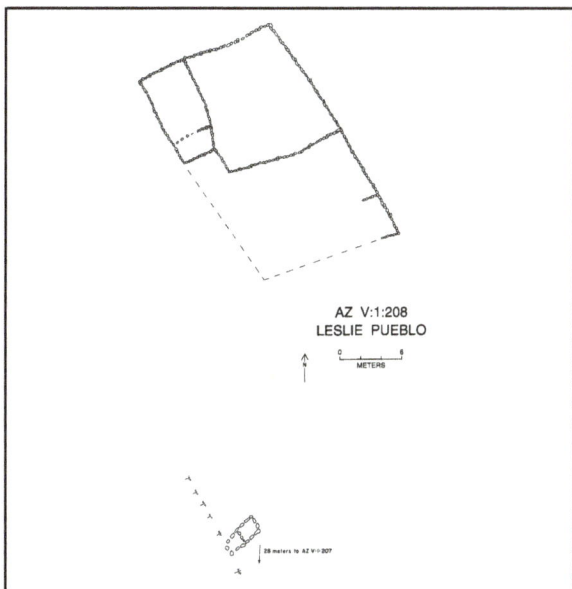

Figure III.7e. Compounds: AZ V:1:208 (ASM)
(2004-1733-image4080)

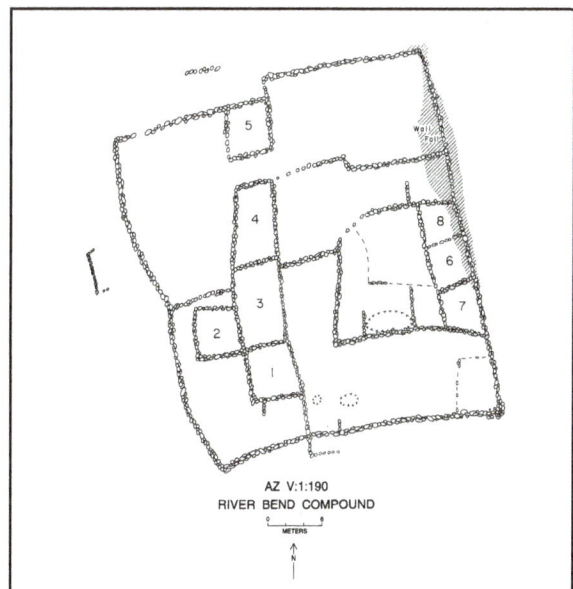

Figure III.7f. Compounds: AZ V:1:190 (ASM)
(2004-1733-image4081)

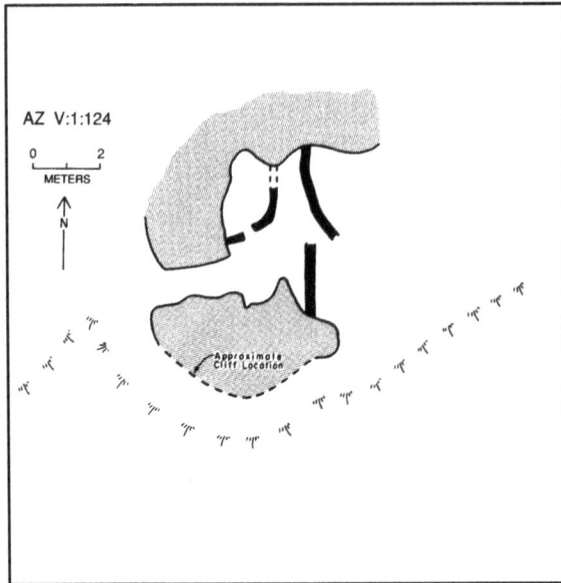

Figure III.8. Small Cliff Dwellings:
AZ V:1:124 (ASM) (2004-1733-image4082)

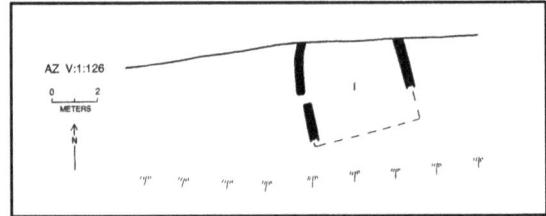

Figure III.9. Small Cliff Dwellings:
AZ V:1:126 (ASM) (2004-1733-image4083)

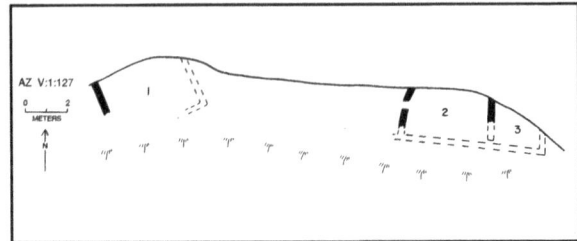

Figure III.10. Small Cliff Dwellings:
AZ V:1:127 (ASM) (2004-1733-image4084)

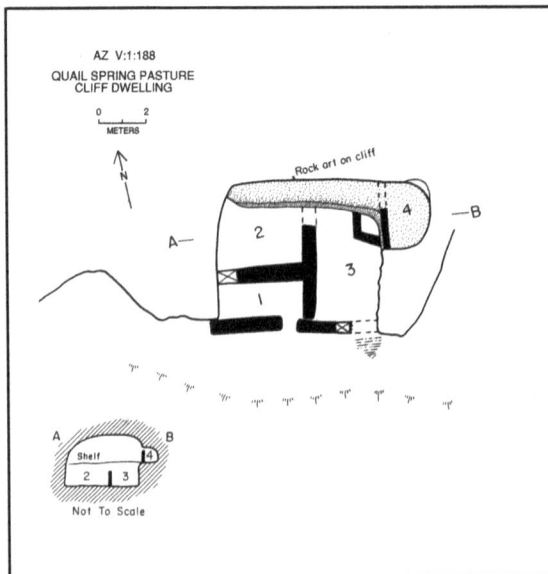

Figure III.11. Small Cliff Dwellings:
AZ V:1:188 (ASM) (2004-1733-image4085)

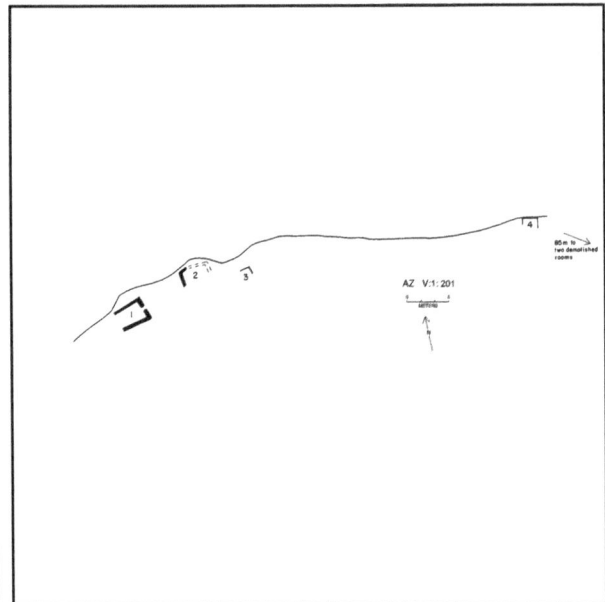

Figure III.12. Small Cliff Dwellings:
AZ V:1:201 (ASM) (2004-1733-image4086)

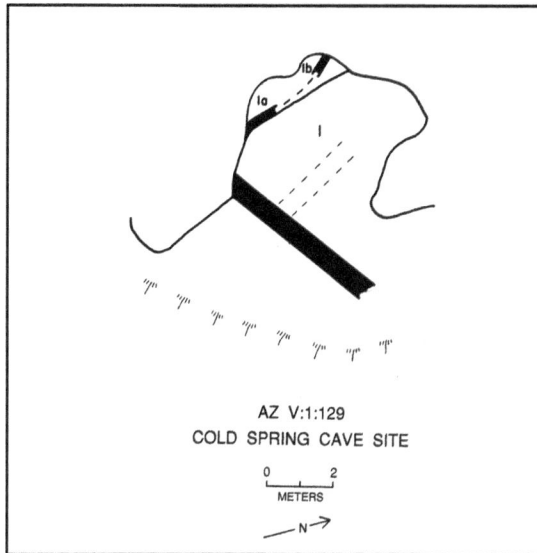

Figure III.13. Small Cliff Dwellings:
AZ V:1:129 (ASM) (2004-1733-image4087)

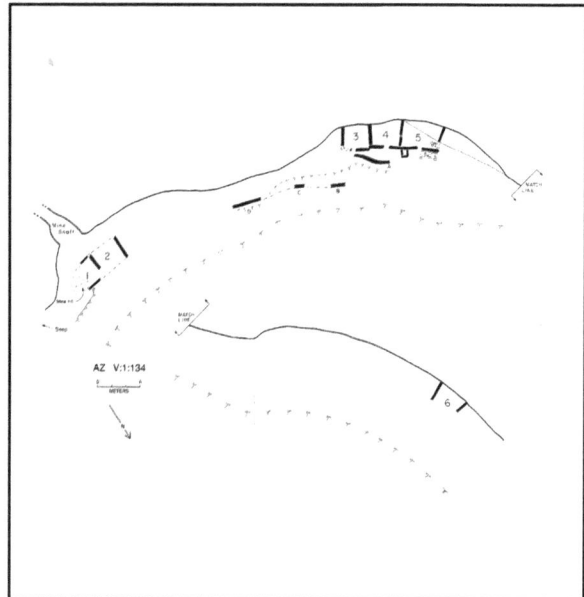

Figure III.14. Small Cliff Dwellings:
AZ V:1:134 (ASM) (2004-1733-image4088)

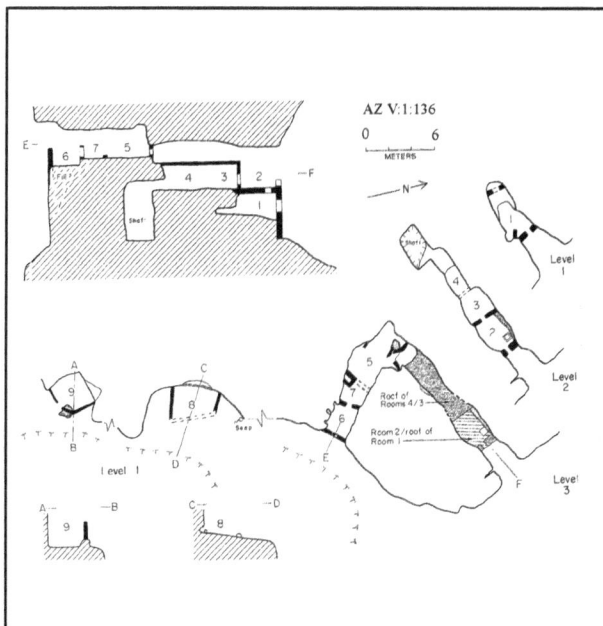

Figure III.15a. Small Cliff Dwellings,
SAP Mapping: AZ V:1:136 (ASM)
(2004-1733-image4089)

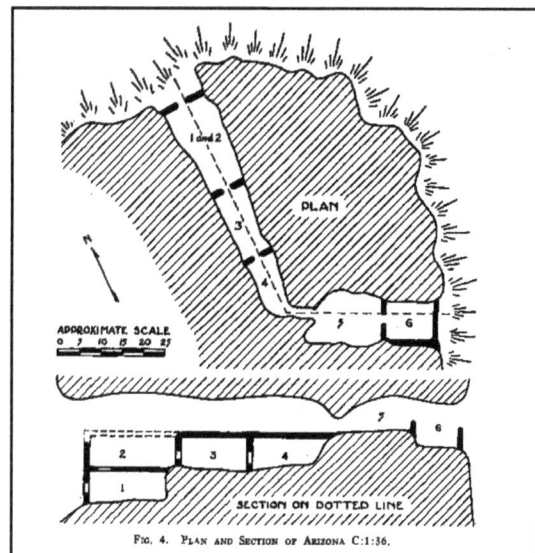

Figure III.15b. Small Cliff Dwellings, Gila Pueblo
Mapping: GP C:1:36 (AZ V:1:136 [ASM]); from
Haury 1934 (2004-1733-image4090)

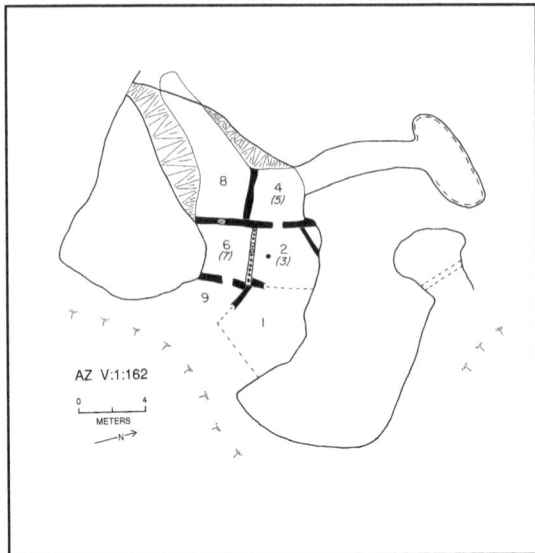

Figure III.16. Small Cliff Dwellings:
AZ V:1:162 (ASM) (2004-1733-image4091)

Figure III.17a. Small Cliff Dwellings, SAP Mapping: AZ V:1:163 (ASM)
(2004-1733-image4092)

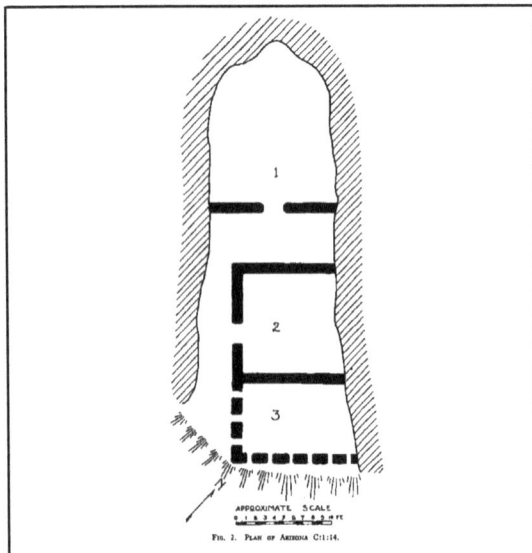

Figure III.17b. Small Cliff Dwellings, Gila Pueblo
Mapping: GP C:1:14   (AZ V:1:163 [ASM]);
from Haury (1934) (2004-1733-image4093)

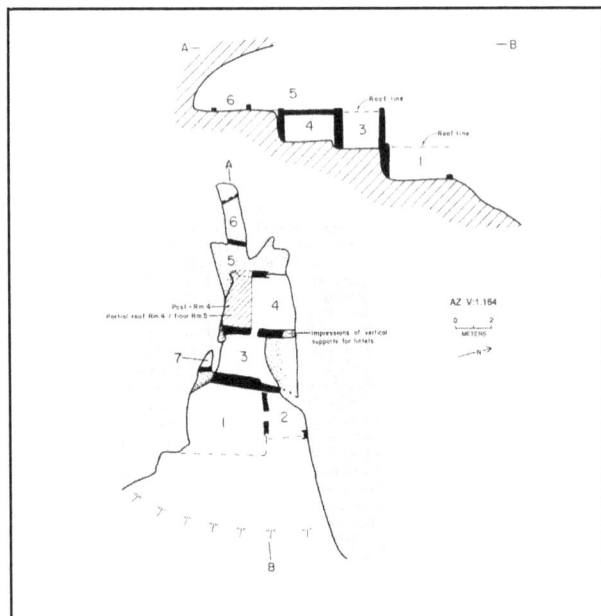

Figure III.18a. Small Cliff Dwellings, SAP Mapping: AZ V:1:164 (ASM)
(2004-1733-image4094)

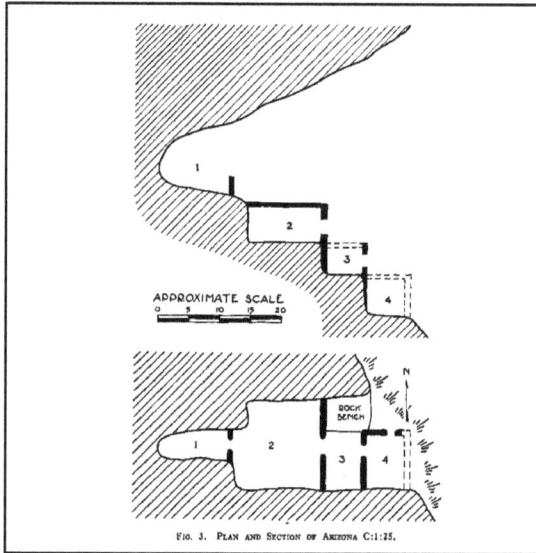

Figure III.18b. Small Cliff Dwellings, Gila Pueblo Mapping: GP C:1:25 (AZ V:1:164 [ASM]); from Haury 1934 (2004-1733-image4095)

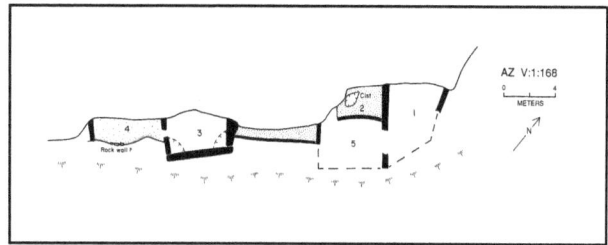

Figure III.19. Small Cliff Dwellings: AZ V:1:168 (ASM) (2004-1733-image4096)

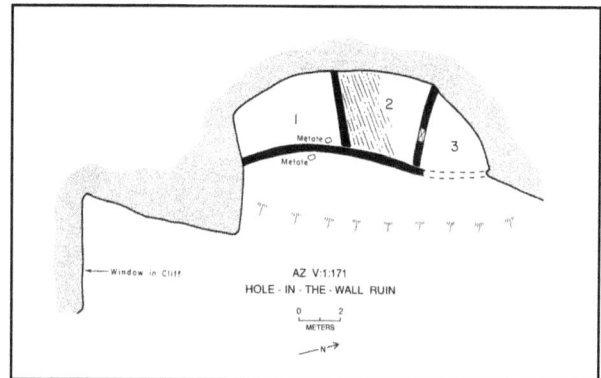

Figure III.20. Small Cliff Dwellings: AZ V:1:171 (ASM) (2004-1733-image4097)

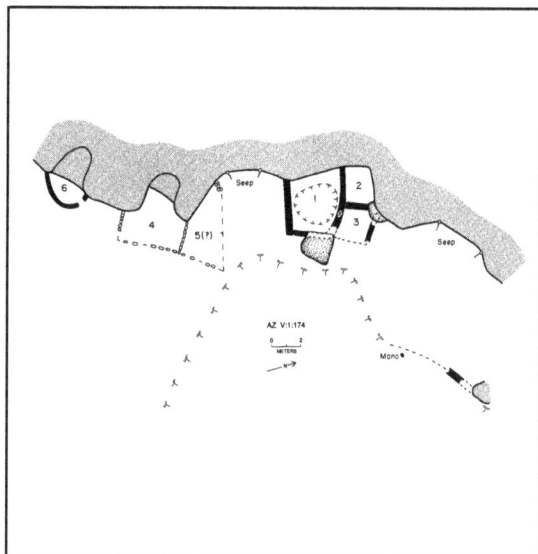

Figure III.21. Small Cliff Dwellings: AZ V:1:174 (ASM) (2004-1733-image4098)

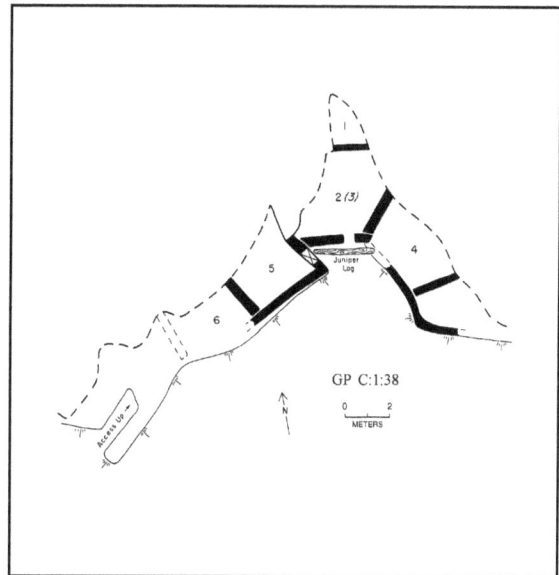

Figure III.22. Small Cliff Dwellings: GP C:1:38 (2004-1733-image4099)

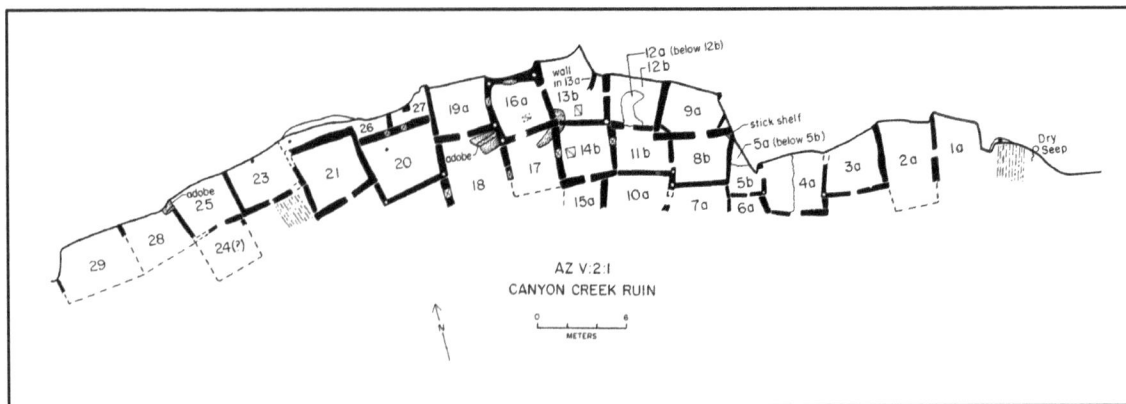

Figure III.23a. Canyon Creek Ruin, SAP Mapping (2004-1733-image4100)

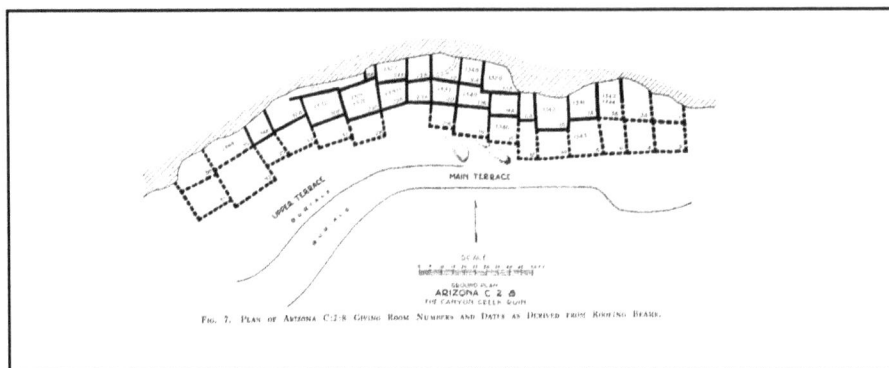

Figure III.23b. Canyon Creek Ruin (GP C:2:8), Gila Pueblo Mapping; from Haury (1934) (2004-1733-image4101)

Figure III.24a. Upper Tonto Ruin, AZ U:15:48 (ASM), SAP Mapping (2004-1733-image4102)

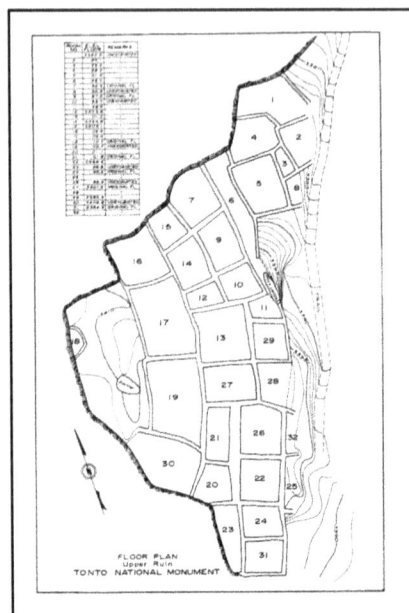

Figure III.24b. Upper Tonto Ruin, from Steen (1962) (2004-1733-image4103)

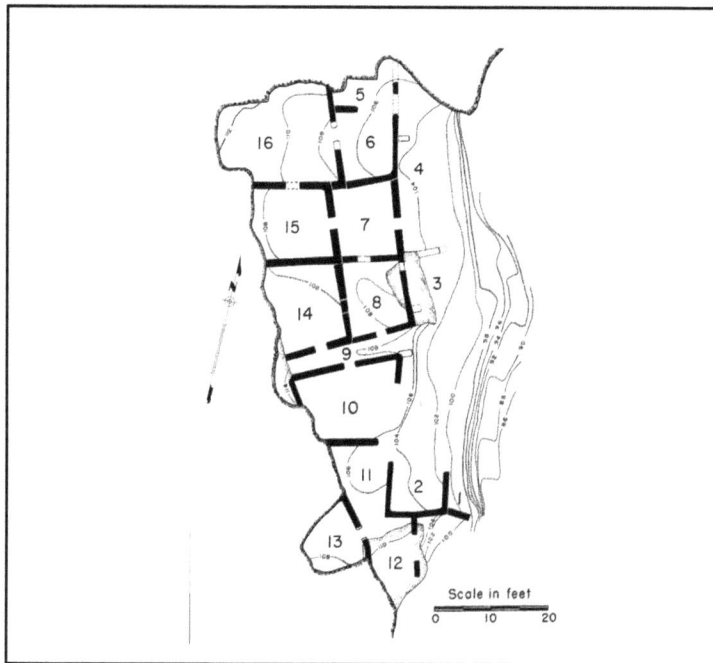

*Figure III.25. Lower Tonto Ruin,
U:15:47 (ASM), from Steen (1962)
(2004-1733-image4104)*

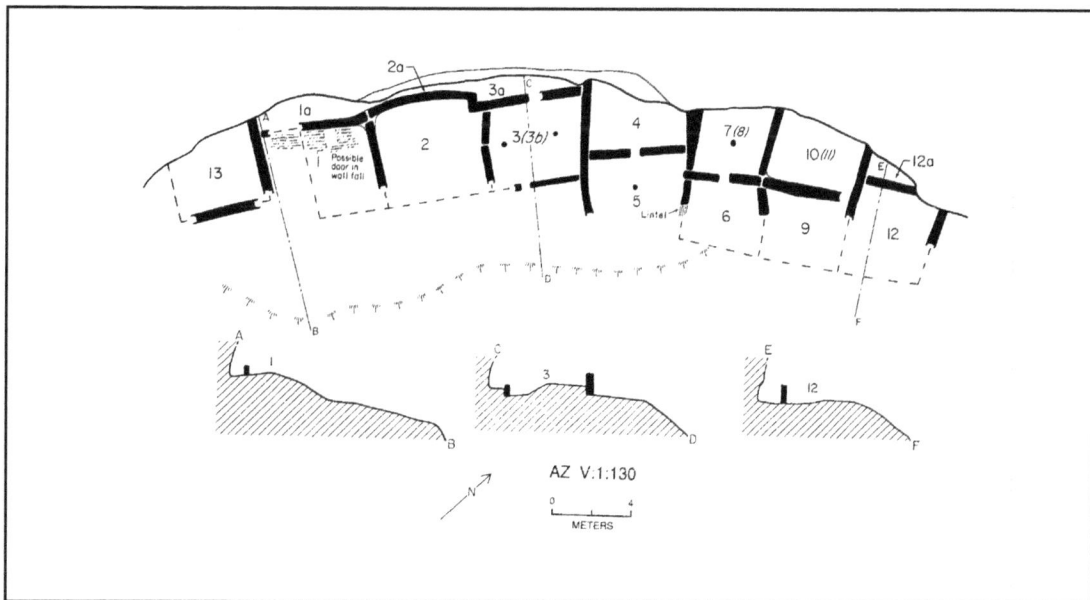

Figure III.26. Large Cliff Dwellings: AZ V:1:130 (ASM) (2004-1733-image4105)

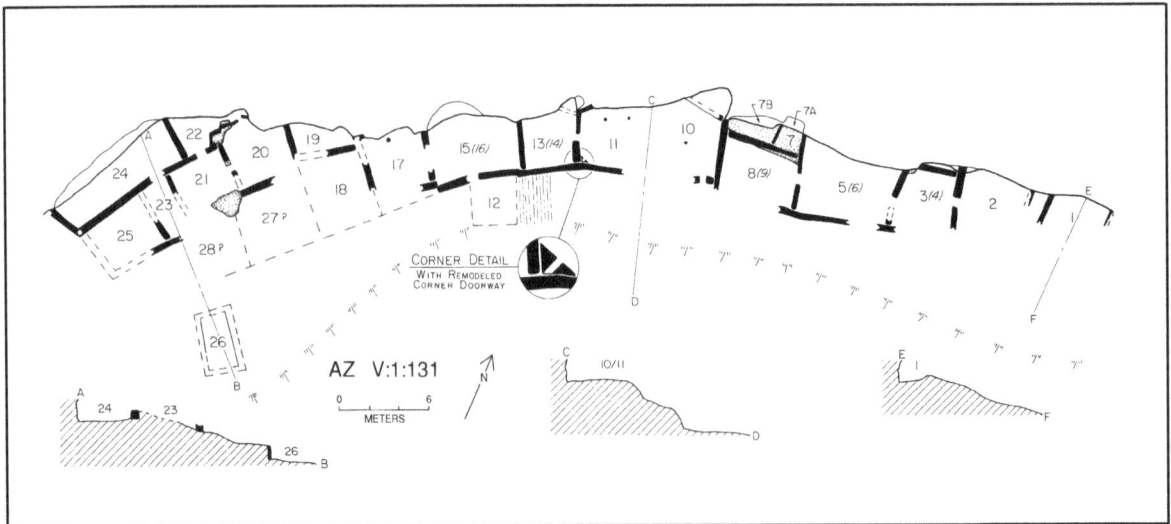

Figure III.27. Large Cliff Dwellings: AZ V:1:131 (ASM) (2004-1733-image4106)

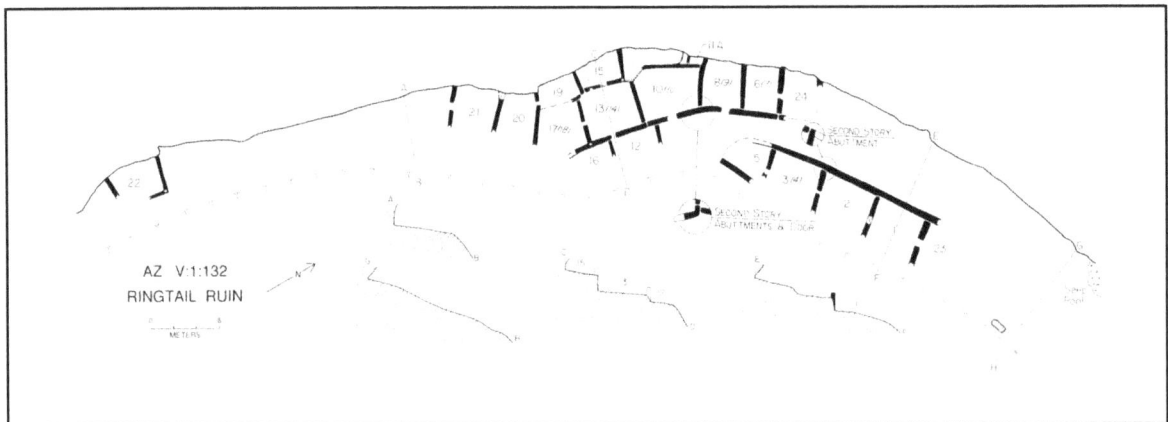

Figure III.28. Large Cliff Dwellings: AZ V:1:132 (ASM) (2004-1733-image4107)

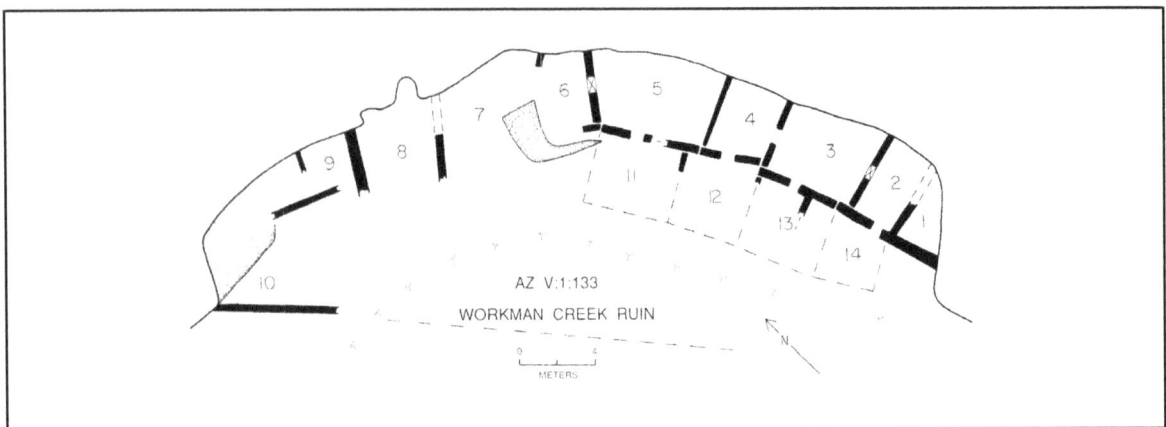

Figure III.29. Large Cliff Dwellings: AZ V:1:133 (ASM) (2004-1733-image4108)

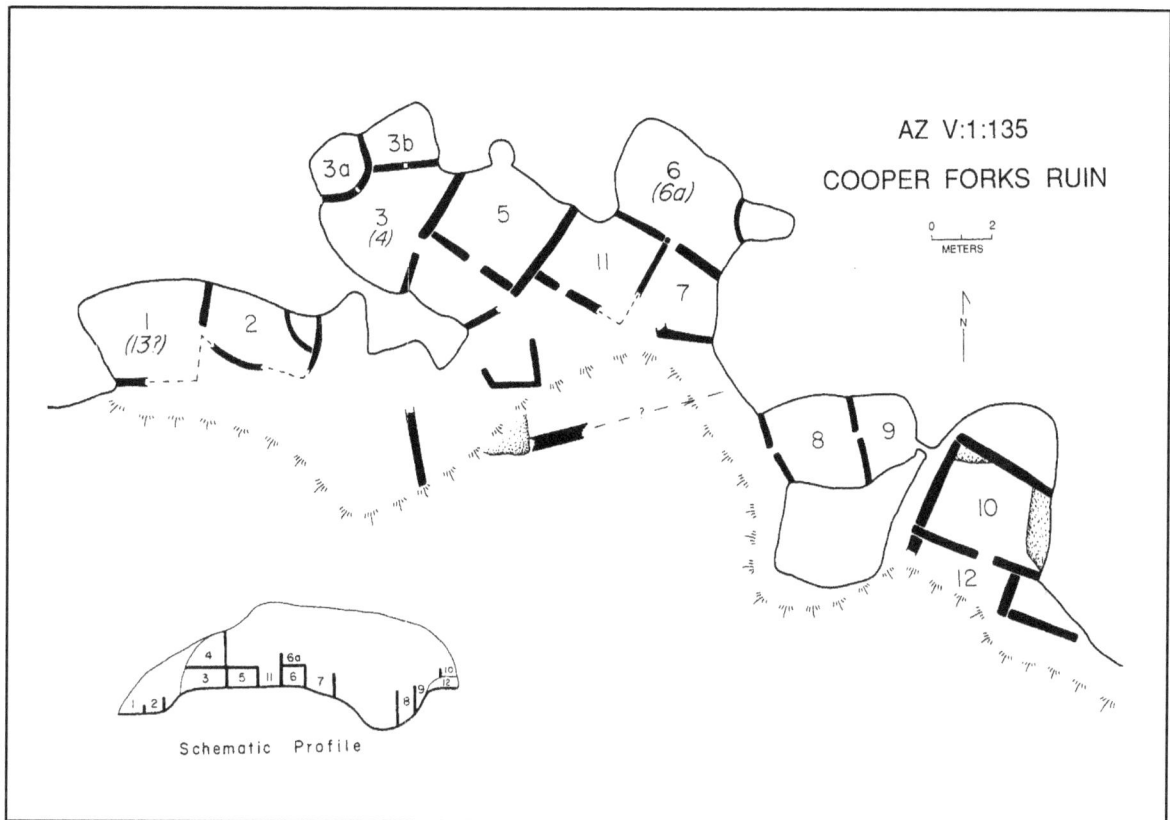

Figure III.30. Large Cliff Dwellings: AZ V:1:135 (ASM) (2004-1733-image4109)

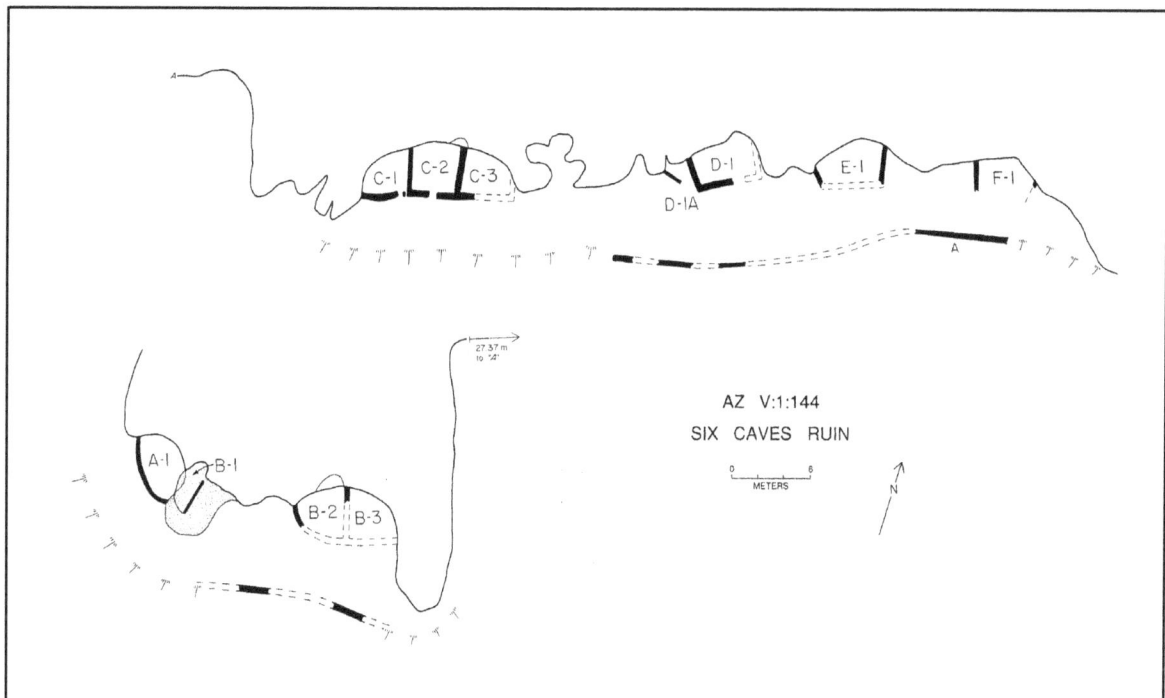

Figure III.31. Large Cliff Dwellings: AZ V:1:144 (ASM) (2004-1733-image4110)

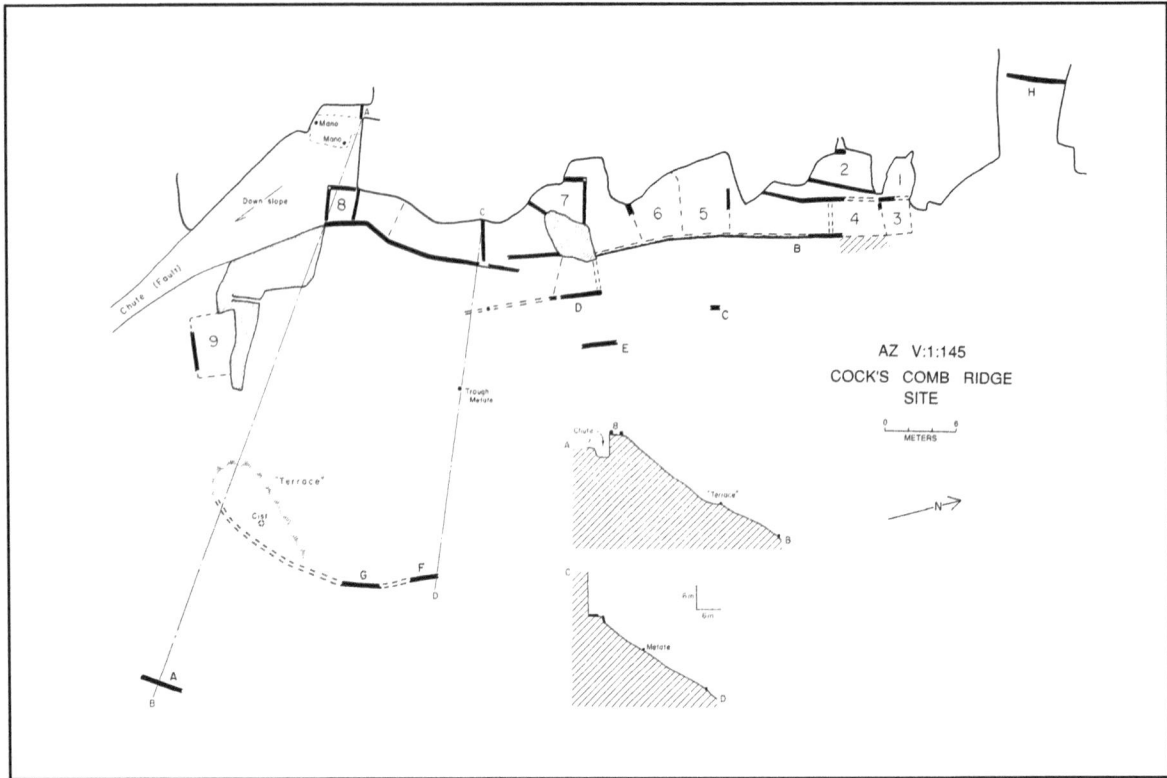

Figure III.32. Large Cliff Dwellings: AZ V:1:145 (ASM) (2004-1733-image4111)

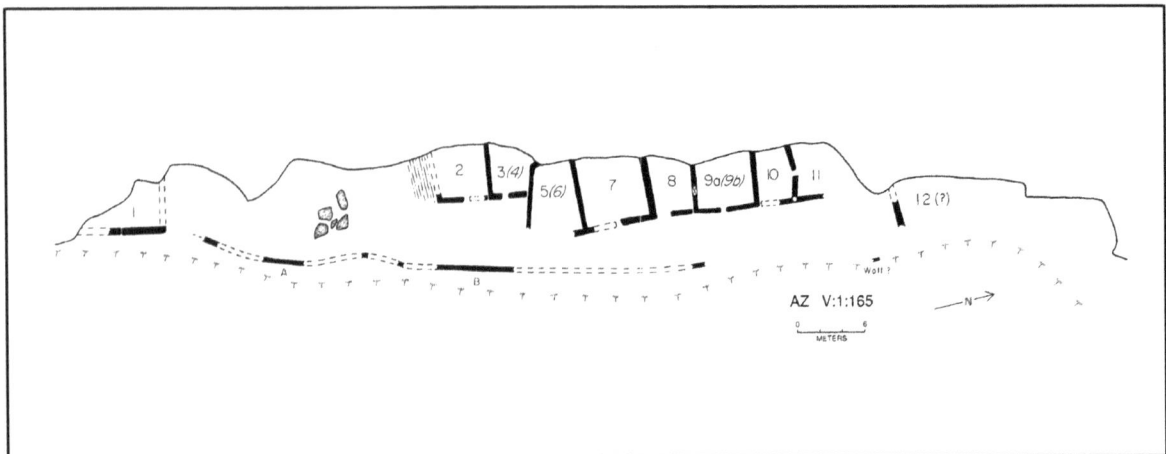

Figure III.33. Large Cliff Dwellings: AZ V:1:165 (ASM) (2004-1733-image4112)

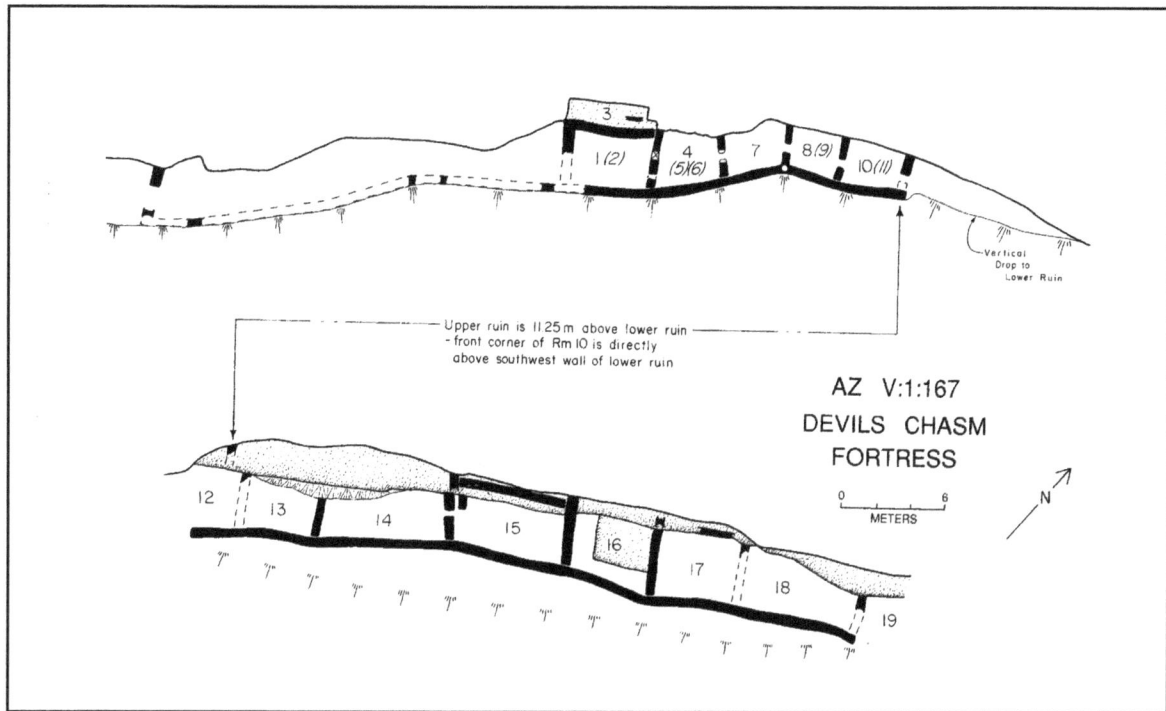

Figure III.34. Large Cliff Dwellings: AZ V:1:167 (ASM) (2004-1733-image4113)

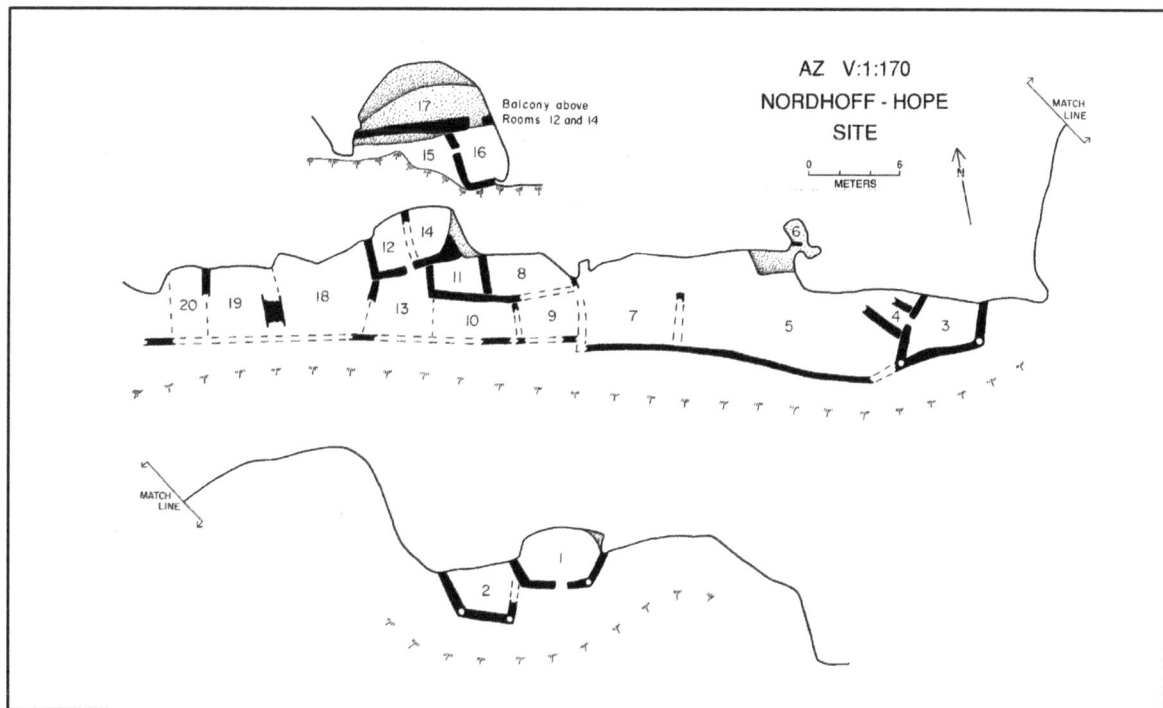

Figure III.35. Large Cliff Dwellings: AZ V:1:170 (ASM) (2004-1733-image4114)

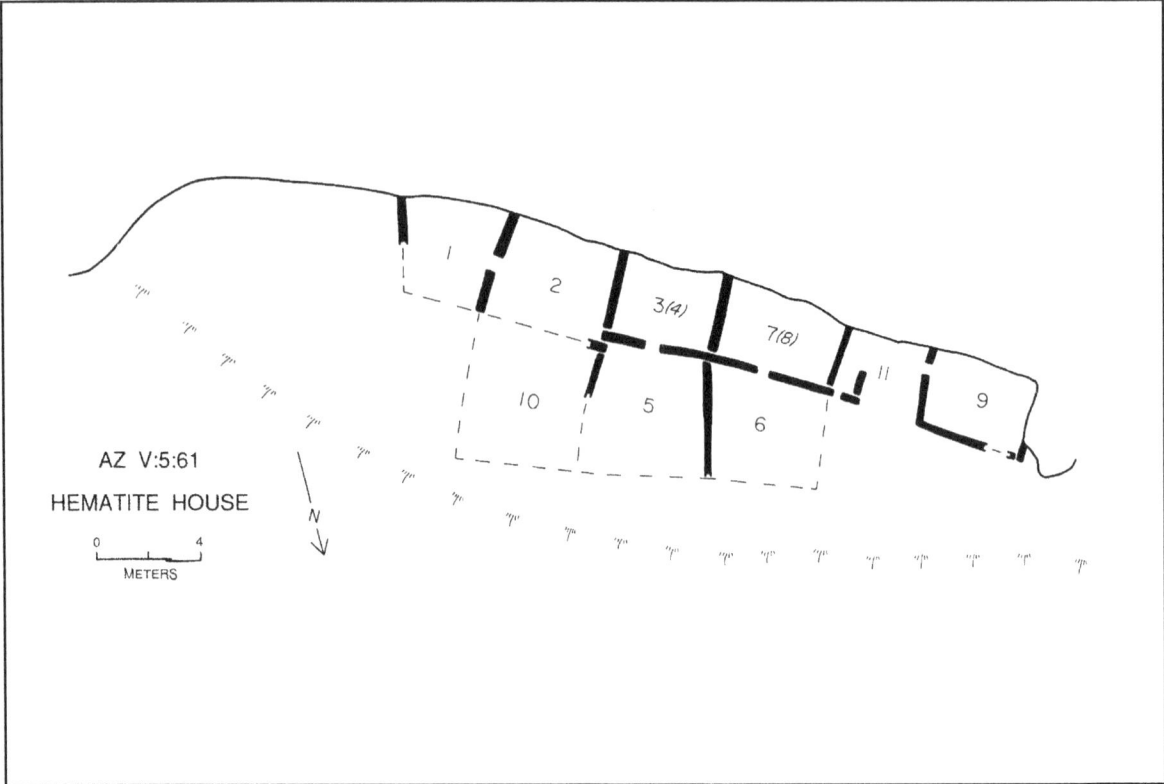

Figure III.36. Large Cliff Dwellings: AZ V:5:61 (ASM) (2004-1733-image4115)

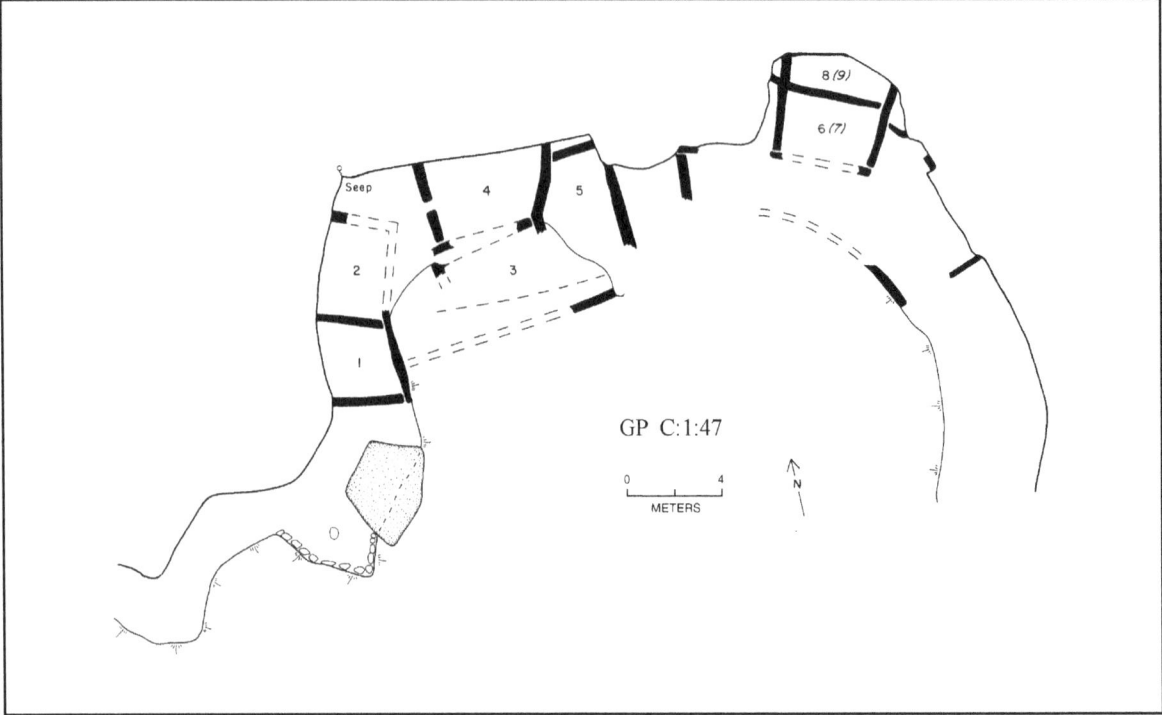

Figure III.37. Large Cliff Dwellings: GP C:1:47 (2004-1733-image4116)

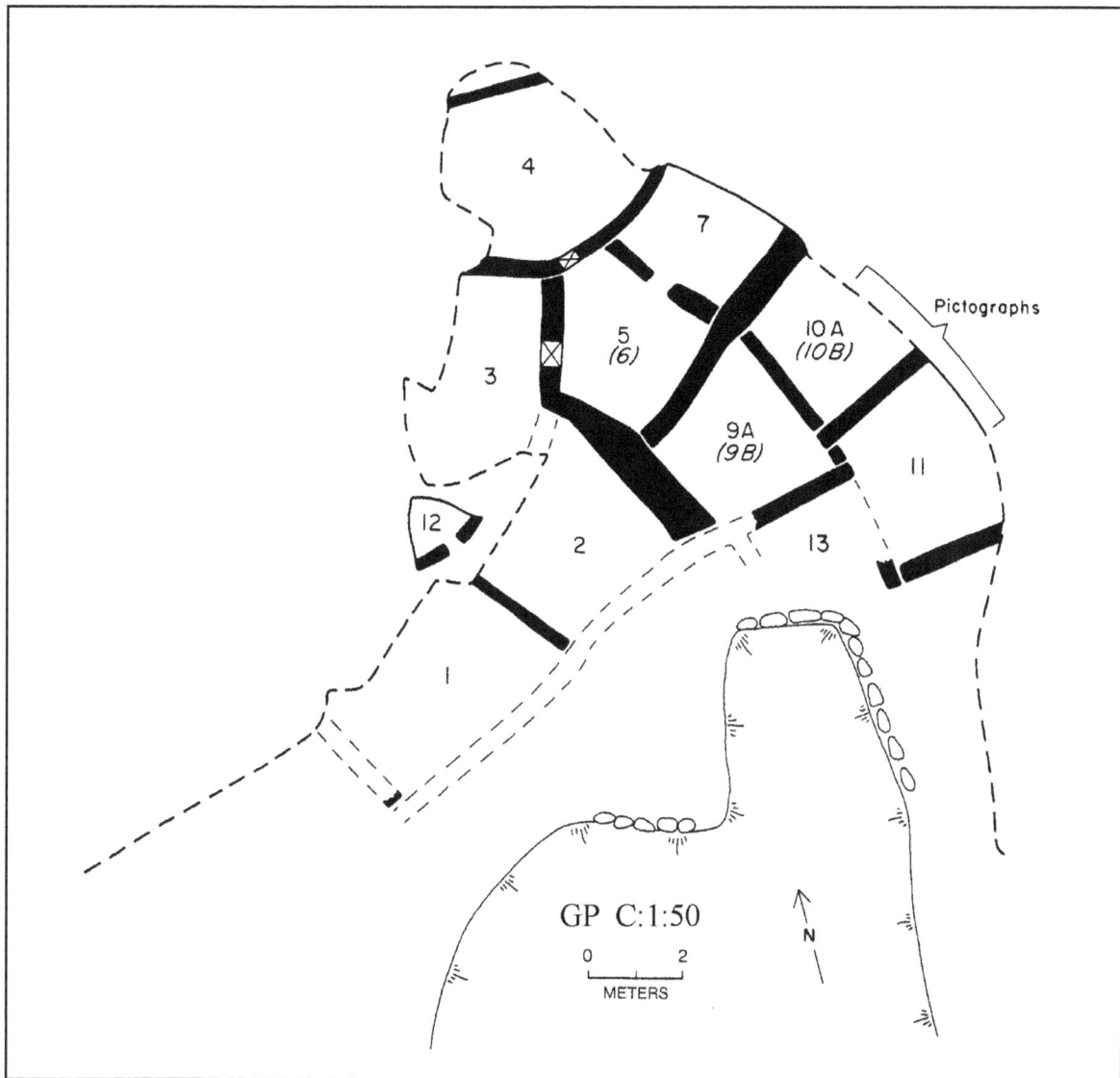

Figure III.38. Large Cliff Dwellings: GP C:1:50 (2004-1733-image4117)

Inventory and Assessment of Research Potential for Plant Remains from Cliff Dwellings in the Sierra Ancha, Arizona

Lisa W. Huckell and Richard C. Lange

INTRODUCTION

Archaeological research in the Cherry Creek drainage of the southeastern Sierra Ancha in central Arizona has produced an assemblage of botanical material that offers additional information on the interaction of people and plants in the area. Work was focused on three tributaries of middle Cherry Creek: Pueblo and Cold Spring canyons, and Devils Chasm. Twenty-eight cliff dwellings were recorded, with surface collections of plant materials made wherever the opportunity presented itself. Most of the sites are located in the same geological unit (see Chapter 3), are south-facing, and occur at an elevation of 5200 ft (1585 m) or more.

Methods

The primary objective of this investigation was to create a basic inventory of the plant materials recovered from the sites. Analysis forms were constructed to record basic aspects of the assemblage. Information categories include taxon, inventory number, ASM site number, intrasite room number where the items were collected, plant part, quantity (number obtained), and whether the item was carbonized, uncarbonized, parched, or scorched; whether the item was unmodified, modified by humans, or modified by non-human agents; and the artifact type. Space was left for com-

ments or additional information recorded on the artifact bag. The coding format and conventions followed for the macrobotanical analysis is Part A of Appendix XX (Lange 2005); the dataset is Part B (Lange 2005:Appendix XX).

For identification purposes, specimens were examined using a binocular stereozoom microscope with a magnification range of 10 to 70 power. Due to the preliminary nature of this study, no recording of measurements or other formal attributes was undertaken.

RESULTS

As is common for perishable material recovered from well-protected environments, virtually all of the material recovered from the sites was in an excellent state of preservation. With few exceptions, the items recovered were uncarbonized. The most significant source of post-depositional adverse impact came from rodents who tended to focus on particular taxa as sources of food and nest components.

Taxa Recovered

The following discussion lists and discusses macrobotanical remains and artifacts recovered by taxa. Notes regarding the potential use of certain plants (food or utilitarian) and their present locations are also included.

Acacia greggii (Catclaw acacia)

A single unmodified seed was obtained from Room 10 at the Cooper Forks Ruin (AZ V:1:135 [ASM]). Although the Southwestern ethnographic record indicates that the seeds of this genus have been used for food, there is a very high probability that this specimen is a post-occupational introduction.

Agave/Yucca

Remains of material attributable to these two genera were commonly recovered from several of the sites in the study area. The most abundant remain is leaf fibers, primarily in the form of quids or wads (macerated and cleaned fibers), and cordage. Other types of remains include knotted fiber bundles and split leaf fragments, stalk bases, and shaft fragments, seeds, self-threaded needles, and sandal fragments.

Large quantities of quids were recovered from several sites. Although he gives no totals, Haury (1934:60) also obtained a number of quids from his work at the Canyon Creek ruin. These compact, fibrous masses are commonly found in protected sites throughout the US Southwest (Reed 1978, Zauderer 1975) and may represent recreational chewing, chewing to extract flavor or nutrients, or in the case of yucca and agave, to macerate the parenchyma tissue from the fibers as a step in the preparation of cordage and other fiber-based items.

Two knotted segments of Agave/yucca were recovered. A swatch of cleaned fibers, connected by means of a square knot, was found at Hematite House (AZ V:5:61 [ASM]) (IN 387; Fig. 8.7f). An incompletely cleaned, knotted segment of an agave leaf was obtained from 6 Caves (AZ V:1:144 [ASM]; IN 204, Fig. 8.7h); the diagnostic marginal teeth are still present. Other knots occur in the assemblage, but are found associated with cordage. The knots were not systematically identified as to type, but square and overhand forms are present. Knotted fibers and leaf segments are commonly encountered in exceptional preservation contexts like caves and cliff dwellings; the full functional range of these artifacts is not yet fully understood. They are likely to represent parts of sandals, carrying baskets and frames, stored bundles of materials, parts of cradles, parts of traps and snares, and other similar items. Similar knotted materials from Canyon Creek Ruin are illustrated by Haury (1934:Plate LVII). Bohrer (1962:89) also shows similar materials from the cliff dwellings at Tonto National Monument.

One partial sandal and two probable fragments were collected. One small piece is from AZ V:1:131 (ASM) (IN 73, Fig. 8.8a). The other is from AZ V:1:164 (ASM)(IN 295, Fig. 8.8b). Both fragments are similar to parts of the more finely-woven sandals illustrated by Pierson (1962:55, Plate 13 D and E) from the Lower Tonto Ruin. The nearly complete specimen was found at the Ringtail Ruin (AZ V:1:132 [ASM]; IN 89, Fig. 8.9). The nearly complete sandal consists of a flat sole with truncated ends. It was constructed by twilled plaiting with an over-one/under-one pattern. The heel area was reinforced by turning the end back on itself and was fastened down to create a pad, similar to some sandals illustrated by Kent (1954:Figs. 22 and 24) from Montezuma Castle and by Pierson (1962:55, Plate 13 A, B, and C) from the Lower Tonto Ruin. A fragment of a tie strap is present near the opposite end.

No attempt was made to distinguish yucca from agave, although this should be done in the future as part of a more detailed study. Many fiber specimens are incompletely processed and still contain epidermal fragments and other potentially diagnostic features. Unprocessed leaf fragments, terminal spines, and knotted leaf segments all offer the possibility of a generic-level identification. A collection of modern comparative specimens of these taxa from the study area would also help in identification efforts.

One additional consideration identifying these fibers is the issue of use of *Apocynum* or Indian hemp. Haury (1934) had samples of fibers from his work at Canyon Creek Ruin identified by the botanist J.J. Thornber, who assigned a significant portion of the material to the genus *Apocynum* (Haury 1934:86, 101-102). The inner bark or bast of this plant yields very fine fibers that can be obtained through a labor-intensive process very similar to that used for flax, involving retting and pounding the stems, then drying the fibers. The modern *Apocynum* sample available to me (Lisa Huckell) indicates that the fine, golden fibers are terete and are lacking the longitudinal groove characteristically found in yucca and agave. They also have clearly visible transverse septae that are not found in agave or yucca. Huckell did not identify any fibers in the assemblage as *Apocynum*. There are some examples of very fine, soft fibers that have been twisted into cordage that appear mechanically damaged as though they had been pounded, a method associated with the retting process for bast fibers. (However, see Lynn Teague's comments on the textiles in this assemblage; she does identify the presence of *Apocynum* in this collection [Appendix V]). Several samples of this twine are red in color—they appear to have been dyed. All of the material has been collectively designated Yucca/agave for the present. Future investigators should consider the possibility of *Apocynum* being present in the assemblage.

Considerable variability can be seen in the fiber assemblage from the Sierra Ancha sites. Several methods of fiber processing have been proposed, based largely on ethnographic evidence, including roasting, pit roasting (steaming), boiling, retting, and pounding, to loose and free the parenchyma or ground tissue, followed by mastication and/or scraping to clean the fibers. Significant variation in the final appearance of processed fiber has been obtained in replicative fiber extraction experi-

ments carried out on yucca (Osborne 1965). Apart from a single leaf with a scorched end (IN 448, Fig. 8.7d), there is no evidence that direct heat was used to process the fibers. However, the large numbers of quids recovered suggest agave was probably pit-roasted and then chewed. Because of the high levels of toxic calcium oxalate crystals present in agave tissue, it must be cooked prior to consumption.

Cordage in the form of short, incomplete fragments was commonly found. It is usually 1- or 2-ply, and is invariably S-spun with a Z-twist. One specimen from AZ V:1:164 (ASM) (IN125, Fig. 8.10b) was made with the agave leaf terminal spine still attached, forming a ready-made, threaded needle. Similar items were found at the Lower Tonto Ruin (Pierson 1962:59) and at Canyon Creek Ruin (Haury 1934: Plate LV).

cf. *Amaranthus* (Pigweed)
A single unmodified amaranth seed (IN 370) was recovered from AZ V:1:168 (ASM). These tiny seeds are commonly recovered macro-remains from prehistoric sites throughout the US Southwest. The ethnographic record indicates continued exploitation of the seeds for food into historic times. It is impossible to determine whether this seed represents a post-occupational introduction, or the use by the site occupants of the seeds for food. The former possibility seems more likely in this instance.

cf. *Cereus gigantea* (Saguaro)
Two unmodified fragments of callus or scar tissue (IN 115) were recovered from AZ V:1:168 (ASM). They match the distinctive layered structure found in the callus formed around saguaro tissue wounds. Saguaros are not present in the immediate site vicinity, but are currently present 2 to 2.5 mi (3.2 to 4.0 km) to the southeast along Cherry Creek. It is possible that a saguaro "boot" was used as a convenient, impromptu disposable container

to convey something up into the site from the lowlands, after which it was discarded.

Celtis reticulata (Net-leaf hackberry)

Half of the boney endocarp of a hackberry fruit (IN 45) was found at the Cooper Forks Ruin (AZ V:1:135 [ASM]). The small, white, spherical structures are often found on archaeological sites located in or near riparian settings, the favored habitat of the tree. Net-leaf hackberry is present in the Cherry Creek and tributary drainages. The small, sweet-tasting fruits are edible raw and have been consumed by several historic Southwestern groups. Their presence in cultural deposits is problematic, as they are usually found uncarbonized. This, coupled with the durability of the thick-walled endocarp, makes it very difficult to accept a cultural explanation for these items unless they are found in very secure cultural contexts. Their popularity with rodents makes this a challenge. Net-leaf hackberry endocarps were also found at both ruins at Tonto National Monument (Bohrer 1962:98).

Compositae (Sunflower/Thistle family)

Two small terminal sprays of leaves and involucres (IN 95) were collected from the Uranium Mine site (AZ V:1:134 [ASM]). Adequate comparative material in the form of herbarium collections or on-site collections could aid in the identification of this material. There are other plant fragments in the Sierra Ancha assemblage that undoubtedly belong to this family. Isolated achenes of various taxa are present in other samples, particularly those that fall into the "miscellaneous" category, an eclectic mixture of plants assembled by rodents. These items were not included in the inventory and will have to be extracted by future investigators with more time available.

Cucurbita sp. (Squash)

Evidence for the use and localized cultivation of squash was found at several sites in the project area, in the form of rind fragments, peduncles or fruit stems, and seeds. With the exception of one rind specimen that bears a possible cut mark (IN395, AZ V:1:164 [ASM]), the remaining items are unmodified. Peduncle morphology is diagnostic to species; all seven specimens in the collection are *C. argyrosperma* (formerly *C. moschata*)(Figure IV.1). For comparison, squash peduncles and rinds from Tonto National Monumen are shown by Bohrer (1962:10). Two peduncles from different sites have been partially scorched (IN 114, AZ V:1:167 [ASM]; IN 390, AZ V:1:164 [ASM]). The 31 rind fragments are thin and display a different cell structure in cross-section from that of bottle gourd (Cutler and Whittaker 1961: Fig. 5). Unfortunately, cross-sectional morphology cannot be used to distinguish squash species; larger fragments than those recovered here display diagnostic surface characteristics that enable species distinctions to be made. The seeds are trickier to differentiate, as the distinctive margins that separate pumpkins (*C. pepo*) from *C. argyrosperma* tend to become very similar in appearance as they weather. However, the margin morphology of one seed (IN 369) from AZ V:1:168 (ASM) suggests that it may belong to *C. pepo*. Haury (1934:59) recovered remains of both *C. pepo* and *C. argyrosperma* during his work in at Canyon Creek Ruin. Both types were widely grown in the prehistoric US Southwest (Bohrer 1962:103; Cutler and Whittaker 1961: Table 2).

Cupressus arizonicus (Arizona Cypress)

Cones and seeds of Arizona cypress (IN 481) were found at AZ V:1:168 (ASM). The two leathery cones and three seeds are unmodified and are very likely of recent origin.

Gossypium hirsutum var. punctatum (Cotton)

Considerable evidence for the local production of cotton was found at several sites. Fibers, in the form of cloth remnants, cordage, and raw fibers, are the most common remains, but seeds and boll fragments are also present, and are good evidence for local production. Local production would have to involve planting on the lowest terraces along Cherry Creek, in the area from just above the modern-day Ellison Ranch downstream. Other areas along Cherry Creek lack the necessary land for planting or do not permit the application of water necessary for cotton production.

Although a fair amount of cotton fiber is present, much of the loose fiber material recovered is obviously from rodent nest contexts and appears to be composed of unraveled cordage or threads from unidentified textiles. Small bits of what appear to be unginned cotton (with seeds) are also present, although most of the seeds have been severely damaged.

Colored fibers are present, with red and gray the two colors represented. Although most US Southwestern aboriginal cotton is white, Bohrer (1962:112) found a wide range of colored cotton at Tonto National Monument; tests revealed that most of it was artificially created rather than natural. Red fibers were found at AZ V:1:164 (ASM) and at the Uranium Mine site (AZ V:1:134 ([ASM]). The rich, rusty red fibers have been dyed, and form a very small component of the cotton assemblage. They are found as small cordage segments (Fig. 8.16c).

Seeds are present, although most are incomplete and unsuitable for measurement. However, the small quantity of intact seeds represents an important source of additional data on seed morphology; measurements from this population could be compared to recently obtained figures for seeds from several prehistoric sites in Arizona (Huckell 1993).

Twenty-five fragments of the boll or capsule that contains the cotton were collected from the Uranium Mine site (AZ V:1:134 [ASM]), Cooper Forks (AZ V:1:135 [ASM]), the Devils Chasm Fortress (AZ V:1:167 [ASM]), and AZ V:1:168 (ASM). Some of the fragments have been crushed or damaged, but, like the seeds, several are intact enough to yield measurements of diagnostic features that could be compared with similar data from other US Southwestern sites (Huckell 1993).

Products manufactured from cotton are represented by cloth and cordage. Small pieces of plainweave cloth were found at several sites: the Ringtail Ruin (AZ V:1:132 [ASM]), the Uranium Mine site (AZ V:1:134 [ASM]), AZ V:1:164 (ASM), and the Devils Chasm Fortress (AZ V:1:167 [ASM]). Most have been badly damaged by rodents. No other types of weave were observed. (For further discussion of the textiles, see Appendix V by Lynn Teague).

Gramineae (Grasses)
Several grasses were obtained from several sites in the study area. Although time was not taken in the present study, there are identifiable vegetative and reproductive materials present that should provide more detailed identifications. Bunch grasses and reed culms constitute most of the material, and most likely represent commonly used roofing materials. For example, part of the closing material (tertiary component, see Chapter 6) in Cooper Forks (AZ V:1:135 [ASM]) Room 3 is densely packed reeds (see Fig. 6.35b).

Juglans major (Native Walnut)
Walnut shells were recovered from two sites: 10 from Cooper Forks (AZ V:1:135 [ASM]) and 5 from AZ V:1:164 (ASM). The extremely durable shells are often found in sites offering access to the riparian habitat favored by the trees. Considerable effort is required to extract the flavorful nutmeats due to the dense shell structure. The nuts are also eagerly sought by animals and birds; some of the shells from V:1:164 have been clearly gnawed by rodents. It is possible that some of them were introduced into the sites by animals. Broken

shells were recovered from several rooms in both the Upper and Lower Tonto Ruins of Tonto National Monument (Bohrer 1962:99).

Juniperus sp. (Juniper)

Half of a juniper seed was recovered from Cooper Forks (AZ V:1:135 [ASM]). Its relationship to the prehistoric occupation of the site must be considered problematic, as both humans and animals have used the fruits for food.

Lagenaria siceraria (Bottle Gourd)

Bottle gourd rind fragments were found at three sites: GP 1:16 (no more specific provenience), AZ V:1:164 (ASM), and Cooper Forks (AZ V:1:135 [ASM]). The pieces are, with one exception, unmodified. A piece from AZ V:1:164 has been scorched. This useful gourd was grown throughout the US Southwest (Cutler and Whittaker 1961: Table 2), where it was converted into water bottles, bowls, rattles, scrapers, scoops, and other utilitarian objects. Peduncles and seeds are rarely found, suggesting the gourds could have been a popular trade item or that they were processed and dried at some distance from habitation areas. In addition to quantities of gourd rinds, Bohrer (1962:109) identified two seeds from the Upper Tonto ruin, which she believed were evidence for the local production of the gourds.

Nolina microcarpa (Beargrass)

Several sites produced remains of beargrass, mainly in the form of leaf fragments. The items include four knotted split leaf bundles, two knotted fiber bundles, 15 longitudinally split leaf splint fragments, and one possible stalk fragment that has been used as the hearth for a fire drill. Of the knots, one has become dissociated, two are square knots, and the others require closer examination. With two exceptions, the leaves are unprocessed apart from being split; their appearance resembles split beargrass leaves favored by Apache basket-makers. Two of the knotted bundles consist of fibers from which much of the leaf ground tissue has been removed. The fire hearth (IN 366, Fig. 8.13a) comes from AZ V:1:168 (ASM), and is made from a vertically split small-diameter flower stalk fragment. It should be noted that the stalk may possibly be agave, as they are very similar in appearance. Anatomically, the two appear to be identical in cross-section; the smaller diameter suggests that it is beargrass, but small agave stalks are also possible.

Presently, beargrass grows along the trail into Pueblo Canyon at the level of the Mescal Limestone, and along the wilderness trails above Pueblo and Cold Spring canyons. Beargrass grows very densely on the slopes below another cliff dwelling (AZ V:1:165 [ASM]), roughly across from Pottery Point.

Opuntia spp. (Cactus)

Four sites contained remains of cactus species. The Uranium Mine site (AZ V:1:134 [ASM]) produced two pieces of the dense, fibrous vasculature that is present inside prickly pear pads. Room 5 at AZ V:1:168 (ASM) also contained two cholla joints. A cholla bud was found in Room 10 at Cooper Forks (AZ V:1:135 [ASM]). AZ V:1:164 (ASM) yielded eight spline clusters that were obtained from a rodent nest in Room 4. With additional time and some familiarity with site vicinity, it might be possible to assign the clusters to a specific taxon. None of the items offered any evidence for their use by humans, who have been known to exploit the fruits, leaves/joints, and buds of various species for food. Animals have also utilized these items for food, and in the case of rodents, for furnishing and defending nests.

Phaseolus vulgaris (Common Bean)

Evidence for the presence of domesticated common bean in the study area comes from the Devils Chasm Fortress (AZ V:1:167 [ASM]), which produced a single bean, and from the

Ringtail Ruin (AZ V:1:132 [ASM]), which yielded a pod fragment. The presence of the pod at the latter site strongly suggests that beans were grown locally, as the beans taken to other areas would logically be shelled prior to being transported. It may have been possible to grow these beans in the trashy midden areas downslope from the cliff dwellings.

Phragmites australis (Reeds)

This grass has already been discussed under Gramineae—those items identified as *Phragmites* in the comments column could be moved here. As indicated before, the long straight culms of this aquatic grass were obtained from several sites, and were used in the construction of roofs {for example, at Cooper Forks Ruin (AZ V:1:135 [ASM])}(Fig. 6.35b). Throughout the US Southwest, the sturdy culms were also a popular material from which to fashion arrowshafts (see Bohrer 1962:84-85; many of these arrows were painted, and were fairly common in the sites). Only one possible fragment of an arrowshaft was found in the SAP sites (IN 299, AZ V:1:164 [ASM]; Fig. 8.14b), and it does not appear to have been painted, at least in the portion recovered. Another common use for this plant is for cane cigarettes. No examples of this were noted at the SAP sites or recovered in the SAP sample.

cf. *Prosopis sp. (Mesquite)*

Seven leguminous leaflets that closely resemble mesquite were obtained from a mouse nest at GP C:1:16. They are still green, and are highly unlikely to be associated with the prehistoric occupation of the site.

Quercus (Oak)

Unmodified pericarp or shell fragments from acorns were obtained from three sites: two from Room 1 at AZ V:1:164 (ASM), one from Room 3 at AZ V:1:168 (ASM), and four from Room 10 at Cooper Forks (AZ V:1:135 [ASM]).

Acorns have been a widely exploited source of food in many parts of the world, but once again, their popularity among animals (particularly rodents), suggests that other explanations besides human use should be considered to account for their presence inside the rooms.

Rumex sp. (Canaigre, wild rhubarb)

The midden slope below the Ringtail Ruin (AZ V:1:132 [ASM]) was the source for 10 canaigre roots. The dessicated roots are unmodified, and their place of recovery strongly suggests a modern origin. Among the Navajo and Tohono-O'odham, the tannin-rich roots have been used to obtain a red dye; it would be interesting to determine whether prehistoric residents used the plant as the dye source for the red cotton and cordage fibers retrieved.

Simmondsia chinensis (Jojoba)

A single jojoba seed was recovered from the Devils Chasm Fortress (AZ V:1:167 [ASM]). It had been gnawed by rodents, and was very likely introduced into the site through rodent activity. The ethnographic record indicates that the nuts have been used for food, being consumed raw or parched and ground. Seeds and husks were recovered from the Lower Tonto Ruin (Bohrer 1962:98).

Wood

Over 100 pieces of wood were obtained from several sites, including bark, stem, and branch wood. Most of this material could be identified to the family or genus level with additional time and a good reference collection of locally available woods. Of the 108 pieces, 35 are carbonized, and 10 have been scorched or burned. Of the 19 modified pieces, one is a miniature bow (Fig. 8.13), three are pieces bent into a knot, and two are impressions in mud; the remainder exhibit cut marks, scraping, deliberate bending, and/or splitting along the long axis, but have no additional clues as to what their intended purpose was. The bow (IN 126) was recovered from AZ V:1:164 (ASM), and is probably a child's toy. It is approximately 30 cm in length; a similar bow (somewhat larger, about 45 cm in length) was found at Tonto National Monument (Bohrer 1962:Plate 3a). The knotted wood fragments come from at least two sites: AZ V:2:79 (ASM) and AZ V:1:164 (ASM). Their function is unknown.

Zea mays (Corn)

The survey produced an excellent collection of maize remains, with cobs predictably the most abundant form, followed by shanks, stalk fragments, tassels, leaf fragments, and dissociated clusters of cupules, the fused vertical ranks of pockets that subtend grain pairs and collectively form the cob. The 442 cobs offer an excellent opportunity to carry out a morphometric study of cob and cupule features for a population from a relatively restricted geographical area and a narrow occupational time period that may be as brief as 40 to 50 years.

Such a study would be an important contribution to the investigation of US Southwestern maize. Much of the information available in the literature consists of largely descriptive treatments that either lack or offer minimal supporting empirical data. The absence of replicable criteria for racial and varietal identifications has resulted in considerable confusion as contemporary archaeobotanists attempt to use and synthesize past studies (Adams 1994). The literature is dominated by the reports of Hugh Cutler, perhaps the most prolific student of prehistoric maize. Over his long career, Cutler came to rely on two features to characterize maize populations: kernel row number and cupule width. His reports contain numerous scattergrams used to portray similarities and differences among populations, trends through time, and define his parameters for various maize races (for examples, see Cutler 1966). Because these two characters are replicable,

they provide an empirical basis for treating cobs and make his extensive body of data the most enduring in terms of usefulness. While a minimal study using row number and cupule width could be informative and allow a general basis for intrasite comparison, the ideal study would focus on a suite of cob and cupule attributes (Bird and Bird 1980).

An increasingly popular view among some paleoethnobotanists is that efforts to assign modern racial names to archaeological cobs are risky and potentially misleading, particularly since many of the characters used to define a race are found in plant parts other than the cob (Sánchez G. and others 1993). Moreover, adequate criteria by which cobs of modern races can be reliably discriminated have yet to be published. The readiness with which maize hybridizes would also have to be acknowledged as an important complicating factor in race recognition. The significant effects of different environments and annual climate regimes on cob and cupule morphology that have been documented in recent experimental studies suggest that they are complex and variable (Adams and others 1999). As a result, the considerable gross morphological variation seen in the Sierra Ancha assemblage is impossible to address in a meaningful manner in terms of race. At this time, it is more prudent to evaluate populations based on metric data rather than poorly supported racial inference. It provides a more objective basis for meaningful comparison within and among populations at local and regional levels, leaving them unencumbered by the limitations and preconceptions imposed by the use of racial names and their associated behaviors that may or may not be appropriate. Genetic data would be the most useful for identifying actual differences within and among populations from different sites, but DNA extraction techniques are in the early stages of development and refinement, and costs are still prohibitive to do this for large numbers of cobs. The creation of a metric database for the Sierra Ancha cobs would be a significant contribution to the small but growing number of similar studies that provide the basis for objective evaluation and comparison of uncarbonized Southwestern maize assemblages.

Miscellaneous
This is a grab-bag category that primarily includes masses of undifferentiated material obtained from rodent nests. Additional time and diligent dissection could yield additional taxa to the inventory presented here, and could provide additional ecological information as well as potentially new information on plants more directly associated with the human occupation of the sites. This category also includes a sample of conifer resin and two samples of what is probably roof plaster.

Unknowns
This is a catch-all category for those items that will require more time and effort to iden-
tify. The items represent variable information potential. Perhaps the most interesting item is a quid (IN 428) from AZ V:1:168 (ASM) that is composed of leafy-looking material that is not agave or yucca.

SUMMARY

The macrobotanical remains collected opportunistically from the cliff dwellings in the southeastern Sierra Ancha represent a diverse assemblage of plants and plant parts used for food, fuel, tools, containers, and architectural elements. More systematic collection and excavation would undoubtedly discover an even richer collection of materials, similar to the types of artifacts recovered by Haury (1934) at Canyon Creek Ruin and described by Bohrer (1962) for the Tonto ruins. The Sierra Ancha collection also presents opportunities for additional studies, particularly of the agave/yucca and Zea (corn) components of this assemblage.

Appendix V

Textiles from AZ V:1:131 (ASM), AZ V:1:134 (ASM), and AZ V:1:136 (ASM)

Lynn S. Teague

Textiles recovered from the Sierra Ancha cliff dwellings AZ V:1:131 (ASM), AZ V:1:134 (ASM) and AZ V:1:136 (ASM) were found in very fragmentary condition. Centuries of rodent activity contributed to the further deterioration of fabrics that were doubtless well worn before they were originally discarded. Specimens include loose fibers, cordage, and seven loom-woven cloth fragments. Together they help to place the Sierra Ancha textile tradition within a regional context.

FIBER

Loose cotton fibers were obtained from AZ V:1:131 (ASM), IN 19, and also from AZ V:1:134 (ASM), IN 95 (Fig. 8.15). In the absence of complete bolls there is little that can be said about these, other than that the fiber length is consistent with Gossypium hirsutum, the species from which all aboriginally-grown cottons of the region are drawn. It is the same species that yields modern "upland" or short staple varieties of commercial cotton. Processed yucca leaf fibers were also found in AZ V:1:134 (ASM), IN 95. All of these fibers probably represent the residue of cordage and fabrics destroyed by rodent activity, rather than raw fiber accumulated for use.

CORDAGE

After the introduction of cotton, native plant fibers became much less popular for fabrics. However, the leaf (yucca, agave) and stem (Indian Hemp or Apocynum, milkweed) fibers retained their appeal for the production of strong cordage. AZ V:1:134 (ASM), IN 486, produced a fragment of cordage that is tentatively identified as Apocynum. It was 2.0mm in diameter and made up of two S-twist yarns plied in a Z- twist. The use of S-twist for the singles yarn is typical of leaf and stem fiber yarns in the region, possibly as a consequence of production using thigh-spinning rather than a handspindle (see Teague 1998a for further discussion of these techniques). Cotton yarn found in IN 95 at the same site shows the Z-twist typical of yarns made from this fiber and spun on a handspindle (Fig. 8.16).

Some of the cordage is colored with red iron oxide pigment. This characteristic is common in cordage from sites below the Mogollon Rim (see Huckell and Lange, Appendix IV, for possible vegetal dyes).

FABRIC

Surviving fragments of cloth were incomplete, and it is not possible to identify the function of the whole fabrics from which the pieces came (Fig. 8.17). Although numerous small fragments of fabric were recovered from the Sierra Ancha cliff dwellings, these were derived from a much smaller number of fabrics that had been disassembled by rodents. Multiple fragments having very similar attributes from single proveniences are treated as single specimens for purposes of this analysis. Only seven independent pieces of cloth appear to be represented.

The fiber used in these woven fabrics is invariably cotton, although yucca was used in loom woven textiles at many sites in the region, most conspicuously at Canyon Creek (Haury 1934). Possible weaving tools are illustrated in Figure 8.12, indicating that cotton was probably grown and processed in the Cherry Creek sites.

Yarns are single-ply and spun with a Z-twist, which is typical of yarns in loom-woven fabrics throughout the southwestern United States. The structure of the fabrics is invariably plainweave, a simple one-over-one-under interlaced fabric. Plain weave is the most common fabric in all post-Archaic assemblages in the region, although there are numerous other fabric structures that also were in use. See Figure 8.17 in this report and Haury (1934) and Steen and others (1962) for comparing fabrics.

In the two cases in which original fabric edges could be observed, no multiple ply cords were used to stabilize the selvage.

Yarn dimensions and densities are also within common ranges (Table V.1). Warp diameters range from 0.5 to 0.8 and weft diameters from 0.7 to 1.0, consistent with the tendency for warp threads to be more tightly spun and finer than weft threads. Warp densities in the Sierra Ancha fabrics range from 7 to 11/centimeter, and weft densities from 6 to 10/centimeter.

In Tables V.2 and V.3, the densities of warps and wefts in fabrics from a variety of archaeological traditions throughout the southwestern United States and northern Mexico are shown. Comparative data are taken from the information assembled for Textiles in Southwestern Prehistory supplemented by additional data from the upper and lower Tonto Ruins, the Point of Pines complex, and southern Arizona (Teague 1996, 1998a, 1998b, 2000, 2003). It can be seen in these tables that the mean densities of warps and wefts in the Sierra Ancha plainweave fabrics are slightly unusual. The mean frequency of warps/centimeter is especially distinctive, the lowest of the archaeological traditions represented. Mean wefts/centimeter are the lowest of any group of assemblages shown, other than those from distant Coahuila in northern Mexico.

However, Figure V.1 shows the distribution of warp and weft frequencies at the Sierra Ancha sites compared to those of textiles at sites identified as Mogollon. The Mogollon sites include unnamed sites in AZ Z:1,2; Doolittle Cave; Sunflower Cave; Painted Cave; Tularosa Cave; Mule Creek Cave; Bear Creek Cave; and Point of Pines. The Point of Pines specimens are from Maverick Mountain Phase contexts, which are consistent in their attributes with other Mogollon assemblages in spite of other evidence at the site pointing toward occupation by northern immigrants. The figure shows that although the Sierra Ancha warp and weft frequencies fall within the lower portions of the distribution of Mogollon specimens, only one Sierra Ancha specimen falls entirely outside the distribution of the Mogollon specimens.

Similarly, Sierra Ancha warp and weft frequencies generally fall within the range found at Canyon Creek Ruin (Fig. V.2). However, the two assemblages could not be mistaken for one another. At Canyon Creek more than 40 percent of fabrics were of yucca, while no yucca cloth was recovered from the Sierra Ancha sites.

Figure V.3 shows a comparison with fabrics from a broad range of Salado sites, including the upper and lower ruins at Tonto National Monument. Again, the Sierra Ancha fabrics fall

Table V.1. Sierra Ancha fabric specimen attributes

Site	IN	Warps/ cm	Warp diam. (mm.)	Wefts/ cm	Weft diam (mm.)	structure	fiber
V:1:136	--	11	0.5	10	0.7	plain	cotton
V:1:134	95	7	0.6	6	1.0	plain	cotton
V:1:134	95	8	0.5	7	1.0	plain	cotton
V:1:134	95	8	0.7	7	1.0	plain	cotton
V:1:134	95	11	1.0	7	0.8	plain	cotton
V:1:134	95	11	0.5	10	0.8	plain	cotton
V:1:134	95	8	0.5	7	0.7	plain	cotton

Table V.2. Comparisons of Number of Warps/Centimeter

Group	Count	Mean	StdDev
Anasazi	1265	10.3115	1.88478
Sierra Ancha	7	8.57143	1.71825
Chihuahua, Sonora, Sinaloa	108	14.1852	5.84254
Coahuila	86	10.3663	1.41264
Hohokam	67	12.6855	3.22505
Mogollon	24	10.1020	3.43766
Salado	351	9.46724	3.13317
Sinagua	50	11.5017	4.12216

Table V.3. Comparisons of Number of Wefts/Centimeter

Group	Count	Mean	StdDev
Anasazi	1264	9.31251	1.42049
Sierra Ancha	7	8.28571	1.97605
Chihuahua, Sonora, Sinaloa	108	8.57963	4.36648
Coahuila	86	3.72650	1.49834
Hohokam	66	9.95120	2.76830
Mogollon	24	9.24996	3.20887
Salado	350	8.79286	2.72514
Sinagua	48	9.44091	2.89797

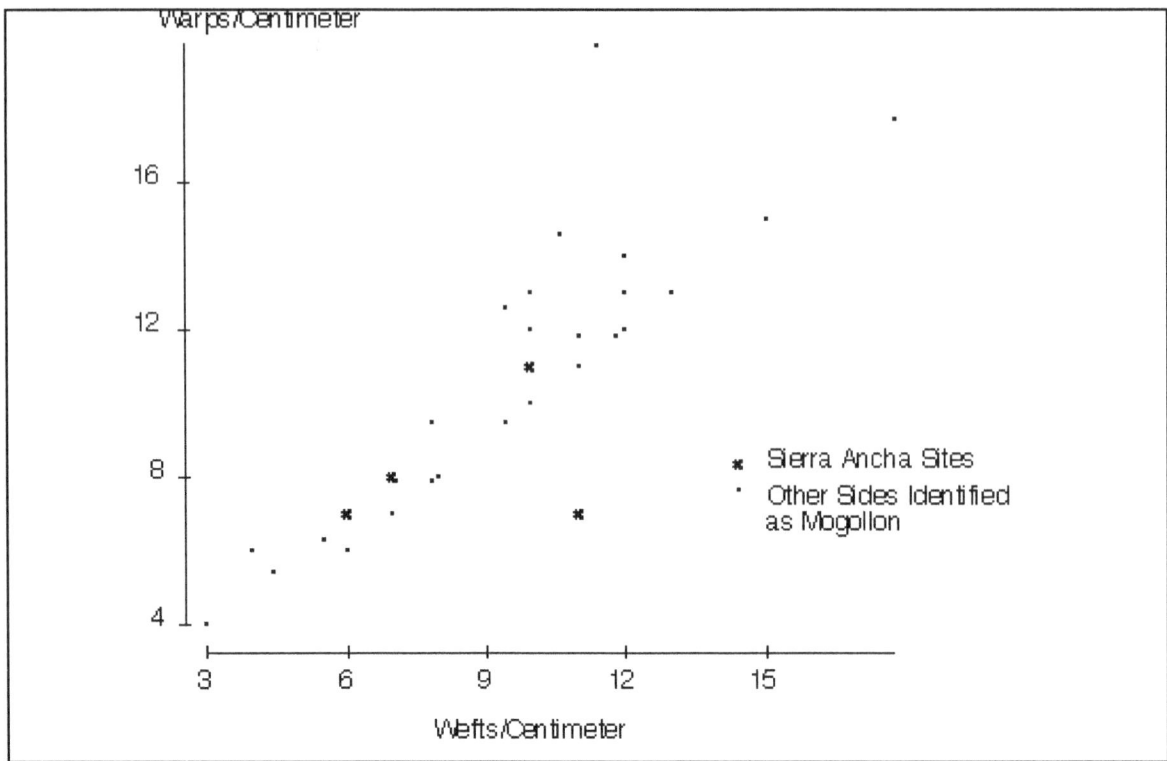

Figure V.1. Warp and Weft frequencies of fabrics from Sierra Ancha Sites and from previously recorded Mogollon sites

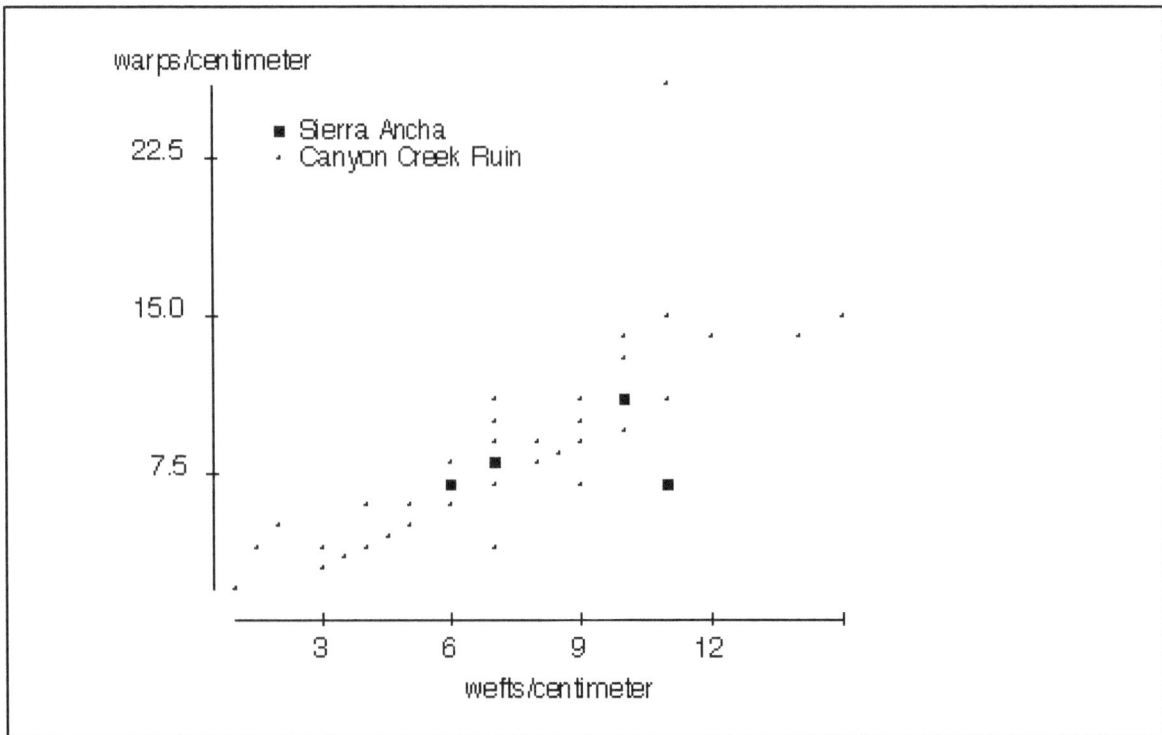

Figure V.2. Warp and weft frequencies at Canyon Creek Ruin and Sierra Ancha sites

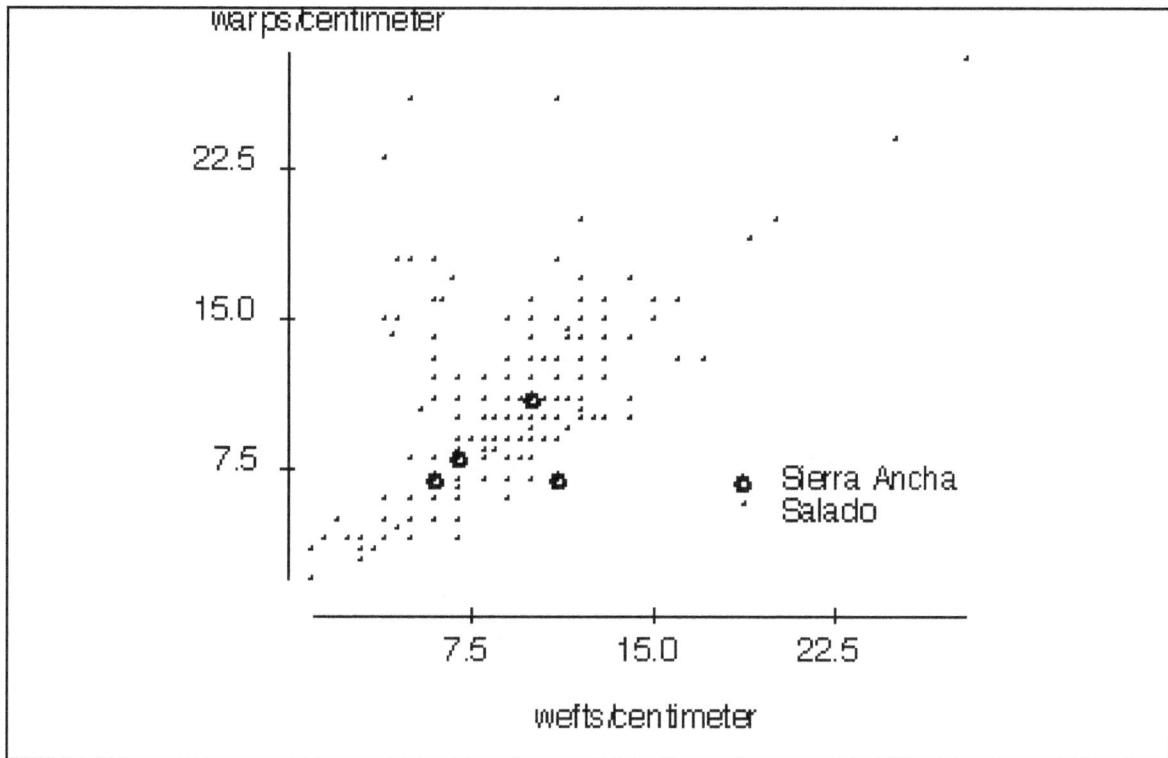

Figure V.3. Warp and weft frequencies at Salado sites and Sierra Ancha sites

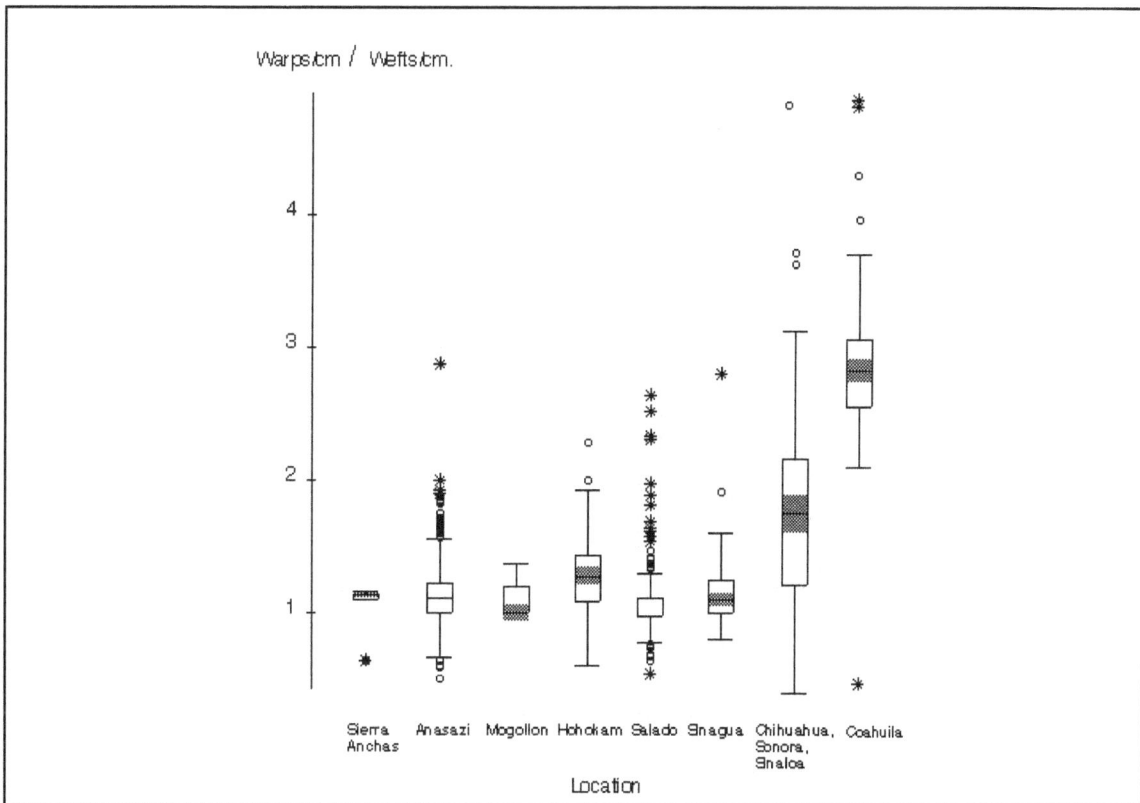

Figure V.4. Warp:weft ratios in plainweaves from major archaeological traditions

Table V.4. Comparing Warp Diameters

Group	Count	Mean	StdDev
Anasazi	23	0.660870	0.318718
Sierra Ancha	7	0.585714	0.121499
Chihuahua, Sonora, Sinaloa	59	0.722881	0.291891
Coahuila	1	0.300000	•
Hohokam	57	0.615789	0.276483
Mogollon	20	0.825000	0.593717
Salado	260	0.810192	0.435958
Sinagua	0	•	•

Table V.5. Comparing Weft Diameters

Group	Count	Mean	StdDev
Anasazi	23	1.20000	0.396576
Sierra Ancha	7	0.885714	0.146385
Chihuahua, Sonora, Sinaloa	59	0.784746	0.299317
Coahuila	1	0.300000	•
Hohokam	56	0.800000	0.269848
Mogollon	20	1.00000	0.881983
Salado	244	0.893648	0.347286
Sinagua	0	•	•

Table V.6. Comparing Ratios of Warps to Wefts in Plainweave Fabrics

Group	Count	Mean	StdDev
Anasazi	1264	1.12131	0.202932
Sierra Ancha	7	1.19524	0.167684
Chihuahua, Sonora, Sinaloa	108	1.81056	0.713360
Coahuila	86	2.92246	0.569975
Hohokam	66	1.31365	0.330214
Mogollon	24	1.10677	0.137138
Salado	350	1.09256	0.254034
Sinagua	48	1.19188	0.310704

within the range of other sites, but only within the lower portion of that range.

It is interesting that the low frequency of warps and wefts at the Sierra Ancha sites is not compensated by the use of yarns of greater diameter to produce a firmer fabric. If anything, the Sierra Ancha yarns are relatively fine (Tables V.4 and V.5).

It is not just the absolute frequency of fabric elements that matter in comparing textile traditions. The relative dominance of warp and weft is often characteristic of broadly defined prehistoric textile traditions in the region (Teague 1998a). The fabrics of Sonora, Sinaloa, Chihuahua, and especially Coahuila are warp-dominant. As one progresses north, traditions with more balanced ratios of warp to weft are found, and in the north on the Colorado Plateau weft-dominant fabrics are a component of assemblages.

Thus it is not unexpected that the ratios of warps to wefts in the plainweave fabrics of the Sierra Ancha are very slightly warp-dominant, and in this are broadly similar to those from the Mogollon and also the Sinagua textile traditions (Table V.6, Figure V.4). They differ from the fabrics of northern Mexico in not being strongly warp-dominant. They are also distinguished from Salado fabrics in this respect. Salado assemblages contain many balanced or nearly balanced specimens, but usually also contain some strongly warp-dominant pieces; these are lacking from the Sierra Ancha assemblage. Ancestral Pueblo assemblages, on the other hand, often contain some strongly weft-dominant pieces, which are also missing from the Sierra Ancha assemblage.

CONCLUSIONS

The textile assemblage from the Sierra Ancha sites is broadly similar to those from other archaeological traditions in the region below the Mogollon Rim and north of what is now Mexico. The people of the Sierra Ancha made cordage from the leaves and stems of native plants and yarn for weaving from cotton. It is likely that cordage was spun using a thigh-spinning technique, while cotton was spun using handspindles.

Fragments of seven plainweave loom-woven fabrics were found. When interpreting these fabrics it is important to remember that six of seven woven specimens were recovered from IN 95 at AZ V:1:134. Although small sample size is a statistical problem, it is even more significant archaeologically that six of the seven fabrics were from a single provenience. The idiosyncrasies of a single weaver could have affected the assemblage.

The seven woven fabrics from the Sierra Ancha sites generally resemble other textiles from the region below the Mogollon Rim and above what is now the Mexican border, and would not be conspicuously different in assemblages from Mogollon sites or from Anasazi, Hohokam, Salado, or Sinagua sites. However, there are differences. No fibers other than cotton were identified in woven fabrics, nor were structures other than plainweave found. The average absolute frequency of warps and wefts is relatively low, but most do not fall outside the ranges that are characteristic of Mogollon sites or later Salado sites in the same area. Yarns are relatively fine, in spite of low element frequencies. The mean ratio of warps to wefts is slightly warp-dominant, which is the prevailing pattern north of what is now Mexico and south of the Mogollon Rim, but the assemblage lacks the strongly warp dominant individual specimens found in some sites.

Only recovery of additional textiles from contemporaneous sites in the Sierra Ancha can shed light on the extent to which the relatively subtle distinctive attributes of these fabrics hold true on a larger scale.

References Cited

Adams, E. Charles
> 1979 Cold Air Drainage and Length of Growing Season in the Hopi Mesas Area. *Kiva* 44(4):285-296.

> 1983 The Architectural Analogue to Hopi Social Organization and Room Use, and Implications for Prehistoric Northern Southwestern Culture. *American Antiquity* 48(1):44-61.

> 2002 *Homol'ovi: An Ancient Hopi Settlement Cluster.* University of Arizona Press, Tucson.

Adams, E. Charles and Andrew I. Duff (editors)
> 2004 *The Protohistoric Pueblo IV World A.D. 1275-1600.* University of Arizona Press, Tucson.

Adams, E. Charles and Charla Hedberg
> 2002 Driftwood Use at Homol'ovi and Implications for Interpreting the Archaeological Record. *Kiva* 67(4):363-384.

Adams, Karen R.
> 1994 A Regional Synthesis of *Zea mays* in the Prehistoric American Southwest. In *Corn & Culture in the Prehistoric New World*, edited by Sissel Johannessen and Christine A. Hastorf, pp. 273-302. Westview Press, Boulder.

Adams, Karen R., Deborah A. Muenchrath and Dylan M. Schwindt
> 1999 Moisture Effects on the Morphology of Ears, Cobs and Kernels of a Southwestern U.S. Maize (*Zea mays* L.) Cultivar, and Implications for the Interpretation of Archaeological Maize. *Journal of Archaeological Science* 26(5):483-496.

Ahlstrom, Richard V.N., Mark L. Chenault, and Kirk C. Anderson
> 1991 *Final Report: The Roosevelt Bajada Survey, Tonto Basin, Gila County, Arizona.* Archaeological Report No. 91-24. SWCA Environmental Consultants, Tucson.

Anderson, Bruce A.
> 1990 *The Wupatki Archeological Survey: Final Report.* Southwest Cultural Resources Center, Professional Paper 35. National Park Service, Santa Fe.

Anderson, Keith M.
> 1988 Part II: Montezuma Castle. In *Archaeological Survey and Architectural Study of Montezuma Castle National Monument*, edited by Susan J. Wells and Keith M. Anderson, pp. 119-229. Publications in Anthropology No. 50. Western Archaeological and Conservation Center, National Park Service, US Department of the Interior, Tucson.

Bandelier, Adolph F.
> 1890 *Final Report of Investigations among the Indians of the Southwestern United States, Carried on Mainly in the Years from 1880 to 1885.* Parts I and II, pp. 1-319 and pp. 1-591. Papers of the Archaeological Institute of America, American Series III and IV. Cambridge.

1971 *The Delight Makers.* Reprinted. Harcourt Brace Jovanovich, Inc., New York. Original publication 1890. Dodd, Mead and Company, New York.

Bannister, Bryant, and William J. Robinson
1971 *Tree-Ring Dates from Arizona U-W, Gila-Salt Rivers Area.* Manuscript on file, Laboratory of Tree-Ring Research, University of Arizona, Tucson.

Barnes, Will C.
1988 *Arizona Place Names.* University of Arizona Press, Tucson.

Bernardini, Wesley
2005 *Hopi Oral Tradition and the Archaeology of Identity.* University of Arizona Press, Tucson.

Bird, Robert McK. and Junius B. Bird
1980 Gallinazo Maize from the Chicama Valley, Peru. *American Antiquity* 45(2):325-332.

Blackiston, A. Hooton
1905 Cliff Dwellings of Northern Mexico. *Records of the Past*, Vol. IV, Part XII: 355-361. Washington, D.C.

1909 Recently Discovered Cliff Dwellings of the Sierras Madres. *Records of the Past*, Vol. VII, Part I: 20-32. Washington, D.C.

Bohrer, Vorsila L.
1962 Nature and Interpretation of Ethnobotanical Materials from Tonto National Monument, 1957. In *Archaeological Studies at Tonto National Monument, Arizona*, by Charlie R. Steen, Lloyd M. Pierson, Vorsila L. Bohrer, and Kate Peck Kent, pp. 75-114. Technical Series No. 2. Southwestern Monuments Association, Globe.

Breheny, Jackie
1988 *LetterReport: Hematite House Pigment Experiment.* Manuscript on file, Sierra Ancha Project, Arizona State Museum, University of Arizona, Tucson.

Breternitz, Cory Dale
1987 *Granite Basin Ruin (AR-03-12-06-70): Repair and Restoration, Tonto National Forest.* Soil Systems Technical Reports No. 87-12. Soil Systems, Inc., Phoenix.

Breternitz, David A.
1966 *An Appraisal of Tree-ring Dated Pottery in the Southwest.* Anthropological Papers of the University of Arizona No. 10. University of Arizona, Tucson.

Bronitski, Gordon
1986 Compressive Testing of Ceramics: A Southwestern Example. *Kiva* 51(2):85-99.

Burton, Jeffery F.
1988 *Prehistoric Rock Art of the Southeast Arizona Uplands, A Formal Record of Fifty-three Rock Art Sites on the Coronado National Forest.* Coronado National Forest, Tucson.

1991 *The Archaeology of Sivu-ovi: The Archaic to Basketmaker Transition at Petrified Forest National Park.* Publications in Anthropology No. 55. U.S. Department of Interior, National Park Service, Western Archeological and Conservation Center, Tucson.

Carlson, Roy L.
1970 *White Mountain Red Ware: A Pottery Tradition of East-Central Arizona and Western New Mexico.* Anthropological Papers of the University of Arizona No. 19. University of Arizona Press, Tucson.

Carter, George F.
1945 *Plant Geography and Cultural History in the American Southwest.* Viking Fund Publications in Archaeology 5, New York.

Cartledge, Thomas R.
1976 Prehistory in Vosberg Valley, Central Arizona. *Kiva* 42(1):95-104.

1977 *Human Ecology and Changing Patterns of Co-Residence in the Vosberg Locality, Tonto National Forest, Central Arizona.* Cultural Resources Report No. 17. U.S. Forest Service, Southwestern Region, Albuquerque.

Chenhall, Robert G.
1971 Random Sampling in an Archaeological Survey. Unpublished Ph.D dissertation, Department of Anthropology, Arizona State University, Tempe.

Christenson, Andrew L.
1991 Microenvironment of Cliffdwellings in Tsegi Canyon, Arizona. *Kiva* 57(1):39-54.

Ciolek-Torrello, Richard S.
1978 A Statistical Analysis of Activity Organization, Grasshopper Pueblo, Arizona. Unpublished Ph.D dissertation, Department of Anthropology, University of Arizona, Tucson.

1979 Late Mogollon Settlement in Central Arizona. Paper presented at the 44th Annual Meeting of the Society for American Archaeology, Vancouver, British Columbia.

1994 Settlement Type and Function. In *The Roosevelt Rural Site Study, Vol. 2, Part 2: Prehistoric Rural Settlements in the Tonto Basin,* edited by Richard Ciolek-Torrello, Steven D. Shelley, and Su Benaron, pp. 623-668. Technical Series No. 28. Statistical Research, Inc., Tucson.

1998 Prehistoric Settlement and Demography in the Lower Verde Region. In *Vanishing River: Lives and Landscapes of the Lower Verde Valley: The Lower Verde Archaeological Project,* edited by Stephanie M. Whittlesey, Richard S. Ciolek-Torrello, and Jeffrey H. Altschul, pp. 531-595. SRI Press, Tucson.

Ciolek-Torrello, Richard S. (compiler)
1999 *Heritage Overview of the Piedmont of the Sierra Ancha, Sierra Ancha, and Cherry Creek Geographic Study Areas.* Technical Report No. 99-65. Statistical Research, Inc., Tucson.

Ciolek-Torrello, Richard S. (editor)
1987 *Archaeology of the Mazatzal Piedmont, Central Arizona,* 2 Vols. Research Paper No. 33. Museum of Northern Arizona, Flagstaff.

Ciolek-Torrello, Richard S. and Richard C. Lange
1979 The Q Ranch Study Area. In *An Archaeological Survey of the Cholla-Saguaro Transmission Line Corridor,* assembled by Lynn S. Teague and Linda L. Mayro, pp. 109-174. Arizona State Museum Archaeological Series 135(1). Arizona State Museum, University of Arizona, Tucson.

1982 Archaeology of the Sierra Ancha: A Synthesis of the Gila Pueblo Survey. In *Introduction and Special Studies, Cholla Project Archaeology,* edited by J. Jefferson Reid, pp. 95-126. Arizona State Museum Archaeological Series 161(1). Arizona State Museum, University of Arizona, Tucson.

1990 The Gila Pueblo Survey of the Southeastern Sierra Ancha. *Kiva* 55(2):127-154.

Ciolek-Torrello, Richard S., and Charles Riggs

1999 *Heritage Resource Survey of the Sierra Ancha and Cherry Creek Fire Analysis Areas. Pleasant Valley and Tonto Basin Ranger Districts, Tonto National Forest, Gila County, Arizona.* Technical Report No. 99-8. Statistical Research Inc., Tucson.

Ciolek-Torrello, Richard S., Steven D. Shelley, Jeffrey H. Altschul, and John R. Welch

1990 *The Roosevelt Rural Sites Study: Research Design.* Technical Series 28. Statistical Research Inc., Tucson.

Ciolek-Torrello, Richard S., Steven D. Shelley, and Su Benaron (editors)

1994 *The Roosevelt Rural Site Study, Vol. 2: Prehistoric Rural Settlements in the Tonto Basin.* Technical Series No. 28. Statistical Research Inc., Tucson.

Ciolek-Torrello, Richard S., Stephanie M. Whittlesey, and John R. Welch

1994 A Synthetic Model of Prehistoric Land Use. In *The Roosevelt Rural Sites Study, Vol. 3: Changing Land Use in the Tonto Basin*, edited by Richard S. Ciolek-Torrello and John R. Welch, pp. 437-472. Technical Series No. 28. Statistical Research, Inc., Tucson.

Clark, Jeffery J.

1995a Domestic Architecture in the Early Classic Period. In *The Roosevelt Community Development Study: New Perspectives on Tonto Basin Prehistory*, edited by Mark D. Elson, Miriam T. Stark, and David A. Gregory, pp. 251-305. Anthropological Papers No. 15. Center for Desert Archaeology, Tucson.

1995b The Role of Migration in Social Change. In *The Roosevelt Community Development Study: New Perspectives on Tonto Basin Prehistory*, edited by Mark D. Elson, Miriam T. Stark, and David A. Gregory, pp. 369-384. Anthropological Papers No. 15. Center for Desert Archaeology, Tucson.

2001 *Tracking Prehistoric Migrations: Pueblo Settlers Among the Tonto Basin Hohokam.* Anthropological Papers No. 65. University of Arizona Press, Tucson.

2004 Domestic Architecture, Site Structure, and Settlement Intensity. In *2000 Years of Settlement in the Tonto Basin: Overview and Synthesis of the Tonto Creek Archaeological Project*, edited by Jeffery S. Clark and James M. Vint, p. 139-193. Anthropological Papers No. 25. Center for Desert Archaeology, Tucson.

Clark, Jeffery J., and Bruce B. Huckell

1998 Introduction to the Slate Creek Section (Draft). In *Tonto Creek Archaeological Project, Archaeological Investigations Along Tonto Creek*, Vol. 2, edited by Jeffery J. Clark and James M. Vint, pp. 157-166. Anthropological Papers No. 22. Center for Desert Archaeology, Tucson.

Clark, Jeffery J. and James M. Vint (editors)

2000 *Tonto Creek Archaeological Project: Archaeological Investigations Along Tonto Creek, Vol. 1: Introduction and Site Descriptions for the Sycamore Creek and Slate Creek Sections.* Anthropological Papers No. 22. Center for Desert Archaeology, Tucson.

Cole, Sally J.

1990 *Legacy on Stone, Rock Art of the Colorado Plateau and Four Corners Region.* Johnson Publishing, Boulder.

1992 *Katsina Iconography in Homol'ovi Rock Art, Central Little Colorado River Valley, Arizona.* Arizona Archaeologist 25. Arizona Archaeological Society, Phoenix.

Colwell-Chanthaphonh, Chip
    2003 Signs in Place: Native American Perspectives of the Past in the San Pedro Valley of Southeastern Arizona. *Kiva* 69(1): 5-29.

Cosner, Aaron J.
    1951 Arrow-shaft Straightening with a Grooved Stone. *American Antiquity* 17(2):147-148.

Courtright, J. Scott, and Esther Morgan
    1997 *An Archaeological Survey of the Buzzard Roost Timber Analysis Area* (Draft). USDA Tonto National Forest, Pleasant Valley Ranger District. Project No. 96-120. On file at Payson Ranger District, Payson.

Craig, Douglas B., and Jeffery J. Clark
    1994 The Meddler Point Site AZ V:5:4/26 (ASM/TNF). In *The Roosevelt Community Development Study, Volume 2: Meddler Point, Pyramid \Point, and Griffin Wash Sites*, by Mark D. Elson, Deborah L. Swartz, Douglas B. Craig, and Jeffery J. Clark, pp. 1-198. Anthropological Papers No. 13. Center for Desert Archaeology, Tucson.

Craig, Douglas B., Mark D. Elson, and J. Scott Wood
    1992 The Growth and Development of a Platform Mound Community in the Eastern Tonto Basin. In *Proceedings of the Second Salado Conference*, edited by Richard C. Lange and Stephen Germick, pp. 22-30. Arizona Archaeological Society Occasional Paper, Phoenix.

Crown, Patricia L.
    1981 Variability in Ceramic Manufacture at the Chodistaas Site, East-Central Arizona. Unpublished Ph.D. dissertation, Department of Anthropology, University of Arizona, Tucson.

    1994 *Ceramics and Ideology: Salado Polychrome Pottery*. University of New Mexico Press, Albuquerque.

Cummings, Byron
    1930 Notes Relating to Early Fieldwork (1906-1933). Arizona State Museum Archives AA-10. University of Arizona, Tucson.

    1931-1936 *Byron Cummings Files: Correspondence Concerning Ruins and Antiquities in Arizona (Prior to 1938)*. Arizona State Museum Archives A-401. University of Arizona, Tucson.

    1940 *Kinishba: A Prehistoric Pueblo of the Great Pueblo Period*. Hohokam Museum Association and the University of Arizona, Tucson.

Curtis, Ross S.
    1990 *Cultural Resources Survey of a 42.7 Mile Long Segment of State Route 288 (The Young to Globe Highway) between the Junction of State Routes 88 and 288, and Young, Gila County, Arizona*. Archaeological Research Services, Tempe.

Cutler, Hugh C.
    1966 *Corn, Cucurbits, and Cotton from Glen Canyon*. Anthropological Papers 80. University of Utah Press, Salt Lake City.

Cutler, Hugh C. and Thomas W. Whittaker
    1961 History and Distribution of the Cultivated Cucurbits in the Americas. *American Antiquity* 26(4):469-485.

Dart, Allen

> 1988 Notes on 88-4. Manuscript on file, Sierra Ancha Project, Arizona State Museum, University of Arizona, Tucson.

> 1997 Fabulous Finds Made at Q Ranch Pueblo. *Old Pueblo Archaeology* 10(1):5-7.

Dean, Jeffrey S.

> 1969 *Chronological Analysis of Tsegi Phase Sites in Northeastern Arizona.* Papers of the Laboratory of Tree-Ring Research No. 3. University of Arizona Press, Tucson.

Deaver, William L., and Richard S. Ciolek-Torrello

> 1995 Early Formative Period Chronology for the Tucson Basin. *Kiva* 60(4):481-529.

Dittert, A.E., Jr.

> n.d. Archaeological Investigations in the Vosberg Locality, Central Arizona. Manuscript on file, Department of Anthropology, Arizona State University, Tempe.

Dockal, James A. and Michael S. Smith

> 2005 Evidence for a Prehistoric Petroglyph Map in Central Arizona. *Kiva* 70(1):413-421.

Doelle, William H.

> 1995 Tonto Basin Demography in a Regional Perspective. In *The Roosevelt Community Development Study: New Perspectives on Tonto Basin Prehistory*, edited by Mark D. Elson, Miriam T. Stark, and David A. Gregory, pp. 201-226. Anthropological Papers No. 15. Center for Desert Archaeology, Tucson.

Doelle, William H., Henry D. Wallace, Mark d. Elson, and Douglas B. Craig

> 1992 *Research Design for the Roosevelt Community Development Study.* Anthropological Papers No. 12. Center for Desert Archaeology, Tucson.

Dorn, Ronald I.

> 1983 Cation-Ratio Dating: A New Rock Varnish Age Determination Technique. *Quaternary Research* 20(1):49-73.

> 2005 Why Testify for the Defense? *La Pintura*, Volume 31, Number 2, February. American Rock Art Research Association, Lemon Grove, California.

Doyel, David E.

> 1976 Revised Phase System for the Globe-Miami and Tonto Basin Areas, Central Arizona. *Kiva* 41(3-4):241-266.

> 1978 *The Miami Wash Project: Hohokam and Salado in the Globe-Miami Area, Central Arizona.* Contribution to Highway Salvage Archaeology in Arizona No. 52. Arizona State Museum, University of Arizona, Tucson.

> 1984 Stylistic and Petrographic Variability in Pueblo II Period Cibola Whiteware from Upper Little Colorado. In *Regional Analysis of Prehistoric Ceramic Variation: Contemporary Studies of the Cibola Whitewares*, edited by Alan P. Sullivan III and Jeffrey L. Hantman, pp. 4-16. Arizona State University Anthropological Papers 31. Arizona State University, Tempe.

> 1985 Summary and Discussion. In *Hohokam Settlement and Economic Systems in the Central New River Drainage, Arizona*, Vol. 1, edited by David E. Doyel and Mark D. Elson, pp. 727-734. Publications in Archaeology No. 4. Soil Systems Inc., Phoenix.

Duff, Andrew I.
   2002 *Western Pueblo Identities*. University of Arizona Press, Tucson.

Effland, Richard W., Jr., and Barbara S. Macnider
   1991 *An Overview of the Cultural Heritage of the Tonto National Forest*. Cultural Resources Report No.
   49. Archaeological Consulting Services, Tempe.

Ellison, Glenn R. "Slim"
   1968 *Cowboys Under the Mogollon Rim*. University of Arizona Press, Tucson.

Elson, Mark D.
   1990 The Use of Argillite as a Ceramic Pigment: A Preliminary Evaluation. *Pottery Southwest* 17(2):1-7.

   1992a Settlement, Subsistence and Cultural Affiliation within the Upper Tonto Basin. In *The Rye Creek Project:
   Archaeology in the Upper Tonto Basin, Vol. 3: Synthesis and Conclusions*, edited by Mark D. Elson and
   Douglas B. Craig, pp. 119-154. Anthropological Papers No. 11. Center for Desert Archaeology, Tucson.

   1992b Temporal Issues in Tonto Basin Prehistory: The Rye Creek Chronology. In *The Rye Creek Project:
   Archaeology in the Upper Tonto Basin, Vol. 3: Synthesis and Conclusions*, edited by Mark D. Elson and
   Douglas B. Craig, pp. 55-78. Anthropological Papers No. 11. Center for Desert Archaeology, Tucson.

   1994 The Pyramid Point Site AZ V:5:1/25 (ASM/TNF). In *The Roosevelt Community Development
   Study, Vol. 2: Meddler Point, Pyramid Point, and Griffin Wash Sites*, by Mark D. Elson, Deborah L.
   Swartz, Douglas B. Craig, and Jeffery J. Clark, pp. 199-295. Anthropological Papers No. 13. Center
   for Desert Archaeology, Tucson.

   1996 A Revised Chronology and Phase Sequence for the Lower Tonto Basin of Central Arizona. *Kiva*
   62(2):117-147.

Elson, Mark D. and Douglas B. Craig (editors)
   1992 *The Rye Creek Project: Archaeology in the Upper Tonto Basin*. Anthropological Papers No. 11.
   Center for Desert Archaeology, Tucson.

Elson, Mark D., and David A. Gregory
   1995 Tonto Basin Chronology and Phase Sequence. In *Roosevelt Community Development Study: New
   Perspectives on Tonto Basin Prehistory*, edited by Mark D. Elson, Miriam T. Stark, and David A.
   Gregory, pp. 61-77. Anthropological Papers 15. Center for Desert Archaeology, Tucson.

Elson, Mark D., David A. Gregory, and Miriam T. Stark
   1995 New Perspectives on Tonto Basin Prehistory. In *The Roosevelt Community Development Study:
   New Perspectives on Tonto Basin Prehistory*, edited by Mark D. Elson, Miriam T. Stark, and David A.
   Gregory, pp. 441-479. Anthropological Papers No. 15. Center for Desert Archaeology, Tucson.

Elson, Mark D. and Michael Lindeman
   1994 The Eagle Ridge Site, AZ V:5:104/1045 (ASM/TNF). In *The Roosevelt Community Development
   Study, Vol. 1, Introduction and Small Sites*, by Mark D. Elson and Deborah L. Swartz, pp. 23-116.
   Anthropological Papers No. 13. Center for Desert Archaeology, Tucson.

Elson, Mark D., Miriam T. Stark, and David A. Gregory (editors)
   1995 *The Roosevelt Community Development Study: New Perspectives on Tonto Basin Prehistory*.
   Anthropological Papers No. 15. Center for Desert Archaeology, Tucson.

English, Nathan B., Julio L. Betancourt, Jeffrey S. Dean, and Jay Quade
   2001 Strontium Isotopes Reveal Distant Sources of Architectural Timber in Chaco Canyon, New Mexico. *Proceedings
   of the National Academy of Sciences of the United States of America* 98(21):11891-11896. Washington, D.C.

Ferg, Alan J.
> 1979 The Petroglyphs of Tumamoc Hill. *Kiva* 45(1-2):95-118.

Ferguson, T.J. and Micah Lomaomvaya
> 1999 *Hoopoq'yaqam niqw Wukoskyavi (Those Who Went to the Northeast and Tonto Basin): Hopi-Salado Cultural Affiliation Study.* Hopi Cultural Preservation Office, The Hopi Tribe, Kykotsmovi.

Fewkes, Jesse Walter
> 1912 Casa Grande, Arizona. *28th Annual Report of the Bureau of American Ethnology, 1906-1907*: 33-179. Bureau of American Ethnology, Washington D.C.

Fish, Paul R. and Suzanne K. Fish
> 1977 *Verde Valley Archaeology: Review and Perspective.* Research Paper No. 8. Museum of Northern Arizona, Flagstaff.

Fisher, Richard D.
> 2003 *Copper Canyon: The Puzzle of Oasis America.* Sunracer Publications, Tucson.

Flannery, Kent V.
> 1972 The Origins of the Village as a Settlement Type in Mesoamerica and the Near East: A Comparative Study. In *Man, Settlement, and Urbanism*, edited by Peter J. Ucko, Ruth Tringham, and Geoffrey W. Dimbleby, pp. 23-53. Schenkman, Cambridge.

Gerald, Rex E.
> 1976 A Conceptual Framework for Evaluating Salado and Salado-Related Material in the El Paso Area. *Kiva* 42(1):65-70.

Germick, Stephen and Joseph S. Crary
> 1989 *Prehistoric Adaptations in the Bajada-Upland Areas of the Tonto Basin: Examples from the A-Cross Road and Henderson Mesa Surveys, Tonto National Forest.* Cultural Resources Inventory Report No. 89-240. Tonto National Forest, Phoenix.

> 1990 *Prehistoric Settlement and Adaptations in the East Piedmont of the Mazatzal Mountains.* Cultural Resources Inventory Report No. 90-200. Tonto National Forest, Phoenix.

> 1998 Settlement Dynamics at the Armer Complex. Paper presented for the Symposium "A Tonto Basin Perspective on Prehistoric Communities in the American Southwest" held at the 63rd Annual Meeting, Society for American Archaeology, Seattle.

Gifford, James C.
> 1980 *Archaeological Explorations in Caves of the Point of Pines Region, Arizona.* Anthropological Papers of the University of Arizona, No. 36. University of Arizona Press, Tucson.

Gilman, Patricia A.
> 1987 Architecture as Artifact: Pit Structures and Pueblos in the American Southwest. *American Antiquity* 52(3):538-564.

Gladwin, Harold S.
> 1957 *A History of the Southwest.* Bond-Wheelwright, Portland, Maine.

Gladwin, Winifred and Harold S. Gladwin
> 1928 *The Use of Potsherds in an Archaeological Survey of the Southwest.* Medallion Papers No. 2. Gila

Pueblo, Globe.

1930 *Some Southwestern Pottery Types: Series I.* Medallion Papers No. 8. Gila Pueblo, Globe.

1934 *A Method for the Designation of Cultures and Their Variations.* Medallion Papers No. 15. Gila Pueblo, Globe.

1935 *The Eastern Range of the Red-on-Buff Culture.* Medallion Papers No. 16. Gila Pueblo, Globe.

Gladwin, Harold S., Emil W. Haury, E.B. Sayles, and Nora Gladwin
1937 *Excavations at Snaketown: Material Culture.* Medallion Papers No. 25. Gila Pueblo, Globe.

Graves, Michael W.
1982 Anomalous Tree-Ring Dates and the Sequence of Room Construction at Canyon Creek Ruin, East-Central Arizona. *Kiva* 47(3):107-131.

Gregory, David A.
1982 Coon Creek, AZ V:5:14. In *Cholla Project Archaeology, Vol. 4: The Tonto-Roosevelt Region,* edited by J. Jefferson Reid, pp. 29-69. Arizona State Museum Archaeological Series 161. Arizona State Museum, University of Arizona, Tucson.

1995 Prehistoric Settlement Patterns in the Eastern Tonto Basin. In *The Roosevelt Community Development Study, Vol. 2: Ceramic Chronology, Technology, and Economics,* edited by James M. Heidke and Miriam T. Stark, pp. 127-184. Anthropological Papers No. 15. Center for Desert Archaeology, Tucson.

Guevara Sánchez, Arturo
1986 *Arqueología del Area de las Cuarenta Casas, Chihuahua.* Colección Científica, Serie Arqueología, Instituto Nacional de Antropología e Historia, México D.F., México.

Haas, Jonathan
1971 *The Ushklish Ruin: A Preliminary Report on Excavations in a Colonial Hohokam Site in the Tonto Basin, Central Arizona.* Arizona Highway Salvage Preliminary Report. Arizona State Museum, University of Arizona, Tucson.

Hack, John T.
1942 *The Changing Physical Environment of the Hopi Indians of Arizona.* Reports of the Awatovi Expedition 1. Peabody Museum, Harvard University, Cambridge.

Halbirt, Carl D. and Steven G. Dosh
1986 *The Late Mogollon Pit House Occupation of the White River Region, Gila and Navajo Counties, Arizona.* Draft Report prepared for Archaeological Investigations, White Mountain Apache Tribe Tribal Development Office, Canyon Day Wastewater Treatment Facility, Fort Apache Indian Reservation, Gila and Navajo Counties, Arizona. Museum of Northern Arizona, Flagstaff.

Harrill, Bruce G.
1967 Prehistoric Burials Near Young, Arizona. *Kiva* 33(2):54-59.

Harris, Myra
1974 An Investigation into Trade Contact at Vosberg, Arizona. Unpublished Master's thesis, Department of Anthropology, Arizona State University, Tempe.

Haury, Emil W.
1932 *Roosevelt 9:6: A Hohokam Site of the Colonial Period.* Medallion Papers No. 11. Gila Pueblo, Globe.

1934 *The Canyon Creek Ruin and Cliff Dwellings of the Sierra Ancha.* Medallion Paper No. 14. Gila

Pueblo, Globe.

1945 *The Excavations of Los Muertos and Neighboring Ruins in the Salt River Valley, Southern Arizona.* Papers of the Peabody Museum of American Archaeology and Ethnology Vol. 24, No. 1. Peabody Museum, Harvard University, Cambridge.

1958 Evidence at Point of Pines for a Prehistoric Migration from Northern Arizona. In *Migrations in New World Culture History*, edited by Raymond H. Thompson, pp. 1-8. University of Arizona Bulletin No. 29(2). Social Sciences Bulletin No. 27. University of Arizona, Tucson.

1976 *The Hohokam: Desert Farmers and Craftsmen.* University of Arizona Press, Tucson.

1986 HH-39: Recollections of a Dramatic Moment in Southwestern Archaeology. In *Emil W. Haury's Prehistory of the American Southwest*, edited by J. Jefferson Reid and David E. Doyel, pp. 55-60. University of Arizona Press, Tucson.

1988 Gila Pueblo Archaeological Foundation: A History and Some Personal Notes. *Kiva* 54(1):1-77.

1989 *Point of Pines, Arizona: A History of the University of Arizona Archaeological Field School.* Anthropological Papers of the University of Arizona No. 50. University of Arizona Press, Tucson.

2004 Cuicuilco Diary: June 11 – September 12, 1925. *Journal of the Southwest* 46(1):55-91.

Heidke, James M.
1995 Overview of the Ceramic Collection. In *The Roosevelt Community Development Study, Vol. 2: Ceramic Chronology, Technology, and Economics*, edited by James M. Heidke and Miriam T. Stark, pp. 7-18. Anthropological Papers No. 14. Center for Desert Archaeology, Tucson.

Herr, Sarah A. (editor)
2004 *Their Own Road: Archaeological Investigations along State Route 260, Payson to Heber – Preacher Canyon Section* (Draft). Technical Report No. 2002-03. Desert Archaeology, Inc., Tucson.

2006 *Their Own Road: Archaeological Investigations along State Route 260, Payson to Heber – Christopher Creek Section* (Draft). Technical Report No. 2003-05. Desert Archaeology, Inc., Tucson.

Hill, W. W.
1982 *An Ethnography of Santa Clara Pueblo, New Mexico.* Edited and annotated by Charles H. Lange. University of New Mexico Press, Albuquerque.

Hohmann, John W.
1990 *Ruin Stabilization and Park Development for Besh-ba-gowah Pueblo.* Studies in Western Archaeology No. 1. Cultural Resource Group, Louis Berger and Associates, Inc., Phoenix.

Hohmann, John W., and Linda B. Kelley
1988 *Erich F. Schmidt's Investigations of Salado Sites in Central Arizona: The Mrs. W.B. Thompson Archaeological Expedition of the American Museum of Natural History.* Museum of Northern Arizona Bulletin No. 56. Museum of Northern Arizona, Flagstaff.

Holbrook Sally J. and Michael W. Graves
1982 Modern Environment of the Grasshopper Region. In *Multidisciplinary Research at Grasshopper Pueblo, Arizona,* edited by William A. Longacre, Sally J. Holbrook, and Michael W. Graves, pp. 5-11. Anthropological Papers of the University of Arizona No. 40. University of Arizona Press, Tucson.

Howard, Jerry B.
  1987 The Lehi Canal System: Organization of a Classic Period Irrigation Community. In *The Hohokam Village: Site Structure and Organization*, edited by David E. Doyel, pp. 211-221. Southwestern and Rocky Mountain Division, American Association for the Advancement of Science, Glenwood Springs.

Huckell, Bruce B.
  1973 The Hardt Creek Site. *Kiva* 39(2):177-197.

  1977 *Arizona U:3:28: The Slate Creek Ruin.* Manuscript on file, Arizona State Museum, University of Arizona, Tucson.

  1978 *The Oxbow Hill-Payson Project: Archaeological Excavations South of Payson, Arizona.* Contribution to Highway Salvage Archaeology in Arizona No. 48. Arizona State Museum, University of Arizona, Tucson.

  1982 *The Distribution of Fluted Points in Arizona: A Review and Update.* Arizona State Museum Archaeological Series 145. Arizona State Museum, University of Arizona, Tucson.

  1998a An Analysis of the Flaked Stone Artifacts. In *Early Farmers of the Sonoran Desert: Archaeological Investigations at the Houghton Road Site, Tucson, Arizona*, edited by Richard Ciolek-Torrello, pp. 80-118. Statistical Research, Inc., Technical Series 72. Tucson.

  1998b The Ground Stone Collection. In *Early Farmers of the Sonoran Desert: Archaeological Investigations at the Houghton Road Site, Tucson, Arizona*, edited by Richard Ciolek-Torrello, pp. 119-126. Statistical Research, Inc., Technical Series 72. Tucson.

Huckell, Bruce B. and James M. Vint
  2000 The Boatyard Site (U:3:286/1352). In *Tonto Creek Archaeological Project, Archaeological Investigations Along Tonto Creek Vol. 1: Introduction and Site Description for the Sycamore Creek and Slate Creek Sections*, edited by Jeffery Clark and James Vint, pp. 161-200. Anthropological Papers No. 22. Center For Desert Archaeology, Tucson.

Huckell, Lisa W.
  1993 Plant Remains from the Pinaleño Cotton Cache, Arizona. *Kiva* 59(2):147-203.

International Movie Database
  2006 Victor L. Ackland. http://imdb.com/name/nm0010065/. Electronic Document. Accessed August 2006.

Jacobs, David F.
  1994 *Archaeology of the Salado in the Livingston Area of Tonto Basin, Roosevelt Platform Mound Study.* Roosevelt Monograph Series No. 3, Anthropological Field Studies No. 32. Office of Cultural Resource Management, Department of Anthropology, Arizona State University, Tempe.

Jernigan, E. Wesley
  1992 *Hour-Glass Rock Art Figures of Southeastern Arizona.* Eastern Arizona College Museum of Anthropology Publication No. 4. Thatcher.

Kaldahl, Eric J., Scott Van Keuren, and Barbara J. Mills
  2004 Migration, Factionalism, and Trajectories of Pueblo IV Period Clusters in the Mogollon Rim Region. In *The Protohistoric Pueblo World A.D. 1275 -1600*, edited by E. Charles Adams and Andrew I. Duff, pp. 85-94. University of Arizona Press, Tucson.

Kent, Kate Peck
  1954 *Montezuma Castle Archeology, Part 2: Textiles.* Southwestern Monuments Association Technical Series 3(2). Globe.

Klucas, Eric E. and Richard S. Ciolek-Torrello

    2005 *The State Route 199—Cottonwood Creek Project*, Vol. 3 (Draft). Technical Series No. 78. Statistical Research Inc., Tucson.

Kolber, Jane

    2004 *A Practical Rock Art Recording Guide.* Edited by Donald E. Weaver, Jr. and Donna Yoder. Bisbee.

Lange, Charles H. and Carroll L. Riley (editors)

    1970 *Southwestern Journals of Adolph F. Bandelier, 1883-1884.* University of New Mexico Press, Albuquerque.

Lange, Richard C.

    1982a Notes from a conversation with Emil Haury. Manuscript on file, Arizona State Museum, University of Arizona, Tucson.

    1982b Steatite: An Analysis and Assessment of Form and Distribution. In *Cholla Project Archaeology*, Vol. 1, edited by J. Jefferson Reid, pp. 167-192. Arizona State Museum Archaeological Series 161. Arizona State Museum, University of Arizona, Tucson.

    1982c AZ V:1:11. In *Cholla Project Archaeology, Vol. 3: The Q Ranch Region*, edited by J. Jefferson Reid, pp. 105-122. Arizona State Museum Archaeological Series 161. Arizona State Museum, University of Arizona, Tucson.

    1989 Baubles and Beads: Prehistoric Use of Soapstone in Central Arizona. In *Reflections: Papers on the Southwestern Culture history in Honor of Charles. H. Lange*, edited by Anne Van Arsdall Poore, pp. 156-172. The Archaeological Society of New Mexico No. 14. Ancient City Press, Santa Fe.

    1992 Pots, People, Politics, and Precipitation: Just Who or What Are the Salado Anyway? In *Proceedings of the Second Salado Conference, Globe, Arizona*, edited by Richard. C. Lange and Stephen Germick, pp. 325-333. Arizona Archaeological Society Occasional Paper, Phoenix.

    1994 *An Archaeological Survey of the Homolovi Ruins State Park Area in Northeastern Arizona, 1985-1989.* Manuscript on file. Arizona State Museum, University of Arizona, Tucson.

    1996 The Little Colorado River, Farming, and Prehistory in the Homol'ovi Area. In *River of Change: Prehistory of the Middle Little Colorado River Valley, Arizona*, edited by E. Charles Adams, pp. 239-258. Arizona State Museum Archaeological Series 185. Arizona State Museum, University of Arizona, Tucson.

    1998 *Prehistoric Land-Use and Settlement of the Middle Little Colorado River Valley: The Survey of Homolovi Ruins State Park, Winslow, Arizona.* Arizona State Museum Archaeological Series 189. Arizona State Museum, University of Arizona, Tucson.

    2001 Tactful Tactical Insights from the Sierra Ancha, East-Central Arizona. In *The Archaeology of Ancient Tactical Sites*, edited by John R. Welch and Todd W. Bostwick, pp. 67-76. Arizona Archaeologist No. 32. Arizona Archaeological Society, Phoenix.

    2005 *Sierra Ancha Project Report.* Manuscript on file, Arizona State Museum, University of Arizona, Tucson.

Lange, Richard C., Alan Ferg, and John Hohmann

    1983 Transcript of a taped interview/conversation with Emil W. Haury. Transcript on file, Arizona State

Museum, University of Arizona, Tucson.

Lange, Richard C. and Barbara A. Murphy
    1982 Transcript of a taped interview/conversation with Travis "Buster" Ellison. Transcript on file, Arizona
    State Museum, University of Arizona, Tucson.

Lange, Richard C., Craig P. Howe, and Barbara A. Murphy
    1993 A Study of Prehistoric Roofing Systems in Arizona Cliff Dwellings. *Journal of Field Archaeology*
    20(4):485-498.

Lengyel, Stacey, and William L. Deaver
    2005 A Chronometric Framework for Evaluating Regional Change in Tonto Basin. In *The State Route
    188—Cottonwood Creek Project, Vol. 3: Conclusions and Synthesis,* (Draft), edited by Eric Eugene
    Klucas and Richard Ciolek-Torrello, pp. 3.1-3.60. Technical Series No. 78. Statistical Research Inc.,
    Tucson.

Lekson, Stephen H.
    1999 *The Chaco Meridian: Centers of Political Power in the Ancient Southwest.* Altamira Press, Walnut Creek.

Leonard, Banks L.
    1996 *Archaeological Testing of Ten Sites along the Young Corridor, Arizona Forest Highway 12 (State
    Route 88), Gila County, Arizona.* Technical Report 96-16. Soil Systems, Phoenix.

Lightfoot, Kent G.
    1979 Food Redistribution Among Prehistoric Pueblo Groups. *Kiva* 44(4):319-339.

Lightfoot, Kent G. and Roberta Jewett
    1984 Late Prehistoric Ceramic Distributions in East-Central Arizona: An Examination of Cibola
    Whiteware, White Mountain Redware, and Salado Redware. In *Regional Analysis of Prehistoric
    Ceramic Variation: Contemporary Studies of the Cibola Whitewares*, edited by Alan P. Sullivan III
    and Jeffrey L. Hantman, pp. 36-73. Arizona State University Anthropological Papers No. 31. Arizona
    State University, Tempe.

Lightfoot, Ricky R.
    1988 Roofing an Early Anasazi Great Kiva: Analysis of an Architectural Model. *Kiva* 53(3):253-272.

Lindauer, Owen
    1992 Architectural Engineering and Variation Among Salado Platform Mounds.In *Proceedings of the
    Second Salado Conference*, edited by Richard C. Lange and Stephen Germick, pp. 50-56. Arizona
    Archaeological Society Occasional Paper, Phoenix.

    1997 *The Archaeology of Schoolhouse Point Mesa, Roosevelt Platform Mound Study.* Roosevelt
    Monograph Series 8, Anthropological Field Studies No. 37. Office of Cultural Resource Management,
    Department of Anthropology, Arizona State University, Tempe.

Lindauer, Owen, Ronna J. Bradley, and Charles L. Redman (editors)
    1991 *The Archaeology of Star Valley, Arizona: Variation in Small Communities.* Anthropological Field
    Studies No. 24. Office of Cultural Resource Management, Department of Anthropology, Arizona State
    University, Tempe.

Love, Marian F.
    1975 A Survey of the Distribution of T-Shaped Doorways in the Greater Southwest. In *Collected Papers in*

Honor of Florence Hawley Ellis, edited by Theodore Frisbie, pp. 296-311. Papers of the Archaeological Society of New Mexico No. 2. Hooper Publishing Co., Norman.

Lowe, Charles H.
1964 *Arizona's Natural Environment*. University of Arizona Press, Tucson.

Lyons, Patrick D.
2003 *Ancestral Hopi Migrations*. Anthropological Papers of the University of Arizona No. 68. University of Arizona Press, Tucson.

Macnider, Barbara S. and Richard W. Effland, Jr.
1989 *Cultural Resources Overview: The Tonto National Forest*. Cultural Resources Report No. 51. Archaeological Consulting Services, Tempe.

Malville, Nancy
2003 Long-distance Transport of Goods in Prehistoric North America. In *Copper Canyon: The Puzzle of Oasis America* by Richard Fisher. Sunracer Publications, Tucson.

Martin, Paul S.
1979 Prehistory: Mogollon. In *Southwest*, edited by Alfonso Ortiz, pp. 61-74. *Handbook of the North American Indians*, Vol. 9, William C. Sturtevant (editor). Smithsonian Institution, Washington, D.C.

Martin, Paul S., John B. Rinaldo, and William A. Longacre
1961 Mineral Creek Site and Hooper Ranch Pueblo, Eastern Arizona. *Fieldiana*: Anthropology 52. Chicago Natural History Museum, Chicago.

McGehee, Ellen
1983 *A Preliminary Report of Dendrochronological Studies in Upper Pueblo Canyon—The Sierra Ancha Wilderness Area*. Manuscript on file, Arizona State Museum, University of Arizona, Tucson.

1983 *A Final Report of Dendrochronological Studies in Upper Pueblo Canyon—The Sierra Ancha Wilderness Area*. Manuscript on file, Arizona State Museum, University of Arizona, Tucson.

McKusick, Charmion R.
1992 Evidences of Hereditary High Status at Gila Pueblo. In *Proceedings of the Second Salado Conference, Globe Arizona*, edited by Richard C. Lange and Stephen Germick, pp. 86-91. Arizona Archaeological Society Occasional Paper, Phoenix.

Mehalic, David S.
2002 Dwelling Upon the Cliffs of the Sierra Ancha: Dendroarchaeological Indicators of Settlement Diversification in the Central Arizona Mountains. Unpublished Master's thesis, Department of Anthropology, University of Arizona, Tucson.

Metzger, Todd R.
n.d. *Ruins Preservation Guidelines: Pecos National Monument, New Mexico* (Draft). Pecos National Monument, National Park Service, Pecos, New Mexico.

Metzger, Todd R., Larry F. Nordby, and Susan F. Eininger
1989 *Wupatki National Monument: Prestabilization Architectural Documentation Manual for Prehistoric Stone Masonry Sites* (Draft). United States Department of the Interior, National Park Service.

Mills, Barbara J.
1999 The Reorganization of Silver Creek Communities from the 11ᵗʰ to the 14ᵗʰ Centuries. In *Living on the Edge of the Rim: Excavation and Analysis of the Silver Creek Archaeological Project 1993-1998*, edited by Barbara J. Mills, Sarah A. Herr, and Scott Van Keuren, pp. 505-511. Arizona State Museum Archaeological Series 192(2). Arizona State Museum, University of Arizona, Tucson.

Mills, Barbara J., Sarah A. Herr, Susan L. Stinson, and Daniela Triadan
1999 Ceramic Production and Distribution. In *Living on the Edge of the Rim: Excavation and Analysis of the Silver Creek Archaeological Project 1993-1998*, edited by Barbara J. Mills, Sarah A. Herr, and Scott Van Keuren, pp. 295-324. Arizona State Museum Archaeological Series 192(2). Arizona State Musem, University of Arizona, Tucson.

Mills, Barbara J., Sarah A. Herr, and Scott Van Keuren (editors)
1999 *Living on the Edge of the Rim: Excavation and Analysis of the Silver Creek Archaeological Project 1993-1998*. Arizona State Museum Archaeological Series 192. Arizona State Museum, University of Arizona, Tucson.

Mindeleff, Victor
1989 *A Study of Pueblo Architecture in Tusayan and Cibola.* Reprinted. Smithsonian Institution Press, Washington, D. C. Originally printed 1891. 8ᵗʰ Annual Report of the Bureau of American Archaeology and Ethnology, 1886-1887. U.S. G.P.O., Washington, D.C.

Minnis, Paul E., and Glen E. Rice
1990 Prehistoric Land Use of the Tonto Basin Landscape: Towards a Synthetic Overview. In *A Design for Salado Research*, edited by Glen E. Rice, pp. 115-121. Roosevelt Monograph Series No.1, Anthropological Series No. 22. Arizona State University, Tempe.

Montgomery, Barbara K.
1992 Understanding the Formation of the Archaeological Record: Ceramic Variability at Chodistaas Pueblo, Arizona. Unpublished Ph.D. dissertation, Department of Anthropology, University of Arizona, Tucson.

Montgomery, Barbara K. and J. Jefferson Reid
1990 An Instance of Rapid Ceramic Change in the American Southwest. *American Antiquity* 55(1):88-97.

Moore, Richard T.
1968 *Mineral Deposits of the Fort Apache Indian Reservation, Arizona.* Arizona State Bureau of Mines Bulletin 177. Arizona State Bureau of Mines, Tucson.

Morgan, Esther
1998 *An Archaeological Survey of the Buzzard Roost Timber Sale, Pleasant Valley Ranger District, Tonto National Forest* (Draft). Project No. 96-137. On file at Payson Ranger District, Payson.

Morris, Donald H.
1969 A Ninth Century Salado (?) Kiva at Walnut Creek, Arizona. *Plateau* 42(1):1-10.

1969 Walnut Creek Village: A Ninth-Century Hohokam-Anasazi Settlement in the Mountains of central Arizona. *American Antiquity* 35(1):49-61.

Newcomb, Joanne M.
1999 Silver Creek Settlement Patterns and Demography. In *Living on the Edge of the Rim: Excavation and Analysis of the Silver Creek Archaeological Project 1993-1998*, edited by Barbara J. Mills, Sarah A. Herr, and Scott Van Keuren, pp. 31-51. Arizona State Museum Archaeological Series 192(1). Arizona

State Museum, University of Arizona, Tucson.

Nordenskiold, Gustaf A.
1973 *The Cliff Dwellers of the Mesa Verde, Southwestern Colorado: Their Pottery and Implements.* Reprinted. Published by AMS Press, Inc., New York for the Peabody Museum of Archaeology and Ethnology, Harvard University, Cambridge. Original publication 1893 as *Ruiner af Klippboningar i Mesa Verde's cañons.* Translated by O. Lloyd Morgan. Royal Printing Office, Stockholm.

Oliver, Theodore H.
1997 *Classic Period Settlement in the Uplands of Tonto Basin: Roosevelt Platform Mound Study Report on the Uplands Complex.* Roosevelt Monograph Series 5, Anthropological Field Studies No. 34. Office of Cultural Resource Management, Department of Anthropology, Arizona State University, Tempe.

2001 Warfare in the Tonto Basin. In *Deadly Landscapes: Case Studies in Prehistoric Southwestern Warfare,* edited by Glen E. Rice and Steven A. LeBlanc, pp. 195-217. University of Utah Press, Salt Lake City.

Oliver, Theodore J., and David F. Jacobs
1997 *Salado Residential Settlements on Tonto Creek: Roosevelt Platform Mound Study.* Roosevelt Monograph Series No. 9, Anthropological Field Studies No. 38. Office of Cultural Resource Management, Department of Anthropology, Arizona State University, Tempe.

Osborne, Carolyn M.
1965 Preparation of Yucca Fibers: An Experimental Study. *Memoirs of the Society for American Archaeology* 19:45-50.

Patterson, Alex
1992 *A Field Guide to Rock Art Symbols of the Greater Southwest.* Johnson Books, Boulder.

Pierson, Lloyd M.
1962 Excavations at the Lower Ruin and Annex, Tonto National Monument. In *Archaeological Studies at Tonto National Monument, Arizona,* by Charlie R. Steen, Lloyd M. Pierson, Vorsila L. Bohrer, and Kate Peck Kent, pp. 33-73. Technical Series Vol. 2. Southwestern Monuments Association, Gila Pueblo, Globe.

Pilles, Peter J., Jr.
1976 Sinagua and Salado Similarities as Seen From the Verde Valley. *Kiva* 42(1):113-124.

Punzmann, Walter R.
1982 A Dendrochronology Report of the Sierra Ancha Cliff Dwellings of the Sierra Ancha Survey Expedition. Unpublished B.A. Honors thesis, Department of Anthropology, University of Arizona, Tucson.

1986 Chronological and Cultural Analysis of C:1:16: A Cliff Dwelling of the Sierra Ancha, East-Central Arizona. Unpublished Master's thesis, Department of Anthropology, University of Arkansas, Fayetteville.

Redman, Charles L.
1993 *People of the Tonto Rim: Archaeological Discovery in Prehistoric Arizona.* Smithsonian Institution Press, Washington, D.C.

Redman, Charles L. and John W. Hohmann (editors)
1986 *Small Site Variability in the Payson Region: The Flex Land Exchange.* Anthropological Studies No. 11. Office of Cultural Resource Management, Department of Anthropology, Arizona State University, Tempe.

Reed, Alan C.
1978 An Analysis of Quids from Hoy House and Lion House. *Southwestern Lore* 44(3):1-22.

Reid, J. Jefferson
1989 A Grasshopper Perspective on the Mogollon of the Arizona Mountains. In *Dynamics of Southwest Prehistory*, edited by Linda S. Cordell and George J.Gumerman, pp. 65-97. Smithsonian Institution Press, Washington, D.C.

Reid, J. Jefferson (editor)
1982a *Cholla Project Archaeology.* Arizona State Musuem Archaeological Series 161, 5 Vols. Arizona State Museum, University of Arizona, Tucson.

1982b *Cholla Project Archaeology: The Q Ranch Region.* Arizona State Museum Archaeological Series 161(3). Arizona State Museum, University of Arizona, Tucson.

1982c *Cholla Project Archaeology: The Tonto-Roosevelt Region.* Arizona State Museum Archaeological Series 161(4). Arizona State Museum, University of Arizona, Tucson.

Reid, J. Jefferson and David E. Doyel (editors)
1986 *Emil W. Haury's Prehistory of the American Southwest.* University of Arizona Press, Tucson.

Reid, J. Jefferson, and Izumi Shimada
1982 Pueblo Growth at Grasshopper: Methods and Models. In *Multidisciplinary Research at Grasshopper Pueblo, Arizona*, edited by William A. Longacre, Sally J. Holbrook, and Michael W. Graves, pp. 12-18. Anthropological Papers of the University of Arizona No. 40. University of Arizona Press, Tucson.

Reid, J. Jefferson, David Tuggle, and Barbara J. Klie
1982 The Q Ranch Sites. In *Cholla Project Archaeology: The Q Ranch Region.* Arizona State Museum Archaeological Series 161(3), edited by J. Jefferson Reid, pp. 33-122. Arizona State Museum, University of Arizona, Tucson.

Reid, J. Jefferson, and Stephanie Whittlesey
1999 *Grasshopper Pueblo: A Story of Archaeology and Ancient Life.* University of Arizona Press, Tucson.

Reynolds, William E.
1981 The Ethnoarchaeology of Pueblo Architecture. Unpublished Ph.D. dissertation, Department of Anthropology, Arizona State University, Tempe.

Rice, Glen E.
1998a The Bureau of Reclamation Archaeology Projects in Tonto Basin. In *A Synthesis of Tonto Basin Prehistory: The Roosevelt Archaeology Studies, 1989-1998*, Chapter 1, edited by Glen E. Rice, pp. 1-9. Roosevelt Monograph Series 12, Anthropological Field Studies No. 41. Arizona State University, Tempe.

1998b Structuring the Temporal Dimension for Tonto Basin Prehistory. In *A Synthesis of Tonto Basin Prehistory: The Roosevelt Archaeology Studies, 1989-1998*, Chapter 2, edited by Glen E. Rice, pp. 11-31. Roosevelt

Monograph Series 12, Anthropological Field Studies No. 41. Arizona State University, Tempe.

1998c The Setting. In *A Synthesis of Tonto Basin Prehistory: The Roosevelt Archaeology Studies, 1989-1998*, Chapter 3, edited by Glen E. Rice, pp. 33-54. Roosevelt Monograph Series 12, Anthropological Field Studies No. 41. Arizona State University, Tempe.

1998d Migration, Emulation, and Tradition in Tonto Basin Prehistory. In *A Synthesis of Tonto Basin Prehistory: The Roosevelt Archaeology Studies, 1989-1998*, Chapter 11, edited by Glen E. Rice, pp. 231-241. Roosevelt Monograph Series 12, Anthropological Field Studies No. 41. Arizona State University, Tempe.

Rice, Glen E. (editor)
1985 *Studies in the Hohokam and Salado of the Tonto Basin.* Report No. 63. Office of Cultural Resource Management, Department of Anthropology, Arizona State University, Tempe.

1990 *A Design for Salado Research.* Roosevelt Monograph Series No.1, Anthropological Field Studies No.22. Office of Cultural Resource Management, Department of Anthropology, Arizona State University, Tempe.

1998 *A Synthesis of Tonto Basin Prehistory: The Roosevelt Archaeology Studies, 1989-1998.* Roosevelt Monograph Series 12, Anthropological Field Studies No. 41. Arizona State University, Tempe.

Rice, Glen E., and Owen Lindauer
1994 Phase Chronology. In *Archaeology of the Salado in the Livingston Area of Tonto Basin, Roosevelt Platform Mound Study*, by David Jacobs, pp. 51-68. Roosevelt Monograph Series 3, Anthropological Field Studies No. 32. Department of Anthropology, Arizona State University, Tempe.

Rice, Glen E. and Theodore J. Oliver
1998 Settlement Patterns and Subsistence. In *A Synthesis of Tonto Basin Prehistory: The Roosevelt Archaeology Studies, 1989-1998*, Chapter 5, edited by Glen E. Rice, pp. 85-104. Roosevelt Monograph Series 12. Anthropological Field Studies 41. Arizona State University, Tempe.

Riggs, Charles R., Jr.
2001 *The Architecture of Grasshopper Pueblo.* University of Utah, Salt Lake City.

2005 Late Ancestral Pueblo or Mogollon Pueblo? An Architectural Perspective on Identity. *Kiva* 70(4):323-348.

Rose, Martin R.
1994 Long Term Drought Reconstructions for the Lake Roosevelt Region. In *The Roosevelt Rural Sites Study, Vol. 3: Changing Land Use in the Tonto Basin*, edited by Richard S. Ciolek-Torrello and John R. Welch, pp. 311-359. Technical Series No. 28. Statistical Research Inc., Tucson.

Rugge, Dale, and David E. Doyel
1980 Petrographic Analysis of Ceramics from Dead Valley. In *Prehistory in Dead Valley, East-Central Arizona: The TG&E Springerville Project*, edited by David E. Doyel and Sharon Debowski, pp. 189-203. Arizona State Museum Archaeological Series 144. Arizona State Museum, University of Arizona, Tucson.

Sánchez G., J. Jesus, Major M. Goodman, and J. O. Rawlings
1993 Appropriate Characters for Racial Classification in Maize. *Economic Botany* 47(1):44-59.

Sanger, Kay K. and Clement W. Meighan
1990 *Discovering Prehistoric Rock Art: A Recording Manual.* Wormwood Press, Calabasa.

Sayles, E.B.
    1945 *The San Simon Branch: Excavations at Cave Creek and in The San Simon Valley, Vol. I: Material Culture*. Medallion Papers No. 34. Gila Pueblo, Globe.

Schaafsma, Polly
    1980 *Indian Rock Art of the Southwest*. School of American Research, Santa Fe. University of New Mexico Press, Albuquerque.

    1992 *Rock Art in New Mexico*. Museum of New Mexico, Santa Fe.

Schoenwetter, James and Frank W. Eddy
    1964 *Alluvial and Palynological Reconstruction of Environments, Navajo Reservoir District*. Museum of New Mexico Papers in Anthropology 13. Museum of New Mexico, Santa Fe.

Schoonover, Grace
    2003 *Millennia of Rock Art at Arrastre Creek*. Arizona Archaeological Society, Desert Foothills Chapter. Cave Creek.

Schoonover, Grace and Christine H. Virden
    1999 Prehistoric Rock Art in the McDowell Mountains Region: A Preliminary Overview of Several Sites. In *McDowell Mountains Archaeological Symposium*, edited by K.J.Schroeder, pp. 231-249. Publication of Papers Presented March 20, 1999, Scottsdale Civic Center Library. Roadrunner Publications in Anthropology 10. Roadrunner Archaeology and Consulting, Tempe.

Shelley, Steven D. and Richard S. Ciolek-Torrello
    1994 Grapevine Recreation and Stockpile Areas. In *Prehistoric Rural Settlements in the Tonto Basin: The Roosevelt Rural Site Study, Vol. 2, Part 1*, edited by Richard S. Ciolek-Torrello, Steven D. Shelley, and Su Benaron, pp. 239-259. Technical Series No. 28. Statistical Research Inc., Tucson.

Simon, Arleyn W., Jean-Cristophe Komorowski, and James H. Burton
    1992 Patterns of Production and Distribution of Salado Wares as a Measure of Complexity. In *Developing Perspectives on Tonto Basin Prehistory*, edited by Charles L. Redman, Glen E. Rice, and Kathryn E. Pedrick, pp. 61-74. Roosevelt Monograph Series 2, Anthropological Field Studies No. 26. Arizona State University, Tempe.

Smith, Watson
    1973 Introduction. In *The Cliff Dwellers of the Mesa Verde, Southwestern Colorado: Their Pottery and Implements*, by Gustav A. Nordenskiold, pp. xi-xiv. Reprinted. Published by AMS Press, Inc., New York for the Peabody Museum of Archaeology and Ethnology, Harvard University, Cambridge. Original published 1893, as *Ruiner af Klippboningar i Mesa Verde's cañons*. Translated by O. Lloyd Morgan. Royal Printing Office, Stockholm.

Snead, James E.
    2001 *Ruins and Rivals: The Making of Southwest Archaeology*. University of Arizona Press, Tucson.

Stark, Miriam T.
    1995 Cultural Identity in the Archaeological Record: The Utility of Utilitarian Ceramics. In *The Roosevelt Community Development Study, Vol. 2: Ceramic Chronology, Technology, and Economics*, edited by James M. Heidke and Miriam T. Stark, pp. 331-362. Anthropological Papers No. 14. Center for Desert Archaeology, Tucson.

Steen, Charlie R.
    1962 Excavations at the Upper Ruin, Tonto National Monument, 1940. In *Archaeological Studies at Tonto National Monument, Arizona* by Charlie R. Steen, Lloyd M. Pierson, Vorsila L. Bohrer, and Kate Peck Kent, pp. 1-30. Technical Series Vol. 2. Southwestern Monuments Association, Gila Pueblo, Globe.

Steen, Charlie R., Lloyd M. Pierson, Vorsila L. Bohrer, and Kate Peck Kent
    1962 *Archaeological Studies at Tonto National Monument, Arizona.* Technical Series Vol. 2. Southwestern Monuments Association, Gila Pueblo, Globe.

Stokes, William L. and Sheldon Judson
    1968 *Introduction to Geology.* Prentice-Hall, Inc., Englewood Cliffs.

Swartz, Deborah L.
    1992 The Deer Creek Site: AZ O:15:52(ASM). In *The Rye Creek Project: Archaeology in the Upper Tonto Basin, Vol. 1: Introduction and Site Descriptions*, by Mark D. Elson and Douglas B. Craig, pp. 93-164. Anthropological Papers No. 11. Center for Desert Archaeology, Tucson.

Swartz, Deborah L. and Brenda G. Randolph
    1994 The Hedge Apple Site, AZ V:5:189/1605 (ASM/TNF). In *The Roosevelt Community Development Study, Vol. 1: Introduction and Small Sites*, by Mark D. Elson and Deborah L. Swartz, pp. 117-139. Anthropological Papers No. 13. Center for Desert Archaeology, Tucson.

Tagg, Martyn D.
    1985 *Tonto National Monument: An Archaeological Survey.* Publications in Anthropology No. 31. Western Archeological and Conservation Center, National Park Service, U.S. Department of the Interior, Tucson.

    1994 Projectile Points of East-Central Arizona: Forms and Chronology. In *Middle Little Colorado River Archaeology: From the Parks to the People*, edited by Anne Trinkle Jones and Martyn D. Tagg, pp. 87-115. The Arizona Archaeologist No. 27. Arizona Archaeological Society, Phoenix.

Teague, Lynn S.
    1996 Textiles from the Upper Ruin. In *Part I: Salvage Excavations at the Upper Ruin AZ U:8:48(ASM) — 1995*, edited by Gregory L. Fox, pp 157-176. Western Archaeological and Conservation Center, Tucson.

    1998a *Textiles in Southwestern Prehistory.* University of New Mexico Press, Albuquerque.

    1998b *Textiles from AZ AA:12:352 (ASM),* Manuscript on file, Arizona State Museum, Tucson.

    2000 Fabrics. In *Archaeological Investigation of Rooms 15 and 16 at the Upper Cliff Dwelling (AZ U:89:48 ASM) Tonto National Monument*, edited by G. L. Fox, pp. 183-195. Publications in Anthropology, Vol. 73. Western Archaeological and Conservation Center, National Park Service, Tucson.

    2003 *Cultural Identity in the Textiles, Traditions, and History of the O'odham and their Neighbors.* Paper presented at the 47th Annual Meeting of the Society for American Archaeology, Minneapolis, 1982.

Teague, Lynn S. and Linda L. Mayro (assemblers)
    1979 *An Archaeological Survey of the Cholla-Saguaro Transmission Line Corridor.* Arizona State Museum Archaeological Series 135. Arizona State Museum, University of Arizona, Tucson.

Thiel, J. Homer
    1995 *Rock Art in Arizona.* Arizona State Historic Preservation Office, Arizona State Parks Board, Phoenix.

Titiev, Mischa
    1992 *Old Oraibi: A Study of the Hopi Indians of Third Mesa.* Reprinted. University of New Mexico Press, Albuquerque. Originally published 1944. Papers of the Peabody Museum of American Archaeology and Ethnology, Vol. 22, No. 1. Harvard University, Cambridge.

Triadan, Daniela

1997 *Ceramic Commodities and Common Containers: Production and Distribution of White Mountain Red Ware in the Grasshopper Region, Arizona.* Anthropological Papers of the University of Arizona No. 61. University of Arizona Press, Tucson.

Triadan, Daniela and Nieves Zedeño

2004 The Political Geography and Territoriality of 14th-Century Settlements in the Mogollon Highlands of East-Central Arizona. In *The Proto-Historic Pueblo World, A.D. 1275-1600*, edited by E. Charles Adams and Andrew I. Duff, pp. 95-107. University of Arizona Press, Tucson.

Troncone, Steven M., Peg Davis, Elinor Large, Man McDonnell, and Ruth Rubenstein

1993 *Archaeological Monitoring of an Arizona Department of Transportation Cattleguard within AZ P:13:7 (ASM) Near Milepost 308 on State Route 288, Young, Gila County.* Report for ADOT Project S-266-505. Archaeological Consulting Services, Ltd., Phoenix.

Tuggle, H. David, and J. Jefferson Reid

2001 Conflict and Defense in the Grasshopper Region of East-Central Arizona. In *Deadly Landscapes: Case Studies in Prehistoric Southwestern Warfare,* edited by Glen E. Rice and Steven A. LeBlanc, pp. 85-107. University of Utah Press, Salt Lake City.

Turner, Christy G. and Jacqueline A. Turner

1999 *Man Corn: Cannibalism and Violence in the Prehistoric American Southwest.* University of Utah Press, Salt Lake City.

Urban, Sharon F.

2004 Rock Art – Why is it so popular? In *Bulletin of Old Pueblo Archaeology Center*, Vol. 39, December. Tucson.

US Department of Commerce

1956 *Climatological Data: Arizona.* Asheville.

US Geological Survey and Arizona Bureau of Mines

1969 *Mineral and Water Resources of Arizona.* Arizona Bureau of Mines Bulletin No. 180. Tucson.

Van West, Carla R.

1994 *River, Rain, or Ruin: Intermittent Prehistoric Land Use Along the Middle Little Colorado River.* Technical Series No. 53. Statistical Research, Inc., Tucson.

1996 Modeling Prehistoric Agricultural Strategies and Human Settlement in the Middle Little Colorado River Valley. In *River of Change: Prehistory of the Middle Little Colorado River Valley, Arizona,* edited by E. Charles Adams, pp. 15-35. Arizona State Museum Archaeological Series 185. Arizona State Museum, University of Arizona, Tucson.

Van West, Carla R., and Jeffrey H. Altschul

1994 Agricultural Productivity and Carrying Capacity in the Tonto Basin. In *The Roosevelt Rural Sites Study, Vol. 3: Changing Land Use in the Tonto Basin*, edited by Richard Ciolek-Torrello and John R. Welch, pp. 361-435. Technical Series No. 28. Statistical Research Inc., Tucson.

Vint, Robert

1993 *Archaeological Stabilization Planning and Interpretive Development for the Sierra Ancha Wilderness Cliff Dwellings, Tonto National Forest: Stabilization Plan.* Technical Report 93-2. Statistical Research

Inc., Tucson.

Wallace, Henry
    1989 *Archaeological Investigations at Petroglyph Sites in the Painted Rock Reservoir Area, Southwestern Arizona*. Technical Report No. 89-5. Institute for American Research, Tucson.

Wallace, Henry D., James M. Heidke, and William H. Doelle
    1995 Hohokam Origins. *Kiva* 60(4):575-618.

Weaver, Jr.,Donald E.
    1991a *Documentation and Evaluation of Two Rock Art Sites Along Pigeon Creek on the Apache-Sitgreaves National Forests, Greenlee County, Arizona.*

    1991b *Documentation and Evaluation of Four Rock Art Sites At Fools Hollow Lake on the Apache-Sitgreaves National Forests, Navajo County, Arizona.*

    1991c *Documentation and Evaluation of Two Rock Art Sites at Chevelon Crossing and Mormon Crossing on the Apache-Sitgreaves National Forests, Coconino County, Arizona.*

    1993 Images on Stone: The Prehistoric Rock Art of the Colorado Plateau. *Plateau* 55(2). Museum of Northern Arizona, Flagstaff.

Welch, John R.
    1994 Environmental Influences on Tonto Basin Agricultural Productivity and Sustainability. In *The Roosevelt Rural Sites Study, Vol. 3: Changing Land Use in the Tonto Basin*, edited by Richard S. Ciolek-Torrello and John R. Welch, pp. 19-39. Technical Series No. 28. Statistical Research Inc., Tucson.

Welch, John R., and Daniela Triadan
    1991 The Canyon Creek Turquoise Mine, Arizona. *Kiva* 56(2):145-164.

Wells, Wesley E.
    1971 *Prehistoric Settlement Patterns of Lower Cherry Creek*. Manuscript on file, Department of Anthropology, Arizona State University, Tempe.

Wendorf, Fred
    1953 *Archaeological Studies in the Petrified Forest National Monument*. Museum of Northern Arizona Bulletin No. 27. Museum of Northwen Arizona, Flagstaff.

Whittlesey, Stephanie M.
    1978 Status and Death at Grasshopper Pueblo: Experiments Toward an Archaeological Theory of Correlates. Unpublished Ph.D. dissertation, Department of Anthropology, University of Arizona, Tucson.

    1982a Examination of Previous Work in the Q Ranch Region: Comparison and Analysis. In *Cholla Project Archaeology: The Q Ranch Region*, edited by J. Jefferson Reid, pp. 123-150. Arizona State Museum Archaeological Series 161(3). Arizona State Museum, University of Arizona, Tucson.

    1982b Vessel Thinning Techniques and Ethnic Identification. *In Cholla Project Archaeology: Ceramic Studies*, edited by J. Jefferson Reid, pp. 18-21. Arizona State Museum Archaeological Series 161(5). Arizona State Museum, University of Arizona, Tucson.

    1994 Ceramics. In *The Roosevelt Rural Sites Study, Vol. 2: Prehistoric Rural Settlements in the Tonto Basin*, Pt. 2, edited by Richard S. Ciolek-Torrello, Steven D. Shelley, and Su Benaron, pp. 337-465.

Technical Series No. 28. Statistical Research Inc., Tucson.

Whittlesey, Stephanie M., and Richard S. Ciolek-Torrello, and Jeffrey H.Altschul
    1998 *Vanishing River: Lives and Landscapes of the Lower Verde Valle:, The Lower Verde Archaeological Project*. Statistical Research Inc., Tucson.

Wilcox, David R.
    1979 The Hohokam Regional System. In *An Archaeological Test of Sites in the Gila Butte-Santan Region, South-Central Arizona*, edited by Glen E. Rice, David R. Wilcox, Kevin Rafferty, and James Schoenwetter, pp. 7-116. Technical Paper No. 3, Anthropological Research Papers No. 18. Arizona State University, Tempe.

    1982 A Set-Theory Approach to Sampling Pueblos: The Implications of Room-Set Additions at Grasshopper Pueblo. In *Multidisciplinary Research at Grasshopper Pueblo, Arizona*, edited by William A. Longacre, Sally J. Holbrook, and Michael W. Graves, pp. 19- 27. Anthropological Papers No. 40. University of Arizona Press, Tucson.

Wilcox, David R., Gerald Robertson, Jr., and J. Scott Wood
    2001a Organized for War: The Perry Mesa Settlement System and Its Central Arizona Neighbors. In *Deadly Landscapes: Case Studies in Prehistoric Southwestern Warfare*, edited by Glen E. Rice and Steven A. LeBlanc, pp. 141-194. University of Utah Press, Salt Lake City.

    2001b Antecedents to Perry Mesa: Early Pueblo III Defensive Refuge Systems in West Central Arizona. In *Deadly Landscapes: Case Studies in Prehistoric Southwestern Warfare*, edited by Glen E. Rice and Steven A. LeBlanc, pp. 109-140. University of Utah Press, Salt Lake City.

Wilcox, David R., Thomas R. McGuire, and Charles Sternberg
    1981 *Snaketown Revisited: A Partial Cultural Resources Survey, Analysis of Site Structure, and an Ethnohistoric Study of the Proposed Hohokam-Pima National Monument*. Arizona State Museum Archaeological Series 155. Arizona State Museum, University of Arizona, Tucson.

Windes, Thomas C. and Peter J. McKenna
    2001 Going Against the Grain: Wood Production in Chacoan Society. *American Antiquity* 66(1):119-140.

Wood, J. Scott
    1976 Appendix. In *An Archeological Survey of the Frog Timber Sale, Pleasant Valley Ranger District, Tonto National Forest: An Experiment in Timber Sale Sampling Design*. Manuscript on file, Tonto National Forest, Phoenix.

    1980 The Gentry Timber Sale: Behavioral Pattern and Prediction In the Upper Cherry Creek Area, Central Arizona. *Kiva* 46(1):99-119.

    1985a The Classic Period in Southwestern Prehistory, 1150-1400: A Quick and Dirty Culture History. Manuscript on file, Sierra Ancha Project Files, Arizona State Museum. Prepared for "Prehistory of the Southwest," a class offered by the Arizona Archaeological Society, Phoenix.

    1985b The Northeastern Periphery. In *Proceedings of the 1983 Hohokam Symposium*, Part 1, edited by A.E. Dittert and Donald E. Dove, pp. 239-262. Arizona Archaeological Society, Phoenix.

    1986 *Vale of Tiers: Tonto Basin in the 14th Century*. Paper presented at the 59th Annual Pecos Conference, Payson.

1987 *Checklist of Pottery Types for the Tonto National Forest: An Introduction to the Archaeological Ceramics of Central Arizona*. The Arizona Archaeologist 21. Arizona Archaeological Society, Phoenix.

1989 *Vale of Tiers, Too: Late Classic Period Salado Settlement Patterns and Organizational Models for Tonto Basin*. Cultural Resources Inventory Report No. 89-12-280. Tonto National Forest, Phoenix.

1992 Toward A New Definition of Salado: Comments and Discussion on the Second Salado Conference. *Proceedings of the Second Salado Conference, Globe, Arizona*, edited by Richard C. Lange and Stephen Germick, pp. 337-344. Arizona Archaeological Society Occasional Paper, Phoenix.

2000 Vale of Tiers Palimpsest: Salado Settlement and Internal Relations in the Tonto Basin Area. In *Salado*, edited by Jeffrey S. Dean, pp. 107-142. University of New Mexico Press, Albuquerque.

Wood, J. Scott and Martin E. McAllister
1984 Second Foundation: Settlement Patterns and Agriculture in the Northeastern Hohokam Periphery, Central Arizona. In *Prehistoric Agricultural Strategies in the Southwest*, edited by Suzanne K. Fish and Paul R. Fish, pp. 271-289. Anthropological Research Papers No. 33. Arizona State University, Tempe.

Zauderer, Jeffrey
1975 A Survey of Typical Antelope House Quids. *Kiva* 41(1):65-70.

Zedeño, Maria Nieves
1994 *Sourcing Prehistoric Ceramics at Chodistaas Pueblo, Arizona: The Circulation of People and Pots in the Grasshopper Region*. Anthropological Papers of the University of Arizona No. 58. University of Arizona Press, Tucson.